Enterprise Information Systems and Advancing Business Solutions:

Emerging Models

Madjid Tavana
La Salle University, USA

Managing Director:	Lindsay Johnston
Senior Editorial Director:	Heather A. Probst
Book Production Manager:	Sean Woznicki
Development Manager:	Joel Gamon
Acquisitions Editor:	Erika Gallagher
Typesetter:	Adrienne Freeland
Cover Design:	Nick Newcomer, Lisandro Gonzalez

Published in the United States of America by
Business Science Reference (an imprint of IGI Global)
701 E. Chocolate Avenue
Hershey PA 17033
Tel: 717-533-8845
Fax: 717-533-8661
E-mail: cust@igi-global.com
Web site: http://www.igi-global.com

Library of Congress Cataloging-in-Publication Data

Enterprise information systems and advancing business solutions: emerging models / Madjid Tavana, editor.
    p. cm.
  Includes bibliographical references and index.
  ISBN 978-1-4666-1761-2 (hardcover) -- ISBN 978-1-4666-1762-9 (ebook) -- ISBN 978-1-4666-1763-6 (print & perpetual access) 1. Management information systems. 2. Business logistics--Technological innovations. I. Tavana, Madjid, 1957-
  HD30.213.E58 2012
  658.4'038011--dc23
          2012002616

British Cataloguing in Publication Data
A Cataloguing in Publication record for this book is available from the British Library.

The views expressed in this book are those of the authors, but not necessarily of the publisher.

Table of Contents

Section 2
Emerging Enterprise Information Technologies

Section 3
Emerging Software Development Technologies

Detailed Table of Contents

Section 1
Emerging Enterprise Resource Planning Strategies

Chapter 1

The implementation of Enterprise Recourse Planning (ERP) systems has grown rapidly, but limited research has been conducted to investigate the utilization of ERP systems. By extending the Technology Acceptance Model, this paper provides a research model for examining the impact of computer self-efficacy and ERP systems design features on the utilization of ERP systems. To test the proposed research model, data are collected through a questionnaire survey distributed among employees in different organizations that have implemented an ERP system in the United Arab Emirates. Structural equation modeling techniques are used in this study to verify the causal relationships between the variables. The results strongly support the extended TAM in understanding employees' utilization of ERP systems. The implications of this study and further research opportunities are also discussed.

Chapter 2

This paper illustrates the results of an analysis of business sectors covered by ERP solutions. The authors answer questions in regards to business sectors supported by ERP solutions, while presenting a list of supported business sectors. Using a statistical analysis, an answer is given to the question of whether there are any business sectors that are supported by a large number of ERP solutions, and whether it is possible to classify business sectors based on the occurrence of the support. Finally, three classifications are described that stem from different statistical views of covering business sectors by ERP solutions, and a suggestion for a unique classification of business sectors is given.

Chapter 3

This research identifies the key skills (e.g., business, team, communication) that industries expect for entry level positions involving enterprise resource planning (ERP) systems. Based on a review of the literature, a number of possible core skills that ERP entry level employees should possess are identified. To identify the relative importance of these specific skills, a web-based survey involving IT professionals from 105 organizations is conducted. Analyzing the findings using exploratory factor analysis and scale reliability analysis indicates four specific and significant factors representing the major key skills that industry expects from entry level ERP positions labeled for this study such as systems analysis and integration, team skills, project management, and business and application understanding. Various common technical skills (e.g., programming, networks) were found to be significantly less important than the business and team skills. This study should assist companies in developing criteria for evaluating potential candidates for entry level positions in ERP systems, as well as universities for evaluating the relevancy of their IT and Business programs.

Chapter 4

The blending of Internet technologies and traditional business concerns impacts all industries and is the latest phase in the ongoing evolution of business. In this changing business environment, the most successful companies are those that leverage their investment in Web-based technologies by implementing e-business solutions supported by sound existing infrastructures based on well-functioning Enterprise Resource Planning (ERP) systems. Companies must also forge tighter links in the supply chain, from raw materials to customers and have increasingly turned to the Internet and Web-based technologies to do so. This paper presents a framework for understanding e-business opportunities within the context of a traditional enterprise and its infrastructure and examines the evolving relationship between e-business and ERP. These developments are moving businesses toward the concept of e-Supply Chain to achieve true supply chain integration. The issues and challenges faced by organizations in moving to such a complete e-business environment are discussed and suggestions are offered for businesses to navigate this challenging transformation.

Chapter 5

Although introducing Enterprise Resource Planning (ERP) to an organization has enormous benefits, it may entail new hazardous challenges if it cannot be well managed. This research focuses on the critical ERP success factors from a case study involving the Esfahan Steel Company, which started ERP implementation in September 2002. An in-depth research of ERP implementation processes and the level of adhering to five chosen ERP critical success factors—project management, top management supports, business process reengineering, and change management and Training—are conducted. Research results revealed that the five critical success factors (CSFs) are highly interdependent and the strengths and weaknesses of each have influenced the quality of ERP implementation to a large extent.

The Implementation of Enterprise Resource Planning (ERP) systems require huge investments while ineffective implementations of such projects are commonly observed. A considerable number of these projects have been reported to fail or take longer than it was initially planned, while previous studies show that the aim of rapid implementation of such projects has not been successful and the failure of the fundamental goals in these projects have imposed huge amounts of costs on investors. Some of the major consequences are the reduction in demand for such products and the introduction of further skepticism to the managers and investors of ERP systems. In this regard, it is important to understand the factors determining success or failure of ERP implementation. The aim of this paper is to study the critical success factors (CSFs) in implementing ERP systems and to develop a conceptual model which can serve as a basis for ERP project managers. These critical success factors that are called "core critical success factors" are extracted from 62 published papers using the content analysis and the entropy method. The proposed conceptual model has been verified in the context of five multinational companies.

Chapter 7

This paper reports the results of an exploratory research that describes the Enterprise Resource Planning (ERP) implementation experiences of Robert Bosch Corporation over a period of time. In this paper, the author highlights a list of factors that could improve ERP implementations such as large resource commitment to the project, adoption of corporate standards that promote process harmonization, making hard yet important decisions that are irreversible, and top management support. The major contribution of this article is in explaining why the ERP implementation experience at Robert Bosch succeeded in 2004 in contrast to its implementation experience during 1992-1999. The resulting practical implications are discussed.

Section 2
Emerging Enterprise Information Technologies

The purpose of this study is to acquire knowledge that will help clarify outsourcing trends in general and an information systems utilization perspective in particular. The authors review recent studies on outsourcing and conduct a nationwide survey. The results of the survey reveal that 60 percent of the respondents are focusing on their supply chain for cost reduction and/or competitive advantages and less than half of the respondents plan to outsource supply chain processes and information systems within the next 5 years. Results also show that major reasons for outsourcing include a lack of ability to handle in house and return on assets, while the largest barrier to outsourcing is cost followed by control concern.

Rebecca Angeles, University of New Brunswick Fredericton, Canada

In this paper, the author looks at the perceived ability of information technology (IT) infrastructure integration and supply chain process integration. In order to moderate the relationship between business process specificity and domain knowledge specificity, the study focuses on two dependent variables; reciprocal investments and relational interaction using the moderated regression procedure. Results show that IT infrastructure integration moderates the relationship between business process specificity and relational interaction, as well as domain knowledge specificity and relational interaction.

João Duarte, Technical University of Lisbon, Portugal
André Vasconcelos, Technical University of Lisbon, Portugal

In the past decade, the rush to technology has created several flaws in terms of managing computers, applications, and middleware and information systems. Therefore, organizations struggle to understand how these elements behave. Even today, as Enterprise Architectures grow in significance and are acknowledged as advantageous artifacts to help manage change, their benefit to the organization has yet to be fully explored. In this paper, the authors focus on the challenge of real-time information systems evaluation, using the enterprise architecture as a boundary object and a base for communication. The solution proposed is comprised of five major steps: establishing a strong conceptual base on the evaluation of information systems, defining a high level language for this activity, extending an architecture creation pipeline, creating a framework that automates it, and the framework's implementation. The conceptual framework proposed avoids imprecise definitions of quality and quality attributes, was materialized in a model-eval-display loop framework, and was implemented using Model Driven Software Development practices and tools. Finally, a prototype is applied to a real-world scenario to verify the conceptual solution in practice.

Dongjin Yu, Hangzhou Dianzi University, China

The evolution of networks and large scale information systems has led to the rise of data sources that are distributed, heterogeneous, and autonomous. As a result, the management of Master Data becomes more complex and of uncertain quality. This paper presents a novel message-based approach to the synchronization of Master Data among multiple autonomous information systems. Different than traditional approaches based on database triggers, the author adopts the optimistic bidirectional strategy with the process of two synchronization phases. By means of data service buses, it propagates synchronized Master Data through messages being passed along star-like cascading routes. Moreover, this approach could resolve possible data conflicts automatically using predefined attribute confidences and deducible current value confidences respectively. Finally, this paper presents the real case about synchronizing datasets among four separate but related systems based on the author's novel message-based approach.

Chapter 12

Cloud computing has spread within enterprise faster than many other IT innovations. In cloud computing, computer services are accessed over the Internet in a scalable fashion, where the user is abstracted in varying degrees from the actual hardware and software and pays only for resources used. This paper examines the adoption of cloud computing in various regions of the world, as well as the potential of cloud computing to impact computing in developing countries. The authors propose that cloud computing offers varying benefits and appears differently in regions across the world, enabling many users to obtain sophisticated computing architectures and applications that are cost-prohibitive to acquire locally. The authors examine issues of privacy, security, and reliability of cloud computing and discuss the outlook for firms and individuals in both developing and developed countries seeking to utilize cloud computing for their computing needs.

Section 3
Emerging Software Development Technologies

Chapter 13

Although ontologies are gaining more and more acceptance, they are often not engineered in a component-based manner due to, among various reasons, a lack of appropriate constructs in current ontology languages. This hampers reuse and makes creating new ontologies from existing building blocks difficult. We propose to apply the notion of roles and role modeling to ontologies and present an extension of the Web Ontology Language OWL for this purpose. Ontological role models allow for clearly separating different concerns of a domain and constitute an intuitive reuse unit.

Chapter 14

Developing new software based on requirements specifications created by business analysts often leads to misunderstanding and lack of comprehension, because of the different backgrounds of the people involved. If requirements specifications instead have a clearly defined structure and comprehensive semantics, this obstacle can be resolved. Therefore, we propose to structure the requirements specifications using existing linguistics-based modeling methods and annotate the used terms with ontologies to enhance the understanding and reuse of these documents during the software engineering process.

Semantic User Interfaces (SUIs), are sets of interrelated, static, domain specific documents having layout and content, whose interpretation is defined through semantic decoration. SUIs are declarative in nature. They allow program composition by the user herself at the user interface level. The operation of SUI based applications follow a service oriented approach. SUI elements referenced in user requests are automatically mapped to reusable service provider components, whose contracts are specified in domain ontologies. This assures semantic separation of user interface components from elements of the underlying application system infrastructure, which allows full separation of concerns during system development; real, application independent, reusable components; user editable applications and generic learnability. This article presents the architecture and components of a SUI framework, basic elements of SUI documents and relevant properties of domain ontologies for SUI documents. The basics of representation and operation of SUI applications are explained through a motivating example.

Chapter 16

XML-based vertical standards are an emerging compatibility standard for describing business processes and data formats in specific industries that have emerged in the past decade. Vertical standards, typically implemented using eXtensible Markup Language (XML), are incomplete products in constant evolution, continually adding functionality to reflect changing business needs. Vertical standards are public goods because they are freely obtained from sponsoring organizations without investing resources in their development, which gives rise to linked collective action dilemmas at the development and diffusion stages. Firms must be persuaded to invest in development without being able to profit from the output, and a commitment to ensure the diffusion of the standard must be secured from enough potential adopters to guarantee success. In this paper, the authors explore organizational drivers for participation in vertical standards development activities for supply- and demand-side organizations (i.e., vendors and end-user firms) in light of the restrictions imposed by these dilemmas.

Vertical standards focus on industry-specific product and service descriptions, and are generally implemented using the eXtensible Markup Language (XML). Vertical standards are complex technologies with an organizational adoption locus but subject to inter-organizational dependence and network effects. Understanding the assimilation process for vertical standards requires that both firm and industry-level effects be considered simultaneously. In this paper, the authors develop and evaluate a two-level model of organizational assimilation that includes both firm and industry-level effects. The study was conducted in collaboration with OASIS, a leading cross-industry standards-development organization (SDO), and with ACORD, the principal SDO for the insurance and financial services industries. Results confirm the usefulness of incorporating firm-level and community-level constructs in the study of complex networked technologies. Specifically, the authors' re-conceptualization of the classical DoI concepts of relative advantage and complexity are shown to be appropriate and significant in predicting vertical standards assimilation. Additionally, community-level constructs such as orphaning risk and standard legitimation are also shown to be important predictors of assimilation.

Chapter 18

Diana M. Sánchez, Rey Juan Carlos University, Spain

César J. Acuña, Rey Juan Carlos University, Spain

José María Cavero, Rey Juan Carlos University, Spain

Esperanza Marcos, Rey Juan Carlos University, Spain

The emerging Semantic Web and, in particular, Semantic Web services (SWS), demands the inclusion of new components in applications involving this technology. Therefore, Web development methodologies must be tailored to support the systematic development of such new components. In previous works we presented a UML profile, which extends the SOD-M method for service oriented Web Information System development of the MIDAS model-driven framework, to address the development of Semantic Web Services using WSMO (Web Service Modeling Ontology). The UML profile allows for the modeling of the new elements required by WSMO Web Services. This paper focuses on studying the possibility of improving the proposed UML profile, including the OCL (Object Constraint Language), for the representation of WSMO logical axioms through three case studies. This would allow developers, whose knowledge does not extend beyond UML, to develop applications that use Semantic Web services.

Chapter 19

César J. Acuña, Rey Juan Carlos University, Spain

Mariano Minoli, Rey Juan Carlos University, Spain

Esperanza Marcos, Rey Juan Carlos University, Spain

Several systems integration proposals have been suggested over the years. However these proposals have mainly focused on data integration, not allowing users to take advantage of services offered by Web portals. Most of the mentioned proposals only provide a set of design principles to build integrated systems and lack in suggesting a systematic way of how to develop systems based on the integration architecture they propose. In previous work we have developed PISA (Web Portal Integration Architecture)—a Web portal integration architecture for data and services—and MIDAS-S, a methodological approach for the development of integrated Web portals, built according to PISA. This work shows, by means of a case study, how both proposals fit together integrating Web portals.

Chapter 20

Kerstin Altmanninger, Johannes Kepler University Linz, Austria

Wieland Schwinger, Johannes Kepler University Linz, Austria

Gabriele Kotsis, Johannes Kepler University Linz, Austria

In collaborative software development, the utilization of Version Control Systems (VCSs) is a must. For this, a multitude of pessimistic as well as optimistic VCSs for model artifacts emerged. Pessimistic approaches follow the lock-edit-unlock paradigm whereas optimistic approaches allow parallel editing of one resource, which are therefore the preferred ones. To be flexible for the ever increasing variety of modeling environments and languages such tools should be independent of the modeling environment and applicable to various modeling languages. Those VCS characteristics may implicate a lack of information for the conflict detection method by virtue of firstly receiving solely the state of an artifact without concrete editing operations and secondly due to unavailable knowledge about the semantics of a modeling language. However, in optimistic VCSs concurrent changes can result in conflicts and inconsistencies. In environment and language independent VCSs inconsistencies would even arise more often due to information losses. Hence, accurate conflict detection methods are indispensable for the realization of such VCSs. To tackle this task, the "Semantically enhanced Model Version Control System" SMoVer is presented. With SMoVer it is possible to specify the semantics of a modeling language, needed for conflict detection in order to provide more accurate conflict reports than other current environment and language independent VCSs. In this work, it is exemplified how semantics of a specific modeling language can be specified in SMoVer, how those specifications can improve the accuracy of conflict reports and finally how those can be presented to modelers.

Preface

This book is dedicated to emerging models in enterprise information systems and advancing business solutions. The book is divided into three sections. The first section presents seven papers that focus on emerging enterprise resource planning strategies. ERP systems are complex, computer-centric systems designed to carry out the most common business functions in organizations, including finance, accounting, human resources, and operations. Such systems enable companies to move from an isolated functional view to a process view of both information system development and business activities. Given their flexibility and applicability to organizations of varying sizes and industrial sectors, and that such systems come embedded with best business processes, ERP systems have become the technology of choice for organizations attempting to reduce waste in their value chain and better integrate functional areas within their organization and members of their supply chain. Much of the value of ERP systems lies in the infrastructure foundation they created for future growth based on information technology. The first part of this foundation is common data. To make an ERP system work in an enterprise, everyone must enter data into ERP systems using the same format. As a result, the data becomes transparent and easy to compare. The second element of this foundation is standardized business processes. ERP requires standardization to reduce the number of process variants that must be supported. Drastic changes are normally needed so that orders can be fulfilled consistently throughout the enterprise. The third part of the foundation is an unconventional leadership structure. Companies implementing ERP systems often learn the need for leadership the hard way in information technology initiatives, rather than conventional line structures.

The second section presents five papers focusing on emerging enterprise information technologies such as enterprise architecture, cloud computing, and autonomous information systems. These papers look at the perceived ability of information technology infrastructure integration and supply chain process integration and show how some new technologies such as cloud computing will take the enterprise architecture discipline a step forward towards the integration of advanced enterprise information technologies.

In the third section, the authors present eight papers that focus on the emerging software development technologies. The Semantic Web is the leading Web development, and domain ontologies are the most important part of semantic Web applications. In recent years, many mainstream and evolutionary methods have been proposed for using software engineering techniques to bring ontology development process closer to wider practitioners' population. This section provides insight into the field of the semantic Web and ontology engineering.

An ERP system is an integrated set of software packages that help organizations integrate their information flow and business processes by using a single database that collects and stores data with a standardized user interface. The implementation of ERP systems by organizations has grown rapidly world-wide in anticipation for achieving better business performance and sustaining competitive advantages. ERP systems can benefit organizations by enabling faster information transactions, increasing productivity, maintaining tightened supply chain links, reducing inventory costs, improving business processes, and increasing customer responsiveness. Researchers have developed different models to study users' perception of information systems. One of the most frequently employed models is the technology acceptance model, which is an adaptation of the theory of reasoned action with a focus on the user acceptance of information systems. Mouakket, in his paper entitled *"Extending the Technology Acceptance Model to Investigate the Utilization of ERP Systems,"* extends the technology acceptance model to investigate employees' utilization of ERP systems. In his proposed model, computer self-efficacy and ERP systems design features affect perceived usefulness and perceived ease of use, which in turn affect ERP system utilization. The goal of this study is to explore these relationships and determine whether the addition of ERP system design features to the technology acceptance model increases its predictive or explanatory power. This study makes valuable contributions to the ERP research and practice. First, Mouakket incorporates computer self-efficacy and ERP systems design features as exogenous factors affecting ERP systems utilization through technology acceptance model's core constructs. Technology acceptance model has been considered a valuable model for tracing the indirect effects of external factors on information system acceptance behavior. Therefore, the results of this study provide further evidence to technology acceptance model's ability to mediate the influence of exogenous factors. Furthermore, most previous research has focused on common and well-known technologies such as spreadsheets, while the present study investigates the utilization of a rather complex and difficult technology, namely ERP systems. Finally, since computer self-efficacy has demonstrated positive direct effect on perceived ease of use and indirect effect on ERP systems utilization, managers should enhance employees' self-efficacy towards the utilization of this technology to improve the perception of ease of use and lessen the perception of system complexity and difficulty. He concludes that managers need to focus on ease of use and emphasize the simplicity of an information system to obtain more favorable attitudes towards system utilization. Providing user support methods such as training sessions can significantly improve users' perception of the information system ease of use.

ERP solutions support general business technology of a certain business sector. Jakupovic et al., in their paper entitled *"A Proposition for Classification of Business Sectors by ERP Solutions Support,"* illustrate the results of their analysis of business sectors covered by ERP solutions. They answer the question of which business sectors are supported by ERP solutions and provide a list of supported business sectors. They use statistical analysis and answer the question whether there are any business sectors supported by large number of ERP solutions, and whether it is possible to classify business sectors based on the occurrence of the support. They study the following characteristics in the existing ERP solution analyses: the average solution implementation cost, the average number of users, the coverage of application areas, the coverage of a certain market segment, applied technology, stability, flexibility, security, documentation, adaptability of the ERP solution, the level of support, upgrade reliability, improvement continuity, and return of investment. They propose unique classifications of business sectors. The first classification suggests that the number of newly supported business sectors increases faster than the number of business sectors where the support is increasing. The second classification shows that the larger number of business sectors are either weakly or excellently supported. The third classification suggests that there is constancy in higher classes of business sectors ERP support, which opens up the problem of maintaining the constancy. The fourth classification illustrates the existence of dynamics between middle classes of supporting business sectors by ERP solutions; i.e. business sectors do not stay long in the second class.

They either go back to the first class or move up to the third class. Each business sector in a class can go through four scenarios: it stays in the same class for an extended period of time (which means that the number of ERP producers supporting it is not changed), it moves up to a higher class (which means that the number of ERP producers supporting it is on the increase), moves down to a lower class (which means than the number of ERP producers supporting it is on the decrease), or completely vanishes from the classification (which means that all ERP producers have renounced their support of this particular business sector). They argue that there are several reasons for classification changes or vanishing of a business sector. Some of these reasons include: (1) non-profitability of business software development, which is the reason why some business sectors never enter the classification (e.g. only a few organizations belong to the particular business sector); (2) business sector is far too complex for supporting it by an business software (gathering knowledge on the business sector is a time-consuming process); (3) business software for a business sector fails (renouncement of the solution happens); and (4) business software for a business sector is profitable so most ERP producers support it (then the business sector moves up to a higher class).

Peslak and Boyle, in their paper entitled "*An Exploratory Study of the Key Skills for Entry-Level ERP Employees,*" explore a series of key information technology skills and determine what skills organizations view as important for entry-level ERP employees. With the critical ERP skills identified, employers can focus on these key areas in recruitment and development activities and improve their success rate for ERP implementation and support. In addition to examining the relative importance of these key skills, they elicits a number of factors that can be used for summary proficiency analysis and help organizations quickly assess employee qualifications for entry level ERP positions. To explore the key skills required for entry-level ERP positions, they develop a Web-based survey. The results of their study suggest that there are four key areas that practitioners view as vital for recent ERP graduates to possess prior to joining their organization. These skills, in order of importance, are: team skills, business and application understanding, project management, and systems analysis and integration. One of the surprising and interesting findings of this study is that technical skills are not found to be the most important skills for ERP graduates, and they do not become of part of the significant factors. Support hardware, networks, operating systems, and support of existing portfolio of applications all are found to be at the bottom of key skills and are not a part of the significant factors. They conclude that it is imperative for the ERP curricula to meet the needs of today's practitioners. They propose that the educators and practitioners together should prepare future ERP knowledge workers and optimize their business implementations and improve organizational performance.

The blending of Internet technologies and traditional business concerns is impacting all industries. The Internet drives the current industry goals of a shorter order-to-delivery cycle, global reach, and personalization. However, without connecting order delivery, manufacturing, financial, human resources, and other back office systems to the Internet, even companies with long track records of innovation are not likely to succeed. Srinivasan, in his paper entitled "*E-Business and ERP: A Conceptual Framework towards the Business Transformation to an Integrated E-Supply Chain,*" argues that the most successful companies will be those that leverage their investment in Web based technologies by implementing e-Business solutions supported by sound existing infrastructures based on well-functioning ERP systems. He argues that today, companies need to forge tighter links up and down the supply chain, from raw materials to customers. Web-based technology puts life and breadth into ERP technology that is large, technologically cumbersome, and does not easily reveal its value. At the same time, ERP allows e-Business to come into fruition, putting real substance behind that flashy webpage. While ERP organizes information within the enterprise, e-Business disseminates information far and wide. In light of the fact that ERP and e-Business technologies supercharge each other, he: (1) presents a framework for understanding e-Business opportunities within the context of a traditional enterprise and its infrastructure; (2) examines the evolving relationship between e-Business and ERP to understand how companies can move ahead to gain competitive advantage (using ERP to leverage and take advantage of the business opportunities opened up by the Internet and e-Business); (3) examines and discusses the role of ERP today and in the context of new business models enabled by e-Business and associated technologies, and that represent the next step in organizational evolution; (4) discusses recent developments in the area of e-supply chain, supply chain integration, and other technological developments; and (5) addresses the issues and challenges faced by organizations in moving to an e-Business environment. This paper is useful to both the research academician and the practicing manager who are interested in understanding the issues, opportunities, and challenges in the ERP and e-Business relationship and how these link to the e-supply chain transformation. More importantly, the paper provides a comprehensive discussion of the factors involved in the complete e-Business enterprise transformation.

Zarei and Naeli, in their paper entitled *"Critical Success Factors in Enterprise Resource Planning Implementation: A Case-Study Approach,"* study the ERP critical success/failure factors by using case study methodology. They aim at recognizing the critical success factors for ERP implementation by reviewing the most critical and relevant literature, examine the level of adhering to the identified success factors in a case study, and investigate the impacts of each critical success factor on ERP implementation and on the other factors in a selected company chosen for the case study. They select five most critical factors from the literatures and show the impacts of each factor on other factors and ERP success in the selected company. They conclude that ERP implementation is a very challenging and risky project for organizations and confirm the impacts of the five selected factors on the success of ERP implementation as mentioned in the literatures. Their results reveal that the five critical success factors are highly interdependent, and the strengths and weaknesses of each of them influence the quality of ERP implementation to a large extent.

The implementation of ERP systems requires huge investments. In spite of that, a considerable number of ERP implementation projects fail or take longer than initially planned. Previous studies have shown that the aim of rapid implementation of such projects has not been successful and the failure of the fundamental goals in these projects has imposed huge costs to investors and shareholders. These failures have reduced overall profits and resulted in skepticism among the managers and investors about the overall benefits of ERP systems. Hence, it is important to understand the factors that determine the success or failure of ERP implementation. Hanafizadeh et al., in their paper entitled *"The Core Critical Success Factors in Implementation of Enterprise Resource Planning Systems,"* study the critical success factors in implementing ERP systems and develop a conceptual model, which can serve as a basis for ERP project managers. These critical success factors, that are "core critical success factors," are extracted from 62 published papers using the content analysis and the entropy method. They verify their conceptual model in the context of five multinational companies.

Sankar, in his paper entitled *"Factors that Improve ERP Implementation Strategies in an Organization,"* presents an exploratory research aimed at identifying factors that led to the success of the enterprise resource planning (ERP) implementation at Robert Bosch GmbH during the period 1992-2004. He records snapshots of the implementation process at two points in time: 2000 and 2004. On each occasion, the Chief Information Officers in Stuttgart, Germany (corporate headquarters) and in Broadview, Illinois (the headquarters of Robert Bosch US) were interviewed. Sankar highlights (1) improving effectiveness of implementation, (2) identifying specific activities that impact the mass of resource endowments, (3) identifying activities that accelerate resource commitment, and (4) identifying the forceful activities that result as the findings of his study. These findings are useful for both academicians who teach and conduct research on ERP implementation strategies, and the practitioners who design and implement them. For practicing managers, he stresses the importance of leadership and communication. He argues that once an organization makes a choice to implement an ERP system, it is easy to make the assumption that the processes in the organization will be automatically streamlined and efficiencies improved. He shows in his case study that the choice of a system is only a part of the equation. Leadership, effective communication, and commitment of the information technology staff are essential to make the system deliver the expected results. He concludes that committing large resources to the project, adopting corporate standards that promote process harmonization, making a few lumpy important decisions that are irreversible, and obtaining support from top management are essential factors to consider when implementing ERP systems.

Outsourcing has become a major trend in various industries and business processes due to globalization and the development of information technology. This trend is not an exception to supply chain management. As logistics service providers become more experienced and sophisticated in their offerings, more and more firms are turning to logistics services providers for such activities as warehousing, packaging, order fulfillment, and transportation. However, the role of information technology and information systems in these outsourced activities is not very clear. In general, there is an agreement that information technology and information systems are the enablers of outsourcing; they help firms control outsourced activities, communicate with outsourced product and/or service providers, and eventually collaborate with third party logistics providers. Sometimes, however, information technology and information systems themselves are subject to outsourcing. What will happen to information technology and information systems when firms outsource supply chain processes? Joo et al., in their paper entitled "*Future State of Outsourcing Supply Chain Information Systems: An Analysis of Survey Results,*" attempt to answer this question by utilizing a survey approach. They show that some firms may utilize internal systems, some may outsource to the provider, while still others may outsource to supply chain management information systems providers. The purpose of their study is to acquire knowledge that will help clarify the direction of outsourcing from an information systems utilization perspective. Their study helps both practitioners and researchers understand outsourcing trends by industries, and in particular, the relationship between outsourced supply chain processes and information technologies/information systems. Their study is especially valuable to the firms that plan on outsourcing supply chain processes and/or information systems. They conclude that the future state of outsourcing supply chain information systems looks promising. They show that as the level of globalization increases, supply chain leaders will emerge, and the necessity for new robust information systems will follow. As outsourcing of supply chain processes grow at an approximate rate of twenty percent annually, outsourcing information systems will increase at about half that (ten percent annually). They argue that all functional areas will need information system support to provide the visibility of supply chain to all participants in the supply chain. The supply chain as a whole will increase in collaboration and communication in the future. Thus, information technology support will be needed to interface supply chain functions with other cross-functional areas, which will call for internal and external system support and maintenance.

Angeles, in her paper entitled "*Effects of Reciprocal Investments and Relational Interaction in Deploying RFID Supply Chain Systems,*" looks at the perceived ability of information technology infrastructure integration and supply chain process integration to moderate the relationship between business process specificity and domain knowledge specificity, and two dependent variables, reciprocal investments and relational interaction using the moderated regression procedure. Her results show that information technology infrastructure integration moderates the relationship between both business process specificity and relational interaction, and domain knowledge specificity and also, relational interaction. Her findings affirm the importance of both the information technology infrastructure integration and supply chain process integration elements that undergird RFID system implementation. She argues that managers need to be aware that current developments directly relate to these elements of the infrastructure environment as their firms seek either or both operational efficiency and market knowledge creation. She also emphasizes that planning for the design or reengineering of business processes to achieve cross-functional process integration and supply chain process integration is a very involved activity as well and one taken seriously by cutting-edge firms. She describes the five levels of business process integration identified in the literature for RFID systems: goal setting assessment, slap and ship, application integration, business process improvement, and collaborative business intelligence. She shows that cross-functional application integration and supply chain process integration are both clear issues in application integration and business process improvement levels. She further argue that managers should be aware of new technologies such as the use of smart RFID networks that would allow the use of event-driven RFID business applications and react to real-time information and assist the movement to business process improvement level. She confirms that complex RFID services could be delivered using real-time events such as pushing alerts to a retail store manager when inventory for a particular product is aging or has reached "stale" status. Finally, considering the scale and scope of RFID systems within a supply chain context, she concludes that managers need to anticipate the processing of the escalating numbers of events created by RFID technologies that will eventually lead to the generation of increasingly complex business rules that will govern the routing and analysis of signals included in the event stream.

The rush to technology has created several flaws when it comes to managing computers, applications, middleware, and information systems. As a result, organizations struggle to understand how all these elements are behaving. As enterprise architectures grow in significance and are acknowledged as advantageous artifacts to help manage change, their benefit to the organization has yet to be fully explored. Duarte and Vasconcelos, in their paper entitled "*Evaluating Enterprise Information Systems: Constructing a Model Processing Framework*," focus on the challenge of real-time information systems evaluation, using the enterprise architecture as a boundary object and a base for communication. They present a parallel between the field of phenomenology (which studies human and group experience and phenomena) and the acts of judging the behavior of architectural components by transforming their observable variables. They further propose an automated cycle of evaluation using the enterprise architecture as the standpoint and communication medium between all parties to help modelers, analysts and every participant in the enterprise community. Their solution is comprised of five major steps: establishing a strong conceptual base on the evaluation of information systems, defining a high level language for this activity, extending an architecture creation pipeline, creating a framework that automates it, and finally, implementing this framework. Their conceptual framework avoids imprecise definitions of quality and quality attributes. This conceptualization is materialized in a model-eval-display loop framework, and is implemented using model driven software development practices and tools. Finally, they apply prototype to a real-world scenario in order to verify the conceptual solution in practice.

The evolution of networks and large scale information systems has led to the rise of data sources that are usually distributed, heterogeneous, and autonomous. Yu, in his paper entitled "*Message-Based*

Approach to Master Data Synchronization among Autonomous Information Systems," presents a novel message-based approach to the synchronization of master data among multiple autonomous information systems. Different from traditional approaches based on database triggers, they adopt the optimistic bidirectional strategy with the process of two synchronization phases. By means of data service buses, they propagate synchronized master data through messages passing along star-like cascading routes. They show that their approach could resolve possible data conflicts automatically using predefined attribute confidences and deducible current value confidences respectively. Finally, they present a real-world case study about synchronizing datasets among four separate but related systems based on their novel message-based approach. They summarize that the message-based data synchronization framework is configured with shared data centers and service buses. It resolves master data conflicts with the help of attribute confidences and current value confidences, respectively. In other words, those from the system with higher confidence values are allowed to overwrite those from the system with lower ones. By means of data service buses, their framework propagates master data through messages passing along star-like cascading routes, and dumps master data in the shared centers. Their approach could ensure the reliable synchronization by message buffering under poor networking condition. They conclude that unlike the traditional trigger-based approaches, their approach is more flexible, extendable, and easier to provide the global data view.

Cloud computing has spread within the enterprise over the last five years much faster than many past information technology innovations. In cloud computing, computer services are accessed over the Internet in a scalable fashion, where the user is abstracted in varying degrees from the actual hardware and software and pays only for resources used. While the technology is increasingly well-understood by the enterprise, few know how to deploy cloud-based systems in the most effective and appropriate way within their specific organization. Arinze and Anandarajan, in their paper entitled "*Factors that Determine the Adoption of Cloud Computing: A Global Perspective*," study the adoption of cloud computing worldwide. They examine the potential of cloud computing to significantly impact computing in developing countries. They also review factors such as privacy rules, technological infrastructure, and regional laws to understand if there are latent factors that determine what types of cloud computing are adopted in various industries and regions. They propose that patterns of cloud computing adoption will vary by industry and by company type. They also suggest that cloud computing offers varying benefits and will appear differently in various regions across the world, enabling many users to obtain sophisticated computing architectures and applications that are cost-prohibitive for many to acquire locally. They scrutinize issues of privacy, security, and reliability of cloud computing and discuss the outlook for firms and individuals in both developing and developed countries seeking to utilize cloud computing for some or all of their computing needs. They conclude that the key to cloud computing is the software that handles user access and resource allocation among user applications, in a transparent manner, to many users, via a mix of computing devices. These devices are shared by multiple users, enabling higher server utilization rates and correspondingly lower user prices than is typically the case in dedicated server environments. They also suggest that such service elasticity and instant provisioning of new resources is a distinguishing feature of cloud computing, as well as increasing levels of reliability for provided services. Users need only pay for services used, so new applications can begin at a price point far lower than would be the case with dedicated private, or even hosted servers. Finally, they propose that cloud services can be brought online much quicker than would be the case in internal computing environments, often in a matter of minutes. This enables firms of all kinds to minimize their involvement in building and maintaining computing infrastructures, and instead, focus on their core competencies.

Ontology languages are emerging as the standard for capturing semantics on the Web. Over the past decade, the research community has focused on addressing how to define reusable ontologies or ontology parts or how to construct ontology from possibly independently developed components. Pradel et al., in their paper entitled *"A Good Role Model for Ontologies: Collaborations"* argue that ontologies are often not engineered in a component-based manner due to a lack of appropriate constructs in current ontology languages. This hampers reuse and makes creating new ontologies from existing building blocks difficult. They propose to apply the notion of roles and role modeling to ontologies and present an extension of the web ontology language for this purpose. Ontological role models allow for clearly separating different concerns of a domain and constitute an intuitive reuse unit. In this article, Pradel et al. introduce role modeling to ontologies. They show how role modeling can bring several benefits to ontologies and ontological modeling including: (1) more natural ontological modeling by separating roles from classes; (2) an appropriate notion and size of reusable ontological components - role models; and (3) separation of concerns by capturing a single concern in a role model. They make the case that role models constitute useful and natural units for component-based ontology engineering. Role models are developed as components and intended to be deployed as such, in contrast to existing approaches aimed at extracting ontological units from ontologies not necessarily designed to be modular. While they argue that modeling with roles is beneficial to ontological modeling and provides a new kind of component not previously considered for ontologies, the transition from object-orientation is not straightforward. Pradel et al. introduce modeling primitives to support roles in ontologies and a discussion of the main differences for role modeling between ontologies and object-oriented models. To convince the research community of the usefulness of role models, they demonstrate their use on two examples. The first example shows separation of concerns, and the second example demonstrates reuse of role models in different contexts. In conclusion, they argue that role models provide an interesting reuse abstraction for ontologies, and roles should be supported as an ontological primitive.

Developing new software based on requirements specifications created by business analysts may lead to misunderstanding because of the different backgrounds of the people involved in the systems analysis and design phase of systems development life cycle. Due to the multidisciplinary nature of systems development, in times of offshoring there are different cultures involved, there are always people with different apprenticeships (business analysts, software engineers, documentation engineers, etc.), which hinders a common understanding of the terms used. This obstacle can be resolved if requirements specifications have a clearly defined structure and comprehensive semantics. Only with the application of linguistics-based modeling methods and a semantic annotation of the terms adopted in requirements specifications can these obstacles be overcome. Lautenbacher et al., in their paper entitled *"Linguistics-Based Modeling Methods and Ontologies in Requirements Engineering,"* propose to structure the requirements specifications using existing linguistics-based modeling methods and annotate the used terms with ontologies to enhance the understanding and reuse of these documents during the software engineering process. In their article, Lautenbacher et al. describe the challenges of current documents and the difference of understanding some data between sender and recipient. They describe their definition of data and how the communication between different persons takes place. They also show how different linguistics-based modeling methods can be used to clarify the underlying meaning of terms. They evaluate several linguistics-based modeling methods and show a summary of their evaluation. They use an example to clarify the application of the modeling methods as well as introduce the process and benefits of semantic annotation through the usage of ontologies. They conclude with the benefits of using linguistics-based modeling methods and ontologies.

Semantic user interfaces are sets of interrelated, static, and domain specific documents with layout and content, whose interpretation is defined through semantic decoration. Semantic user interfaces are declarative in nature as they allow program composition by the users themselves at the user interface level. The operation of semantic user interface-based applications follow a service-oriented approach where their elements referenced in user requests are automatically mapped to reusable service provider components, whose contracts are specified in domain ontologies. This assures semantic separation of user interface components from elements of the underlying application system infrastructure. Tilly and Porkoláb, in their paper entitled *"Semantic User Interfaces,"* present the architecture and components of a semantic user interface framework along with the basic elements of semantic user interface documents and their relevant properties of domain ontologies. They also explain the representation and operation of semantic user interface applications through a motivating example. They conclude with the following important advantages of the semantic user interface documents: (1) separation of concerns between stakeholders; (2) platform and device independence; (3) user interaction simplification; (4) learnability; and (5) reusability.

Standards play a major role in a firm's operational effectiveness and often make the difference between success and failure. A new class of compatibility standards known as vertical standards has emerged in the last decade. Vertical standards focus on business processes and data formats specific to individual industries and are generally implemented using the eXtensible Markup Language (XML) due to its flexibility and extensibility. Mendoza and Ravichandran in their paper entitled *"Drivers of Organizational Participation in XML-Based Industry Standardization Efforts"* explore the motivation for participation in the development of vertical standards for supply-side (i.e. vendors) and demand-side (i.e. end-users) organizations in the face of these linked dilemmas. They test two linear regression models using constructs that explore the effect of resource and interest heterogeneity in the participation of supply-side and demand-side firms in XML-based vertical standards development activities. Their results provide evidence of the existence of passive adopters in vertical standards development activities, and highlight the need for further work to understand the extent of supply-side influence in development activities. Their results also show there may be greater vendor influence in vertical standards development than previously understood, even as end-users retain strategic control of the development path. While supply-side participation seems driven by commercial business interests, demand-side participation is motivated by protecting compatibility with existing investments in business processes and data formats, while minimizing investment. Their data provides an empirical confirmation of the presence of passive adopters in vertical standards development. This is an important finding for supply-side organizations, because it confirms their participation in standards development efforts can generate business opportunities before standards completion. Suppliers can become sources of expertise to demand-side organizations to help them understand the applicability and functionality of the emerging standard and reducing barriers to later diffusion. Confirmation of the existence of passive adopter behavior is also important for demand-side organizations, because passive adoption may allow supply-side firms to take control of the strategic direction of vertical standards development activities, or to manipulate vertical standards compatibility to introduce switching costs, as has been observed with physical products. They conclude that these findings should be of interest to standards-developing organizations, because they show that it is possible to exploit industry standards based on open technologies, such as XML, for competitive advantage during the development cycle, and not only during or after the adoption stage. They propose that additional research is necessary to determine how standards-developing organizations solve resource problems when faced with passive adopters. It is possible passive adopters withhold participation and resources in exchange for a commitment to adopt the end result, without which the adoption stage may fail.

In a follow-up paper, entitled "*An Empirical Evaluation of the Assimilation of Industry-Specific Data Standards Using Firm-Level and Community-Level Constructs,*" Mendoza and Ravichandran show that vertical standards are complex technologies with an organizational adoption locus, but subject to inter-organizational dependence and network effects. They argue that understanding the assimilation process for vertical standards requires that both firm- and industry-level effects be considered simultaneously. They develop and evaluate a two-level model of organizational assimilation that includes both firm- and industry-level effects. The study was conducted in collaboration with OASIS, a leading cross-industry standards-development organization, and with ACORD, the principal standards-development organization for the insurance and financial services industries. Their results confirm the usefulness of incorporating firm-level and community-level constructs in the study of complex networked technologies. Specifically, their reconceptualization of the classical diffusion of innovations theory concepts of relative advantage and complexity are shown to be appropriate and significant in predicting vertical standards assimilation. Additionally, they show community-level constructs such as orphaning risk and standard legitimation to be important predictors of assimilation.

Many different Web development methodologies have been proposed to address different aspects of Web application development. Applications involving Semantic Web service technology require the inclusion of new components. Therefore, Web development methodologies must be tailored to support the systematic development of such new components. Sánchez et al., in their paper entitled "*Toward UML-Compliant Semantic Web Services Development,*" focus on the study of object constraint language as a tool to refine the unified modeling language profile in order to represent the axiom definition using a language closer to the perspective of software developers. As part of unified modeling language family, they consider object constraint language to be a good choice as a means to represent logical expressions. They also validate the adoption of object constraint language for the representation through several case studies.

Several systems integration proposals have been suggested over the years. However, most of these proposals have do not allow users to take advantage of services offered by Web portals. Most of them only provide a set of design principles to build integrated systems and lack in suggesting a systematic way of how to develop systems based on the integration architecture they propose. Acuña et al., in their paper entitled "*Integrating Web Portals with Semantic Web Services: A Case Study,*" review a Web portal integration architecture called PISA, and a Web portal integration architecture for data and services, called MIDAS-S. They present a case study to show how both architectures fit together integrating Web portals.

The utilization of version control systems is a prerequisite in successful collaborative software development. Over the past decade, a multitude of pessimistic as well as optimistic version control systems has emerged for model artifacts. Pessimistic approaches follow the lock-edit-unlock paradigm, whereas optimistic approaches allow parallel editing of one resource. The optimistic approaches are preferred to the pessimistic ones. Such tools should be independent of the modeling environment and applicable to various modeling languages to be flexible for the ever increasing variety of modeling environments and languages. Those version control systems characteristics may implicate a lack of information for the conflict detection method by virtue of firstly receiving solely the state of an artifact without concrete editing operations and secondly due to unavailable knowledge about the semantics of a modeling language. However, in optimistic version control systems concurrent changes can result in conflicts and inconsistencies. In environment and language independent version control systems inconsistencies would even arise more often due to information losses. Therefore, accurate conflict detection methods are indispensable for the realization of such version control systems. Altmanninger et al., in their paper entitled "*Semantics for Accurate Conflict Detection in SMoVer: Specification, Detection and Presentation by Example*," tackle this task by proposing the semantically enhanced model version control system (SMoVer). They show that With SMoVer it is possible to specify the semantics of a modeling language, needed for conflict detection in order to provide more accurate conflict reports than other current environment and language independent version control systems. They show how semantics of a specific modeling language can be specified in SMoVer, how those specifications can improve the accuracy of conflict reports, and finally how those can be presented to modelers.

Madjid Tavana
La Salle University, USA

Section 1
Emerging Enterprise Resource Planning Strategies

Chapter 1
Extending the Technology Acceptance Model to Investigate the Utilization of ERP Systems

Samar Mouakket
University of Sharjah, UAE

ABSTRACT

The implementation of Enterprise Recourse Planning (ERP) systems has grown rapidly, but limited research has been conducted to investigate the utilization of ERP systems. By extending the Technology Acceptance Model, this paper provides a research model for examining the impact of computer self-efficacy and ERP systems design features on the utilization of ERP systems. To test the proposed research model, data are collected through a questionnaire survey distributed among employees in different organizations that have implemented an ERP system in the United Arab Emirates. Structural equation modeling techniques are used in this study to verify the causal relationships between the variables. The results strongly support the extended TAM in understanding employees' utilization of ERP systems. The implications of this study and further research opportunities are also discussed.

INTRODUCTION

The implementation of Enterprise Resource Planning (ERP) systems by organizations has grown rapidly world-wide in recent years in the aim of achieving better business performance and sustaining competitive advantages (Mabert et al.,

2000; Van Everdingen et al., 2000; Olhager & Selldin, 2003; Lin et al., 2006). An ERP system is an integrated set of software packages that help organizations integrate their information flow and business processes by using a single database that collects and stores data with a standardized user interface (Gable, 1998; Aladwani, 2001; Abdinnour-Helm et al., 2003; Shih, 2006; Osei-Bryson et al., 2008). ERP systems can benefit organizations in

DOI: 10.4018/978-1-4666-1761-2.ch001

different ways such as enabling faster information transactions, increasing productivity, maintaining tightened supply chain links, reducing inventory costs, improving business processes, and increasing customer responsiveness (Li, 1999; Davenport, 2000; Abdinnour-Helm et al., 2003; Umble et al., 2003; Calisir & Calisir, 2004).

Despite the growth in ERP system implementation, research shows a growing dissatisfaction with ERP systems arguing that they have failed to deliver the anticipated benefits (Holland, et al., 1998; Gable, et al., 1998, Bingi et al., 1999). ERP systems are found to be difficult to learn and use, very costly, and time consuming to implement (Davenport, 1998; Mabert et al, 2000; Bagchi et al., 2003). These findings show that research in the different factors that enable a successful adoption of this type of information systems is very essential.

Researchers have developed different models to study users' perception of information systems (IS). One of the most frequently employed models is the Technology Acceptance Model (TAM) (Davis, 1989), which is an adaptation of the Theory of Reasoned Action (TRA) (Fishbein & Ajzen, 1975; Ajzen & Fishbein, 1980) but with more focus on user acceptance of information systems (IS). Because a considerable body of work on IS acceptance and adoption has been conducted as a result of TAM, it has become an important model when investigating user acceptance of a new information technology (Adams et al., 1992; Taylor & Todd, 1995; Yi & Hwang, 2003; Bueno & Salmeron, 2008; Hernandez et al., 2008; Hamner & Qazi, 2009).

TAM posits that perceived ease of use of a technology (PEOU) and perceived usefulness (PU) determine a person's behavior towards the technology. But PEOU and PU are also influenced by exogenous variables, which vary according to the context. Thus, Davis (1989) and later Davis (1993) have suggested adding exogenous variables to TAM as a way of improving the original model. Accordingly, the main objective of this research is to investigate the influence of exogenous variables on TAM and IS acceptance.

In this paper, we are extending TAM to investigate employees' utilization of ERP systems in the United Arab Emirates (UAE). In our proposed model, computer self-efficacy (CSE) and ERP systems design features affect perceived usefulness and perceived ease of use, which in turn affect ERP system utilization. The goal of this paper is to explore these relationships to determine whether the addition of CSE and ERP systems design features to the TAM increases its predictive or explanatory power.

Although the rate of ERP implementation failure has been rather high (Amaoko-Gyampah & Salam, 2004; Chang et al., 2008; Bueno & Salmeron, 2008; Youngberg et al., 2009), IS researchers have paid little attention to this technology. Thus, we feel that research into employees' utilization of ERP systems should be investigated and studied further. In addition, most published research conducted on ERP systems has been undertaken in America and western countries with limited knowledge of ERP system utilization in the Gulf region, particularly in the UAE. In fact, we believe that our research is the only one attempting to investigate the utilization of ERP systems in the UAE, and we hope the findings will contribute to the body of knowledge in that specific area.

The remainder of the paper is organized as follows: The second section summarizes previous research on ERP systems. The third section proposes the research model and presents the hypotheses. The fourth section introduces the research methodology to be used in this work, the analysis of the data collected and the results reached. The data has been analyzed using structural equation modeling (SEM) to evaluate the strength of the hypothesized relationship. The conclusion and practical implications of the research are presented in the fifth section. The article concludes with presenting the limitations and directions for further research.

PREVIOUS RESEARCH ON THE APPLICATION OF TAM ON ERP SYSTEMS

Recently, researchers have applied TAM to study and explain user's adoption of ERP systems (Amoako-Gyampah & Salam, 2004; Gefen, 2004; Nah et al., 2004; Hwang, 2005; Amoako-Gyampah, 2007; Wu & Wang, 2007; Sun et al., 2009; Younberg et al., 2009, Calisir et al., 2009). Sun et al. (2009) have extended TAM to include one dimension of the technology task fit model, which is perceived work compatibility, to investigate users' IS usage intention, actual usage, and performance of 138 users of ERP systems in 62 organizations in China. They have found that perceived work compatibility can be a valuable diagnostic tool for companies wanting to evaluate the extent to which their internal operations are compatible with the rest of the industry.

The study by Younberg et al. (2009) examined technology acceptance variables for highly educated, professional users of an ERP component to understand significant variables' correlation and predictive effects on perceived usefulness and usage constructs. They have found that job relevance, output quality and perceived ease of use influence users' perception of technology usefulness. Bueno and Salmeron (2008) have extended TAM to test the influence of specific critical success factors (CSFs) on ERP implementation. The members of the sample are information systems directors from organizations that have decided to implement an ERP system. The findings show the importance of the role of top management support, communication, cooperation, training, and technological complexity systems on the behavioral intention to use ERP systems.

Amoako-Gyampah (2007) has investigated the influence of perceived usefulness, user involvement, argument for change, prior usage and ease of use on the behavioral intention to use an ERP system. A mail survey has been used to collect data in a specific organization that has implemented an ERP system. He has found that users' perception of perceived usefulness, ease of use of the ERP system, and the users' level of intrinsic involvement all affect their intention to use this technology. The results seem to suggest that managerial efforts aimed at increasing the users' perceptions of usefulness and personal relevance of this technology will contribute to system implementation success.

Bradely and Lee (2007) focus on the effect of training and training satisfaction on the acceptance of an ERP system in a mid-size university. They have found that post implementation training satisfaction is related to perceived ease of use, while current training satisfaction and user participation are related to perceived usefulness. They conclude that although training is important when implementing a new ERP system, training budget in reality is usually cut as projects face problems in cost and time.

In summary, the application of TAM to ERP systems implementation appears to be a complex issue, since we need both organizational and individual points of view. Thus, more research is needed to understand the factors behind making ERP systems work successfully.

RESEARCH MODEL AND HYPOTHESES

In this research, we have investigated the effect of computer self-efficacy and ERP systems design features on TAM. Figure 1 presents the proposed model showing the suggested exogenous factors affecting PEOU and PU which in turn affect employees' utilization of ERP systems.

Computer Self-Efficacy (CSE)

Computer self efficacy is defined as the ability of an individual to use the computer to perform a specific task (Compeau & Higgins, 1995; Marakas et al., 1998). Studies of computer self-efficacy

Figure 1. The proposed research model

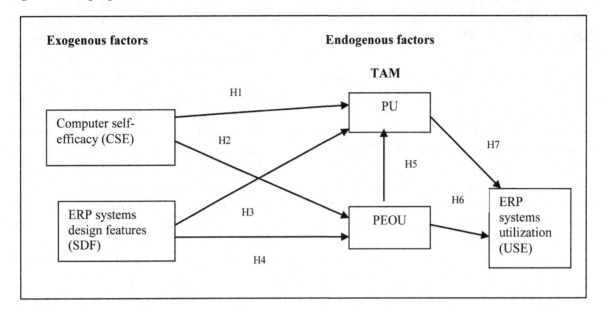

suggest that computer self-efficacy is a significant determinant of an individual's decision to use computers through ease of use and usefulness (Venkatesh & Davis, 1996; Igbaria & Livari, 1995; Venkatesh & Davis, 2000; Hung & Liang, 2001). For example, Venkatesh and Davis (2000) have found that computer self-efficacy strongly influence PEOU, and suggest that training is important to improve user computer self-efficacy which will consequently lead to user acceptance of the IS. Wang et al. (2003) have found that computer self-efficacy has a positive effect on both perceived ease of use and perceived usefulness, which consequently affects the intention to use online banking in Taiwan.

Within the context of ERP systems, the study of Shih (2006) reveals that computer self-efficacy is an important factor in explaining the ERP usage behavior, as he has found that computer self-efficacy significantly, positively and directly affects PEOU and PU. Similarly, Shih and Huang (2009) have shown that computer self-efficacy has a significant influence on perceived usefulness when implementing ERP systems. Thus, the following hypotheses are formulated:

Hypothesis 1: Computer self-efficacy positively influences perceived usefulness.
Hypothesis 2: Computer self-efficacy positively influences perceived ease of use.

ERP Systems Design Features

Design features can be defined as any information, components, and features used in developing IS. These elements can be an influential factor in determining users' perceptions and attitudes toward IS. Many studies have identified the design elements that can be considered significantly essential to users of IS (Henderson et al., 1995; Zhang & Dran, 2000, 2001, 2002; Aladwani & Palvia, 2002; Jaspers et al., 2004; Shergill & Chen, 2005; Ozen & Basoglu, 2007; Seneler et al., 2008). Nielsen (1999) points out the following important elements of design that determine the success or failure of a Web site: speed, quality of a search mechanism, clarity of structure and navigation. Another important factor affecting quality of service is system speed. Nielsen (1997) believes that speed must be the overriding design criterion, and argues that users need a response time of less than one second, moving from one page to another. Hausman and Siekpe (2009) believe that improved website design can encourage users to complete transactions smoothly and attract them to revisit the website, while bad design would hinder their movement in the website and eventually discourage them from revisiting the website.

Within the context of ERP systems, limited research has focused on understanding the ways in which users interact with this technology and the influence of design features on users' attitudes towards it. Eason (1988) argues that users will become less willing to put up with difficult interfaces of ERP systems and search for alternatives when IS development fails to meet user needs. Calisir and Calisir (2004) examine the effects of interface usability characteristics (namely system capability, compatibility, flexibility, user guidance, learnability, and minimal memory load) on end-user satisfaction with ERP systems in a study with 51 users in 24 companies. They have found that interface usability characteristics have a strong impact on perceived usefulness which in turn affects end-user satisfaction. They recommend that ERP system designers should pay more attention to user requirements analysis to determine their expectations for the content of ERP systems.

Singh and Wesson (2009) believe that the complexity of ERP systems user interfaces negatively affects the usability of these systems. A case study approach was used to verify a set of proposed usability heuristics in terms of their ability to identify the potential usability issues with a specific ERP system, namely SAP. The suggested usability heuristics have been adapted from Nielson's set of heuristics. The heuristic evaluation was conducted using a task-based approach, involving the use of three usability experts working at SAP Research in South Africa. The experts were asked to complete two scenarios (add a customer and process a sales order) on SAP. The case study shows that the proposed ERP heuristics not only supported the usability issues identified with Nielsen's ten heuristics but also identified new usability issues that were not identified with them. The researchers believe that the combined set of ERP heuristics can be applied to improve the usability of existing ERP systems.

This study believes that employees in the UAE will consider ERP systems design features to be an important factor affecting PEOU and PU. Thus, the following hypotheses are proposed:

Hypothesis 3: ERP systems design features positively influence perceived usefulness.
Hypothesis 4: ERP systems design features positively influence perceived ease of use.

PEOU and PU

According to TAM, user's attitude towards the use of information systems (IS) is determined by perceived usefulness (PU) and perceived ease of use (PEOU). The TAM considers these two factors to be of great importance for any acceptance of a new information system (Davis, 1989). PEOU is defined as the degree to which the user expects the information system to be easy to use (Davis, 1989). In other words, the easier one finds the IS, the more likely he or she will use it. PU, on the other hand, considers user's attitude towards an IS will increase his or her performance (Davis, 1989). As suggested by TAM, PEOU is seen to have a significant direct effect on PU and attitude (Davis et al., 1989; Venkatesh & Davis, 2000). In other words, the less effort it takes an individual to use a system, the more useful it can be to him/her, which in turn can increase his/her performance. Calisir and Calisir (2004) have examined the effects of interface usability characteristics, perceived usefulness, and perceived ease of use on end-user satisfaction with ERP systems in a study with 51 users in 24 companies. They have found that perceived ease of use has an indirect effect on satisfaction via perceived usefulness, indicating that users consider ERP systems less useful if they find them difficult to use. In their study of the factors that influence the ERP system users' acceptance and use, Bueno and Salmeron (2008) have found that perceived usefulness of an ERP system depends on the perceived ease of use. Similar results have been reached by Shih (2006), Hwang (2005), Amoako-Gyampah (2007), and Calisir et al. (2009). Thus, the current research investigates the following hypothesis:

Hypothesis 5: Perceived ease of use positively influences perceived usefulness.

In addition, evidence has shown that PEOU and PU have an influence on user's attitude towards IS (Davis et al., 1989; Venkatesh & Davis, 1996; Venkatesh & Morris, 2000). Chang (2008) has applied TAM to identify consumers' acceptance of intelligent agent (IA) technology for the automation of auction websites. He has found that perceived usefulness is the most influential factor in promoting intention to use an auction website. Hwang (2005) has found that both perceived ease of use and perceived usefulness positively influence user's attitude towards ERP systems. Similarly, a study of Amoako-Gyampah (2007) in a large global organization that was implementing an ERP system, specifically SAP, have revealed that perceived usefulness and ease of use have direct positive and significant effects on behavioral intention towards this system. Consistent with previous findings, this research suggests that:

Hypothesis 6: Perceived ease of use positively influences ERP systems utilization.

Hypothesis 7: Perceived usefulness positively influences ERP systems utilization.

RESEARCH METHODOLOGY

Instrument Development and Subjects

According to our proposed model, we have extended TAM with Computer self-efficacy and ERP systems design features constructs. A five point

Likert type scale ranging from one being "strongly agree" to five being "strongly disagree" is used to collect data on each of the following constructs: CSE, ERP systems design features, PU, PEOU, and ERP systems utilization.

This research uses the survey method to test its hypotheses. A questionnaire consisting of six parts has been developed and administered. The questionnaire is composed of 33 questions, unambiguous and easy for respondents to complete. The first part (eight questions) involves demographic questions designed to solicit information about the respondent. The next four parts include 25 items divided as the following: four items are used to measure computer self-efficacy (CSE), six items are used to measure perceived ease of use (PEOU), five items are used to measure perceived usefulness (PU), seven items are used to measure the ERP systems design feature (SDF), and three items are used to measure employee's utilization of ERP systems (USE).

The items of the questionnaire have been constructed based on an extensive review of the literature in the area of information system implementation. The scales to measure PU, PEOU and ERP systems utilization have been taken from previously validated IS related studies on TAM (Davis, 1989; Wang et al., 2003; Shergill & Chen, 2005; Al-Somali et al., 2009), which have established their reliability and validity. The measures of CSE have been also adapted from validated IS related studies on TAM (Wang et. al, 2003; Hu et al., 2003; Shih, 2006; Shih & Huang, 2009), which have established their reliability and validity. The measures of ERP systems design features have been drawn from previously related IS studies on TAM (Jaruwachirathanakul & Fink, 2005; Shergill & Chen, 2005; Ha & Stoel, 2009), which have also established their reliability and validity. The questionnaire items used to measure each construct are presented in Table 1.

The questionnaire has been administered by hand to a convenient sample of 550 employees (UAE nationals and non-UAE nationals) working

Table 1. Summary of the measurement scales

Construct	Measurement items
Computer self-efficacy (CSE)	CSE1 - I can usually deal with most difficulties I encounter when using the ERP system
	CSE2 - I am very confident in my abilities to use the ERP system
	CSE3 - I am confident in using the ERP system if somebody shows me how to use it first
	CSE4 - I am confident in using the ERP system even if I have only online instructions for reference
Perceived ease of use (PEOU)	PEOU1 - Learning to use the ERP systems is easy for me
	PEOU2 - It is easy to do what I want to do using the ERP system
	PEOU3 - Using the ERP system is clear and understandable
	PEOU4 - Interaction with the ERP system is clear and understandable
	PEOU5 - It is easy to become skillful at using ERP system
	PEOU6 - Using the ERP system is easy
Perceived usefulness (PU)	PU1 - Using the ERP system enables me to complete my work more quickly
	PU2 - Using the ERP system has made my work easy
	PU3 - Using the ERP system saves me time
	PU4 - I find using the ERP system useful in my work
	PU5 - Using the ERP system has increased my job productivity
ERP system design features (SDF)	SDF1 - I face no problems with using the services of the ERP system
	SDF2 - The ERP system does not contain any technical-oriented jargon which are not explained
	SDF3 - The ERP system executes transactions quickly and efficiently
	SDF4 - The ERP system design and navigation makes it comfortable to conduct a transaction
	SDF5 - The ERP system presents the information clearly
	SDF6 - Steps to complete the ERP system transactions are too easy
	SDF7 - The information is quick to download
Utilization of ERP systems (USE)	USE1 - I have used the ERP system
	USE2 - I strongly recommend the use of the ERP system
	USE3 - I will increase my use of the ERP system

in different medium and large size, private and public organizations in two major cities in the UAE, namely Dubai and Abu-Dhabi. The study samples target organizations which have implemented an ERP system. After gaining permission from the officials of the organizations, the questionnaire has been distributed by hand on the premises and later was collected also by hand from the employees who filled the questionnaire. 365 responses have been received. After eliminating incomplete responses, we selected 344 usable responses as the final sample. The final response rate is 62.54%, which is acceptable for research purpose.

Demographic data, with single item questions, are gathered about the participants. Detailed descriptive statistics of the respondents' characteristics are shown in Table 2. As Table 2 indicates, the sample is almost evenly split between males (51.2%) and females (48.8%). The percentage of non-UAE nationals is relatively higher (64.3% to 35.7%) because, according to the latest UAE government statistics, UAE nationals constitute less than 20% of the total UAE population. 58.4% of the employees hold a university degree, while

41.6% do not hold a university degree. 56.4% of the employees are either managers or administrators while 39.5% work in technical related jobs. 57.3% of the employees who participate in this survey are between the age 36 and 45. More than 50% of the employees who participate in this survey earn between 76,000 and 149,999 Dirham a year (The dirham=$3.68). The majority of the employees who participate have used either SAP (37.2%) or Oracle application (34.0%). Finally, the proportion of employees from private companies is higher than that in public institutions (57.3% to 42.7%).

Analysis Results

A statistical analysis has been performed to test the relationships between the different research variables using structural equation modeling (SEM), which is the preferred approach for analyzing interactions between multiple independent and dependent variables, such as the ones used in our model. First, the measurement model is estimated to assess reliabilities and validities of the different variables. Second, the structural model is estimated to test the relationships among CSE, ERP systems design features, PU, PEOU, and ERP systems utilization.

Measurement Model

A confirmatory factor analysis (CFA) using SPSS-AMOS is performed to test the measurement model. As suggested by Hair et al. (2006), a factor should have a minimum of two items and each item factor loading should be greater than 0.35 for a sample size of 250. As a result of the confirmatory factor analysis, the following five items have been excluded due to low factor loadings (less than 0.35): one item has been removed from CSE, one item has been removed from PEOU, two items have been removed from PU, and one item has been removed from SDF. A new measurement model, containing 20 use-

Table 2. Descriptive statistics of respondents' characteristics

Item	Percentage (%)
Gender	
176 male	51.2
168 female	48.8
Nationality	
123 (UAE national)	35.7
221 (Non-UAE national)	64.3
University Degree	
201 (Yes)	58.4
143 (No)	41.6
Job category	
106 (Managerial)	30.8
88 (Administrative)	25.6
136 (Technical)	39.5
14 (Other)	4.1
Age	
4 (< 25)	1.2
112 (26-35)	32.5
197 (36- 45)	57.3
29 (46-55)	8.4
2 (>55)	0.6
Average yearly income (UAE Dirham)	
13 (<=49,999)	3.8
63 (50,000-75,999)	18.4
120 (76,000-99,999)	34.0
81 (100,000-149,999)	23.6
67 (>=150,000)	20.2
ERP systems used	
117 (Oracle Applications)	34.0
38 (Microsoft Dynamics)	11.0
59 (PeopleSoft)	17.2
128 (SAP)	37.2
2 (Baan)	0.6
Organization type	
147 (Public)	42.7
197 (Private)	57.3

ful items, has been derived after conducting the CFA. Table 3 shows the factor loadings and the fit indices of the improved measurement model. All the standardized factor loadings are significant and are above the acceptable level of 0.35.

The fit of the indicator to the construct and construct reliability and validity have been tested for the measurement model. First, the reliability of each measurement scale is computed by applying the Cronbach's alpha. The overall measures are reported in Table 3. As shown in Table 3, the

Table 3. CFA factor loadings of improved scale

Construct	Measures	Factor loading
Computer self-efficacy (CSE) Composite reliability= 0.915 Variance extract= 0.785 Cronbach's α= 0.801	CSE1	.795
	CSE2	.842
	CSE3	.681
Perceived ease of use (PEOU) Composite reliability= 0.936 Variance extract= 0.732 Cronbach's α=.766	PEOU1	.779
	PEOU2	.803
	PEOU3	.635
	PEOU4	.725
	PEOU5	.713
Perceived usefulness (PU) Composite reliability= 0.937 Variance extract= 0.833 Cronbach's α=.730	PU1	.891
	PU2	.874
	PU3	.765
System design features (SDF) Composite reliability= 0.947 Variance extract= 0.751 Cronbach's α=.841	SDF1	.761
	SDF2	.717
	SDF3	.841
	SDF4	.855
	SDF5	.792
	SDF6	.771
Utilization of ERP systems (USE) Composite reliability= 0.917 Variance extract= 0.787 Cronbach's α=.757	USE1	.766
	USE2	.820
	USE3	.748

reliability coefficients range from 0.730 to 0.841, which is higher than the acceptable level of 0.70 agreed in the literature (Nunnally, 1978; Nunnally & Bernstein, 1994; Hair et al., 2006). Second, the composite reliability and average variance extracted for each construct is evaluated. Table 3 shows that all constructs have shown acceptable composite reliability and average variance by exceeding the 0.50 suggested value by Fornell and Larcker (1981). The results in Table 3 confirm that the scales used in this study are both reliable and valid.

The proposed model shows an acceptable level of fit with the sample data, based on the assessment criteria of several common model-fit measurements. Table 4 shows that the value of CMIN/DF (766.852/175) is 4.382, which is acceptable. The

value of GFI is .918, which is above the suggested value of 0.90. The values of the normalized and the comparative fit indices NFI and CFI are .908 and .912, which are above the suggested estimates of 0.90, and finally the value of RMSEA is 0.04 (the suggested value <= 0.05).

Structural Model

The structural model suggested in this study has been tested using SPSS/AMOS. The results (Table 4) show an acceptable fit of the proposed structural model with relative chi-square (CMIN/DF) = 4.456, root mean square residual (REMSEA) = 0.04, goodness-of-fit index (GFI) = 0.912, normed-fit-index (NFI) = 0.904, and the comparative fit index (CFI) = 0.910. Table 5 shows that hypothesis tests support all postulated paths except for one, namely H1. Figure 2 displays the standardized path coefficients and significance levels.

Hypotheses 1 and 2 examine the impact of computer self-efficacy (CSE) on perceived ease of use (PEOU) and perceived usefulness (PU). The results indicate that CSE has a significant impact on PEOU (ß=0.291), while CSE has no significant impact on PU (ß=0.088). Thus, we conclude that H1 has not been supported, while H2 has been supported.

Hypotheses 3 and 4 test the relationship between ERP systems design features and the following variables: PEOU and PU. Results show that ERP systems design features positively influence both PEOU (ß=0.584) and PU (ß=0.394). Thus, the two hypotheses are supported.

Hypotheses 5, 6 and 7 investigate the associations between PU, PEOU, and utilization of ERP systems. The findings reveal that employees' utilization of ERP systems is influenced by both PEOU (ß=0.471) and PU (ß=0.213). In addition, the results indicate that PEOU has a significant impact on PU (ß=0.349). We conclude that all three hypotheses have been supported.

Table 4. Measures of the overall fit for the measurement and the structural models

	CMIN/DF (chi square/degree of freedom ratio) (<=5)	Goodness-of-fit (GFI) (>.90)	Normed fit index (NFI) (>.90)	Comparative fit index (CFI) (>.90)	Root mean square residual (RMSEA) (<=.05)
The measurement model	4.382	0.918	0.908	0.912	0.04
The structural model	4.456	0.912	0.904	0.910	0.04

DISCUSSION AND IMPLICATIONS

This study empirically investigates the indirect effects of two exogenous factors, computer self-efficacy and ERP systems design features, on determinants of IS acceptance as outlined in TAM. The aim is to provide useful and interesting results regarding employee utilization of ERP systems. The results provide strong support for both the suitability of TAM for explaining ERP systems utilization and the extension of TAM with computer self-efficacy and ERP systems design features constructs to enhance the original model. The findings also suggest new and promising areas for further research in employee's utilization of ERP systems.

The study has found that computer self-efficacy positively and directly affects PEOU but surprisingly has no effect on PU. Since, CSE has demonstrated a positive direct effect on perceived ease of use; we can suggest that it has an indirect positive effect on utilization of ERP systems. This supports the suggestion that TAM provides

a basis for mapping the effects of exogenous factors (Davis, 1989). Many studies have addressed the relationship between CSE and perceived ease of use (Venkatesh & Davis, 1996; Chau, 2001; Ma & Liu, 2004, Thong et al., 2002; Luarn & Lin 2005; Hasan, 2006, 2007; Amin, 2007). Hu et al. (2003) have found that CSE has a positive effect on perceived ease of use before and after 130 school teachers attended an intensive training program on Microsoft PowerPoint. Ong et al. (2004) have found that CSE has a significant effect on perceived ease of use when investigating the acceptance of an e-learning system among 140 engineers.

As a result of the positive relationship between CSE and PEOU, many researchers have suggested training as an important method of improving CSE (Gist et al., 1987; Compeau & Higgins, 1995; Salanova et al., 2000; Chou, 2001; Torkzadeh & van Dyk, 2001). Venkatesh and Davis (1996) have proposed that training programs aiming at improving computer self-efficacy can be effective in increasing system use. Torkzadeh and van Dyke

Table 5. Summary of results of the hypothesis testing (S: Supported, NS: Not supported)

Hypothesis	Result of testing
H1: *Computer self-efficacy positively influences perceived usefulness.*	NS
H2: *Computer self-efficacy positively influences perceived ease of use.*	S
H3: *ERP systems design features positively influence perceived usefulness.*	S
H4: *ERP systems design features positively influence perceived ease of use.*	S
H5: *Perceived ease of use positively influences perceived usefulness.*	S
H6: *Perceived ease of use positively influences ERP systems utilization.*	S
H7: *Perceived usefulness positively influences ERP systems utilization.*	S

Figure 2. Summary of standardized path coefficients and significance levels. Insignificant path is dotted

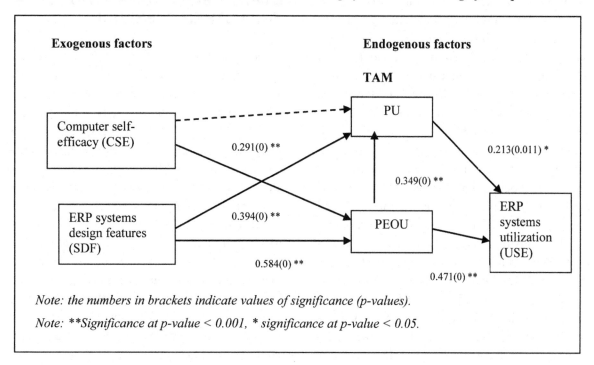

Note: the numbers in brackets indicate values of significance (p-values).

Note: **Significance at p-value < 0.001, * significance at p-value < 0.05.

(2001) have demonstrated that computer training has significantly improved the CSE of males and females. Shih (2004) and Laughlin (1999) have also shown that training may be considered the most widely recognized critical success factor. Therefore, we suggest that managers put more efforts on system training which will increase employees' utilization of ERP systems.

The study has also found that CSE does not significantly influence perceived usefulness, which is consistent with the results of previous studies which have reported a negative and insignificant relationship between the two constructs (Igbaria & Iivari, 1995; Chau, 2001). One explanation may be that individuals with low level of self-efficacy cannot understand the usefulness of the system because they are more concerned about their ability to learn how to use the system (Kuo et al., 2004).

The findings of this research have also shown that ERP design features have great impact on perceived ease of use and perceived usefulness, which in turn affect employee utilization of this

service. Similar findings have been reached by other researchers in IS studies (Suganthi et al., 2001; Hausman & Siekpe, 2009). Thong et al. (2002) have pointed out the importance of interface or system characteristics of an information system as a determining factor of users' adoption behavior. Thus, the results should be of interest to IS designers who want their products to be eventually accepted and used. IS designers should pay attention not only to usefulness and ease of use of the system, but also to its design features. Hence, vendors need to improve ERP systems designs and navigation, and increase the ease with which employees can browse through different modules. The more the employee feels comfortable with the features of the website, the more they are likely to utilize ERP systems.

With respect to the relationships among the constructs of the TAM, the result of this study shows that perceived ease of use has significant influence on perceived usefulness. This result is in line with previous studies in IS (Shih, 2006;

Ramayah & Aafaqi, 2004; Amin, 2007), which indicates that if employees find ERP systems easy to use, they will find them useful to use in their work. Furthermore, the study has found that both perceived ease of use and perceived usefulness have positive effect on utilization of ERP systems. Similar findings have been reached by other researchers (Ramayah & Jantan, 2004; Ramayah & Aafaqi, 2004; Hasan, 2007). This shows that employees' utilization of ERP systems depends on both their perception of its usefulness and how easy it is to use. The findings provide an additional support to the validity of the TAM core model.

This study makes valuable contributions to IS research and practice. First, the current study has incorporated CSE and ERP systems design features as exogenous factors affecting ERP systems utilization through TAM's core constructs. TAM has been considered a valuable model for tracing the indirect effects of external factors on IS acceptance behavior. Thus, the results of this study provide further evidence to TAM's ability to mediate the influence of exogenous factors. Furthermore, most previous research has focused on easy and well known technologies such as Microsoft Word and Excel (Doll et al., 1998). The present study, in contrast, has investigated the utilization of a rather complex and difficult technology, namely ERP systems. Finally, since CSE has demonstrated positive direct effect on PEOU and indirect effect on ERP systems utilization, managers should enhance employees' self-efficacy towards the utilization of this technology to improve perceptions of ease of use and reduce perceptions of system complexity and difficulty. Managers need to focus on ease of use and emphasize the simplicity of an IS to obtain more favorable attitudes toward system utilization. Providing user support methods such as training sessions (Igbaria et al., 1996) can be useful in improving users' perceptions of the easiness of the IS.

LIMITATIONS AND DIRECTIONS FOR FUTHER RESEARCH

Although the findings of this study contribute to better understanding of the factors that influence the utilization of ERP systems, our study is not without limitations that should be acknowledged and considered when interpreting the results. More studies are needed to validate, expand and generalize these results. First, the findings discussed above and their implications are derived from one single study in one country, thus we need to be careful when generalizing our findings to other countries in the Gulf region. A similar study examining the same model in a broader sample of companies located in different Gulf region countries could help in extending and enhancing the findings of the study. Second, testing the research model against one data set concerning one type of IS represents one limitation. Thus, it is essential that the research model be tested against other technologies. Finally, we have focused on examining the impact of only two exogenous factors, CSE and ERP systems design features. We suggest incorporating other factors which may provide better understanding of employees' utilization of ERP systems.

REFERENCES

Abdinnour-Helm, S., Lengnick-Hall, M., & Lengnick-Hall, C. (2003). Pre-implementation attitudes and organizational readiness for implementing and Enterprise Resource Planning system. *European Journal of Operational Research, 146*(2), 258–273. doi:10.1016/S0377-2217(02)00548-9

Adams, D. A., Nelson, R. R., & Todd, P. A. (1992). Perceived Usefulness, Ease of Use and Usage Information Technology. *Management Information Systems Quarterly, 16*(2), 227–250. doi:10.2307/249577

Ajzen, I., & Fishbein, M. (1980). *Understanding Attitudes and Predicting Social Behavior*. Englewood Cliffs, NJ: Prentice-Hall.

Al-Somali, S. A., Gholami, R., & Clegg, B. (2009). An investigation into the acceptance of online banking in Saudi Arabia. *Technovation*, *29*(2), 130–141. doi:10.1016/j.technovation.2008.07.004

Aladwani, A. (2001). Change management strategies for successful ERP implementation. *Business Process Management Journal*, *7*(3), 266–275. doi:10.1108/14637150110392764

Aladwani, M. A., & Palvia, P. C. (2002). Developing and validating instrument for measuring user perceived web quality. *Information & Management*, *39*(6), 467–476. doi:10.1016/S0378-7206(01)00113-6

Amin, H. (2007). Internet banking adoption among young intellectuals. *Journal of Internet Banking and Commerce*, *12*(3), 1–13.

Amoako-Gyampah, K. (2007). Perceived usefulness, user involvement and behavioral intention: an empirical study of ERP implementation. *Computers in Human Behavior*, *23*(3), 1232–1248. doi:10.1016/j.chb.2004.12.002

Amoako-Gyampah, K., & Salam, A. F. (2004). An extension of the technology acceptance model in an ERP implementation environment. *Information & Management*, *41*(6), 731–745. doi:10.1016/j.im.2003.08.010

Bagchi, S., Kanungo, S., & Dasgupta, S. (2003). Modeling use of enterprise resource planning systems: A path analytic study. *European Journal of Information Systems*, *12*(2), 142–158. doi:10.1057/palgrave.ejis.3000453

Bingi, P., Sharma, M., & Godla, J. (1999). Critical issues affecting an ERP implementation. *Information Systems Management*, *16*(3), 7–14. doi:10.1201/1078/43197.16.3.19990601/31310.2

Bradely, J., & Lee, C. C. (2007). ERP and user satisfaction: A case study. *International Journal of Enterprise Information Systems*, *3*(4), 33–50.

Bueno, S., & Salmeron, J. L. (2008). TAM-based success modeling in ERP. *Interacting with Computers*, *20*(6), 515–523. doi:10.1016/j.intcom.2008.08.003

Calisir, F., & Calisir, F. (2004). The relation of interface usability characteristics, perceived usefulness, and perceived ease of use to end-user satisfaction with enterprise recourse planning (ERP) systems. *Computers in Human Behavior*, *20*(4), 505–515. doi:10.1016/j.chb.2003.10.004

Calisir, F., Gumussoy, C. A., & Bayram, A. (2009). Predicting the behavioral intention to use enterprise resource planning systems: An exploratory extension of the technology acceptance model. *Management Research News*, *32*(7), 597–613. doi:10.1108/01409170910965215

Chang, H.-H. (2008). Intelligent agent's technology characteristics applied to online auctions task: A combined model of TTF and TAM. *Technovation*, *28*(9), 564–577. doi:10.1016/j.technovation.2008.03.006

Chang, M.-K., Cheung, W., Cheng, C.-H., & Yeung, J. H. Y. (2008). Understanding ERP system adoption from the user's perspective. *International Journal of Production Economics*, *113*(2), 928–942. doi:10.1016/j.ijpe.2007.08.011

Chau, P. Y. K. (2001). Influence of computer attitude and self-efficacy on IT usage behavior. *Journal of End User Computing*, *13*(1), 26–33.

Chou, H. W. (2001). Effects of training method and computer anxiety on learning performance and self-efficacy. *Computers in Human Behavior*, *17*(1), 51–69. doi:10.1016/S0747-5632(00)00035-2

Compeau, D. R., & Higgins, C. A. (1995). Computer Self-Efficacy: Development of a Measure and Initial Test. *Management Information Systems Quarterly*, *19*(2), 89–211. doi:10.2307/249688

Davenport, T. H. (1998). Putting the enterprise into the enterprise system. *Harvard Business Review*, *76*(4), 121–131.

Davenport, T. H. (2000). *Mission critical: realizing the promise of enterprise systems*. Boston: Harvard Business School Press.

Davis, F. D. (1989). Perceived usefulness, perceived ease of use, and user acceptance of information technology. *Management Information Systems Quarterly*, *13*(3), 319–340. doi:10.2307/249008

Davis, F. D. (1993). User acceptance of information technology: System characteristics, user perceptions and behavioural impacts. *International Journal of Man-Machine Studies*, *38*(3), 475–387. doi:10.1006/imms.1993.1022

Davis, F. D., Bagozzi, R. P., & Warshaw, R. P. (1989). User acceptance of computer technology: A comparison of two theoretical models. *Management Science*, *35*(8), 982–1003. doi:10.1287/mnsc.35.8.982

Doll, W. J., Hendrickson, A., & Deng, X. (1998). Using Davis's perceived usefulness and ease of-use instruments for decision making: A confirmatory and multi group invariance analysis. *Decision Sciences*, *29*(4), 840–869. doi:10.1111/j.1540-5915.1998.tb00879.x

Eason, K. (1988). *Information technology and organizational change*. London: Taylor & Francis.

Fishbein, M., & Ajzen, I. (1975). *Belief, attitude, Intention and behavior: An introduction to research and theory*. Reading, MA: Addison-Wesley.

Fornell, C., & Larcker, D. (1981). Structural equation models with unobservable variables and measurement error. *JMR, Journal of Marketing Research*, *18*(1), 39–50. doi:10.2307/3151312

Gable, G. (1998). Large package software: A neglected technology. *Journal of Global Information Management*, *6*(3), 3–4.

Gable, G., Scott, J., & Davenport, T. H. (1998, September 29-October 2). Cooperative ERP life cycle knowledge management. In *Proceedings of the 9th Australasian Conference on Information Systems*, Sydney, Australia (pp. 227-240).

Gefen, D. (2004). What makes an ERP implementation relationship worthwhile: linking trust mechanisms and ERP usefulness. *Journal of MIS*, *21*(1), 263–288.

Gist, M. E. (1987). Self-efficacy: implications for organizational behavioral and human resource management. *Academy of Management Review*, *12*(3), 472–485. doi:10.2307/258514

Ha, S., & Stoel, L. (2009). Consumer e-shopping acceptance: Antecedents in a technology acceptance model. *Journal of Business Research*, *62*(5), 565–571. doi:10.1016/j.jbusres.2008.06.016

Hair, J. F., Black, W., Babin, B., Anderson, R. E., & Tatham, R. L. (2006). *Multivariate Data analysis*. Upper Saddle River, NJ: Prentice-Hall.

Hamner, M., & Qazi, R. U. R. (2009). Expanding the technology acceptance model to examine personal computing technology utilization in government agencies in developing countries. *Government Information Quarterly*, *26*(1), 128–136. doi:10.1016/j.giq.2007.12.003

Hasan, B. (2006). Delineating the effects of general and system-specific computer self-efficacy beliefs on IS acceptance. *Information & Management*, *43*(5), 565–571. doi:10.1016/j.im.2005.11.005

Hasan, B. (2007). Examining the Effects of Computer Self-Efficacy and System Complexity on Technology Acceptance. *Information Resources Management Journal, 20*(3), 77–88.

Hausman, A. V., & Siekpe, J. S. (2009). The effect of web interface features on consumer online purchase intentions. *Journal of Business Research, 62*(1), 5–13. doi:10.1016/j.jbusres.2008.01.018

Henderson, R., Podd, J., Smith, M., & Varela-Alvarez, H. (1995). An examination of four user-based software evaluation methods. *Interacting with Computers, 7*(4), 412–432. doi:10.1016/0953-5438(96)87701-0

Hernandez, B., Jimenez, J., & Martin, M. J. (2008). Extending the technology acceptance model to include the IT decision-maker: A study of business management software. *Technovation, 28*(3), 112–121. doi:10.1016/j.technovation.2007.11.002

Holland, C., Light, B., & Gibson, N. (1998, August 14-16). Global ERP implementation. In *Proceedings of the American Conference of Information Systems (AMCIS '98), Global Information Technology and Global Electronic Commerce Mini-Track*, Baltimore, MD.

Hu, P. J. H., Clark, T. H. K., & Ma, W. W. (2003). Examining technology acceptance by school teachers: A longitudinal study. *Information & Management, 41*(2), 227–241. doi:10.1016/S0378-7206(03)00050-8

Hung, S. Y., & Liang, T. P. (2001). Effect of computer self-efficacy on the use of executive support systems. *Industrial Management & Data Systems, 101*(5), 227–237. doi:10.1108/02635570110394626

Hwang, Y. (2005). Investigating enterprise systems adoption: uncertainty avoidance, intrinsic motivation, and the technology acceptance model. *European Journal of Information Systems, 14*(2), 150–161. doi:10.1057/palgrave.ejis.3000532

Igbaria, M., & Iivari, J. (1995). The effects of self-efficacy on computer usage. *Omega, 23*(6), 587–605. doi:10.1016/0305-0483(95)00035-6

Igbaria, M., Parasuraman, S., & Baroudi, J. (1996). A motivational model of microcomputer usage. *Journal of Management Information Systems, 13*(1), 127–143.

Jaruwachirathanakul, B., & Fink, D. (2005). Internet Banking Adoption Strategies for a Developing Country: The Case of Thailand. *Internet Research, 15*(3), 295–311. doi:10.1108/10662240510602708

Jaspers, M. W. M., Steen, T., Bos, C. V. D., & Geenen, M. (2004). The think aloud method-a guide to user interface design. *Medical Informatics, 73*(11-12), 781–795. doi:10.1016/j.ijmedinf.2004.08.003

Kuo, F. Y., Chu, T. H., Hsu, M. H., & Hsieh, H. S. (2004). An investigation of effort–accuracy trade-off and the impact of self-efficacy on Web searching behaviors. *Decision Support Systems, 3*(3), 331–342. doi:10.1016/S0167-9236(03)00032-0

Laughlin, S. P. (1999). An ERP game plan. *The Journal of Business Strategy, 20*(1), 32–37. doi:10.1108/eb039981

Li, C. (1999). ERP packages: What's next? *Information Systems Management, 16*(3), 31–36. doi:10.1201/1078/43197.16.3.19990601/31313.5

Lin, H.-Y., Hsu, P.-Y., & Ting, P.-H. (2006). ERP Systems Success: An Integration of IS Success Model and Balanced Scorecard. *Journal of Research and Practice in Information Technology, 38*(3), 215–228.

Luarn, P., & Lin, H. H. (2005). Toward an understanding of the behavioral intention to use mobile banking. *Computers in Human Behavior*, *21*(6), 873–891. doi:10.1016/j.chb.2004.03.003

Ma, Q., & Liu, L. (2004). The technology acceptance model: A meta-analysis of empirical findings. *Journal of Organizational and End User Computing*, *16*(1), 59–72.

Mabert, V. A., Soni, A., & Venkataramanan, M. A. (2000). Enterprise resource planning survey of U.S. manufacturing firms. *Production and Inventory Management Journal*, *41*(2), 52–58.

Marakas, G. M., Yi, M. Y., & Johnson, R. D. (1998). The multilevel and multifaceted character of computer self-efficacy: toward clarification of the construct and an integrative framework for research information. *Information Systems Research*, *9*(2), 126–163. doi:10.1287/isre.9.2.126

Nah, F. F., Tan, X., & The, S. H. (2004). An empirical investigation on end-user's acceptance of enterprise systems. *Information Resources Management Journal*, *17*(3), 32–53.

Nielsen, J. (1997). *The need for speed*. Retrieved from http://www.useit.com/alertbox/ 9703a.html

Nielsen, J. (1999). User interface directions for the Web. *Communications of the ACM*, *42*(1), 65–72. doi:10.1145/291469.291470

Nunnally, J. C. (1978). *Psychometric Theory*. New York: McGraw Hill.

Nunnally, J. C., & Bernstein, I. H. (1994). *Psychometric theory* (3rd ed.). New York: McGraw Hill.

Olhager, J., & Selldin, E. (2003). Enterprise resource planning survey of Swedish manufacturing firms. *European Journal of Operational Research*, *146*(2), 365–373. doi:10.1016/S0377-2217(02)00555-6

Ong, C. S., Lai, J. Y., & Wang, Y. S. (2004). Factors affecting engineers' acceptance of asynchronous e-learning systems in high-tech companies. *Information & Management*, *41*(6), 795–804. doi:10.1016/j.im.2003.08.012

Osei-Bryson, K.-M., Dong, L., & Ngwenyama, O. (2008). Exploring managerial factors affecting ERP implementation: An investigation of the Klein-Sorra model using regression splines. *Information Systems Journal*, *18*(5), 499–527. doi:10.1111/j.1365-2575.2008.00309.x

Ozen, C., & Basoglu, N. (2007, August 5-9) Exploring the Contribution of Information Systems User Interface Design Characteristics to Adoption Process. In *PICMET 2007 Proceedings*, Portland, OR (pp. 951-958).

Ramayah, T., & Aafaqi, B. (2004). Role of self-efficacy in e-library usage among student of a public university in Malaysia. *Malaysia Journal of Library and Information Science*, *9*(1), 39–57.

Ramayah, T., & Jantan, M. (2004). Internet usage among Malaysian students: The role of demographic and motivational variables. *PRANJANA: The Journal of Management Awareness*, *7*(2), 59–70.

Salanova, M., Grau, R. M., Cifre, E., & Llorens, S. (2000). Computer training, frequency of usage and burnout: The moderating role of computer self-efficacy. *Computers in Human Behavior*, *16*(6), 575–590. doi:10.1016/S0747-5632(00)00028-5

Seneler, C. O., Basoglu, N., & Daim, T. A. (2008, July 27-31). Taxonomy for Technology Adoption: A Human Computer Interaction Perspective. In *PICMET 2008 Proceedings*, Cape Town, South Africa (pp. 2208-2219).

Shergill, G. S., & Chen, Z. (2005). Web-based shopping: Consumers' attitudes towards online shopping in New Zealand. *Journal of Electronic Commerce Research*, *6*(2), 79–94.

Shih, Y.-Y. (2004). A case study of the critical success factors in implementing enterprise resource planning. *Journal of Ming Hsin Institute of Technology, 30,* 159–169.

Shih, Y.-Y. (2006). The effect of computer self-efficacy on enterprise resource planning usage. *Behaviour & Information Technology, 25*(5), 407–411. doi:10.1080/01449290500168103

Shih, Y.-Y., & Huang, S.-S. (2009). The actual usage of ERP systems: An extended technology acceptance perspective. *Journal of Research and Practice in Information Technology, 41*(3), 263–276.

Singh, A., & Wesson, J. (2009, October 12-14). Evaluation Criteria for Assessing the Usability of ERP Systems. In *Proceedings of the 2009 Annual Research Conference of the South African Institute of Computer Scientists and Information Technologists (SAICSIT'09),* Riverside, Vanderbijlpark, South Africa (pp. 87-95).

Suganthi, B., Balachandher, K. G., & Balachandran, S. (2001). Internet banking patronage: an empirical investigation of Malaysia. *Journal of Internet Banking and Commerce, 6*(1). Retrieved from http://www.arraydev.com/commerce/jibc/0103_01.htm.

Sun, Y., Bhattacherjee, A., & Ma, Q. (2009). Extending technology usage to work settings: The role of perceived work compatibility in ERP implementation. *Information & Management, 46*(6), 351–356. doi:10.1016/j.im.2009.06.003

Taylor, S., & Todd, P. A. (1995). Understanding Information Technology Usage: A Test of Competing Models. *Information Systems Research, 6*(2), 144–176. doi:10.1287/isre.6.2.144

Thong, J. Y. L., Hong, W. H., & Tam, K. R. (2002). Understanding user acceptance of digital libraries: What are the roles of interface characteristics, organizational context, and individual differences? *International Journal of Human-Computer Studies, 57*(3), 215–242. doi:10.1016/S1071-5819(02)91024-4

Torkzadeh, G., & van Dyke, T. P. (2001). Development and validation of an Internet self-efficacy scale. *Behaviour & Information Technology, 20*(4), 275–280. doi:10.1080/01449290110050293

Umble, E. J., Haft, R. R., & Umble, M. M. (2003). Enterprise resource planning: implementation procedures and critical success factors. *European Journal of Operational Research, 146*(2), 241–257. doi:10.1016/S0377-2217(02)00547-7

Van Everdingen, Y., Van Hillegersber, J., & Waarts, E. (2000). ERP adoption by European midsize companies. *Communications of the ACM, 43*(4), 27–31. doi:10.1145/332051.332064

Venkatesh, V., & Davis, F. D. (1996). A model of the antecedents of perceived ease of use: Development and test. *Decision Sciences, 27*(3), 451–481. doi:10.1111/j.1540-5915.1996.tb01822.x

Venkatesh, V., & Davis, F. D. (2000). A Theoretical Extension of the Technology Acceptance Model: Four Longitudinal Field Studies. *Management Science, 46*(2), 186–204. doi:10.1287/mnsc.46.2.186.11926

Venkatesh, V., & Morris, M. G. (2000). Why Do Not Men Ever Stop to Ask for Directions? Gender, Social and their Role in Technology Acceptance and Usage Behaviour. *Management Information Systems Quarterly, 24*(1), 115–139. doi:10.2307/3250981

Wang, Y. S., Wang, Y. M., Lin, H. H., & Tang, T. I. (2003). Determinants of User Acceptance of Internet Banking: An Empirical Study. *International Journal of Service Industry Management, 14*(5), 501–519. doi:10.1108/09564230310500192

Wu, J. H., & Wang, L. (2007). Measuring ERP success: the key-users' viewpoint of the ERP to produce a viable IS in the organization. *Computers in Human Behavior, 23*(3), 1582–1596. doi:10.1016/j.chb.2005.07.005

Yi, M., & Hwang, Y. (2003). Predicting the use of web-based information systems: self-efficacy, enjoyment, learning goal orientation, and the technology acceptance model. *International Journal of Human-Computer Studies, 59*(4), 431–449. doi:10.1016/S1071-5819(03)00114-9

Yougberg, E., Olen, D., & Hauser, K. (2009). Determinants of professionally autonomous end-user acceptance in an enterprise resource planning systems environment. *International Journal of Information Management, 29*(2), 138–144. doi:10.1016/j.ijinfomgt.2008.06.001

Zhang, P., & Dran, G. (2000). Satisfiers and dissatisfiers: A two-factor model for website design and evaluation. *Journal of the American Society for Information Science American Society for Information Science, 51*(14), 1253–1268. doi:10.1002/1097-4571(2000)9999:9999<::AID-ASI1039>3.0.CO;2-O

Zhang, P., & Dran, G. (2001, January 3-6). Expectations and Rankings of Website Quality Features: Results of Two Studies on User Perceptions. In *Proceedings of the 34th Annual Hawaii International Conference on System Sciences (HICSS-34)* (Volume 7).

Zhang, P., & Dran, G. (2002). User expectations and ranking of quality factors in different web site domains. *International Journal of Electronic Commerce, 6*(2), 9–33.

This work was previously published in International Journal of Enterprise Information Systems, edited by Madjid Tavana, pp. 38-54, Volume 6, Issue 4, copyright 2010 by IGI Publishing (an imprint of IGI Global).

Chapter 2
A Proposition for Classification of Business Sectors by ERP Solutions Support

Alen Jakupovic
Polytechnic of Rijeka, Croatia

Mile Pavlic
University of Rijeka, Croatia

Neven Vrcek
University of Zagreb, Croatia

ABSTRACT

This paper illustrates the results of an analysis of business sectors covered by ERP solutions. The authors answer questions in regards to business sectors supported by ERP solutions, while presenting a list of supported business sectors. Using a statistical analysis, an answer is given to the question of whether there are any business sectors that are supported by a large number of ERP solutions, and whether it is possible to classify business sectors based on the occurrence of the support. Finally, three classifications are described that stem from different statistical views of covering business sectors by ERP solutions, and a suggestion for a unique classification of business sectors is given.

INTRODUCTION

Information and telecommunication technology is unstoppably entering all segments of human activities by changing processes which run in them (Čerić, 2001). This paper is interested in business sectors which are currently supported by Enterprise Resource Planning (ERP) solutions.

Generally, an organization can be defined as: "..a deliberate association of people whose common goal is to fulfil certain tasks using suitable means and least possible effort in whichever area of social life" (Sikavica et al., 1993). When business is seen as an area of social life, business organization emerges.

DOI: 10.4018/978-1-4666-1761-2.ch002

Each business organization, no matter if it is a profit or not for profit organization, accomplishes its goals and tasks by performing a group of connected activities which build connected business processes. A group of business processes belonging to a business organization is called business technology of the given business organization. Goals and tasks which every business organization strives to accomplish by performing a group of business processes, belong to one or more business sectors. Business technology of a certain business sector is a group of business processes used to achieve the goals and tasks of the concerned business sector.

If the number of business process inputs and outputs of a certain business sector (i.e., business technology of a given business sector) is large, i.e., the number of data that needs to be considered in order to create information is large, and if the algorithm for converting data into information is complex and the time needed to supply the information is short, then business processes, i.e., business technology is supported by complex business software. A special kind of business software is the ERP solution (Fertalj et al., 2004; Koch, 2008; Vukšić et al., 2005).

ERP solutions support general business technology of a certain business sector. The producers of ERP solutions speak of the "best practice" method in creating general business technology of a business sector. The creation of "best practice" is not explored to a satisfying degree in scientific literature. The article "The creation of 'best practice' software: Myth, reality and ethics" attempts at giving the answer to the question "How are 'best practices' created and embedded in new ERP software?" through the presentation of case studies in which follows the creation of the ERP product destined to be marketed as a best practice solution for higher education institutions (Wagner et al., 2006).

The purpose of this paper is to answer the question which business sectors are supported by ERP solutions, are there any business sectors which are supported by a large number of ERP solutions, and is it possible to classify business sectors based on the occurrence of the support.

In the existing ERP solution analyses, the following characteristics were studied: the average solution implementation cost, the average number of users, the coverage of application areas, the coverage of a certain market segment, applied technology, stability, flexibility, security, documentation, adaptability of the ERP solution, the level of support, upgrade reliability, improvement continuity, return of investment, etc. (Abas Business Software, 2003; Burns, 2006; Burns, 2008).

The article "Novel Approach to BCG Analysis in the Context of ERP System Implementation", published in the journal Advances in Information Systems Development, shows an analysis of business processes within different business sectors and industries. The article describes the relationship between gap and BCG analysis through nine large projects of deploying ERP solutions in which the SPIS methodology is applied – a methodology for strategic planning of information systems. From the conducted analysis of business processes, conclusions on individual business sectors and industries are synthesized (Vrček et al., 2007).

As opposed to existing ERP solutions analyses, this paper observes business sectors which existing ERP solutions support, but the aim is not to evaluate ERP solutions, but rather the primary concern of the paper is to evaluate business sectors. The same analysis served as the basis for a suggestion of classification of ERP solution producers which is represented in the article "Analysis and Classification of ERP Producers by Business Operations", published in the Journal of Computing and Information Technology (Jakupović et al., 2009).

Figure 1. Model of the conducted business sectors analysis

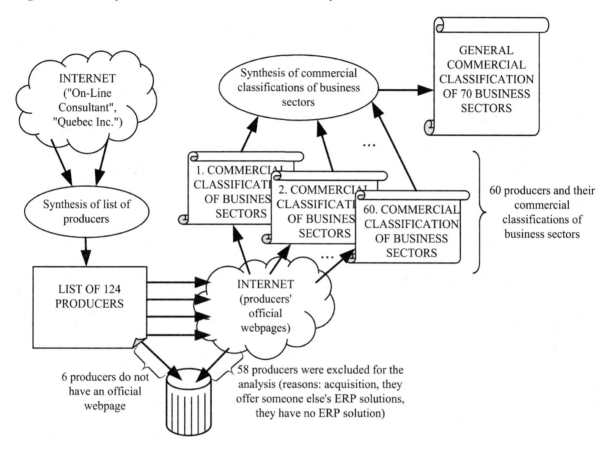

International Data Corporation (IDC) defines ERP solution as an business software for at least three of the following four segments of business: (IDC, 2000)

- Accounting
- Manufacturing
- Material management/distribution
- HR management, payroll

Besides ERP solutions, there are other specific business software which support some business sectors (e.g., business software for healthcare services), but which do not meet the requirements stated by the definition, and due to that, do not belong to the class of ERP solutions. Such business software is not presented in this paper.

THE ANALYSIS OF BUSINESS SECTORS COVERED BY SPECIALIZED ERP SOLUTIONS

The analysis was conducted over 124 foreign ERP solutions producers, whose list emerged as a combination of two main producers' lists, published on web pages of "On-Line Consultant" (a list of 44 producers) (On-Line Consultant, 2009) and "Quebec Inc." (a list of 97 producers) (Quebec Inc., 2007). The operation of both these companies is the development of a method for the choice of business software. The "Software Finder" (Software Finder, 2009) (the service for finding the producers of business software) was used to track down the official web pages of certain companies. Figure 1 shows the model which served as a basis for the analysis of business sectors.

Table 1. A part of analyzed ERP solution producers

Producer	Official Web page	ERP specialized solution
Cedar Group	http://www.cedaropenaccounts.com/	CedarOpenAccounts
Ceecom, Inc.	http://www.ceecom.com/	Ceecom ERP System
Cincom Systems	http://www.cincom.com/us/eng/index.jsp?loc=usa	Cincom CONTROL
Epicor	http://www.epicor.com/www/	Enterprise, iScala, Vantage, Vista, CRS Retail Suite
Europa Telecom Group	http://www.europa-telecom.co.uk/index.cfm?uuid=D6EFFE7693	ETG-ERP, ETG-ERM, ETG-ECM
Glovia International	http://www.glovia.com/html/	Extended ERP
IBM	http://ibm.com	grupa proizvoda (Lotus, Websphere)
Microsoft	http://www.microsoft.com/en/us/default.aspx	grupa proizvoda Microsoft Dynamics
Oracle	http://www.oracle.com/index.html	PeopleSoft Enterprise applications, JD Edwards EnterpriseOne, E-Business Suite
Sage Software	http://www.sagesoftware.com/	Sage Accpac ERP, Sage BusinessVision, Sage MAS 500 ERP, Sage MAS 90 ERP, Sage MAS 200 ERP, Sage PFW ERP...
SAP	http://www.sap.com/index.epx	grupa proizvoda SAP Business Suite, SAP Business One
SYSPRO	http://www.syspro.com/corporate/Global_Region.asp?region=US	grupa proizvoda Syspro ERP
Technology Group International	http://www.tgiltd.com/	Enterprise 21

Out of 124 companies, six of them do not have an official web page, and a certain number of companies is under the composition of other companies or offers ERP solutions of other producers (like SAP, Navision, etc). In effect, these companies were not considered. Finally, the number of analyzed companies offering their own ERP solution came to 91. Table 1 shows a part of analyzed producers of ERP solutions.

Out of 91 producers, 60 of them (i.e., 66%) have a specialized ERP solution for a certain business sectors.

The remainder of 31 producers offer ERP solution which is not connected to any business sector. These are general ERP solutions which application in a business sector demands additional activities (in this case, the verticalization of ERP solutions is introduced). The verticalization of ERP solution can be defined as a process of expanding, modifying or adjusting the general ERP solution by enforcing specific qualities of a certain business sector. The result of this procedure is a specialized ERP solution which supports business processes of the given business sector.

Existing classifications of business sectors are not appropriate for conducting an analysis of their support by ERP solutions (e.g., Eurostat, 2009; Maitland et al., 2002). Due to that, a new, more appropriate classification was created by analysing commercial classifications of business sectors of the aforementioned 60 ERP solution producers (e.g., Microsoft, 2009; SAP, 2009). This resulted in a general commercial classification of business sectors of ERP solution producers. A list of

Table 2. General commercial classification of business sectors

Financial and Public Services	Manufacturing	Service
1. Banking	Aerospace & Defense	*48. Logistics Services*
2. Capital Markets	*13. Aerospace and Defense Manufacturers*	Media
3. Insurance	*14. Airline Management*	*49. Broadcasting*
Defense & Security	*15. MRO/M&E Service Providers*	*50. Entertainment*
4. Defense Logistics	Automotive	*51. Newspapers and Magazines*
5. Public Security	*16. Automotive OEMs*	*52. Premium Content Publishers*
Healthcare	*17. Sales and Service Organizations*	*53. Postal Services*
6. Healthcare Payers	*18. Automotive Suppliers*	*54. Professional Services*
7. Healthcare Providers	*19. Chemicals*	*55. Railways*
Education & Research	*20. Shipbuilding*	*56. Marine Transportation*
8. Schools	*21. Agricultural*	*57. Retail*
9. Higher Education	Consumer Products	*58. Facilities Management*
10. Research	*22. Apparel and Footwea*	*59. Not for Profit & Charities*
Public Sector	*23. Beverage*	*60. Rental*
11. Government	*24. Consumer Durables and Home Appliances*	*61. Hospitality*
12. Public Security	*25. Food*	*62. Real Estate*
	26. Home and Personal Care	*63. Telecommunications*
	27. Industrial Machinery & Components	Utilities
	High Tech	*64. Generation*
	28. Business, Medical, and Consumer OEMs	*65. Retail*
	29. Electronics Manufacturing Service Providers	*66. Transmission and Distribution*
	30. Semiconductor and Component Manufacturers	*67. Gas*
	31. Software Providers	*68. Waste*
	32. Industrial Machinery & Components	*69. Water*
	Life Sciences	*70. Wholesale Distribution*
	33. Pharmaceuticals	
	34. Biotechnology/Biopharmaceuticals	
	35. Medical Device/Scientific Instruments	
	Mill Products	
	36. Building Materials	
	37. Fabricated Metal Products	
	38. Furniture	
	39. Packaging	
	40. Plastics	
	41. Primary Metals	
	42. Pulp and Paper	
	43. Textile	
	44. Rubber	
	45. Timberlands and Solid Wood	
	46. Mining	
	47. Oil & Gas	

business sectors for each and every producer was based on the data of supported business sectors of every producer (the data used from their official web page). After the analysis of all producers, the resulting commercial classifications of business sectors have been aligned in order to avoid overlapping. Finally, these were integrated into a final list of business sectors. This way a list emerged, showing 70 business sectors to which specialized ERP solutions can be applied (see Table 2).

CLASSIFICATION OF BUSINESS SECTORS

An analysis was conducted, showing how many ERP solution producers support a certain business sectors (Table 3). The analysis was conducted based on the created General Commercial Classification of Business Sectors (see Table 2) and the data showing which business sectors from the General Business Classification are supported by the observed ERP producer (these data are found on the official webpages of ERP producers). The final result of gathering data is shown in Table 10, Table 11, and Table 12, which can be found in the Appendix A. The gathered data were statistically analysed, and the goal of the analysis was to determine the support of business sectors by ERP solutions. Based on the calculated coverage, a classification was created by using graphical method for representing data, graphical method for viewing data frequency, grouping data into four groups based on quartiles, and by applying arithmetic mean to limit values of given classifications.

Table 3 shows that the support of business sectors by ERP solution is between 1 and 25 producers. It can be seen that the best supported sector is *70. Wholesale Distribution* (25 ERP producers support it, i.e., around 42%), and the least supported sectors are *53. Postal Services, 56. Marine Transportation,* and *68. Waste (Utilities)*. Only 1 ERP solution producer supports these. There is a relatively large number of business sectors with weak support. Total of 33 business sectors or 47% of them are relatively weakly supported (under 10% of producers support them, i.e., less than 6 of them). 21 business sectors or 30% of them have relatively good support (more than 20% of ERP producers support them, i.e., over 13).

The analysis of commercial classifications of ERP solutions producers resulted in three basic classes of business sectors belonging to the same business function, these being: financial and public services (12 business sectors) manufacturing (35 business sectors) and service (23 business sectors) (see Table 2).

If all observed business sectors are classified into three basic types (financial and public services, manufacturing and service), then the results of support are shown in Table 4.

As one can see from Table 4, the larges number of business sectors are service (76.67%), and manufacturing (68,33%), while business sectors from the area of financial and public services are

fewer (38,33%). However, certain sectors from the area of finance (banking and insurance) are well supported. It needs to be said that a weaker support of a business sector by an ERP solution does not necessarily mean that this business sector is poorly supported by some other business software, because for the observed business sector, there can be specialized business software which do not enter the class of ERP solution, and this paper does not describe these.

CLASSIFICATION OF BUSINESS SECTORS ACCORDING TO ERP SOLUTION SUPPORT

Figure 2 graphically illustrates business sectors and their support by ERP solutions. The X axis shows the numerical codes of business sectors, which are listed in the first column of Table 3. The Y axis represents total number of ERP producers which, by their ERP solutions, support a given business sector.

The illustration of business sectors supported by ERP solutions (Figure 2) shows three breaking points (marked with A, B and C) where the graph starts growing steeply. It is visible that every business sector belongs to exactly one area bounded by points A, B and C. The same ERP producer can be in different areas, which means that it covers business sectors belonging to different groups. However, the graph does not show a certain ERP producer, but the total number of the group ERP producer which supports a certain business sector.

Business sectors in the interval to point A (30 of them) are supported by 1 to 5 producers of ERP solution (the size of ERP producers interval is 5). The interval from A to B holds the total of 23 business sectors which are supported by 5 to 13 ERP solution producers (interval size is 13 − 5 = 8). The interval from B to point C holds 13 business sectors, supported by 14 to 18 producers (interval size is 18 − 14 = 4). And finally, the last

Table 3. Business sectors supported by ERP solutions

No.	Business sector	Type of business sector	Number of producers	% of supporting
1	53. Postal services	Service	1	1,67%
2	56. Maritime transportation	Service	1	1,67%
3	68. Waste (Utilities)	Service	1	1,67%
4	5. Public Security	Financial and public services	2	3,33%
5	12. Public Security (Public Sector)	Financial and public services	2	3,33%
6	44. Rubber (Mill Products)	Manufacturing	2	3,33%
7	58. Facilities Management	Service	2	3,33%
8	62. Real Estate	Service	2	3,33%
9	4. Defense Lofistics (Defense & Security)	Financial and public services	3	5,00%
10	21.Agricultural	Manufacturing	3	5,00%
11	36. Building Materials (Mill Products)	Manufacturing	3	5,00%
12	67. Gas (Utilities)	Service	3	5,00%
13	10. Research (Education & Research)	Financial and public services	4	6,67%
14	20. Shipbuilding	Manufacturing	4	6,67%
15	38. Furniture (Mill Products)	Manufacturing	4	6,67%
16	39. Packaging (Mill Products)	Manufacturing	4	6,67%
17	42. Pulp and Paper (Mill Products)	Manufacturing	4	6,67%
18	43. Textile (Mill Products)	Manufacturing	4	6,67%
19	45. Timberlands and Solid Wood (Mill Products)	Manufacturing	4	6,67%
20	46. Mining	Manufacturing	4	6,67%
21	49. Broadcasting (media)	Service	4	6,67%
22	60. Rental	Service	4	6,67%
23	6. Healthcare Payers (Healthcare)	Financial and public services	5	8,33%
24	14. Airline Management (Aerospace & Defence)	Manufacturing	5	8,33%
25	31. Software Providers (High Tech)	Manufacturing	5	8,33%
26	34. Biotechnology/Biopharmaceuticals (Life Sciences)	Manufacturing	5	8,33%
27	50. Entertainment (Media)	Service	5	8,33%
28	51. Newspapers and Magazines (Media)	Service	5	8,33%
29	55. Railways	Service	5	8,33%
30	69. Water (Utilities)	Service	5	8,33%
31	8. Schools (Education & Research)	Financial and public services	6	10,00%
32	52. Premium Content Publishers (Media)	Service	6	10,00%
33	64. Generation (Utilities)	Service	6	10,00%
34	2. Capital Markets	Financial and public services	7	11,67%
35	9. Higher Education (Education & Research)	Financial and public services	7	11,67%
36	61. Hospitality	Service	7	11,67%
37	18. Automotive Suppliers (Automotive)	Manufacturing	8	13,33%
38	66. Transmission and Distribution (Utilities)	Service	8	13,33%
39	17. Sales and Service Organizations (Automotive)	Manufacturing	9	15,00%

continued on following page

Table 3. Continued

No.	Business sector	Type of business sector	Number of producers	% of supporting
40	47. Oil & Gas	Manufacturing	9	15,00%
41	48. Logistics Services	Service	9	15,00%
42	65. Retail (Utilities)	Service	9	15,00%
43	35. Medical Device/Scientific Instruments (Life Sciences)	Manufacturing	10	16,67%
44	40. Plastics (Mill Products)	Manufacturing	10	16,67%
45	63. Telecommunications	Service	10	16,67%
46	7. Healthcare Providers (Healthcare)	Financial and public services	11	18,33%
47	22. Apparel and Footwear (Consumer Products)	Manufacturing	12	20,00%
48	32. Industrial Machinery & Components	Manufacturing	12	20,00%
49	59. Not for Profit & Charities	Service	12	20,00%
50	3. Insurance	Financial and public services	13	21,67%
51	15. MRO/M&E Service Providers (Aerospace & Defence)	Manufacturing	13	21,67%
52	24. Consumer Durables and Home Appliances (Consumer Products)	Manufacturing	13	21,67%
53	26. Home and Personal Care (Consumer Products)	Manufacturing	13	21,67%
54	1. Banking	Financial and public services	14	23,33%
55	27. Industrial Machinery & Components	Manufacturing	15	25,00%
56	33. Pharmaceuticals (Life Sciences)	Manufacturing	16	26,67%
57	41. Primary Metals (Mill Products)	Manufacturing	16	26,67%
58	57. Retail	Service	16	26,67%
59	28. Business, Medical, and Consumer OEMs (High Tech)	Manufacturing	17	28,33%
60	29. Electronics Manufacturing Service Providers (High Tech)	Manufacturing	17	28,33%
61	30. Semiconductor and Component Manufacturers (High Tech)	Manufacturing	17	28,33%
62	11. Government (Public Sector)	Financial and public services	18	30,00%
63	13. Aerospace and Defense Manufacturers (Aerospace & Defense)	Manufacturing	18	30,00%
64	19. Chemicals	Manufacturing	18	30,00%
65	23. Beverage (Consumer Products)	Manufacturing	18	30,00%
66	37. Fabricated Metal Products (Mill Products)	Manufacturing	18	30,00%
67	16. Automotive OEMs (Automotive)	Manufacturing	19	31,67%
68	25. Food (Consumer Products)	Manufacturing	20	33,33%
69	54. Professional Services	Service	21	35,00%
70	70. Wholesale Distribution	Service	25	41,67%

Table 4. The share of sectors according to type

Basic type	The number of ERP producers	Share (%)
Financial and public sector	23	38,33%
Manufacturing	41	68,33%
Sevice	46	76,67%

interval from point C, holds 4 business sectors, supported by 19 to 25 ERP solution producers (interval size is 25 – 19 = 6).

Such observed areas of different graph steepness, can be the basis for developing a relative classification of business sector support. Let the area up to point A be called Class I, area between point A and point B Class II, the area between point B and point C Class III, and the area following point C be Class IV. Then it can be said that a business sector belongs to Class I if less than 10% of ERP solution producers supports it, belongs to Class II if it is supported by 10% to 22%, to Class III if it is supported by 22% to 30%, and Class IV if it is supported by more than 30% of ERP solution producers.

Unlike Class I, Class II and Class III, Class IV does not have a well defined upper interval limit, so it covers a vast area of 70% (Class I covers 10%, Class II covers 12% and Class III covers 8%). In order to avoid such a leap, new classes are introduced: Class V, Class VI and Class VII, which are defined as follows.

Class VII covers area which is as wide as the area of Class I, Class VI covers area which is as wide as area of Class II, and Class V covers area which is as wide as area of Class III. This corrects the width of area belonging to Class IV. So, the upper limit of Class VII is 100%, and the lower limit is 100% - 10% = 90% (10% is area width of Class I). By analogy, the upper limit of Class VI is 90%, and the lower limit is 90% - 12% = 78% (12% is the area width of Class II). The upper limit of Class V is 78%, and the lower limit is 78% - 8% = 70% (8% is the area width of Class III). And finally, the lower limit of Class IV is 30%, and the upper limit is 70%. The width of area covered by Class IV is 40% (before, it was 70%). Table 5 shows the number and percentage of business sectors in each class, i.e., the number

Figure 2. Graphic illustration of business sectors supported by ERP solutions

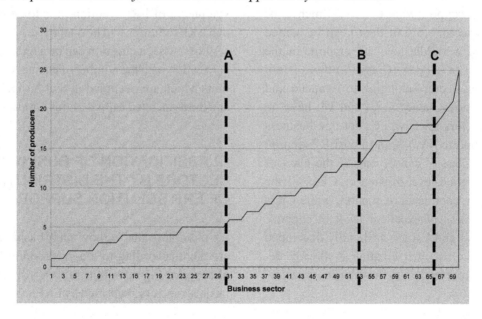

Figure 3. The distribution of business sectors supported by ERP solutions

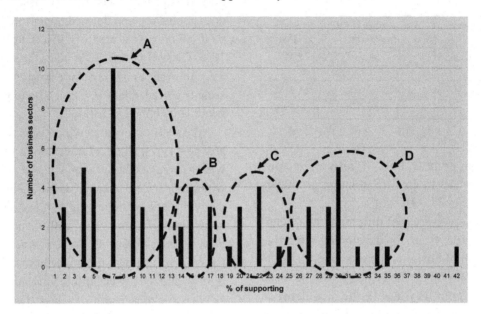

and percentage of business sectors in a given group of sectors.

Table 5 shows that the largest number of business sectors (30% or 43% of them) is in Class I, which can be also named the class of a weak level of support. Class II, which holds 23 business sectors (33% of them) can be named the class of a sufficient level of support, Class III, which holds 13 business sectors (19% of them) the class of a good level of support, while Class IV, which holds 4 business sectors (5% of them) can be named the class of a middle level of support. In the middle level of support (Class IV) there is not one business sector belonging to financial and public services. Classes V, VI and VII have no business sectors for now, i.e., not one business sector is supported by 70% and more ERP solution producers. Class V can be named the class of sufficiently good level of support, Class VI the class of very good level of support, while Class VII is the class of excellent level of support. Classes V, VI and VII are artificially developed (the procedure of their creation is already described) in order to classify those business sectors

which might eventually become supported by a large number of ERP producers.

By analyzing historic data of the emergence of ERP solutions and their spreading on new business sectors, estimation could be reached, concerning when very good and excellent support will emerge and which business sectors will be excellently supported. If the market holds same factors of influence on the investment in the development of ERP solution, it is to be expected that ERP solutions will be on the rise in the area of services. Also, a question can be asked – is this in correlation with the number of business organizations which are occupied in that business sector and the associated capital of this industry branch.

CLASSIFICATION OF BUSINESS SECTORS BY THE DISTRIBUTION OF ERP SOLUTION SUPPORT

It is possible to analyse how many business sectors are there according to a corresponding average of support. Figure 3 illustrates a distribution of business sectors supported by ERP solutions. The

Table 5. Distribution of business sectors according to classes

Class	Class (level of support)	Definition (% of supporting)	Total	Financial and public services	Manufacturing	Service
Class I	Weak	<0, 10>	30 (43%)	5 (42%)	13 (37%)	12 (52%)
Class II	Sufficient	[10, 22>	23 (33%)	5 (42%)	10 (29%)	8 (35%)
Class III	Good	[22, 30>	13 (19%)	2 (16%)	10 (29%)	1 (4%)
Class IV	Middle	[30, 70>	4 (5%)	0 (0%)	2 (5%)	2 (9%)
Class V	Sufficiently good	[70, 78>	0 (0%)	0 (0%)	0 (0%)	0 (0%)
Class VI	Very good	[78, 90>	0 (0%)	0 (0%)	0 (0%)	0 (0%)
Class VII	Excellent	[90, 100>	0 (0%)	0 (0%)	0 (0%)	0 (0%)
TOTAL			70 (100%)	12 (100%)	35 (100%)	23 (100%)

Table 6. Definition of supported business sectors classes based on distribution of ERP support

Class	Definition (% of supporting)	Total	Financial and public services	Manufacturing	Service
Class A	<0, 12]	36 (51%)	8 (67%)	13 (37%)	15 (65%)
Class B	<12, 17]	9 (13%)	0 (0%)	5 (14%)	4 (17%)
Class C	<17, 24]	9 (13%)	3 (25%)	5 (14%)	1 (4%)
Class D	<24, 76]	16 (23%)	1 (8%)	12 (35%)	3 (14%)
Class E	<76, 83]	0 (0%)	0 (0%)	0 (0%)	0 (0%)
Class F	<83, 88]	0 (0%)	0 (0%)	0 (0%)	0 (0%)
Class G	<88, 100]	0 (0%)	0 (0%)	0 (0%)	0 (0%)
TOTAL		70 (100%)	12 (100%)	35 (100%)	23 (100%)

X axis represents averages, and Y axis represents the number of business sectors with the associated average of supporting.

If, as a basis for determining a new possible classification of business sectors from the distribution graph of business sectors supported by ERP solutions (Figure 3), we use the protruding peaks and groupings around these, then we can observe 4 classes which represent distributions of support. These classes are marked by letters A, B, C and D. The distribution of support within a certain class has a shape of normal distribution.

On the graph in Figure 3, there are borders between classes A, B, C and D. These borders are: Class A = <0, 12], Class B = <12, 17], Class C = <17, 24] and Class D = <24,100]. Again, a class emerges (in this case Class D) which stands out with the width of the area it covers (the width

is 76%). If we apply the aforementioned way of changing the area width (see previos chapter), in order to make the classification appropriate for future enlarged number of ERP solution, then 3 new classes emerge: Class E, Class F and Class G.

Table 6 illustrates the definition of business sectors class areas according to the distribution of ERP solution support. The table also shows the number of member of a certain class distributed according to the type of business sector, and the total number of members.

Table 6 shows that only Class B has got no business sectors from financial and public services, while all other classes have business sectors belonging to various branches. It is interesting that this classification shows the most business sectors (51% of them) are weakly supported (Class A) – similar to the classification in Table 5, but also that 16 business sectors (23% of them) have middle support – unlike the classification in Table 5 where only 4 business sectors (5% of them) have middle support. Also, it can be observed that Classes B and C have the least number of business sectors. This leads to a conclusion that when a business sector moves from the lowest class (Class A) to a higher class (Class B and C), it stays there for a relatively short period of time. It either goes back to the lowest class (Class A) or moves to a higher class (Class D). If this would not be the case, than Classes B and C would have more members than Class D, i.e., business sector would stay longer in classes B and C. Classes E, F and G have no members for now, i.e., there are no business sectors which are supported by more than 76% of producers.

CLASSIFICATION OF BUSINESS SECTORS ACCORDING TO THE DISTRIBUTION OF ERP SUPPORT BASED ON QUARTILES

It is possible to suggest another classification based on quartiles (Bailey et al., 2004). Table 7 shows a distribution of business sectors supported by ERP on four groups same in number.

The border of the first data group (first quartile) is a number to which 25% of data is less than or equal to it. The border of the second data group (first quartile) is the median (the middle data value that divides a group into two equal parts), while the border of the third data group is a number to which 75% of data is less than or equal to it. (Bailey et al., 2004)

First table row shows the numerical codes of business sectors (it responds to the first column of Table 3), while the second row shows the level of support (it responds to the last column of Table 3).

As it can be seen from Table 7, the first quartile is 6,67%, the second is 11,67% and the third one is 21,67%. If quartiles are rounded to whole numbers (that is, 7%, 12% and 22%), and used for defining class borders of business sectors supported by ERP, then it is possible to get four classes. The last class (Class IV) has a wide area as well. By applying the described procedure for decreasing width new classes emerge: Class V, Class VI and Class VII. Table 8 shows a definition of business sector classes according to the distribution of ERP solution support and quartiles, number of members for each class assorted by the type of business sector, and the total number of members.

Table 8 illustrates that classes defined in this way (except new classes V, VI and VII) have business sectors from all branches (financial and

Table 7. Distribution of business sectors supported by ERP solutions based on quartiles

1. quartile   **2. quartile (median)**   **3. quartile**

1	2	3	4	5	6	7	8	9	10	11	12	13	14	15	16
1,67	1,67	1,67	3,33	3,33	3,33	3,33	3,33	5,00	5,00	5,00	5,00	6,67	6,67	6,67	6,67
17	**18**	**19**	**20**	**21**	**22**	**23**	**24**	**25**	**26**	**27**	**28**	**29**	**30**	**31**	**32**
6,67	6,67	6,67	6,67	6,67	6,67	8,33	8,33	8,33	8,33	8,33	8,33	8,33	8,33	10,00	10,00
33	**34**	**35**	**Median**	**36**	**37**	**38**	**39**	**40**	**41**	**42**	**43**	**44**	**45**	**46**	**47**
10,00	11,67	11,67	11,67	11,67	13,33	13,33	15,00	15,00	15,00	15,00	16,67	16,67	16,67	18,33	20,00
48	**49**	**50**	**51**	**52**	**53**	**54**	**55**	**56**	**57**	**58**	**59**	**60**	**61**	**62**	**63**
20,00	20,00	21,67	21,67	21,67	21,67	23,33	25,00	26,67	26,67	26,67	28,33	28,33	28,33	30,00	30,00
64	**65**	**66**	**67**	**68**	**69**	**70**									
30,00	30,00	30,00	31,67	33,33	35,00	41,67									

public services, manufacturing and service). Such a classification has managed to successfully spread business sectors by classes. Classes contain almost a constant number of business sectors (the third column of Table 8), and if branches of business sectors are observed as well, that constancy is mostly maintained (the fourth, fifth and sixth column of Table 8). What is interesting is that all classes (except class II, and new classes V, VI and VII) contain the largest number of business sectors belonging to manufacturing. Here, classes V, VI and VII have no members as well, i.e., there are no business sectors which are supported by more than one out of 78% of producers.

A PROPOSITION FOR A UNIQUE CLASSIFICATION OF BUSINESS SECTORS

Figure 4 shows the interrelationship of class definitions which are illustrated in previous chapters. The Y axis holds various kinds of classifications, these being: Classification I is related to a classification based on business sectors supported by ERP solutions (see Table 5), Classification II is related to a classification based on the distribution of supporting business sectors by ERP solutions (see Table 6) and Classification III is related to a classification based on quartiles applied to the distribution of supporting business sectors by ERP solutions (see Table 8).

Table 8. Definition of classes of business sectors support based on the distribution of ERP solution support and quartiles

Class	Definition (% of supporting)	Total	Financial and public services	Manufacturing	Service
Class I	<0, 7]	22 (32%)	4 (33%)	10 (29%)	8 (35%)
Class II	<7, 12]	14 (20%)	4 (33%)	3 (8%)	7 (30%)
Class III	<12, 22]	17 (24%)	2 (17%)	10 (29%)	5 (22%)
Class IV	<22, 78]	17 (24%)	2 (17%)	12 (34%)	3 (13%)
Class V	<78, 88]	0 (0%)	0 (0%)	0 (0%)	0 (0%)
Class VI	<88, 93]	0 (0%)	0 (0%)	0 (0%)	0 (0%)
Class VII	<93, 100]	0 (0%)	0 (0%)	0 (0%)	0 (0%)
TOTAL		70 (100%)	12 (100%)	23 (100%)	35 (100%)

Table 9. A proposition of a unique classification of business sectors

Class	Definition (% of supporting)	Total	Financial and public services	Manufacturing	Service
Class I	<0, 10.25]	33 (47%)	6 (50%)	13 (37%)	14 (61%)
Class II	<10.25, 21.25]	16 (23%)	3 (25%)	7 (20%)	6 (26%)
Class III	<21.25, 30]	17 (24%)	3 (25%)	13 (37%)	1 (4%)
Class IV	<30, 70]	4 (6%)	0 (0%)	2 (6%)	2 (9%)
Class V	<70, 78.75]	0 (0%)	0 (0%)	0 (0%)	0 (0%)
Class VI	<78.75, 89.75]	0 (0%)	0 (0%)	0 (0%)	0 (0%)
Class VII	<89.75, 100]	0 (0%)	0 (0%)	0 (0%)	0 (0%)
TOTAL		70 (100%)	12 (100%)	35 (100%)	23 (100%)

Figure 4. The interrelationship of different class definitions

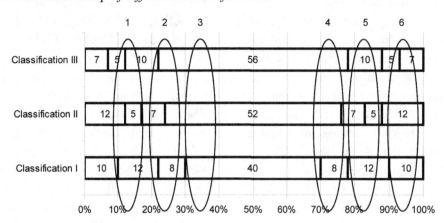

Figure 4 shows 6 groups which make interval borders of the given classifications. The borders of the interval are calculated using the arithmetic mean of a given group. This results in:

- for border 1: $(10 + 12 + 7 + 12) / 4 = 10,25\%$
- for border 2: $(22 + 17 + 24 + 22) / 4 = 21,25\%$
- for border 3: 30%
- for border 4: 70%
- for border 5: $(78 + 76 + 83 + 78) / 4 = 78,75\%$
- for border 6: $(90 + 88 + 88 + 93) / 4 = 89,75\%$

A final definition of business sectors class borders which is an arithmetic mean of borders belonging to different classifications, described in previous chapters, is shown in Table 9.

Table 9 illustrates that the largest number of business sectors (the third column) is in Class I, and the least number in Class IV. New classes V, VI and VII have no members, i.e. there are no business sectors which are supported by more than 70% of producers. It is visible that a larger number of business sectors from Manufacturing is in a higher class (Class III and Class IV), which can be explained by the fact that ERP solutions were firstly used to support business sectors from Manufacturing (see Vukšić et al., 2005).

Figure 5 shows the interrelationship between four classifications of business sectors which are defined in previous chapters.

Classification I illustrates business sectors which are classified according to their support by ERP solution. This classification clearly shows that a larger number of business sectors is in a lower class, and that this number rapidly decreases in value in higher classes. This classification suggests that the number of business sectors which are just in the process of applying support by ERP solutions is the largest, and that this number linearly decreases from class to class.

Figure 5 shows the interrelationship between four classifications of business sectors which are defined in previous chapters.

Classification II represents classifying business sectors based on the distribution of ERP support. This classification, unlike Classification I, suggests that a larger number of business sectors which are in the process of support by ERP solutions is in a lower class, then this number decreases (Class II), but then, in higher classes, is again on the rise. One could come to a conclusion that a larger number of business sectors is either weakly or excellently supported, and that a smaller number of business sectors is in a "transition stage" of moving to a higher or lower class.

Classification III classifies business sectors based on quartiles and the distribution of supporting business sectors. It is visible that this classification suggests that there is a larger number of business sectors that have just started to be

Figure 5. The relationship between classes of different classifications of business sector

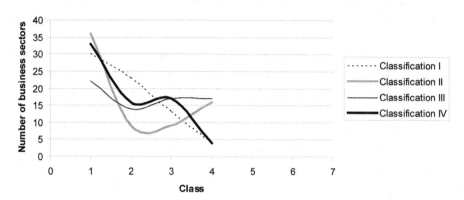

supported by ERP solutions, then this number slightly decreases in higher classes, and after that increases again, but after that stays constant (Classes III and IV). The constancy in the highest classes shows that the number of business sectors which are most frequently supported by ERP solutions either rarely changes or the change is specific, i.e., the change is such that maintains the constancy (e.g., incoming and outgoing business sectors in Classes III and IV are equal).

Classification IV is a combination of Classifications I, II and III. This classification suggests that the largest number of business sectors is just starting to get ERP support. The number of business sectors which are most frequently supported by ERP solutions is extremely small (Class IV). What is interesting is the dynamics that exists between Classes II and III (i.e., a larger number of business sectors is in Class III than the one in Class II), and it shows that business sectors do not stay long in Class II, but either go back to Class I or move to a higher Class III.

CONCLUSION

The paper analyzes ERP solutions and which business sectors these support. Four classifications of business sectors based on their ERP solution support are represented. The first three classifications are based on different views on

gathered data on support of business sectors by ERP solutions (graph of support, distribution of support and the application of quartiles), while the fourth one is a combination of the first three. Each of the described classifications shows a view to business sectors.

Classification I suggests that the number of newly supported business sectors increases faster than the number of business sectors where the support is increasing (i.e., incoming business sectors in Class I is larger than the incoming business sectors in other classes).

Classification II shows (unlike Classification I) that the larger number of business sectors is either weakly or excellently supported.

Classification III suggests that there is constancy in higher classes of business sectors ERP support, which opens up the problem of maintaining the constancy (few changes or changes with specific characteristics).

Classification IV illustrates the existence of dynamics between middle classes of supporting business sectors by ERP solutions, i.e., business sectors do not stay long in Class II; they either go back to Class I or move up to Class III. Business sectors from Class I are supported by a small number of ERP solutions. This can happen for more reasons: non-profitability of the specific business sector, a high sophistication of work process or a small number of potential buyers.

Classification IV suggests that many business sectors have moved to Class III, which can mean that it would be most acceptable to built in business processes of those business sectors which are now in Class II into the ERP solution (e.g., capital market, education, automotive, oil, logistics, retail, telecommunication, healthcare, etc).

Each business sector which is in a class can go through four scenarios: it stays long in the class (which means that the number of ERP producers supporting it is not changed), it moves up to a higher class (which means that the number of ERP producers supporting it is on the increase), moves down to a lower class (which means than the number of ERP producers supporting it is on the decrease) or completely vanishes from the classification (which means that all ERP producers have renounced their support of this particular business sector).

There are several reasons why business sectors change classes or completely vanish from the classification. Some of these reasons are: non-profitability of business software development, which is the reason why some business sectors never enter the classification (e.g., only a few organizations belong to the particular business sector), business sector is far too complex for supporting it by an business software (gathering knowledge on the business sector is a time-consuming process), business software for a business sector fails (renouncement of the solution happens), business software for a business sector is profitable so most ERP producers support it (then the business sector moves up to a higher class).

Described classifications represent relative classifications of business sectors, since these are based on the current level of business sector support by ERP solutions. In order to obtain an absolute classification (or, a classification closer to absolute), the analysis of business sectors, supported by ERP solutions, needs to be repeated periodically.

In the earlier work of the authors (see Jakupovic et al., 2009) an analysis of business sectors supported by ERP solutions was conducted, and it was intended for ERP solution producers, business organizations, and the scientific community. Further conclusions follow.

Alongside the existing list of business sectors which are supported by ERP producers, business organizations have the possibility to see whether a specialized ERP solution already exists for their business sector, which can serve as additional information in the process of decision making concerning the acquisition of a new business software. Also, the information on the existence of business software for a certain business sector can be of meaning in reaching the final decision on the choice of business sector a business organization will undertake in the process of foundation.

On the other hand, such information can help existing, as well as future ERP producers during the choice of business sector they will support.

Finding out which business sectors are supported by specialized ERP solutions, a set of new questions emerge for the scientific community, such as: which factors influence the lack of support for certain business sectors, which factors influence the dynamics of spreading the support to new business sectors, do some business sectors stand out in relation to the number of different specialized ERP solutions which support them, etc.

The distribution of knowledge, based on ERP producers, about certain business sectors, provides business organizations with additional information on ERP producers, which can be used in the process of decision making concerning the choice of producer and its business software. It is possible that it would be better to leave the acquisition of business software to a producer which is specialized in a certain business sector, because this means the producer is better acquainted with the business technology of a given business sector. However, this should not be the sole criterion in making the choice.

To ERP producers, existing ones or the new ones, the distribution of knowledge gives insight into the weight under which ERP producers operate. The information on the weight that existing ERP producers carry can serve as a guideline to existing or new producers, telling them how much knowledge they must have to enter the market. It is obvious that the analysis of entering the market cannot be based solely on such information.

The scientific community, through the distribution of knowledge, gets an insight into the weight carried by ERP producer, as well as a set of new questions: which factors influence the weight; factors of increase, decrease or invariability of weight, is there an interrelationship between observed factors, what is the dynamics of this weight, etc...

REFERENCES

Abas Business Software. (2003). *ERP Survey 2003/2004.* Retrieved from ftp://ftp.abas.de/pub/marketing/download/eng_konradin2003.pdf

Bailey, R. (2004). *Mathematics – Applications and Concepts (Course 2).* New York: McGraw-Hill.

Burns, M. (2006). *Accounting System/ERP Customer Survey.* Retrieved from http://www.180systems.com/ERPCustomerSurvey.php

Burns, M. (2008). *Accounting/ERP Comparison.* Retrieved from http://www.180systems.com/ERPsystem-comparison.php

Čerić, V. (2001). Building the Knowledge Economy. *Journal of Computing and Information Technology, 9*(3), 177–183. doi:10.2498/cit.2001.03.02

Eurostat. (2009). Retrieved from http://ec.europa.eu/eurostat/ramon/index.cfm?TargetUrl=DSP_PUB_WELC

Fertalj, K., & Kalpić, D. (2004). ERP Software Evaluation and Comparative Analysis. *Journal of Computing and Information Technology, 12*(3), 195–209. doi:10.2498/cit.2004.03.02

IDC. (2000). *The Integrated Enterprise Resource Management Software Application Market in Croatia, 1999-2004.* Czech Republic: IDC East Central Europe.

Jakupović, A., Pavlić, M., & Fertalj, K. (2009). Analysis and Classification of ERP Producers by Business Operations. *Journal of Computing and Information Technology, 17*(3), 239–258.

Koch, C. (2008). *The ABCs of ERP.* Retrieved from http://www.cio.com/article/40323/ERP_Definition_and_Solutions

Maitland, M., & Blitzer, D. M. (2002). *A GICS Overview for Standard & Poor's U.S. Indices.* Retrieved from www2.standardandpoors.com/spf/pdf/index/GICSIndexDocument.PDF

Microsoft. (2009). Retrieved from: http://www.microsoft.com/industry/default.mspx

On-Line Consultant. (2009). Retrieved from http://www.health-infosys-dir.com/top%20ERP%20vendors.htm

Quebec Inc. (2007). Retrieved from http://templates.rfp-builder.com/ERP1/ERPvendors.htm

SAP. (2009). Retrieved from http://www.sap.com/industries/index.epx

Sikavica, P., & Novak, M. (1993). *Poslovna organizacija.* Zagreb, Croatia: Informator.

Software Finder. (2009). Retrieved from http://softwarefinder.mbtmag.com/

Vrček, N., Dobrović, Ž., & Kermek, D. (2007). Novel Approach to BCG Analysis in the Context of ERP System Implementation. In Župančič, J. (Ed.), *Advances in Information Systems Development* (*Vol. 1*, pp. 47–60). New York: Springer. doi:10.1007/978-0-387-70761-7_5

Vukšić, V. B., & Spremić, M. (2005). ERP System Implementation and Business Process Change: Case Study of a Pharmaceutical Company. *Journal of Computing and Information Technology, 13*(1), 11–24. doi:10.2498/cit.2005.01.02

Wagner, L. E., Scott, V. S., & Galliers, D. R. (2006). The creation of 'best practice' software: Myth, reality and ethics. *Information and Organization, 16*(3), 251–275. doi:10.1016/j.infoandorg.2006.04.001

APPENDIX

Figures 6, 7 and 8 show data which were used in the analysis of business sectors supported by ERP producers. The first column shows producer's name, and other columns show numerical codes of certain business sectors from the general commercial classification.

Figure 6. ERP producers and business sectors from group Financial and Public Services

Producer	Financial and Public Services												TOTAL
	1	2	3	4	5	6	7	8	9	10	11	12	
3i Infotech	√	√	√								√		4
Add+On Software													0
Advanced Software Development Corp													0
American Business Systems, Inc.													0
Aperum	√	√	√								√		4
BatchMaster Software Inc													0
Cedar Group	√		√				√				√		4
Cincom Systems	√		√			√	√	√	√		√		7
CMS Manufacturing Systems, Inc													0
COSS Systems													0
Cougar Mountain Software											√		1
CSB-System													0
CYMA											√		1
Datacor													0
Datamodes													0
Deltek Systems											√		1
EMR Innovations													0
Enhanced Systems & Services													0
Epicor	√	√	√										3
eTek International													0
Europa Telecom Group	√		√				√	√	√		√		6
Evolucion e Inovacion Empresarial SC	√												1
EXEControl Global Solutions													0
FlexiInternational	√	√	√			√							4
Glovia International													0
GMA Infosys													0
IFS													0
iLatina B2B Business Services													0
Intacct Corp													0
Intentia International	√		√				√	√	√		√		6
Intuit													0
IQMS													0
iSoft							√						1
JDH Business Systems													0
Maconomy, Inc										√			1
Made2Manage Systems													0
Microsoft	√	√	√				√	√	√	√	√		8
Mincom				√							√		2
MYOB US													0
NetSuite													0
Open System, Inc													0
Oracle	√	√	√	√	√	√	√	√	√	√	√	√	12
QAD													0
Ramco Systems	√		√								√		3
Red Wing Software, Inc.													0
Relevant Business Systems													0
Ross Systems													0
Sage Software							√				√		2
SAP	√		√	√	√		√		√	√	√	√	9
SYSPRO													0
Tailor Made Systems (TMS)													0
Verticent													0
Vigilant Business Software, Inc.											√		1
Ceecom, Inc.													0
i2													0
IFS													0
ProfitKey International													0
Technology Group International													0
Eshbel							√				√		2
IBM	√	√	√				√	√	√	√	√		9

Figure 7. ERP producers and business sectors from group Manufacturing

Producer	Manufacturing																																			TOTAL
	13	14	15	16	17	18	19	20	21	22	23	24	25	26	27	28	29	30	31	32	33	34	35	36	37	38	39	40	41	42	43	44	45	46	47	
3i Infotech																																				0
Add+On Software																																				0
Advanced Software Development Corp																																				0
American Business Systems, Inc.																																				0
Aperum (novo ime infor)	√		√	√	√	√	√	√		√	√	√	√	√		√	√	√	√	√	√				√			√	√							21
BatchMaster Software Inc							√				√		√	√								√														5
Cedar Group															√																					1
Cincom Systems																																				0
CMS Manufacturing Systems, Inc	√		√	√						√		√	√	√		√	√	√							√			√								12
COSS Systems	√			√																		√			√	√			√				√			7
Cougar Mountain Software																																				0
CSB-System							√				√		√	√								√														5
CYMA																																				0
Datacor							√																													1
Datamodes							√						√									√														3
Deltek Systems	√																	√			√															3
EMR Innovations							√				√		√	√								√														5
Enhanced Systems & Services	√							√							√									√	√											5
Epicor																																				0
eTek International															√																					1
Europa Telecom Group																														√						1
Evolucion e Inovacion Empresarial SC																																				0
EXEControl Global Solutions																																				0
FlexiInternational																																				0
Glovia International			√													√	√	√		√																5
GMA Infosys																																				0
IFS	√	√	√	√	√	√	√	√	√		√		√			√	√	√			√	√		√		√		√	√	√					√	22
iLatina B2B Business Services																																		√		1
Intacct Corp																																				0
Intentia International	√		√	√			√			√	√	√	√				√	√		√	√		√		√	√		√	√		√	√		√	√	21
Intuit															√																					1
IQMS			√																					√				√								3
iSoft																																				0
JDH Business Systems			√												√										√	√										4
Maconomy, Inc																																				0
Made2Manage Systems	√																√	√		√					√			√	√							7
Microsoft			√	√	√	√				√	√	√	√				√			√		√													√	12
Mincom	√		√	√	√												√								√				√				√			8
MYOB US																																				0
NetSuite									√																											1
Open System, Inc																																				0
Oracle	√	√	√	√	√	√	√	√		√	√	√	√	√		√	√	√	√		√	√	√	√	√	√	√	√	√	√	√		√	√	√	31
QAD			√							√	√	√	√	√		√	√	√			√	√			√			√								13
Ramco Systems			√				√				√		√												√			√						√		7
Red Wing Software, Inc.								√																												1
Relevant Business Systems	√		√												√																					3
Ross Systems							√				√	√	√	√							√	√		√	√		√		√				√			12
Sage Software															√																					1
SAP	√	√	√	√	√	√	√	√		√	√	√	√	√	√	√	√	√	√	√	√	√	√	√	√	√	√	√	√	√	√		√	√	√	32
SYSPRO	√		√	√			√			√	√	√	√	√		√	√	√			√	√		√		√		√	√			√				19
Tailor Made Systems (TMS)																																				0
Verticent																									√			√								2
Vigilant Business Software, Inc.																																				0
Ceecom, Inc.										√	√		√		√	√	√	√				√														8
i2	√			√						√	√	√	√	√		√	√	√			√				√			√								13
IFS	√	√	√	√	√	√	√	√	√		√		√			√	√	√			√	√		√		√		√	√	√					√	22
ProfitKey International	√			√													√	√	√					√												6
Technology Group International							√		√		√	√	√	√	√		√	√	√				√													11
Eshbel	√		√	√	√	√	√			√		√				√	√	√	√					√							√					14
IBM	√	√	√	√	√	√	√			√	√	√	√	√		√	√	√	√			√	√											√		19

Figure 8. ERP producers and business sectors from group Service

Producer	48	49	50	51	52	53	54	55	56	57	58	59	60	61	62	63	64	65	66	67	68	69	70	TOTAL
3i Infotech																								0
Add+On Software																						√		1
Advanced Software Development Corp							√						√											2
American Business Systems, Inc.										√												√		2
Aperum (novo ime infor)										√	√			√		√		√			√	√		7
BatchMaster Software Inc																								0
Cedar Group										√		√		√										3
Cincom Systems										√		√				√								3
CMS Manufacturing Systems, Inc																								0
COSS Systems			√	√	√																			3
Cougar Mountain Software										√		√												2
CSB-System	√									√														2
CYMA												√												1
Datacor																								0
Datamodes																						√		1
Deltek Systems							√					√												2
EMR Innovations																								0
Enhanced Systems & Services	√																√							2
Epicor							√					√		√				√				√		5
eTek International							√															√		2
Europa Telecom Group																√								1
Evolucion e Inovacion Empresarial SC																								0
EXEControl Global Solutions							√						√					√				√		4
FlexiInternational							√								√									2
Glovia International							√									√								2
GMA Infosys																						√		1
IFS	√						√	√								√	√		√	√		√		8
iLatina B2B Business Services																								0
Intacct Corp							√			√			√	√								√		5
Intentia International	√											√						√				√		4
Intuit							√					√		√				√				√		5
IQMS																								0
iSoft																								0
JDH Business Systems													√									√		2
Maconomy, Inc							√					√												2
Made2Manage Systems							√																	1
Microsoft		√	√		√		√							√			√	√	√			√		9
Mincom	√							√		√									√					4
MYOB US																						√		1
NetSuite							√			√		√	√	√				√				√		6
Open System, Inc							√			√		√										√		4
Oracle		√	√	√	√		√									√		√	√	√	√	√		11
QAD																								0
Ramco Systems	√									√												√		3
Red Wing Software, Inc.																								0
Relevant Business Systems							√																	1
Ross Systems																								0
Sage Software							√					√			√							√		4
SAP	√	√	√	√	√	√	√	√		√						√	√	√	√		√	√		15
SYSPRO							√															√		2
Tailor Made Systems (TMS)				√	√																	√		3
Verticent																								0
Vigilant Business Software, Inc.										√												√		2
Ceecom, Inc.																						√		1
i2	√									√														2
IFS	√						√	√								√	√		√	√		√		8
ProfitKey International																								0
Technology Group International																						√		1
Eshbel							√			√	√					√						√		4
IBM		√	√	√	√		√			√						√	√	√	√			√		11

This work was previously published in International Journal of Enterprise Information Systems, edited by Madjid Tavana, pp. 59-86, Volume 6, Issue 3, copyright 2010 by IGI Publishing (an imprint of IGI Global).

Chapter 3

An Exploratory Study of the Key Skills for Entry-Level ERP Employees

Alan R. Peslak
Penn State University, USA

Todd A. Boyle
St. Francis Xavier University, Canada

ABSTRACT

This research identifies the key skills (e.g., business, team, communication) that industries expect for entry level positions involving enterprise resource planning (ERP) systems. Based on a review of the literature, a number of possible core skills that ERP entry level employees should possess are identified. To identify the relative importance of these specific skills, a web-based survey involving IT professionals from 105 organizations is conducted. Analyzing the findings using exploratory factor analysis and scale reliability analysis indicates four specific and significant factors representing the major key skills that industry expects from entry level ERP positions labeled for this study such as systems analysis and integration, team skills, project management, and business and application understanding. Various common technical skills (e.g., programming, networks) were found to be significantly less important than the business and team skills. This study should assist companies in developing criteria for evaluating potential candidates for entry level positions in ERP systems, as well as universities for evaluating the relevancy of their IT and Business programs.

INTRODUCTION

Enterprise Resource Planning (ERP) systems are complex, computer-centric systems designed to carry out the most common business functions in an organization, including finance, accounting, human resources, and operations. Such systems enable companies to move from an isolated or stove-pipe functional view to a process view of both IS development and business activities. Although originally designed for large organizations (e.g., mySAP ERP, Oracle Applications), there currently exist a number of ERP systems designed for organizations with as few as 10 users

DOI: 10.4018/978-1-4666-1761-2.ch003

(e.g., SYSPRO, SAP Business One). Given their applicability to organizations of varying sizes and industrial sectors, and that such systems come embedded with best business processes, it is not surprising that ERP systems have become the technology of choice for organizations attempting to reduce waste in their value chain and better integrate functional areas within their organization and members of their supply chain.

The growing popularity of ERP systems, combined with the shortage of recent IT graduates and the commoditization and subsequent outsourcing of many of the technical aspects of IT (e.g., programming, technical support), have caused organizations to question the key skills that they should expect from entry-level ERP employees. This research explores a series of key IT skills and determines what skills organizations view as important for entry-level ERP employees. With the critical ERP skills identified, employers can focus on these key areas in recruitment and development activities and improve their success rate for ERP implementation and support. Though there has been much work done on entry level skills necessary for information systems and technology graduates, little work has been none for entry-level ERP employees. In addition to examining the relative importance of these key skills, this research elicits a number of factors that can be used for summary proficiency analysis and help organizations quickly assess employee qualifications for entry level ERP positions.

ENTERPRISE RESOURCE PLANNING

There has been significant work done in the general information systems area of enterprise resource planning systems. One area of enterprise resource planning systems that has received some attention in the literature is the success or failure rate of ERP implementations. Enterprise resource planning systems are so comprehensive and as a result so complex that they require coordination across many disciplinary areas in an organization and often take multiple years to implement. They have had an uneven record of success in organizations. Estimates vary widely on the success rate of ERP implementations. Barker and Frolick (2003) suggest that 50% of ERP implementations succeed. Hong and Kim (2002) estimate a 25% success rate. Others suggest failure rates up to 90% (Scott & Vessey, 2002; Martin, 1998). Ho, Wu, and Ta (2004) have reported that currently there are relatively few successes. Overall, there is insufficient research into enterprise resource planning systems. As one author suggests, "research in the ERP area is still lacking and the gap in the ERP literature is huge" (Al-Mashari, 2003).

The essential parts of an enterprise resource planning system are integrated modules that allow business process that cross business functional areas; one large real-time database that allows for a single entry and repository for information across business functions; and seamless business transactions across business functions (Miller, 2003).

Okrent and Vokurka (2004) note six core processes that are streamlined in ERP systems: quote to cash, procure to pay, plan to perform, manufacturing operations, product life cycle, and financial management. McAdam and Galloway (2005) suggest ERP systems allow "standardising business processes, ensuring integrity of data, and removing the number, complexity, and expense surrounding old independent legacy systems."

ERP systems had their origins in materials requirements planning (MRP) that evolved to a more comprehensive system with a name coined by the Gartner Group in 1990. (Yu, 2005). ERP systems coordinate business functions and processes, are designed to lower costs "in its entire supply chain by either shortening throughput times; lowering inventory or by providing quality service" (Gupta, Priyadarshini, Massoud, & Agrawal, 2004). McAdam and Galloway (2005) suggest that ERP systems can play an "increasingly important role in sustaining 'leading edge' competitiveness.

ERP systems sales are estimated at $12 billion (Arc Advisory Group, 2003) to $30 billion (King, 2005). Market penetration is estimated at 70% of the Fortune 1000 (Bingi, Sharma, & Godla, 1999). In addition there has been a great deal of work done that has explored the gap between information systems training and the needs of practitioners. Kim, Hsu, and Stern (2006) suggest that there continues to be a skills gap between information systems curriculum and skills need by entry level IS/IT employers. They note that project management is not "adequately covered". Other skills that need more attention include security and ERP. Peslak (2005b) notes that business processes and functions are not sufficiently included in IS and IT curricula. Boyle (2007) also suggests "grounding in business functions" is essential. Muscatello and Chen (2008) in a large scale industry study found that "firms now realize that business process changes and project management are strongly linked to the success of the ERP implementation". Tesch, Braun, and Crable (2008) found teamwork to be highest variable sought in interpersonal skills for entry-level IT professionals. McMurtrey, Downey, Zeltmann, and Friedman (2008), the "most important skills for new IT professionals were soft skills, specifically the personal attributes of problem-solving, critical thinking, and team skills. However, the study also found that technical skills were essential…"

Trauth, Farwell, and Lee (1993) performed an oft-cited study that reviewed data from IS managers, consultants, professors, and end-users and identified many areas where "there is an 'expectation gap' between industry needs and academic preparation". Some of the areas that deserve attention include information access and security, re-engineering business processes, and especially systems integration. Lee and Fang (2008) recently studied this gap and found current gaps between employers and students on nearly all skill levels. Aken and Michalisin (2007) grouped their entry

level IT gap analysis in four areas soft skills, business skills, technical skills, and programming skills. Lee and Han (2008) found entry level "programmer/analysts in the Fortune 500 are expected to fulfill a combination of roles from computer program writers to technical experts as well as businessmen." Merhout, Hvelka, and Hick (2009) have found a growing trend toward soft skills for entry-level MIS graduates.

But there has been little work done on the precursor to ERP success, obtaining the right employees to implement and maintain these systems and especially little with regard to entry-level professionals. In their review of research into ERP critical success factors (CSF), Pairat and Jungthirapanich (2005) found nearly every study saw ERP teamwork and composition as a critical success factor. Employees are key. As a result, hiring of new employees with the proper skills and attributes is essential. There has been published research that has suggested content for ERP curricula, and thus potential skills needed for entry-level ERP employees, including Hawking, Ramp, and Shackleton, (2001), Hawking (1999), Becera-Fernandez, Murphy, and Simon (2000), Peslak (2005a), Antonucci et al. (2004), Hayen, Holmes, and Cappel (2000), Davis and Comeau (2004), Boykin and Martz (2004), and Watson and Schneider (1999). But none of these studies have empirically tested how these skills and content are viewed by practitioners.

RESEARCH OBJECTIVES AND METHODOLOGY

To explore the key skills required for entry-level ERP positions, a web based survey is developed. The overall research objectives were to find the key skill factors that were desired in entry-level ERP workers. To develop the survey, various skills that one would expect of entry-level IS professionals were first identified (e.g., Lee et al., 1995; Stewart & Rosemann, 2001). Next, entry-level skills more specific to ERP systems were added to the list. Given the lack of research in the area, for the latter category, we examined among other things, research on content recommendations for ERP courses and programs (e.g., Hawking et al., 2001; Peslak, 2005a; Watson & Schneider, 1999). This process resulted in a total of 27 potential entry-level ERP skills, with these skills loosely placed into three categories, as identified in Table 1.

To determine the key skills required by industry, 455 ERP professionals involved in SAP (e.g., R/3, mySAP ERP) implementation, management or support activities were asked to complete the web-based focused on the key skills that they would like a recent graduate / new hire to have was conducted in mid-2005. To control for the ERP software used in the organizations under study, SAP was chosen given the company's domination in large organizations, and its recent move into the mid-sized ERP market. Of the 455 ERP professionals invited to participate in the study, 105 usable surveys were returned resulting in a usable response rate of 23.1%.

Table 1. Potential skills of entry-level ERP employees

Technical Skills	Support end user computing Support the existing portfolio of applications Support hardware Networks Operating systems Systems analysis Systems design/integration Systems life cycle management Relational databases ERP related programming language (e.g., ABAP, JAVA) Data management (e.g., data modeling) Decision support systems
Business Skills	Knowledge of business functions Willingness to learn in detail a specific business functional area of the organization Ability to quickly understand the needs of customers Ability to understand the business environment Ability to interpret business problems Ability to develop appropriate technical solutions to business problems Knowledge of ERP concepts Ability to learn new technologies Ability to focus on technology as a means, not an end Ability to understand technological trends
Team & Soft Skills	Ability to work cooperatively in a team environment Ability to work in a collaborative environment Ability to plan projects Ability to lead projects Ability to deal with uncertainty Ability to accomplish assignments Ability to write effective reports / memos / documents Ability to deliver effective presentations Ability to be proactive Ability to be sensitive to organizational culture Ability to teach others

RESULTS

The specific IT professionals represented in this study included IT managers and project managers (i.e., n = 35), technical specialists (i.e., n = 36), and IT consultants (i.e., n = 34). As each of these three groups have different job responsibilities, they may also differ in what ERP skills they deem important for entry-level ERP positions. To examine if any such differences do in fact exist between these three groups, multivariate analysis of variance (MANOVA) is applied. Results of performing MANOVA indicates that no differences exists between the groups (i.e., Wilks' Λ = .451, F (66, 140) = 1.036, p = .423). Subsequently, the data from the three groups can be combined and analyzed together, with the relative importance of each skill presented in Table 2.

To elicit the core skill factors, exploratory factor analysis (EFA) with varimax rotation is applied. A number of variables were discarded after a few attempts at EFA, but 25 variables remained and were found to measure five unique factors. These components are shown in Table 3 and Table 4. Table 3 shows that five factors exceeded an Eigenvalue of 1 which is used for acceptable cutoff (Moore, 2000). The five factors represent a high 65% of the variance explained. In addition scale reliability was performed on the factors and four factors were well above .70, the minimum for acceptability (Nunnally, 1978). There are shown along with the factors and Varimax rotation in Table 4. These factors are systems analysis and integration, team skills, project management, decision analysis, and business and application understanding. For this and subsequent analyses, similar to Chow (2004) and Taylor and Wright (2004), factor loadings over 0.50 were used to identify factors contributing to a factor cluster.

Two key statistical tests were performed on the data and shown in Table 5. The Kaiser-Meyer-Olkin test which measures sampling adequacy was .83. This is well above .7 which is seen as the cutoff for adequacy of factor analysis (de Vaus, 1991). Bartlett's test of sphericity suggests that the variables are not correlated at p < .001.

After the factors were determined, scale reliability was performed to determine the reliability of the factors. Items were excluded if the alpha could be improved. As a result four factors were determined to be reliable, utilizing 20 of the original variables. These were business and application understanding, team skills, project management, and systems analysis and integration. All showed extremely high alpha values of .871, .841, .889, and .787. The final factor originally found (4 decision analysis), was not supported by scale reliability analysis.

DISCUSSION

Business and Application Understanding

The first factor deals with what is commonly called soft skills (Table 6). Overall, it is suggested that an enterprise resource planning graduate have a broad business and application understanding of organizational needs and requirements. The alpha for this seven item factor was .871. As shown in Table 7, the alpha is not improved if any item is deleted. The variables associated with this factor included: business functions, organizational culture, and using technology as a means to an end. This business and application understanding was seen as a key factor needed for ERP graduates. The overall group mean of all these items was high at 7.68 on a scale of one to nine with nine being the highest score.

Team Skills

The second factor is one that is often mentioned by practitioners for any information technology project. The skill is broadly known as team skills. It is suggested that an enterprise resource plan-

Table 2. Relative importance of key skills

Skill Description	Mean
Ability to understand the business environment	8.129
Ability to work cooperatively in a team environment	8.127
Ability to accomplish assignments	8.097
Ability to be proactive	7.975
Ability to work in a collaborative environment	7.973
Knowledge of business functions	7.829
Ability to interpret business problems	7.776
Ability to focus on technology as a means, not an end	7.717
Ability to learn new technologies	7.705
Ability to deal with uncertainty	7.679
Knowledge of ERP concepts	7.58
Ability to quickly understand the needs of customers	7.435
Ability to write effective reports / memos / documents	7.322
Willingness to learn in detail a specific business functional areas of the organization	7.268
Systems analysis	7.212
Ability to develop appropriate technical solutions to business problems	7.191
Ability to be sensitive to organizational culture	7.183
Ability to deliver effective presentations	7.16
Ability to plan projects	7.057
Ability to understand technological trends	7.026
Ability to teach others	6.849
Systems design/integration	6.764
Data management (e.g., data modeling)	6.714
Systems life cycle management	6.665
Support end user computing	6.556
Ability to lead projects	6.343
Decision support systems	6.25
Relational databases	5.812
ERP related programming language (e.g., ABAP)	5.721
Support the existing portfolio of applications	5.689
Operating systems	4.388
Networks	4.16
Support hardware	3.542

ning graduate have knowledge and experience in working in teams. The collaborative environments experienced in organizations today are essential for enterprise resource planning graduate success. The Alpha for this five-item factor was 0.841. The Alpha is not improved by an exclusion of any item as shown in Table 9. The variables associated with this factor as shown in Table 8 included: the ability to work cooperatively in a team environment, the ability to work in collaborative environments, and the ability to accomplish assignments. The overall group mean of these items was very high at 7.92 on the scale of one to nine with nine of being the highest score.

Project Management

The next factor is another general business area. The enterprise resource planning graduate should have specific project management expertise and experience. The variables associated with this factor included the ability to deliver effective presentations, the ability to teach others, the ability to write effectively, and the ability to both plan and lead projects. The Alpha associated with this five item factor was very high at 0.889. As shown in Table 11 the Alpha could not be improved by deletion of any item. Table 10 shows the item statistics for each of the five variables. It should be noted that the overall group mean of these items though still high at 6.95 was lower than the other two factors thus far.

Systems Analysis and Integration

The final factor which emerged from the study was the more traditional systems analysis and integration (Table 12). Interestingly, the group mean for this factor was the lowest of all four at 6.88. This three items factor had an overall Alpha of 0.785. The variables associated with this factor included systems analysis, systems design and integration,

Table 3. Total variance explained

Component	Initial Eigenvalues			Extraction Sums of Squared Loadings			Rotation Sums of Squared Loadings		
	Total	% of Variance	Cumulative %	Total	% of Variance	Cumulative %	Total	% of Variance	Cumulative %
1	9.660	37.154	37.154	9.660	37.154	37.154	3.985	15.328	15.328
2	2.571	9.890	47.043	2.571	9.890	47.043	3.919	15.073	30.401
3	1.877	7.219	54.263	1.877	7.219	54.263	3.229	12.420	42.821
4	1.515	5.826	60.089	1.515	5.826	60.089	3.084	11.861	54.682
5	1.252	4.815	64.904	1.252	4.815	64.904	2.658	10.221	64.904
6	.999	3.843	68.747						
7	.954	3.671	72.418						
8	.924	3.554	75.971						
9	.871	3.348	79.319						
10	.679	2.611	81.930						
11	.617	2.373	84.303						
12	.511	1.965	86.268						
13	.463	1.779	88.047						
14	.404	1.552	89.600						
15	.359	1.380	90.980						
16	.329	1.267	92.247						
17	.325	1.249	93.496						
18	.304	1.171	94.667						
19	.295	1.136	95.803						
20	.226	.871	96.674						
21	.217	.836	97.510						
22	.207	.796	98.306						
23	.135	.521	98.827						
24	.119	.459	99.286						
25	.108	.417	99.703						
26	.077	.297	100.000						

and systems lifecycle management. The variables are shown in Table 13 and shows that the Alpha is not improve if any item is deleted. A preliminary review of this factor showed that four items (the addition of programming languages were over .5 in factor loading. But as shown in Table 14, the elimination of this variable improved scale reliability.

CONCLUSION AND IMPLICATIONS FOR PRACTITIONERS

Overall, the results of this study suggest that there are four key areas that practitioners view as vital for recent ERP graduates to posses prior to joining their organization. These skills in order of group mean are Team Skills, Business and Application Understanding, Project Management, and Systems Analysis and Integration. The study empirically

Table 4. Rotated component matrix

	Component				
	1	**2**	**3**	**4**	**5**
Systems Analysis	.150	.120	.028	.144	**.723**
Systems life cycle management	.124	.157	.174	.056	**.775**
Operating systems	.098	.051	.044	**.568**	.447
ERP related programming language (e.g., ABAP)	-.011	.025	.066	.047	**.608**
Ability to accomplish assignments	.020	**.776**	.116	.211	.249
Ability to quickly understand the needs of customers	.248	**.606**	.433	-.044	.055
Ability to work in a collaborative environment	.168	**.797**	.088	.181	.117
Ability to be proactive	.269	**.777**	.220	-.040	.073
Ability to work cooperatively in a team environment	.183	**.639**	.131	.185	.296
Ability to deal with uncertainty	.234	.409	.316	.261	-.197
Ability to plan projects	.142	-.019	**.534**	.695	.092
Ability to lead projects	.270	.076	**.600**	.566	.095
Ability to write effective reports / memos / documents	.194	.295	**.757**	.055	.243
Ability to deliver effective presentations	.293	.262	**.759**	.227	-.013
Ability to teach others	.257	.318	**.513**	.560	.055
Knowledge of business functions	**.566**	.229	.574	-.068	.184
Ability to understand the business environment	**.718**	.039	.470	-.142	.176
Willingness to learn in detail a specific business functional areas of the organization	**.746**	.060	.283	.105	-.028
Ability to be sensitive to organizational culture	**.612**	.387	.096	.206	-.110
Ability to interpret business problems	**.794**	.269	.174	.225	-.015
Ability to develop appropriate technical solutions to business problems	.452	.071	.226	.410	.248
Ability to focus on technology as a means, not an end	**.524**	.356	.171	.162	.219
Systems design/integration	-.154	.255	-.044	.374	**.660**
Decision support systems	.015	.174	.005	**.636**	.149
Ability to learn new technologies	**.539**	.482	-.091	.406	.098
Ability to understand technological trends	.461	.305	.003	**.590**	.140

confirms what has been proposed by theoretical researchers. Chaing and Mookerjee (2004) explicitly suggest "the problem of managing a software project is related to the problem of coordinating a team to produce a common goal." Team skills are essential. Peslak (2005b) suggests that business understanding is the missing element in information systems and technology education. Nah and Delgado (2006) saw project management as a critical success factor for enterprise resource planning implementation and upgrade success. Systems analysis was seen as essential for ERP success by both Boykin, Martz, and Mensching (1999) and Nah and Delgado (2006). One of the surprising and interesting findings of this study was that technical skills were not found to be the most important skills for ERP graduates and they did not become of part of the significant factors. Support hardware, networks, operating systems, and support of existing portfolio of applications

Table 5. KMO and Bartlett's Test

Kaiser-Meyer-Olkin Measure of Sampling Adequacy		.830
Bartlett's Test of Sphericity	Approx. Chi-Square	1553.250
	df	325
	Sig.	.000

Table 6. Item statistics

	Mean	Std. Deviation	N
Knowledge of business functions	7.82	1.472	101
Ability to understand the business environment	8.13	1.206	101
Willingness to learn in detail a specific business functional areas of the organization	7.28	1.680	101
Ability to be sensitive to organizational culture	7.20	1.530	101
Ability to interpret business problems	7.81	1.391	101
Ability to focus on technology as a means, not an end	7.77	1.216	101
Ability to learn new technologies	7.72	1.415	101

Table 7. Item-total statistics

	Scale Mean if Item Deleted	Scale Variance if Item Deleted	Corrected Item-Total Correlation	Cronbach's Alpha if Item Deleted
Knowledge of business functions	45.91	40.602	.704	.844
Ability to understand the business environment	45.60	43.362	.703	.847
Willingness to learn in detail a specific business functional areas of the organization	46.46	39.430	.651	.854
Ability to be sensitive to organizational culture	46.53	41.311	.627	.856
Ability to interpret business problems	45.92	40.254	.781	.834
Ability to focus on technology as a means, not an end	45.96	45.218	.568	.862
Ability to learn new technologies	46.01	43.910	.537	.867

Table 8. Item statistics

	Mean	Std. Deviation	N
Ability to accomplish assignments	8.10	1.181	105
Ability to quickly understand the needs of customers	7.43	1.675	105
Ability to work in a collaborative environment	7.97	1.417	105
Ability to be proactive	7.97	1.228	105
Ability to work cooperatively in a team environment	8.12	1.080	105

Table 9. Item-total statistics

	Scale Mean if Item Deleted	Scale Variance if Item Deleted	Corrected Item-Total Correlation	Cronbach's Alpha if Item Deleted
Ability to accomplish assignments	31.50	18.829	.676	.803
Ability to quickly understand the needs of customers	32.16	16.214	.603	.833
Ability to work in a collaborative environment	31.62	16.334	.769	.772
Ability to be proactive	31.62	18.930	.628	.814
Ability to work cooperatively in a team environment	31.47	20.021	.616	.819

Table 10. Item statistics

	Mean	Std. Deviation	N
Ability to write effective reports / memos / documents	7.34	1.550	103
Ability to deliver effective presentations	7.15	1.746	103
Ability to plan projects	7.07	1.800	103
Ability to lead projects	6.34	2.126	103
Ability to teach others	6.86	1.847	103

Table 11. Item-total statistics

	Scale Mean if Item Deleted	Scale Variance if Item Deleted	Corrected Item-Total Correlation	Cronbach's Alpha if Item Deleted
Ability to write effective reports / memos / documents	27.42	41.814	.666	.880
Ability to deliver effective presentations	27.61	38.220	.756	.860
Ability to plan projects	27.69	38.295	.720	.867
Ability to lead projects	28.42	33.618	.788	.853
Ability to teach others	27.89	37.410	.741	.862

Table 12. Item statistics

	Mean	Std. Deviation	N
Systems design/integration	6.77	1.746	102
Systems Analysis	7.21	1.702	102
Systems life cycle management	6.67	2.007	102

Table 13. Item-total statistics

	Scale Mean if Item Deleted	Scale Variance if Item Deleted	Corrected Item-Total Correlation	Cronbach's Alpha if Item Deleted
Systems design/integration	13.87	11.182	.578	.762
Systems Analysis	13.44	10.724	.660	.681
Systems life cycle management	13.98	9.049	.655	.686

Table 14. Item-total statistics before excluding programming languages

	Scale Mean if Item Deleted	Scale Variance if Item Deleted	Corrected Item-Total Correlation	Cronbach's Alpha if Item Deleted
Systems Analysis	19.08	18.214	.624	.635
Systems life cycle management	19.63	16.334	.611	.636
Systems design/integration	19.52	18.452	.586	.655
ERP related programming language (e.g., ABAP)	20.59	20.904	.346	.785

all were found to be at the bottom of key skills and were not a part of the significant factors. Even a specific ERP language (ABAP) did not remain as a variable in the systems factor.

The importance of successful implementation and operation of ERP system is paramount. Many researchers have attempted to determine critical success factors and important issues associated with ERP success. Many have proposed that people are one of the most important variables in a winning ERP strategy. Many academic researchers have attempted to develop a curriculum that emphasized key skills that graduates should have as they enter ERP related positions. This manuscript attempts to bridge the gap and provide a fresh platform for practical ERP success as well as core components and skills that are essential to an ERP curriculum. The study has determined that there are four key areas that have been deemed critical by practitioners namely systems analysis and integration skills, project management, team skills, and overall business and organizational analysis. It is imperative that ERP curricula be reviewed to meet the needs of today's practitioners and modify their courses to meet these requirements. Together educators and

practitioners can prepare future ERP knowledge workers to optimize their business implementations and improve organizational performance.

ACKNOWLEDGMENT

The authors wish to thank the anonymous reviewers for their insightful suggestions and input. This manuscript has been greatly enhanced by their efforts.

REFERENCES

Aken, A., & Michalisin, M. (2007) The Impact of the Skills Gap on the Recruitment of MIS Graduates. In *Proceedings of the 2007 ACM SIGMIS CPR conference on Computer personnel research: The global information technology workforce* (pp. 105-111).

Al-Mashari, M. (2003). Enterprise resource planning (ERP) systems: A research agenda. *Industrial Management + Data Systems, 103*(1-2), 22-27.

Antonucci, Y., Corbitt, G., Stewart, G., & Harris, A. (2004). Enterprise systems education: where are we? Where are we going? *Journal of Information Systems Education, 15*(3), 227–234.

ARC Advisory Group. (2003). *ERP Market Opportunities Change While Remaining Strong Overall at $8.9 Billion.* Retrieved from http://www.arcweb.com/Community/arcnews/arcnews.asp?ID=328

Barker, T., & Frolick, M. (2003). ERP implementation failure: a case study. *Information Systems Management, 20*(4), 43–49. doi:10.1201/1078/43647.20.4.20030901/77292.7

Becerra-Fernandez, I., Murphy, K. E., & Simon, S. J. (2000). Enterprise resource planning: Integrating ERP in the business school curriculum. *Communications of the ACM, 43*(4), 41. doi:10.1145/332051.332066

Bingi, P., Sharma, M., & Godla, J. (1999). Critical Issues Affecting an ERP Implementation. *Information Systems Management, 16*(3), 7–14. doi:10.1201/1078/43197.16.3.19990601/31310.2

Boykin, R., & Martz, W. Jr. (2004). The integration of ERP into a logistics curriculum: applying a systems approach. *Journal of Enterprise Information Management, 17*(1), 45–55. doi:10.1108/09576050410510944

Boykin, R., Martz, W., & Mensching, J. (1999). The integration of enterprise information systems in the operations management curriculum. *Journal of Computer Information Systems, 39*(4), 45–55.

Boyle, T. (2007). Technical-Oriented Enterprise Resource Planning (ERP) Body of Knowledge for Information Systems Programs: Content and Implementation. *Journal of Education for Business, 82*(5), 267–274. doi:10.3200/JOEB.82.5.267-275

Chiang, I. R., & Mookerjee, V. S. (2004). A fault threshold policy to manage software development projects. *Information Systems Research, 15*(1), 3–21. doi:10.1287/isre.1040.0012

Chow, W. (2004). An exploratory study of the success factors for extranet adoption in e-supply chain. *Journal of Global Information Management, 12*(1), 60–67. doi:10.4018/jgim.2004010104

Davis, C., & Comeau, J. (2004). Enterprise integration in business education: Design and outcomes of a capstone ERP-based undergraduate e-business management course. *Journal of Information Systems Education, 15*(3), 287–299.

deVaus, D. (1991). *Surveys in Social Research* (3rd ed.). Sydney, Australia: Allen and Unwin.

Gupta, O., Priyadarshini, K., Massoud, S., & Agrawal, S. (2004). Enterprise resource planning: a case of a blood bank. *Industrial Management + Data Systems, 104*(7), 589-603.

Hawking, P. (1999). The teaching of enterprise resource planning systems (SAP R/3) in Australian Universities. In *Proceedings Pan-Pacific Conference XVI*, Fiji.

Hawking, P., Ramp, A., & Shackleton, P. (2001). IS'97 model curriculum and enterprise resource planning systems. *Business Process Management Journal, 7*(3), 225–233. doi:10.1108/14637150110392700

Hayen, R., Holmes, M., & Cappel, J. (2000). A framework for SAP R/3 enterprise software instruction. *Journal of Computer Information Systems, 40*(2), 79–85.

Ho, C., Wu, W., and Tai, W. (2004). Strategies for the adaptation of ERP systems. *Industrial Management + Data Systems, 104*(3-4), 234-251.

Hong, K., & Kim, Y. (2002). The critical success factors for ERP implementation: an organizational fit perspective. *Information & Management, 40*(1), 25–40. doi:10.1016/S0378-7206(01)00134-3

Kim, Y., Hsu, J., & Stern, M. (2006). An Update on the IS/IT Skills Gap. *Journal of Information Systems Education, 17*(4), 395–402.

King, W. (2005). Ensuring ERP implementation success. *Information Systems Management, 22*(3), 83–84. doi:10.1201/1078/45317.22.3.20050601/88749.11

Lee, C., & Han, H. (2008). Analysis of Skills Requirement for Entry-Level Programmer/Analysts in Fortune 500 Corporations. *Journal of Information Systems Education, 19*(1), 17–27.

Lee, D., Trauth, E., & Harwell, D. (1995). Critical skills and knowledge requirements of IS professionals: A Joint Academic/Industry Investigation. *Management Information Systems Quarterly, 19*(3), 313–340. doi:10.2307/249598

Lee, S., & Fang, X. (2008). Perception Gaps About Skills Requirement for Entry-Level IS Professionals Between Recruiters And Students: An Exploratory Study. *Information Resources Management Journal, 21*(3), 39–63. doi:10.4018/irmj.2008070103

Martin, M. (1998). An electronics firm will save big money by replacing six people with one and lose all the paperwork, using enterprise resource planning software. But not every company has been so lucky. *Fortune, 137*(2), 149–151.

McAdam, R., & Galloway. (2005). Enterprise resource planning and organizational innovation: a management perspective. *Industrial Management + Data Systems, 105*(3), 280-290.

McMurtrey, M., Downey, J., Zeltmann, S., & Friedman, W. (2008). Critical Skill Sets of Entry-Level IT Professionals. *An Empirical Examination of Perceptions from Field Personnel Journal of Information Technology Education, 7*, 101–120.

Merhout, J., Havelka, D., & Hick, S. (2009). Soft Skills versus Technical Skills: Finding the Right Balance for an IS Curriculum. In *Proceedings of Americas Conference on Information Systems (AMCIS) AMCIS 2009* (pp. 1-8).

Miller, B. (2003). "What is ERP?" *CIO*. Retrieved from http://www2.cio.com/analyst/report2003.html

Moore, J. (2000). One Road to Turnover: An Examination of Work Exhaustion in Technology Professionals. *Management Information Systems Quarterly, 24*(1), 141–168. doi:10.2307/3250982

Muscatello, J., & Chen, I. (2008). Enterprise Resource Planning (ERP) Implementations: Theory and Practice. *International Journal of Enterprise Information Systems, 4*(1), 63–78. doi:10.4018/jeis.2008010105

Nah, F., & Delgado, S. (2006). Critical Success Factors for Enterprise Resource Planning Implementation and Upgrade. *Journal of Computer Information Systems, 46*(5), 99–114.

Nunnally, J. C. (1978). *Psychometric Theory* (2nd ed.). New York: McGraw-Hill.

Okrent, M., & Vokurka, R. (2004). Process mapping in successful ERP implementations. *Industrial Management + Data Systems, 104*(8-9), 637-643.

Pairat, R., & Jungthirapanich, C. (2005). A Chronological Review of ERP Research: An Analysis of ERP Inception, Evolution, and Direction. In *Proceedings of Engineering Management Conference, 2005 IEEE International* (Vol. 1, pp. 288-292).

Peslak, A. (2005a). A twelve-step, multiple course approach to teaching enterprise resource planning. *Journal of Information Systems Education, 16*(2), 147–155.

Peslak, A. (2005b). Incorporating Business Processes and Functions: Addressing The Missing Element In Information Systems Education. *Journal of Computer Information Systems, 45*(4), 56–61.

Scott, J., & Vessey, I. (2002). Managing risks in enterprise implementations. *Communications of the ACM, 45*(4), 74–81. doi:10.1145/505248.505249

Stewart, G., & Rosemann, M. (2001). Industry-oriented design of ERP-related curriculum - An Australian initiative. *Business Process Management Journal, 7*(3), 234–242. doi:10.1108/14637150110392719

Taylor, W., & Wright, G. (2004). Organizational readiness for successful knowledge sharing: challenges for public sector managers. *Information Resources Management Journal, 17*(2), 22–37. doi:10.4018/irmj.2004040102

Tesch, D., Braun, G., & Crable, E. (2008). An Examination of Employers' Perceptions and Expectations of IS Entry-level Personal and Interpersonal Skills. *Information Systems Education Journal, 6*(1), 3–16.

Trauth, E. M., Farwell, D. W., & Lee, D. (1993). The IS expectation gap: Industry expectations versus academic preparation. *Management Information Systems Quarterly, 17*(3), 293–308. doi:10.2307/249773

Watson, E., & Schneider, H. (1999). Using ERP systems in education. *Communication of the Association for Information Systems, 1*(9). Retrieved from http://cais.isworld.org/articles/?vol=1&art=9

Yu, C. (2005). Causes influencing the effectiveness of the post-implementation ERP system. *Industrial Management + Data Systems, 105*(1-2), 115-132.

This work was previously published in International Journal of Enterprise Information Systems, edited by Madjid Tavana, pp. 1-14, Volume 6, Issue 2, copyright 2010 by IGI Publishing (an imprint of IGI Global).

Chapter 4

E-Business and ERP:
A Conceptual Framework toward the Business Transformation to an Integrated E-Supply Chain

Mahesh Srinivasan
The University of Akron, USA

ABSTRACT

The blending of Internet technologies and traditional business concerns impacts all industries and is the latest phase in the ongoing evolution of business. In this changing business environment, the most successful companies are those that leverage their investment in Web-based technologies by implementing e-business solutions supported by sound existing infrastructures based on well-functioning Enterprise Resource Planning (ERP) systems. Companies must also forge tighter links in the supply chain, from raw materials to customers and have increasingly turned to the Internet and Web-based technologies to do so. This paper presents a framework for understanding e-business opportunities within the context of a traditional enterprise and its infrastructure and examines the evolving relationship between e-business and ERP. These developments are moving businesses toward the concept of e-Supply Chain to achieve true supply chain integration. The issues and challenges faced by organizations in moving to such a complete e-business environment are discussed and suggestions are offered for businesses to navigate this challenging transformation.

INTRODUCTION

Traditional companies must embrace the Internet to survive, but, at the same time, pure Internet companies benefit from the assets and infrastructure of their "bricks-and-mortar" counterparts. The blending of Internet technologies and traditional

business concerns is impacting all industries and is really the latest phase in the ongoing evolution of business. Today, the Internet is driving the current industry goals of a shorter Order-To-Delivery (OTD) cycle, global reach and personalization. However, without connecting order delivery, manufacturing, financial, human resources, and other back office systems to the Internet, even companies with long track records of innovation

DOI: 10.4018/978-1-4666-1761-2.ch004

are not likely to succeed. The most successful companies will be those that leverage their investment in Web based technologies by implementing e-Business solutions supported by sound existing infrastructures based on well-functioning Enterprise Resource Planning (ERP) systems.

Today companies need to forge tighter links up and down the supply chain, from raw materials to customers. Of late, companies have increasingly turned to the Internet and Web-based technologies to accomplish this. But what they have found is that without ERP software, sharing accurate information with their trading partners is impossible. Web-based technology puts life and breadth into ERP technology that is large, technologically cumbersome, and does not easily reveal its value. At the same time, ERP allows e-Business to come into full flower, putting real substance behind that flashy web page. While ERP organizes information within the enterprise, e-Business disseminates information far and wide. In short, ERP and e-Business technologies supercharge each other.

In light of the above, the objectives of this paper are to:

- Present a framework for understanding e-Business opportunities within the context of a traditional enterprise and its infrastructure.
- Examine the evolving relationship between e-Business and ERP, and to understand how companies can move ahead to gain competitive advantage by using ERP to leverage and take advantage of the business opportunities opened up by the Internet and e-Business.
- To examine and discuss the role of ERP today and in the context of new business models those are enabled by e-Business and associated technologies and that represent the next step in organizational evolution.
- To discuss recent developments in the area of e-Supply Chain and Supply

Chain integration and other technological developments.
- Understand the issues and challenges faced by organizations in moving to an e-Business environment.

This article will be useful to both the research academician and the practicing manager who are interested in understanding the issues, opportunities and challenges in the ERP and e-Business relationship and how these link to the e-supply chain transformation. More importantly, the paper provides a comprehensive discussion of the factors involved in the complete e-Business enterprise transformation and some suggestions as to how to navigate the same. The complete e-Business enterprise transformation involves leveraging web-based technologies (including web-based ERP) to manage the major enterprise business functions and in this case we specifically focus on the supply chain function.

This paper is organized as follows: In the next section, we provide a brief literature review of ERP and e-Business and how these are linked to a broader idea of the e-supply chain. In the following section, we discuss some of the key developments in the evolving relationship between e-Business and ERP followed by a discussion of "web-enabled" ERP. This leads to our discussion of "e-supply chains" and how ERP and e-Business technologies can be leveraged to achieve supply chain integration. The last section discusses the issues involved in moving towards an e-Business environment, followed by a conclusion.

Before we move on to a further discussion of the subject matter, it is important to clearly define what we mean by ERP and e-Business. A formal definition for the same is provided here:

ERP: Kumar and Van Hillegersberg (2000) define ERP systems as "configurable information systems packages that integrate information and information-based processes within and across functional areas in an organization". In this sense, ERP systems are designed to integrate business functions and allow data to be shared across many boundaries and divisions within the company.

- **e-Business:** Electronic business encompasses three stages: e-Commerce, e-Business, and e-Partnering. The early stages of a company's e-business activity are almost always focused on reaching the customer, the later stages on streamlining value-chain activities to deliver more value to the customer (Norris et al., 2000).
  - **e-Commerce** either leverages an Internet-based sales channel to enhance marketing and sell products or services, or leverages the Internet to make purchasing more efficient. Electronic Data Interchange (EDI) is one technology that has enabled B2B e-commerce for many years; however due to the technological developments and improvements like XML, today's Web-based technologies can do away with the necessity for EDI.
  - **e-Business** improves business performance by using electronic information technologies and open standards to connect suppliers and customers at all steps along the value chain.
  - **e-Partnering** is an intense relationship between businesses that utilize e-Business capabilities to create an environment for shared business improvements, mutual benefits, and joint rewards. e-Partnering is a strategic relationship in which companies work together to optimize an overall value chain.

Literature Review

The majority of papers related to the ERP literature pertain to issues associated with ERP implementation. A review of the functionalities of ERP systems (Biehl & Kim, 2003) reveals that most packages offer a full set of supply chain capabilities, including the planning and execution of marketing activities (the demand side), shop floor and inventory management, ordering, billing, and invoicing, with the potential of delegating ordering and receiving to the end-user. In addition, most packages schedule and optimize distribution through functionality such as management of logistics suppliers or transportation planning. Also, ERP systems are now capable of internet integration and, in extension, enterprise application integration through XML and customized interfaces. Baker (2005) discusses the objectives of using XML in B2B e-commerce, reviews the technical structure of XML, and discusses ways that data integrity can be maintained and security enhanced while engaging in B2B e-commerce. The internet integration facilitates online ordering and sales; the linking of suppliers' and customers' ERP systems to the firm's; online analytical processing to create (near-) real time processing and promising of orders and increase inventory visibility; access to financial clearinghouses for online financial transactions; collaborative sourcing and contract negotiation, and a variety of pricing procedures such as auctions and dynamic pricing. (Biehl, 2005). Burca, Fynes and Marshall (2005) examine how small to medium-sized organizations are responding to the challenge of harnessing ERP and internet technologies to enhance performance and improve competitiveness and aims to identify the barriers preventing organizations from harnessing these technologies. Successful twenty-first century organizations will typically have embraced enterprise resource planning (ERP) systems to integrate e-business processes within the organization and to underpin the creation of integrated inter-organizational systems (Burn & Ash, 2005). This frequently results in new business processes, organizational structures, human resource skill requirements, management roles and knowledge management systems (Robey et al., 2002; Chang et al., 2003; Ash & Burn, 2003; Okrent & Vokurka, 2004; McAdam & Galloway, 2005). To be successful in this new climate, however, organizations have to learn new approaches to planning for collaborative systems and to manage e-business enabled cycles of innovation (Wheeler, 2002; Zahra & Gerard, 2002). Few studies have explored the dynamics of e-business strategic planning and scant information is available on how to implement new paradigms successfully and how to ensure more effective e-business performance as a result (Damanpour, 2001; Kallio et al., 2002). This paper attempts to fill this gap. Bendoly and Kaefer (2004) illustrate how both the product and the process of ERP system implementation can facilitate and increase the effectiveness of future e-commerce projects, such as B2B e-procurement.

There have been a number of papers that have foreseen the integration of Supply Chain Management (SCM) functionality within ERP packages as a logical progression. The future of ERP is all about improving the supply chain and promotion greater collaboration across multiple enterprises (Alwabel, Zairi & Gunasekaran, 2006). SCM systems have two important system functions, maintaining timely information sharing across the overall supply chain and facilitating the synchronization of the entire supply chain. The philosophy of SCM is that a firm has the right product in the right place, at the right price, at the right time, and in the right condition. Under this assumption, an enterprise requires not only the free flow of information within its organizational boundary, but also the timely sharing of the right information with the right business partners. The reason is that the success of a firm's SCM would depend upon the accuracy and velocity of the information which every business partner provides (Zheng et al., 2000). A review of the literature shows that numerous approaches regarding the evolution and type of SCM are to be found. Some analysts, such as Burnes (1996) and LaLonde (1998) support a three-phase evolutionary process. In recent years,

the focus of SCM has shifted from the engineering and improvement of individual functional processes to the co-ordination of the activities of a dynamic supply chain network. The tremendous transformations fostered by e-business have called for further SCM research in this area (Grieger, 2002). Electronic supply chain management (e-SCM) is the collaborative use of technology to enhance business-to-business processes and improve speed, agility, real-time control and customer satisfaction. Folinas et al., 2004 use five dimensions (business strategy, partnership relationships, information/decision-making, technology and logistics functions) to illustrate the evolution of e-SCM. However it is seen that enterprises have not been able to achieve the full potential of the e-SCM concept. The reasons for this are many. Moller (2005) concludes that ERP is an institutionalized component of enterprise infrastructure. It is necessary to rethink the concept of enterprise systems and to gain a deeper insight into the business impact of ERP, which ERP II (essentially componentized ERP, e-business and collaboration in the supply chain) may provide the conceptual framework for. In many cases the scope of e-SCM has not be fully defined and is misunderstood. This paper links the idea of the SCOR model to clearly define and identify the true potential of the e-SCM. It also discusses the issues involved in the complete e-Business transformation (e-SCM is considered part of the larger e-Business) and how companies may navigate this transformation.

The Evolving Relationship Between E-Business and ERP: Key Developments

ERP is the latest in a number of manufacturing and financial information systems that have been devised since the late 1940s to streamline the information flow that parallels the physical flow of goods, from raw materials to finished products (Norris et al., 2001). The traditional focus of production-management information systems (MRP, MRPII and ERP) has been on the movement of information within an enterprise. On the other hand, Web-based technologies facilitate the movement of information between businesses and from business to consumer, as well as vice-versa. Such web-based technologies may also aid in the exchange of information from business to employees and from business to shareholders/partners.

However, it is necessary to have an internal enterprise transaction engine, independent of the supplier and customer facing front ends, for any company large enough to be considered an enterprise. To date, the best of these internal transaction engines are driven by ERP software. The issue, then, is far more complex than the e-Business evangelists make it out to be. e-Business simply does not work without clean internal processes and data. Hence it is necessary for organizations to devote resources to both technologies that facilitate transaction processing and the communication capabilities of e-nabling technologies.

Retrieving and Using Information from the Value-Chain

Today competitive advantage occurs from the ability of companies to relay information quickly through the value chain. What drives the maximum value for the customers is the ability of each organization to retrieve information from a tightly integrated value chain and to use that information to drive decisions within the organization. A company that combines ERP technology with Web-based technology looks something like Figure 2.

With the e-Buy/ERP/e-Sell enterprises extended across the value chain, companies can create tightly linked extended enterprises. Because information is more easily available using Web-based technology to connect both suppliers and customers, the opportunity exists for an enterprise to create new business strategies based on transforming a value chain into an integrated value network. By assembling a network of partners that specialize and excel in the links of the value chain, it is possible for organizations to achieve

Figure 1. The principle connections required to conduct e-Business. (Adapted from Norris, et al., "E-Business and ERPNorris, et al., "E-Business and ERP: Transforming the Enterprise", John Wiley and Sons, Inc. 2000)

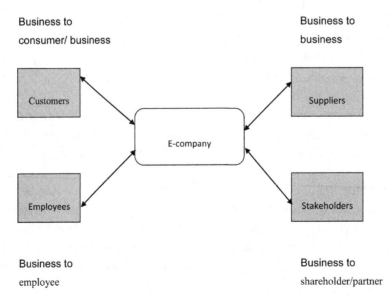

new levels of quality, flexibility and cost savings (Alwabel, Zairi & Gunasekaran, 2006).

The e-Business Potential Aided by ERP

In today's highly competitive environment, it is not enough to just communicate with partners in the supply chain and with customers in the demand chain. Coordination between value-chain partners is the key in this highly competitive business environment. There is a need for businesses to work together to create seamless information flows. And this is where web-based technologies prove to be indispensable. Web-based technology affords the enterprise the ability to get more information to more places more easily. ERP technology affords an enterprise, its business partners in the supply chain, and its customers in the demand chain the ability to coordinate the information they have and to determine how they present it to others. ERP and e-business are not competitive systems. Their greatest benefits can only be achieved when they are used in agreement, completing each other. Thus, without successful ERP system the e-business systems would have only little to present, as in today's new business environment, power has shifted toward consumers who demand intelligent products that deliver new dimensions of value time and content in addition to the current ones price and quality (Aldrich & Douglas, 1999).

Complementary Technologies of ERP and e-Business

ERP and Internet technologies are rapidly coming together. ERP is the internal technological hub of a single enterprise. Web-based technology extends each enterprise's internal information infrastructure into the external environment. While ERP technology supports current business strategy, e-Business opens the door to new strategic opportunities. Today's ERP systems, when fully

Figure 2. ERP and web-based technology together extend the enterprise (Adapted from Norris, et al., "E-Business and ERPNorris, et al., "E-Business and ERP: Transforming the Enterprise", John Wiley and Sons, Inc. 2000)

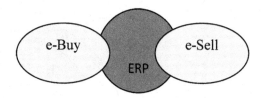

installed as integrated suites, can be thought of as central repositories of internal corporate information. ERP software helps organizations to effectively and efficiently manage all their internal information resources to meet overall goals. On the other hand, Web-based technology provides connections via the Internet to a host of external parties. Figure 3 depicts how ERP and Internet/Web-based technologies can come together and complement each other.

It should be noted that knowledge management is not associated with any one technology. Rather, it is depicted as a process that requires an organization to tap the data in all information channels and consolidate that information so that it is meaningful to the business.

Software Provider Challenges

ERP software providers face a number of challenges when reinventing themselves for e-Business. Because ERP applications manage internal business transactions, they generate assumptions about how business processes are managed, the chief among them being that they are controlled by one organization, transactional information should be combined into large totals and that only certain people participate in specific processes (Callaway, 2000).

The fundamental design of traditional ERP systems thus inherently conflicts with the outwardly focused, interactive, event-driven model

Figure 3. Complementary technologies of ERP and e-business (Adapted from Norris, et al., "E-Business and ERPNorris, et al., "E-Business and ERP: Transforming the Enterprise", John Wiley and Sons, Inc. 2000)

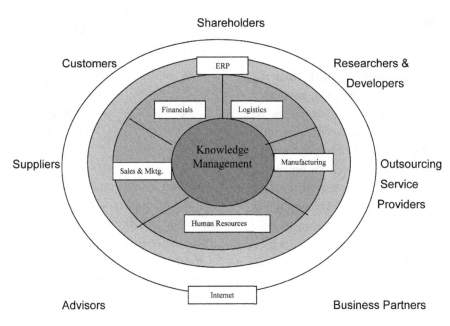

of e-Business. e-Business operates chiefly under the assumptions that control of business processes can be shared or dispersed among many organizations, that people need access to small quantities of some transactional data in real time and that many people participate in a variety of processes. Hence it is necessary that ERP software providers overcome this core conflict. It is suggested that this can be done in one of three ways:

1. They (ERP software vendors) must redesign the interfaces, processes, and underlying architecture of their systems to operate in a multi-tier, thin-client environment tailored for a variety of users who require flexibility.
2. ERP software suppliers must learn to use a new set of Web-based technologies and incorporate Web-based features into their software offerings.

3. They must make their transactional systems more compatible with front-office applications – a difficult task because core ERP software operates differently from ERP extensions. ERP systems providers must reconcile and integrate their disparate data models and execution engines, which may require separating the ERP extensions from the central ERP database.

ERP software providers often begin Web enabling their products by making them accessible via a Web browser. Web enabling an application is significantly different from reengineering it to leverage Internet technology. ERP software vendors must go beyond Web enabling their products. In order to compete with next-generation Web-based software, ERP providers must add more than a Web browser interface to their packages. They must rebuild the extended products that the

Internet makes possible. Among other things, they need to provide: quick, simple reconfiguration of business processes, intuitive interfaces that require no training, real-time or near real-time data access, interactive and collaborative features such as real-time chat and white boarding (which is the ability to electronically sketch out ideas or pictures for real-time interaction), real-time analysis and open access to any internal or external user.

N-Tier Architecture

Adding a browser interface to an ERP system does not enable any extended functions because the Client-Sever architecture of the product is not changed. Vendors must rebuild their software to provide next-generation e-Business capabilities. Using a multi-tiered architecture – often referred to as an n-tier architecture – distributes the applications across a thin front end, a Web server, an application server, and a database. Such an arrangement is shown in Figure 4.

Following are some of the main benefits of an n-tiered architecture:

- The application can be designed to access only certain pieces of data from the ERP system, enabling safe operation by a range of external users.

- The application's performance, availability, and response time improve because users do not directly access the ERP system.
- Developers can redesign the application interface to present data and functions in a simple, more logical manner.
- The application is more scalable and reliable because of techniques that can be used in the Web application server, such as process clustering, load balancing, and high-availability failover.

Some of the user benefits include: faster implementation, faster response to process and organizational change, flexible software use, improved system maintenance, simpler integration with other software, tighter integration with supply chain partners, faster introduction of new applications, improved scalability and less exposure to technological change. N-tiered based ERP systems are suited for best e-Business, allowing companies that have already purchased ERP systems to leverage their investment.

ERP and e-Commerce

Software vendors including ERP vendors are trying to position themselves as e-Business companies by providing e-commerce software. These

Figure 4. N-tier architecture

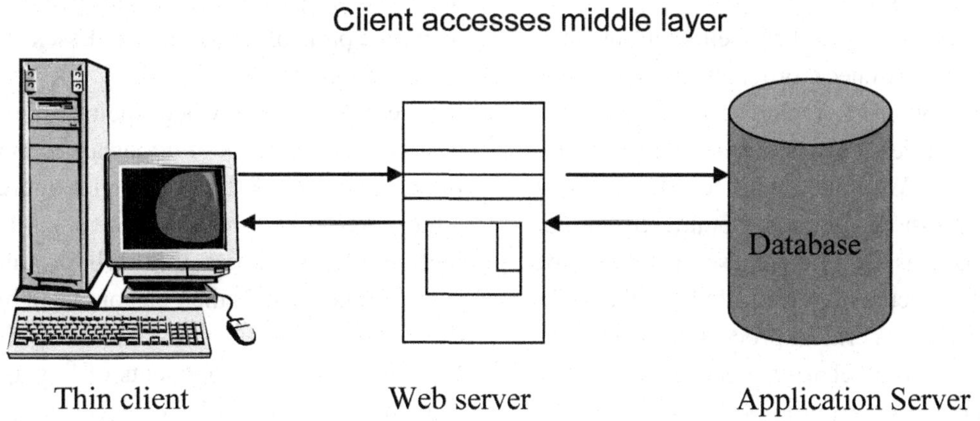

Client accesses middle layer

Thin client   Web server   Application Server

software providers and ERP vendors are moving to capitalize on the growing e-commerce frenzy by facilitating their customers' needs to buy and sell online.

E-commerce software and back-end systems, including ERP software, must be integrated for companies to manage the fulfillment process seamlessly. Back-end integration helps companies track the transactions they conduct on the Web. Companies can then coordinate the data they collect from online transactions with information they gather from other channels, such as telephone, traditional retail stores, and in-person interactions. Integrating e-commerce sites with back-office systems allows companies to present an organized, professional image to their trading partners and customers. Tight integration enables the company to recognize online customers because their histories, including data gathered from other channels, reside in one location – thus enabling the company to provide superior and improved customer service. Providing this continuity is critical for e-Business success. Without it, customers loose their sense of security and trust when conducting business on a Web site; they cannot be sure the company is effectively managing its information.

As of today, there are a number of ERP systems vendors who are providing e-Commerce applications too. Most ERP software providers currently focus on six types of e-Commerce applications: B2B selling, B2C storefronts, Commerce engines, Self-service applications, Internet based procurement and Portals.

ERP applications for B2B selling allow business partners to check order status, pay bills, and initiate orders to replenish inventory. B2C storefront applications enable companies to create retail-like Web sites with features such as catalogs and shopping carts. Commerce engines (also known as e-commerce servers) separate activity that occurs on a Web site from the back-end systems. This critical process protects internal systems from security breaches and usage spikes that can interrupt important transactions.

Self-service applications allow users to access information or transactions that would typically require additional assistance – like obtaining purchase orders, checking inventory levels, checking order status, etc.

Out of these, Internet based procurement and Portals are by far the most important and is discussed in the next sub-section.

Is it predicted that the strategies and products itself being offered by some of the ERP vendors will change rapidly during the coming few years. Hence buyers need to carefully examine their options before selecting an e-commerce software provider.

Portals

A portal is a Web site that houses a collection of information related to a specific theme or topic and provides visitors with access to related services and information sources. Portals also typically include the ability to conduct transactions (Callaway, 2000). Figure 5 describes how Portals provide web access to collections of information. Today many business portals are being designed and launched for business applications. Today, ERP software providers are designing their portals primarily for business users. Many companies have become interested in business-oriented portals because of their potential benefits, which range from simplifying information access to streamlining business processes to sharing information across otherwise functionally and geographically disparate parts of the company (Essex, 1999).

Marketplace Portals: Many ERP providers have created portals where their customers can access extensive lists of goods and service suppliers. The ERP software supplier aggregates – either directly or through partners – a large collection of companies that sell products and services and enables their customers to buy from them. Large ERP vendors, including SAP and Oracle, are strong proponents of this approach. They believe that their extensive customer bases

Figure 5. Portals provide web access to collections of information

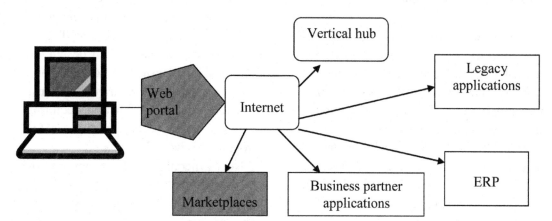

will attract a significant number of sellers to the market.

The Corporate/ Desktop Portal: Portals can also be used to give employees easy access to the typically disparate and disconnected business systems they need to complete their jobs. Via desktop or enterprise portals, which are also referred to as corporate portals, employees can access both internal and external software and systems. Desktop portals are Web-based interfaces that give users access to all the disparate applications through one screen on their PC. Many ERP providers are designing enterprise portals.

The Vertical Hub: Vertical hub portals target specific groups of companies in the same industry. Unlike marketplace portals, which offer more generic commerce services, vertical hubs such as PlasticsNet.com and ChemNet provide services, transactions, and other content tailored to the needs of a specific industry. Few ERP providers currently provide industry-specific portals, but some like SAP have announced intentions to do so.

The Business Case for Portals: Enterprise portals facilitate accessing a variety of internal and external applications and information sources. In a traditional client-server environment, users must sign onto the system many times to access different applications. An entire application may need to be loaded onto their computers, even

though they may use only a small portion of that software. Employees are limited to applications that run in a client-server or windows computing environment and in addition to that, they can use only applications and databases that exist within he physical location of their company. Maintaining desktop environments is also expensive and cumbersome because individual applications must be installed on each machine.

Enterprise portals, on the other hand, allow users to access both internal and external applications and information sources simultaneously via a single, customized, browser-based interface to meet their specific needs. Enterprise portals are easier to maintain because they deliver applications to multiple users via a centrally located server, accessing only those specific components of particular applications related to their jobs.

Linking Portals to ERP Systems: Companies require an Enterprise Application Integration (EAI) tool or framework to connect the disparate systems they want to access via their portals. EAI tools are necessary as long as companies create portals that access both ERP software and external systems, even if they use portals offered by their ERP software provider. Figure 6 illustrates this. Also data integration capabilities will be required to gather data from structured and unstructured data sources.

INTERNET PROCUREMENT

In addition to e-Commerce and portals, ERP software providers are expanding into the areas of Internet-based procurement or e-Procurement. e-Procurement is more than just a system for making purchases online. A properly implemented system can connect companies and their business processes directly with suppliers while managing all interactions between them. This includes management of correspondence, bids, questions and answers, previous pricing, and multiple e-mails sent to multiple participants (Burt et al., 2003). e-Procurement can take place in an e-marketplace (defined as "marketplaces implemented by use of telematics, which means mechanisms of market-typical exchange of goods and services, which support all phases of the transaction" (Schmid, 1993) or directly between two organizations and the software automates the purchasing process using internet technologies. Requisitioners can access the system via a standard browser where they are routed to company approved catalogues either internal or external.

Traditional ERP software includes purchasing functions that allow users to create P.O.s and requisitions, receive invoices, and log spending, for example. Because of their design, however, traditional ERP systems made a single administrator or set of administrators responsible for the entire purchasing function, requiring every employee with purchasing requests to funnel through that channel.

Next-generation ERP systems manage purchasing differently. By using Internet technology and leveraging the component-based architectures of newer software, many ERP package vendors are opening the purchasing function, making it easier for employees to participate in the purchasing process. This is illustrated in Figure 7.

Internet-based procurement systems give the purchaser control over the shopping by providing access to online catalogs, which may be buyer managed, seller managed or third party managed. ERP software providers may use one or a combination of these catalog management tools.

Earlier in the section on "Interactive relationships with Value-Chain Partners" we saw how

Figure 6. Using Integration Software (EAI) to link portals to ERP

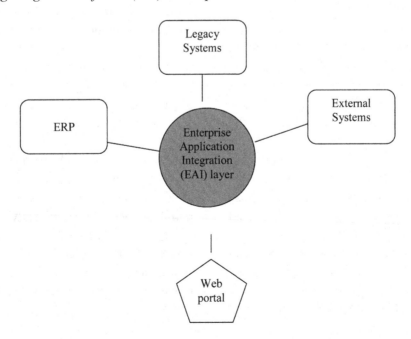

Figure 7. Internet and component technology opens the purchasing process

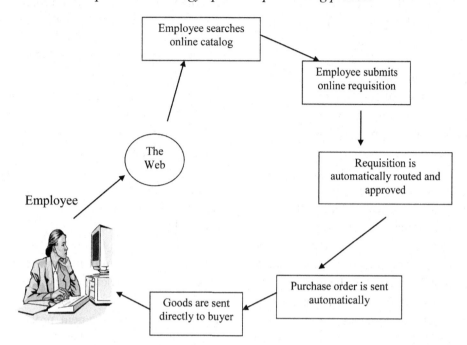

information is more easily available using Web-based technology to connect both suppliers and customers, and how this creates the opportunity for an enterprise to create new business strategies based on transforming a value chain into an integrated value network. This concept is discussed in detail in the following section.

E-Supply Chain and Supply Chain Integration

Supply Chain Management (SCM) has been defined as "the systemic, strategic coordination of the traditional business functions and the tactics across these business functions within a particular company and across businesses within the supply chain, for the purposes of improving the long term performance of the individual companies and the supply chain as whole". (Mentzer et al., 2001, p. 18). The core of ERP, an integrated set of applications that link together back-office operations, will become a subclass of a much larger and broader enterprise business system.

The integration of ERP and SCM is expected to create a new spectrum in the information industry, i.e. the integration of all core business processes through one comprehensive information system and the cooperation among multiple parties and trading partners in the value chain to create a collaborative business and operational environment (Tarn, Yen & Beaumont, 2002).

In this context, e-SCM focuses on the management of information flows and represents a philosophy of managing technology and processes in such a way that the enterprise optimizes the delivery of goods, services and information from the supplier to the customer. As organizations enter a new era of global competitiveness, e-SCM becomes a tremendous catalyst for achieving and maintaining a competitive advantage by enhancing and fostering operational agility and lower cost structure, product/service differentiation, increased market share and profitability (Folians et al., 2004). However, for organizations to take advantage of e-SCM capabilities they must ensure that their own ERP systems are implemented correctly beforehand. Without properly functioning ERP systems, e-SCM may do nothing more than create upstream and downstream problems at internet speed (Norris et al., 2001). Sarkis and Sundarraj (2000) suggest that e-SCM provides organizations with significantly increased strategic options for achieving long-term flexibility and adaptability. With the growth of e-commerce, customers are demanding faster turnaround and greater customization than ever before (Van Hoek, 2001). At the same time, organizations are looking for innovative ways to make their businesses more consumer-centric. They need to improve their relationships with customers to create customer loyalty and e-SCM is perceived as the vehicle to achieve this. e-SCM also levels the playing field between large and small organizations, allowing any size enterprise to access suppliers and customers around the world. (Burca et al., 2005)

E-Supply Chain

e-SCM is about cultural change and changes in management policies, performance metrics, business processes, and organizational structures across the supply chain (Norris et al., 2000).

Information visibility across the supply chain can become a substitute for inventory; therefore, information must be managed as inventory is managed today – with strict policies, discipline, and daily monitoring. Integrating the supply chain more tightly, both within a company and across an extended enterprise made up of suppliers, trading partners, logistics providers, and the distribution channel, is the vision implied in the snapshot of the e-Business panorama, value chain integration.

Visibility, access and timeliness lie at the core of value-chain integration. Essentially, value-chain integration helps avoid mis-match within the supply and demand functions by facilitating real-time synchronization of supply and demand. The enabler to support an organization in its efforts to become part of an extended enterprise, e-SCM requires companies to develop collaborative business systems and processes that can span across multiple enterprise boundaries.

The e-supply chain consists of six components: Supply-chain replenishment- which encompasses the integrated production and distribution processes that utilize real-time demand and strategic partner alignment to improve customer responsiveness.; Collaborative Planning, which requires buyers and sellers to develop a single shared forecast of demand and plan of supply to support this demand, and to update it regularly; Collaborative Product Development, which involves the use of product-design and product-development techniques across multiple companies, using e-Business; E-Logistics, which is the use of Web-based technologies to support the warehouse and transportation management processes; Internet Procurement and Web Portals, which have been discussed in detail in earlier sections of this paper.

So the next question is: How exactly would an e-Supply Chain work? A model of such a concept of e-Supply Chain is given in Figure 8.

Here is how the e-Supply Chain would ideally operate. Consider that company B is a major retailer having a retail chain network across the country and company A is one of its major suppliers. When a consumer purchase occurs at company B, the data is fed to the retail chain's ERP system. The retail chain (company B) then moves the updated demand data to the Extranet. At this time the critical data is automatically fed into the company A's ERP system. This system runs and makes the appropriate quantity and schedule adjustments. The key output is copied to the extranet set up between company A and its suppliers. This data might include updated Inventory snapshots as well as updated forecasted demand and orders for materials. Based on the data company A's suppliers see on the extranet, they automatically replenish company A's Inventory and adjust their own ERP gross requirements to meet demands. The end result is the real-time

Figure 8. Model of an e-supply chain

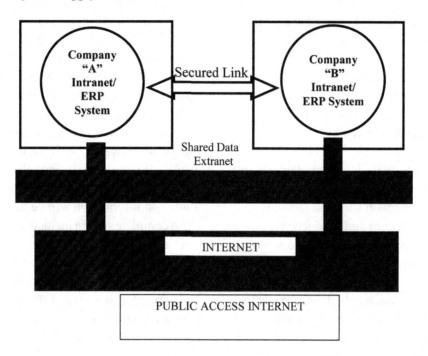

update of demands from the consumer to the raw material supplier. Thus the e-Supply Chain creates a seamless environment that stretches from customers right through to suppliers. Hence with the e-Supply Chain, organizations will be able to manage the supply chain to achieve the right balance of customer responsiveness and low inventory levels with an aggressive cycle time.

As can be seen, there is tremendous scope and a great opportunity for ERP in the operation of an e-Supply Chain. In fact this is where companies and major ERP vendors are moving and this is where the true value of ERP lies. However the following key limitations of ERP systems in providing effective SCM support emerge from an exploratory study by Akkermans et al. (2003): (1) their insufficient extended enterprise functionality in crossing organizational boundaries; (2) their inflexibility to ever-changing supply chain needs, (3) their lack of functionality beyond managing transactions, and (4) their closed and non-modular system architecture.

Integrating the Supply Chain to Reap the Rewards: SCOR Model:

No discussion on e-Supply Chain will be complete without the discussion of the SCOR Model. The Supply Chain Operations Reference (SCOR) Model was developed and endorsed by the Supply Chain Council (SCC). The SCOR-model provides a unique framework that links business process, metrics, best practices and technology features into a unified structure to support communication among supply chain partners and to improve the effectiveness of supply chain management and related supply chain improvement activities.

The SCOR Model includes:

- All customer interactions, from order entry through the paid invoice.
- All physical material transactions, from the supplier's supplier to the customer's customer, including equipment, supplies, spare parts, bulk product, software, etc.

- All market interactions, from the understanding of aggregate demand to the fulfillment of each order (Ptak & Schragenheim, 1999).

The four distinct processes for the SCOR model are source, make, deliver, and plan. The supply chain configuration is driven by:

- "Deliver" channels, inventory deployment, and products.
- "Make" production sites and methods
- "Source" locations and products
- "Plan" levels of aggregation and information sources.

The real results from supply chain management come from the integration of processes throughout the entire supply chain from the supplier's supplier to the customer's customer – as has been illustrated by Figure 9.

The big return on ERP investment and the future revenue and profit growth come from integrating the enterprise to its entire supply chain. Technology will need to continue to develop that will enhance and speed the information linkages. Some companies have decided that they wish to implement only a supply chain software system and not implement the supporting ERP management processes. This is like building a house on quick sand. Without adequate control of the internal processes, an integrated supply chain is truly only as strong as its weakest link. The integration of the supply chain is an area where the speed and accessibility of technology will make a large impact. This technology can include EDI, E-commerce, Internet, or a variety of other possibilities. However, without the accurate data feeding this technology and robust business processes supporting the strategy, the risk is that the same bad information will be the result.

A complete system includes both planning and execution management. This is the point where ERP can be so effective as a tool. The fact remains, plans will change but to fail to plan is planning to fail. The planning side of the integrated system uses soft data. Changes and variability are expected events. The more quickly an enterprise can react; the less cost is incurred by the operation. This is where a robust and reliable ERP system could be of immense value.

Moving to an E-Business Environment: Technology, Processes and People

Moving to an e-Business environment involves a major organizational change. Prior studies on ERP

Figure 9. Integration of processes throughout the entire supply chain (Supply Chain Council Inc. available: http://www.supply-chain.org/)

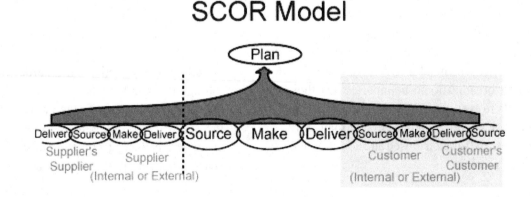

implementation increasingly identifying people and organizational issues as critical features to be addressed for successful systems integration (Southwick & Sawyer, 1999; Markus & Markus; Bunker, 2000; Bhattacherjee, 2000. A. Bhattacherjee, Beginning SAP R/3 Implementation at geneva Pharmaceuticals. Communications of the Association for Information Systems 4 2 (2000). Bhattacherjee, 2000). We argue that e-Business forces change to occur to three corporate domains – technology, processes, and people – at both a strategic and an operational level. Figure 10 illustrates where within these domains and levels all of the various issues fall when a company engages in a comprehensive e-Business effort.

STRATEGIC ISSUES

Technology: Strategic technological issues are, for the most part, similar to the issues that face any company implementing ERP. The first thing that needs to be put in place is an optimal system architecture in line with our discussions before. Management of technology is also an important factor that deserves due consideration at the strategic planning level. Every enterprise should develop what is called as "technology fit factors" that include the factors of scalability, flexibility and cost. Since these are factors that have long-term implications, they are strategic in nature. The bottom-line is that technology should not be allowed to drive the enterprise: rather, technology should "fit" the enterprise. A winning technology strategy requires a strong and enduring partnership with key hardware and software suppliers to achieve the fit with respect to the three mentioned factors. The integrator also plays an important role which extends beyond managing technology and more importantly involves managing process and people issues as well.

Process: e-Business being a new business model in itself may require enterprises to engineer new processes or reengineer old ones. In interest of maintaining accountability, each process needs to have an enterprise-wide owner, accountable for the process's performance, the budget to execute the process, and the quality of all process deliverables. A well-established and understood process to quickly resolve conflicts is also necessary.

People: People can and often do effectively block the success of major technology integration

Figure 10. ERP/ e-Business organizational issues – domain and level matrix

efforts. The "people" issue is the most important in change management associated with an e-Business transformation and depending on how this issue is handled can make or break a company's move to e-Business. People barriers remain unchanged – and in some instances are heightened – by the Internet. The ability to manage change is a litmus test for any form of business success. And as in any change and implementation process, executive sponsorship is the key. Effective communication about the reason for the change and enlisting support for the change is very important. Providing employees training on the new processes and putting in place a system to collect and implement constructive employee feedback is also necessary.

OPERATIONAL ISSUES

Operational Issues revolve around getting e-Business initiatives up and running in a timely fashion, adhering to schedules and budgets 'to avoid cost and deadline overruns, and maintaining downfield vision. Again the three factors of technology, process and people become important at the operational level too and needs to be proactively managed.

Technology: In this area, one needs to manage a number of operational concerns including: product selection, defining product support requirements, defining performance expectations, coordinating the implementation schedule, ensuring good budget planning and ensuring security and data integrity. One suggestion is to develop a multi-function team that would evaluate various e-Business front end packages with respect to the "fit" factors developed at the strategic planning level. This will also ensure that the expected level of performance is achieved and ensures buy-in from employees in the future. Also at this stage it is necessary to coordinate the implementation schedule, conduct product training, and manage product installations. Also with respect to budget

planning, developing contingency plans for unexpected cost overruns is useful.

Processes: At the operational level, the main objective is meeting the objectives and timeliness determined at the strategic level for engineering or reengineering the feeder processes that build up to create the end-to-end processes. This can be achieved through an effective change-control mechanism that ties in with the operational controls that were established at the strategy level. Process implementation teams with their clear authority and accountability with respect to delivering on process metrics should be established.

People: At the operational level, the typical problems faced by managers include: organizational scope, change complexity, political resistance, cultural change and change capability. The manager associated with the e-Business initiative is tasked with the job of recruiting and retaining individuals with the required skill levels. Knowledge transfer and knowledge management should be the responsibility of each team member and needs to be institutionalized enterprise wide.

CONCLUSION

To date, e-Business is still an integrated modular architecture. ERP vendors are all banking on portals to one extent or another. They see this strategy, as well as that of offering alternative models of providing ERP – through outsourcing or ASP relationships – as an opportunity to continue gaining either installed base or renters, and to continue their growth. If companies want to connect with each other, to pass robust information back and forth and make their extra-enterprise relationships more efficient and effective, they will need to settle on a language, grammar and syntax for data. Those ERP software providers that develop the most open systems, which make it easier for companies to work together, will be the winners.

Herein we presented a framework for understanding e-Business opportunities within the context of a traditional enterprise and its infrastructure and also examined the evolving relationship between e-Business and ERP. These developments are moving business towards the concept of e-Supply Chain to achieve true supply chain integration. However the ideal of true e-SCM is far from realized. Clearly there is a dearth of research on what is required for the transformation from ERP systems to enable a true e-SCM model. This paper could be seen as a step in that direction. The issues and challenges faced by organizations in moving to such a complete e-Business environment revolve around technology, processes and people. These were discussed in detail and suggestions for businesses to navigate this challenging transformation were offered. Hopefully more work in this important area will follow.

e-Business requires tight collaboration among trading partners, but most ERP systems are not yet technically prepared to facilitate this. Today, ERP vendors are at different stages in transforming themselves for the Web-enabled world. No single application will provide or create competitive advantage. Currently, an integration of vendor-supplied ERP, decision support tools, middleware, customer development, and Web sites among trading partner communities are all required to achieve the promised benefits of e-Business. However, the bottom line is that, companies best positioned to succeed at e-Business are those that have solid business infrastructures utilizing ERP-based software and capabilities.

REFERENCES

Alwabel, S. A., Zairi, M., & Gunasekaran, A. (2006). The Evolution of ERP and Its Relationship with e-Business. *International Journal of Enterprise Information Systems, 2*(4), 58–76.

Ash, C., & Burn, J. M. (2003). Strategic framework for the management of E-ERP change. *European Journal of Operational Research, 46*(2), 374–387. doi:10.1016/S0377-2217(02)00556-8

Baker, R. (2005). Enterprise Information Systems and B2B E-Commerce: The Significance of XML. *International Journal of Enterprise Information Systems, 1*(1), 53–64.

Bendoly, E., & Schoenherr, T. (2005). ERP system and implementation-process benefits: implications for B2B e-procurement. *International Journal of Operations & Production Management, 25*(4), 304–319. doi:10.1108/01443570510585516

Bhattacherjee, A. (2000). Beginning SAP R/3 Implementation at Geneva Pharmaceuticals. *Communications of the Association for Information Systems, 4*(2).

Biehl, M. (2005). Selecting internal and external supply chain functionality: the case of ERP systems versus electronic marketplaces. *Journal of Enterprise Information Management, 18*(4), 441–457. doi:10.1108/17410390510609590

Biehl, M., & Kim, H. (2003). Electronic marketplaces versus enterprise resource planning: a comparison and decision methodology for supply chain management. International Journal of Technology. *Policy & Management, 3*(3/4), 262–284.

Bunker, D. (2000). *Enterprise Resource Planning System Tools: The Context of their Creation and Use within the Technology Transfer Process.* Paper presented at the Americas Conference on Information Systems, AMCIS, Long Beach, CA.

Burn, J., & Ash, C. (2005). A dynamic model of e-business strategies for ERP enabled Organizations. *Industrial Management & Data Systems, 105*(8), 1084–1095. doi:10.1108/02635570510624464

Burnes, J. (1996). *Using ISCM to create a competitive edge in the year 2000.* Cambridge, MA: MIT Center for Transportation Studies.

Burt, D. N., Dobler, D. W., & Starling, S. L. (2003). *World-Class Supply Management: The Key to Supply Chain Management.* New York: McGraw-Hill.

Callaway, E. (2000). *ERP – The Next Generation: ERP is Web Enabled for E-business.* Charleston, SC: Computer Technology Research.

Chang, K., Jackson, J., & Grover, V. (2003). E-commerce and corporate strategy: an executive perspective. *Information & Management, 40*(7), 663–675. doi:10.1016/S0378-7206(02)00095-2

Damanpour, F. (2001). E-businesse e-commerce evolution: perspective and strategy. *Managerial Finance, 27*(7), 16–34. doi:10.1108/03074350110767268

de Búrca, S., Fynes, B., & Marshall, D. (2005). Strategic technology adoption: extending ERP across the supply chain. *Journal of Enterprise Information Management, 18*(4), 427–440. doi:10.1108/17410390510609581

Douglas, A. F. (1999). *Mastering the digital marketplace: practical strategies for competitiveness in the new economy.* New York: John Wiley & Sons.

Essex, D. (1999). Get into Web Portal. Computerworld. Retrieved April 15, 2010, from http://www.informationweek.com

Folinas, D., Vlachopoulou, M., Manthou, V., & Sigala, M. (2004). Modeling the e-volution of supply chain: Cases and best practices. *Electronic Networking Applications and Policy, 14*(4), 274–283. doi:10.1108/10662240410555298

Grieger, N. (2002). Electronic marketplaces: a literature review and a call for supply chain management research. *European Journal of Operational Research, 144,* 280–294. doi:10.1016/S0377-2217(02)00394-6

Kallio, J., Saarinen, T., & Tinnila, M. (2002). Efficient change strategies. *Business Process Management Journal, 8*(1), 80–93. doi:10.1108/14637150210418647

Kumar, K., & Van Hillegersberg, J. (2000). ERP experiences and evolution. *Communications of the ACM, 43*(4), 22–26. doi:10.1145/332051.332063

LaLonde, B. (1998). Supply chain evolution by the numbers. *Supply Chain Management Review, 2*(1), 7–8.

Markus, M. L., Tanis, C., & Fenema, P. (2000). Multisite ERP implementations. *Communications of the ACM, 43*(4), 42–46. doi:10.1145/332051.332068

McAdam, R., & Galloway, A. (2005). Enterprise resource planning and organisational innovation: a management perspective. *Industrial Management & Data Systems, 105*(3), 280–290. doi:10.1108/02635570510590110

Mentzer, J. T., DeWitt, W., Keebler, J. S., Min, S., Nix, N. W., & Smith, C. D. (2001). Defining supply chain management. *Journal of Business Logistics, 22*(1), 1–25.

Møller, C. (2005). Unleashing the Potential of SCM: Adoption of ERP in Large Danish Enterprises. *International Journal of Enterprise Information Systems, 1*(1), 39–52.

Noekkenved, C. (2000). *Collaborative processes in e-supply networks: towards collaborative community B2B marketplaces.* New York: PricewaterhouseCoopers.

Norris, G., Hurley, J. R., Hartley, K. M., & Dunleavy, J. R. (2000). *E-Business and ERP: Transforming the Enterprise.* London: John Wiley & Sons Inc.

Okrent, M. D., & Vokurka, R. J. (2004). Process mapping in successful ERP implementations. *Industrial Management & Data Systems, 104*(8), 637–643. doi:10.1108/02635570410561618

Ptak, C. A., & Schragenheim, E. (1999). *ERP – Tools, Techniques and Applications for Integrating the Supply Chain*. Boca Raton, FL: St. Lucie Press/ APICS.

Robey, D., Ross, J. W., & Boudreau, M. (2002). Learning to implement enterprise systems: an exploratory study of the dialectics of change. *Journal of Management Information Systems, 19*(1), 17–46.

Sarkis, J., & Sundarraj, R. P. (2000). Factors for strategic evaluation of enterprise information technologies. *International Journal of Physical Distribution & Logistics Management, 30*(3/4), 196–220. doi:10.1108/09600030010325966

Schmid, B. F. (1993). Electronic markets. *Wirtschaftsinformatik, 35*(5), 465–480.

Southwick, R., & Sawyer, S. (1999). Critical Views of Organization, Management, and Information Technology: Applying Critical Social Theory to Information System Research. Paper presented at the Americas Conference on Information Systems, Milwaukee, WI.

Tarn, J. M., Yen, D. C., & Beaumont, M. (2002). Exploring the rationales for ERP and SCM integration. *Industrial Management & Data Systems, 102*(1), 26–34. doi:10.1108/02635570210414631

Van Hoek, S. (2001). E-Supply chains – virtually non-existing. *Supply Chain Management: An International Journal, 6*(1), 21–28. doi:10.1108/13598540110694653

Wheeler, B. C. (2002). NEBIC: a dynamic capabilities theory for assessing net-enablement. *Information Systems Research, 13*(2), 125–146. doi:10.1287/isre.13.2.125.89

Zahra, S. A., & Gerard, G. (2002). The net-enabled business innovation cycle and the evolution of dynamic capabilities. *Information Systems Research, 13*(2), 147–151. doi:10.1287/isre.13.2.147.90

Zheng, S., Yen, D. C., & Tarn, M. J. (2000). The new spectrum of the cross-enterprise solution: the integration of supply chain management and enterprise resource-planning systems. *Journal of Computer Information Systems*, 84–93.

This work was previously published in International Journal of Enterprise Information Systems, edited by Madjid Tavana, pp. 1-19, Volume 6, Issue 4, copyright 2010 by IGI Publishing (an imprint of IGI Global).

Chapter 5

Critical Success Factors in Enterprise Resource Planning Implementation:
A Case–Study Approach

Behrouz Zarei
University of Tehran, Iran

Mina Naeli
University of Tehran, Iran

ABSTRACT

Although introducing Enterprise Resource Planning (ERP) to an organization has enormous benefits, it may entail new hazardous challenges if it cannot be well managed. This research focuses on the critical ERP success factors from a case study involving the Esfahan Steel Company, which started ERP implementation in September 2002. An in-depth research of ERP implementation processes and the level of adhering to five chosen ERP critical success factors—project management, top management supports, business process reengineering, and change management and Training—are conducted. Research results revealed that the five critical success factors (CSFs) are highly interdependent and the strengths and weaknesses of each have influenced the quality of ERP implementation to a large extent.

INTRODUCTION

Today's the globalization phenomena, market expansion, increased customers' expectations and competition among firms, and business complexities, forced companies to investigate more on information systems in an attempt to improve their business practices and procedures. One of these systems which is receiving an universal attention from many companies all over the world is ERP that meets companies' requirement for more integrated and flexible business processes.

"The key underlying idea of ERP is the use of information technology to achieve the capability to plan and integrate enterprise-wide resources" (Kumar et al., 2003). ERP integrates the processes and applications of various functions of an orga-

DOI: 10.4018/978-1-4666-1761-2.ch005

nization such as design, production, purchasing, marketing, and finance (Kumar et al., 2003).

ERP implementation can both gain enormous advantages for successful companies and at the same time be a disaster for those companies which cannot manage its implementation successfully. ERP implementation projects are the most difficult development projects for organizations due to its complexity, enterprise wide scope and fundamental organizational changes needed to align with the new system and business processes (Wilder & Davis, 1998). Therefore, as emphasized by Holland and Light (1999) all managers who want to implement ERP have to ask two important questions of "How can ERP systems be implemented successfully?" and "What are the critical success factors for ERP implementation?"

This paper has three main objectives. Recognizing the critical success factors for ERP implementation by reviewing the most critical and relevant literature, examining the level of adhering to the identified success factors in the selected case study; and investigating the impacts of each critical success factor on ERP implementation and on the other factors in the selected case study.

LITERATURE REVIEW

Since ERP implementation is an expensive and risky venture, many authors have identified different factors which, to a great extent, influence successful implementation. Holland and Light (1999) created a model which classifies the CSFs into strategic and tactical factors. Strategic factors include legacy system, business vision, ERP strategy, top management support and project plans. Tactical factors were represented as client consultation, personnel, business process change and software configuration, client acceptance; and monitoring. The Holland model has been used in many other studies. For example, Allen, Kern, and Havenhand (2002) in addition to independently identifying strategic and tactical CSFs in Holland

model added, in their paper, a set of contextual CSFs for ERP implementation in public sectors

Nah, Lau, and Kuang (2001) identified 11 critical success factors for ERP implementation based on structured literature search. Later Nah, Zuckweiler, and Lau (2003) surveyed 54 CIOs of 1000 companies in which they were asked to evaluate the importance of each CSFs. Somers and Nelson's (2001) research was based on a large scale meta-study of the case study literature, from among which they identify twenty-two critical success factors. Also, they asked US executives to rank the ERP CSFs, through which they produced top ten CSFs in terms of the mean score. Somers and Nelson (2004) grouped these factors into the key player and key activities and describe that these factors are having different degree of importance in the different stages of ERP project life cycle. Key players are people or groups of people whom are affected by ERP implementation to a great extent. They defined key players as top management support, project champion, steering committee, implementation consultants, project team, vendor-customer partnership, venders' tools, and vender support. Key activities are those activities during the implementation that have vital impact on the success of ERP implementation. Including user training and education, management of expectations, selection of appropriate package, project management, customization, data analysis and conversion, business process reengineering, architecture definition, dedicating resources, change management, establishing clear goals and objectives, education on new business processes, interdepartmental communication, and interdepartmental cooperation (Somers & Nelson, 2004).

Feeny and Willcocks (1998) maintained that in order to reach success in ERP implementation, 9 core IT capabilities are required. These are IT leadership, business systems thinking, relationship building, architecture planning, technology fixing, informed buying, contract facilitation, contract monitoring, and supplier development.

Gargeya and Brady (2005) searched more than 100 articles and books and suggested six critical success factors for ERP implementation: (1) Working with functionality/maintained scope; (2) Project team/Management support/Consultants; (3) Internal Readiness/Training; (4) Dealing with organizational diversity; (5) Planning/Development/Budgeting; (6) Adequate testing.

Also Nah and Delgado (2006) organized the CSFs suggested by the previous literatures into seven categories: business plan and vision; change management; communication; ERP team composition; skills and compensations; management support and championship; project management; system analysis, selection and technical implementation.

From among all the mentioned factors, Project management, Top management support, Business process reengineering (BPR), Change management and Education and training, are selected to be investigated in the selected case study because they are addressed frequently in the literature by researchers. The factors are employed for our case study according to the following discussion.

Project Management

Project management consists of organizing, directing and controlling activities in addition to motivating the most expensive resource in organization, that is, 'people' (Al-Mashari, 2003). Umble (2003) explained that project management includes an obvious definition of project objectives and the development of both clear work plan and resource plan. Also Trepper (1999) believes that the single most influential factor in ERP adoption success is project manager's knowledge, skills, abilities and experience. Kumar (2003) in a research asked project managers of 20 Canadian organizations to list the criteria used for the selection of the project manager. Project management skills, functional experiences and IT management experience, in order gained the highest percentages.

Success of any project undoubtedly depends, to a large extent, on its team members. Because of its enterprise-wide scope, ERP requires a cross-functional and multi-skilled implementation team because both business and technical knowledge is essential for success (Sumner, 1999; Davenport, 2000). Also, Wee (2000) explained that the project team's devotion of their full time to the ERP implementation project should be their priority. Meanwhile, he believes that putting the team in one location in such a way that they can see each other facilitates team working. The team's workload should be manageable, and giving them incentives and compensation will help successful implementation on time and within the allocated budget. On the other hand in different stages of ERP implementation, the involvement of consultants is necessary (Somers & Nelson, 2001).

Based on the above discussion the following factors are examined in the case of Esfahan Steel Company.

1. The project manager should have the required project management skills; and functional and IT management experience.
2. The ERP team should be cross-functional and multi-skilled.
3. The team should devote their full time to ERP implementation.
4. The team's workload should be manageable.
5. The ERP team should be given appropriate compensation and incentives.
6. Objectives and expectation of the new system should be clearly defined.
7. Clear work and resource plan should take place.
8. Consultants should have an in-depth knowledge of the software and have industry-specific knowledge.
9. Consultants should be involved in different stages of implementation.

Top Management Support

Top management should have involvement in the project and allocate valuable resources to the implementation process (Holland, 1999). Establishing new goals, roles, responsibilities, policies and organizational structure; exhibiting strong commitment to the successful introduction of information technology (IT); and communicating the corporate IT strategy to all employees are the responsibilities of top management in IT implementation. Also, mediation between parties should be done in times of conflict (McKersie & Walton, 1991; Roberts & Barrar, 1992).

Therefore, the following sub-factors are studied in the selected case:

1. Strong support and approval of the top management is required during the implementation.
2. Senior management should justify the necessity of ERP for employees and communicate reasonable goals of the new system to them.
3. Senior management must be committed, with its involvement and allocating valuable resources, to the implementation process.
4. New organizational structures and policies should be established and communicated to the employees.
5. In the case of conflict between the old and new system, managers should mediate properly.

Business Process Reengineering (BPR)

The structures, tools and processes which are provided by the ERP system are not entirely compatible with the current organizational structure and processes (Umble, 2003). No enterprise can exactly fit to the ready-made world class business processes which ERP will introduce; therefore, in order to get the maximum benefits of ERP, all organizations have to reengineer the whole or

some part of their business processes (Al-Mashari, 2003). The organization should try to change the business process in a way that fit the software with minimal customization as aligning the business process with the software implementation is critical (Holland et al., 1999). Based on five CSFs of BPR presented by Al Mashari and Zairi (1999), the following sub factors for success of BPR in ERP projects are employed:

1. Appropriate change management strategies should be established
2. Top management commitment and leadership is critical.
3. A new organizational structure should be established and communicated.
4. Effective planning for reengineering processes should be established. Also current and future business process model should be clearly identified.
5. Adequate resources should be allocated.

Change Management

Even the most flexible ERP systems force its own logic to the organization's structure, strategies, and culture, and may result in establishing new business processes and/or reengineering the key business processes (Umble, 2003). It is emphasized that one of the considerable mistakes of chief executives is accepting ERP as simply a software system and perceiving implementation of ERP as a primarily technological challenge. They ignore the fact that ERP causes fundamental changes in the way the organization operates.

Aladwani (2001) suggested a conceptual framework consisting of three phases to help top management deal with employee's resistance to change in ERP implementation. The three suggested phases are:

1. 'Knowledge formation phase': 'identify and evaluate the attitudes of individual users and influential groups.'

2. 'Strategy implementation phase': by using the information from the previous stage organization should develop and implement the strategies for overcoming users' resistance to the system.
3. 'Status evaluation phase': Continuous monitoring and evaluating the progress of change management efforts.

Based on Aladwani's suggested framework, the following sub-factors for "Change management" are defined:

1. Identifying the attitudes of individual users and influential groups.
2. Communicating ERP benefits to the employees.
3. Explaining the general ERP operation to the employees.
4. Involving employees in defining the aims of the ERP system.
5. Involving employees in different ERP implementation phases.
6. Setting education as a priority for the beginning of the project, and allocating money and time to various forms of education and training.
7. Getting the support of opinion leaders who have influence on attitudes toward the new system.
8. Ensuring that the organization and people are ready for fundamental changes resulted from introducing ERP.

Education and Training

As mentioned previously, training is one of the main change management strategies, and establishing an appropriate plan for the education and training of the end-user is a big challenge for the organization. The project team is mostly trained by sending them to the venders' training center, and executives and employees who will use the system use vender training facilities and in-house

programs (Kumar et al., 2003). Some of the most critical sub-factors of Education and training for further study in the selected case are:

1. Establishment of an appropriate plan for the education and training of the end-users.
2. Allocating sufficient time, money and facilities to training efforts as well as expecting underestimating training requirement.
3. Having enough computer expert users.
4. Establishing continuous vender training facilities to meet users' needs after installation.

RESEARCH METHODOLOGY

The single case study approach has been selected since the main objective of this research is analysis of new information on the implementation of ERP and comparing our case critical success factors and those in the literature. An in-depth study of the selected case enable the researcher to confirm or challenge the role of the five discussed CSFs.

The primary source of data collection in this study is a semi-structured interview. The researcher designed a set of questions to be covered during the interview but kept the interview flexible, omitted some questions in particular interviews, changed the order of questions depending on the flow of conversation or used additional questions. Also, documentation was used as the second source of evidence in this research in an attempt to increase the reliability of the study.

EMPIRICAL DATA

Esfahan steel company (ESCO) is the first and the largest manufacturer of steel products in Iran. Its capacity has expanded to 1,900,000 tons annually since 1990, and it is now producing 2,200,000 tones. It is managed by the government of Iran and comprises approximately 10000 direct employees. ERP implementation in ESCO started in

September 2002 and completed in October 2003. GTS from UAE and Basa from Iran were selected to cooperate with ERP implementation in ESCO.

In this section the five chosen ERP critical success factors are investigated in the project of ERP implementation in ESCO. As mentioned in addition to the company's documents, examining these factors is primary done through interviewing with project manager, finance key user, human resource key user, and a number of end users. These interviews conducted based on an open questionnaire created using the sub-factors identified in the literature review section. Although there is other important factors which have influenced ERP implementation in ESCO, because of limited scope of this project only the following factors are studied.

Project Management

The ESCO project team for the implementation of ERP consisted of 15 members from GTS, 17 members from Basa, 11 members in project management team, 110 ESCO specialists familiar with processes and functions in different sections of the company and 35 operators for data entry.

"Defining clear goals for the project was the most critical part of the job" the project manager said. He told the researcher before starting ERP implementation; the steering committee; the project management team and the specialist from GTS and Basa had different meetings to define the ERP objectives and expectations. The scope of the project, clear work, and resource plan were defined in the definition phase of the implementation. The project manager said "Any changes in scope of the project, the agreed-upon functionality, or the approved project plan were managed through change requests and approved by both ESCO and BASA/GTS project managers"

The project manager selection criteria were also suggested by Oracle. One of the key users told the researcher that the selected project manager had three main privileges: He had ERP implementation

experience as he had worked for SAP in Germany for one year, he was familiar with business processes in ESCO, and he was young and naturally more energetic and risk taking.

All the respondents emphasized the crucial role of key users in ERP implementation success. Key users are responsible for ERP in their department and select their own team to help ERP implementation. They are also the best functional consultants for the project team because they know the business processes of their department. The project manager selected one key user for each department and key Users meeting were held on a weekly basis to assess the progress of each team member and to plan for the following week(s). Also the fifteen consultants from GTS had, in addition to technical knowledge, enough business knowledge as they had the experience of implementing ERP in another steel production company in UAE and the seventeen consultants from Basa were also completely familiar with ESCO business processes since they had cooperation with ESCO in other IT projects. Consultants were involved in all phases of ERP implementation

Except for key users who had other responsibilities in addition to ERP implementations, team members devoted all their time to ERP. The members of the project team were also given awards and one of the responsibilities of key users was dedicating awards to those employees who had a positive role in ERP implementation. However, in no case were compensations used.

Top Management Support

"The steering committee and on top of them the senior manager of ESCO were interested in updating the current IT setup with the available latest technology in the industry. They investigated different options and decided to introduce ERP system to the organization" said the project manager. All respondents claimed that the top management support during implementation and adoption was excellent and they believed that during implementation, ERP was the priority for the top manager. The project manager also emphasized that the senior manager ask the project team to provide him with continuous reports on the progress of ERP. And during the ERP implementation period, regular meetings were held to inform top management and the steering committee about overall project progress, risks and problems. Also in order to provide more support for the project team, the top manager assigned one of the members of steering committee as the ERP project sponsor and defined the following responsibilities which are mentioned in the project leading documents of ESCO:

- Confirms project objectives fit with the overall ESCO program strategy.
- Conflict management.
- Lead the project Steering Committee meetings.
- Manage and resolve contractual issues with the vendors.
- Ensure a proper strategy for know-how transfer.

On the other hand, most of the respondents believed that the top manager and the steering committee could not successfully establish and communicate the new organizational structure and business processes. The project manager said: "ERP in ESCO would be much more successful if new and proper organizational structures were successfully established". Finance and Human resource key users also believed that the top manager could not successfully communicate ERP benefits to employees. "The senior manager had to allocate more time for communicating with middle managers and employees in order to make them ready for change and gain their support" said the Human resource key user. Also confliction occurred many times between the advocators of the old and the new systems. The project sponsor, the top manager and the steering committee had a mediator role in times of conflict.

Business Process Reengineering (BPR)

"Changing the business processes was the most difficult part of the job" said the project manager. He said "The Consultants worked with us to identify which customization and/or additional functionality needed to be developed. Since we did not undertake any hard customization and just a number of soft customizations were implemented, we had to start business process reengineering in order to align the current business processes with standard processes introduced by ERP." The Finance key user said "Although current business processes, future process model, and high level gap analyses were identified and developed respectively in RD.020 and BP.080 and BR.010 documents, and appropriate solutions for changing and reengineering business processes were established in the meeting between ESCO executives and GTS/BASA consultants, we could not successfully reengineer our processes." The reasons they stated were mainly:

- ESCO Organizational culture.
- Middle managers resistance to change.
- Weak change management strategies.
- Top manager and steering committee's inability to efficiently establish and communicate new business processes.
- Top management and steering committee's weaknesses to successfully overcome political, organizational, and economic barriers were against the BPR.
- In some cases, lack of budget.

Change Management

"Although we made a great effort to make the organization ready for change through training, advertisement and seminars and publishing many papers about ERP in the company's internal magazine, I strongly believe we failed to successfully gain employees' readiness" Said the project manager. He emphasized that ESCO could have reduced employees' resistance to change by allocating more time and money to this phase. Almost all the respondents believed there was the need to do more for improving the employees' readiness for accepting change.

In order to involve employees in ERP implementation processes, the project manager selected key users and communicated the ERP benefits and difficulties to them and asked them to give their suggestions and ideas for better implementation. "Since all the key users were opinion leaders, they were the most qualified persons to communicate ERP advantages to other employees, gain their support and involvement, and decrease their resistance to the changes" Said the project manager. The other strategy for communicating ERP benefits was publishing articles about ERP in the internal magazine of ESCO during the ERP implementation.

Training facilities were provided for employees. But, according to respondents' words, these facilities were not adequate and efficient. "One of our serious weaknesses in change management was poor training" said the finance key user. Also the Finance key user emphasized an interesting fact. He claimed the resistance was intensified by reduction of employees' workload. He told the researcher that key users had to create new responsibilities for their employees and fill their extra time with additional activities like research.

Education and Training

To gain in-depth information about the training schema, its quality and challenges, interviews were conducted with the project manager, the key user of finance department, and three end user employees, two from finance and one from human resource department. Almost all the respondents believed that training activities were not efficient and they suffer, to a great extent, from poor training. Finance key user said the number of training sessions were not adequate and trainers were not qualified

enough to teach us. Also another main problem was trainers' language. "Trainers were speaking in English and since they were Indians and spoke very quickly, we could hardly understand their lectures" said one of the end users. When the researcher asked the finance key user: "how did you solve this problem?" he said: "fortunately my ERP team and I had enough computer knowledge so we worked with the new system all the day and learned its operations through trial and error, and then we could teach other finance employees how to work with the ERP finance modules. But, it was a very hard and time-consuming job". The researcher also found out that after implementing all the ERP modules and reaching the go-live status, no more training facilities were provided for the project team members, key users and end user employees.

FINDING ANALYSIS

The analytical technique which is used in this research is "Pattern matching". The pattern matching technique is suggested by Yin (1994) and it compares empirically based pattern with the predicted one (Yin, 1994). In the literature review section of this research, among all the critical success factors, five factors are selected. The primary prediction is that these factors largely affect the success of ERP implementation in our case study. The empirical data collected in the last sections is used to identify the main strengths and weaknesses of each of these factors and their effects on the success or failure of ERP implementation in ESCO. This analysis is tabulated and shows the level of adhering to each of five CSFs and is used for more analysis on the interdependency of the factors in the selected case (see Table 1).

Factors Interdependency

The research findings reveal that project management and Top management support have

Table 1. Major strengths and weaknesses of ERP implementation in ESCO

WEAKNESSES	STRENGTHS	FACTORS
1. Since key users had many responsibilities they could not allocate all their time to ERP implementations. 2. Compensations were not used in required cases.	1. Clear definitions of objectives and expectations of ERP have been established before starting the implementation. 2. Clear work and resource plans have been established. 3. A qualified project manager has been selected. 4. Project team members' responsibilities have been clearly defined. 5. ERP implementation team consisted of multi-skilled members. 6. Team members assigned their full time to the project 7. Team work load was manageable. 8. ERP members were given incentives. 9. Consultants had both technical and the industry-related knowledge. 10. Consultants were involved in all phases of ERP implementation.	Project Management
1. Top manager and steering committee could not successfully establish and communicate a new organizational structure and business processes. 2. Top manager did not adequately communicate ERP goals and advantages to employees.	1. Top manager intensively supported ERP implementation. 2. Top manager allocated needed resources to the project. 3. Top manager and project sponsor had middle roles in times of conflicts.	Top management support
1. Needed change management strategies were not successfully established and implemented in order to make the organization ready for fundamental changes. 2. A new organizational structure was not successfully established and communicated. 3. Political, organizational and economic barriers against BPR could not be completely overcome. 4. Lack of budget.	1. No hard customization to the ERP software package has been undertaken.2.Current business processes, future process model and high level gap analysis were identified and developed in order to establish an appropriate plan for business processes reengineering.	Business Process Reengineering (BPR)
1. The attitudes of individual groups and influential groups were not completely identified. 2. Adequate time and money were not allocated for communication with employees. 4. Employees were not asked to get involved in defining ERP objectives. 5. Training facilities were not adequate and efficient.	1. Involvement of employees in different ERP implementation phases. 2. Getting support of key users as opinion leaders who can influence their colleagues' attitudes toward new systems. 3. Establishing two influential communication strategies: Assigning key users to communicate ERP goals, benefits and general operation to employees. And, publishing articles about ERP in the ESCO internal magazine.	Change Management
1. The training plan was not defined appropriately 2. Insufficient time and money allocated for training efforts. 3. Trainers were not qualified enough. 4. Trainers used to speak in English, and most employees could not understand them. 5. Training activities were not continuous.	1. Having enough computer expert users.2.Establishing clear training plan for project team, key users and end users.	Training

more strengths than weaknesses, although their weaknesses cannot be ignored, they are the most considerable privileges of ERP implementation in ESCO. On the other hand, BPR, Change management, and Training suffer from considerable weaknesses which have negative influences on the success of ERP implementation in the company.

These five factors are interdependent, and strengths and weaknesses of each of them have influenced other factors and general ERP success in ESCO. The followings are some of the main impacts of strengths and weaknesses of each factor on the others:

- Constituting cross-functional and multi-skilled project team has largely support changing current business processes because fundamental changes in business processes need experts who have enough business specific knowledge to identify and develop current and future business processes model.

- Involving key users has had an undeniable impact on change management process in ESCO. As mentioned in the previous chapter, these leaders can gain the support and involvement of the employees. Also, since they know the business process of their department in detail and are the most experienced members of the project team, their guidance is valuable for establishing BPR strategies.

- Top management and the steering committee could not successfully establish and communicate the new organizational structure. According to respondents, this weakness seems to be the main cause of BPR failure.

- Top management although having positive impacts on Change management by showing support from ERP and taking a mediator role in times of conflict, could not take a role in reducing resistance of employees and making them ready for change because they were not successful in communicating ERP goals and advantages to the employees.

- Lack of budget has been one of the serious constrains for BPR, Change management and Training activities.

- Change management and Training are highly interdependent. While poor training basically harmed Change management and gave rise to the objections of employees, the involvement of employees in different ERP implementation phases and publishing articles about ERP in the internal mag-

azine of ESCO increased their knowledge of and experience with ERP.

- Failure in making the organization adequately ready for change harmed BPR and caused resistance of groups of employees and middle managers to fundamental changes needed for successfully establishing ERP in the organization.

CONCLUSION

Enterprise resource planning (ERP) system integrates and organizes enterprise-wide resources and it is gaining universal attention from most companies all over the world. Implementing ERP is a very challenging and risky project, and instead of gaining expected benefits for the organization, it can be changed to a disaster for those cannot manage it properly. Therefore, critical factors which are vital to ERP success should be identified and studied in order to help managers with implementing ERP successfully with minimum drawbacks. This research studied the ERP critical success/failure factors by using case study methodology. Five most critical factors were selected from the literatures, and the impacts of each factor on other factors and ERP success in the selected company were shown. This research concluded that ERP implementation is a very challenging and risky project for organizations and confirmed the impacts of the five selected factors on the success of ERP implementation as mentioned in the literatures. The results revealed that the five CSFs are highly interdependent and the strengths and weaknesses of each of them have influenced the quality of ERP implementation to a large extent.

REFERENCES

Al-Mashari, M. (2003). Enterprise Resource Planning (ERP) systems: a research agenda. *Industrial Management & Data Systems, 103*(1), 22–27. doi:10.1108/02635570310456869

Al-Mashari, M., & Zairi, M. (1999). BPR implementation process: an analysis of key success and failure factors. *Business Process Management Journal, 5*(1), 87–112. doi:10.1108/14637159910249108

Aladwani, A. M. (2001). Change management strategies for successful ERP implementation. *Business Process Management Journal, 7*(3), 266–275. doi:10.1108/14637150110392764

Allen, D., Kern, T., & Havenhand, M. (2002). ERP critical success factors: an exploration of the contextual factors in public sector institutions. In *Proceeding of the 35th Hawaii International Conference on System Sciences.*

Davenport, T. H. (2000). *Mission critical: Realizing the promise of Enterprise Systems.* Boston: Harvard Business School press.

Feeny, D., & Willcocks, L. (1998). Core IS capabilities for exploring IT. *Sloan Management Review, 39*(3), 9–21.

Gargeya, V. B., & Brady, C. (2005). Success and failure factors of adopting SAP in ERP system implementation. *Business Process Management Journal, 11*(5), 501–516. doi:10.1108/14637150510619858

Holland, D., Light, B., & Gibson, N. (1999). A critical success factors model for ERP implementation. *IEEE Software, 16*(3), 30–36. doi:10.1109/52.765784

Kumar, V., Maheshwari, B., & Kumar, U. (2003). An investigation of critical Management issues in ERP implementation: empirical evidence from Canadian organizations. *Technovation, 23,* 793–807. doi:10.1016/S0166-4972(02)00015-9

McKersie, R. B., & Walton, R. E. (1991). Organizational Change. In Morton, M. S. S. (Ed.), *The Corporation of the 1990s: Information Technology and Organizational Transformation* (pp. 244–277). New York: Oxford University press.

Nah, F. F., & Delgado, S. (2006). Critical success factors for enterprise resource planning implementation and upgrades. *Journal of Computer Information Systems, 46*(5), 99–113.

Nah, F. F., Lau, J. L., & Kuang, J. (2001). Factors for successful implementation of enterprise systems. *Business Process Management Journal, 7*(3), 285–296. doi:10.1108/14637150110392782

Nah, F. F., Zuckweiler, K., & Lau, J. L. (2003). ERP implementation: chief information officers' perceptions of critical success factors. *International Journal of Human-Computer Interaction, 16*(1), 5–22. doi:10.1207/S15327590IJHC1601_2

Roberts, H. J., & Barrar, P. R. N. (1992). MRP II implementation: key factors for success. *Computer Integrated Manufacturing Systems, 5*(1), 31–38. doi:10.1016/0951-5240(92)90016-6

Somers, T. M., & Nelson, K. G. *(2001).* The impact of critical success factors across the stages of Enterprise Resource Planning implementations. *In* Proceeding of the 34th Hawaii International Conference on Systems Sciences.

Somers, T. M., & Nelson, K. G. (2004). A taxonomy of players and activities across the ERP project life cycle. *Information & Management, 41*(3), 257–278. doi:10.1016/S0378-7206(03)00023-5

Sumner, M. (1999). Critical success factors in enterprise wide information management systems projects. In *Proceedings of the Americas Conference on Information Systems (AMCIS)* (pp. 232-234).

Trepper, C. (1999). *ERP project management is key to a successful implementation.* Retrieved from http://www.erphub.com/strategy

Umble, E. J., Haft, R. R., & Umble, M. M. (2003). Enterprise Resource Planning: Implementation procedures and critical success factors. *European Journal of Operational Research, 146*, 241–257. doi:10.1016/S0377-2217(02)00547-7

Wee, S. (2000). *Juggling toward ERP success: keep key success factors high.* Retrieved from http://www.erpnews.com/erpnews/erp904/02get.html

Wilder, C., & Davis, B. (1998). False starts, Strong finishes. *Informationweek, 711*, 41–53.

Yin, R. K. (1994). *Case Study Research: Design and Methods* (5th ed.). Fort Worth, TX: Dryden press.

This work was previously published in International Journal of Enterprise Information Systems, edited by Madjid Tavana, pp. 48-58, Volume 6, Issue 3, copyright 2010 by IGI Publishing (an imprint of IGI Global).

Chapter 6
The Core Critical Success Factors in Implementation of Enterprise Resource Planning Systems

Payam Hanafizadeh
Allameh Tabataba'i University, Iran

Roya Gholami
Aston University, UK

Shabnam Dadbin
Allameh Tabataba'i University, Iran

Nicholas Standage
Aston University, UK

ABSTRACT

The Implementation of Enterprise Resource Planning (ERP) systems require huge investments while ineffective implementations of such projects are commonly observed. A considerable number of these projects have been reported to fail or take longer than it was initially planned, while previous studies show that the aim of rapid implementation of such projects has not been successful and the failure of the fundamental goals in these projects have imposed huge amounts of costs on investors. Some of the major consequences are the reduction in demand for such products and the introduction of further skepticism to the managers and investors of ERP systems. In this regard, it is important to understand the factors determining success or failure of ERP implementation. The aim of this paper is to study the critical success factors (CSFs) in implementing ERP systems and to develop a conceptual model which can serve as a basis for ERP project managers. These critical success factors that are called "core critical success factors" are extracted from 62 published papers using the content analysis and the entropy method. The proposed conceptual model has been verified in the context of five multinational companies.

DOI: 10.4018/978-1-4666-1761-2.ch006

BACKGROUND

An Enterprise Resource Planning (ERP) system is an integrated solution, which makes the organization capable of effectively and efficiently using its resources (e.g., materials, human resource, capital, information and so on) (Nah, Lou, & Kuang, 2001). The Implementation of ERP projects take considerable time and needs huge amounts of resources to be consumed from the organization. The growing popularity of ERP systems in multinational corporations (MNCs) and subsequently the increased expenditure in financial and human resources has motivated researchers to focus on implementation of ERP project and related issues (AMR Research, 1999).

Despite the fact that the implementation of an ERP system can have tangible and intangible benefits for the organization, there is some evidence indicating the failure of these projects. The project managers often emphasize on technical and financial aspects of the project and ignore the non-technical aspects such as human and organizational aspects. Therefore, in order to succeed in implementing an ERP project and avoid the failures, organizations need to know the critical success factors. Each success factor has their own specific effect, while they are not independent of each other (Esteves, Casanovas, & Pastor, 2003; Zairi, 2003).

The Implementation of ERP systems not only requires a huge amount of time and a flexible budget but can also lead to a state of confusion in the organizational culture; and sometimes such systems end in exploitation rate fall and a decrease of customer satisfaction in the short run. According to the research done by Standish group, over 90% of ERP implementations exceed their initially allocated budget and time. As a result, it is essential to study the factors resulting in the success of such systems (Parr, 2000; Umble, 2003).

METHODOLOGY

Extracting Core CSFs

In this study, after extracting CSFs from published literature, those CSFs which were most commonly mentioned in previous research were given higher priority and were selected as the core success factor. 62 papers from international journals and conference proceeding were selected, which were published during 2000 -2009.

In the next step, 60 CSFs were extracted from these articles. Since the core CSFs are those that have been identified by the majority of previous papers, the frequency of CSFs (the number of times that a CSF appears in the selected articles) is an appropriate criterion for extracting them. Thus, content analysis, a quantitative approach—counting the frequency of phenomena within a case in order to gauge its importance compared with other cases (Walliman, 2001), was employed. The Entropy method which quantifies the frequency of CSFs to the values that can be used for determining their degree of importance was utilized in the next step. In other words, when a CSF has been frequently identified by previous studies, it must be highly correlated with the level of importance and can be selected as a candidate for the core CSFs. We should also mention that, two CSFs with different titles but the same definition were assumed identical.

Developing the Conceptual Model

Determining Importance Coefficient of CSFs Based on Frequency

In this step, a CSF-Researcher matrix is constructed and then by using the entropy method, the importance coefficients of CSFs is calculated (Saaty, 1990). The main reason for which the entropy method is important in the probabilistic and algorithmic information theories is that it converts the probability of events to the values that can be used for ranking them (Kinsner, 2007). The Entropy method has the obvious advantage of being blindly applicable to any event without the use of any prior knowledge (Denoual & Imag, 2006). The CSF-Researcher matrix is shown in Table 1 theoretically as well as in Table 1A. in which the real data is inserted(the appendix).

For each a_{ij} in the presented CSF-Researcher matrix (Table 1) P_{ij} can be estimated as the probability of CSF_i appearing in article j (Shannon, 1948):

$$P_{ij} = \frac{a_{ij}}{\sum_{j=1}^{62} a_{ij}} \quad i = 1,...,60 \quad j = 1,...,62$$

(1)

In a sense, P_{ij} is the normalized value for a_{ij} and $\sum_{j=1}^{62} p_{ij} = 1$. After defining P_{ij}, we can now explain entropy. Entropy is a concept in physical science, information theory and, even in social sciences that was originally proposed by Shannon (Shannon, 1948; Jaynes, 1954; Cover & Thomas, 1991). Since an outcome includes certain information content, the information content of the normalized outcomes of the attribute can be measured by means of an entropy value (Kenevissi, 2006). It measures the amount of uncertainty existent in the content of information in a message denoted by E_i and defined as in the following:

$$E_i = -\kappa \times [\sum_{j=1}^{62} (p_{ij} \times \ln p_{ij})] \quad i = 1,...,60$$

(2)

ln stands for a Neperian logarithm and *k* is a positive constant defined as $\circ = \dfrac{1}{\ln(62)}$, which is a normalizing positive constant to maintain $0 \leq E_i \leq 1$. Finally, the importance coefficient

of each CSF was calculated using the following formula:

$$\text{»}'_i = \frac{E_i}{\sum_{i=1}^{60} E_i} \quad i = 1,...,60$$

(3)

CSFs' importance coefficients based on entropy is shown in *Table 2[1]*. For example for the first index (i.e., HR and capability management), calculations are as follows:

$$\sum aij = 8$$

Pij=1/8=0.125

K=1/Ln62=0.242

$$E= -0.24 \sum_{j=1}^{62} (0.125 Ln 0.125) = 0.5032$$

λ_i=0.5032/23.3004=0.0215

After measuring the weight of factors using entropy method and sorting weighs, the Scree plot of CSFs has been drawn as shown in *Figure 1*.

As shown in the Scree plot, the plot is kinked after the 7th factor, therefore, we consider the factors lying before the kinked point, as core CSFs, which have the maximum weight.

In the next step, using the core CFSs suggested by the Scree plot, the following conceptual model is proposed (*Figure 2*).

Top Management Commitment and Support: It is one of the two most widely cited CSFs. This concept refers to the need to have committed leadership at the top management level. In addition, this concept refers to the need for management to anticipate any glitches that might be encountered and the need for senior management who would be involved in the strategic planning, but who are also technically orientated. Sarker and Lee (2003)

Table 1. The CSF-Researcher matrix

Researcher CSF	M_1	M_2	...	M_{62}	Index Frequency
i_1	a_{11}	a_{12}	...	$a_{1\,62}$	$r_1 = \sum_{j=1}^{62} a_{1i}$
i_2	a_{21}	a_{22}	...	$a_{2\,62}$	$r_2 = \sum_{j=1}^{62} a_{2i}$
.	.	.	.	.	.
i_{60}	$a_{60\,1}$	$a_{60\,2}$	...	$a_{60\,62}$	$r_{60} = \sum_{j=1}^{62} a_{60i}$

empirically proved that strong and committed leadership at the top management level is essential to the success of an ERP implementation.

Project Management: Project management refers to the ongoing management of the implementation plan. Therefore, it involves not only the planning stages, but also the allocating of responsibilities to various players, the definition of milestones and critical paths, training and human resource planning, and finally the determination of measures of success (Nah, Lou, & Kuang, 2001). Somers and Nelson (2001) also advocate the need to establish a steering committee comprised of senior management from different corporate functions, senior project management reps, and ERP end-users. Steering committee members should be involved in ERP selection, monitoring dur-

Figure 1. Scree Plot of CSFs and their weights

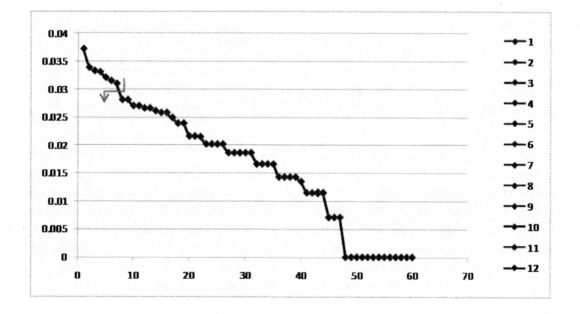

Table 2. Importance Coefficient of CSFs

Critical Success Factor	λ_i	Critical Success Factor	λ_i
HR & Capability Management	0.0215	Ease of Use	0.0143
Cross Functional Coordination	0.0239	Shared Beliefs	0.0115
Software Configuration	0.0202	Personal Relevance of Technology	0
System Development	0	Organizational Fit to ERP	0.0258
Project Management	**0.0315**	Company wide Support	0.0202
Change Management	**0.0339**	Minimum Customization	00.0239
Leadership	0.0115	Accuracy & Reliability	0.0186
Operational Process Discipline	0.0143	Relationship with Vendor & Lower-level User	0.0143
Internal Team	0.0115	System Flexibility	0.0143
End User Acceptance	0.0216	Participation by Manager, Stockholder & Team	0.0281
Top Management Support	**0.0372**	Adaption Mechanism	0.0071
Qualified Consultant	0.0266	Monitoring & Feedback	0.0249
Integration Management	0.0258	Top Management Awareness	0
Time Management	0.0202	Problem Solving Meeting	0
Cost Management	0.0266	Re-Skilling	0.0143
Quality Management	0.0071	Clarity Goal & Strategy	0.0166
Communication	**0.0321**	Software Development Testing & Troubleshooting	0.0216
Risk Management	0.0186	Software Product Skill	0
Procurement Management	0	Empowered Decision Maker	0.0166
Change strategy Development & Deployment	0.0186	Effective Utilization	0
Business Process Reengineering	**0.0333**	Project Meeting	0
Software Selection	0.0166	Stockholder Commitment	0.0186
Training & Education	**0.0331**	CRM	0
Job Redesign	0.0071	Data Warehouse	0.0166
Project Team	**0.0310**	SCM	0
Project Champion	0.0261	Control	0.027
Visioning & Planning	0.027	Linking with Strategy	0.0186
IT Infrastructure	0.0202	Project Usefulness	0.0135
Culture	0.0281	System Security	0
Moral & Motivation	0.0115	Post Implementation	0

ing implementation and management of outside consultants.

Change Management: Change management is the other most widely cited critical success factor. This concept refers to the need for the implementation team to formally prepare a change management program (Nah, Lou, & Kuang, 2001) and be conscious of the need to consider the implications of such a project. One key task is to build user acceptance of the project and a positive employee attitude. This might be accomplished through education about the benefits and need for an ERP system (Somers & Nelson, 2001). Part of this building of user acceptance should also involve securing the support of opinion leaders throughout the organization. There is also a need

Figure 2. Conceptual Model of core CSFs

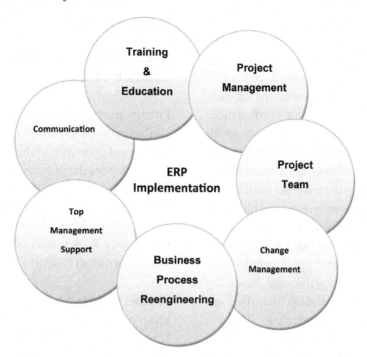

for the team leader to effectively negotiate between various political turfs. Wood and Caldas (2001) further stress that in planning the ERP project; it must be looked upon as a change management initiative not an IT initiative.

Project Team: It has also been repeatedly mentioned throughout the literature that there is a critical need to put in place a solid, core implementation team that is comprised of the organization's best and brightest individuals. These individuals should have a proven reputation and there should be a commitment to "release" these individuals to the project on a full-time basis. Soh et al. (2000) has also cited the need for the team to possess the necessary skills to probe for details when conducting the planning phase of the implementation. Once the team has been established, it might then be necessary to train the individuals.

Training and Education: The completeness, length and detail, timing, and even who to train is an ongoing concern for companies implementing an ERP system. To begin with, training represents a high component of the implementation budget.

Training users for a longer period might be cost-prohibitive. Training users too early might lead to forgetfulness. Other implementation activities might hinder an organization's ability to wait till just before implementation to train users. In fact, the number of users that might need to be trained makes this extremely difficult. At the same time it is important that both user-managers and end-users have a common understanding of the purpose of the training, the training mechanisms, the length and the detail of training that is provided as part of the implementation process. Before user-managers can design an appropriate training program they need to understand how their perceptions about what is being proposed differ from the perceptions of end-users. Training during technology implementation is important because of the potential of training to influence user attitudes, behavior, performance and acceptance of the technology. As indicated earlier, training has been identified as one of the important critical success factors for ERP implementation success. Thus, if gaps exist in the perceptions of end-users and user-managers on the adequacy of the training, managers have to become aware of these differences and take measures to address these differences so that favorable attitudes that lead to the acceptance of technology can be developed (Finney & Cotbett, 2007).

Communication: ERP systems are very expensive and, therefore, the decision to adopt these technologies is very likely to come from senior managers. Once managers make that decision they have to use communication to explain and justify their actions. Presenting the business justification for the ERP system is usually not difficult. What is important is how that justification is translated to lower level employees so that they feel motivated to go along with the implementation and not resist the changes that will occur, hence the need for greater communication than perhaps occurs in other project environments. Since the outcome of this communication, the ability to influence behavior, is dependent on factors such as the frequency and accuracy of information, it is expected that perceptions about the usefulness of the technology will also be dependent on the amount and perceived quality of communication that is provided. Additionally, communication is one of the key enablers for process change.

The implementation of an ERP system requires a lot of process changes. Effective communication will lead to the development of trust and exchange of information needed for those process changes and ultimately the acceptance of the technology. Finally, there are several "unknowns" in an ERP implementation environment and improved communication can lead to more acceptances of these unknowns and the reduction of needless anxiety (Al-Mashiri & Zairi, 2000).

Business Process Re-Engineering: It is the fundamental rethinking and radical redesign of business processes to achieve dramatic improvements in critical, contemporary measures of performance, such as cost, quality, service and speed. ERP systems are built on best practices that are followed in the industry. Implementing an ERP system must involve re-engineering the existing business processes to align the best business standards (Finney & Cotbett, 2007).

Model Verification by Five Case Studies of ERP Implementation

Finally, in order to verify the conceptual model and to propose practical implications, five international companies which have implemented ERP solutions have been examined. The CSFs identified in all five companies were compared with reference to the conceptual model.

Company A: A Case of Bad Communication

Profile: Company A is one of China's largest cosmetic companies and is headquartered in Beijing. It is a multinational that operates in more than thirty countries worldwide. Having established a huge growth in its business, the company had decided to update its current software systems and replace them with an ERP solution. A Swedish company was selected as the appropriate vendor to deploy this solution at a total price 98,320 USD. The implementation of the system in this case was deemed as a failure for a variety of reasons including business standards and language differences that were not considered in the development phases (Xue & Ma, 2008).

ERP Implementation Issues Faced: There were several implementation issues faced which impacted on the total success of the portal. However the main reason for which this implementation was a failure was due to bad *communication* between the client and the vendor.

To begin with, the Swedish ERP vendor at the time had been carrying out all implementations in the English language: given that the main language in Chinese business was Mandarin the system had to be translated into this language. The vendor had attempted to translate the system but did leave key words in English. The fact that the system was operating with a two language format has confused the employees of Company A.

Secondly, the format of accounting and financial tables such balance sheets and the profit and loss table is somewhat different in China than the one used in major European countries. As the version implemented differed, this is something that caused further confusion to the Chinese employees. Moreover minor technical issues such as overlapping numbers and the placement of arithmetical symbols were not desired results for the local workforce, who eventually began to show their disappointment.

Probably the most crucial factor was the inefficient relationship between the vendor and the client company. After the appearance of the technical issues described previously, the company has asked the vendor to make the necessary corrections, but the vendor had failed to act effectively upon them, which resulted in a very poor relationship between them. The end result of this transaction was for the client company to take the vendor to court and obtain financial compensation for the decrease in productivity and general disruptions caused by the product.

Critical Success Factors that Arise From This Case:

- Language and translation concerns are of key significance in international ERP applications. These aspects should be addressed early in the implementation process.
- The difference in international business standards should be taken into account when developing international platforms. Several governmental bodies enforce different regulations to those in the home country of the vendor. These differences may be in financial table formats or even in the way the entire business process is carried out.
- The client-vendor relationship is a defining factor in the overall success of the project. Minor technical issues and training and

support of how to use the system should be proactive. Had these issues been dealt with in the case of Company A the entire outcome of the implementation would have been more desirable.

Company B: The Importance of Change Management and Business Process Re Engineering

Profile: Company B is a privately owned multinational aircraft engine's provider. The company operates in thirteen countries and collaborates with a number of other multinational corporations. Having restructured recently, the company's executive board has decided to upgrade its information technology initiative as they believed it would better facilitate the interests of the organizations key stakeholders. At the time, the company operated its own in house developed legacy systems which were largely inefficient and unable to cope with contemporary business requirements. Another key issue is that these legacy systems supported a heavily decentralized management style as they all operated in isolations thus creating the so called 'Information Silos'. These Silos had formed the basis of several inventory control problems and did not facilitate communication between various manufacturing departments and the accounting department. Finally it is worth noting that the company had recently outsourced its IT department in an attempt to focus on core competencies (Yusuf, Gunasekaran, & Abthorpe, 2004).

ERP Implementation Issues Faced: As the new integrated portal would introduce interoperability between the different departments of the company, there was a need to prepare the workforce and support the change in the business environment. This type of change management was addressed by making the employees aware of the overall improvements that the new system will bring to the organization. The technical training and awareness was deployed by both internal and external consultants and was carried out in the form of seminars.

A Business Process Re engineering (BPR) initiative had to be applied in the company as there was a need to form a strong unified business model. The approach was carried out by firstly identifying the current business processes, then identifying problems that exist amongst these processes, followed by trying to fit in these problems into the ERP system and then finally to adapt all of the processes into the system. The IT vendor deemed it was appropriate to initially apply a 'Vanilla ERP' version of the system to the company. This version minimized costs and made the installation much simpler.

The final set of issues that needed to be dealt with was of a technical nature. A huge amount of data had to be recovered from the system currently in use. Having this in mind, the vendor company developed specialized software that would facilitate the transfer of data between the two systems. Furthermore, the developers ensured that all potential software to be installed will be fully compatible with the ERP system provided by an authorization process that had to be further justified by business related reasons.

A pilot approach was employed before entirely activating the new system. The overall result was a successful implementation which amongst others had also improved customer response time.

Critical Success Factors that Arise From the Case:

- Preparing the workforce and forming an environment for cultural change. It is not only necessary to provide technical training but also to ensure that users will be aware of the benefits that the system will introduce. High user involvement in the early stages of the development of the project is one way of achieving the above.

- For the system to adequately address the requirements of its stakeholders and to make full use of the abilities of the IT

vendor it is essential that in the development team there are representatives of both sides, namely vendor and client.

- Business Process Reengineering is essential in adapting old business methodologies to the newly proposed system. BPR is of further use when adopting a Vanilla ERP approach as applying old business formats to the new system may result in time consuming and costly situations.

- Technical issues involving data transfer, compatibility, usage, support and updates of the system should be addressed by the supplying vendor and there needs to be a transfer of knowledge and competencies to the client company's IT departments where applicable.

- The implementation approach may be in the form of prototyping, piloting by parts or simply by a big bang change over. In cases where large multinationals such as company B are involved, step by step approaches or piloting are more advisable as they can significantly reduce the chances of further costs and distress the entire organization.

Company C: Top Management Support and Efficient Project Management are Key Elements to Success

Profile: Company C is a designer, manufacturer and marketer for casual footwear. The company engages in international business by licensing and distributing to over 130 markets worldwide. The company at the time had been using old legacy systems which gave out inaccurate information and were extremely time consuming. An ERP system solution appeared to be the ideal step forward to assist business growth and to improve current internal operations. With the involvement of senior management and a new management initiative, Company C managed to successfully implement a resource planning system and enjoyed the added benefits provided by it. An external ERP vendor was assigned to develop and deploy the system (Motwani, Mirchandani, & Gunasekaran, 2002)

ERP Implementation Issues Faced: Company C adopted a step by step approach of installing the system by gradually deploying it into specific business modules such as the marketing department. In order to assemble an effective project team the company carried out various meeting informing employees and discussing various other options they had at the time. After the team had been formed the implementation approach was then decided.

The entire project was planned and distinct milestones were set by top management as a project management initiative. Furthermore, before making the portal operational intense 'White Box' and 'Black Box' testing was carried out. The company had also taken into account previous implementations of ERP systems in other organizations and had successfully prevented obstacles that would occur in common situations. A high user involvement was also encouraged, extensive training was carried out and all of the employees had access to further training resources. To facilitate this type of training the external vendor had trained the in- house IT department which in turn transferred the knowledge to the rest of the employees. The fact that the implementation was carried out in phases enabled the latter departments to learn and improvise from the experiences of the departments that the system has been initially deployed to, this had also significantly reduced potential risks that could have developed into serious problems for the entire project. This type of project management was crucial to the success of the entire implementation.

At the same time a strong and effective relationship with the vendor ensured that all obstacles that appeared during the implementation were immediately dealt with. A cautious change of management scheme was also enforced by the company's senior management. In this particular case, the high involvement of senior and middle

management is worth noting. In addition to the above, team based working enabled open communication amongst employees at different levels of the organization, which enabled continuous feedback and knowledge transfers between them.

Critical Success Factors that Arise From the Case:

- High senior management involvement is essential for the entire implementation of the system as it triggers the continuous interest of all stakeholders involved.
- Strong relationships with the external ERP vendor ensure the effective overcoming of potential obstacles.
- A step by step installation approach can also significantly reduce obstacles. A deuteron learning concept is also facilitated by using such an approach.
- High user involvement and the provision of adequate training is a crucial factor that ensures the ongoing use of the system in the most beneficial manner.
- A change management plan positively affects the culture of the organization and guarantees the preparation of the employees for the business process change that will follow.

Company D: Knowledge Transfer (Training and Education) and Top Management Support

Profile: Company D is an OEM (original equipment manufacturer) that operates in China and has recently been acquired by an American firm. The company at the time had a low IT budget and was using its IT department as a supportive role. Company D also operated old legacy systems and aimed to replace them by an ERP system as time consuming operations with inaccurate outputs were often evident in the day to day use of these systems. Senior management at the same time aimed to improve business process efficiency and reduce production and operating costs. An incremental approach was used to install the system by using the financial modules as a starting point (Chuck & Ngai, 2007).

ERP Implementation Issues Faced: Due to the fact that the in house IT department had not been highly experienced in complex projects such as ERP systems there were some initial difficulties when placing the IT managers in the driving seat. The risk of resistance to the changes imposed had been reduced by the strong involvement of senior management and an IT executive. This had also contributed to the high acceptance that the system had across all of the functional modules of the organization. Furthermore, it encouraged a high user involvement throughout the implementation process which ensured that all stakeholder needs were addressed. Finally the ERP package selected was the ideal solution for the current business requirements, something that made issues such as business process reengineering and business process redesign much simpler. In this case the transfer of knowledge to the in house IT department and the solid education provided to the users of the system ensured a smooth change over. As with previous cases the evidence of Top management support throughout the entire project provided the guiding source for the transition.

Critical Success Factors that Arise From the Case: Strong senior management support which ensured that the necessary attention was given to the implementation issues faced.

- Business process redesign. As the new solution will impose a large amount of change in the way the business currently operates, a need to carefully examine current business processes and translate them onto the new portal is highly evident.
- Selection of the appropriate ERP package. Before selecting a specific package there needs to be a close examination of the current business needs and the market supply. Selecting a system which does not fulfill

the business requirements would not only be an instant financial loss but will form an opportunity cost for the organization.

- Adequate authority must be granted to the developers and the in-house IT department by the general management so that they can operate more efficiently and effectively.
- High user involvement should be encouraged from the start thus ensuring that all major interests of the various stakeholders involved are represented. This will also increase operational efficiency as less training and support would be required in the long term.
- A transfer of knowledge from the external consultants to the company's IT department is essential for the ongoing operational success of the system. This department will be the guidance and supporting actor for the functional phase of the system and they should therefore be more than comfortable in manipulating it.

Company E: The Structure of the Project Team

Profile: Company E is a British based multinational that operates in thirty countries worldwide. The company operates in the engineering industry and as with some of the previous cases they have also decided to upgrade their current legacy systems with an ERP solution. In this case a smooth transition took place with considerable top manager support, however the structure of the project team and the way that particular tasks were divided and allocated were of equal importance to the overall success (Newell, Huang, & Tansley, 2006).

ERP implementation issues faced: In this case particular emphasis was placed upon human resources (HR). A senior HR manager was appointed as a key project manager in the implementation team. A rather collective work load was allocated with at least two people in charge of any particular task. All members involved in the project were also encouraged to express the ideas before selecting the actual enterprise resource planning package. This ensured high user involvement and at the same time development a notion of ownership. Furthermore the IT consultants of the project team managed to gain a holistic view of the project as they were also involved in areas other than programming and development.

Although the project team members originated from a variety of backgrounds the team bonding and bridging that took place facilitated in taking advantage of the full potential that this diverse project team carried.

Overall the successful outcome of this implementation enabled numerous benefits, such as reducing procurement costs, for the entire organization after the system had been launched. This success was attributed to knowledge integration amongst the project team.

Critical Success Factors that Arise From the Case:

- A strong Top management support was evident from the pre selection stages of the ERP package. The appointment of senior HR into a project manager role clearly demonstrates the commitment the top management had in this initiative.
- A diverse project team which spanned expertise from HR and IT. This gave the team multiple capabilities and understandings of various concepts. However is it the openness and the encouragement of expressing ideas that enabled this team to take advantage of its potential?
- The high user involvement in the overall project. IT consultants where involved in issues other than IT development this enabled them gain a higher understanding of the holistic picture of the project. Not only where these consultants gaining a broader understanding but at the same time knowledge regarding the basic functionalities of

the system were transferred to the rest of the members.
- The knowledge sharing amongst the project team and team bonding enabled the team members to trust each other and develops a feeling of unity. Furthermore this facilitates the expression of new ideas and further helps in resolving potential conflicts in interests that various stakeholders may face.

Comparison of CSFs Proposed by Conceptual Model and the Five Case Studies

According to the conceptual model, the seven CSFs are extracted as follows: (1) Top Management Support, (2) BPR, (3) Training, (4) Communication, (5) Change Management, (6) Project Management, and (7) Project Team.

In agreement with the proposed conceptual model, there is an emphasis on communication in all five cases; communication between employees and management, stockholders and between internal team and employees. One more factor proposed by the conceptual model is change management which is highly evident in company B. BPR has been mostly mentioned in the case of company B as well. Furthermore Top Management support has been evident in almost all cases. The most evident cases of Top management support were Company C and Company D. Training and education has been identified in the first three companies (i.e., A, B, and C). Finally Project Management and the Project Team played a vital role in the case of Company E.

All of the seven factors identified in the conceptual model have been verified by the five company cases presented above. This leads to solid proof that these factors have real time practical influences.

DISCUSSION AND CONCLUSION

The fact that a number of CSF was not applicable in the context of some companies was a major limitation. To overcome this limitation and reach a consensus on core CSFs, the previous studies relied on expert opinion and questionnaires. But, due to the high number of extracted CSF (60 CSFs), this method was not very practicable in this instance. In this article, the main criterion for selecting core CSF was the frequency of CSFs in the reported literature. In the adoption of such a criterion, first of all, there is no need for data to extract core CSFs; second, since higher priority was assigned to those CSFs which were employed in more studies, researchers' opinions were utilized as proxies for experts' opinions—indirectly without the use of questionnaires. Hence, the problems with and limitations of obtaining experts' opinions were avoided; in addition, a broad range of experts and researchers' opinions (62) were taken into consideration.

Therefore, the meta-heuristic methodology presented in this paper can be a valuable and simple tool for improving the existing set of CSFs. Also, since our core CSFs represents a convergence of CSFs of the literature, the experienced researchers have consensus on them. This introduces them as a standard set and a basis for benchmarking those CSFs considered to be of the highest significance for ERP implementation. However, all firms are not at the same level or have well-developed in terms of ICT maturity.

The five companies that were reviewed come to reinforce those critical success factors to which the conceptual model concludes to. These cases confirm that the implementation of enterprise resource planning systems is an area to which more attention needs to be given. In both successful and unsuccessful installations, organizational culture issues appear to significantly impact the overall outcome.

While several studies so far have attempted to identify various critical success factors, most lack the proposition of a unique methodology for successfully implementing these systems. The conceptual model can be considered as an early attempt to propose a specific plan that can guarantee the accomplishment of key stakeholder objectives.

At this point it is also worth noting that there is room for significant further research. A possible area that may be researched upon is the formation of strategic relationships between clients and vendors. This article has shown that the quality of this relationship can define the overall success of the system and prevents huge financial losses. It is therefore strongly advisable that a model of establishing and maintaining such strategic relationships is established.

Finally, organizations must learn how to identify and manage the issues that uniquely relate to their own specific cases. A possible way of doing this will be to examine the factors in the model one by one and attempt to find the application of this factor in their own environment. An ERP system will not offer competitive advantage just by simply installing it: it is the strategic use of this tool and its complete application in all areas of the company that will assist it in succeeding against its competitors.

REFERENCES

Achanga, P., Shehab, E., Rajkumar, R., & Nelder, G. (2006). Critical success factors for lean implementation within SMEs. *Journal of Manufacturing Technology Management*, *4*(17), 460–471. doi:10.1108/17410380610662889

Al-Mashari, M., & Al-Mudimigh, A. (2003). ERP implementation: lessons from a case study. *Information Technology & People*, *1*, 21–33. doi:10.1108/09593840310463005

Al-mashari, M., Al-mudimigh, A., & Zairi, M. (2003). Enterprise Resource Planning: A Taxonomy of Critical Factors. *European Journal of Operational Research, 146*(1), 352–364. doi:10.1016/S0377-2217(02)00554-4

Al-Mudimigh, A. (2007). The role and impact of business process management in enterprise systems implementation. *Business Process Management Journal, 6*(13), 866–874. doi:10.1108/14637150710834604

Amoako-Gyampah, K. (2004). ERP implementation factors A comparison of managerial and end-user perspectives. *Business Process Management Journal, 2*(10), 171–183. doi:10.1108/14637150410530244

Boon, O., Wilkin, C., & Corbitt, B. (2003). *Towards A Broader Based Is Success Model – Integrating Critical Success Factors and the Deleon AND McLean's Is Success Model*. Retrieved from www. deakin.edu.ac

Bozarth, C. (2006). ERP implementation efforts at three firms Integrating lessons from the SISP and IT-enabled change literature. *International Journal of Operations & Production Management, 11*, 1223–1339. doi:10.1108/01443570610705836

Carton, F., Frederic, A., & Sammon, D. (2007). Project management: a case study of a successful ERP implementation. *International Journal of Managing Projects in Business, 1*(1), 106–124. doi:10.1108/17538370810846441

Chuang, M.-L., & Shaw, W. H. (2008). An empirical study of enterprise resource management systems implementation From ERP to RFID. *Business Process Management Journal, 5*(14), 675–693. doi:10.1108/14637150810903057

Chuck, C. H., & Ngai, E. W. T. (2007). ERP systems adoption: An exploratory study of the organizational factors and impacts of ERP success. *Information & Management, 44*, 418–432. doi:10.1016/j.im.2007.03.004

Cover, T. M., & Thomas, J. A. (1991). *Elements of information theory*. New York: John Wiley and Sons Inc. doi:10.1002/0471200611

David, C., & Coker, W. (2006). *Lessons Learned from the Army's Largest ERP Implementation*. Retrieved from khyde@corpcomminc.com

Denoual, E., & Imag, C. G. (2006). A method to quantify corpus similarity and its application to quantifying the degree of literality in a document. *International Journal of Technology and Human Interaction, 2*, 51–66.

Donovan, R. M. (n.d.). Retrieved from www. rmdonovan.com

El Sawah, S., El Fattah, T., Assem, A., & Rasmy, M. H. (2008). A quantitative model to predict the Egyptian ERP implementation success index. *Business Process Management Journal, 3*(14), 288–306. doi:10.1108/14637150810876643

Esteves, J., Casanovas, J., & Pastor, J. (2003). Modeling with Partial Least Squares Critical Success Factors Interrelationships in ERP Implementations. In *Proceedings of the Ninth Americans conference on Information systems*.

Esteves, J., & Pastor, J. (2001). Analysis of Critical Success Factors Relevance along SAP Implementation Phases. In *Proceedings of the Seventh Americas Conference ON Information Systems*.

Finney, S., & Corbett, M. (2007). ERP implementation:a compilation and analysis of critical success factors. *Business Process Management Journal, 3*(13), 329–347. doi:10.1108/14637150710752272

Fui, F., Nah, H., Zuckweiler, K. M., Lee, J., & Lau, S. (2003). ERP Implementation: Chief Information Officers' Perceptions of Critical Success Factors. *International Journal of Human-Computer Interaction, 1*(16), 5–22.

Gargeya, V. B., & Brady, C. (2005). Success and failure factors of adopting SAP in ERP system implementation. *Business Process Management Journal, 5*(11), 501–516. doi:10.1108/14637150510619858

Grant, G. G. (2003). Strategic alignment and enterprise systems implementation: the case of Metalco. *Journal of Information Technology, 18*, 159. doi:10.1080/0268396032000122132

Ha¨kkinen, L., & Hilmola, O.-P. (2008). Life after ERP implementation Long-term development of user perceptions of system success in an after-sales environment. *Journal of Enterprise Information Management, 3*(21), 285–309. doi:10.1108/17410390810866646

Her Wu, J., & Min Wang, Y. (2006). Measuring ERP success: the ultimate users' view. *International Journal of Operations & Production Management, 8*(26), 882–903.

Hong, K. K., & Kim, Y. G. (2002). The Critical Success Factors for ERP Implementation: An Organizational Fit Perspective. *Information & Management, 40*, 25–40. doi:10.1016/S0378-7206(01)00134-3

Huang, S.-M., Chang, I.-C., Han, L. S., & Tong, M. (2004). Assessing risk in ERP projects: identify and prioritize the factors. *Industrial Management & Data Systems, 8*(104), 681–688. doi:10.1108/02635570410561672

Iidaka, T., Matsumoto, A., Nogawa, J., Yamamoto, Y., & Sadato, N. (2006). *Front parietal Network Involved in Successful Retrieval from Episodic Memory. Spatial and Temporal Analyses Using fMRI and ERP*. Oxford, UK: Oxford University Press.

ERP Implementation Guidelines. (2002). *ERP Executive Steering Committee.*

Jaynes, E. T. (1954). Information theory and statistical mechanics. *Physical Review, 106*, 620–630. doi:10.1103/PhysRev.106.620

Karsak, E., & O' zogul, O. (2009). An integrated decision making approach for ERP system selection. *Expert Systems with Applications, 36*, 660–667. doi:10.1016/j.eswa.2007.09.016

Katerattanakul, P., Hong, S., & Lee, J. (2006). Enterprise resource planning survey of Korean manufacturing firms. *Management Research News, 12*(29), 820–837. doi:10.1108/01409170610717835

Ke, W., & Wei, K. K. (2008). Organizational culture and leadership in ERP implementation. *Decision Support Systems, 45*, 208–218. doi:10.1016/j.dss.2007.02.002

Kenevissi, F. (2006). *Multi-criteria decision making (Tech. Rep.)*. Newcastle Upon Tyne, UK: Newcastle University, Newcastle Engineering Design Centre.

Kim, Y., Lee, Z., & Gosain, S. (2005). Impediments to successful ERP implementation process. *Business Process Management Journal, 2*(11), 158–170. doi:10.1108/14637150510591156

Kinsner, W. (2007). Is entropy suitable to characterize data and signals for cognitive informatics? *International Journal of Cognitive Informatics and Natural Intelligence, 1*, 34–57.

Kumar, V., Maheshwari, B., & Kumar, U. (2002). ERP systems implementation: best practices in Canadian government organizations. *Government Information Quarterly, 19*, 147–172. doi:10.1016/S0740-624X(02)00092-8

Kwahk, K.-Y., & Lee, J.-N. (2008). The role of readiness for change in ERP implementation: Theoretical bases and empirical validation. *Information & Management, 45*, 474–481. doi:10.1016/j.im.2008.07.002

Law, C. H., & Ngai, E. W. T. (2007). An investigation of the relationships between organizational factors, business process improvement, and ERP success. *Benchmarking: An International Journal, 3*(14), 387–406. doi:10.1108/14635770710753158

Lian, J. (2001). *A study of Prerequisites for Successful ERP Implementations From The project Management, Perspective.* Retrieved from www.canias.com/enterprise/articles/20080604

Lois, F., & Gerald, J. (2003). *The Role of Governance in ERP System Implementation.* Retrieved from www.elsevier.com.

Marnewick, C. (2005). A conceptual model for enterprise resource planning (ERP). *Information Management & Computer Security, 2*(13), 144–155. doi:10.1108/09685220510589325

Metaxiotis, K., Zafeiropoulos, I., Nikolinakou, K., & Psarras, J. (2005). Goal directed project management methodology for the support of ER implementation and optimal adaptation procedure. *Information Management & Computer Security, 1*(13), 55–71. doi:10.1108/09685220510582674

Mirzaee, M. (2007). ERP Experiment in Unilever Company. In *Proceedings of the second conference of experiment on ERP implementation.* Retrieved from www.irerp.com.

Motwani, J., Mirchandani, D., & Gunasekaran, A. (2002). Successful implementation of ERP projects: Evidence from two case studies. *International Journal of Production Economics, 75,* 83–96. doi:10.1016/S0925-5273(01)00183-9

Muscatello, J. R., Small, M. H., & Chen, I. J. (2003). Implementing enterprise resource planning (ERP) systems in small and midsize manufacturing firms. *International Journal of Operations & Production Management, 8*(23), 850–871. doi:10.1108/01443570310486329

Nah, F., Lou, J., & Kuang, J. (2001). Critical Factors for Successful Implementation of Enterprise Systems. *Business Process Management Journal, 3*(7), 285–296. doi:10.1108/14637150110392782

Newell, S., Huang, J., & Tansley, C. (2006). ERP Implementation: A knowledge Integration Challenge for the Project Team. *Knowledge and Process Management, 4*(13), 227–238. doi:10.1002/kpm.262

Ngai, E. W. T., Law, C. C. H., & Wat, F. K. T. (2008). Examining the critical success factors in the adoption of enterprise resource planning. *Computers in Industry, 59*(58), 548–564. doi:10.1016/j.compind.2007.12.001

Okren, M. D., & Vokurka, R. J. (2004). Process mapping in successful ERP implementations. *Industrial Management & Data Systems, 8*(104), 637–643. doi:10.1108/02635570410561618

Parr, A. N., & Shanks, G. (2000). A Taxonomy of ERP Implementation Approaches. In *Proceedings of the 33rd Hawaii International Conference on System Sciences.*

Peslak, A. R. (2006). Enterprise resource planning success. *Industrial Management & Data Systems, 9*(106), 1288–1303. doi:10.1108/02635570610712582

Ramayah, T., & Chiun Lo, M. (2007). Impact of shared beliefs on "perceived usefulness" and "ease of use" in the implementation of an enterprise resource planning system. *Management Research New, 6*(30), 40–431.

Remus, U. (2007). Critical success factors for implementing enterprise portals A comparison with ERP implementations. *Business Process Management Journal, 4*(13), 538–552. doi:10.1108/14637150710763568

Research, A. M. R. (n.d.). *AMR Research Predicts ERP Market will Reach $66.6 Billion by 2003.* Retrieved May 5, 2008 from http://www.amrresearch.com/Content/View.asp?pmillid=13280

Saaty, L. (1990). *Decision making for leaders.* Pittsburgh, PA: RWS publications.

Sarker, S., & Lee, A. S. (2003). Using a case study to test the role of three key social enablers in ERP implementation. *Information & Management, 40,* 414–425. doi:10.1016/S0378-7206(02)00103-9

Schniederjans, M. J., & Kim, G. C. (2003). Implementing enterprise resource planning systems with total quality control and business process reengineering Survey results. *International Journal of Operations & Production Management, 4*(23), 418–429. doi:10.1108/01443570310467339

Seng Woo, H. (2007). Critical success factors for implementing ERP: the case of a Chinese electronics manufacturer. *Journal of Manufacturing Technology Management, 4*(18), 431–442.

Shannon, C. E. (1948). A mathematical theory of communication. *The Bell System Technical Journal, 27,* 623–656.

Sharma, A. (n.d.). *Risks in ERP implementation.* Retrieved from www.AshutoshSharma.gov.in

Snider, B., da Silveira, G. J. C., & Balakrishnan, J. (2009). ERP implementation at SMEs: analysis of five Canadian cases. *International Journal of Operations & Production Management, 1*(11), 4–29. doi:10.1108/01443570910925343

Soh, C., Kien, S. S., & Tay-Yap, J. (2000). Cultural fits and misfits: is ERP a universal solution?",Association for Computing Machinery. *Communications of the ACM, 43,* 47. doi:10.1145/332051.332070

Soja, P. (2006). Success factors in ERP systems implementations: lessons from practice. *Journal of Enterprise Information Management, 6*(19), 646–661. doi:10.1108/17410390610708517

Soja, P. (2008). Examining the conditions of ERP implementations: lessons learnt from adopters. *Business Process Management Journal, 1*(14), 105–121. doi:10.1108/14637150810849445

Somers, T., & Nelson, K. (2001). The Impact of Critical Success Factors across the Stage of Enterprise Resource Planning Implementations. In *Proceeding of the 34th Hawaii International Conference on System Sciences.*

Son Yu, C. (2005). Causes influencing the effectiveness of the post-implementation ERP system. *Management & Data Systems, 1*(105), 115–131.

The Checklist for Successful ERP Implementation. (2002). Retrieved from www.buker.com

Trimmer, K. J., Pumphry, L. D., & Wiggins, C. (2002). ERP implementation in rural health care. *Journal of Management in Medicine, 2/3*(16), 113–132. doi:10.1108/02689230210434871

Umble, E. J., Haft, R. R., & Umble, M. M. (2003). Enterprise Resource Planning: Implementation Procedures and Critical Success Factors. *European Journal of Operational Research, 146,* 241–257. doi:10.1016/S0377-2217(02)00547-7

Verville, J., Bernadas, C., & Halingten, A. (2005). So you're thinking of buying an ERP? Ten critical factors for successful acquisitions. *Journal of Enterprise Information Management, 6*(118), 667–685.

Walliman, N. (2001). *Your research project.* London: Sage Publications.

Wei Chou, S., & Chieh Chang, Y. (2008). The implementation factors that influence the ERP (enterprise resource planning) benefits. *Decision Support Systems, 46,* 149–157. doi:10.1016/j.dss.2008.06.003

Wood, T., & Caldas, M. P. (2001). Reductionism and Coplex thinking during ERP implementation. *Business Process Management Journal, 5*(7), 387–393. doi:10.1108/14637150110406777

Xu, Q., & Ma, Q. (2008). Determinants of ERP implementation knowledge transfer. *Information & Management*, *45*, 528–539. doi:10.1016/j.im.2008.08.004

Yen, R. H., Li, E. Y., & Niehoff, B. P. (2008). Do organizational citizenship behaviors lead to information system success? Testing the mediation effects of integration climate and project management. *Information & Management*, *45*, 394–402. doi:10.1016/j.im.2008.04.004

Yusuf, Y., Gunasekaran, A., & Abthorpe, M. (2004). Enterprise Information systems project implementation: A case study of ERP in Rolls-Royce. *International Journal of Production Economics*, *87*, 251–266. doi:10.1016/j.ijpe.2003.10.004

Zairi, M. (2003). *You're ERP Project Won't Fail. CAN YOU SEE it?* Retrieved from www.ibm.com

Ziaee, M., Fathian, M., & Sadjadi, S. J. (2006). A modular approach to ERP system selection. *Information Management & Computer Security*, *5*(14), 485–495. doi:10.1108/09685220610717772

ENDNOTE

[1] See also Jose, Salvatore and Matthias, 2005, Kenevissi, 2006, Tang, Leung and Lam, 2006. Chan, Koa and Wu M,1999. Macwan and Katti,2006. Semere, 2005.Ding and Liang, 2005.

APPENDIX

Figure 3.

Researcher / CSF	Kim,etal,2005	Snider,etal,2009	Fergal,etal,2007	Al-Mashari,etal,2003	Karsak,2009	Finney&sherry,2007	Amoako,2004	El Sawah,2008	Ha'kkinen,2008	Bozarth,2006	Bozarth,2006	Wei Chou,2008	Trimmer,2002	Metaxiotis,2005	Soja,2006	Katerattanakul,2006	Okren,2004	Xu,2008	Son Yu,2005	Schniederjans,2003	Kwahk,2008	sum
HR& Capability Management	√		√											√								3
Cross Functional Coordination	√											√										2
Software Configuration	√					√												√				3
System Development	√																					1
Project Management	√	√	√	√		√		√	√					√	√							9
Change Management	√			√		√			√		√						√			√		7
Leadership	√																					1
Operational Process Discipline		√																				1
Internal Team		√																				1
End user Acceptance		√						√														2
Top Management Support		√				√		√	√				√		√				√	√		8
Qualified Consultant		√		√									√			√						4
Integration Management			√			√				√			√									4
Time Management			√			√							√		√							4
Cost Management			√			√							√									3
Quality Management			√							√												2
Communication			√	√		√	√										√	√				6

Figure 4.

Researcher / CSF	Soja,2006	Remus,2007	Ramayah,2007	Soja,2008	Rebecca,2008	Her Wu,2006	Verville,eatl,2005	Wooad,2001	Gargeya,2005	Peslak,2006	Ngai,2008	Muscatello,2003	Ke&Wei,2004	Law,2007	Chuang,2008	AlMudimigh,2007	Achanga,2006	David,2006	Sharma	Donovan	Iidaka,2006	Sum
HR& Capability Management								√						√					√			3
Cross Functional Coordination																						0
Software Configuration											√	√										2
System Development																						0
Change Management									√		√			√		√		√			√	6
Leadership												√					√					2
Operational Process Discipline							√				√								√			3
Internal Team																						0
End user Acceptance		√					√												√			3
Top Management Support	√	√							√		√		√	√	√	√				√	√	10
Qualified Consultant														√								1
Integration Management		√			√	√					√											4
Time Management					√	√																2
Cost Management										√	√							√	√			4
Quality Management																						0
Communication		√			√				√		√				√			√				6

Figure 5.

CSF \ Researcher	ERP Implementation Guidelines.(2002)	Mirzaee,2007	Fui,2003	Marrnewick,2005	Ziaee,2006	Huang,2004	Remus,2007	SengWoo,2007	Boon,2003	Wall,2003	Hong,2002	Nah,2001	Somers,2001	Esteves,2001	Lian,2001	Buker.Com,2002	Almashari,2003	Umble,2003	Loisfitz,2003	Zairi,2003	Sum
HR& Capability Management	√	√																			2
Cross Functional Coordination											√	√	√	√	√	√	√		√		8
Software Configuration	√				√																2
System Development																					0
Project Management		√	√			√	√	√													5
Change Management	√		√	√				√			√	√	√	√	√		√	√	√	√	13
Leadership																					0
Operational Process Discipline																					0
Internal Team		√	√																		2
End user Acceptance	√				√		√														3
Top Management Support	√	√	√			√	√	√	√	√	√	√	√	√	√	√	√	√	√	√	18
Qualified Consultant		√								√	√	√	√	√			√	√			8
Integration Management											√	√	√							¥	4
Time Management					√																1
Cost Management					√							√	√			√	√			√	6
Quality Management																					0
Communication			√			√		√			√	√	√	√	√		√			√	10

Figure 6.

Researcher CSF	Kim,etal,2005	Snider,etal,2009	Fergal,etal,2007	Al-Mashari,etal,2003	Karsak,2009	Finney&sherry,2007	Amoako,2004	El Sawah,2008	Ha"kkinen,2008	Bozarth,2006	Bozarth,2006	Wei Chou,2008	Trimmer,2002	Metaxiotis,2005	Soja,2006	Katerattanakul,2006	Okren,2004	Xu,2008	Son Yu,2005	Schniederjans,2003	Kwahk,2008	Sum
Risk Management			√																			1
Procurement Management			√																			1
Change Strategy Development &Deployment				√																		1
Business Process Reengineering				√		√							√			√		√		√		6
Software Selection					√																	1
Training &Education						√	√					√			√			√		√		6
Job Redesign						√																1
Project Team						√					√			√	√					√		5
Project Champion																						0
Visioning &Planning															√	√						2
IT Infrastructure						√									√							2
Culture								√	√													2
Moral& Motivation						√							√		√							3
Ease of use							√														√	2
Shared beliefs							√													√		2
Personal Relevance of Technology							√															1
Organizational Fit to ERP								√				√				√						3

Figure 7.

Researcher / CSF	Soja,2006	Remus,2007	Ramayah,2007	Soja,2008	Rebecca,2008	Her Wu,2006	Verville,eatl,2005	Wooad,2001	Gargeya,2005	Peslak,2006	Ngai,2008	Muscatello,2003	Ke&Wei,2004	Law,2007	Chuang,2008	AlMudimigh,2007	Achanga,2006	David,2006	Sharma	Donovan	Iidaka,2006	sum
Risk Management																						0
Procurement Management																						0
Change Strategy Development &Deployment																						0
Business Process Reengineering	√						√	√		√	√				√				√			7
Software Selection	√												√									2
Training &Education					√			√			√		√				√	√				6
job Redesign																						0
Project Team			√		√			√		√								√				5
Project Champion								√					√									2
Visioning &Planning								√														1
IT Infrastructure							√			√	√				√						√	5
Culture	√							√		√		√					√					5
Moral& Motivation																						0
Ease of use		√		√																		2
Shared beliefs		√																				1
Personal Relevance of Technology																						0
Organizational Fit to ERP												√	√									2

Figure 8.

Researcher / CSF	ERP Implementation	Mirzaee,2007	Fui,2003	Marnewick,2005	Ziaee,2006	Huang,2004	Remus,2007	SengWoo,2007	Boon,2003	Wall,2003	Hong,2002	Nah,2001	Somers,2001	Esteves,2001	Lian,2001	Buker.Com,2002	Almashari,2003	Umble,2003	Loisfitz,2003	Zairi,2003	Sum
Risk Management												√	√			√	√			√	5
Procurement Management																					0
Change Strategy Development &Deployment																					0
Business Process Reengineering			√				√					√	√	√	√	√	√	√	√	√	11
Software Selection		√					√														2
Training &Education						√		√	√		√	√	√	√	√	√	√	√	√	√	13
Job Redesign						√															1
Project Team						√		√	√		√	√	√	√	√			√	√		10
Project Champion			√								√		√		√		√		√		6
Visioning &Planning			√							√	√	√	√	√		√	√	√	√	√	11
IT Infrastructure																					0
Culture			√			√					√	√				√	√	√	√		8
Moral& Motivation																					0
Ease of use																					0
Shared beliefs																					0
Personal Relevance of Technology																					0
Organizational Fit to ERP											√	√	√	√			√	√		√	7

Figure 9.

Researcher / CSF	Kim etal,2005	Snider,etal,2009	Fergal,etal,2007	Al-Mashari,etal,2003	Karsak,2009	Finney&sherry,2007	Amoako,2004	El Sawah,2008	Ha¨kkinen,2008	Bozarth,2006	Bozarth,2006	Wei Chou,2008	Trimmer,2002	Metaxiotis,2005	Soja,2006	Katerattanakul,2006	Okren,2004	Xu,2008	Son Yu,2005	Schniederjans,2003	Kwahk,2008	sum
Company Wide Support								√														1
Minimum Customization										√					√							2
Accuracy &Reliability											√				√							2
Relationship with Vendor &Lower-level User											√				√							2
System Flexibility										√												1
Participation by Manager, Stockholder &Team											√				√							2
Adaption Mechanism												√		√								2
Monitoring &Feedback						√									√							2
Top Management Awareness															√							1
Problem Solving Meeting																√						1
Re skilling																√	√					2
Clarity Goal &Strategy																						0
Software Development Testing & Troubleshooting																						0
Software Product Skill																						0
Empowered Decision Maker						√																1
Effective Utilization																						0

Figure 10.

Researcher / CSF	Soja,2006	Remus,2007	Ramayah,2007	Soja,2008	Rebecca,2008	Her Wu,2006	Verville,eatl,2005	Wooad,2001	Gargeya,2005	Peslak,2006	Ngai,2008	Muscatello,2003	Ke&Wei,2004	Law,2007	Chuang,2008	AlMudimigh,2007	Achanga,2006	David,2006	Sharma	Donovan	Iidaka,2006	Sum
Company Wide Support																						0
Minimum Customization		√							√		√											3
Accuracy &Reliability						√	√				√				√							4
Relationship with Vendor &Lower-level User	√														√							2
System Flexibility						√														√		2
Participation by Manager, Stockholder &Team	√					√	√			√	√	√										6
Adaption Mechanism																						0
Monitoring &Feedback	√								√			√										3
Top Management Awareness																						0
Problem Solving Meeting																						0
Re skilling											√											1
Clarity Goal &Strategy				√	√						√			√								4
Software Development Testing & Troubleshooting									√		√											2
Software Product Skill															√							1
Empowered Decision Maker																						0
Effective Utilization					√																	1

Figure 11.

Researcher / CSF	ERP Implementation	Mirzaee,2007	Fui,2003	Marnewick,2005	Ziaee,2006	Huang,2004	Remus,2007	SengWoo,2007	Boon,2003	Wall,2003	Hong,2002	Nah,2001	Somers,2001	Esteves,2001	Lian,2001	Buker.Com,2002	Almashari,2003	Umble,2003	Loisfitz,2003	Zairi,2003	sum
Company Wide Support											√	√			√	√			√	√	6
Minimum Customization	√												√	√				√	√		5
Accuracy &Reliability																					0
Relationship with Vendor &Lower-level User																					0
System Flexibility	√																				1
Participation by Manager, Stockholder &Team											√	√		√	√	√	√		√		7
Adaption Mechanism																					0
Monitoring &Feedback		√									√	√				√	√	√			6
Top Management Awareness																					0
Problem Solving Meeting																					0
Re skilling												√									1
Clarity Goal &Strategy							√														1
Software Development Testing & Troubleshooting			√								√	√		√			√			√	6
Software Product Skill																					0
Empowered Decision Maker												√		√	√					√	4
Effective Utilization																					0

Figure 12.

CSF \ Researcher	Kim etal,2005	Snider,etal,2009	Fergal,etal,2007	Al-Mashari,etal,2003	Karsak,2009	Finney&sherry,2007	Amoako,2004	El Sawah,2008	Ha¨kkinen,2008	Bozarth,2006	Bozarth,2006	Wei Chou,2008	Trimmer,2002	Metaxiotis,2005	Soja,2006	Katerattanakul,2006	Okren,2004	Xu,2008	Son Yu,2005	Schniederjans,2003	Kwahk,2008	Sum
Project Meeting																	√					1
Stockholder Commitment										√												1
CRM																√						1
Data Warehouse																√						1
SCM																√						1
Control											√			√								2
Linking with Strategy															√							1
Project Usefulness									√													1
System Security																						0
Post Implementation																						0

Figure 13.

CSF \ Researcher	Soja,2006	Remus,2007	Ramayah,2007	Soja,2008	Rebecca,2008	Her Wu,2006	Verville,eatl,2005	Wooad,2001	Gargeya,2005	Peslak,2006	Ngai,2008	Muscatello,2003	Ke&Wei,2004	Law,2007	Chuang,2008	AlMudimigh,2007	Achanga,2006	David,2006	Sharma	Donovan	Iidaka,2006	Sum
Project Meeting																						0
Stockholder Commitment																						0
CRM																						0
Data Warehouse											√							√	√			3
SCM																						0
Control						√																1
Linking with Strategy	√																					1
Project Usefulness		√				√																2
System Security																			√			1
Post implementation																			√			1

This work was previously published in International Journal of Enterprise Information Systems, edited by Madjid Tavana, pp. 82-111, Volume 6, Issue 2, copyright 2010 by IGI Publishing (an imprint of IGI Global).

Chapter 7

Factors that Improve ERP Implementation Strategies in an Organization

Chetan S. Sankar
Auburn University, USA

ABSTRACT

This paper reports the results of an exploratory research that describes the Enterprise Resource Planning (ERP) implementation experiences of Robert Bosch Corporation over a period of time. In this paper, the author highlights a list of factors that could improve ERP implementations such as large resource commitment to the project, adoption of corporate standards that promote process harmonization, making hard yet important decisions that are irreversible, and top management support. The major contribution of this article is in explaining why the ERP implementation experience at Robert Bosch succeeded in 2004 in contrast to its implementation experience during 1992-1999. The resulting practical implications are discussed.

INTRODUCTION

In today's volatile business climate, market behavior no longer seems to guarantee an eventual equilibrium in which both supply and demand are satisfied. Rather, if a company makes a move at the right moment, this can initiate a positive snowball

effect that gives that company an exponentially growing lead over its rivals (Baets, 1998). If a company makes a move at the wrong moment, it might join the likes of Circuit City, Linens-n-Things, and Lehman Brothers in bankruptcy (Newman, 2008). Organizations are experiencing environments that are not only changing more rapidly but are increasingly subject to sudden irregularities (Ellis, 1988). In environments that are non-linear

DOI: 10.4018/978-1-4666-1761-2.ch007

and dynamic, traditional strategic theories such as SWOT analysis (Hill & Westbrook, 1997) may have to be supplemented by new approaches such as dynamic strategies to explain the factors that can help in effective implementation of ERP systems (Baets, 1998; Ghemawat & Cassiman, 2005; Erat & Kavadias, 2006; McGuinness & Morgan, 2005; Paquin & Koplyay, 2007; Yuksel & Dagdeviren, 2007; Allen et al., 2002).

SWOT analysis is one of the primary tools of choice to identify effective IT strategies. Several groups have put this tool to effective use: Shuai (2008) uses a SWOT analysis to provide policy recommendations to the Chinese government on whether they should contribute to the World Food Programme. Arslan and Er (2008) use a SWOT analysis to formulate a strategy concerned with the safe carriage of bulk liquid chemicals in maritime tankers. Guerrero, Lozano, and Rueda-Canutuche (2008) use a SWOT analysis to identify eight strategic measures aimed at providing policymakers with key guidelines to minimize negative social, economic, and environmental impacts due to a mine collapse in Spain. Uscher-Pines et al. (2008) apply a SWOT analysis to a domestic shortage of influenza vaccine to identify lessons learned and to generate effective solutions for future public health rationing emergencies. Mauerhofer (2008) analyzes several conceptual figures describing the relationship between environmental, social, and economic sustainability by using a SWOT analysis. Other applications for SWOT analyses are determining international distribution centers (Lee & Lin, 2008); renal allograft rejection strategies (Mengel et al., 2007); outsourcing of airlines' maintenance, repair, and overhaul activities (Alkaabi et al., 2007); energy planning (Terrados et al., 2007); planning support systems (Vonk et al., 2007); urban development planning (Halla, 2007); and evaluating nuclear energy strategies (Lee et al., 2007). Once an effective IT strategy has been decided on, what other tools can be used to enhance the success of implementation strategies?

This study is an exploratory research aimed at identifying factors that led to the success of the enterprise resource planning (ERP) implementation at Robert Bosch GmbH during the period 1992-2004. We recorded snapshots of the implementation process at two points in time: 2000 and 2004. On each occasion the companies's Chief Information Officers in Stuttgart, Germany (corporate headquarters) and in Broadview, IL (the headquarters of Robert Bosch US) were interviewed. Comparing the sets of data gathered for the two different time periods revealed very different strategies and personalities leading the implementation effort. In particular, it was educational to examine why the SAP R/3 implementation at Robert Bosch GmbH ran into problems during 1999 and how these problems were resolved by 2004.

We analyzed the strategy used in the ERP implementation process using a SWOT analysis during 1999 and shared the results with the company. In a subsequent meeting with the CIOs during 2004, we noticed that that the company had actually used substantially different strategies and that the SAP R/3 implementation was nevertheless proceeding successfully in the company. A literature search for a theory that could explain the implementation experiences of Robert Bosch GmbH identified the Force Field Analysis approach suggested by Paquin and Koplyay (2007) as a promising candidate for depicting dynamic strategic situations (Ghemawat, 1999, 2006). This paper applies a modified version of this theory to explain the ERP implementation experiences of Robert Bosch GmbH. Thus, the *study objective* is:

- *Identify the factors that made it possible for the ERP implementation experiences at Robert Bosch GmbH to succeed in 2004 in contrast to its implementation experience in 1999*

The next section reviews the relevant literature and discusses gaps in our understanding of successful ERP implementation experiences. We go on to discuss the role dynamic analysis theory—especially Force Field Analysis—can play in explaining ERP implementation experiences, derive a possible research framework, and describe the research methodology used. The Robert Bosch GmbH ERP implementation experience is then described, followed by an analysis of the implementation using the research framework and a discussion of the findings. The limitations of the research and future research issues are then discussed. The paper concludes by discussing the implications for practice.

ERP IMPLEMENTATION EXPERIENCES

Total cost of ownership (TCO) of an ERP system, including hardware, software, professional services, and internal staff costs, averages $15 million (Koch 2007). However, ERP implementation failures and less-than-satisfactory productivity improvements are common, and many firms have difficulties with ERP implementation (King, 2005; Akkermans & van Helden, 2002). Although the transition to an ERP framework is often a long, difficult, and costly process due to the nature and complexity of ERP systems (Jones and Young 2006), senior IT managers believe that the integration and application of ERP systems is one of the most important issues that they are currently facing (Cox, 2007; Luftman & McLean, 2004).

The challenges inherent in implementing ERP systems include business process change versus system customization, change resistance, communication, and project management (Caruso & King, 2002). The total cost of implementation of ERP systems is relatively high; Robert Bosch GmbH budgeted around $1 billion for its ERP implementation (Sankar & Rau, 2006). The early adopters of integrated ERP modules found them to be incredibly risky to implement. Although failures to deliver projects on time and within budget were an old IT story, enterprise systems represent even higher risks and may even be a "bet-our-company" type of failure (Brown & Vessey, 2003).

End-users' reluctance or unwillingness to adopt or use the newly implemented ERP system is often cited as one of the main reasons for ERP failures (Nah & Tan, 2004). Xue et al. (2005) report that language, report and table format, Business Process Reengineering (BPR), economic reform impact, cost-control systems, human resource problems, price issues, and connection with ERP service companies were the main reasons for the failure of eight ERP implementations in China. Nah, Lau, and Kuang (2001) identify eleven factors that are critical to ERP implementation success – ERP teamwork and composition, changing management programs and culture, top management support, business plan and vision, business process reengineering with minimum customization, good project management, monitoring and evaluation of performance, effective communication, software development, testing and troubleshooting, project championing, and appropriate business and IT legacy systems. Holland and Light (1999) recommend that an effective IT infrastructure is essential for an ERP implementation. Teo and coworkers (Teo et al., 1997; Teo & Ang, 1999, 2000) identify top management support, clear-cut corporate plan, user-IS relationship, qualified personnel, and anticipating changes in IT as the Critical Success Factors in IS planning. Other researchers find that delivery of good services, alignment of IS priorities with those of the whole organization, support from senior management, effective communication, measurement metrics, training, organization's size, quality of vendor/consultant, culture, structure, internal IT support, and ensuring that IS services evolve to meet organizational needs are the most important critical success factors for IT executives (Allen & Helms, 2006; Ifinedo, 2008; Allen, 2008; Soja, 2008; Pollalis, 2003; Pollalis & Frieze, 1993; DeLone & McLean, 2003; Lin, 2007; Tsai et al., 2007).

ERP IMPLEMENTATION EXPERIENCES: POSSIBLE RESEARCH FRAMEWORK

Strategic planning is the method by which a community continuously creates artifactual systems to serve extraordinary purposes (Cook, 2000). Yuksel and Dagdeviren (2007) point out that SWOT analysis provides neither an analytical means with which to determine the importance of identified factors nor the ability to assess decision alternatives according to these factors. They consider that SWOT analysis suffers from deficiencies in measuring and evaluating the value of system implementations. Another issue with SWOT analysis is its inability to consider uncertain and two-sided factors, its lack of prioritization of the factors and strategies, and its inclusion of too many extractable strategies (Ghazinoory et al., 2007). Even though the shortcomings of SWOT analysis are well documented, this method is commonly used to analyze projects and implementations (Lai & Rivera, 2006; Yuksel & Dagdeviren, 2007). It may be important to use other research models in addition to the SWOT analysis to better explain ERP implementations.

Ghemawat and Cassiman (2005) highlight the need for dynamic perspective in strategy formulations. A fully dynamic approach to strategy demands a theory that is not only limited to linking what the organization did yesterday (that is, in the past) to what it can do well today, but also links what it does today to what it can do well tomorrow (that is, in the future) (Ghemawat, 1999).

The research framework derived for this study is based on a modification of the Force Field Analysis theory (Paquin & Koplyay, 2007). In their analysis, dynamics are introduced into business strategy by treating it as a force field. They used the factors of resource mobilization and market potential to explain the forceful activities that may result. The concept of resources mobilization represents the organization's capacity to muster material, financial, human, organizational,

managerial, and informational resources at a given time. The concept of market potential accounts for the organization's potential in launching and exploiting new products, new technologies, and new business practices.

We modified their theory to opine that the two factors of mass of resource endowments and acceleration of resource commitments may explain the forceful activities that result in effective ERP implementation (Figure 1). The forceful activities are those that change the direction of the organization significantly, leading to the development of new product/system/process capabilities, significant growth, major changes to systems/processes, expanded R&D functions, enhanced manufacturing, and/or the development of superior human relations functions. The mass of resource endowments are those that an organization deploys, comprising the size of the company, the size of the system being deployed, the corporate standards being adopted, the number of people using the product/system, and the size of the team implementing the change. The acceleration of the resource commitments made by the organization are composed of one or more "lumpy" important decisions, large changes in the resource endowments allocated to the project, the irreversibility of these commitments/decisions, changes in performance measurements, and the focus and involvement among implementation team members. The next section describes the rationale for the selection of the case study methodology to test the research framework.

METHODOLOGY

The case study is an excellent way of gathering and organizing data when the phenomenon under study is not linear and represents dynamic realities (Yin, 2003; Maxwell, 2005; Schultze, 2000; Stake, 1994; Gruman, 2006; Baets, 1998; Ellis, 1988; Lucas, 2002; Alcacer, 2006). Multiple-case studies, including two or more cases within the

Figure 1. Possible dynamic strategy framework

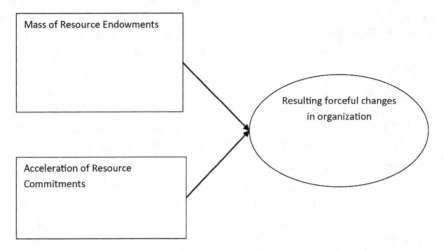

same study, can be used very effectively to test a theoretical model. These multiple cases need to be selected so that they replicate each other – either predicting similar results or contrasting results for predictable reasons (Yin, 2003). Some authors view the case study as a particular type of ethnographic (interpretive) research that involves intensive and detailed study of one individual or of a group as an entity, through observation, self-reports, and any other means (Langenbach et al., 1994; Tesch, 1990; Mertens, 2005). Many different research strategies (collecting data through document study, interviews, observation or participation and analyzing data using hermeneutics, phenomenology or grounded theory) can be used to build an interpretive understanding (Caroll & Swatman, 2000). Case research is particularly appropriate for certain types of problems, namely those in which research and theory are at their early, formative stages, and sticky, practice-based problems where the experiences of the actors are important and the context of action is critical (Benbasat et al., 1987). Given that ERP implementations are complex and the impact is felt corporate-wide, we decided to test the proposed framework using several well-documented case studies on the implementation of ERP systems in

a single company, Robert Bosch GmbH (Sankar & Rau, 2006).

Interview data, observation notes, and press release documents were used as information sources for the case study. Figure 2 provides a summary of the interviews conducted with company officers. The data set collected through the case studies was analyzed in order to test the research framework.

IT STRATEGIES USED BY ROBERT BOSCH GMBH: 1992-2004

Background on Robert Bosch GmbH

The company was founded in 1886, when Robert Bosch opened his "Workshop for precision and electric engineering." The following year he met Gottlieb Daimler and was commissioned to develop a low-voltage magneto for Daimler's internal-combustion engine for stationary machines (Heuss et al., 1994). From that humble beginning, Robert Bosch GmbH has grown to become a 44 billion Euro company, with about 258,000 associates worldwide. By 2008, the Bosch Group had become the world's largest automotive supplier in terms of sales (Robert Bosch, 2008).

Figure 2. Interview summary

	Period 1: 1992-1999	**Period 2: 2000-2004**
Number of interviews	- Multiple interviews at Robert Bosch GmbH, Germany with CIO - Multiple interviews at Robert Bosch US, USA with CIO	- Multiple interviews at Robert Bosch GmbH, Germany with CIO - Multiple interviews at Robert Bosch US, USA with CIO
Time frame	2 months	1 month
Research output	2 case studies documenting ERP implementation at headquarters and at USA; an analysis of strategies using SWOT analysis	1 case study documenting ERP implementation at head quarters and at USA; predictions about new SAP R/3 implementations appropriate for Robert Bosch GmbH
Verification of case study data	Written approval by the CIO	Written approval by the CIO

IT STRATEGIES USED BY ROBERT BOSCH: 1992-1999

During 1992, Robert Bosch's Board of Management established a new IT division, with a corporate-wide responsibility for IT, known as QI. The ERP package SAP was being implemented in Robert Bosch world-wide, but the top management of Bosch was not satisfied with how the implementation was going. In an attempt to address this, QI developed new concepts to standardize and harmonize the company's business processes, as well as defining a standardized systems solution. Don Chauncey, the CIO at Robert Bosch US (RBUS), had inherited multiple information systems that did not communicate with each other seamlessly (Figure 3). In a 1999 interview, he explained the evolution of information systems at different locations as follows:

When I was hired, RBUS had implemented PRMS in the smaller divisions, and I helped finish the implementation in the UO organization, a part of the business that sold to heavy-duty and automotive Original Equipment Manufacturers. Today we are running our factories on PRMS. There are some modules of PRMS that are very innovative, but it is basically an MRP II system.

The major plants of UO are in Charleston and Anderson, South Carolina. I hired Krish Kumar, who is now the Director of Corporate Information Technology for UO. I sent Krish to the Charleston plant because he was a PRMS expert. We implemented it successfully. The UA division wanted software that would fully meet their requirements and selected the J.D. Edwards System that fit the distribution needs of their division.

Also RBME was moving to PRMS from a mainframe, as had the UO organization in the US. So PRMS is used extensively in our company and we have significant expertise in its implementation.

PRMS was the Bosch standard here as well as in other parts of the world and the QI standards allow Bosch businesses to remain on PRMS. However when new ERP systems become necessary to replace PRMS, the new standard will be SAP.

Krish Kumar, another CIO at a plant in the U.S. who directly reported to Don Chauncey,

Figure 3. IT applications in Robert Bosch US - 1997

```
• IT Applications (examples)

    SBPT and K1: SAP R/3 (except F/A: Computron)

    UA: J.D.Edwards

    UO-Plants: PRMS (UO-Version)

    RBME: PRMS (RBME-Version)

    DTUS: PRMS (HR/Payroll Peoplesoft)

    Financials mainly centralized: GL, F/A, A/P (Computron), A/R (MSA)

    Human Resources centralized: HR/Payroll (MSA)
```

UO – Business that sold to heavy-duty and automotive Original Equipment Manufacturers
RBME – Robert Bosch Mexico
DTUS – Diesel Technology Company
SAP R/3, J.D. Edwards, PRMS, Peoplesoft – Vendors of different ERP systems
GL, F/A, A/P, A/R, HR – Components of SAP R/3 systems (financial and human resource)

wanted to align the information systems in UO with business processes in order to support the requirements of his end-users. In another of the 1999 interviews he told us:

There are many projects ongoing already here and in Germany. If you look at this complexity there is no way that I can address the business requirements with the existing systems. The only way I can accomplish this is with a clear strategy of understanding the future business processes and aligning the system configuration accordingly.

Exploiting the information systems is where I see the benefit of the entire investment for Bosch in IT. Take for example the process of receiving an item, storing it, moving it to an assembly, and understanding the transaction costs of this process. Today we use multiple systems for these steps. With the current systems, I can't tie together some of the critical pieces of information. The existing systems are not aligned with the automotive vertical market. The result is that within the IT organization we are fighting fires constantly. The software does not accommodate the growing

and changing business requirements and we have to tell our customers that the system can't deliver the information they want.

Our end-users are asking for real-time information. I cannot have the IT associates function as program generators and developers anymore; they have to become business minded people helping their users by actively working with them and resolving their business issues.

Pressure to Standardize Systems

QI created a project to define and use a common system throughout the Robert Bosch (RB) plants in the automotive equipment business sector (UBK - Unternehmensbereich Kraftfahrzeugausrüstung) and the EW division (Elektrowerkzeuge - power tools). The QI-Newsletter of July 1999 stated that standardization is one of the most important goals within QI:

Standardization is the focus of our attention these days with the RB/3W project, one of the largest projects in the history of Robert Bosch GmbH. RB/3W is the standardized IT product for UBK plant logistics, developed for and by Bosch on the basis of SAP R/3. Today's IT systems, which are meeting requirements in the plants well, are now outdated. The main reason for renewal is, however, the need for standardizing our processes throughout the company. Our primary goal is to remain the strategic partner for our customers. And that implies shaping our internal and external processes so that we can act fast and purposefully, at the lowest possible cost.

Responding to this pressure for standardization, Don Chauncey, the CIO of RBUS developed a proposal for implementing SAP R/3 for the RBUS operations. A summary of the process he used to develop the proposal is as follows:

- During 1998, RBUS created a proposal for implementing an HR solution with PeopleSoft. It was not accepted by QI, who asked RBUS to implement this function using SAP R/3. QI agreed with Don Chauncey that financials (FI) should also be implemented.
- During March 1999, Don Chauncey started work on a proposal to include financial/ controls (FI/CO) and Human Relations (HR).
- During August 1999, he worked with Krish Kumar to include the logistics function of UO (Automotive Original Equipment Division).
- During October 1999, Don Chauncey started revising the proposal so that it could be presented to the North American Operating Committee (NAOC), thereby making it possible for the SAP R/3 implementation to proceed at RBUS.

After hearing the presentation, the NAOC opted to put the project proposal on hold.

Analysis of the Strategies

We developed detailed case studies based on the interviews and had them approved by the CIOs. We chose to analyze the strategies used by Robert Bosch using SWOT analysis since it was the dominant methodology used by academicians to analyze company strategies. We made the following recommendations to the company:

The company is positioning itself to maximize its local responsiveness and this can be classified as the company using a multi-domestic strategy. It brings both skills and products to the company's foreign markets, but is customizing its skills and products for each individual foreign market. Given this strategic direction, it might be worthwhile for the company to implement ERPs in each country independently, without insisting that they all work together. This strategy might be the best fit given the current corporate strategy. The advantages of this strategy are that different countries will be able to use different systems depending on their investments and returns. For example, some of the divisions at RBUS might decide not to change their current systems and this might be beneficial from the local business point of view. Even if QI were to provide economic incentives for the domestic units to standardize across the company, they may prefer this approach as it preserves the independence and autonomy of the country-wide operations.

The disadvantage is that it may not be feasible to close the books in five days, the Bosch board's stated goal, if SAP R/3 is not implemented fully across the divisions. The concept of top-down design, where the best processes are identified and implemented uniformly across the organization, is a good concept. A major issue is whether the end-users will be willing to buy into the best process concept, when for a long time they have been used to their own systems.

Review of the policies showed that other reasons for the limited success in the first period were the limited resources committed, the disagreements, and the indecisive central IT management. When we revisited the company in 2004 for a follow-up study, we found that the company had implemented the SAP R/3 system across many countries successfully.

IT STRATEGIES USED BY ROBERT BOSCH: 2000-2004

During the period 2000-2004, many changes took place in Robert Bosch. In 2000, the CIO of Robert Bosch in Stuttgart, Dr. Eggensperger, resigned and was replaced by Mr. Gerd Friedrich. Mike Bieganski was appointed as Vice President, Information Technology, for RB North America and was driving the process of implementing SAP R/3 in RB North America. Don Chauncey became the VP for Data Security. Krish Kumar left the company.

Status of ERP Implementation at RBUS

In August 1999 a proposal was presented to the NAOC to implement the SAP R/3 system. This proposal was put on hold by the decision makers. However, the implementation of SAP R/3 in K1, known as Chassis Systems, continued. In 2000 and 2001 a great deal of the standardization relating to data structures and business processes was completed. The automotive sector led the ERP implementation. Other sites were included based on the experience of implementing SAP R/3 in the Chassis Systems division. Finally, a single R/3 instance for the automotive business was implemented, with about 6,000 users across North America. This project cost $30 million. The company followed a phased approach, with the first step costing $13 million. During this stage,

eleven sites were converted in only 18 months, following an aggressive schedule in order to accommodate the elimination of data centers and legacy applications left over from business acquisitions. The second stage, costing $17 million, included conversion to the SAP ERP at six manufacturing locations and an engineering/sales headquarters site, and also included implementation of the HR/Payroll modules at all corporate and automotive sites. In addition to the implementation of SAP R/3, from a technical perspective the infrastructure across the US was now aligned. The data centers in both the automotive and non-automotive businesses were consolidated, thus drastically reducing personnel and costs while at the same time improving the quality of the processes.

To implement such a major project successfully, the right organization was critical. In order to manage the project, managers for the different areas, such as logistics, quality and finance, were appointed. For integration purposes a program manager was named who focused on business processes, and, rather than having key users, business process leaders were appointed. By implementing these changes, the managers were able to match their business macro model to SAP modules. By mid-2003, about 13 legacy systems had been eliminated and this also made integration easier. The PRMS system and Computron were retired and HR-Payroll was also harmonized as far as possible, taking into account differences in union vs. non union plants, local union rules, and differences in state taxes. A separate R/3 instance was implemented for all of North America for HR-Payroll, integrated via Application Liking Enabling (ALE) links to the necessary elements of the ERP system.

When the complex system structures originally discussed in 1999 are compared with the actual systems architecture being used in 2004, the results show a relatively easier and clearer structure (Figure 4) composed of four SAP R/3 systems interconnected by ALE scenarios.

Figure 4. R/3 systems architecture in Robert Bosch North America

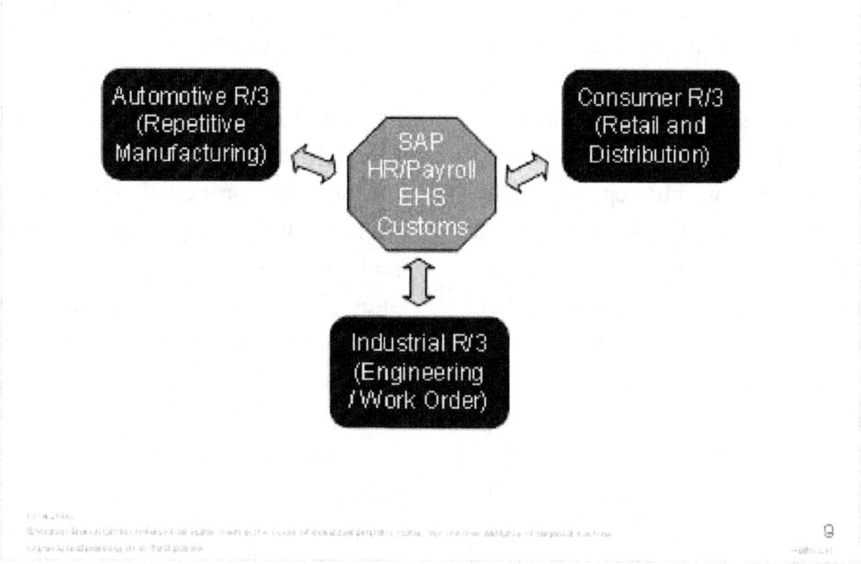

Status of ERP Implementation at RB

Three major changes were initiated at Robert Bosch GmbH during 2000-2004. They were:

- **A change in focus from production (plant) to value chain (division):** The focus moved from "how we produce" to "how we support the whole lifecycle of products." It was no longer a question of how many products a plant produced, but rather how much value the plant added to the product, which was controlled on product-group level. The previous key performance measure was the operating result of the plant, and this totally changed to a concept of value-based management. As a result, the company's key organizational unit became the division, as it was responsible for the whole value-chain starting with the product development, including manufacturing, and ending with sales. Convincing people that it was not necessary to have a plant system, but instead a system based on the products offered by divisions took

about six months. QI offered a Bosch version of R/3 to each division, where the Bosch processes were customized and could be used to roll out to a division. The division was then able to take the customized version and implement it at the plants.

- **Increased importance of process harmonization:** In order to facilitate the harmonization process, representatives from each of the divisions were temporarily seconded to the QI harmonization team. For instance, for the purchasing process each division was represented in the purchase process harmonization team by its purchase process owner. To address the issue of changes in the business requests, a change request process was initiated to enable the harmonization team to discuss and decide how a request fit into the harmonization strategy and how the requests should be implemented according to the version policy. In addition to the harmonization of the systems to be used in the divisions, this ensured that implementers and end-users were speaking the same language.

- **A single development system for the roll-out:** QI adopted a single development system for the entire automotive business and took this as the basis for the rollout to the divisions. With regard to the structuring issue within the R/3 system, Bosch decided that each division would be represented by a separate R/3 company code and have a separate R/3 instance; the diesel systems had a company code, gasoline systems had another company code, etc. Each plant in every European country had its own company code; in a big plant like the one in Bamberg, Germany, products for several different divisions may be produced. Bamberg will thus have an R/3 plant code in the diesel R/3 system and another plant code in the R/3 instance of the gasoline division. From the R/3 system viewpoint, it was decided to handle the common services of the plant facility via the ERP solution.

One of the reasons why the changes initiated in 2000-2004 were successful was that the direction of the board of management relating to IT had changed tremendously. When Gerd Friedrich joined QI as the CIO, he elevated the discussion about process-standardization and ERP implementation strategies to the level of the board of management of Robert Bosch. The main strategy was discussed and agreed with two members of the board, namely the CFO and Dr. Dais, who was responsible for IT. Gerd Friedrich had first to convince them that it was necessary both to separate the harmonization process from implementation and rollout and to implement a separate project organization. In order to reduce the complexity, the project focused on the automotive business, which comprises about two third of the Bosch business. The board wanted to start there because the advantages expected were substantial. To convince the board, it was essential to have sufficient backing to take it to the next level. This top-down approach was essential in making the project a success.

Bosch defined three different organizational entities that would be in charge of the following: (1) defining, standardizing, and harmonizing the business processes and data structures; (2) implementing the processes in the R/3 system; and (3) rolling out the product in the different sites. The different divisions were invited to send representatives to work with the first group in order to accurately define the business processes. If divisions chose not to participate, they were forced to accept the processes as defined by others. Based on the processes defined by the first group, the IT people in the second group implemented the processes in the R/3 System to produce a version that was ready to roll out. The third group was responsible for the education and training of all the people impacted, setting up the production R/3 instance for the division, and so on. These three groups were coordinated by a board which reported directly to two members of the board of management. Less than 20% of the total costs for the ERP systems were spent by the IT implementation group; the bulk of the funds were used by the other two groups to create change in the company, change business processes, educate employees, etc.

Gerd Friedrich, the CIO, serves on the board that coordinates the three organizations. He was, in addition, responsible for the IT implementation, so the CIO was not only responsible for IT but also (via the board) for the whole process (defining, implementing, and rollout). If any of the implementations were not successful, the CIO was thus immediately aware of the problem. In a 2004 interview with us, Gerd Friedrich commented that he knew of no other big company that operates this way. He believes that this helped the business units cooperate with each other to achieve the goals of the company.

ANALYSIS OF THE ROBERT BOSCH CASE STUDIES USING THE RESEARCH FRAMEWORK

As shown in the earlier section, our analysis of the IT strategies utilized during the period 1992-1999 led to a recommendation to implement ERP in each country independently, without insisting that they all work together. This strategy seemed to be consistent with the strategic vision of the management team at the time (1999) which was looking toward implementing incremental change. However, when we compared this recommendation with the actual situation in 2004, we found that the company actually pursued a strategy of a single development system for the rollout and a standardized master data to enable a high degree of integration. Explaining these changes required us to enhance the SWOT analysis and investigate dynamic strategic analysis models. Based on research, we derived the research framework (Figure 2) as shown in Section 3. In this section, this new framework will be used to analyze how the IT implementation strategy improved for Robert Bosch.

Analysis of IT Strategies During 1992-1999

During the period 1992-1999, Robert Bosch had substantial resource endowments. It was a large company with 250 subsidiaries and affiliated companies in 48 countries, and 185 production plants worldwide. It already had 20,000 SAP R/3 users in its European divisions by 1999, although more than 11 information systems were still being used by RBUS to manage its operations. Therefore, the mass of resource endowments was substantial enough during this period.

The next step in the analysis to determine whether the company had sufficient acceleration in resource commitments to make substantial changes. On several occasions QI issued statements such as, "it is efficiency that is essential for QI, neither the total costs nor the number of employees." When RBUS developed a proposal to make incremental changes during 1999, the NAOC put the proposal on hold and asked for "must do" items, emphasizing the need for a corporate standard and the need to improve processes. There were also difficulties in agreeing to a definition of single instance. Mike Bieganski, the VP for IT for K1/ISY2 North America, scrutinized the proposal made by Don Chauncey, at the time the CIO of RBUS, and came up with a variety of recommendations. In a 1999 interview with us, Mike described the process as follows:

We are trying to figure out how you build SAP in one big instance in the US so everybody uses the same configuration based upon the QI SAP model. Or do you organize it by business units with consolidation points for reporting at RBUS? And that's what we are trying to determine. Why are we starting a system and getting bids and trying to do all these things when we don't have the very basic elements of how to harmonize? The first tasks are agreement on a specific chart of accounts, on the cost component layout, and on customer and vendor numbering. We don't have an RBUS harmonization model with RB in Germany.

Don Chauncey had concerns about Mike's recommendations, explaining:

As we go through this, what Mike is suggesting is that we try to leverage K1's implementation for UO but keep them separate, as separate businesses. Well, his idea is to manage consolidations and track corporate initiatives through the use of a business warehouse. And yet, that's not what QI and RBUS have in mind. RBUS needs enough control to drive standardization into the businesses. If we're not standardizing when we do this, we will have lost a major opportunity. In order to ensure this standardization and to centralize cash control, RBUS will need, at a minimum, to have a consolidation ledger, accounts payable, cash disbursement and a fixed asset system for external reporting. I believe that the centralization of accounts receivable is also a major opportunity for the future. Then for reporting at the North American level, there will need to be some business warehouse capability to look at total business with customers and suppliers – unless this can be done in the primary system.

RBUS came up with four different alternate structures for implementing SAP R/3 and there was no agreement among the CIOs of the different divisions on which structure should be implemented. Overall, the agreements among the IT groups in RB GmbH and RBUS in selecting a common strategy were inconsistent.

When the components that make up the acceleration variable are analyzed, we note that there were no large resource endowments allocated to this project and the changes planned for the system were incremental and reversible. The CIOs at the different divisions at RBUS did not agree with each other, the CIOs at RB GmbH, head quarters at Germany and RBUS did not have the same vision, and the involvement of the IT team to the project was not strong. The combination of all these factors resulted in a deceleration in the rate of change during this period.

It is no wonder the forceful activities that resulted in 1999 were not strong. Only a few systems at RBUS were converted to SAP R/3, partial standards were implemented across the company, and a common shared IT strategy was not implemented. Therefore, we can depict the IT strategies deployed during 1992-1999 in Figure 5.

ANALYSIS OF ROBERT BOSCH CASE STUDY: 1999-2004

The changes that occurred over the period 1999-2004 were substantial. The mass of resource endowments allocated to IT increased since Gerd Friedrich, the new CIO, convinced the board that the company was at the end of the life cycle of their major IT systems and there was a need for major investment. The project cost for the changeover in RBUS was $30 million during 2001, while the company as a whole planned to invest $1 billion in the standardized systems, processes, and procedures during 2002-2008.

The rate of change in resource commitments increased substantially as the company appointed new CIOs at both their headquarters and their US division. The CIOs of these divisions were now working together much more closely and strongly endorsed the concept of harmonizing the business processes and data structures. The alignment between QI and top management also improved once the CIO became a member of the board that coordinated the three groups that were implementing the SAP R/3 processes across the company. He was now not only responsible for IT, but also for the process as a whole, including defining, implementing, and roll-out. If anything went wrong, he was immediately aware of the problem.

When the components that make up the acceleration variable are analyzed, we note that there were major resources allocated to this project and the changes planned for the system were massive and irreversible. RBUS alone spent $30 million during 2001. RB GmbH also made major changes in the focus of plants from "how we produce" to "how we support the whole lifecycle of products." The company's key organizational unit became the division instead of plant. A single development system for the entire automotive business was rolled out to all the divisions. The bulk of the expenditure was used by groups to create change in the company, change business processes, and educate employees. In addition, the CIO at RB GmbH was provided a seat at the board, thereby ensuring that the rate of change would be accelerated. He also appointed people who had already implemented SAP R/3 systems in RBUS and RB Mexico thereby ensuring that implementation in these countries moved rapidly. During our inter-

Figure 5. Analysis of strategies used during 1992-1999

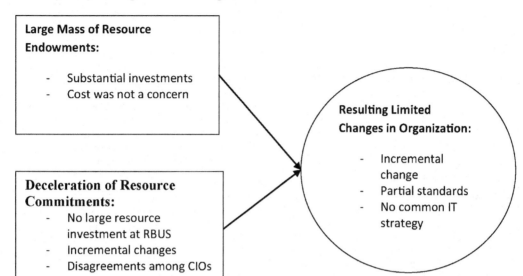

views with the executives, we sensed that they were involved in the changeover and committed to the project. This was very different from the meetings during 1999, where the disagreements among the CIOs were evident. All these resulted in acceleration in the rate of change during the 1999-2004 periods.

The resultant forceful activities that took place were unprecedented. Data centers were consolidated, resulting in significant reductions in personnel and substantial, cost savings, as well as in quality improvements in the processes. Thirteen legacy systems were eliminated and a single R/3 instance was implemented for all of North America. RBUS also worked with QI to harmonize the business globally. The system structures used in 1999 were simplified and made clearer, with four SAP R/3 systems interconnected by ALE scenarios and a major change in focus, as described in Section 5.3.1.

A single development system was implemented for the entire automotive business and used as the basis for the rollout to the divisions, with each division being represented by a separate R/3 company code and a separate R/3 instance. The European IT project covered 70% of the business,

and the rest 30% covered harmonized systems on a regional basis. This was also true for Brazil and the U.S., where the implementation approach was basically the same, but the customizing of the system was different. It became possible to obtain consolidated financial results on an RB level by using an SAP BW (Business Warehouse) solution.

In summary, the forceful activities that were in progress by 2004 were very strong and significant. Therefore, we can depict the IT strategies during 2000-2004 in Figure 6.

FINDINGS

The above discussion shows that the research framework is able to explain why even though the implementations during 1992-1999 were not successful, the subsequent changes resulted in a successful implementation during 2000-2004. The findings of this study discuss: (i) improving effectiveness of implementation, (ii) identifying specific activities that impact the mass of resource endowments, (iii) identifying activities that accelerate resource commitment, and (iv) identifying the forceful activities that result. These findings

Figure 6. Analysis of strategies used during 1999-2004

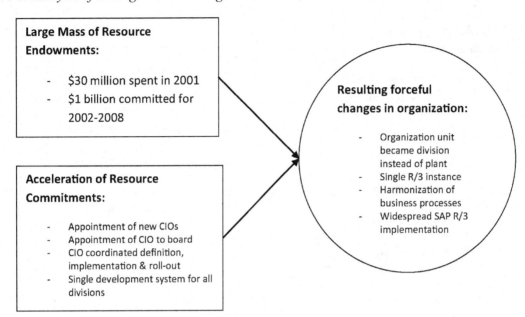

are likely to be helpful to both academicians who teach and research ERP implementation strategies and the practitioners who design and implement them.

Improving Effectiveness of ERP Implementation

The SWOT model seems to be helpful in selecting the appropriate IT strategy, but does not help in formulating strategies for its effective implementation. The force field analysis framework seems to explain how the implementation of the selected strategy could be improved through the commitment of more resources, better/ clear decision making, and organization for using these resources.

Identifying Activities that Impact the Mass of Resource Endowments

1. **Proper Investment of Resources:** The framework suggests that the resources allocated for the ERP decision must be sub-

stantial. This has not previously been identified as an important critical success factor in the literature (Nah et al., 2001; Holland & Light, 2001). One reason for this omission might be that many companies do not disclose the amounts of funds that are used for developing ERP systems. Robert Bosch decided to invest close to one billion dollars during 2001 to 2008 in order to implement its ERP system. Similarly, the funds invested at Oracle Corporation were substantial when it implemented its E-Business suite software in its own business (Sauer & Willcocks, 2003), while Cisco's ERP system initially cost over $15 million and the company spent another $100 million connecting it to the Internet (Davenport, 2000). These examples show that a company implementing an ERP system must be willing to devote substantial resources to the effort.

2. **Adoption of corporate standards:** During 1999, various divisions of the company could not agree on a corporate standard. The scenario changed in 2004, when the

new CIO team took over the operations of the IT division. In a 2004 interview with us, Gerd Friedrich, the CIO, explained:

The board does not accept excuses not to use the standardized and harmonized processes. If a division is not willing to accept the standardized processes, we will bring it up to the board and then the division has to show figures which make it clear that their business will be damaged if they use the standardized processes. It is not only a question of whether they like the standardized systems or not, they really have to show the negative impact on the business by using a standardized process. The board has come up with such a process to resolve disagreements, but I have to admit that up to now no division has used this escalation process.

Standardization improves the implementation speed. For example, several universities have realized substantial gains by using a single instance of financial software for their institutions (Caruso & King, 2002). This is emphasized by Brown and Vessey (2003), who state that change management must be rigorously planned and generously resourced. When a company is faced with faltering ERP implementation, a question to ask might be: are the different departments/divisions willing to standardize their operations? If the answer is negative, then it may indicate reasons why the limited resource endowments may not result in forceful results.

Identifying Activities that can Accelerate Resource Commitments

1. **Making difficult, irreversible commitments/ decisions:** RBUS moved quickly and spent $30 million during 2000-2002, converted 11 sites in 18 months, followed an aggressive schedule to eliminate data centers and legacy applications left over

from business acquisitions. Robert Bosch as a corporation changed the focus from "how we produce" to "how we support the whole lifecycle of products." These changes can be classified as lumpy important decisions that were irreversible and provided the acceleration that produced forceful results. Other organizations wanting to make successful ERP implementations may also need to make such lumpy decisions. Past studies on critical success factors in ERP implementation have not identified this as a factor (Nah et al., 2001; Dong, 2008; Ifinedo, 2008; Allen, 2008).

2. **Enlisting top management support:** Effective communication and teamwork among the people implementing the ERP system and top management support provided the acceleration needed to ensure the success of the SAP R/3 implementation at Robert Bosch. This result confirms the findings from earlier research, which list team work, project management, and top management support as critical success factors (Fui-Hoon et al., 2003; Garcia-Sanchez & Perez-Bernal, 2007).

Identifying the Resultant Forceful Activities

1. **Increasing ability to embrace newer technologies such as Service Oriented Architecture (SOA):** An organization that has successfully implemented ERP systems appears to advance by developing Service Oriented Architectures and other measures to integrate the operations. At Robert Bosch GmbH, for example, QI decided to adopt a single development system for the entire automotive business and take this as the basis for the rollout to the divisions. Before Bosch went through the harmonization process, the implemented systems looked superficially similar but were actually quite different from

each other, leading to a set of incompatible development systems. During 2001-2002, Bosch realized that standardizing master data is essential in order to achieve a high degree of integration. In the U.S., and Europe, Bosch is on track to reach a high degree of integration.

2. **Significant growth by successful mergers/acquisitions with other companies:** An organization that has successfully implemented an ERP system seems to be successful in its ability to merge with or acquire other companies. This process moves faster once clear organizational standards are established. Sales at Robert Bosch GmbH had grown from 16 billion Euros in 1989 to 26 billion Euros in 1998 to 35 billion Euros in 2002 to 44 billion Euros in 2006 (The numbers are approximate since Deutsche Marks have been converted to Euros for comparison purposes). The sales growth over the period 1989-1998 was 62%, increasing to 69% over the period 1998-2006.

3. **Ability to Reassign Personnel to Other Divisions:** It is the human factors and not the technology that makes the difference between commercial success and failure, and between acceptance and rejection of a system (Angell & Smithson, 1991). Standardized systems ensure that people in different divisions speak the same language. For example, a purchase clerk from Bosch's Reutlingen plant, which produces semiconductors and engine control units, can talk to his or her colleague in the Hildesheim plant, where car radios are manufactured, and get help in using the SAP R/3 system and fixing a problem. From a company point of view, moving people from one division to the other has also become much easier. They understand each other even though the products are different, and are thus able to help each other (Sankar & Rau, 2006).

LIMITATIONS AND FUTURE RESEARCH

As with other studies based on case study research methodology, the research framework will be more robust once it has been tested with other ERP implementations. Also, using the framework to predict future scenarios and then comparing the actual outcomes with the predictions will make it possible to adjust the framework to improve its reliability.

A valuable avenue for future research should be to identify a series of metrics through which the variables in Figure 2 can be further operationalized. Another research project is to study the implementation of SAP R/3 at RB GmbH again and compare those results with the earlier ones. Such a project will provide an opportunity to verify the validity of the framework. The SAP R/3 implementation at Robert Bosch cost about one billion dollars over a 10-year period. These are normally reported in balance sheets and rarely studied by academicians. Faculty members in history departments study the evolution of society, but business faculty members do not commonly study implementations of large systems in companies. This paper shows a need for studying such massive implementations and encouragement from academic administrators to provide credit to faculty members for documenting these implementations.

IMPLICATIONS FOR PRACTICE AND CONCLUSIONS

The case study and the search for an appropriate framework to depict the changing conditions at Robert Bosch lead to the following suggestions for practitioners:

1. **Importance of leadership and communication:** Once an organization makes a choice to implement an ERP system, it is easy to

Figure 7. Important factors to be considered when implementing ERP systems in developing this article

- Committing large resources to the project
- Adopting corporate standards that promote process harmonization
- Making a few lumpy important decisions that are irreversible
- Obtaining support from top management

make the assumption that the processes in an organization will be automatically streamlined and efficiencies improved. This case study shows that choice of a system is only a part of the equation. Leadership, effective communication, and commitment of the IT staff are essential to make the system deliver the expected results.

2. **Top managers need to go beyond resource provision to promoting an IS:** The top management at RB GmbH did not wait to perform a thorough cost-benefit analysis before investing vast sums of money to implement SAP R/3 in their organizations. They trusted their CIO team to make the necessary changes and appointed the CIO at RB GmbH to the board.

3. **Effective ERP implementations require lumpy decisions that tend to be irreversible:** The study shows that the organization has to make lumpy important decisions so that the change is irreversible and provides the necessary acceleration. Dong (2008) stresses this point when he states that top managers need to adapt their level and content of support rather than rely on solely on training and technical assistance during large-scale system implementations.

The major contribution of this article lies in explaining the forces that made it possible for the ERP implementation experiences at Robert Bosch to succeed in 2004 in contrast to its implementation experience in 1999. The paper also highlights a list of factors that must be considered by CIOs when implementing ERP systems (Figure 7).

These factors make it possible for the mass of resource endowments to be significant and acceleration to be positive so that the resulting forceful activities in the organization make the implementation experience a success and beneficial to the company.

ACKNOWLEDGMENT

I acknowledge the strong contribution of Dr. Karl-Heinz Rau, Pforzheim University, who collaborated with me in developing the Robert Bosch case studies. In addition, thanks are due to the executives at Robert Bosch GmbH and Robert Bosch US who provided information that was used.

REFERENCES

Akkerman, H., & Van Helden, K. (2002). Vicious and Virtuous Cycles in ERP Implementation: A Case Study of Interrelations Between Critical Success Factors. *European Journal of Information Systems*, *11*(1), 35–46. doi:10.1057/palgrave/ejis/3000418

Al-kaabi, H., Potter, A., & Naim, M. (2007). An Outsourcing Decision Model for Airlines MRO Activities. *Journal of Quality in Maintenance Engineering*, *13*(3), 217–227. doi:10.1108/13552510710780258

Alcacer, J. (2006). Location Choices Across the Value Chain: How Activity and Capability Influence Collocation. *Management Science*, *52*(10), 1457–1471. doi:10.1287/mnsc.1060.0658

Allen, D., Kern, T., & Mattison, D. (2002). Culture, Power, and Politics in ICT Outsourcing in Higher Education Institutions. *European Journal of Information Systems, 11*, 159–173. doi:10.1057/palgrave/ejis/3000425

Allen, R. S., & Helms, M. M. (2006). Linking Strategic Practices and Organizational Performance to Porter's Generic Strategies. *Business Process Management Journal, 12*(4), 433–454. doi:10.1108/14637150610678069

Angell, I., & Smithson, S. (1991). *Information Systems Management*. London: Macmillan Information Systems Series.

Arslan, O., & Er, I. D. (2008). SWOT Analysis for Safer Carriage of Bulk Liquid Chemicals in Tankers. *Journal of Hazardous Materials, 154*(1-3), 901–913. doi:10.1016/j.jhazmat.2007.10.113

Baets, W. R. J. (1998). *Organizational Learning and Knowledge Technologies in a Dynamic Environment*. Norwell, MA: Kluwer Academic Publishers. doi:10.1007/978-1-4615-5773-9

Benbasat, I., Goldstein, D. K., & Mead, M. (1987). The Case Research Strategy in Studies of Information Systems. *Management Information Systems Quarterly, 11*(3), 368–386. doi:10.2307/248684

Black, J. A., & Farias, G. (2000). Dynamic Strategies: Emergent Journeys. *Emergence, 2*(1), 101–113. doi:10.1207/S15327000EM0201_07

Brown, C. V., & Vessey, I. (2003). Managing the Next Wave of Enterprise Systems: Leveraging Lessons from ERP. *MIS Quarterly Executive, 2*(1), 65–77.

Caruso, J., & King, P. (2002). *Enterprise Systems at Three University Systems: California State University, University System of Georgia, University of Wisconsin System*. Boulder, CO: Educase Center for Applied Research.

Cook, W. J. (2000). *Strategies: The Art of Science of Holistic Strategy*. Westport, CT: Quorem.

Cox, J. (2007, May 8). ERP, Security Among Top Concerns for Higher-Ed IT Pros. *CIO*.

Davenport, T. H. (2000). *Mission Critical: Realizing the Promise of Enterprise Systems*. Boston: Harvard Business School Press.

DeLone, W. H., & McLean, E. R. (2003). The DeLone and McLean Model of Information Systems Success: A Ten-Year Update. *Journal of Management Information Systems, 19*(4), 9–30.

Dong, L. (2008). Exploring the Impact of Top Management Support of Enterprise Systems Implementation Outcomes. *Business Process Management Journal, 14*(2), 204–218. doi:10.1108/14637150810864934

Ellis, R. J. (1988). *Managing Strategy in the Real-World: Conclusions and Frameworks for Field Studies of Business Practice*. Lexington, MA: Lexington Books.

Erat, S., & Kavadias, S. (2006). Introduction of New Technologies to Competing Industrial Customers. *Management Science, 52*(11), 1675–1688. doi:10.1287/mnsc.1060.0561

Fui-Hoon Nah, F., Zuckweiler, K. M., & Lee-Shang, J. L. (2003). ERP Implementation: Chief Information Officer's Perceptions of Critical Success Factors. *International Journal of Human-Computer Interaction, 16*(1), 5–22. doi:10.1207/S15327590IJHC1601_2

Garcia-Sanchez, N., & Perez-Bernal, L. E. (2007). Determination of Critical Success Factors in Implementing an ERP System: A Field Study in Mexican Enterprises. *Information Technology for Development, 13*(3), 293–309. doi:10.1002/itdj.20075

Ghazinoory, S., Zadeh, A. E., & Memariani, A. (2007). Fuzzy SWOT Analysis. *Journal of Intelligent and Fuzzy Systems, 18*(1), 99–108.

Ghemawat, P. (1999). *Strategy and the Business Landscape*. Reading, MA: Addison-Wesley.

Ghemawat, P. (2006). *Strategy and the Business Landscape* (2nd ed.). Upper Saddle River, NJ: Pearson Education, Inc.

Ghemawat, P., & Cassiman, B. (2005). Special Issue on Strategic Dynamics: Call for papers. *Management Science*. Retrieved January 2, 2007, from http://mansci.pubs.informs.org/special_issues/Special_Issue_on_Strategic_Dynamics.pdf

Gruman, G. (2006, December). Four Stages of Enterprise Architecture. *CIO Magazine*, 67-76.

Guerrero, F. M., Lozano, M., & Rueda-Cantuche, J. M. (2008). Spain's Greatest and Most Recent Mine Disaster. *Disasters, 32*(1), 19–40. doi:10.1111/j.1467-7717.2007.01025.x

Halla, F. (2007). A SWOT Analysis of Strategic Urban Development Planning: The Case of Dar es Salaam city in Tanzania. *Habitat International, 31*(1), 130–142. doi:10.1016/j.habitatint.2006.08.001

Heuss, T., Gillespie, S., & Kapczynski, J. (1994). *Robert Bosch: His Life and Achievements*. New York: Henry Holt & Co.

Hill, T., & Westbrook, R. (1997). SWOT Analysis: It's Time for a Product Recall. *Long Range Planning, 3*, 46–52. doi:10.1016/S0024-6301(96)00095-7

Holland, C. P., & Light, B. (1999). A Critical Success Factors Model for ERP Implementation. *IEEE Software, 16*(3), 30–36. doi:10.1109/52.765784

Ifinedo, P. (2008). Impacts of Business Vision, Top Management Support, and External Expertise on ERP Success. *Business Process Management Journal, 14*(4), 551–568. doi:10.1108/14637150810888073

Jones, M. C., & Young, R. (2006). ERP Usage in Practice: An Empirical Investigation. *Information Resources Management, 19*(1), 23–42. doi:10.4018/irmj.2006010102

King, W. R. (2005). Ensuring ERP Implementation Success. *Information Systems Management, 22*(3), 83–84. doi:10.1201/1078/45317.22.3.20050601/88749.11

Koch, C. (2007). *Getting Started with Enterprise Resource Planning (ERP): CIO*. Retrieved December 5, 2007, from www.cio.com/article/40323/3

Lai, C. A., & Rivera, J. C. Jr. (2006). Using a Strategic Planning Tool as a Framework for Case Analysis. *Journal of College Science Teaching, 36*(2), 26–30.

Langenbach, M., Vaughn, C., & Aagaard, L. (1994). *An Introduction to Educational Research*. Needham Heights, MA: Allyn & Bacon.

Lee, K., & Lin, S. (2008). A Fuzzy Quantified SOWT Procedure for Environmental Evaluation of an International Distribution Center. *Information Sciences, 178*(2), 531–549. doi:10.1016/j.ins.2007.09.002

Lee, T. J., Lee, K. H., & Oh, K. (2007). Strategic Environments for Nuclear Energy Innovation in the Next Half Century. *Progress in Nuclear Energy, 49*(5), 397–408. doi:10.1016/j.pnucene.2007.05.002

Lin, H.-F. (2007). Measuring Online Learning Systems Success: Applying the Updated DeLone and McLean Model. *Cyberpsychology & Behavior, 10*(6), 817–820. doi:10.1089/cpb.2007.9948

Lucas, H. C. Jr. (2002). *Strategies for Electronic Commerce and the Internet*. Cambridge, MA: MIT Press.

Luftman, J., & McLean, E. (2004, June). Key Issues for IT Executives. *MISQ Executive*, 269-295.

Mauerhofer, V. (2008). 3-D Sustainability: An Approach for Priority Setting in Situation of Conflicting Interests towards a Sustainable Development. *Ecological Economics, 64*(3), 496–506. doi:10.1016/j.ecolecon.2007.09.011

Maxwell, J. A. (2005). *Qualitative Research Design: An Interactive Approach.* Thousand Oaks, CA: Sage Publications Inc.

McGuinness, T., & Morgan, R. E. (2005). The Effect of Market and Learning Orientation on Strategy Dynamics. *European Journal of Marketing, 39*(11-12), 1306–1326. doi:10.1108/03090560510623271

Mengel, M., Sis, B., & Halloran, P. F. (2007). SWOT Analysis of Banff: Strengths, Weaknesses, Opportunities, and Threats of the International Banff Consensus Process and Classification System for Renal Allograft Pathology. *American Journal of Transportation, 7*(1), 2221–2226. doi:10.1111/j.1600-6143.2007.01924.x

Mertens, D. M. (2005). *Research and Evaluation in Education and Psychology.* Thousand Oaks, CA: Sage Publications, Inc.

Nah, F. F., Lau, J. L.-S., & Kuang, J. (2001). Critical Factors for Successful Implementation of Enterprise Systems. *Business Process Management Journal, 7*(3), 285–296. doi:10.1108/14637150110392782

Nah, F. F., & Tan, X. (2004). An Empirical Investigation on End-users' Acceptance of Enterprise Systems. *Information Resources Management Journal, 17*(3), 32–53. doi:10.4018/irmj.2004070103

Newman, R. (2008, November 11). *Here Comes a Bankruptcy Boom.* Retrieved January 23, 2009, from http://www.usnews.com/blogs/flowchart/2008/11/11/here-comes-a-bankruptcy-boom.html

Paquin, J.-P., & Koplyay, T. (2007). Force Field Analysis and Strategic Management: A Dynamic Approach. *Engineering Management Journalm, 19*(1), 28–37.

Pollalis, Y. A. (2003). Patterns of Co-Alignment in Information-Intensive Organizations: Business Performance Through Integration Strategies. *International Journal of Information Management, 23*, 469–492. doi:10.1016/S0268-4012(03)00063-X

Pollalis, Y. A., & Frieze, I. H. (1993). A New Look at Critical Success Factors in IT. *Information Strategy: The Executive's Journal, 10*(1), 24–34.

Robert Bosch Gmb, H. (2008). *Structure and business sectors.* Retrieved October 15, 2008, from http://www.bosch.com/content/language2/html/2153.htm

Sankar, C. S., & Rau, K. (2006). *Implementation Strategies for SAP R/3 in a Multinational Organization.* Hershey, PA: Idea Group Inc. doi:10.4018/978-1-59140-776-8

Sauer, C., & Willcocks, L. (2003). Establishing the Business of the Future: The Role of Organizational Architecture and Information Technologies. *European Management Journal, 21*(4), 497–508. doi:10.1016/S0263-2373(03)00078-1

Schultze, U. (2000). A Confessional Account of an Ethnography about Knowledge Work. *Management Information Systems Quarterly, 24*(1), 3–41. doi:10.2307/3250978

Shuai, C. (2008). China's New Cooperation Strategy with the World Food Programme: a SWOT Analysis. *Outlook on Agriculture, 37*(2), 111–117. doi:10.5367/000000008784648898

Soja, P. (2008). Examining the Conditions of ERP Implementations: Lessons Learnt from Adopters. *Business Process Management Journal, 14*(1), 105–123. doi:10.1108/14637150810849445

Stake, R. E. (1994). Case Studies. In Denzin, N. K., & Lincoln, Y. S. (Eds.), *Handbook of Qualitative Research* (pp. 236–247). Thousand Oaks, CA: Sage.

Teo, T. S. H., & Ang, J. S. K. (1999). Critical Success Factors in the Alignment of IS Plans with Business Plans. *International Journal of Information Management, 19*, 173–185. doi:10.1016/S0268-4012(99)00007-9

Teo, T. S. H., & Ang, J. S. K. (2000). How Useful are Strategic Plans for Information Systems? *Behaviour & Information Technology, 19*(4), 275–282. doi:10.1080/01449290050086381

Teo, T. S. H., Ang, J. S. K., & Pavri, F. N. (1997). The State of Strategic IS Planning Practices in Singapore. *Information & Management, 33*, 13–23. doi:10.1016/S0378-7206(97)00033-5

Terrados, J., Almonacid, G., & Hontoria, L. (2007). Regional Energy Planning through SWOT Analysis and Strategic Planning Tools: Impact on Renewables Development. *Renewable & Sustainable Energy Reviews, 11*(6), 1275–1287. doi:10.1016/j.rser.2005.08.003

Tesch, R. (1990). *Qualitative Research Analysis: Types and Software Tools*. New York: Falmer.

Tsai, W.-H., Fan, Y.-W., Leu, J.-D., Chou, L.-W., & Yang, C.-C. (2007). The Relationship Between Implementation Variables and Performance Improvements of ERP Systems. *International Journal of Technology Management, 38*(4), 350–373. doi:10.1504/IJTM.2007.013406

Uscher-Pines, L., Barnett, D. J., Sapsin, J. W., Bishai, D. M., & Balicer, R. D. (2008). A Systematic Analysis of Influenze Vaccine Shortage Policies. *Public Health, 122*(2), 183–191. doi:10.1016/j.puhe.2007.06.005

Vonk, G., Geertman, S., & Schot, P. (2007). A SWOT Analysis of Planning Support Systems. *Environment & Planning, 39*(7), 1699–1714. doi:10.1068/a38262

Xue, Y., Liang, H., Boulton, W. R., & Snyder, C. A. (2005). ERP Implementation Failures in China: Case Studies With Implications for ERP Vendors. *International Journal of Production Economics, 97*(3), 279–295. doi:10.1016/j.ijpe.2004.07.008

Yin, R. K. (2003). *Applications of Case Study Research*. Thousand Oaks, CA: Sage.

Yuksel, I., & Dagdeviren, M. (2007). Using the Analytic Network Process (AHP) in a SWOT Analysis: A Case Study for a Textile Firm. *Information Sciences, 177*, 3364–3382. doi:10.1016/j.ins.2007.01.001

This work was previously published in International Journal of Enterprise Information Systems, edited by Madjid Tavana, pp. 15-34, Volume 6, Issue 2, copyright 2010 by IGI Publishing (an imprint of IGI Global).

Section 2
Emerging Enterprise Information Technologies

Chapter 8

Future State of Outsourcing Supply Chain Information Systems:
An Analysis of Survey Results

Seong-Jong Joo
Colorado State University, Pueblo, USA

Ik-Whan G. Kwon
Saint Louis University, USA

Chang Won Lee
Hanyang University, South Korea

ABSTRACT

The purpose of this study is to acquire knowledge that will help clarify outsourcing trends in general and an information systems utilization perspective in particular. The authors review recent studies on outsourcing and conduct a nationwide survey. The results of the survey reveal that 60 percent of the respondents are focusing on their supply chain for cost reduction and/or competitive advantages and less than half of the respondents plan to outsource supply chain processes and information systems within the next 5 years. Results also show that major reasons for outsourcing include a lack of ability to handle in house and return on assets, while the largest barrier to outsourcing is cost followed by control concern.

INTRODUCTION

In recent years, outsourcing has become a major trend in various industries and business processes due to globalization and the development of information technology. This trend is not an exception to supply chain management. As logistics service providers become more experienced and sophisticated in their offerings, more and more firms are turning to logistics services providers for such activities as warehousing, packaging, order fulfillment, and transportation. What is not so clear, however, is the role of information technology and

DOI: 10.4018/978-1-4666-1761-2.ch008

information systems (IT/IS) in these outsourced activities. In general, we understand that IT/IS are the enablers of outsourcing. IT/IS help firms control outsourced activities, communicate with outsourced product and/or service providers, and eventually collaborate with third party logistics providers. Sometimes, however, IT/IS themselves are subject to outsourcing. When firms outsource supply chain processes, what will happen to IT/IS?

This paper attempts to answer this question by utilizing a survey approach that will take facts from practitioners throughout the United States. Some firms may utilize internal systems, some may outsource to the provider, while still others may outsource to supply chain management information systems providers. The purpose of this study is to acquire knowledge that will help clarify the direction of outsourcing from an information systems utilization perspective. This study will help both practitioners and researchers understand outsourcing trends by industries and, in particular, the relationship between outsourced supply chain processes and information technologies/ information systems. This study will be especially valuable to the firms that plan outsourcing supply chain processes and/or information systems. This study is limited to the presentation of the survey results along with some discussions and is not intended to provide statistical inferences to the findings. The remainder of this study consists of a literature review on outsourcing, survey design and data collection, results and discussion on the survey followed by a conclusion that addresses a summary of findings and future directions.

LITERATURE REVIEW

This section includes outsourcing trends identified by a literature review. Although the literature review is not exhaustive, it will show the recent trends by industries and products. In addition, the study covers activities outsourced, outsourcing trends (past, current, and future), and key driv-

ers for retaining or outsourcing internal systems, technological capabilities for outsourcing, and enablers and barriers to outsourcing.

Outsourcing by Industry

Aerospace

About fifty years ago, the aerospace industry was a typical example of vertically integrated firms. American manufacturers, which the aerospace industry belongs to, outsource their business between 50 and 70 percent in terms of total value added to their products (Rossetti & Choi, 2005). According to Rossetti and Choi, companies can achieve their maximized collective market presence and profitability with strategic partnership or outsourcing. However, Rossetti and Choi argue that outsourcing can result in abusing partners by focusing on reducing price excessively and repeatedly, extending payment terms, and forcing them to reduce inventory level to an acceptable level.

Automobile

Volkswagen (VW) in Brazil, which produces trucks and buses, has implemented the pure modular consortium model, which is radical outsourcing in that module suppliers have the responsibility of assembling their modules directly on VW's assembly line (Collins et al., 1997; Pires, 1998). VW prepares the plant and assembly line, and takes the responsibility of plant coordination and final testing. Only 200 workers out of 1,350 employees required for the full capacity of the plant will be directly hired by VW. In addition, VW maintains seven module suppliers instead of 400 traditional suppliers. As a result, VW can save twenty percent of its cost and at least ten percent of assembly time.

Like Volkswagen, Volvo actively implements an outsourcing policy of internal activities such as allowing parts of final assembly of components by suppliers (Svensson, 2001). Accordingly, Volvo tends to be a brand owner by outsourcing manufacturing and assembly processes to suppliers. As a result, Volvo expects to enhance competitiveness in the global market and profitability.

A case study of Chrysler Jeeps WIPERs identifies issues related to outsourcing components such as interface compatibility, which can be solved by modularization and standardization (Mikkola, 2003). Product complexity is found to be a determinant of outsourcing in the automobile industry (Novak & Eppinger, 2001). That is, higher product complexity will lead a firm to in-house production.

According to an in-depth case study on a major European auto maker and its suppliers, outsourcing decisions on automotive components, which may transfer competencies from original equipment manufacturers (OEM) to suppliers, should not alter the leadership of auto makers within the supply chain as long as the auto makers maintain a strong competence as system integrator and create a new way of developing supply chain management (Caputo & Zirpoli, 2002).

The SMART car produced by Mercedes-Benz consists of five main modules that are outsourced to a small number of first tier suppliers in sequence for final assembly (Hoek, 1998). In fact, the modular design of products facilitates outsourcing decision and customization in the market (Mikkola & Skjott-Larson, 2004).

Chemical

Outsourcing in the chemical industry is not a rare incident. To cope with residual liability due to outsourcing chemical products to partners, product stewardship is suggested for chemical manufacturers (Snir, 2001).

The upstream of supply chains in the bulk chemical industry heavily pursues efficiency with economies of scale. BP Chemicals, a primary producer of bulk chemicals for secondary chemical manufacturers, is a good example of this case. To achieve efficiency with economies of scale, primary chemical producers seldom outsource

their conversion processes. However, secondary producers such as DuPont for agricultural crop protection chemicals outsource parts of their business (e.g., product development) to save time to market and cost (Collins & Bechler, 1999). DuPont tries to outsource processes up to the penultimate stage while keeping the final stage in the synthesis of biologically active molecules in their business.

One of the other types of outsourcing in the chemical industry is the use of an outside service for facility operations. Seuring (2003) introduced outsourcing facility operations in the German chemical industry. Facility operators defined as "site-bound providers of services aiming to support companies on site" (Seuring, 2003) allow chemical manufacturers to focus on their core business.

Electronic

Shortened product life cycles and increased global competition force electronic manufacturing companies to focus on their core competencies such as product design and development while they opt to outsource other processes such as the actual manufacturing of products (Mason et al., 2002). Honeywell Consumer Products Limited in Hong Kong, a manufacturer of consumer electronics, decided to keep a part of its product to save new technology investment (Choy & Lee, 2002).

A company that produces various printed circuit boards decided to implement a strategy for outsourcing parts of its assembly processes to suppliers (Sislian & Satir, 2000). Its primary purpose of outsourcing was not to pursue cost effectiveness but to achieve competitive advantage that can add differentiated features to the products.

Information Technology (IT)

Fine (2000) discusses modularization and outsourcing in the computer industry. Mercury Computer Systems is a provider of modularized computer components for various computer systems such as medical imaging systems for General

Electric, Marconi, Philips, and Siemens. In addition, Mercury Computer Systems can provide signal-processing technology that increases base station capacity for wireless service providers such as Ericsson, Lucent, Motorola, and Nortel. The increased base station capacity will enable the wireless service providers to run the Internet base applications that require higher data transfer rates.

Hewlett-Packard's mobile phone testing equipment operations is a successful case of outsourcing in the IT industry (Lonsdale, 1999). Hewlett-Packard (HP) has continuously defined and redefined its critical activities for outsourcing for the past 15 years and has achieved competitive advantages. HP keeps an emphasis on the final assembly of products such as configuration management, comprehensive solution to measurement, testing equipment, and research and development. Other processes are actively outsourced. By keeping only high value-added core activities in house, HP enjoys reduced cycle time and increased responsiveness to customer requirements. HP also moved to outsourcing notebook computers, servers, and workstations (Parker & Anderson, 2002). Due to a short product life cycle, HP sources its notebook products from Asian manufacturers. Similarly, HP sources servers and workstations from contract manufacturers to cope with severe price competition.

According to the literature survey by Mason et al. (2002), production through outsourcing in the electronic manufacturing industry is around 20 percent for integrated devices as of year 2001 and continues to increase about 25 percent per year. The major factors for the outsourcing trend in the industry are to shorten product life cycles, increasing global competition, cost reduction with economies of scale, and better utilization of expensive capital investment. They further argue that a firm cannot compete with other companies under the current business environment that requires aforementioned major factors from companies.

Rather, the companies must leverage the strengths of their supply chains to be agile in the market.

Dell and Cisco extensively outsource their manufacturing and product development. Dell's core competencies are quality, customization, and responsiveness at prices that other manufacturers cannot match (Leavy, 2001). With outsourcing, Dell and Cisco maintain higher growth rates than their highly integrated predecessors.

Logistics

As third party logistics (3PL) providers increase their services, outsourcing various logistics activities become more popular than ever. Logistics functions that are frequently outsourced include shipment consolidation, warehouse management/operations, logistic information systems, carrier selection, and rate negotiation (Spalding, 1998). According to a survey, about seventy-one percent of respondents currently involved in outsourcing activities are collaborating with 3PL providers in at least two logistics functions (Rabinovich et al., 1999).

A four-wheel-drive tractor manufacturer has developed successful partnerships for warehouse management (Ding & Stoner, 2004). The partnership includes a materials service center near the manufacturing facility, which performs warehouse functions from receiving to part kitting to component sub-assembly. The company can increase inventory accuracy by outsourcing warehouse management and can run its factory without interruption due to inventory shortage. Companies like John Deere, Case-New Holland, and Mitsubishi Motors also use 3PL providers for outsourcing warehouse management.

Food

Outsourcing in the food industry is often limited to warehousing and shipment activities (Hoek, 1999). Unilever-Sagit, which is Unilever's Italian foodstuff subsidiary producing frozen and deep frozen foods, has implemented the strategy for outsourcing its distribution system to save mainly personnel costs (Calza & Passaro, 1997).

Financial Service

Outsourcing trends in the financial service industry follow closely those in the manufacturing sector. Outsourcing functions in the financial service industry include check clearing and payment processing in retail banking, settlement in the trading industry, credit rating in the lending industry, and custody of assets in the investment management industry (Tas & Sunder, 2004).

Toy

Most toys are fashion products with a strong seasonal demand and a short life cycle. Accordingly, requirements in logistics support are highly volatile and subject to outsourcing. In addition, because toy companies consider design as a core competency, manufacturing is also frequently outsourced. Toy companies such as Hasbro and Mattel can handle huge seasonal volumes and avoid traditional capital commitment by outsourcing their production and logistics processes (Johnson, 2001).

Other Industries

A survey of the facility management industry in the United Kingdom shows an increasing trend on outsourcing facility management functions such as service of production equipment, post services, delivery services, energy optimization, copying/printing, security, education/training, and work environment/furnishing (Brochner, Adolfsson, & Johansson, 2002). The companies outsourcing facility management can take advantage of lowered expenses, due to economies of scale.

Outsourcing Trends

Information Technology (IT)

Lee et al. (2003) summarized outsourcing trends in the IT industry into five different periods: 1960s, 1970s, 1980s, 1990s, and the future. In the 1960s, because computers were large and costly, firms outsourced time-sharing or processing services to the external vendors. In the 1970s, the major outsourcing activity was contract programming. In the 1980s, most IT related activities were performed in house. Thus, outsourcing was limited to standardization. In the 1990s, facility management and system integration were targets to be outsourced. The authors forecast that the form of future outsourcing in the IT industry will be application service providers or ASP, which include hardware vendors, network providers, software vendors, and system integrators.

Automobile

A survey reveals that automakers and suppliers have not increased outsourcing in the past decade when measuring the degree of outsourcing with dollar amount spent in procurement in terms of turnover (Corswant & Fredriksson, 2002). According to the survey, automakers will demand suppliers to take more responsibility for development and assembly of systems and modules in the future.

Technologies Being Used by Customers and 3PLs

A survey on the use of IT at 3PLs, which includes 126 3PLs in Singapore, shows information technologies being used by 3PLs in conjunction with logistics services (Piplani, Pokharel, & Tan, 2004). Logistics activities performed with the use of IT are order processing and accounting for transportation; order processing, workflow, and bar coding for warehouses; electronic data interchange (EDI), workflow, and order processing for freight forwarding; EDI, workflow, and wireless communication for container depot.

A survey study that includes sixty companies out of the 500 largest manufacturers in the United States, based on annual sales revenue, shows that two-third of the companies, which are users of 3PL, are either committed to implementing radio frequency identification (RFID) technology in their supply chain or actively considering its application (Lieb & Bentz, 2005).

Drivers for Outsourcing Internal Supply Chain Systems

A case study of the telecommunication industry identifies five reasons or drivers for outsourcing such as (1) the most competent source that is the best available internal or external source to a company; (2) increased flexibility; (3) reduced risk exposure; (4) cost reduction; and (5) supplier management (McIvor, 2003). Meanwhile, Khan and Fitzgerald (2004) suggest cost reduction, reduced time cycle, and access to highly skilled professionals as drivers for offshore outsourcing.

A study on small businesses in New Zealand reveals various drivers for outsourcing. The top ten drivers in the order of importance are: (1) access to experts; (2) to have quality services from outsourcer; (3) access to new technology; (4) to have more flexible and responsive systems; (5) to have more time to focus on core business competency; (6) to reduce costs; (7) to reduce risk and uncertainty; (8) to reduce project completion time; (9) to gain competitive advantage; and (10) lack in-house capability (Al-Qirim, 2003).

Based on literature and observations, Heikkila and Cordon (2002) summarized reasons to outsource such items as scarcity of capital, lack of know-how, flexibility and the need for quick response or small production, speed or time to market, asset utilization or spare capacity, and economies of scale. In addition, reducing costs, improving quality, service, and delivery, improv-

ing organizational focus, increasing flexibility, and facilitating change are considered as commonly cited reasons for outsourcing (Fan, 2000).

Scale economies and strategic sourcing are two major drivers for outsourcing products and/or services (Kakabadse & Kakabadse, 2000). Scale economies are about cost savings and cost-effective access to resource, knowledge, and technology. Strategic sourcing includes sourcing into strategy formulation that consists of strategic repositioning, core competence enhancement, greater service integration, and/or higher value creation.

For outsourcing information systems (IS), Smith, Mitra, and Narashimhan (1998) classify major drivers for outsourcing into five categories such as cost reduction, focus on core competence, cash need, IS capability factors, and environment factors. McFarlan and Nolan (1995) suggest several pressures to outsource: (1) general managers' concerns about costs and quality; (2) breakdown in IT performance; (3) simplified general management agenda; (4) financial factors; (5) corporate culture; elimination of an internal irritant; and (6) other factors.

A study of outsourcing logistics functions summarizes drivers or reasons to outsource in the five key factors: (1) centrality of the logistics functions to the firm's core competency; (2) risk liability and control; (3) cost/service tradeoffs in operations; (4) information and communications systems; and (5) market relationships (Rao & Young, 1994).

Barriers to Outsourcing

One study of small to medium-sized firms in New Zealand, Al-Qirim (2003) suggests fourteen problems of outsourcing, which are also barriers to outsourcing. Five of them are identifying right suppliers, right choice from diverse products, non-performance/under-performance of suppliers, insufficient funds, and exceeding the planned budget. Heikkila and Cordon (2002) identifies several potential drawbacks or barriers to outsourcing such as transfer of know-how that encourages new competitors; changes in the balance of power in the industry; dependency, confidentiality, and security issues, and fear of opportunism.

SURVEY DESIGN AND DATA COLLECTION

The survey targeted the functional areas of Consulting, Distribution, Engineering, Information System/Information Technology, Merchandising, Operations/Production, and Purchasing. A total of 3,851 email questionnaires were distributed nationwide in the U.S. to each functional area based on the target percentage noted in Table 1. Among those sent, 996 responses (25.9% return rate) were collected during the week of October 23, 2006 through October 30, 2006.

To authenticate the validity of our returns, a filter question was asked to limit analysis to professionals directly involved in logistics and supply chain areas within their organizations. Among 996 respondents, twenty-two percent of them actually were knowledgeable of and/or involved in their current supply chain functions and systems. These professionals are the industry gauges for the future of Logistics and Supply Chain systems.

The response demographics in Figure 1 illuminate a great picture of the context in which our professionals were representing. Sixty-nine percent of our respondents represent Service Industries (Logistics, Health Care, Financial, Service Operational, etc.), Non-Profit (Religious Organizations, Foundations, etc.), Consultative, and Manufacturing Organizations. While the remaining thirty-four percent represent Research and Development (R&D), Engineering, Government/Utility, Distribution, Wholesale, and Retail Organizations.

Organization sizes are measured with three categories in companies' annual revenues such as over five-hundred million dollars, between one

Table 1. Distribution of Questionnaires

Functional Area	Percentage
Operations/Production	30%
Purchasing	22%
Merchandising	15%
Distribution	14%
Consulting	7%
Engineering	7%
IS/IT	5%

* Sample size (N) = 996

hundred and five-hundred million dollars, and less than one-hundred million dollars. Sixty-six percent of our respondents represent organizations making less than one-hundred million U.S. dollars in annual revenues, while eighteen percent make over five-hundred million dollars in annual revenue. The remaining sixteen percent of companies have their annual revenues between one hundred- and five-hundred million dollars.

SURVEY RESULTS AND DISCUSSION

Eleven questions are administered for understanding outsourcing trends. The questions and results are discussed within appropriate subtitles.

Recognition of the Supply Chain Contributions

The first and the second questions (Q1 and Q2) in our survey are "Does your company recognize the supply chain as an area of focus for cost reductions within the next five years?" and "Does your company recognizes the supply chain as an area of focus for competitive advantages within the next five years?", respectively. Respondents indicated a lack of control or focus on logistics and supply chain processes. Table 2 reveals that around sixty percent of all respondents are focusing on their

Figure 1. Response Demographics by Business Types

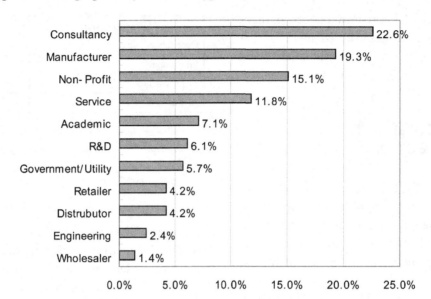

supply chain for cost reductions and/or competitive advantages within some levels. These respondents were primarily with organizations that made less than one hundred million U.S. dollars in annual revenues. Forty-one percent of respondents even do not recognize supply chain management as an area of focus for competitive advantages within the next five years. As globalization is intensified and supply chain management costs rise on account of capacity shortages and extended lead times, it is inevitable to institute supply chain systems to manage capacity shortage and costs increase.

As logistics and supply chain costs rise and a lack of control surfaces, there will be a surge in organizations looking for ways to better manage their supply chain functions and information systems. Information technologies surrounding supply chain functions and processes will be in high demand, and more will be demanded from logistics service providers. As the focus of organizations begin shifting to their supply chain activities for competitive advantages and cost savings, they will see a large opportunity gap that currently exists. As shown in Figure 2 for the third question (Q3): "How would you currently rate the supply chain performance of your organization?", sixty-five percent of the respondents rate their supply chain performance at a level of average or below, while only seven percent rate their performance as excellent.

Table 2. Recognition of the Supply Chain Contributions

Response	Q1: Does your company recognize the supply chain as an area of focus for cost reductions within the next five years?	Q2: Does your company recognize the supply chain as an area of focus for competitive advantages within the next five years?
Yes	43%	43%
Somewhat	19%	15%
No	38%	41%

* Sample size (N) = 996

Figure 2. Rating Supply Chain Performance

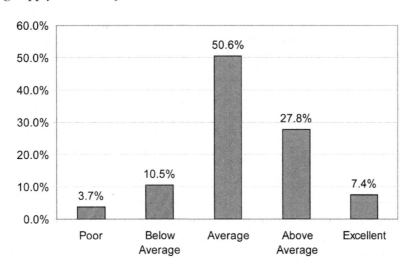

Outsourcing Plan

Although many of the respondents consider their supply chain performance as average at best, the majority of the respondents do not plan to outsource supply chain management. The fourth and fifth questions (Q4 and Q5) are "Which, if any, supply chain functions do you plan to outsource within the next five years?" and "Which, if any, supply chain information systems do you plan to outsource within the next five years?" respectively. Table 3 shows that less than half of respondents plan to outsource supply chain functions or processes within the next five years (Q4). Likewise, only twenty-nine percent of the respondents answer that they have a plan to outsource supply chain information systems within the next five years (Q5). Among those who plan to outsource their supply chain functions, off-shore manufacturing, customer relationship management, order processing, transportation and warehousing management are listed as most likely candidates. Of the information technology outsourcing, off-shore manufacturing, order processing, advanced planning, inventory planning and management, transportation and warehousing management are listed as most likely candidates.

Over half of all respondents noted that they did not plan on outsourcing any supply chain functions or systems in the next 5 years. These respondents were evenly divided between companies that have recognized supply chain and logistics as an area for cost savings and competitive advantages, as well as those that have not recognized logistics and supply chain as an area for cost savings and competitive advantages. Smaller companies that have not focused on logistics and supply chain do not have immediate reason to outsource any functions or systems, and those that have focused on logistics and supply chain typically have internal processes and barriers preventing them from outsourcing.

As to the reasons for outsourcing supply chain systems (Question No. 6), Figure 3 shows various reasons for outsourcing supply chain information systems. For those organizations that choose to outsource, we found that they do so for two primary reasons, a lack of ability to handle in house (23.2%) and concern on return on assets (23.6%). Among the specified reasonsw, flexibility is ranked at the third place for the reasons of outsourcing.

Table 3. Outsourcing Plans within the Next Five Years

	Q4: Which, if any, supply chain functions do you plan to outsource within the next five years?	Q5: Which, if any, supply chain information systems do you plan to outsource within the next five years?
Advanced Planning	4%	7%
Asset Tracking	4%	2%
Customer Relationship Management	7%	4%
Forecasting	5%	2%
Inventory Planning and Management	4%	6%
Manufacturing	7%	8%
Order Processing	6%	6%
Procurement	5%	3%
Transportation Management	7%	6%
Warehouse Management	7%	6%
Other	4%	5%
None	65%	71%

*Due to multiple selections, the sum of total may exceed 100%; Sample size (N) = 996.

Changes in Outsourcing in the Past Five Years

The seventh question was "Compared to the past five years, how has your outsourcing of supply chain functions changed?" The eighth question was "Compared to the past five years, how has your outsourcing of supply chain information systems changed?" Table 4 displays the responses to the two questions.

Over three-fourths of respondents outsource the same or less supply chain functions, and ninety percent outsource the same or less supply chain information systems. Data indicates that,

as we progress in future supply chain focuses; the bulk of industries will likely maintain the status quo. Increased outsourcing will continue at a trend of about ten to twenty percent over the next five years, but it appears that majority organizations will not hand over their supply chain functions or systems to third party providers.

Barriers to Outsourcing

Barriers to outsourcing are quite normal and prevalent in today's market (Al-Qirim, 2003; Heikkila and Cordon, 2002). When asked, "Which barriers to outsourcing do you encounter within

Table 4. Outsourcing Trends Compared to the Past Five Years

Response	Q7: Compared to the past five years, how has your outsourcing of supply chain functions changed?	Q8: Compared to the past five years, how has your outsourcing of supply chain information systems changed?
We outsource less	14%	13%
We outsource same	64%	77%
We outsource more	22%	10%

* Sample size (N) = 996

Figure 3. Reasons for Outsourcing Supply Chain Information Systems

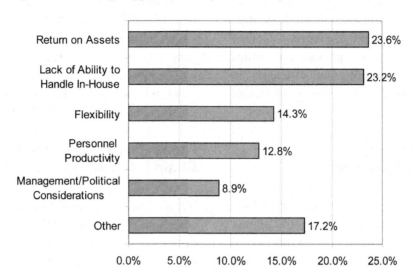

your firm (Question 9 or Q9)," the largest barrier was that of cost (23.9%) which is followed by control issue (17.8%) and management issue (15.5%) respectively. Among the specific reasons, control concerns, which are about fear to loose control over outsourced activities and services, are

the second major barrier to outsourcing. Figure 4 illustrates major barriers to outsourcing.

It is interesting to note that twenty-one percent of respondents did not encounter barriers to outsourcing. While outsourcing appears to be a continuing trend, some manageable barriers such as political, cost, and privacy barriers will need to

Figure 4. Barriers to Outsourcing

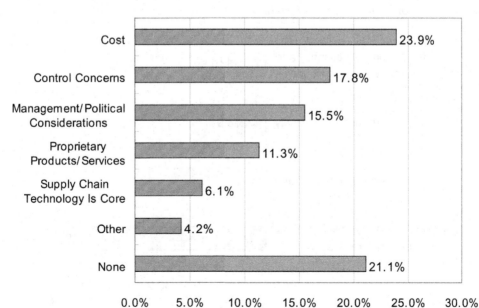

be resolved or reduced before significant increases will be noticed. Information technology may provide great solutions to these barriers. Robust technological systems will provide companies with the privacy, flexibility, and efficiency to improve supply chain functions and reduce costs simultaneously.

Maintenance of Supply Chain Software Systems

When asked, "How supply chain software systems were currently maintained (Question 10)," almost fifty percent of the respondents reported not having any supply chain systems in their organization. Figure 5 shows the responses to Q10.

The respondents that did not have systems were the same respondents that had not identified their supply chain as an area for cost reductions or competitive advantages. We call these organizations as the Supply Chain Followers (SCF). Supply Chain Followers are smaller in revenue (less than one hundred million dollars), haven't focused on logistics or supply chain for cost savings or competitive advantages, and do not have supply

chain information systems or software. Supply Chain Leaders (SCL), on the other hand, are the larger entities that are focusing on logistics and supply chain in this survey. SCL organizations will be those that are demanding better and more robust systems, while improving their supply chain functions both internally and externally.

Areas for Outsourcing Supply Chain Information Systems

Supply Chain Information System outsourcing covers all of the key supply chain and logistics functions. Order Processing will likely be the highest growth area, while Asset, Inventory, Transportation, and Warehouse management systems will steadily increase as well. The last and eleventh question (Q11) is "Which areas do you plan to outsource for supply chain management information systems?" Figure 6 summarizes the answers to Q11.

Outsourcing these key information systems allows organizations to receive third party expertise and management, as well as information technology and system support for improvement

Figure 5. Maintenance of Supply Chain Information Systems

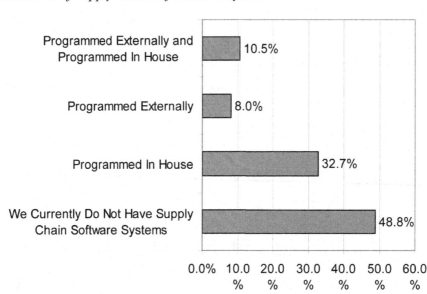

Figure 6. Areas for Supply Chain Information System Outsourcing

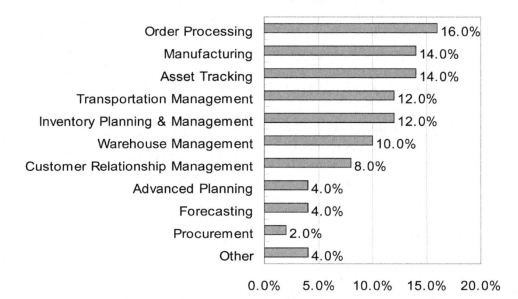

initiatives. Internally designed systems face the same political anti-change barriers to improvement as do their functional counterparts. Organizations are slowly realizing that outsourced systems and functions are forced by competition to continuously improve as a proactive attempt to grow business. When systems and functions are externally outsourced, the third party market empowers organizations to transfer operations or information systems from one vendor to another based on vendor offerings, capacity, specialty, and capabilities.

CONCLUSION

This paper explored the future state of the outsourcing trend of supply chain management in general and of supply chain information systems in particular. Pertinent literature review indicated active outsourcings of products/services in different industries. Based on our survey results, we are able to summary the following findings:

- Sixty percent of all respondents are focusing on their supply chain for cost reduction and/or competitive advantages within some levels
- Less than half of respondents plan to outsource supply chain processes and information systems within the next five years
- Major reasons for outsourcing are a lack of ability to handle in house and return on assets
- The largest barrier to outsourcing is cost followed by control concern, especially for outsourcing information systems.

The future state of outsourcing supply chain information systems looks promising. As the level of globalization increases, Supply Chain Leaders will emerge, and the necessity for new robust information systems will follow. As outsourcing of supply chain processes grow at an approximate rate of twenty percent annually, outsourcing information systems will increase at about half (ten percent annually). All functional areas will need information system support to provide the visibility of supply chain to all participants in the supply chain. The supply chain as a whole will increase in collaboration and communication in the future. Thus, information technology support will be needed to interface supply chain functions with other cross-functional areas, which will call for internal and external system support and maintenance.

The major limitation of this study is the straightforward presentation of survey results. In the future study, it is desirable to provide results based an inferential statistical analysis.

ACKNOWLEDGMENT

This research project is partially supported by a research fund provided by the Center for Supply Chain Management Studies at St. Louis University

REFERENCES

Al-Qirim, N. A. (2003). The strategic outsourcing decision of IT and eCommerce: the case of small businesses in New Zealand. *Journal of Information Technology Cases and Applications*, *5*(3), 32–56.

Brochner, J., Adolfsson, P., & Johansson, M. (2002). Outsourcing facilities management in the process industry: a comparison of Swedish and UK patterns. *Journal of Facilities Management*, *1*(3), 265–271. doi:10.1108/14725960310807953

Calza, F., & Passaro, R. (1997). EDI network and logistics management at Unilever-Sagit. *Supply Chain Management*, *2*(4), 158–170. doi:10.1108/13598549710191322

Caputo, M., & Zirpoli, F. (2002). Supplier involvement in automotive component design: outsourcing strategies and supply chain management. *International Journal of Technology Management*, *23*(1, 2, & 3), 129-154.

Choy, K. L., & Lee, W. B. (2002). A generic tool for the selection and management of supplier relationships in an outsourced manufacturing environment: the application of case based reasoning. *Logistics Information Management*, *15*(4), 235–253. doi:10.1108/09576050210436093

Collins, R., & Bechler, K. (1999). Outsourcing in the chemical and automotive industries: choice or competitive imperative? *Journal of Supply Chain Management*, *35*(4), 4–10. doi:10.1111/j.1745-493X.1999.tb00239.x

Collins, R., Bechler, K., & Pires, S. (1997). Outsourcing in the automotive industry: from JIT to modular consortia. *European Management Journal*, *15*(5), 498–508. doi:10.1016/S0263-2373(97)00030-3

Corswant, F., & Fredriksson, P. (2002). Sourcing trends in the car industry: a survey of car manufacturers' and suppliers' strategies and relations. *International Journal of Operations & Production Management*, *22*(7/8), 741–758. doi:10.1108/01443570210433526

Ding, F., & Stoner, A. (2004). An evaluation procedure for material service centers. *Supply Chain Management*, *9*(2), 197–203. doi:10.1108/13598540410527088

Fan, Y. (2000). Strategic outsourcing: evidence from British companies. *Marketing Intelligence & Planning*, *18*(4), 213–220. doi:10.1108/02634500010333398

Fine, C. H. (2000). Clockspeed-based strategies for supply chain design. *Production and Operations Management*, *9*(3), 213–221. doi:10.1111/j.1937-5956.2000.tb00134.x

Heikkila, J., & Cordon, C. (2002). Outsourcing: a core or non-core strategic management decision. *Marketing Intelligence & Planning*, *11*(4), 183–193.

Hoek, R. I. (1998). Logistics and virtual integration postponement, outsourcing and the flow of information. *International Journal of Physical Distribution & Logistics Management, 28*(7), 508–523. doi:10.1108/09600039810247498

Hoek, R. I. (1999). Postponement and the reconfiguration challenge for food supply chains. *Supply Chain Management, 4*(1), 18–34. doi:10.1108/13598549910255068

Johnson, M. E. (2001). Learning from toys: lessons in managing supply chain risk from the toy industry. *California Management Review, 43*(3), 106–123.

Kakabadse, N., & Kakabadse, A. (2000). Critical review-outsourcing: a paradigm shift. *Journal of Management Development, 19*(8), 670–728. doi:10.1108/02621710010377508

Khan, N., & Fitzgerald, G. (2004). Dimensions of offshore outsourcing business models. *Journal of Information Technology Cases and Applications, 6*(3), 35–50.

Leavy, B. (2001). Supply strategy what to outsource and where. *Irish Marketing Review, 14*(2), 46–52.

Lee, J., Hyunh, M. Q., Kwok, R. C., & Pi, S. (2003). IT outsourcing evolution-past, present, and future. *Communications of the ACM, 46*(5), 84–88. doi:10.1145/769800.769807

Lieb, R., & Bentz, B. A. (2005). The use of third-party logistics services by large American manufacturers: the 2004 survey. *Transportation Journal, 44*(2), 5–15.

Lonsdale, C. (1999). Effective managing vertical supply relationships: a risk management model for outsourcing. *Supply Chain Management, 4*(4), 176–183. doi:10.1108/13598549910284499

Mason, S. J., Cole, M. H., Ulrey, B. T., & Yan, L. (2003). Improving electronics manufacturing supply chain agility through outsourcing. *International Journal of Physical Distribution & Logistics Management, 32*(7), 610–620. doi:10.1108/09600030210442612

McFarlan, F. W., & Nolan, R. L. (1995). How to manage an IT outsourcing alliance. *Sloan Management Review, 36*(2), 9–23.

McIvor, R. (2003). Outsourcing: insights from the telecommunications industry. *Supply Chain Management, 8*(3/4), 380–394.

Mikkola, J. H. (2003). Modularity, component outsourcing, and inter-firm learning. *R & D Management, 33*(4), 439–454. doi:10.1111/1467-9310.00309

Mikkola, J. H., & Skjott-Larson, T. (2004). Supply-chain integration: implications for mass customization, modularization, and postponement strategies. *Production Planning and Control, 15*(4), 352–361. doi:10.1080/0953728042000238845

Novak, S., & Eppinger, S. D. (2001). Sourcing by design: product complexity and supply chain. *Management Science, 47*(1), 189–203. doi:10.1287/mnsc.47.1.189.10662

Parker, G. G., & Anderson, E. G. Jr. (2002). From buyer to integrator: the transformation of the supply-chain manager in the vertically disintegrating firm. *Production and Operations Management, 11*(1), 75–91. doi:10.1111/j.1937-5956.2002.tb00185.x

Piplani, R., Pokharel, S., & Tan, A. (2004). Perspective on the use of information technology at third party logistics service providers in Singapore. *Asia Pacific Journal of Marketing and Logistics, 16*(1), 27–41. doi:10.1108/13555850410765113

Pires, S. R. I. (1998). Managerial implications of the modular consortium model in a Brazilian automotive plant. *International Journal of Operations & Production Management, 18*(3), 221–232. doi:10.1108/01443579810368290

Rao, K., & Young, R. (1994). Global supply chains: factors influencing outsourcing logistics functions. *International Journal of Physical Distribution & Logistics, 24*(6), 11–19. doi:10.1108/09600039410066141

Robinovich, E., Windle, R., Dresner, M., & Corsi, T. (1999). Outsourcing of integrated logistics functions: an examination of industry practices. *International Journal of Physical Distribution & Logistics Management, 29*(6), 353–373. doi:10.1108/09600039910283587

Rossetti, C., & Choi, T. Y. (2005). On the dark side of strategic sourcing: experiences from the aerospace industry. *The Academy of Management Executive, 19*(1), 46–60.

Seuring, S. A. (2003). Outsourcing into service factories: an exploratory analysis of facility operators in the German chemical industry. *International Journal of Operations & Production Management, 23*(10), 1207–1223. doi:10.1108/01443570310496634

Sislian, E., & Satir, A. (2000). Strategic sourcing: a framework and a case study. *Journal of Supply Chain Management, 36*(3), 4–11. doi:10.1111/j.1745-493X.2000.tb00246.x

Smith, M. A., Mitra, S., & Narashimhan, S. (1998). Information systems outsourcing: a study of pre-event firm characteristics. *Journal of Management Information Systems, 15*(2), 61–93.

Snir, E. M. (2001). Liability as a catalyst for product stewardship. *Production and Operations Management, 10*(2), 190–206. doi:10.1111/j.1937-5956.2001.tb00078.x

Spalding, J. O. (1998). Transportation industry takes the right-of-way in the supply chain. *IIE Solutions, 30*(7), 24–28.

Svensson, G. (2001). The impact of outsourcing on inbound logistics flows. *International Journal of Logistics Management, 12*(1), 21–35. doi:10.1108/09574090110806208

Tas, J., & Sunder, S. (2004). Financial services business process outsourcing. *Communications of the ACM, 47*(5), 50–52. doi:10.1145/986213.986238

This work was previously published in International Journal of Enterprise Information Systems, edited by Madjid Tavana, pp. 1-16, Volume 6, Issue 3, copyright 2010 by IGI Publishing (an imprint of IGI Global).

Chapter 9

Effects of Reciprocal Investments and Relational Interaction in Deploying RFID Supply Chain Systems

Rebecca Angeles
University of New Brunswick Fredericton, Canada

ABSTRACT

In this paper, the author looks at the perceived ability of information technology (IT) infrastructure integration and supply chain process integration. In order to moderate the relationship between business process specificity and domain knowledge specificity, the study focuses on two dependent variables; reciprocal investments and relational interaction using the moderated regression procedure. Results show that IT infrastructure integration moderates the relationship between business process specificity and relational interaction, as well as domain knowledge specificity and relational interaction.

INTRODUCTION

This study looks at the perceived ability of two variables, information technology(IT) infrastructure integration and supply chain process integration, to moderate the relationship between the independent variables, business process specificity and domain knowledge specificity and two dependent variables, reciprocal investments and relational interaction in anticipated radio frequency identification (RFID) system deployment initiatives in the supply chain.

Though not yet at the expected speedy rate of diffusion, RFID system implementation initiatives are still a major consideration in improving supply chains across industries. It has been a number of years now since landmark mandates have been issued by institutions like the U.S. Department of Defense, U.S. Federal Food and Drug Administration, and the global retailer Wal-Mart and others like Target, Tesco, Metro Stores, among others, for their trading partners to use RFID at the case and pallet levels (Lee, Feng, & Ying, 2009; Barratt & Choi, 2007; Songini, 2007).

DOI: 10.4018/978-1-4666-1761-2.ch009

Firms worldwide continue to experiment with its use and although the signs are encouraging and positive in exceptional cases such as in Wal-Mart's, more firms tread the path cautiously and are still mainly driven by "hub" firms who require their trading partners use it, even if only on a tentative basis. University of Arkansas' RFID Research Center has reported that RFID-enabled inventory systems in the Wal-Mart test stores improved inventory count accuracy by 13 percent, thus reducing the need to hold unnecessary inventory (Blanchard, 2008). In an earlier set of findings, the Center reported that the initial 16 percent reduction in out-of-stock instances was reassessed only to show an actual 30 percent reduction for items selling 0.1 to 15 units daily. The percentage is even higher at 62 percent for faster moving items selling at 7 to 15 units daily (Manufacturing Business Technology, 2006). For the most part, however, firms still hesitate to use RFID because the touted benefits and possible implementation problems are not yet clear or definitive from both the industrial and academic research perspectives (Zhou, 2009).

More research studies have been conducted since, that give us an indication of more important things to consider when implementing RFID in the supply chain. This study closes up specifically on RFID as it relates to the concepts of IT infrastructure integration, supply chain process integration, business process specificity, domain knowledge specificity, reciprocal investments, and relational interaction. The following are selected studies that help highlight the salience of these concepts in RFID implementation within the supply chain.

Kim et al. (2008) found, in their study of 70 American and 87 Korean retailers, that the IT infrastructure supporting RFID is critical in improving inventory management, store operations, and demand management, and boosting business strategic performance. The American retailers specifically valued the hardware/software applications needed for inventory management,

whereas the Korean retailers valued parts of the IT infrastructure that supported efficient store operations and demand management. For inventory management, both groups of retailers recognized the importance of data system automation in enabling interfirm sharing of accurate data pertinent to inventory control, real-time inventory, reduced shrinkage, visibility of orders, etc. Cannon et al. (2008), however, argue that the presence of an IT infrastructure alone does not guarantee that it will add to the firm's competitiveness. In order to extract maximum value from RFID, there has to be "high IT embeddedness" or an environment that more fully integrates IT into the firm's critical decision making (Powell & Dent-Micalieff, 1997; Chatfield & Yetton, 2000) and making asset-specific investments with an electronic trading partner.

Suggested IT infrastructure support for RFID in current technology environments has been described in numerous studies. The more recent ones include the following. Chang, Cheng, and Lin (2007) describe the web services-enabled architecture for an RFID environment. Jankowska, Kurbel, and Schreber (2007), on the other hand, introduced the architecture for agent-based mobile supply chains using RFID and other mobile technologies that links supply chain planning and execution. Lee and Park (2008), working along the same lines, also provide a dynamic tracing task model for an RFID-based SCM architecture intended to enhance the traceability range beyond simple distribution channels.

Streamlining business processes to align with the requirements of RFID initiatives is needed for supply chain process integration among trading partners. Sabbaghi and Vaidyanathan (2008) consider RFID to be critical in the following four business processes in the supply chain: demand management, order fulfillment, manufacturing flow management, and return management. Mobile and ubiquitous commerce add reach and complexity to extended supply chains that include the

IT environments of material and service suppliers and channel supply partners such as wholesalers, distributors, retailers, customers, etc. Keen and Mackintosh (2001) present the concept of "process freedoms" that RFID promises to manage such value webs by supporting the mobility of critical SCM elements such as business activities, people, information, documents, and communications. An important prerequisite to make this work, though, is a panoramic vision that encompasses all related business processes that need to be reengineered so that they recognize the intricate interdependencies and electronic linkages involved (Sabbaghi & Vaidyanathan, 2008).

In transaction cost theory, the concept of asset specificity of investments made by trading partners in each other is a substantial concern as use of these investments could not be transferred to other trading partners (Heide, 1994; Joshi & Stump, 1999). In this study, these asset-specific investments are referred to as "reciprocal investments." Cannon et al. (2008) claim that making such reciprocal investments in RFID initiatives is much riskier when the relationship with one's trading partner is for a longer term and when there is a high level of environmental uncertainty. Thus, firms will be likely to make such investments only with highly trusted trading partners and only with those firms who have notable reputations to protect, as a built-in governance measure against opportunistic behavior.

When it comes to the hub firm-trading partner arrangement, Ferguson (2006) argues that current RFID mandates spurred by powerful hub firms skew the benefits of the implementation initiatives in favor of the hub firms, thus, raising the asset-specific costs of their less powerful trading partners and exposing the latter to greater risks. Relational interaction can be used to overcome such difficulties in the imbalances of power valence among supply chain partners and enable the relationship.

There is great need for relational interaction among trading partners involved in RFID systems in order to negotiate the complex issues involved in such initiatives. Fortunately, more research studies are coming out that shed more light on delicate issues such as cost sharing among trading partners. In their study of a number of business cases involving firms using RFID, Ju, Ju, and Sun (2008) established the criticality of trading partners' interacting so that they could negotiate important issues such as cost sharing, accountability, responsibility, data standards, hardware standards, among other concerns. Less powerful trading partners, of course, have reason to express concern about inequitable distribution of cost responsibilities. Some hub firms such as Wal-Mart mandate that their trading partners shoulder these costs and accept financial responsibility for them (Kinsella, 2003; Tierney, 2003; Elliott, 2005; Roberti, 2005). Wal-Mart penalizes suppliers that do not comply with the mandate at US$2 per pallet (Logistics Today, 2008). Collaboration among trading partners is highly encouraged because even delicate issues like cost shifting could be managed reasonably and creative solutions have been arrived at (Ju, Ju, & Sun, 2008). For instance, RFID costs shouldered by distributors could be recouped later using premier pricing strategies and from revenue from offering RFID-enabled value added services such as the logistics services offered by TNT Express (Tierney, 2003). Some academics are working on more equitable ways of sharing the costs of the RFID tags. In their simulation of item-level RFID use in the supply chain, Gaukler, Seifert, and Hausman (2007) make recommendations about the appropriate allocation of RFID costs under manufacturer-dominant and retailer-dominant scenarios in order to optimize supply chain profit for both parties.

Certain RFID system deployments may require that a trading partner's key business processes such as operating processes, administrative processes, and quality-control processes be very unique and specific to the needs of another trading partner --- this is referred to as "business process specificity" (Subramani & Venkatraman, 2003). In this scenario involving supply chain partners, the ability of one party to provide critical information and expertise may also be needed for important decisions in this specific relationship --- this, in turn, is referred to as "domain knowledge specificity" (Subramani & Venkatraman, 2003).

The demands on supply chain partners that will be participating in these RFID initiatives will be significant enough for these firms to consider using relational interaction routines and reciprocal investments to support business process specificity and domain knowledge specificity. Reciprocal investments are transaction-specific investments made by supply chain trading partners in a business exchange intended to cement the relationship beyond what is ordinarily delivered by contractual agreements. Relational interaction routines are a combination of formal and informal mechanisms used to facilitate the exchange of information and knowledge between a focal firm and its trading partners.

The IT infrastructure and business process support that should undergird RFID systems are a great concern considering how supply chains are getting more complex and more international in their geographic scope (Simchi-Levi, Kaminsky, & Simchi-Levi, 2004).

This study uses the moderated regression procedure to test the ability of both IT infrastructure integration and supply chain process integration to moderate the relationship between the independent and dependent variables using data gathered from 115 firms using an online survey.

LITERATURE REVIEW

The following discussion features the review of the literature for the independent, dependent, and moderator variables used in this study.

Independent Variables

Business Process Specificity

A business process is a set of one or more linked activities which are designed to achieve a specific business objective by taking inputs which are, then, converted to outputs valued by customers or markets (WfMC, 1999; Hammer & Champy, 1993; Davenport, 1993). Business process specificity refers to "…the degree to which critical business processes of one firm are specific to the requirements of the other firm in an interorganizational relationship" (Subramani & Venkatraman, 2003, p. 49).

Business processes could be designed and arranged to meet the idiosyncratic needs of a specific business partner and could revolve around those that involve new product introduction, customer service, inventory management, and quality control, for instance (Subramani & Venkatraman, 2003). In Subramani's fieldwork study, a mattress manufacturer changed its production processes significantly in a number of its plants to put in place a customized build-to-order system that would allow one of its retailers to support a more efficient inventory maintenance system. The intangible and idiosyncratic investments made by this mattress manufacturer apply only to this one retailer. The considerable costs to the mattress manufacturer of accommodating this retailer's unique needs are offset by the fairly high exit barriers for the retailer, which is now highly dependent on this system for its smooth inventory operations (Subramani & Venkatraman, 2003). These unique business processes are normally not transferable to activities a firm conducts with its other trading partners.

A number of recent research studies and papers have highlighted the importance of the business process focus in supply chain management systems, particularly using emerging technologies like RFID.

Radhakrishnan, Zu, and Grover (2008) argue that investments in information technology should be leveraged because of its major impact on a firm, which is more evident when viewed from the business process level. They name five operational process capabilities that reflect the critical primary activities of the value chain: (1) production and operational process capability; (2) product and service enhancement process capability; (3) sales and marketing process capability; (4) supplier relations process capability; and (5) customer relationship process capability. In their study of IT focal firms in North America, they found strong evidence that firms that focused on IT and took measures to effectively diffuse, absorb, manage, and use IT at the process level enjoyed differential business value. Thus, they highly encourage the development of core organizational process capabilities and ensuring that IT innovations and organizational process changes are conducted together.

These findings are echoed by those of McCormack and Johnson (2001) but within the context of a supply chain of electronic trading partners. In their observations of leading edge firms, they have found that investments in IT, by themselves, do not improve supply chain performance. Top performing firms were found to be those that invested in IT that directly supported a business process orientation in designing and maintaining the firms' supply chains. In their study of 90 firms, Lockamy III and McCormack (2004) reiterate the significant relationship between supply chain management maturity and performance. They pursue the concept of supply chain "process maturity" as embodied in the Supply Chain Operations Reference (SCOR) model, one adopted by the Supply Chain Council as a cross-industry standard diagnostic tool for supply chain management.

Supply chain "process maturity" purports that business processes in a supply chain have a life cycle indicated by the extent to which they are defined, managed, measured, and controlled. The SCOR model has the following five levels

of process maturity, with each level representing a certain degree of predictability, capability, control, effectiveness, and maturity. The first one is the "Ad Hoc" level where business practices of value chain partners are unstructured, unpredictable, undefined, and not measured. At this level, supply chain costs are high, there is little horizontal interorganizational linkage, and customer satisfaction is low. The second level is called "Defined," where basic SCM business processes are defined and documented, process performance is predictable, and targets defined but often missed. SCM costs are still high and customer satisfaction improved, though still low. The third level is called "Linked" represents the breakthrough level. There is now evidence of strategic intent in setting out SCM goals, cross-company teams representing customers, suppliers, and others share SCM measures, process performance is predictable, and targets are achieved. SCM costs are declining and customer satisfaction largely improves. The fourth level is "Integrated" where value chain members work collaboratively at the process level. Practices like collaborative forecasting and planning start to emerge. Process performance is predictable and set by cross-firm teams and targets are met most of the time. SCM costs plummet and customer satisfaction achieved to the level of it being a source of competitive advantage. The fifth and highest level is "Extended" where supply chains compete against each other. There is a clear horizontal, customer-oriented, collaborative culture that bonds all supply chain members. Investments in and measurements of process performance of the extended system are both shared among participants, and the benefits are reaped and distributed among them.

Domain Knowledge Specificity

"Domain knowledge specificity" is the degree to which a supplier's critical expertise such as competitive analysis and strategy formulation and new-product development are particular to the requirement of the focal firm in the relationship (Subramani & Venkatraman, 2003). Within a supply chain context, expertise in retail distribution channel management, for instance, would be meaningful to a retailer who might look up to a supplier for guidance in competitive analysis, strategy formulation, and new product conception. Usually, the basis of domain knowledge is "... specialized knowledge [that] is created through social processes that encourage the validation, refinement, and enrichment of knowledge in the context of action..." (Nonaka, 1994).

In Subramani's fieldwork study, for instance, a retailer of women's clothing reported how their supplier's analysis of their retail sales figures helped them better understand varying patterns in size and color customer preferences by region. This, in turn, led to the creation of regional size profiles and more accurate and useful store-level merchandise forecasts for their products. Once again, domain knowledge specificity as demonstrated by this knowledgeable supplier that invested in mining important retailer sales figures in order to extract meaningful insights useful to the retailer in making critical decisions and planning for innovation created a high exit barrier for this specific retailer (Dyer & Singh, 1998).

In so applying its domain knowledge to a specific trading partner, the supplier is really exerting to understand the patterns and rules particular to a specific context. This, in turn, cultivates a supplier's ability to undertake problem diagnosis and resolution with greater sensitivity to its retailer's needs. The resulting knowledge of one's retailer trading partner's unique supply chain needs is subsequently shared among the key personnel of the interacting firms.

In transaction cost theory, resources that need to be dedicated to such specialized business processes are referred to as "relationship-specific investments." Within a supply chain context, greater business process specificity and domain knowledge specificity usually indicate that the supplier is committed to a particular retailer, for instance,

and, thus, would differentiate itself favourably against other competing suppliers. When there is a greater degree of business process specificity and domain knowledge specificity involved, suppliers are even more motivated to include the retailer in joint decision making activities that may favour them (Milgrom & Roberts, 1986), and by interacting more intensively, suppliers could identify opportunities for improving the deployment of their relationship-specific business processes and domain expertise (Dyer & Singh, 1998). Doing so would not only prolong the relationship, but also safeguard the relationship-specific investments the supplier has to make in order to deliver idiosyncratic services and thus, would discourage opportunistic and disloyal behavior on the part of the retailer, who is now accruing increasingly higher switching costs. Performance of interfirm relationships could be strengthened and enhanced by both business process and domain knowledge specificity (Dyer, 1996; Mukhopadhyay & Kekre, 2002; Zaheer & Venkatraman, 1994).

Dependent Variables

Reciprocal Investments

This study focuses on the use of reciprocal investments in inter-organizational relationships involved in supply chain integration where different forms of IT are used to enable coordination-intensive electronic linkages. Integrated supply chain systems require high levels of commitment in order to put in place the right IT infrastructure consisting of aligned business processes, networking connections, global data schema, shared business applications, etc... (Grover & Saeed, 2007). Interfacing processes between and among firms could be highly idiosyncratic to allow a seamless sharing of both information and business applications across the supply chain. Eventually, trading partners will have to face the choice of making reciprocal investments, which are transaction-specific investments made by trading partners in a business exchange relationship (Artz, 1999). In transaction cost theory, reciprocal investments are also associated with the concept of "asset specificity" which refers to "...durable investments that are undertaken in support of particular transactions...." (Williamson, 1985, p. 55). Asset specific investments or reciprocal investments may take various forms --- financial, physical, or relationship-based resources (Morgan & Hunt, 1994). Examples of such investments could include modification of internal manufacturing processes to accommodate a specific customer's product design requirements or configuring an information systems, such as vendor-managed inventory or continuous replenishment systems for high value customers (Zhao, Huo, Flynn, & Yeung, 2008). Reciprocal investments usually signal the intention of trading partners to commit to a stable, long-term relationship (Moore, 1998; Anderson &Weitz, 1992). Since the resources are idiosyncratic and unique to the electronic relationship, these transaction-specific assets are difficult, if not impossible to redeploy elsewhere if the relationship ceases to exist (Joshi & Stump, 1999; Heide, 1994).

Williamson (1996) suggested that a mutual reliance relationship develops when both parties invest assets in each other and put them at risk, thus, discouraging the occurrence of opportunistic behaviors on either side. Thus, reciprocal investments appear to reduce the transaction costs associated with writing, monitoring, and enforcing contractual agreements (Bromiley & Cummings, 1991) and encourage long-term, stable cooperative relationships (Zaheer & Venkatraman, 1995). When a focal firm makes such investments in a small number of business exchange partners, the intention to commit is even more credible (Bakos & Brynjolfsson, 1993).

Relational Interaction

Relational interaction routines are defined as a combination of both formal and informal mecha-

nisms used to facilitate the exchange of information and knowledge between a focal firm and its trading partners (Patnayakuni, Rai, & Seth, 2006). Organizational routines are a formalized set of procedures put in place so that the firms in the relationship could explore opportunities for improvement by promoting predictable task performance and enabling coordination patterns, process configurations, and communication processes that support the sharing of information and knowledge (Davenport & Prusak, 2000; Grant, 1996). One such opportunity lies in planning and coordinating supply chain activities using information flows (Okhuysen & Eisenhardt, 2002). Siemnieniuch et al. (1999) in fact, found that the integration of information flows between supply chain partners, in fact, resulted when the firms focused on know-how involved in collaborative planning. Within a supply chain context, organizational practices usually dictate the collective and distributed capability of coordinating among trading partners (Orlikowski, 2002).

There is evidence of the continuing relevance of relational interaction in interorganizational supply chain based relationships. In their study of business units of enterprises embedded in customer and channel partner ties in the high-tech and financial services industries, Saraf, Langdon, and Gosain (2007) found that knowledge sharing with channel partners and business process coupling with customers were both significantly associated with business performance. In their study of supply chain integration between 617 Chinese manufacturers and their customers, Zhao, Huo, Flynn, and Yeung (2008) found that customers committed to their suppliers more readily cooperate with them by sharing information and integrating inter-organizational business processes. Customer integration appeared to be more readily achieved using these relational interaction routines when there existed a congruence in values and norms between customers and manufacturers and an intrinsic desire to invest in a long-term relationship. Among the multiple results of the Wang and

Wei (2007) study of 150 large- and medium-sized Taiwanese firms, it was found that building an aligned supply chain relationship based on trust facilitates information exchange that leads to information visibility, which, in turn, enables greater supply chain flexibility.

A survey of 819 manufacturing and service industry supply chain professionals from North America, Europe, and Asia focused on four key issues under the umbrella of strategic supplier relationship management as a way of maximizing and optimizing buyer-supplier interactions (Day & Webb, 2006). One of these issues was management of different types of supply chain relationships and the relational interaction routines with specific segments of a firm's supplier base that were deemed very important. Of particular interest was how to manage "breakthrough" partners or suppliers (no more than 10 firms) and "development suppliers" (from 10 to 40 firms). Breakthrough suppliers have a significant impact on the customer firm success. Development suppliers are still important and customer firms have a high expectation of a continuing relationship building up towards closer interdependence and integration. Relational interaction routines would need to be in place to pursue the design of relationship management strategies requiring negotiations over such delicate concerns as performance measurement using balanced scorecards, setting target goals, sharing performance benefits, among others.

Moderator Variables

Information Technology (IT) Infrastructure Integration Capability

IT infrastructure integration is defined as the degree to which a focal firm has established IT capabilities for the consistent and high-velocity transfer of supply chain-related information within and across its boundaries. This study closely looks at the IT infrastructure integration requirements needed to support the use of RFID within a supply chain context. The formative construct introduced by Rai, Patnayakuni, and Seth (2006) was adopted in this study and used both conceptually and in the instrumentation as well. They define IT infrastructure integration in terms of two subconstructs, data consistency and cross-functional SCM application systems integration. The IT infrastructure needed to support RFID systems should be able to provide real-time information visibility, made possible by collecting data at much lower levels of granularity made possible by RFID. The criticality of data consistency is underlined by this quote: "... having good, usable, uniform data is the foundation for sharing and processing data to achieve a collaborative, tighter, supply chain" (Pagarkar et al., 2005, p. 19). Also, initiatives like Global Data Synchronisation (GDS) will facilitate the achievement of data consistency by synchronizing master data that uniquely describe the product or services being exchanged among trading partners (Patni Americas, Inc., 2008; Holloway, 2006; Pagarkar et al., 2005). The expected "data overload" that will occur with the collection of RFID data only amplifies the need for data consistency. Other data consistency issues include: 1) missing data attributes: some data attributes needed by retailers, for instance, are not being provided by their suppliers; 2) dissimilar data characteristics: lack of data similarity may be due to a variety of things --- different field sizes, different data formats, etc.; 3) varying data nomenclature used: trading partners use different data field names so much so that even if the data entity contains all required attributes, valid data being transmitted from one trading partner might still be rejected by the RFID system of another trading partner --- a major problem if specific values for certain fields are expected to trigger downstream transaction processing (Shutzberg, 2004).

1. **Data consistency:** The extent to which data has been commonly defined and stored in consistent form in databases linked by supply chain business processes is referred to as

data consistency (Rai, Patnayakuni, & Seth, 2006). Data consistency is a key requirement in creating a data architecture that defines the structure of the data and the relationships among data entities that is fundamental in establishing inter-organizational data sharing (Van Den Hoven, 2004). Simchi-Levi, Kaminsky, and Simchi-Levi (2004) note that recently, many suppliers and retailers observed that despite the lack of variation in customer demand for products, inventory and back-order levels vary, nevertheless, across many supply chains, oddly enough. This observed variability up and down the supply chain is called the "bullwhip effect" (Moyaux & Chaib-draa, 2007; Simchi-Levi, Kaminsky, & Simchi-Levi, 2004). Sharing consistent data upstream and downstream in the supply chain is one major solution to overcoming the bullwhip effect.

Data from legacy systems of supply chain trading partners need to be accessed to produce useful, integrated data, and to be able to transport this data into various dataware-house structures. Often, data from diverse sources is inconsistent and unusable for the integration purposes required for supply-chain wide initiatives.

2. **Cross-functional SCM application systems integration:** Cross-functional supply chain management applications systems integration is defined by Malhotra, Gosain, and El Sawy (2005) as the level of real-time communication of a hub firm's functional applications that are linked within an SCM context and their exchanges with enterprise resource planning (ERP) and other related inter-enterprise initiatives like customer relationship management (CRM) applications. At the lowest level, an ERP system is essential in enabling the seamless integration of information flows and business process across functional areas of a focal firm --- this

is normally referred to as "ERP I" (Law & Ngai, 2007). ERP functionalities are important control and management mechanisms that are connected with the ERP systems of the firm's trading partner --- referred to as "ERP II". ERP implementations are growing more extensive and interconnected among firms in linked value chains. Karimi, Somers, and Bhattacherjee (2007) found that ERP projects with greater functional, organizational, or geographic scope result in higher positive shareholder returns.

To obtain optimum results, supply chain trading partners have to inevitably approach a collaborative posture in their relationships which would rely heavily on cross-functional interenterprise integration. To facilitate the realization of this goal, the Supply Chain Council (SCC), a not-for-profit corporation, has endorsed the Supply Chain Operations Reference Model (SCOR) as the cross-industry standard for supply chain management (Holloway, 2006).

The SCOR model encompasses the business processes involved in five distinct areas: 1) demand/supply planning and management; 2) sourcing stocked, make-to-order, and engineer-to-order products; 3) make-to-stock, make-to-order, and engineer-to-order production execution; 4) order, warehouse, transportation and installation management for stocked, make-to-order, and engineer-to-order products; and 5) return of raw materials (to suppliers) and receipt of returns of finished goods (from customers), including defective products, maintenance, operations, and repair products, and excess products (Holloway, 2006). This model is used as a reference model by firms in order to address, improve, and communicate supply chain management practices among trading partners. Collaborative supply chain endeavours that involve coordinating inter-firm business processes to achieve supply chain wide integration are facilitated by tools like the SCOR model.

Supply Chain Process Integration Capability

In this study, supply chain process integration is defined following the construct used by Malhotra, Gosain, and El Sawy (2005): the degree to which a hub firm has integrated the flow of information (Lee, Padmanabhan, & Whang, 1997), physical materials (Stevens, 1990), and financial information (Mabert & Venkatraman, 1998) with its value chain trading partners. This formative construct has three subconstruct components: information flow integration, physical flow integration, and financial flow integration (Mangan, Lalwani, & Butcher, 2008).

Information has the potential to reduce variability in the supply chain, enable suppliers to make better forecasts (i.e., more accurately accounting for effects of promotions and market changes, for instance), enable the coordination of manufacturing and distribution strategies, enable lead time reduction, and enable retailers to service their customers better by providing preferred items and avoiding out of stock situations (Simchi-Levi, Kaminsky, & Simchi-Levi, 2004).

This study uses the construct, information flow integration, to mean the degree to which a firm exchanges operational, tactical, and strategic information with its supply chain trading partners (Malhotra, Gosain, & El Sawy, 2005). The instrument used in this study measures the sharing of production and delivery schedules, performance metrics, demand forecasts, actual sales data, and inventory data, for information flow integration.

Malhotra, Gosain, and El Sawy (2005) define physical flow integration as the level to which the hub firm uses global optimization with its value chain partners to manage the flow and stocking of materials and finished goods. Raw materials, subassemblies, and finished goods constitute downstream physical flows, whereas returned products for defects or repairs make up the upstream physical flows. In this study, physical flow integration is measured in terms of multi-echelon

optimization of costs, just-in-time deliveries, joint management of inventory with suppliers and logistics partners, and distribution network configuration for optimal staging of inventory (Malhotra, Gosain, & El Sawy, 2005).

Financial flow integration is defined as the level to which a hub firm and its trading partners exchange financial resources in a manner driven by workflow events (Malhotra, Gosain, & El Sawy, 2005). Value chain participants that do not have well-designed business processes often do not have consistent views of important financial downstream flows such as prices, invoices, credit terms and upstream financial flows that could include payments and account payables (McCormack & Johnson, 2003).

Accurate financial flows are enabled by event-based workflow systems that trigger electronic payments, for instance, upon delivery of goods. Interacting business processes within a value chain should be reengineered so that participating firms can experience the following benefits: (1) reduce the costs of billing, payment processing, and dispute handling; (2) shorten the invoicing and receivables cycle time; (3) accelerate the rate of payments; (4) make relevant financial information accessible for high-level decision making; (5) improve customer relationships by gathering information on customer preferences with billing and invoicing transactions; and (6) positively influence revenue growth by improving cash flow availability for various reasons like production ramp-up with spikes in customer demand or develop new products/services for innovation (Greenfield, Patel, & Fenner, 2001).

In this study, the financial flow integration items measure the automatic triggering of both accounts receivables and accounts payables (Malhotra, Gosain, & El Sawy, 2005). Waiman, Chu, and Du (2009) view RFID as a technology solution that could help reduce the latency gaps between material and information flows in the supply chain, which move along separate paths in the supply chain. Physical flow of materials trigger data capturing from the relevant node in the business chain and product movement information is filtered into a repository stored in an Internet-based repository via a portal which is accessible to all authorized trading partners. RFID tags can help logistics service providers, for instance, get real-time logistics and distribution, field service, warehousing, shipping, and transportation data from its trading partners participating in their value chain. The synchronization of the two flows, in turn, will lead to competent make-to-order or engineering-to-order manufacturing, efficient vendor management inventory, and better customer demand management.

HYPOTHESES TO BE TESTED

This study purports to test the following hypotheses:

H1: The positive relationship between business process specificity and reciprocal investments will be moderated by IT infrastructure integration --- i.e., the higher the level of IT infrastructure integration, the greater the positive relationship between business process specificity and reciprocal investments.

H2: The positive relationship between domain knowledge specificity and reciprocal investments will be moderated by IT infrastructure integration --- i.e., the higher the level of IT infrastructure integration, the greater the positive relationship between domain knowledge specificity and reciprocal investments.

H3: The positive relationship between business process specificity and reciprocal investments will be moderated by supply chain process integration --- i.e., the higher the level of supply chain process integration, the greater the positive relationship between business process specificity and reciprocal investments.

H4: The positive relationship between domain knowledge specificity and reciprocal investments will be moderated by supply chain process integration --- i.e., the higher the level of supply chain process integration, the greater the positive relationship between domain knowledge specificity and reciprocal investments.

H5: The positive relationship between business process specificity and relational interaction will be moderated by IT infrastructure integration --- i.e., the higher the level of IT infrastructure integration, the greater the positive relationship between business process specificity and relational interaction.

H6: The positive relationship between domain knowledge specificity and relational interaction will be moderated by IT infrastructure integration --- i.e., the higher the level of IT infrastructure integration, the greater the positive relationship between domain knowledge specificity and relational interaction.

H7: The positive relationship between business process specificity and relational interaction will be moderated by supply chain process integration --- i.e., the higher the level of supply chain process integration, the greater the positive relationship between business process specificity and relational interaction.

H8: The positive relationship between domain knowledge specificity and relational interaction will be moderated by supply chain process integration --- i.e., the higher the level of supply chain process integration, the greater the positive relationship between domain knowledge specificity and relational interaction.

RESEARCH METHODOLOGY

Data for this pilot research study was collected using a survey questionnaire administered online to members of the Council of Supply Chain

Management Professionals (CSCMP). The data analyzed for this paper was drawn from a convenience sample of 115 firms that responded to a certain part of the survey questionnaire --- these are organizations that had not yet implemented RFID but are knowledgeable about it or may be implementing RFID in the future. The specific items used for business process specificity and domain knowledge specificity were borrowed from Subramani (2004), while the items for IT infrastructure integration (i.e., data consistency and cross-functional application integration) and supply chain process integration were borrowed from Rai, Patnayakuni, and Seth (2006). The items for reciprocal investments were borrowed from Son, Narasimhan, and Riggins (2005), while the items for relational interaction were borrowed from Patnayakuni, Rai, and Seth (2006).

Since the organizations have not yet implemented RFID, the survey respondent was asked to indicate their perceptions of the importance of the business process specificity, domain knowledge specificity, reciprocal investments, and relational interaction. The same approach was used in anticipating their perceptions of the use of the RFID system in achieving data consistency, cross-functional application integration, and supply chain process integration. Seven-point Likert scales were used with minimum-maximum anchoring points appropriate to the construct being measured. The computer program SPSS version 15 was used in conducting a series of simple regression data analyses and their associated moderated regression analysis runs.

Data Measurement Properties

The internal consistency of the items constituting each construct was assessed using Cronbach's alpha and the results are in conformance with Nunnally's (1978) guidelines of getting values of .70 or above. Generally speaking, the items have internal consistency with values beyond the .70 threshold recommended. The different variables

used in the study showed the following reliability results: business process specificity (Cronbach alpha=.954); domain knowledge specificity (Cronbach alpha=.948); reciprocal investments (Cronbach alpha=.964); relational interaction (Cronbach alpha=.962); data consistency (Cronbach alpha=.944); cross-functional application integration (Cronbach alpha=.930); financial flow integration (Cronbach alpha=.820); physical flow integration (Cronbach alpha=.975); and information flow integration (Cronbach alpha=.965).

To establish convergent and divergent validity, the item-to-total correlations of the constructs were examined and, in general, the specific items have a stronger correlation with the construct than with other items (Rai, Patnayakuni, & Seth, 2006).

Sample Profile Description

The convenience sample consists of a total of 115 firms from the membership of the Council of Supply Chain Management Professionals that responded to a certain part of the survey questionnaire --- these were the firms that constitute the convenience sample of organizations that are knowledgeable about RFID or may be implementing RFID in the future. About 51.06 percent of the firms had 1,000 or less employees and 32.62 percent had more than 1,000 employees. The following profile shows the membership of the firms in different industry sectors: service (78.57 percent), manufacturing (21.43 percent).

Moderated Regression Procedure

Moderated regression analysis tests whether the relationship between two variables changes depending on the value of another variable (i.e., interaction effect) (Aguinis, 2004). The moderator variable explains changes in the nature of independent variable to the dependent variable effect, and provides information concerning the conditions under which an effect or relationship is likely to be stronger.

Regression analysis was conducted to test the hypotheses presented in this study. The moderated regression procedure requires testing first order effects, which in this study, will be referred to as "model 1." A model 1 simple regression tests the direct effects of a predictor variable on a dependent variable. Simple regressions, therefore, were run between the independent variables, business process specificity and domain knowledge specificity, and each of the dependent variables, reciprocal investments and relational interaction. The variance in the dependent variable on account of the independent variable is noted using the R^2 value. Then, the regression procedure testing second order effects is conducted, which will be referred to as "model 2" in this study. A model 2 regression duplicates the model 1 regression equation and adds the product term which includes the hypothesized moderator variable.

It is important to determine how large the change in R^2 should be in order to qualify as "practically significant" or one that should merit serious attention (Aguinis, 2004). After conducting a Monte Carlo simulation, Evans (1985) stipulated that "...a rough rule would be to take 1% variance explained as the criterion as to whether or not a significant interaction exists in the model...." (p. 320). Evans found that in conducting the simulation, when the population scores included a moderating effect, results based on samples consistently demonstrated an R^2 change that was 1 percent or higher. On the other hand, when the population scores did not include a moderating effect, the change in R^2 was usually smaller than 1 percent. In conclusion, empirical and simulation results appear to indicate that a statistically significant R^2 change of about 1 percent to 2 percent demonstrates an effect size worthy of consideration. The results in this study include significant R^2 change values within the range with a maximum value of 5.7 percent and a smaller value of 2.3 percent, which indicate considerable significant moderating effects of IT infrastructure integration and supply chain process integration.

SPSS was used to run the regression equations and model 1 was specified for block 1 and model 2 was specified for block 2. The resulting R^2 values need to be noted for models 1 and 2. If the R^2 value is greater for model 2 than for model 1, then, the moderator variable included in the product term is demonstrating a moderating effect.

FINDINGS

Both IT infrastructure integration and supply chain process integration more effectively moderate the relationship between business process specificity and domain knowledge specificity and only one of the two dependent variables, relational interaction. Between IT infrastructure integration and supply chain process integration, however, the former was able to moderate the relationship between both business process specificity and domain knowledge specificity and the dependent variable, relational interaction.

RFID System Dependent Variables: Reciprocal Investments and Relational Interaction

IT Infrastructure Integration Capability as Moderator Variable

More substantial results are shown here based on the percent R^2 change resulting from the introduction of a product term, ITIntegrate3Cat1, in the regression equation. This is the nominal variable that represents the mean of data consistency and cross-functional process integration, the two components of IT infrastructure integration. Tables 1 through 8 show the results of running two regression models: model 1 (column two of all tables) showing the relationships between the two independent variables, business process specificity and domain knowledge specificity, and the two dependent variables, reciprocal investments and relational interaction, without the product term, and model 2 (column three of all tables), the regression results with the inclusion of the product term.

Table 1 shows the results with business process specificity as independent variable, reciprocal investments as the dependent variable. IT infrastructure integration, in this case, the proposed moderator variable, in fact, does not effectively moderate the relationship between the independent and dependent variables. The percentage variance explained by the moderator variable with the product term as shown in model 2 (column 3) is a miniscule 0.1 percent and is insignificant. The table column labelled "% Variance Explained by Moderator with Product Term" indicates the contribution of the product term --- which is the product of the moderator variable, in this case, IT infrastructure integration and the specific predictor variable. And so, for instance, in the case of Table 1, the product term would be the product of business process specificity and IT infrastructure integration (i.e., BusProcSpec3XITCat1). The next column label shows "F Value of Model 2 (degrees of freedom), which means that the F value of model 2 which includes the product term is shown along with the degrees of freedom for that regression model. The significance of the F change from model 1 to model 2 is indicated by the last column. In the case of Table 1, the significance of F change (0.1 percent) is p<.695, indicating an insignificant result.

The relationships between the predictor and the dependent variables as moderated by IT infrastructure integration should be interpreted accordingly. Let's take the case of Table 1 once again. About 39.5 percent of the variance in reciprocal investments is explained by business process specificity and IT infrastructure integration as indicated by model 1 in Table 1. Model 2 is, then, introduced by including the product term (i.e., BusProcSpec3X-ITCat1) which represents the interaction between business process specificity and IT infrastructure integration, and the R^2 value here changes to 39.6 percent. As shown on Table 1, the addition of the product term resulted in a very small R^2 change of 0.1 percent, $F(3, 111) = 24.208$, p<.695. This result supports the absence of a moderating effect by IT infrastructure integration.

Table 5, which depicts the relationship between domain knowledge specificity and reciprocal investments, shows a similar result with that of Table 1--- IT infrastructure integration does not moderate the relationship significantly in this case as well (p < .819).

The situation changes, however, when relational interaction is the dependent variable.

Table 3 shows a significant moderating effect by IT infrastructure integration between business process specificity and relational interaction (p<.02). This means that the higher the level of IT infrastructure integration, the higher the level of relational interaction needed in RFID

Table 1. Moderated regression for reciprocal investments with IT infrastructure integration as moderator (N=115)

IV: Business Process Specificity					
DV: Reciprocal Investments					
Moderator Variable: ITIntegrate3Cat1 (Nominal variable for the mean of data consistency and cross-functional process integration – IT infrastructure integration)					
Independent Variable	**Model 1: R2 Without Product Term**	**Model 2: R2 With Product Term**	**% Variance Explained by Moderator with Product Term**	**F Value of Model 2 (degrees of freedom)**	**Significance of F Change**
Business Process Specificity	.395	.396	0.1%	24.208 (3,111)	P<.695

Table 2. Moderated regression for reciprocal investments with supply chain process integration as moderator (N=115)

IV: Business Process Specificity					
DV: Reciprocal Investments					
Moderator Variable: SCMIntegrate3Cat1 (Nominal variable for the mean of information flow integration, physical flow integration, and financial flow integration)					
Independent Variable	**Model 1: R2 Without Product Term**	**Model 2: R2 With Product Term**	**% Variance Explained by Moderator with Product Term**	**F Value of Model 2 (degrees of freedom)**	**Significance of F Change**
Business Process Specificity	.369	.379	1%	23.216 (3,114)	P<.178

systems requiring business process specificity. IT infrastructure integration, when introduced in the product term, contributes 3.7 percent to the variance in relational interaction when in relationship with business process specificity. In other words, the moderating effect of IT infrastructure integration explains 3.7 percent of the variance in the increase of relational interaction over and above the variance explained by business process specificity and IT infrastructure integration as separate independent variables.

Table 7 exhibits a similar finding: IT infrastructure integration effectively and significantly (p<.002) moderates the relationship between domain knowledge specificity and relational interaction. Similarly, the higher the level of IT infrastructure integration, the higher the level of

relational interaction needed in RFID systems requiring domain knowledge specificity.

RFID System Dependent Variables: Reciprocal Investments and Relational Interaction

Supply Chain Process Integration Capability as Moderator Variable

As Table 2, Table 4, Table 6, and Table 8 show, supply chain process integration does not have as much impact as IT infrastructure integration in moderating the relationships between the predictor and dependent variables.

Table 2 shows the relationship between business process specificity and reciprocal investments, which is not significantly moderated by

Table 3. Moderated regression for relational interaction with IT infrastructure integration as moderator (N=115)

IV: Business Process Specificity					
DV: Relational Interaction					
Moderator Variable: ITIntegrate3Cat1 (Nominal variable for the mean of data consistency and cross-functional process integration – IT infrastructure integration)					
Independent Variable	**Model 1: R2 Without Product Term**	**Model 2: R2 With Product Term**	**% Variance Explained by Moderator with Product Term**	**F Value of Model 2 (degrees of freedom)**	**Significance of F Change**
Business Process Specificity	.270	.307	3.7%	16.415 (3,111)	P<.017

Table 4. Moderated regression for relational interaction with supply chain process integration as moderator (N=115)

IV: Business Process Specificity					
DV: Relational Interaction					
Moderator Variable: SCMIntegrate3Cat1 (Nominal variable for the mean of information flow integration, physical flow integration, and financial information flow integration – supply chain process integration)					
Independent Variable	**Model 1: R2 Without Product Term**	**Model 2: R2 With Product Term**	**% Variance Explained by Moderator with Product Term**	**F Value of Model 2 (degrees of freedom)**	**Significance of F Change**
Business Process Specificity	.369	.379	1%	23.216 (3,114)	P<.178

Table 5. Moderated regression for reciprocal investments with IT infrastructure integration as moderator (N=115)

IV: Domain Knowledge Specificity					
DV: Reciprocal Investments					
Moderator Variable: ITIntegrate3Cat1 (Nominal variable for the mean of data consistency and cross-functional process integration – IT infrastructure integration)					
Independent Variable	**Model 1: R2 Without Product Term**	**Model 2: R2 With Product Term**	**% Variance Explained by Moderator with Product Term**	**F Value of Model 2 (degrees of freedom)**	**Significance of F Change**
Domain Knowledge Specificity	.353	.353	0%	20.209 (3,111)	P<.819

supply chain process integration. Model 1 in this regression, which depicts business process specificity and supply chain process integration as independent predictors, account for 36.9 percent in the variance of reciprocal investments. Adding the product term (i.e., BusProcess3XSCMCat1) in model 2 leads to the 1 percent variance explained by the moderator with the product term (i.e., R^2 = .379), but is insignificant (p<.178). Table 6 shows a similar result for domain knowledge specificity as the predictor variable and reciprocal investments as dependent variable. Model 1 in this table shows that domain knowledge specificity and supply chain process integration account for 34.3 percent in the variance of reciprocal investments. The introduction of the product term in model 2 ever so slightly improves the R^2 to 34.5 percent, accounting for only 0.2 percent

variance explained by the moderator with the product term, which happens to be insignificant (p<.646).

Supply chain process integration successfully moderates the relationship between domain knowledge specificity and relational interaction, however (Table 8). As independent predictor variables, domain knowledge specificity and supply chain process integration explain 27.3 percent of the variance in relational interaction (i.e., model 1). With the addition of the product term, the R^2 increases to 29.6 percent (i.e., model 2), thus indicating that the moderator with the product term explained an additional 2.3 percent in the variance of relational interaction. Moreover, the F change is significant at the .10 level (p<.057). Thus, the higher the level of supply chain process integration, the higher the level of relational inter-

Table 6. Moderated regression for reciprocal investments with supply chain process integration as moderator (N=115)

IV: Domain Knowledge Specificity					
DV: Reciprocal Investments					
Moderator Variable: SCMIntegrate3Cat1 (Nominal variable for the mean of information flow integration, physical flow integration, and financial flow integration – supply chain process integration)					
Independent Variable	Model 1: R2 Without Product Term	Model 2: R2 With Product Term	% Variance Explained by Moderator with Product Term	F Value of Model 2 (degrees of freedom)	Significance of F Change
Domain Knowledge Specificity	.343	.345	0.2%	19.984 (3,114)	P<.646

Table 7. Moderated regression for relational interaction with IT infrastructure integration as moderator (N=115)

IV: Domain Knowledge Specificity					
DV: Relational Interaction					
Moderator Variable: ITIntegrate3Cat1 (Nominal variable for the mean of data consistency and cross-functional process integration – IT infrastructure integration)					
Independent Variable	Model 1: R2 Without Product Term	Model 2: R2 With Product Term	% Variance Explained by Moderator with Product Term	F Value of Model 2 (degrees of freedom)	Significance of F Change
Domain Knowledge Specificity	.311	.368	5.7%	21.577 (3,111)	P<.002

action needed in RFID systems requiring domain knowledge specificity.

Table 4, however, shows that supply chain process integration does not significantly moderate the relationship between business process specificity and relational interaction. In model 1 of this regression, business process specificity and supply chain process integrated accounted for 36.90 percent in the variance of relational interaction, as independent variables. With the introduction of the product term (i.e., BusProcess3XSCMCat1) in model 2, the R^2 increases to 37.90 percent or a 1 percent increase in the variance explained by the moderator. However, the change in F is not significant for model 2 (p<.178).

DISCUSSION OF FINDINGS

Only hypotheses 5, 6, and 8 were positively confirmed in this study. IT infrastructure integration has been effective in moderating the relationship between both business process specificity and relational interaction, and domain knowledge specificity and also, relational interaction. This means that the higher the level of IT infrastructure integration, the higher the level of relational interaction needed in RFID systems requiring both business process specificity and domain knowledge specificity. On the other hand, supply chain process integration has effectively moderated the relationship between domain knowledge specificity and relational interaction. Similarly, this means that the higher the level of supply chain process integration, the higher the level of

Table 8. Moderated regression for relational interaction with supply chain process integration as moderator (N=115)

IV: Domain Knowledge Specificity					
DV: Relational Interaction					
Moderator Variable: SCMIntegrate3Cat1 (Nominal variable for the mean of information flow integration, physical flow integration, and financial flow integration – supply chain process integration					
Independent Variable	**Model 1: R2 Without Product Term**	**Model 2: R2 With Product Term**	**% Variance Explained by Moderator with Product Term**	**F Value of Model 2 (degrees of freedom)**	**Significance of F Change**
Domain Knowledge Specificity	.273	.296	2.3%	15.989 (3,114)	P<.057

relational interaction needed in RFID systems requiring domain knowledge specificity.

The study findings clearly indicate the salience of relational interaction more so than reciprocal investments. The descriptive data shows that the reported means for relational interaction items were greater than the means for reciprocal investments: 1) relational interaction (item 1 mean = 4.65; item 2 mean=4.61; item 3 mean=4.84; item 4 mean-4.61; overall mean for relational interaction = 4.6775); reciprocal investments (item 1 mean= 3.67; item 2 mean= 3.93; item 3 mean = 4.00; overall mean for reciprocal investments = 3.8667). A one sample T test indicates a significant difference between the relational interaction and reciprocal investments means (p<.000). It appears that the relationships between the respondent firms and their trading partners (TP) are in the early stages of development as study respondents are not yet confident that their TPs would make the reciprocal investments needed for education in the use of RFID, initial support in developing RFID linkages, and exchanging business documents using the RFID linkages within a long-term partnership context. Study participants expressed more self-assurance that both their firm and their TPs would have relational interaction routines that would put in place organizational mechanisms that would facilitate information exchange, encourage quality and improvement initiatives, sharing of best practices, and learning about new technolo-

gies and markets. It is important to note that it is not necessary to make asset specific and trading partner-specific reciprocal investments in order to put these relational interaction routines in place. Firms could use digital and electronic linkages that already have in place in dealing with other supply chain trading partners to support relational interaction coordination mechanisms.

IMPLICATIONS FOR MANAGERS AND STUDY LIMITATIONS

These findings affirm the importance of both the IT infrastructure integration and supply chain process integration elements that undergird RFID system implementation. Managers also need to be aware current developments directly relate to these elements of the infrastructure environment as their firms seek either or both operational efficiency and market knowledge creation. In one of the later meetings of GS1, a nonprofit organization that coordinates the development of standards for technologies like barcodes and RFID, a key issue was "data synchronization" or the ability to share accurate data throughout the supply chain which would require data consistency (Roberti, 2008). Planning for the design or reengineering of business processes to achieve cross-functional process integration and supply chain process integration is also a very involved activity as well and one taken seriously by leading-edge firms. Anthony Bigornia, IBM Consulting Services, indicated that firms that will drive the most learning from their RFID implementations are those that address business process issues directly (Wasserman, 2005). ChainLink Research, a research and consulting firm focusing on supply chains, found that more than 40 percent of the manufacturing firms participating in their study are implementing RFID to pursue process improvement goals specifically in the following areas: manufacturing and plant-floor operations; outbound shipping; distribution and logistics; invoice and dispute resolution; service and support; supply chain and custody tracking (which includes e-pedigrees, or electronic documents used to trace a product's manufacturing and distribution history); recall and product expiration; and asset and capital-equipment tracking (Bacheldor, 2006). About five levels of business process integration have been identified for RFID systems: level 1 (goal setting assessment); level 2 (slap and ship); level 3 (application integration); level 4 (business process improvement); and level 5 (collaborative business intelligence) (Blossom, 2005). Cross-functional application integration and supply chain process integration are both clear issues in levels 3 and 4. Application integration must be planned for carefully because of the need to use preprogrammed adapters or plug-ins that will need to deliver RFID data to enterprise resource planning (ERP), customer relationship management (CRM), supply chain management (SCM), other files, databases, and systems (Blossom, 2005). Managers should also be aware of new technologies such as the use of smart RFID networks that would allow the use of event-driven RFID business applications and react to real-time information and assist the movement to level 4 or the improvement of business processes (Bhargava, 2007). Complex RFID services could be delivered using real-time events such as pushing alerts to a retail store manager when inventory for a particular product is aging or has reached "stale" status.

Considering the scale and scope of RFID systems within a supply chain context, managers need to anticipate the processing of the escalating numbers of events created by RFID technologies that will eventually lead to the generation of increasingly complex business rules that will govern the routing and analysis of signals included in the event stream (Blossom, 2005).

The study has a number of limitations. First of all, study participants that were knowledgeable about RFID or may be implementing RFID in the future were asked to report their perceptions of the importance of IT infrastructure integration and supply chain process integration, relational interaction, reciprocal investments, business process specificity, and domain knowledge specificity. A future study should capture these perceptions from firms that have actually implemented RFID systems. Second, the data was gleaned from a convenience sample of 115 firms. A random sample is needed in order to arrive at representative implications and generalizations.

REFERENCES

Aguinis, H. (2004). *Regression Analysis for Categorical Moderators*. New York: The Guilford Press.

Anderson, E., & Weitz, B. (1992). The use of pledge to build and sustain commitment in distribution channels. *JMR, Journal of Marketing Research, 29*(1), 18–34. doi:10.2307/3172490

Artz, K. W. (1999). Buyer-Supplier Performance: The Role of Asset Specificity, Reciprocal Investments and Relational Exchange. *British Journal of Management, 10*, 113–126. doi:10.1111/1467-8551.00114

Bacheldor, B. (2006). Process Improvement Drives Manufacturers' RFID Implementations. *RFID Journal*. Retrieved July 1, 2008, from http://www.rfidjournal.com/article/articleview/2903/1/1/

Bakos, J. Y., & Brynjolfsson, E. (1993). Information technology, incentives, and the optimal number of suppliers. *Journal of Management Information Systems, 10*(2), 37–53.

Barratt, M., & Choi, T. (2007). Mandated RFID and institutional responses: cases of decentralized business units. *Production and Operations Management, 16*(5), 569–585.

Bhargava, H. (2007). Building Smart RFID Networks. *RFID Journal*. Retrieved July 7, 2008, from http://www.rfidjournal.com/article/articleview/3387/1/82/

Blanchard, D. (2008, May). Wal-Mart Lays Down the Law. *Industry Week*, 71–74.

Blossom, P. (2005, January 24). Levels of RFID Maturity, Part 2. *RFID Journal*. Retrieved July 5, 2008, from http://www.rfidjournal.com/article/articleview/1347/1/82/

Bromiley, P., & Cummings, L. L. (1991). *Transaction Costs in Organizations with Trust (Tech. Rep.)*. University of Minnesota, Department of Strategic Management and Organization.

Cannon, A. R., Reyes, P. M., Frazier, G. V., & Prater, E. L. (2008). RFID in the contemporary supply chain: multiple perspectives on its benefits and risks. *International Journal of Operations & Production Management, 28*(5), 433–545. doi:10.1108/01443570810867196

Chang, Y., Cheng, Y., & Lin, B. (2007). An efficient web services –enabled architecture for radio frequency identification environment. *International Journal of Mobile Communications, 5*(6), 646–660. doi:10.1504/IJMC.2007.014179

Chatfield, A. T., & Yetton, P. (2000). Strategic payoff from EDI as a function of EDI embeddedness. *Journal of Management Information Systems, 16*(4), 195–224.

Davenport, T. H. (1993). *Process Innovation: Reengineering Work Through Information Technology*. Boston, MA: Harvard Business School Press.

Davenport, T. H., & Prusak, L. (2000). *Working Knowledge: How Organizations Share What They Know*. Boston, MA: Harvard Business School Press.

Day, M., Magnan, G., Webb, M., & Hughes, J. (2006, April). Strategic Supplier Relationship Management. *Supply Chain Management Review*, 40-48.

Dyer, J. H. (1996). Does governance matter? Keiretsu alliances and asset specificity as sources of Japanese competitive advantage. *Organization Science, 7*, 649–666. doi:10.1287/orsc.7.6.649

Dyer, J. H., & Singh, H. (1998). The Relational View: Cooperative Strategy and Sources of Interorganizational Competitive Advantage. *Academy of Management Review, 23*(4), 660–679. doi:10.2307/259056

Elliott, M. (2005). Yellow light, green light. *Industrial Engineer, 37*, 6.

Evans, M. G. (1985). A Monte Carlo study of the effects of correlated method variance in moderated multiple regression analysis. *Organizational Behavior and Human Decision Processes, 36*, 302–323. doi:10.1016/0749-5978(85)90002-0

Ferguson, R. B. (2006). RFID loses reception: high tag costs are still putting the kibosh on returns on investment. *e-Week, 23*(10), 11-12.

Gaukler, G. M., Seifert, R. W., & Hausman, W. H. (2007). Item-level RFID in the retail supply chain. *Production and Operations Management, 16*(1), 65–76.

Grant, R. (1996, July/August). Prospering in dynamically competitive environments: Organizational capability as knowledge integration. *Organization Science, 7*(4), 375–387. doi:10.1287/orsc.7.4.375

Greenfield, A., Patel, J., & Fenner, J. (2001). Online Invoicing for Business-to-Business Users. *Information Week, November, 863,* 80-82.

Hammer, M., & Champy, J. (1993). *Reengineering the Corporation: A Manifesto for Business Revolution.* London: N. Brealey.

Heide, J. B. (1994). Interorganizational governance in marketing channels. *Journal of Marketing, 58*(1), 71–85. doi:10.2307/1252252

Holloway, S. (2006). *Potential of RFID in the Supply Chain.* Chicago, IL: Solidsoft Ltd.

Jankowska, A. M., Kurbel, K., & Schreber, D. (2007). An architecture for agent-based mobile supply chain management. *International Journal of Mobile Communications, 5*(3), 243–258. doi:10.1504/IJMC.2007.012393

Joshi, A. W., & Stump, R. L. (1999). Determinants of commitment and opportunism: Integrating insights from transaction cost analysis and relational exchange theory. *Canadian Journal of Administrative Sciences, 16*(4), 334–352.

Ju, T. L., Ju, P. H., & Sun, S. Y. (2008). A strategic examination of Radio Frequency Identification in Supply Chain Management. *International Journal of Technology Management, 43*(4), 349–436. doi:10.1504/IJTM.2008.020555

Karimi, J., Somers, T. M., & Bhattacherjee, A. (2007). The Impact of ERP Implementation on Business Process Outcomes: A Factor-Based Study. *Journal of Management Information Systems, 24*(1), 101–134. doi:10.2753/MIS0742-1222240103

Keen, P., & Mackintosh, R. (2001). *The freedom economy: Gaining the m-commerce edge in the era of wireless internet.* New York: Osborne-McGraw Hill.

Kim, E. Y., Ko, E., Kim, H., & Koh, C. E. (2008, October). Comparison of benefits of radio frequency identification: Implications for business strategic performance in the U.S. and Korean retailers. *Industrial Marketing Management, 37*(7), 797–806. doi:10.1016/j.indmarman.2008.01.007

Kinsella, B. (2003). The Wal-Mart factor. *Industrial Engineer, 35,* 32.

Law, C. C. H., & Ngai, E. W. T. (2007). ERP systems adoption: An exploratory study of the organizational factors and impacts of ERP success. *Information & Management, 44,* 418–432. doi:10.1016/j.im.2007.03.004

Lee, D., & Park, J. (2008). RFID-based traceability in the supply chain. *Industrial Management & Data Systems, 108*(6), 713–725. doi:10.1108/02635570810883978

Lee, H. L., Padmanabhan, V., & Whang, S. (1997). Information Distortion in Supply chain: The Bullwhip Effect. *Management Science, 43*(4), 546–558. doi:10.1287/mnsc.43.4.546

Lee, Y. M., Feng, C., & Ying, T. L. (2009, February). A quantitative view on how RFID can improve inventory management in a supply chain. *International Journal of Logistics: Research & Applications, 12*(1), 23–43. doi:10.1080/13675560802141788

Lockamy, A. III, & McCormack, K. (2004). The development of a supply chain management process maturity model using the concepts of business process orientation. *Supply Chain Management: An International Journal, 9*(4), 272–278. doi:10.1108/13598540410550019

Logistics Today. (2008, March). Wal-Mart Says Use RFID Tags or Pay Up. 4.

Mabert, V. A., & Venkatraman, M. A. (1998). Special Research Focus on Supply Chain Linkages: Challenges for Design and Management in the 21st Century. *Decision Sciences, 29*(3), 537–550. doi:10.1111/j.1540-5915.1998.tb01353.x

Malhotra, A., Gosain, S., & El Sawy, O. A. (2005, March). Absorptive Capacity Configurations in Supply Chains: Gearing for Partner-Enabled Market Knowledge Creation. *Management Information Systems Quarterly, 29*(1), 145–187.

Mangan, J., Lalwani, C., & Butcher, T. (2008). *Global Logistics and Supply Chain Management.* Hoboken, NJ: John Wiley & Sons, Inc.

Manufacturing Business Technology. (2006, August). RFID really does reduce stock-outs. 52.

McCormack, K., & Johnson, B. (2001, October). Business process orientation, supply chain management, and the e-corporation. *IIE Solutions,* 33-37.

McCormack, K. P., & Johnson, W. C. (2003). *Supply Chain Networks and Business Process Orientation.* Boca Raton, FL: St. Lucie Press.

Milgrom, P., & Roberts, J. (1986). Relying on the information of interested parties. *The Rand Journal of Economics, 17,* 18–32. doi:10.2307/2555625

Moore, K. R. (1998). Trust and relationship commitment in logistics alliances: a buyer perspective. *International Journal of Purchasing and Materials Management, 34*(2), 211–237.

Morgan, R. M., & Hunt, S. D. (1994). The commitment-trust theory of relationship marketing. *Journal of Marketing, 58*(3), 20–38. doi:10.2307/1252308

Moyaux, T., & Chaib-draa, B. (2007, May). Information sharing as a coordination mechanism for reducing the bullwhip effect in supply chain. *IEEE Transactions on Systems, Man, and Cybernetics, 37*(3), 396–409. doi:10.1109/TSMCC.2006.887014

Mukhopadhyay, T., & Kekre, S. (2002, October). Strategic and Operational Benefits of Electronic Integration in B2B Procurement Processes. *Management Science, 48*(10), 1301–1313. doi:10.1287/mnsc.48.10.1301.273

Nonaka, I. (1994). Dynamic theory of organizational knowledge creation. *Organization Science, 5,* 14–37. doi:10.1287/orsc.5.1.14

Nunnally, J. C. (1978). *Psychometric Theory.* New York: McGraw-Hill.

Okhuysen, G. A., & Eisenhardt, K. M. (2002, August). Integrating knowledge in groups: How formal interventions enable flexibility. *Organization Science, 13*(4), 370–386. doi:10.1287/orsc.13.4.370.2947

Orlikowski, W. J. (2002, May/June). Knowing in practice: Enacting a collective capability in distributed organizing. *Organization Science, 13*(3), 249–273. doi:10.1287/orsc.13.3.249.2776

Pagarkar, M., Natesan, M., & Prakash, B. (2005). *RFID in Integrated Order Management Systems.* Chennai, India: Tata Consultancy Services.

Patnayakuni, R., Rai, A., & Seth, N. (2006). Relational Antecedents of Information Flow Integration for Supply Chain Coordination. *Journal of Management Information Systems, 23*(1), 13–49. doi:10.2753/MIS0742-1222230101

Patni Americas, Inc. (2008). *Thought Paper: Global Data Synchronization: A Foundation Block for Realizing RFID Potential.* Cincinnati, OH: Patni Americas, Inc. Retrieved July 24, 2008, from http://www.patni.com/resource-center/collateral/RFID/tp_RFID_Global-Data-Synchronization.html

Powell, T. C., & Dent-Micaleff, A. (1997). Information technology as competitive advantage: the role of human, business, and technology resources. *Strategic Management Journal, 18*(5), 375–405. doi:10.1002/(SICI)1097-0266(199705)18:5<375::AID-SMJ876>3.0.CO;2-7

Radhakrishnan, A., Zu, X., & Grover, V. (2008). A process-oriented perspective on differential business value creation by information technology: An empirical investigation. *Omega, 36*, 1105–1125. doi:10.1016/j.omega.2006.06.003

Rai, A., Patnayakuni, R., & Seth, N. (2006, June). Firm Performance Impacts of Digitally Enabled Supply Chain Integration Capabilities. *Management Information Systems Quarterly, 30*(2), 225–246.

Roberti, M. (2005). Wal-Mart to expand RFID tagging requirement. *RFID Journal.* Retrieved April 9, 2007, from http://www.rfidjournal.com/article/articleview/1930/1/1/

Roberti, M. (2008). Laying the Foundation for RFID. *RFID Journal.* Retrieved August 10, 2008, from http://www.rfidjournal.com/article/articleview/3524/1/435/

Sabbaghi, A., & Vaidyanathan, G. (2008). Effectiveness and efficiency of RFID technology in supply chain management: Strategic values and challenges. *Journal of Theoretical and Applied Electronic Commerce Research, 3*(2), 71–81. doi:10.4067/S0718-18762008000100007

Saraf, N., Langdon, C. S., & Gosain, S. (2007, September). IS Application Capabilities and Relational Value in Interfirm Partnerships. *Information Systems Research, September, 18*(3), 320-339.

Shutzberg, L. (2004). Radio Frequency Identification (RFID). In *Consumer Goods Supply Chain: Mandated Compliance or Remarkable Innovation*? Norcross, GA: Rock-Tenn Company.

Siemnieniuch, C. E., Waddell, F. N., & Sinclair, M. A. (1999, April). The role of 'partnership' in supply chain management for fast-moving consumer goods: A case study. *International Journal of Logistics, 2*(1), 87–101. doi:10.1080/13675569908901574

Simchi-Levi, D., Kaminsky, P., & Simchi-Levi, E. (2004). *Managing the Supply Chain: The Definitive Guide for the Business Professional.* New York: McGraw-Hill.

Somers, K. J., & Bhattarcherjee, T. M. (2007). The Role of Information Systems Resources in ERP Capability and Business Process Outcomes. *Journal of Management Information Systems, 24*(2), 221–260. doi:10.2753/MIS0742-1222240209

Son, J., Narasimhan, S., & Riggins, F. J. (2005). Effects of Relational Factors and Channel of Climate on EDI Usage in the Customer-Supplier Relationship. *Journal of Management Information Systems, 22*(1), 321–353.

Songini, M. L. (2007, February). Wal-Mart Shifts RFID Plans. *Computerworld, 26*, 14.

Stevens, G. C. (1990). Successful Supply Chain Management. *Management Decision, 28*(8), 25–30. doi:10.1108/00251749010140790

Subramani, M. (2004, March). How Do Suppliers Benefit From Information Technology Use in Supply Chain Relationships. *Management Information Systems Quarterly, 28*(1), 45–73.

Subramani, M. R., & Venkatraman, N. (2003). Safeguarding Investments in Asymmetric Interorganizational Relationships: Theory and Evidence. *Academy of Management Journal, 46*(1), 46–62. doi:10.2307/30040675

Tierney, S. (2003). Exciting times --- but what about all the data RFID generates? *Frontline Solutions, 12*, 50.

Van Den Hoven, J. (2004). Data architecture standards for the effective enterprise. *Information Systems Management, 21*(3), 61–64. doi:10.1201/1078/44432.21.3.20040601/82478.9

Waiman, C., Chu, S. C., & Du, T. C. (2009). A technology roadmap for RFID adoption in supply chains. *International Journal of Electronic Business, 7*(1), 44–57. doi:10.1504/IJEB.2009.023608

Wang, E. T. G., & Wei, H. L. (2007, November). Interorganizational Governance Value Creation: Coordination for Information Visibility and Flexibility in Supply Chains. *Decision Sciences, 38*(4), 647–674.

WFMC. (1999). *Terminology & Glossary* (Document Number WFMC-TC-1011, 3.0).

Williamson, O. E. (1985). *The Economic Institutions of Capitalism*. New York: The Free Press.

Zaheer, A., & Venkatraman, N. (1994). Determinants of Electronic Integration in the Insurance Industry: An Empirical Test. *Management Science, 40*(5), 549–566. doi:10.1287/mnsc.40.5.549

Zaheer, A., & Venkatraman, N. (1995). Relational Governance as an Interorganizational Strategy: An Empirical Test of the Role of Trust in Economic Exchange. *Strategic Management Journal, 16*, 373–392. doi:10.1002/smj.4250160504

Zhao, X., Huo, B., Flynn, B. B., & Yeung, J. H. Y. (2008). The impact of power and relationship commitment on the integration between manufacturers and customers in a supply chain. *Journal of Operations Management, 26*, 368–388. doi:10.1016/j.jom.2007.08.002

This work was previously published in International Journal of Enterprise Information Systems, edited by Madjid Tavana, pp. 35-57, Volume 6, Issue 2, copyright 2010 by IGI Publishing (an imprint of IGI Global).

Chapter 10
Evaluating Information Systems:
Constructing a Model Processing Framework

João Duarte
Technical University of Lisbon, Portugal

André Vasconcelos
Technical University of Lisbon, Portugal

ABSTRACT

In the past decade, the rush to technology has created several flaws in terms of managing computers, applications, and middleware and information systems. Therefore, organizations struggle to understand how these elements behave. Even today, as Enterprise Architectures grow in significance and are acknowledged as advantageous artifacts to help manage change, their benefit to the organization has yet to be fully explored. In this paper, the authors focus on the challenge of real-time information systems evaluation, using the enterprise architecture as a boundary object and a base for communication. The solution proposed is comprised of five major steps: establishing a strong conceptual base on the evaluation of information systems, defining a high level language for this activity, extending an architecture creation pipeline, creating a framework that automates it, and the framework's implementation. The conceptual framework proposed avoids imprecise definitions of quality and quality attributes, was materialized in a model-eval-display loop framework, and was implemented using Model Driven Software Development practices and tools. Finally, a prototype is applied to a real-world scenario to verify the conceptual solution in practice.

INTRODUCTION

Laudon and Laudon (2009) describe the importance of knowledge and knowledge management in the today's enterprises. Even though humans have the innate trait of self-awareness through

consciousness, organizations — becoming more and more living complex social organisms — fail to automatically develop similar capabilities of sensing and learning. This task then falls upon the individuals, who must work together, interact and share knowledge and, therefore, engage the task of sense-making as to improve the collective self-awareness.

DOI: 10.4018/978-1-4666-1761-2.ch010

To transfer knowledge, communication must be done through known shared boundary objects that are described using a set of concepts and with a semantics which cannot be ambiguous.

The need for Organizational Knowledge is already a widely accepted fact, and in order to improve the holistic view of the Organizational Structure, Enterprise Architectures have been proposed as valuable artifacts due to their communicative nature (Magalhães et al., 2008).

With mechanisms to represent organization blueprints, easy-to-use notations to describe high-level requirements and real-time processing, enterprises will become increasingly aware of themselves and their ecosystem, and will be able to make quicker, smarter and better informed decisions.

To increase the collective organizational knowledge, information has to be applied, which in turn can only be produced by processing relevant data in the first place (Ackoff, 1989). The ability to collect more data from more organizational sources is there unavoidably valuable. We will focus on the use of data produced by operation systems, middleware, applications and other technological elements to better understand how the technology and information layers of deployed enterprise architectures behave in real-time.

Regarding architectural representations as boundary objects, we intend to take advantage of their creation and maintenance to encourage stakeholders in an enterprise to discuss, define and perform evaluation through the definition of quality attributes.

This research therefore addresses today's inability to evaluate systems in real-time through the "eyes" of Enterprise Architectures.

The rest of the paper is organized into four sections. Next section provides an overview of related work regarding Enterprise Architectures, quality evaluation and modelling instrumentation. The following section presents the proposed solution: the conceptual abstraction, the Model Processing Framework and its implementation.

Next we present a case study of the implementation of the developed prototype in the Telecommunication industry. The final section presents the conclusions and the future work suggestions.

ENTERPRISE ARCHITECTURES AND EVALUATION TECHNIQUES OVERVIEW

Enterprise Architectures

As stated in the previous section, enterprise architectural representations allow enterprises to make quicker, smarter and better informed decisions. These enterprise architecture meta models are usually constructed in layers that separate, for example, hardware and software from human actors and even information.

The Unified Enterprise Architecture Modelling Language (and LEAN) (Khoury, 2007), is a highly conceptual metamodel for enterprise modelling based on a societal metaphor. It can be understood as meta-metamodel for Enterprise description, from where concepts of Organisation Engineering Center Framework (CEOF) (Vasconcelos et al., 2008) or ArchiMate (Lankhorst et al., 2005) (for example) can be specialized.

The CEOF stems from the academic domain of Organisational Engineering and defines a clear hierarchy of concepts for Enterprise Architectures, views for different desires, and provides structural metrics for TO-BE architecture comparison.

The ArchiMate language stems from a mix of academic and organisational environments and defines a taxonomy along with views that target different stakeholders. Regarding evaluation, ArchiMate also focuses on evaluation of TO-BE architectures, but instead provides analysis of their dynamic behaviour.

What all have yet to provide is the ability to, once the architecture is deployed, perform evaluation of behaviour of this architecture, using real-time data and events. To be able to execute this action, the authors expect to make available the following benefits to the architecture life cycle:

- By executing real-time evaluation, we assert the deviation from the before (model) and the implementation, for events specified using model elements and so we perform a "reality-check";
- Perform observations on how the architecture actually behaves after implementation, so that the evaluations such as ArchiMate's can be corroborated (along the temporal axis).
- Understand changes in behaviour, either from infrastructure degradation or unknown change in practices, habits or processes.

Evaluating Information Technology: Metrics And Measuring Qualities

Robert E. Filman (1999) describes the steps towards achieving "ilities" - typical attributes of systems such as reliability, performance, availability and maintainability - in compositional architectures. These concepts exist in a myriad of domains ranging from Networking to Software Development - and recently, Enterprise Architectures. Even within a given domain, these definitions are not clear. For example, in multimedia domains, the notion of quality of service is subjective since there is not a widely accepted QoS Framework (Aurrecoechea et al., 1996) and QoS must be always understood in the context of the domain or framework used to measure it.

Filman then states that there is more than one definition for concepts such as reliability; to define reliability is to specify the requirements established in a certain environment and by certain people to attain reliability. The consequence of this looseness is therefore an impossibility to uniquely and globally define *ilities*. Nevertheless, for one to be able to measure the behaviour of an information system according to a set of qualities,

the definition of the set of functional, aesthetic, systematic and combinatory requirements must be accomplished by stakeholders.

Regarding Enterprise Architectures, as we presented in the previous section, CEOF (Vasconcelos et al., 2008) provides structural metrics, while ArchiMate focuses on predicting behaviour. Archimate's evaluation, however, is not built on a well defined structured of metrics.

Instrumentation

Considering that the solution proposed in this paper uses models and we wish to provide users with an executable representation of the enterprise architecture, we identified several requirements for these tools, such as: i) The support for metamodels and metamodel extensions is essential since Enterprise Architecture Frameworks are metamodel level entities. ii) To augment portability and mobility of the solution, import and export of models is also desirable. iii) One way of performing validations is through the verification of constrains on the model; for UML, the OCL performs this function and therefore it is required for the tool not only syntax validation of the constraint language but also execution. iv) The last but equally important feature is the ability to chain model transformation actions, since we are going to perform model edition, validation and execution of custom tasks.

After comparing some modelling tools, regarding these features, the authors opted for extending openArchitectureWare[1] for supporting these requirements. Also, by being Open Source, we have the possibility of extending the tool for adjust to our needs.

On Providing Quality Views Over Information System Architectures

In this section we were able to verify that Enterprise Architecture Metamodels and Frameworks are not prepared for real-time evaluation of deployed architectures. This feature has potential benefits such as helping to reduce the gap between reality and the modelled architecture, provide real-time feedback on its behaviour and, finally, reduce the time to assert the need for change.

In the next section, we will take Gerald Khoury's work on the Lightweight Enterprise Architecture Notation and CEOF Architecture Metamodel and construct a conceptual framework for processing models to perform real-time evaluation. Next, we will take openArchitectureWare and provide an implementation of this framework so that we can attest its feasibility.

A MODEL PROCESSING FRAMEWORK FOR IS EVALUATION

In order to address the problem of evaluating systems in real-time using enterprise architectures as a boundary object and a base for communication, the authors propose a solution comprised of five major steps: establishing a strong conceptual base on the evaluation of systems, defining a high level language for this activity, extending an architecture creation pipeline, creating a framework that automates it and finally implementing this framework. These steps are next described.

Establishing The Phenomenological Setting

Recker and Niehaves (2008) explained the relevance of philosophy in Information System research by linking several philosophical disciplines such as Ontology, Methodology and Epistemology to IS research paradigms (e.g., positivism, interpretivism). By understanding how we perceive others, what we observe and how we judge, we were able to come up with unified, global, overview of the concepts that are involved when performing evaluation of Information Systems and, therefore, be able to model this domain.

Society has been established as a proper metaphor for enterprises. In order to accomplish our goal, we set out to find a parallel between experiencing, judging, perceiving-capable agents since, inherently, these activities occur inside society and consequently within the metaphor.

Phenomenology is the "study of structures of consciousness as experienced from the first-person point of view" (Stanford 2009). Its key concepts are: intentionality (experience always is directed at something or is about something), qualia (sensory data), bracketing (putting aside the question of the existence of a real world) and consciousness itself. We found this philosophical discipline and these concepts to have a profound link to the Information Systems and Information System research area (Recker & Niehaves, 2008). In the following paragraphs we describe the mentioned concepts, and then move on to determine in what way the phenomenological dialectic fits the problem at hand.

Since *Phenomenology* imposes subjectivity upon the world, we can place its rationale within the *interpretivist* trend (López-Garay, 2003; Mingers, 2001). Considering that the phenomenological concepts and their relations apply to society, we then propose that they can also be mapped into the society metaphor and therefore its target (enterprise systems).

The act of perceiving (*noesis*) the enterprise structure allows the detection of its meaning, therefore producing the boundary object (*noema*) referred in the Organisational Engineering domain as Enterprise Architecture. And by determining what manifestations are observable on this architecture, we perform the *phenomenological bracketing*, for the assumption develops that objects will always be perceived as modelled, regardless of the particularities relative to their nature.

This construction of an enterprise architecture allows the specification of enterprise elements as simply 'being there' - or *noumena* - while by describing their manifestations we define how they appear before the senses - *phenomena.*

By modelling evaluation as an activity that is inherently dependent on observations - *qualia* - we establish a link to the *intentionality* aspect of experience, according to phenomenology. And, finally, by having agents record manifestations as observed (from the first person standpoint) we construct the observed objects' *facticity.*

Considering this "phenomenological ontology" in a level of abstraction greater than the target of our desired metaphor, we were able to assert its validity and also construct a parallel between evaluation of Information Systems and the philosophical discipline of phenomenology. Many of the central concepts of this domain can be understood under the scope of agent interaction, should they be systems, humans, communities and organisations.

Producing a High-Level Language Extension

We began by performing the following changes on the LEAN (Khoury, 2007) node pairings: (1) added an "observes" relationship between an **Agent and a Resource**, (2) add the **Agent → Resource** and **Agent → Rule** to the "produces" pairing. These two changes reflect the necessity on bringing Agents and Resources closer. This necessity arose from our closer inspection of the philosophical notions of experience. This close binding also supports the approach of modelling what can be observed on an entity and how to measure that entity's actions.

With a proper metaphor for the act of evaluation, we proceeded to construct our Model Processing Framework (MPF). The next (brief) sub-section defines the setting on which the MPF operates.

Revisiting The Information System Architecture Building Pipeline

The solution this paper proposes further extends ISA creation pipeline (improved in Vasconcelos et al., 2008), so that systems can be monitored from the perspective of the final **(AS-IS) ISA**. The revisited pipeline (Figure 1) includes an extra cycle located at its end that feeds the ISA artifact, the manifestations and measurements into a processing framework. This framework is able to evaluate the state of the deployed ISA regarding defined metrics.

Defining A Model Processing Framework

In OMG (2005) the concept of Model Processing is described as a set of tasks, namely creating a model and performing analysis techniques that are put together in the form of a Model Processing Framework (MPF) (Figure 2). In the following paragraphs we describe each of the MPF's components used as a base for our research. We explain their tasks and input/outputs and how they are connected. In order to separate the conceptualization of our framework and the tool support (described in section *"Implementing the Model Processing Framework"*), we have kept out all the implementation aspects.

The Model Editor supports the creation and edition of models, with proper lexicon and syntactic validation (according to an Enterprise Architecture meta-model). These meta-models must encompass the four concepts of the Lightweight Enterprise Architecture Notation (LEAN): agent, action, resource and rule. The creation and edition of models must be fully supported by the tool, not obligating the user to understand lower-level programming concepts.

As we explained in section *"Establishing the Phenomenological setting"*, evaluation occurs by observing agents while they are performing actions. Therefore, object representation is necessary

Figure 1. Proposal for pipeline with Information Systems evaluation

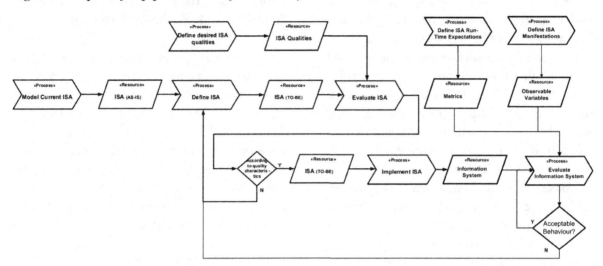

so that individual characteristics can be modelled. Objects as "things" must be reified within the tool, so that Object diagrams or similar representations of object-level schemas are possible.

The Model Converter's purpose is to act like a pre-processor, transforming the modelled architecture into a format that can be consumed by the Model Analyser. The converter, loaded with the Enterprise Architecture meta-model, has the capacity to navigate a model and generate the

code needed to capture the values of monitoring points defined by the modeller.

The core of this MPF is the Model Analyser. It is responsible for performing the evaluation of the Information Systems based on the enterprise architecture model (along with manifestations and measurement specifications) that were defined in the Model Editor (Figure 3). The Model-Level Analyser acts upon metrics that are defined within the meta-model (not requiring user intervention) and, on the other hand, the Object Level Analyser

Figure 2. Model Processing Framework

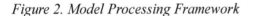

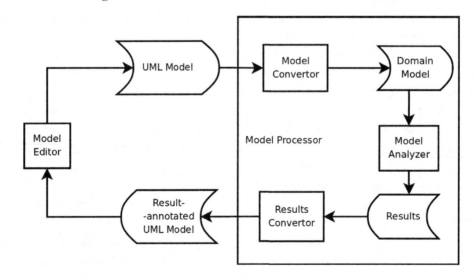

Figure 3. Expanded view of the Model Analyzer

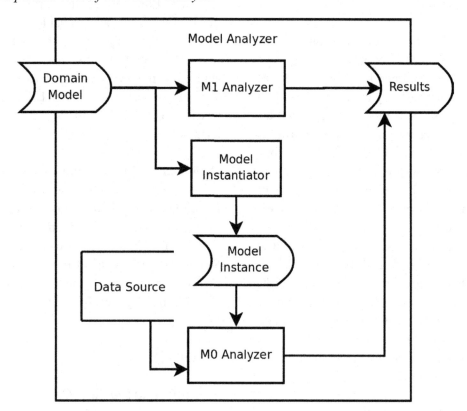

uses continuously stored data and user-defined metrics to judge instance behaviour.

The final stage in the MPF cycle, executed by the Results Converter, is the transportation of information produced by the Model Analyser back into the visual representation of the model, as in the Model Editor. The values (of data collected) are displayed in each of the objects' manifestation attributes and the generated warnings by the Model Analyser are displayed to the user.

Implementing The Model Processing Framework

This section describes a possible implementation for the MPF using an existing architecture meta-model and an UML tool.

The aim is to construct a model driven evaluation framework for the real-time manifestations of deployed enterprise architectures. For this implementation is assumed to exist an infrastructure comprised of a central repository and agents that capture (through its senses) certain dynamic attributes.

Extending The Meta-Model

The framework chosen was the Center of Organisational Design and Engineering[2] Framework (CEOF) since it draws a clear line along the several layers of the Enterprise Architecture, and describes the entities that belong to each layer.

In this research this framework was extended at the Information System Architecture level, through its Block and Service elements (for further detail on CEOF concepts please refer to Vasconcelos (2006)) since, in this architecture, the concept of agent as action-performer entity does not exist.

Monitoring Point

Thinking back to our LEAN extension and Vasconcelos et al. (2008) taxonomy, Blocks closely represent Agents and therefore we must define how (or through what) they manifest themselves in reality. For this meta-model, we changed the manifestation semantics slightly in order to better align out concepts with CEO's. The ODE loop (Matos, 2007) shows the concepts "Variables" and "Monitoring Points" as the meta-level inputs for Domain Monitoring. To better suite ODE's syntax we used the latter concept "Monitoring Points" to refer to the observation standpoint of a certain variable of an Agent's behaviour. Monitoring points are therefore the equivalent of the Manifestations, but add a perspective semantic to it. This characteristic is useful due to the nature of the Case Study monitoring platform that relies on monitoring agents located near systems that observe their manifestations.

Definition: A Monitoring Point is a dynamic property of a Block that can be observed over time.
Relations: This primitive has the following associations: Block - the Monitoring Point exist within Block (see Vasconcelos, 2006).
Semantics: Monitoring Point primitives represent observable variables of information system components (see Table 1).

UML Definition

Metric

Looking back into the ODE loop, Domain Analysis is performed adding models (structure) and metrics (evaluation) to the results of Domain Monitoring (observable data). Essentially the Metric concept represents an expectancy that is based on collected data from Monitoring Points.

In CEO Framework, the Service is a collection of operations made available by architectural blocks. We therefore apply the metric concept to the Service element; so that we can evaluate actions, using manifestations from the actor, according to LEAN and our LEAN extension (see section "*Producing a High-Level Language Extension*").

Definition: A Metric represents a behavioural expectancy of a Service.
Relations: This primitive has the following associations: Service - Metric primitives exist within Service (see Vasconcelos et al., 2007)
Semantics: represents an expectation based on collected data from Monitoring Points. Monitoring (see Table 2).

UML Definition

Instrumenting the MPF Cycle

The tool selected was openArchitectureWare (oAW) since it supports: graphical interface, UML2, UML Profiles, Code Generation, XMI import and export, OCL checking and for being Open Source, as described in section "*Instrumentation*".

The Model Editor requires easy-to-use, UML2 class and object diagram support as well as support for UML profiles. openArchitectureWare includes the Graphical Modelling Framework[3] (from the Eclipse Modelling Project) that provides this tool with a graphical environment for creating diagrams. The prototype implemented the Information System Architecture of the CEO framework on a UML Profile (using a Profile diagram in the graphical interface), added with the meta-model extension in this diagram, by creating two Stereotypes named *Monitoring Point* and *Metric* as described in the previous subsection. After defining the CEOF profile and

Table 1. Monitoring point primitives represent observable variables of information system components

Well Formed-ness Rule	A Monitoring Point can only exist within the context of a given Block context Monitoring_Point inv Monitoring_Point_Relations: self.class.oclISKindOf (Block)
Notation	Monitoring Point follows the standard UML representation for Attributes
UML Profile diagram (partial)	

its extension, the authors created an UML model (using the Class Diagram), applied the profile, and modelled an architecture with the correct taxonomy. To model object instances in oAW, the eclipse UML2 implementation supplies the uml::InstanceSpecification element, which is a M1-level representation of the M0 object.

The next block in the MPF workflow (see Figure 2), the Model Converter, plays the role of converting the UML model into a format than can be used by the Model Analyzer. An XMIReader component was used (so that other components can manipulate the UML model) along with the Generator component to perform code generation. The CEOF meta-model was recreated in Ruby using an Object Oriented approach so that, when the Generator is invoked, it creates two ruby source files: one for the model and another for the instances, and each level is supported by the upper.

For the core of this MPF, the Model Analyser, openArchitectureWare supports OCL expressions and validations. These are used to calculate Service metrics by navigation InstanceSpecifications, accessing Monitoring Point values in Blocks,

performing calculations and finally comparing the output with a threshold which warns the user. They are also used to perform checks at the model-level for ill-formedness, according to the meta-model.

Finally, the Results Converter transforms the manipulated model (now possessing values for the monitoring points) back into UML. This processing block also has the responsibility to guarantee that the end of the processing cycle leaves the openArchitectureWare in a state where the process can be run again. To be able to show the user the values used for calculating metrics, the model UML(.uml) file is rewritten, and special care is given so that in subsequent executions of the workflow only changes these values.

AN IT EVALUATION CASE STUDY

In this section we explain how the MPF proposed in this paper was applied to a real-world situation. This research was developed in an enterprise context; therefore, our test bed consisted of the Portu-

Table 2. The metric follows the standar UML representation for operations

Well Formed-ness Rule	A Metric can only: Exist within the context of a given Service context Metric inv Metric_Relations: self.class.oclISKindOf (Service)
Notation	Metric follows the standard UML representation for Operations
UML Profile diagram (partial)	![metaclass Operation inheriting to stereotype Metric]

guese Telecom enterprise (PT-Comunicações, or PT-C) and its technological infrastructure.

PT-C has been concerned over the years with measuring IT performance, availability and errors. For that purpose, the Pulso platform was developed to sustain mechanisms of near-real-time measuring, monitoring and storing basic performance indicators for major systems that support key business processes (Alegria et al., 2004).

However, the evaluation procedures are still *ad-hoc* since there is no technical or conceptual framework that allows - in a simple, declarative and semantically robust way - to define what entities are being targeted and how to specify and calculate the relevant indicators for either Quality of Service, Quality of Protection or even Quality of Maintenance.

The EDS[4] division of PT-Comunicações is responsible for this monitoring platform and, as such, provided an environment that was both resourceful and accessible for us to experiment with our solution since we were given access to an infrastructure of monitoring, data collector agents attached to every relevant server, database and network link. By "relevant set" we mean the entities that are, at the time of this writing, critical to the business.

In this section we describe a "proof-of-concept" implementation of an existing scenario. We start by describing the Pulso platform, namely its architecture, its infrastructure of monitoring agents, and its current evaluation mechanisms. Our purpose is to demonstrate the steps needed to construct a cycle of the MPF using the implementation described in previous. For this we describe a fraction of PT-C Call Center system (enough for the purpose of this case study) and an evaluation scenario using the CEOF metamodel and the openArchitectureWare implementation.

Pulso Architecture

The Pulso monitoring framework (Alegria et al. 2004) is comprised of system monitoring agents (e.g., Linux, Windows, HP-UX, Oracle) and network probes (client-server and server-server).

Agents are system-specific software whose job is to periodically capture basic behaviour readings of their hosts. For instance, Linux agents capture observable variables such as CPU usage, CPU load (for 1, 5 and 15 minutes) and memory usage. For databases, agents designed for Oracle DBMS capture waiting times for query processing queues. Depending on the business demands, the agents are further developed to produce more observable variables.

Probes passively monitor network traffic between both servers and clients or between servers. They capture data regarding bandwidth consumption and protocol-specific traffic (e.g., SQL transaction requests and errors, IIS communication).

In the Pulso platform the definition of Enterprise entities (ranging from disk partitions to business processes) is constructed using a graph of "things" and the links between then. Therefore, there are no classes, no type hierarchy and no architectural layers. This approach provided some benefits due to the lack of constrains on the evaluation process, making it faster to implement. However, by allowing any entity to be related to another and by providing full flexibility and no constraints, this solution has also been proven to be hard to maintain as systems grow in complexity. Since there are no *a priori* validations that can be performed on the Technology Infrastructure model, the structures evolve into large graphs, inherently difficult to debug and complex to change in the long term.

To store the data produced by agents and probes a centralized repository was created in the form of a database, where all events are dispatched after being sent to a central logging server. These events have a common header format that includes an identification of the monitored entity, what is observed attribute and the timestamp of the event. The header helps a dispatcher determine where to insert the event in a database where the time series for each event type are stored, for future analysis.

Call Center IS Evaluation

As a case study, we analyse a part of the Helpdesk Call Center that provides assistance to PT's internet, television and phone customers. The infrastructure that supports it consists of:

- **Interactive Voice Response:** interactive technology that allows a computer to detect voice and keypad inputs. It is used to channel the client to the correct pool of call center agents by a telephone key driven menu;
- **Automatic Call Distributor:** device or system that distributes incoming calls to a specific group of terminals which are used by agents;
- **Computer Telephony Integration:** allows interactions on a telephone and a computer to be integrated or co-ordinated;
- **Customer Relationship Management:** manages client data such as personal information and account data. It is supported by Siebel software.

The typical flow of a client's call starts when the client dials the number and is picked up by the IVR. The client is asked to specify one of the pre-selected classes of problems and, after the IVR has the necessary data, it transfers the call to the ACD. The distributer selects an available agent, from the correct pool of agents, and afterwards the conversation can begin.

Setting Up OpenArchitectureWare

Our first step of the implementation was to create an openArchitectureWare project and properly configure it. This involves (1) creating an empty openArchitectureWare project and configuring it for UML2, (2) loading the CEOF profile and (3) creating an empty UML model and a UML Class diagram.

Having set up the base project, we started modelling the Call Center into the oAW application. The creation of the Information System Architecture is essential to our modelling of the phenomena produced by these systems and so our next step was to describe it. While modelling this fraction of the ISA we only included the blocks and services we were able to identify from the existing documentation and, therefore, elements

such as databases or even software components were possibly left out (the resulting Class diagram can be seen in Figure 4).

To stereotype either classes (Blocks) or interfaces (Services), the context menu of that element provides an "Apply Stereotype" entry where only the appropriate stereotypes can be applied (e.g., Block stereotypes cannot be applied to interfaces).

Figure 4. UML Class diagram for the ISA with added Monitoring Points and a Metric

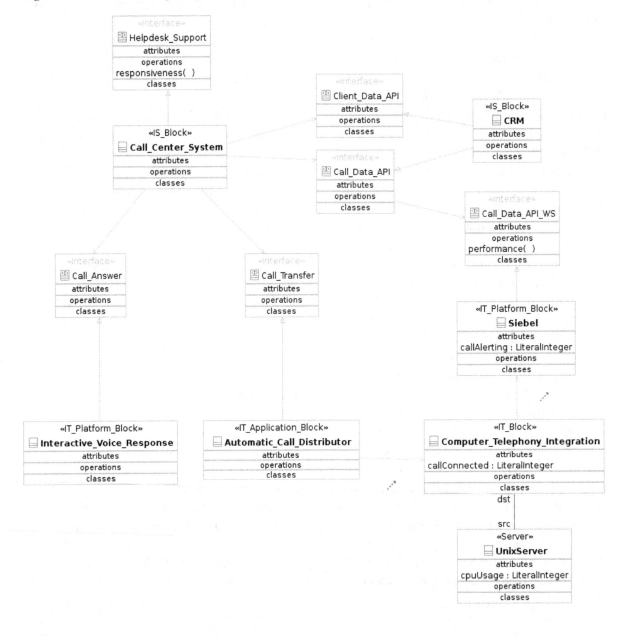

Since what we need to capture the dynamic behaviour of this architecture, we also need to construct the corresponding Object diagram. This diagram contains the instances of the Class diagram that exist and will be the target of our evaluation.

To add the Object diagram onto our solution, we used the existing UML Class diagram where we added the representation of the objects through UML's InstanceSpecification primitive and "Usage" relationships (the resulting object diagram can be seen in the MPF execution below, Figure 5).

The next step of the configuration was to establish what we can observe on each of the Blocks and how do we wish to evaluate the services on which they are implemented. As observable variables of the existing blocks we have (1) "callAlerting" on the Computer Telephony Interaction IT Block, (2) "callConnected" on the Siebel Platform Bock and (3) "cpuUsage" on the Unix-Server.

We chose to model the measurements as expectancies (that evaluate to true or false) for this fits better with the OCL paradigm and provides a way to warn the user of this MPF if an expectation is not met.

The *responsiveness* metric was created to calculate the difference between the two moments of the call alerting and the moment the operator picks up the call. For the purpose of this proof-of-concept, we assume the last timestamp of each moment and the metric simply determines if the difference is greater than a certain number. Since most of the systems are on automatic answering, we do not want them to be greater than 1 second. The *performance* metric is a simple threshold checker to see if the UNIX server's cpu is not being overused, degrading the system's performance. The following code listing shows how this performance and responsiveness metrics was defined, using oAW's implementation of OCL. The metrics are defined using the model-level elements and also the thresholds that define if the metric passes or fails according to the expectations for the instances.

Resulting ISA and Execution

Adding monitoring points to Blocks is done by adding an attribute to a Block stereotyped Class and applying the CEOF::Monitoring Point. Similarly, adding operations to Services defines metrics, after applying the stereotype (of the same name). We applied three Monitoring Point and the two Metrics to the existing ISA (Figure 4).

Having our class and object diagrams, manifestations and metrics modelled, we were able to execute the Model Processing Framework's workflow and observe its output. As presented in Figure 5, at the end of the cycle, the instances that contain monitoring points now have values associated, and the Console View at the bottom of the oAW screen has launched a warning since the last registered call took 1 second to be answered (the difference of timestamps between the two moments).

Using this prototype, supported on openArchitectureWare, and on the MPF proposed in the previous section, PT-Comunicações, besides being able to compute the simple metrics introduced in this paper, manage to configure new (more complex) metrics, taking advantage of the observed IT manifestations provided from existing system monitoring agents and network probes.

CONCLUSION AND FUTURE WORK

The Information System Research is still in a very immature state. Several contributions have started to emerge during the last 20 years and the interest on the topics such as Information System modelling, Enterprise Architectures and Organisational Engineering and Design are growing fast.

In this paper the authors further develop the research of Khoury (2007), Vasconcelos et al. (2001, 2004, 2007, 2008) by providing some insight on how to perform architecture-centric, ontologically supported, evaluation of Information System behaviour. This research began by finding the appropriate mindset to approach this problem

Figure 5. Results after a run of the MPF cycle

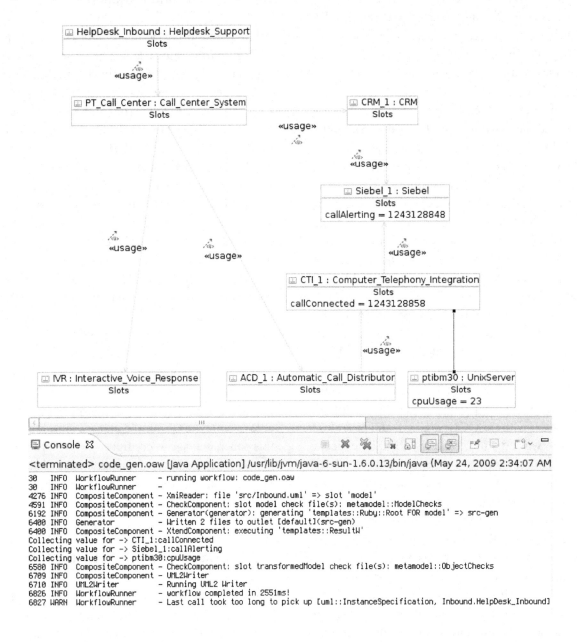

through a higher level abstract analogy to our problem. We turned into the metaphorical view of societies as a superset of enterprise systems, and searched within this metaphor for guidelines on how to model a solution.

This paper presents a parallel between the field of Phenomenology (that studies human and group experience and phenomena) and the acts of judg-

ing the behaviour of architectural components by transforming their observable variables.

To help modellers, analysts and every participant in the enterprise community, the authors propose an automated cycle of evaluation using the Enterprise Architecture as the standpoint and communication medium between all parties.

Listing 1. Responsiveness and Performance Metrics

```
context Instance Specification if hasMetric (this, "responsiveness")
WARNING "Last call took too long to pick up ":
(getValue (this, "Computer_Telephony_Integration", " callConnected ") -
getValue (this, "Siebel", "callAlerting")) < 1 ;
context InstanceSpecification if hasMetric (this, " performance ")
WARNING "Last call took too long to pick up":
getValue (this, "UnixServer ", "cpuUsage") < 9 5 ;
```

The MPF is an architecture-centric evaluation framework of the real-time behaviour of information systems, made of four major components: Model Editor, Model Converter, Model Analyser, and Results Converter.

The authors also implemented a MPF prototype using the openArchitectureWare tool, and applied it to a real-world enterprise example, being able to measure simple metrics from observed manifestations. In this implementation the authors: (a) extended an Enterprise Architecture Framework (the CEO Framework) to support the ontology proposed; (b) used the primitives of the framework to populate an oAW's profile diagram; (c) created a template project on oAW that implements each step of the MPF, along with an automation workflow that executes the full cycle of the MPF.

Nevertheless, the Model Processing Framework implementation has some limitations that are expected to be overcome as future work:

- The cycle cannot be repeated automatically (the user has to press the "Run" button again). Investigation has already been done (also the community forum is very active) regarding this issue, and it can be solved with a Java Ant task that executes the workflow as a normal Java application;
- The helper functions that abstract the metric design from the Eclipse/Ecore model navigation can be further developed to provide a friendlier experience;

- The presentation of negatively evaluated metrics can be improved by, for example, marking the diagram elements with colour codes;
- Not all meta-model integrity checks of the CEO framework were implemented.

Finally, being "unified" an aspect of our ontology extension and conceptual MPF; we did not attempt to apply our solution to another architecture meta-model such as, for example, Archimate. However, the authors consider the MPF proposed to be perfectly compatible with Archimate, for it also has a well-defined notation. OpenArchitectureWare is also prepared to handle such flexible notations as Javabeans-based models and XML-based models, so this is expected to be addressed in the future.

ACKNOWLEDGMENT

The case study research presented in this paper was possible thanks to the support of Portugal Telecom – Comunicações.

REFERENCES

Ackoff, R. L. (1989). From data to wisdom. *Journal of Applied Systems Analysis, 16*, 3–9.

Alegria, J., Carvalho, T., & Ramalho, R. (2004). *Uma experiência open source para tomar o pulso e ter pulso sobre a função sistemas e tecnologias de informação*. Paper presented at the 5ª CAPSI, Conferência da Associação Portuguesa de Sistemas de Informação, Lisboa, Portugal.

Aurrecoechea, C., Campbell, A., & Hauw, L. (1996). A survey of qos architectures. *Multimedia Systems Journal, 6*, 138–151. doi:10.1007/s005300050083

Filman, R. E. (1999). *Achieving ilities*. Paper presented at the Workshop on Compositional Software Architectures, Monterey, CA.

Khoury, G. R. (2007). *A unified approach to enterprise architecture modeling.* Unpublished doctoral dissertation, Faculty of Information Technology, University of Technology, Sydney.

Lankhorst, M., et al. (2005). *Enterprise Architecture at Work - Modelling, Communication, and Analysis.* New York: Springer. ISBN-10: 3-540-24371-2

Laudon, J., & Laudon, K. (2009). *Management Information Systems: Managing the Digital Firm* (10th ed.). Upper Saddle River, NJ: Prentice Hall. ISBN-10: 013607846X

López-Garay, H. (2003). Extending checkland's phenomenological approach to information systems. In *Critical reflections on information systems: a systemic approach* (pp. 46-64). ISBN: 1-59140-040-6

Magalhães, R., Sousa, P., & Tribolet, J. (2008). The role of business processes and entreprise architectures in the development of organizational self-awareness. *TECKNE - Revista de Estudos Politecnicos, 6*(9), 9-30.

Matos, M. (2007). Organizational engineering: An overview of current perspectives. Unpublished master's thesis, Instituto Superior Técnico, Technical University of Lisbon, Lisbon, Portugal.

Mingers, J. (2001). Embodying information systems: the contribution of phenomenology. *Information and Organization, 11*(2), 103–128. doi:10.1016/S1471-7727(00)00005-1

OMG. (2005). *UML profile for schedulability, performance, and time specification.* Needham, MA: Object Management Group.

Recker, J., & Niehaves, B. (2008). Epistemological perspectives on ontology-based theories for conceptual modeling. *Applied Ontology, 3*(1/2), 111-130. ISSN: 1570-5838

Stanford University. (2009). *Stanford encyclopedia of philosophy.* Retrieved June 2009, from http://plato.stanford.edu/

Vasconcelos, A. (2006). *CEO Framework for Information System Architecture: An UML profile* (Tech. Rep.). Retrieved from http://web.ist.utl.pt/ist14250/reports/CEOF_UML_Profile_v1_2.pdf

Vasconcelos, A., Caetano, A., Neves, J., Sinogas, P., Mendes, R., & Tribolet, J. (2001). *A Framework for Modeling Strategy, Business Processes and Information Systems.* Paper presented at the 5th International Enterprise Distributed Object Computing Conference EDOC, Seattle.

Vasconcelos, A., Mendes, R., & Tribolet, J. (2004). Using Organizational Modeling to Evaluate Health Care IS/IT Projects. In *Proceedings of the 37th Annual Hawaii International Conference on System Sciences (HICCS37),* HI.

Vasconcelos, A., Sousa, P., & Tribolet, J. (2007). Information System Architecture Metrics: an Enterprise Engineering Evaluation Approach. *The Electronic Journal Information Systems Evaluation, 10*(1), 91-122. ISSN: 1566-6379

Vasconcelos, A., Sousa, P., & Tribolet, J. (2008). Enterprise Architecture Analysis: An Information System Evaluation Approach. *International Journal of Enterprise Modelling and Information Systems Architectures, 3*(2), 31-53. ISSN: 1860-6059

ENDNOTES

[1] http://www.openarchitectureware.org/

[2] Center of Organisational Design and Engineering (CODE) was formerly known as CEO (Centro de Engenharia Organizacional, in Portuguese, or Center for Organization Engineering)

[3] http://www.eclipse.org/modeling/gmf/

[4] Eficiência, Disponibilidade e Segurança de sistemas (in Portuguese), or Efficiency, Availability and Security in Systems

This work was previously published in International Journal of Enterprise Information Systems, edited by Madjid Tavana, pp. 17-32, Volume 6, Issue 3, copyright 2010 by IGI Publishing (an imprint of IGI Global).

Chapter 11
Message–Based Approach to Master Data Synchronization among Autonomous Information Systems

Dongjin Yu
Hangzhou Dianzi University, China

ABSTRACT

The evolution of networks and large scale information systems has led to the rise of data sources that are distributed, heterogeneous, and autonomous. As a result, the management of Master Data becomes more complex and of uncertain quality. This paper presents a novel message-based approach to the synchronization of Master Data among multiple autonomous information systems. Different than traditional approaches based on database triggers, the author adopts the optimistic bidirectional strategy with the process of two synchronization phases. By means of data service buses, it propagates synchronized Master Data through messages being passed along star-like cascading routes. Moreover, this approach could resolve possible data conflicts automatically using predefined attribute confidences and deducible current value confidences respectively. Finally, this paper presents the real case about synchronizing datasets among four separate but related systems based on the author's novel message-based approach.

INTRODUCTION

The evolution of networks and systems of data management has led to the rise of multiple wide scale information systems with data sources of very different kinds. Indeed, these sources can be distributed, heterogeneous and autonomous. Consequently, the lack of consistent and accurate reference information becomes the major issues

confronting IT applications today. It is not uncommon to come across multiple sets of redundant and inconsistent data on customers and other items of primary focus in an organization (Piprani, 2009). Master Data Management (MDM) is an emerging discipline focusing on integrating data split in multiple systems by defining a master repository formatted as a data warehouse (Menet & Lamolle, 2009). Here, Master Data basically refer to the key business information which may include reference data about customers, products,

DOI: 10.4018/978-1-4666-1761-2.ch011

employees, materials, suppliers, etc. Master Data often turn out to be non-transactional in nature. In this regard, Master Data can support transactional processes and operations, and more often, relate with comprehensive analytics and reporting.

Data synchronization is an automated action to make the distributed Master Data be consistent with each other and up-to-date (Lee, Kim, & Choi, 2004). Through synchronization, the inconsistent, or stale Master Data, could be replaced with the right ones timely and automatically. Synchronization is different with backups, though they all involve data duplication. Backing up one disk to the other refers to make an exact copy of first disk onto to the other, thus preserving all the data on first one. By synchronization, however, the information from one dataset will be copied to the other, so each dataset will have the same information.

Data synchronization usually occurs between two or more autonomous information systems with locally administrated data stores. Under some complicated circumstances, synchronization would even involve tens of systems. Synchronization generally happens continually because distributed Master Data always keep changing. In order to synchronize data in a faster mode, only the shared information needs to be copied instead of duplicating the whole datasets. Since the data synchronization may involve large amount of data transferred under wide area networks, it however tolerates moderate time delay. In other words, data are never fully synchronized and synchronization just helps the distributed inconsistent data to be more consistent.

Synchronizing distributed Master Data is unavoidable under some circumstances. Case studies have revealed the significance of adoption of data synchronization for large organizations (Fuller, Sankar, & Raju, 2009; Zucker & Wang, 2009). For instance, the enterprise global data view could be only constructed with the data collected from multiple autonomous systems distributed inside the organization. Meanwhile, for the sake of business collaboration, different applications also need to be coupled with the underlying data swapping across system boundaries. In both cases, Master Data from different systems representing the same entity may be inconsistent because they are supervised under different domains and in different ways.

Current research issues related with data synchronization mainly focus on its performance, flexibility and methods of data conflict resolution. This paper presents the data synchronization framework, called MDSIF. MDSIF provides the coherent data snapshots for all related datasets by sending, receiving, and storing Master Data encapsulated in messages. Furthermore, MDSIF resolves data conflicts by setting Attribute Confidences and Current Value Confidences respectively. The Attribute Confidence, determined beforehand by data managers, indicates the reliability of all values of certain attribute created from certain dataset. Meanwhile, the Current Value Confidence, set automatically according to its own original Attribute Confidence, represents the present confidence of each shareable value. When the conflict is detected, the value with higher Current Value Confidence is allowed to overwrite that with lower one. Different with the traditional approaches such as triggers-based framework, MDSIF allows optimistic bidirectional synchronization, and is therefore more flexible, extendable and easier to be administrated.

The rest of the paper is organized in the following manner. The next section presents the architecture of synchronization framework based on messages, i.e., MDSIF. Following the overall introduction of conflict resolving strategy, the resolving method in the formal way, and its evaluation metrics are given. The successfully implemented case is then illustrated afterwards. After presenting related works, the paper finally provides concluding remarks and offers future research directions.

MDSIF AND ITS FRAMEWORK

The management rights of Master Data are generally isolated from enterprise systems (Luh, Pan, & Wei, 2008). Hence, the synchronization of Master Data should be achieved independently of existent systems. The star-like synchronization framework presented in this paper, named as the Message-based Data Synchronization and Integration Framework, or simply MDSIF, interacts with the underlying participating datasets (Figure 1). Beside the star-like topology, the framework might otherwise adopt peer to peer (P2P) topology without any synchronization centers, which would avoid performance bottlenecks (Endo, Miyamoto, Kumagai, & Fujii, 2004). However, in P2P architecture, every dataset should connect directly with the other remaining ones. Hence, the number of data swapping paths would increase dramatically with more datasets involved, which eventually made the framework too complicated to be administrated. In addition, as it lacks the centers dumped with shared data, it would be rather hard to form the global data view which is usually required for enterprise-level decision support.

MDSIF is constructed based on distributed Data Service Buses. Here, the nodes connected by the same bus belong to one group, called domain. The nodes represented by D in Figure 1, are the participating datasets whose Master Data need to be synchronized. On the other hand, the nodes of administrative data centers, represented by R in Figure 1, are responsible for the data synchronization inside their own administrating regions. In addition, the data centers also keep the copies of synchronized Master Data for future reference. Due to limited capacity of storage under certain circumstances, however, only the data center directly connected with participating datasets through Data Service Bus (Level 1) would keep the copies of Master Data in its domain. In this way, the indexes to actual datasets are nevertheless required for global data view, since data are not physically integrated. The Data Service Bus then connects neighboring domains to form a larger one. Thus, MDSIF would be easily extended to make different domains coupled by cascading service buses. If synchronization involves datasets outside a domain, multiple buses would join to decide the nodes where data should be updated.

Figure 1. Cascade synchronization framework based on messages

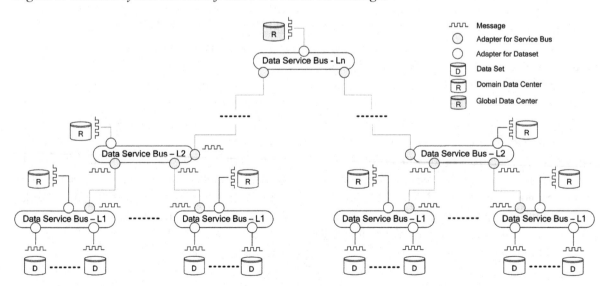

Due to the networking instability in the wide area distributed environment, MDSIF introduces the asynchronous communication model based on messages. When implementing MDSIF, the Message-Oriented Middleware (MOM) is actually employed. MOM is the traditional infrastructure focused on sending and receiving messages that increases the interoperability of an application by allowing the application to be distributed over heterogeneous platforms (Goel, Sharda, & Taniar, 2003). It typically supports asynchronous calls between the client and server by the message queues which provide temporary storage when the destination program is busy or not connected.

In MDSIF, the message itself encapsulates both the control information and the data. The adapters reside in all participating datasets and data centers, as message senders or message receivers. When asked to synchronize data, the message is created and kept in local output queue, and later the adapter, or the messages sender, would send the message when appropriate. In this way, the adapter could continue to execute its own task with no need to wait for the response from message receiver. On the other hand, the message receiver is not required to handle the request immediately once it receives the data. The messages would be kept in the input queue until they are consumed or handled eventually. Thus, the data integrity and consistence would be fully guaranteed in terms of application-level when the network breaks down,

although it does not support rollbacks or commits in terms of database transactions.

For each node of destination, MDSIF assumes messages from one node arrive and be consumed in the same order as they are sent. However, MDSIF does not require messages from all different nodes arrive and be consumed in sequence. This condition could be easily guarded by most of state-of-the-art MOM products.

RESOLVING DATA CONFLICTS

In distributed complicated environments, Master Data conflicts usually occur when the values from two or more participating datasets differ with each other although they represent the same entity. Master Data conflicts bring ambiguity, and dramatically decreases qualities of data.

Traditionally, database triggers are adopted to resolve Master Data conflicts (Figure 2). Once the data source detects operations of value insertion, deletion or modification, it executes predefined triggers to redo the same operations in the targets through database links. However, the trigger-based approach only allows the execution of fixed and unidirectional synchronization, which transfers the data in the predefined source to the predefined target. In fact, however, data in the datasets other than the predefined source may need to be synchronized with the data in target, when the data in the predefined source are temporary absent

Figure 2. Synchronization flows in the trigger-based approach

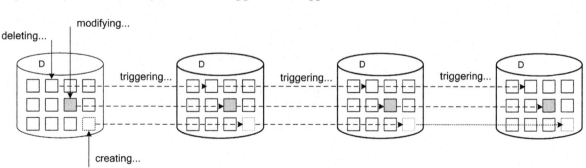

or lost. Under other circumstances, the data in source are even allowed to be replaced by the data in target if the source data are null or could be simply ignored, which leads to the bidirectional synchronization.

In MDSIF, the data conflict would be resolved automatically by predefined data confidence values which denote the extent of data reliability. Different with the traditional approach based on database triggers, MDSIF does not predefine sources or targets of data synchronization. For the values on same attribute of same entity, those from the dataset with higher or equal confidence value are all allowed to overwrite those from the dataset with lower one (Figure 3). For some more complicated scenarios, different confidence values may need to be set for different attributes, but not single value for the whole record.

There are two kinds of confidences in MDSIF:

1.   AC: Attribute Confidences

Every shareable attribute in each dataset has its own Attribute Confidence to indicate the reliability of all values of the attribute created from this dataset. Attribute Confidences are determined before the synchronization happens by the data managers who are familiar with and in charge of the data's business value.

Attribute Confidences are stored in the Attribute Confidence Table. Moreover, Attribute Confidences are fixed and could not be changed after setting.

2.   CVC: Current Value Confidences

The Current Value Confidence represents the present confidence of each shareable value. Since the Current Value Confidence is set automatically according to the Attribute Confidence of the corresponding attribute in its original dataset, it may be different with its own Attribute Confidence.

Current Value Confidences are stored in Current Value Confidence Table. Different with Attribute Confidences, Current Value Confidences may change during the whole synchronization process.

MDSIF duplicates and spreads above confidence tables to different datasets and data centers for local reference in order to reduce synchronization time. Therefore, the confidence tables are also required to be synchronized.

Figure 3. Synchronization flows in the MDSIF approach

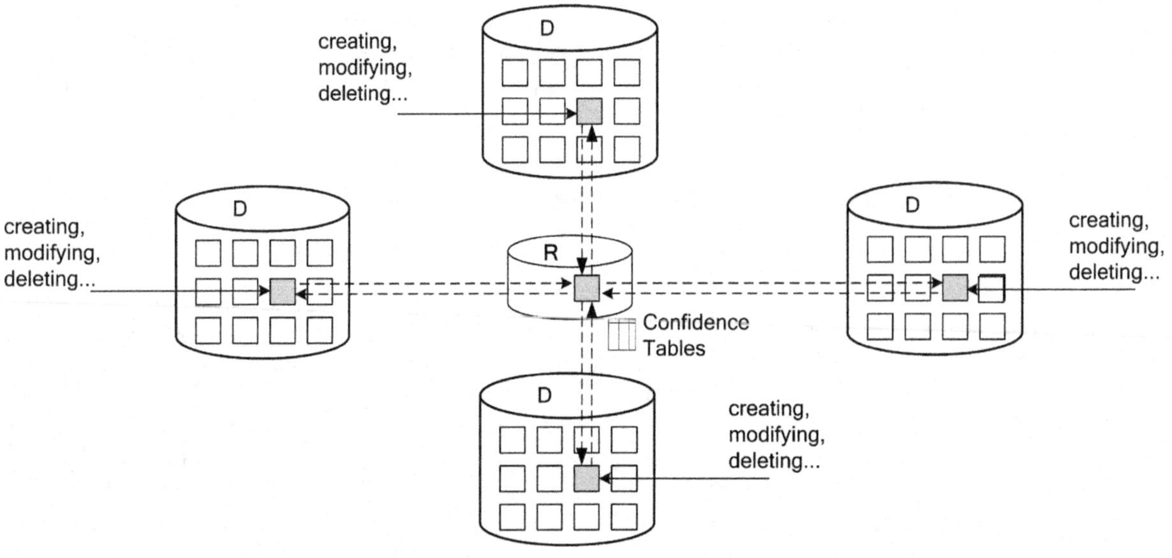

Generally, two kinds of data are involved during synchronization, i.e. Master Data, or Reference Data, and Non-Master Data. Master Data are the shared entity data with two or more input or modification points, such as the basic information of entities like companies, persons, etc. The synchronization of Master Data is somewhat sophisticated, as the confidences of conflicting ones should be compared to decide the most reliable one. On the other side, Non-Master Data are generally referred to the specific entity's business status managed by one system, but also interested by some other systems. Because there exists just one input or modification point, i.e. the owner, the synchronization of Non-Master Data is relatively easy. Modification of Non-Master Data issued from the owner is allowed and then directly propagated to other participating nodes. However, any modification of existing Non-Master Data not issued from the owner is rejected, simply because the owner has the full confidence, while the others have no confidences at all.

Figure 4 shows the conflict resolving approach for both Master Data and Non-Master Data. In essence, the synchronization method for Non-Master Data is the special case for Master Data. Here, the buffer of conflicting data is introduced for the processing of Master Data synchronization. Only those have higher confidence values in the buffer could be sent to the shared data center and then ready to be used by other systems.

SYNCHRONIZATION METHODS

This section describes the method in detail to get data consistent through synchronizing unmatched values among different datasets in MDSIF. For simplicity, the method described here is limited in just one domain.

Definition 1: *The distributed Data Synchronization Framework is denoted as a quadruple E, i.e.* $E = \{D, U, R, T\}$, *in which:*

Figure 4. Different approaches to Master Data and non-Master Data synchronization

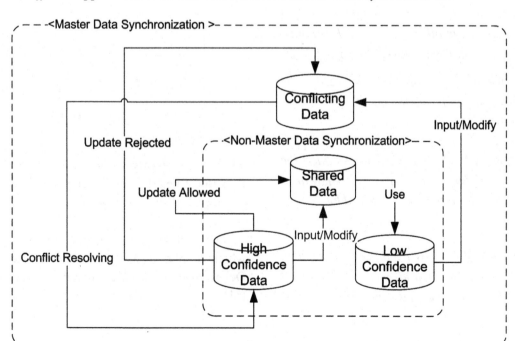

$D = \left\{ D_0, D_1, ..., D_{n-1} \right\}, n \geq 2$, *is the combination of all participating datasets, named as the Synchronized Datasets, or simply Datasets.*

$U = \left\{ u_0, u_1, ..., u_{k-1} \right\}, k \geq 1$, *is the Set of Attributes on which values should be kept consistent in D.*

$R = R^{u_0} \bigcup R^{u_1} \bigcup ... \bigcup R^{u_{k-1}}$, *is the Shared Dataset Center, or simply Data Center, formed by synchronizing all the values on attribute set in U.*

$T = \left\{ T_0, T_1, ...T_{m-1} \right\}$, *is the Set of Synchronization Rules.*

Definition 2: *For the attribute u, the extent of reliability of dataset D_i compared with other datasets in E is called the Attribute Confidence (AC) of D_i for attribute u, represented as C_i^u, where $0 \leq C_i^u \leq 1$. The higher the reliability, the bigger C_i^u.*

Definition 3: *For the shared value $r = r_i^{u_j}$ on attribute u_j in D_i, the extent of reliability compared with its replicas in other datasets in E is called the Current Value Confidence (CVC) of $r_i^{u_j}$ in D_i, represented as $V_i^{r_{u_j}}$ where $0 \leq V_i^{r_{u_j}} \leq 1$. The higher the reliability, the bigger $V_i^{r_{u_j}}$.*

Definition 4: *If $C_i^u = 1$, then D_i is called the Dataset with Full Confidence, or Determined Dataset, in E for attribute u, denoted by M^u.*

Definition 5: *If $C_i^u = 0$ the dataset D_i is called the Dataset with No Confidence, or Ignored Dataset, in E for attribute u, denoted by I^u.*

With the above definitions, the synchronization method in the framework E could be described as following two phases.

Phase I: Initial Synchronization

Step 1: Sort Attribute Confidences

For each attribute u, reorder all the datasets in D, except the *Determined Dataset M^u* according to their *Attribute Confidences* from high to low. Assume the result is:

$$D^T = \left\langle D_{i_0}, D_{i_1}, ...D_{i_{n-1}} \right\rangle, \qquad (\text{T0})$$
$$C_{i_0}^u \geq C_{i_1}^u \geq ... \geq C_{i_{n-1}}^u$$

Note there is always only one *Determined Dataset* at most for each shared attribute.

Step 2: Construct the Data Center R

Let R^u denote the shared dataset for attribute u, then:

$$R^u = \begin{cases} \left(r^u, v^r \right) \middle| r^u \in M^u \bigcup \left(D_{i_0}^u - M^u \right) \\ \bigcup \left(D_{i_1}^u - D_{i_0}^u - M^u \right) \bigcup ... \\ \bigcup \left(D_{i_{n-1}}^u - D_{i_{n-2}}^u - ... - D_{i_0}^u - M^u \right), \\ v^r = \max \left(C_i^u \middle| r^u \in D_i^u \right) \end{cases} (\text{T1})$$

where v^r represents the *Current Value Confidence* for value r, i.e., the highest *Attribute Confidence* among all *Synchronized Datasets* containing r^u.

In particular, (T1) could be simplified as (T2), which simply means that all datasets except the Determined Dataset are Ignored Datasets for attribute u.

$$R^u = \left\{ \left(r^u, v^r \right) \middle| r^u \in M^u, v^r = 1.0 \right\},$$
$$C_{i_0}^u = C_{i_1}^u = ... = C_{i_{n-1}}^u = 0 \tag{T2}$$

Thus *Data Center* R could be constructed as following:

$$R = \bigcup R^u, u = u_0, u_1, ..., u_{k-1} \tag{T3}$$

Step 3: Duplicate the shared data

Copy the shared data from the *Data Center* R to all related datasets:

$$D_i^{u_j} = \left\{ r \middle| r \in R^{u_j} \right\}, i = 0, 1, ..., n-1;$$
$$j = 0, 1, ..., k-1 \tag{T4}$$

Phase II: Usual Synchronization

After the initial synchronization, all Master Data in distributed datasets are regarded as consistent. Subsequent synchronization occurs when any data manipulation, such as inserting, updating, and deleting, may introduce the inconsistency.

1. Synchronization of Dataset Caused by Local Data Manipulations

To create the record which contains shared value
$$r_{u_0}, r_{u_1}, ..., r_{u_j}, ...r_{u_{k-1}}$$
on attributes $u_0, u_1, ..., u_j, ..., u_{k-1}$ respectively in D_i:

Step 1: Make sure that the same record has not been added yet. If not, reject creating and terminate synchronization.
Step 2: Add the record in D_i, and set the CVCs of its attribute values:

$$V_i^{r_{u_0}} = C_i^{u_0}, V_i^{r_{u_1}} = C_i^{u_1}, ...,$$
$$V_i^{r_{u_j}} = C_i^{u_j}, ..., V_i^{r_{u_{k-1}}} = C_i^{u_{k-1}}.$$

Step 3: Create a new piece of message with information of newly added record and its related CVCs, and keep it in the output queue to *Data Center*.

To update existing value $r_i^{u_j}$ on attribute u_j in D_i:

Step 1: If $C_i^{u_j} < V_i^{r_{u_j}}$, reject the modification and terminate synchronization.
Step 2: Modify $r_i^{u_j}$ in D_i, and promote its CVC to $C_i^{u_j}$.
Step 3: Create a new piece of message with information of updated value $r_i^{u_j}$ and its related CVC of $C_i^{u_j}$, and keep it in the output queue to *Data Center*.

To delete the record which contains shared value $r_{u_0}, r_{u_1}, ..., r_{u_j}, ...r_{u_{k-1}}$ on attributes $u_0, u_1, ..., u_j, ..., u_{k-1}$ respectively in D_i:

Step 1: If $\exists u_j, C_i^{u_j} < V_i^{r_{u_j}}$, reject the deletion and terminate synchronization.
Step 2: Set:

$$V_i^{r_{u_0}} = V_i^{r_{u_1}} = ... = V_i^{r_{u_j}} = ... = V_i^{r_{u_{k-1}}} = 0.$$

Step 3: Create a new piece of message with information of deleted record, and keep it in the output queue to *Data Center*.

2. Synchronization of Data Center

Take each piece of message in the input queue of *Data Center* in sequence, and repeat data manipulations as it indicates.

To create a record:

- Make sure that the same record has not been added yet. If not, go to the updating steps.

- Add the record in R, and set CVCs of its attribute values as message indicates.
- Create a new piece of message with the information of newly added record and its related CVCs, and keep it in the output queue to all participating *Datasets* except the originating one.

To update existing value r^{u_j} on attribute u_j :

- If $V_i^{r_{u_j}} < V^{r_{u_j}}$, create a new piece of message with roll-back information, keep it in the output queue to the originating *Dataset*, and terminate synchronization. Here, $V^{r_{u_j}}$ refers to CVC of existing value r^{u_j} in *Data Center*, and $V_i^{r_{u_j}}$ refers to CVC which message indicates.

- Update r^{u_j} , and promote its CVC to $V_i^{r_{u_j}}$.
- Create a new piece of message with information of updated value r^{u_j} and its related CVC, and keep it in the output queue to all participating *Datasets* except the originating one.

To delete the record which contains shared value $r_{u_0}, r_{u_1}, ..., r_{u_j}, ... r_{u_{k-1}}$ on attributes $u_0, u_1, ..., u_j, ..., u_{k-1}$ respectively:

- If the record not existed, terminate synchronization.
- If $\exists u_j, V_i^{r_{u_j}} < V^{r_{u_j}}$, create a new piece of message with roll-back information, keep it in the output queue to the originating *Dataset*, and terminate synchronization.
- Set:

$$V^{r_{u_0}} = V^{r_{u_1}} = ... = V^{r_{u_j}} = ... = V^{r_{u_{k-1}}} = 0.$$

- Create a new piece of message with deleting information, and keep it in the output queue to all participating *Datasets* except the originating one.

3. Synchronization of Datasets Caused by Remote Data Manipulations

Take each piece of message in the input queues of datasets in sequence, and repeat data manipulations as it indicates. The procedures are similar with those for synchronization of *Data Center*.

The above synchronization method may also be illustrated by state diagram. Figure 5 gives the example, which shows the promotion routes of CVS for some shared value with 3 possible CVCs, where $C_{i_1}^u < C_{i_2}^u < C_{i_3}^u$. The shared value could be created with CVC of $C_{i_1}^u$, $C_{i_2}^u$, or $C_{i_3}^u$. Moreover, it could be promoted with CVC from $C_{i_1}^u$ to $C_{i_2}^u$ or $C_{i_3}^u$, or from $C_{i_2}^u$ to $C_{i_3}^u$ as the result of modification.

EVALUATION

The overhead of MDSIF could be measured in terms of storage space of extra confidence tables. Suppose there are p entities with attributes of $u_0, u_1, ..., u_{k-1}$, needing to be synchronized, among n nodes including one data center. If the identity has 10 bits and the confidences are graded into 4 scales using 2 bits, the extra storage space of AC tables and CVC tables, in bits, could be calculated as:

$$
\begin{aligned}
M &= M_{AC} + M_{CVC} \\
&= (10+2)kn + (10+2)kpn \\
&= 12kn(p+1)
\end{aligned}
\tag{1}
$$

On the other hand, the storage space of Master Data is calculated as (2), where m_i stands for the storage space of attribute u_i, in bits. Here, suppose the identity has 10 bits.

$$M_{MD} = pn\left(10 + \sum_{i=0}^{i=k-1} m_i\right) \tag{2}$$

Figure 5. The state diagram showing promotion route of CVS for some shared value with three possible CVCs

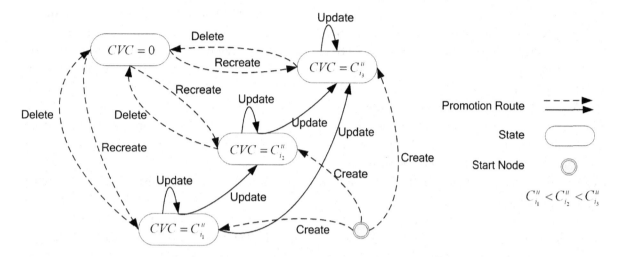

Thus, storage overhead, Q, could be evaluated as the ratio of extra storage of confidence tables to that of Master Data being synchronized, as in (3).

$$Q = \left(M_{AC} + M_{CVC} \right) / M_{MD}$$
$$= 12k\left(p+1\right) \Big/ \left(10p + p \sum_{i=0}^{i=k-1} m_i \right) \quad (3)$$

For huge volume data synchronization where p is big enough, (3) could be further simplified to (4) in which $\bar{m}$ stands for the average bits of one attribute value.

$$Q = 12k / \left(10 + k\bar{m} \right) \quad (4)$$

According to our survey, $\bar{m}$ is around approximately 160 bits. Therefore, the storage overhead of MDSIF is no more than 7.5%.

Another metric is the synchronization latency. In MDSIF, the latency is the sum of time taken to compare confidences, transfer and update data. Here, the communication time accounts for the major part of latency. Since updated data are first forwarded to *Data Center*, and then dispatched to each participant node, the synchronization latency

of MDSIF is determined by the longest transferring delay between *Data Center* and participant nodes as (4) illustrates.

$$T = T_{compare} + T_{transfer} + T_{update}$$
$$\approx T_{transfer} = t_{D_i,R} \quad (5)$$
$$+ \max \left(t_{R,D_j} \,\Big|\, j = 0,1,...,n-1, j \neq i \right)$$

In (5), $t_{D_i,R}$ represents the communication time between D_i and *Data Center R*, and t_{R,D_j} represents the communication time between *Data Center R* and D_j.

CASE STUDIES

MDSIF has been successfully implemented for the construction of regional Labor and Social Security Data Center (LSSDC) (Figure 6). Here, IBM Websphere MQ (International Business Machines Corp., 2009) is adopted as the Message Oriented Middleware (MOM) to send, receive and store the swapped data encapsulated in messages. Currently, data are stored in Oracle databases, while the copies of Attribute Confidence tables and Current Value tables are kept in the center node and the participating datasets.

LSSDC collects data from separate information systems including Social Security System (SSS, Node #1), Professional Training System (PTS, Node #2), Employment System (ES, Node #3) and Job Recommendation System (JRS, Node #4). Master Data, such as profiles of individual and employers, are used by several functional groups and stored in the above different systems across an organization; therefore, the possibility exists for duplicate and/or inaccurate Master Data. Regarding the information of individual profiles, SSS has the most accurate records of basic information such as name, age and gender. Besides, PTS keeps the most current information of education background since it deals with training affairs. ES, however, knows exactly if one is employed or jobless. Finally, JRS is only a utility application system for the introducing of occupation. Accordingly, the information managed by JRS is regarded as least accurate.

Figure 7 illustrates the Attribute Confidence Table and Current Value Confidence Table for the case. Here, the updatable status could be deduced according to the related values in the Attribute Confidence Table and Current Value Confidence Table. For example, the value of birthdate (denoting the individual's birth date) for Record 1001 could be replaced with new value created from Node #1 or Node #2, but not the value from Node #3, because its Current Value Confidence (10) is bigger than the corresponding Attribute Confidence in Node #3 (01), but smaller than or equal to that in Node #1 (11) and Node #2 (10).

The synchronization case involved records of approximately 190,000 organizations and 4,230,000 individuals, among which 5 organizational attributes and 6 individual attributes are required to keep consistent. The initial round took approximately 3 hours to complete, and the subsequent synchronization happens on demand and is achieved within 3 seconds when operations of participant systems reach peaks between 10 and 11 in the morning, and 2 and 3 in the afternoon. The actual storage overhead is approximately 7.4%.

Figure 6. The data in four autonomous information systems are synchronized to build up the LSSDC. Front-end data swapping pools are introduced to avoid the interference of transactional processing.

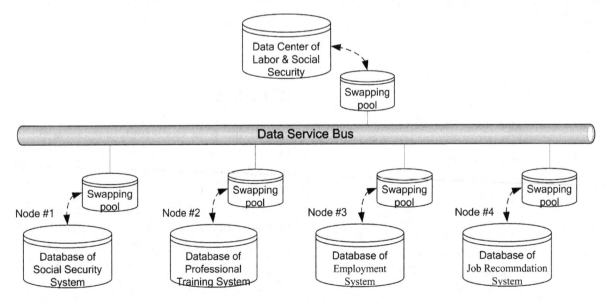

Figure 7. The Attribute Confidence Table and Current Value Confidence Table for the case

1) Attribute Confidence Table

Attribute	Node ID.	AC
PersonID	#1	11
Birthdate	#1	*11*
Birthdate	#2	*10*
Birthdate	#3	01
Degree	#1	10
Degree	#2	11
Income	#1	10
Income	#3	11
Income	#4	01
...	...	...

AC: Attribute Confidence

2) Current Value Confidence Table

Record ID.	Attribute	CVC
1001	PersonID	11
1001	*Birthdate*	*10*
1001	Degree	10
1001	Income	01
1002	PersonID	11
1002	Birthdate	11
1002	Degree	11
1002	Income	11
...	...	...

CVC: Current Value Confidence

RELATED WORKS

The problem of data synchronization attracts many researchers' attention. The related topics include incremental replication methods, synchronization strategy, synchronization in mobile environments, synchronization performance and scalability, and so on.

Many synchronization models have been proposed. For instance, Li and Wang (2007) propose an active differential data synchronal model in which the change of the source data is listened actively and the update of the destination data is done synchronously through a monitor. Foster, Greenwald, Kirkegaard, Pierce, and Schmitt (2007) implement a generic synchronization framework, called Harmony, which can be used to build state-based synchronizers for a wide variety of tree-structured data formats. A novel feature of this framework is that the synchronization process—in particular, the recognition of conflicts—is driven by the schema of the structures being synchronized.

There is a significant body of established research on data synchronization in mobile environments. The Coda distributed file system implements a comprehensive approach to file system synchronization in a weakly connected environment (Satyanarayanan & Kistler, 1992). In order to adapt synchronization to bandwidth and resource constraints, the concept of item relationships might be adopted to synchronize only the items relevant to the user (Koskimies, 2005). Under some circumstances, the recent-data-win policy is adopted as the resolution rule in the mobile environment (Lee et al., 2004). Lindholm, Kangasharju, and Tarkoma (2009) present a middleware, called Syxaw (Synchronizer with XML-awareness), for synchronization of structured data in a mobile and resource-constrained environment. Syxaw distinguishes itself from related proposals in that it interoperates transparently with resources on the World Wide Web, and by exhibiting a model of synchronization that is both easy to understand and well suited for weak devices in a mobile and ubiquitous environment.

Manual intervention is usually unavoidable for resolving conflicts occurred in different datasets. For example, Yesilbas and Lombard (2004) propose the elements of a synchronized repository are determined by identifying involved static knowledge and the formalizing protocols driven by actors. Similarly, Endo et al. (2004) present the method which needs administrators to manage whether they permit changes by other peers with consistency. Nevertheless, Heumer, Schilling, and Latoschik (2005) achieve the automatic data exchange and synchronization by integrating an extra central knowledge component. It handles the incoming possibly conflicting changes and treats different data formats uniformly based on the declarative attribute representation concept. MDSIF, however, conducts a fully automatic synchronization process, after data managers manually define the Attribute Confidences before synchronization begins.

Davidson, Garcia-Molina, and Skeen (1985) classify database consistency strategies as pessimistic or optimistic. It is widely agreed that pessimistic approaches are inappropriate in a network with possibly disconnected data storages (Cohen, 2000; Terry, Theimer, Petersen, Demers, Spreitzer, & Hauser, 1995). MDSIF adopts optimistic strategies of data consistency. Instead of preventing conflicts by limiting availability of data, MDSIF allows replicas to be updated independently, detecting and resolving any resulting conflicts. In this way, the synchronization processes could sometimes be suspended in case of network breakdown.

Many focus on how to improve the performance and scalability for synchronizing large replicated datasets among distributed systems. Exploiting parallelism, omitting transfer of unnecessary metadata, synchronizing at a block level rather than a file level, using sophisticated compression methods are all feasible ways to achieve these goals (Schutt, Schintke, & Reinefeld, 2003). Frequent synchronization leaves only a small amount of stale data, but might result in high cost. Dey, Zhang, and De (2006) examine the trade-off between the synchronization and staleness costs and derive the optimal synchronization frequency. Furthermore, Italiano and Ferreira (2006) present a framework that uses parameter sets to define the most suitable synchronization options in order to decrease the update time between the transactional and analytical systems.

Because data synchronization would bring about huge business profits, the industrial track has also developed many related products. Promoted as the platform-independent data sync industrial standard, SyncML (Synchronization Markup Language), currently referred to as Open Mobile Alliance Data Synchronization and Device Management, is the generic framework of information exchange for all devices and applications over any network (Open Mobile Alliance Ltd., 2009). MNCRS, or Mobile Network Computing Reference Specification, is another industrial mobile data synchronization framework specification (Cohen, 2000). The framework, with a persistent synchronization store as its core, is designed to accommodate memory-limit devices and unreliable and expensive connections. Typical commercial products include Oracle Streams, which have many advantages over traditional synchronous and asynchronous replication methods (Yan, Diao, & Jiang, 2008). However, the data sync requirements from commercial and industrial societies are still far from satisfaction (Bowling, Licul, & Hammond, 2007).

CONCLUSION AND FUTURE WORKS

How to resolve Master Data conflicts effectively and efficiently among multiple disparate autonomous systems often challenges the engineers who engage in system coupling. The message-based data synchronization framework, MDSIF, is configured with shared data centers and service buses. It resolves Master Data conflicts with the help of Attribute Confidences and Current Value Confidences respectively. In other words, those from the system with higher confidence values are allowed to overwrite those from the system with lower ones. By means of data service buses, MDSIF propagates Master Data through messages passing along star-like cascading routes, and dumps Master Data in the shared centers. It could ensure the reliable synchronization by message buffering under poor networking condition. Different with traditional trigger-based approaches, MDSIF is more flexible, extendable, and easier to provide the global data view.

MDSIF currently does not support synchronization in batch mode. However, the update of one object during synchronization sometimes involves a set of related operations on several other objects. Masud and Kiringa (2007) resolve this issue to some extent by setting synchronization chains to propagate related conflicts in series. Similarly, we are also considering extending MDSIF to accommodate batch synchronizations, which would be probably achieved through message compositions.

In addition, current MDSIF needs a holistic quantitative evaluation framework. Possible metrics may include synchronization latency, storage overhead of confidence tables, rate of data consistency, and its impact on participant systems. Hereby, future research would also focus on the comprehensive evaluation of MDSIF and its optimization of performance in more complicated environments.

ACKNOWLEDGMENT

The work is supported by the Foundation of Zhejiang Provincial Key Science and Technology Projects (No. 2008C11099-1), the Science Foundation of the Hangzhou Dianzi University (No. KYS055608069, No. KYS055608057), and the Natural Science Foundation of Zhejiang province of China (No. Y6090312). Many have contributed to the work demonstrated in this paper. The requirement and initial idea was promoted by Prof. Shixin Feng from Hangzhou Information Center of Labor and Social Security. Dr. Wanqing Li helped construct the earlier version of MDSIF. Dr. Dominik Slezak, the Chief Scientist at Infobright, presented many valuable suggestions. Special thanks are dedicated to the above mentioned ones and all reviewers of the paper.

REFERENCES

Bowling, T., Licul, E. D., & Hammond, V. (2007). *Global Data Synchronization: Building a flexible approach*. Retrieved December 12, 2009, from ftp://ftp.software.ibm.com/software/integration/wpc/library/ge-5103990.pdf

Cohen, N. H. (2000). A Java Framework for Mobile Data Synchronization. In O. Etzion & P. Scheuermann (Eds.), *Cooperative Information Systems* (LNCS 1901, pp. 287-298). Berlin: Springer.

Davidson, S. B., Garcia-Molina, H., & Skeen, D. (1985). Consistency in partitioned networks. *ACM Computing Surveys*, *17*, 341–370. doi:10.1145/5505.5508

Dey, D., Zhang, Z. J., & De, P. (2006). Optimal synchronization policies for data warehouses. *Journal on Computing*, *18*(2), 229–242.

Endo, S., Miyamoto, T., Kumagai, S., & Fujii, T. (2004). A Data Synchronization Method for Peer-to-Peer Collaboration Systems. In *Proceedings of International Symposium on Communications and Information Technologies* (pp. 368-373). Washington, DC: IEEE.

Foster, J. N., Greenwald, M. B., Kirkegaard, C., Pierce, B. C., & Schmitt, A. (2007). Exploiting schemas in data synchronization. *Journal of Computer and System Sciences*, *73*, 669–689. doi:10.1016/j.jcss.2006.10.024

Fuller, M., Sankar, C. S., & Raju, P. K. (2009). Design and development of the data synchronization case study. *Computers in Education Journal*, *19*(4), 22–31.

Goel, S., Sharda, H., & Taniar, D. (2003). Message-Oriented-Middleware in a Distributed Environment. In T. Böhme, G. Heyer, & H. Unger (Eds.), *Innovative Internet Community Systems* (LNCS 2877, pp. 93-103). Berlin: Springer.

Heumer, G., Schilling, M., & Latoschik, M. E. (2005). Automatic data exchange and synchronization for knowledge-based intelligent virtual environments. *IEEE Virtual Reality*, 43-50.

International Business Machines Corp. (2009). *WebSphere MQ*. Retrieved December 12, 2009, from http://www-01.ibm.com/software/integration/wmq/

Italiano, I. C., & Ferreira, J. E. (2006). Synchronization options for data warehouse designs. *Computer, 39*(3), 53–57. doi:10.1109/MC.2006.104

Koskimies, O. (2005). Using data item relationships to adaptively select data for synchronization. In L. Kutvonen & N. Alonistioti (Eds.), *Distributed Applications and Interoperable Systems* (LNCS 3543, pp. 220-225). Berlin: Springer.

Lee, Y. S., Kim, Y. S., & Choi, H. (2004). Conflict resolution of data synchronization in mobile environment. In A. Laganà, M. L. Gavrilova, V. Kumar, Y. Mun, C. J. K. Tan, & O. Gervasi (Eds.), *Computational Science and its Applications* (LNCS 3044, pp. 196-205). Berlin: Springer.

Li, X. M., & Wang, H. (2007). The Model of the Active Differential Data Synchronization for the Heterogeneous Data Source Integration Systems. In *Proceedings of the First International Symposium on Information Technologies and Applications in Education* (pp. 572-574). Washington, DC: IEEE.

Lindholm, T., Kangasharju, J., & Tarkoma, S. (2009). Syxaw: Data Synchronization Middleware for the Mobile Web. *Mobile Networks and Applications, 14*(5), 661–676. doi:10.1007/s11036-008-0146-1

Luh, Y. P., Pan, C. C., & Wei, C. R. (2008). An Innovative Design Methodology for the Metadata in Master Data Management System. *International Journal of Innovative Computing, Information and Control, 4*(3), 627–637.

Masud, M. M., & Kiringa, I. (2007). Collaborative Data Synchronization in an Instance-Mapped P2P Data Sharing System. In R. Meersman, Z. Tari, P. Herrero, et al. (Eds.), *On the Move to Meaningful Internet Systems* (LNCS 4805, pp. 7-8). Berlin: Springer.

Menet, L., & Lamolle, M. (2009). A Model Driven Engineering Approach Applied to Master Data Management. In R. Meersman, P. Herrero, & T. Dillon (Eds.), *On the Move to Meaningful Internet Systems* (LNCS 5872, pp. 19-28). Berlin: Springer.

Open Mobile Alliance Ltd. (2009). *Data Synchronization Working Group*. Retrieved December 12, 2009, from http://www.openmobilealliance.org/Technical/DS.aspx

Piprani, B. (2009). A Model for Semantic Equivalence Discovery for Harmonizing Master Data. In R. Meersman, P. Herrero, & T. Dillon (Eds.), *On the Move to Meaningful Internet Systems* (LNCS 5872, pp. 649-658). Berlin: Springer.

Satyanarayanan, M., & Kistler, J. (1992). Disconnected operation in the Coda file system. *ACM Transactions on Computer Systems, 10*(1), 3–25. doi:10.1145/146941.146942

Schutt, T., Schintke, F., & Reinefeld, A. (2003). Efficient synchronization of replicated data in distributed systems. In P. M. A. Sloot et al. (Eds.), *Computational Science (ICCS 2003)* (LNCS 2657, pp. 274-283). Berlin: Springer.

Terry, D. B., Theimer, M. M., Petersen, K., Demers, A. J., Spreitzer, M. J., & Hauser, C. H. (1995). Managing update conflicts in Bayou, a weakly connected replicated storage system. In *Proceedings of the fifteenth ACM symposium on Operating systems principles* (pp. 172-182). New York: ACM.

Yan, H., Diao, X. C., & Jiang, G. Q. (2008). Research on Data Synchronization in Oracle Distributed System. In *Proceedings of 2008 International Seminar on Future Information Technology and Management Engineering* (pp. 540-542). Washington, DC: IEEE.

Yesilbas, L. G., & Lombard, M. (2004). Towards a knowledge repository for collaborative design process: focus on conflict management. *Computers in Industry, 55*(3), 335–350.

Zucker, S. G., & Wang, S. H. (2009). The impact of data synchronization adoption on organizations: A case study. *Journal of Electronic Commerce in Organizations, 7*(3), 44–64.

This work was previously published in International Journal of Enterprise Information Systems, edited by Madjid Tavana, pp. 33-47, Volume 6, Issue 3, copyright 2010 by IGI Publishing (an imprint of IGI Global).

Chapter 12
Factors that Determine the Adoption of Cloud Computing:
A Global Perspective

Bay Arinze
Drexel University, USA

Murugan Anandarajan
Drexel University, USA

ABSTRACT

Cloud computing has spread within enterprise faster than many other IT innovations. In cloud computing, computer services are accessed over the Internet in a scalable fashion, where the user is abstracted in varying degrees from the actual hardware and software and pays only for resources used. This paper examines the adoption of cloud computing in various regions of the world, as well as the potential of cloud computing to impact computing in developing countries. The authors propose that cloud computing offers varying benefits and appears differently in regions across the world, enabling many users to obtain sophisticated computing architectures and applications that are cost-prohibitive to acquire locally. The authors examine issues of privacy, security, and reliability of cloud computing and discuss the outlook for firms and individuals in both developing and developed countries seeking to utilize cloud computing for their computing needs.

INTRODUCTION

Cloud computing is a computing paradigm shift in which server hardware and software are not located onsite, but instead, accessed over the Internet on demand in a dynamically scalable and virtualized form.

According to the Gartner Group, cloud services revenue is forecast to exceed $68 billion in 2010

DOI: 10.4018/978-1-4666-1761-2.ch012

– a 16.6% increase from 2009 (DeFelice & Leon, 2010). The number of people subscribing to mobile cloud apps is also forecasted to rise from 71 million to nearly a billion by 2014 (Cherry, 2009).

These back-end resources exist in a "cloud", namely a mix of typically remote computing resources that are accessed through the Internet (Hayes, 2008; Mell & Grance, 2010). Cloud-based services present an abstraction layer to the user that eliminates the need for the user to configure specific devices (see Figure 1).

Figure 1. Cloud computing

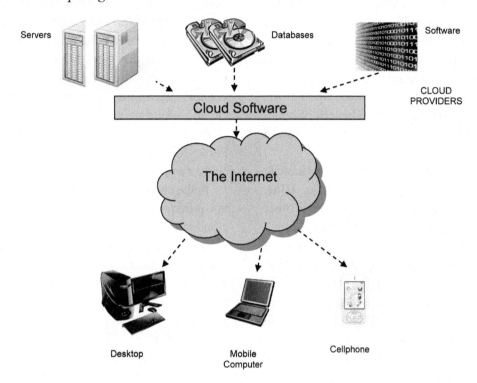

Using virtualization, clients share a mix of servers, hard drives, data communications devices, and memory (Cervone, 2010). In additions, such services are monitored, with the user paying for only what computing resources they use, in a metered fashion. The cloud appears as a single point of access for all the users' needs.

The growing popularity of the new phenomenon stems from the attractiveness of the organization not having to maintain computing infrastructures in-house. IT can now use new software or IT infrastructure services on the fly without having to pay for in-house software or hardware. This drastically reduces the cost of deploying applications (Cusumano, 2010; Durkee, 2010)

These subscription or pay-per-use services can help to reduce implementation times for even large systems and extend the IT capabilities of the firm in a flexible fashion (King, 2010).

The New York Times offers a prime example of enterprise cloud computing. Having digitized over a century's worth of newspaper pages, it converted them to browser-friendly PDF format and deployed them to the cloud in a matter of days (Golden, 2009).

Additionally, organizations can gain access to computing power they cannot afford to buy. Universities and biotech companies for example, often lack in-house massive computing power to conduct certain types of research. Many are now looking beyond the walls of their institutions and turning to cloud computing as a solution (May, 2010; Thilmany, 2009)

There are generally understood to be three types of cloud computing, namely software (or applications), platforms, and infrastructure. They are known respectively as SaaS – software as a service; PaaS – platform as a service; and IaaS – infrastructure as a service.

At the low end of cloud computing are the email services that millions are familiar with, such as Yahoo mail, Gmail and Hotmail. The email servers and users' email are stored on the cloud via the Internet, managed by Yahoo, Google, and Microsoft. Access takes place through the Internet and consumers get the benefit of email service without handling hardware or software installation and maintenance issues.

The major cloud computing providers include Hewlett Packard, Microsoft, Amazon, IBM, Salesforce and Google. They and many other vendors are investing billions of dollars in cloud computing (Golden, 2009). Many providers of shrink-wrapped software, ranging from enterprise software to office productivity software – who would be losers as cloud computing spreads – are quickly moving to deliver their applications using cloud computing.

It is not only the US that has its sights set on cloud computing. The government of Taiwan plans to invest NT $24 billion in cloud computing over the next 5 years (Chiu, 2010). IBM has also developed two cloud computing centers in South Africa and another China, and in 2010, opened another in Poland.

The Rise of the Cloud

Cloud computing's recent rise has been brought about by parallel developments in various types of information and communications technologies. The first of these is the sophisticated software that manages the cloud resources (e.g., servers, operating systems, memory, clusters, and storage area networks) and ensures smooth multi-tenancy for all the users.

This management software is the key distinguishing element of cloud computing, enabling thousands of users to share computing resources transparently and incorporating such features as failover, security, and load balancing (Armbrust et al., 2010; Barnes, 2010). Creeger (2010) describes how virtualization challenges the traditional binding of infrastructural services to physical devices.

Cloud software is highly complex (Barnes, 2010) and there is no standard for managing clouds. Rather, the software is usually proprietary to the vendors offering the services. Amazon's EC2, Google's AppEngine, and Microsoft's Azure Services Platform, The IBM Cloud and Salesforce's Force are examples of commercially available cloud computing platforms.

In the cloud computing literature, the distinction is frequently made between *public* and *private* cloud offerings. Public cloud services are offered by third parties, firms such as Google that service the needs of diverse firms. Thus, the applications and data from multiple firms share the same cloud infrastructure, depending on the cloud software to maintain data and application privacy.

Some authors, e.g., Armbrust et al. (2010), exclude private cloud computing from consideration as true cloud offerings, citing their inelastic resource limits and the need for capital outlays on in-house hardware and software. However, given a large organization of several tens of thousands of employees, a private cloud may actually serve more "customers" than a public cloud provider. So it may be just a matter of scale.

A study conducted by VersionOne (2009) found that 41% of senior IT professionals don't know what cloud computing is and two-thirds of senior finance professionals are confused by the concept. In addition, a recent report by McKinsey & Co identified twenty-two different definitions for cloud computing (Woo, 2010).

The focus of this paper is on how cloud computing is being adopted across various types and sizes of industries, and across developing and developed countries. This is an exploratory study that analyzes emerging data on cloud use to begin to identify patterns of adoption by different types of industries across different countries.

The results of this initial study will be to identify patterns of adoption and describe the factors affecting firms' selection of cloud computing alternatives in different regions of the world. The result is a better understanding of cloud computing that can assist the IT manager seeking to make the best use of the new technology to support IT and wider business objectives of their organization.

CLOUD COMPUTING INFRASTRUCTURES

Cloud computing is related to other computing architectures and concepts that have featured along its evolutionary path. Some of these concepts, like grid computing, or utility computing are often wrongly confused with cloud computing, although cloud computing shares some of their features.

Grid Computing: This form of distributed computing parcels out parts of a large computing task to multiple, loosely-coupled computers. The "grid" uses parallel processing to perform the task.

Utility Computing: The idea behind utility computing is making computing resources available to users in the same way as electricity utility supplies electricity. The service is metered or "pay-per-use", just like electricity or water is metered and charged (Brynjolfsson et al., 2010).

Client-Server Computing: In client/server computing, a client computer makes requests over a network to a server computer, which provides computational or data-related services.

Application Service Provider (*ASP*): An ASP provides access by customers over the Internet to remote applications that support the organization's business activities.

Virtualization: ASPs have operated using virtualization for many years. This enables them to co-host multiple websites and user applications on a single server, so that the cost of a server is shared by multiple users. VMWare and Citrix server lead in the server virtualization arena, with Citrix's Xen software used by Amazon for its EC2 cloud offering.

There are in fact, three types of systems architectures associated with the term, cloud computing, as shown in Figure 2. They are:

Software as a Service (SaaS): This is the most popular form of cloud computing, where the user accesses and uses commercially available applications remotely. The user cannot typically access the operating system or servers, but requires only the functionality of the application. Salesforce.com's CRM, Google Apps, and Netsuite's ERP application are examples of public cloud SaaS or On-Demand applications Nevin, 2009).

Platform as a Service (PaaS): Instead of providing an application, PaaS vendors e.g., Rackspace, provide users a computing platform that is usually virtual. The customer then installs their own applications on this virtual platform. These virtual servers use cloud software to share resources across multiple servers and storage units.

Infrastructure as a Service (IaaS): In this form of cloud computing, the vendor rents the hardware and networking equipment used to support the customer's operations or business services. The client then pays on a per-use basis. With IaaS, the type of application the client runs does not matter—any application can be created or any shrink-wrapped software can be deployed on an IaaS platform.

PRIVATE VS. PUBLIC CLOUDS

Another major distinguishing characteristic of various types of cloud computing is the ownership and location of the cloud. There are private and public clouds. A public cloud is owned and operated by a third-party cloud firm that provides cloud services to an array of customers. They share the hardware, software and communications of the cloud and have access to on-demand, utility-based cloud services.

There are also private cloud architectures in which an organization chooses to use a SaaS, PaaS, or IaaS strategy to satisfy its information

Figure 2. Three types of cloud computing

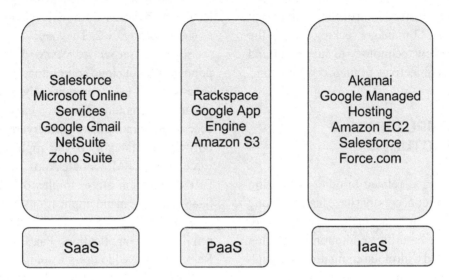

processing needs. Critics of the term "private cloud" argue that cloud computing excludes private clouds due to the finite resources available for overall processing and the need of the using company to purchase new IT resources if existing resources are being fully utilized – unlike true cloud computing that would simply provision more resources on the fly.

Certainly, this argument has merit, but in the largest organizations, often comprising hundreds of thousands of computer users and thousands of applications, one can certainly imagine a private cloud infrastructure that consolidates dispersed servers across the organization. The main benefit would then simply be the higher resource utilization that comes from sharing by many (internal) clients.

THE CLOUD VS. TRADITIONAL COMPUTING MODELS

The emerging view of cloud computing is that it is evolutionary in regard to the types of infrastructure that preceded it, such as the ASP computing model, grid computing, client/server computing and vir-

tualization. It certainly borrows key elements of many of these technologies and infrastructures.

However, it is also correct in the view of many, to view cloud computing as revolutionary for businesses, enabling an entirely new business model for the IT function in the organization. Prior to the cloud, organizations had two major options, including (a) locally hosting and managing their server infrastructure, or (b) leasing a remote server via and Application Service Provider (ASP) to run the organization's applications.

Local hosting means creating an in-house computing infrastructure – allocating facilities for computing equipment, procuring and installing servers and software, storage and backups, power management and uninterruptible power supplies (UPSs). In addition, the organization is responsible for hardware upgrades, software patches and upgrades and security.

Internal IT operations also require the organization to hire and maintain an IT staff to run and manage the infrastructure. All these capital and recurrent costs can be prohibitive for the small or medium enterprise (or SME) who wants to focus on their core competency and not on running IT operations.

Using a remote server, as with a local server, involved server setup and management, and did not allow for elastic growth in capacity. Scalability was coarse-grained, as any growth beyond local or remote capabilities necessitated a server replacement or addition.

The other part of this equation was that the new server (additional or replacement) could not be brought online immediately; it had to be purchased, delivered, and installed, a process that might take days or even weeks.

With the cloud however, resources are elastic and provisioning is fine-grained (Lucky, 2009). Using the cloud software and fabric, each user can be provisioned exactly the amount of resources they need in real time and the user billed for it. By spreading user processing amid multiple processors, servers and storage area networks (SANs), cloud providers obtain higher resource utilization on average than the typical single server.

BUSINESS MODELS AND BENEFITS

Businesses are quickly turning to cloud computing for a variety of reasons, which this part of the paper now explores

Lower Costs

Multiplexing the computing needs of hundreds or thousands of customers reduces the cost to cloud providers and makes cloud computing cheaper for the customer. Leveraging this higher computer utilization makes cloud computing an attractive option for both the vendors and users of cloud computing services. In September 2009, an Aberdeen Group study (2009) found that disciplined companies achieved on average an 18% reduction in their IT budget from cloud computing and a 16% reduction in data center power costs.

Pay-as-you-Grow/ No Initial Financial Outlays

For the new organization with an untested concept or product, cloud computing allows their computing resources to grow elastically from 5 customers to say, 500,000, paying only for resources used at all times (Greengard & Kshetri, 2010). This means that large initial outlays for servers and storage and so on are no longer needed. The company only pays for computation and storage for five users at the launch of their new product/service and for new users as they are added. They are therefore freed from large outlays on staff and equipment.

Instant-On Services

Development time for the launch of a new service or product can be dramatically reduced or eliminated through the use of cloud computing as virtual web servers can be immediately provisioned and brought online in the cloud. This is superior to the setup times for infrastructure that is part and parcel of in-house or even hosted systems.

Business Agility

Cloud computing clients enjoy unprecedented business agility as a result of deploying new and experimental concepts and products/services to the web in record time and at minimal cost. This allows faster test feedback as to the workability of new ideas and innovations that are rapidly deployed. The other benefit is that firms can spend more time on their core competency, which may not be developing and maintaining IT infrastructure.

Cloud Computing Cons: Privacy, Reliability, Security and Cost

Despite the touted advantages of cloud computing and the massive movement towards the cloud by companies large and small, there are still criticisms of cloud computing discussed in the press.

A major concern with cloud computing is privacy. There are still many corporations that will not entrust their data or processing logic to the cloud due to privacy concerns. When an organization migrates applications and data to the cloud, then the cloud vendor can monitor the inputs, outputs and data of both the client and users.

Government intrusion, such as the United States' National Security Agency's now-disclosed covert monitoring program, can also violate privacy. Vendors such as Amazon are trying to address such concerns, by deploying infrastructure in regions such as the EU, but privacy remains a sore spot for cloud critics (Gatewood, 2009).

Security is also raised frequently as a risk item for cloud computing (Wang et al., 2010). In 2009, Ma.gnolia, an online bookmarking service, suffered a catastrophic data failure in which many of its users irretrievably lost their bookmarks. Also in 2009, users of T-Mobile Sidekick also lost data due to a server error at Danger, a Microsoft subsidiary.

In 2008, the Linkup, a cloud vendor with over 20,000 paying customers lost most of their customer's data after a system crash. Blaming their problems on a partner storage company was cold comfort to customers who had no recourse after The Linkup went out of business following the crash.

Reliability is related to security and relates to uptime and system availability. A company has few options if their cloud vendor's infrastructure goes down or suffers from degraded service. However, many of the top cloud vendors such as Rackspace and Amazon for example, offer impressive Service Level Agreements (SLAs). Cloud customers want vendors to incorporate the factors below in their SLAs:

- What happens if the cloud service goes down?
- What happens if network connectivity to/ from the cloud goes down?
- Is there data backup in the event a server instance goes down?
- Does the vendor have redundancy in place in the event network connectivity to the cloud goes down?
- Does a secondary cloud exist in the event the entire cloud goes down?

Some have made the counter argument that cloud computing potentially provides a level of reliability that exceeds that of all but the largest firms. By distributing computing resources and divorcing hardware from applications, cloud computing users are rarely affected by the failure of any single server or storage device. Thus, the reliability argument against cloud computing weakens as the technology advances.

SMEs vs. Larger Firms

Small and medium enterprises stand to gain the most from cloud computing improvements, as the cloud enables them to deploy applications cheaper and quicker than they could afford on their own. The cost models are also more advantageous as there are no minimums for software licenses – small numbers of users and customers obtain the same performance benefits as larger numbers. In Creeger (2010), one discussion centers on how SMEs led the initial wave of cloud computing in the enterprise, larger firms being followers to cloud technology.

As cloud computing has become more robust and reliable, with better SLAs, larger firms have begun to move to the web and to explore cloud possibilities. The future will likely hold as much growth in large company usage of cloud computing as with smaller companies.

Cloud Computing in Developing Countries

The major focus of this paper is to examine the adoption of cloud computing not only in the

United States, but also in other regions of the world. The United States and other parts of the developed world have the greatest levels of adoption of cloud computing, but other parts of the world have possibly even more to gain than the developed world, with the possibility of changes to the world's economy possible by the adoption of cloud computing.

Greengard (2010) describes how powerful in-house computing infrastructures are beyond the reach of most individuals and even corporations in developing countries. In these countries, cloud computing offers a unique opportunity to obtain the use of powerful and sophisticated computing infrastructures and applications at minimal cost. Thus, cloud computing has a special significance for the developing world.

As one example, Greengard (2010) describes the cloud-based trading software created by the Apparel Export Promotion Council that serves 11,000 of its members. He also describes the widespread use of Google Apps and Smartphone apps in developing countries across the world. Greengard projects that cloud computing will grow in India from a $50 million industry in 2009 to a $15 billion industry, as more small businesses jump on the cloud bandwagon.

In a sense, cloud computing is beginning to serve as the great "leveler" as companies small and large in developed and developing nations alike gain the same access to sophisticated and powerful applications in the cloud. We will examine next how cloud computing can indeed become a game changer in developing countries, the significance to developing country economies and how they can take the biggest advantage of cloud computing opportunities.

Issues Surrounding Cloud Computing in the Developing World

For cloud computing to be effectively adopted and utilized in developing countries, several issues must be addressed. Some of the key issues are

technology-related, while others relate to the law and to ecommerce. These issues are as follows:

Reliable Connections to the Internet. A key requirement for cloud computing is a reliable connection to the Internet. In many developing countries, the reliable connections of the developed world are not yet available for personal computing and businesses alike. In others, reliable business-rated broadband connections are still prohibitively expensive for the SMEs.

Today's cloud computing applications mostly require broadband access and the ability of developing nations to take full advantage of cloud computing will be determined by the future costs and reliability of Internet transmissions.

The good news is that Internet access is spreading rapidly in the developing world, notably India, China, Africa, and South America. Table 1 shows dramatic increases in Internet usage in the various continents. Africa, for example, experienced 2357% increase in Internet users between 2000 and 2010, with the Middle East experiencing a 1,825% increase during the same period.

The availability of broadband in developing nations is significant in relation to cloud computing, as most cloud applications are designed to work with rich media that are only available using broadband. Therefore, expensive satellite communications to businesses are quickly being replaced by DSL and WIMAX connections in many developing countries.

Some problems remain in parts of Africa, Asia and South America, where there is a lack of fixed lines to the inner regions, meaning that most new DSL connections are primarily deployed in large cities, especially coastal cities where new undersea fiber-optic cables terminate.

The ITU (2009) describes how, due to few fixed networks in many developing countries, where wired access is often restricted to major urban centers, it is mobile broadband that has taken the lead in expanding high-speed Internet access to the wider population. Mobile cellular networks are extremely widespread in developing nations and

Table 1. Levels of global internet access

WORLD INTERNET USAGE AND POPULATION STATISTICS						
World Regions	**Population (2010 Est.)**	**Internet Users Dec. 31, 2000**	**Internet Users Latest Data**	**Penetration (% Population)**	**Growth 2000-2010**	**Users % of Table**
Africa	1,013,779,050	4,514,400	**110,931,700**	10.9%	2357.3%	5.6%
Asia	3,834,792,852	114,304,000	**825,094,396**	21.5%	621.8%	42.0%
Europe	813,319,511	105,096,093	**475,069,448**	58.4%	352.0%	24.2%
Middle East	212,336,924	3,284,800	**63,240,946**	29.8%	1825.3%	3.2%
North America	344,124,450	108,096,800	**266,224,500**	77.4%	146.3%	13.5%
Latin America/ Caribbean	592,556,972	18,068,919	**204,689,836**	34.5%	1032.8%	10.4%
Oceania / Australia	34,700,201	7,620,480	**21,263,990**	61.3%	179.0%	1.1%
WORLD TOTAL	6,845,609,960	360,985,492	**1,966,514,816**	**28.7%**	444.8%	100.0%

Source: Adapted from Internetworldstats.com, 2010

are now used increasingly for data applications (SMS, MMS, M-Commerce and M-Banking). Many of these new applications are cloud-based applications.

The ITU describes mobile phone penetration in developing countries reaching 68% in 2010—higher than any other technology before. It sees developing countries as being innovative in adapting mobile technology to their needs and predicts greater benefits from broadband once adequate and affordable access is available. (ITU, 2010)

New 'Tethering functions, allow the use of 3G or 4G Smartphones as 'hotspots' or Wi-Fi access points. This offers users in LDCs the opportunity to use their Smartphones as replacements for routers and gain broadband access on their PCs. This technology will become more common as cellphone technology spreads.

Cherry (2009) states that by 2014, mobile devices will send and receive more data per month than they did in all of 2008.

ANALYSIS

Deployment of cloud computing continue to take place at differing paces in various parts of the world. The fastest deployments are taking place in the United States, followed by OECD countries, and then by less developed countries. In this section, we look at what cloud computing will mean for various categories of users in each of the three regions.

We also examine issues unique to each region relating to legal, privacy, contract enforcement, and security, and how these will affect the growth of cloud computing in each of the regions.

United States

Most of the major and second-tier cloud vendors are located in the United States, which is where, not surprisingly, the greatest advertising and use of cloud computing is taking place.

It is in the US, with pervasive broadband, that the greatest uptake in corporate cloud computing is taking place. Small businesses are taking to the cloud in large numbers, viewing it as an opportunity to leverage powerful computing assets at a fraction of the price.

The popularity of such cloud offerings as Salesforce.com (SaaS) and cloud hosting services (e.g., Rackspace and Amazon) is testimony to the confidence enjoyed by small businesses in the reliability of the technology.

Larger businesses have been slower to adopt cloud computing, but this is changing, with large corporations going beyond experimental projects to deploying first, non mission-critical applications and then, mission-critical applications to the web.

The introduction of Service-Level Agreements by the larger cloud vendors is also playing a major part in easing the way for these larger companies to become cloud computing users.

Another major development for corporate cloud computing users in the U.S. is adoption of the private cloud model. Many organizations, for which privacy and security are overriding concerns, are choosing private cloud architectures, to take advantage of server virtualization and cloud infrastructure, but in a private setting.

While many cloud "purists" do not agree that the private or enterprise cloud is indeed a cloud, the reality is that larger organizations are beginning to implement this technology, regardless of nomenclature.

For individual entrepreneurs, cloud computing is a boon and is already in widespread use for entrepreneurial projects of all varieties. Cloud computing has given these entrepreneurs access to the same technologies as larger corporations at a much lower cost. In the near future, most of the data and applications of entrepreneurs that are traditionally hosted will migrate to the cloud.

At the consumer level, users already use a multitude of cloud based applications, including email services such as yahoo mail and hotmail. They also upload photos to the web, use Google Apps for their documents and increasingly use cloud based social networks and applications like cloud based computer backups. US individual users are already very comfortable with the web and the next few years will likely see an explosion in individual use of cloud services as reliability grows.

OECD/ASEAN Countries

Countries that fall into the OECD share many of the same characteristics as the U.S. They sport widespread broadband availability, typically higher than the U.S., and enjoy the legal protection of contracts and intellectual property found there.

However, cloud computing faces formidable obstacles in Europe and the wider OECD as strict privacy laws there place rigid limits on the movement of information beyond the borders of the 27-country European Union (Bristow et al., 2010).

European governments seek to protect personal information from aggressive marketers and cybercriminals after it leaves the jurisdictions of individual EU members. This hinders cloud computing, which depends on a free flow of information.

Gartner estimates global sales of cloud services to reach $102 billion by 2012 (Gartner Group 2010). However, Europe is expected to account for only $18 billion in 2010, or only 26% of the global total. By 2012, Gartner sees Europe's share of global cloud sales rising to 29%, even though the EU's economy is larger than that of the United States.

The European Data Privacy Directive, the main body of European law governing international data transfers, is another obstacle to cloud computing in the EU, as it prohibits the movement of E.U. data outside the union's borders.

The EU has approved only the United States, Argentina and Canada to provide cloud computing services. Israel and Andorra have pending applications to serve as computing centers for EU customers.

Companies seeking to process EU data in unapproved countries, such as offshoring hubs, India and Malaysia must negotiate and enter into binding service level agreements with data processors that ensure personal information of EU citizens will be handled in accordance with E.U. regulations (O'Brien, 2010).

The U.S. businesses with the greatest stake in cloud computing — primarily Microsoft, Google, H.P. and Oracle — are using a three-pronged approach, involving: (a) lobbying the E.U. to looses the restrictions on the movement of data within the cloud, (b) devising encryption approaches to protect the privacy of users' data within the cloud, and (c) building cloud infrastructures located in the EU that serve primarily EU based customers and obey EU rules.

In other words, in the EU, the promise exists for the growth of cloud computing, but it currently lags its potential for organizational deployment of mission-critical applications that will enable corporations to obtain similar benefits to their U.S. counterparts. This may change in the future.

The research firm IDC estimates the market for cloud computing in Asia outside Japan will grow to about $1.3 billion in 2010 and will continue to grow at a rate of about 40% a year until 2014. While the rate of growth is impressive, it is still a miniscule amount compared to the US and the EU.

The major brakes of cloud computing in Asia are regulations, concerns about data security and poor Internet connections. However, the landscape is being transformed by improved technology and the phenomenal growth in broadband experienced by Asian countries.

Some countries, such as Singapore, South Korea, and Hong Kong, have more highly developed telecommunication infrastructures, leading to their new status as cloud computing hubs within the region (Fitzimmons, 2010). What is clear is that while tight data regulations in countries like China and poor infrastructure in India limit growth, cloud computing will be massively adopted in Asia in the next few years.

For small organizations and individual entrepreneurs, while the pace of adoption is slower than the EU and the United States, cloud computing is poised to transform computing in Asia, with more applications likely to be delivered through Smartphones in many countries, in addition to the desktop.

Less Developed Countries (LDCs)

LDCs have the greatest limitations to the spread of cloud computing, but paradoxically, offer the greatest benefits to corporations and individuals. Cloud computing business users in LDCs have the opportunity to access and use applications well beyond their ability to purchase or even use on a hosted basis.

The lower price point of many cloud applications will be beneficial to both corporations and small business users in much of Africa, South America and poorer countries in South Asia.

The major limitation facing the spread of cloud computing in LDCs is the widespread availability of "traditional" broadband, or broadband to the desktop via landlines. It is becoming clear that in parts of the world such as Sub Saharan Africa there will likely never be the same amount of fixed lines laid to homes and businesses as is the case in richer countries.

The amount that would have to be spent on laying cable would be cost-prohibitive for poorer countries. However, many such countries are skipping this technological phase of telecommunications and going directly to broadband wireless technologies, such as 3G and 4G. In many sub Saharan countries, up to half the populations have access to broadband via mobile phones while less than 5% of their populations have access to landlines (Cleverley, 2009).

Developers of cloud computing in LDCs will need to ensure that their services can be delivered over Smartphones through microbrowsers, which are many times more widespread than computers. With 3G and 4G services, that becomes very feasible. Vendors like Salesforce.com already deliver Smartphone-ready interfaces to their CRM applications. Also, basic services like email are in use by millions in LDCs who are thus already familiar with the cloud concept.

From a very slow start therefore, it would seem that cloud computing has a bright future, though over a longer-term deployment schedule in LDCs. Millions in these countries would likely trust externally hosted clouds to support their applications than internally hosted applications.

Using an external host in a country such as the US, small firms would view themselves as protected from poor power supply conditions and low physical security that would characterize their own locally-developed infrastructures.

The availability of much lower price points that traditionally hosted solutions would also be very attractive to users in countries with a much lower GDP than rich countries. Legal issues and privacy concerns are also likely to be less of an obstacle to LDCs taking advantage of cloud offerings located outside their borders.

SUMMARY AND CONCLUSION

Cloud computing is proving to be a transformational technology with huge impact for businesses and individual computer users across the world. Using such technologies as server virtualization, the Internet and worldwide web, grid computing, utility computing, and client/server computing, services are delivered over the Internet by this new form of computing infrastructure.

The key to cloud computing is the software that handles user access and resource allocation among user applications in a transparent manner to many users via a mix of computing devices. These devices are shared by multiple users, enabling higher server utilization rates and correspondingly lower user prices than is typically the case in dedicated server environments.

Such service elasticity and instant provisioning of new resources is a distinguishing feature of cloud computing, as well as increasing levels of reliability for provided services. Users need only pay for services used, so new applications can begin at a price point far lower than would be the case with dedicated private, or even hosted servers.

In addition, cloud services can be brought online much quicker than would be the case in internal computing environments, often in a matter of minutes. This enables firms of all kinds to minimize their involvement in building and maintaining computing infrastructures and instead, focus on their core competencies.

The growth of cloud computing, forecast to be a $102 billion market in 2014, has been fastest in the United States, followed by other OECD members and then Asian countries. Legal restrictions and poor broadband have limited growth in these two regions, but once these issues are adequately handled, cloud computing use is likely to grow massively as users take advantage of the new technologies.

In LDCs, cloud computing will take a different direction as more services will likely be delivered over cell-based broadband networks to Smartphones on 3G and 4G networks and not via rare landlines.

Small businesses across all regions will gain more than larger businesses that can afford their own powerful and sophisticated computing infrastructures. Individual entrepreneurs will gain even more in being able to leverage powerful infrastructures to test their ideas in the marketplace. This revolution in computing is therefore likely to be very transformative globally over the next decade.

REFERENCES

Aberdeen Group. (2009). *Business Adoption of Cloud Computing*. Boston: Author.

Armbrust, M., Fox, A., Griffith, R., Joseph, A., Katz, R., & Konwinski, A. (2010). A View of Cloud Computing. *Communications of the ACM, 53*(4), 50. doi:10.1145/1721654.1721672

Arnold, W. (2010, October 10) Regulations and Security Concerns Hinder Asia's Move to Cloud Computing. *The New York Times*.

Barnes, F. (2010). Putting a lock on Cloud-Based Information. *Information Management Journal, 44*(4), 26–30.

Bristow, R., Dodds, T., Northam, R., & Plugge, L. (2010). Cloud Computing and the Power to Choose. *EDUCAUSE Review, 45*(3), 14.

Brynjolfsson, E., Hofmann, P., & Jordan, J. (2010). Economic and Business Dimensions Cloud Computing and Electricity: Beyond the Utility Model. *Communications of the ACM, 53*(5), 32. doi:10.1145/1735223.1735234

Cervone, F. H. (2010). An overview of virtual and cloud computing. *OCLC Systems & Services, 26*(3), 162–165. doi:10.1108/10650751011073607

Cherry, S. (2009). Forecast for Cloud Computing: Up, Up, and Away. *IEEE Spectrum, 46*(10), 68. doi:10.1109/MSPEC.2009.5268002

Chiu, Y. (2010). Taiwan Sees Clouds in Its Forecast. *IEEE Spectrum, 47*(8), 13. doi:10.1109/MSPEC.2010.5520615

Cleverley, M. (2009). Emerging Markets How ICT Advances Might Help Developing Nations. *Communications of the ACM, 52*(9), 30. doi:10.1145/1562164.1562177

Creeger, M. (2010). Moving to the Edge: A CTO Roundtable on Network Virtualization. *Communications of the ACM, 53*(8), 55. doi:10.1145/1787234.1787251

Cusumano, M. (2010). Technology Strategy and Management Cloud Computing and SaaS as New Computing Platforms. *Communications of the ACM, 53*(4), 27. doi:10.1145/1721654.1721667

Deelman, E. (2010). Grids and Clouds: Making Workflow Applications Work in Heterogeneous Distributed Environments. *International Journal of High Performance Computing Applications, 24*(3), 284. doi:10.1177/1094342009356432

DeFelice, A., & Leon, J. (2010). Cloud Computing. *Journal of Accountancy, 210*(4), 50–55.

Durkee, D. (2010). Why Cloud Computing Will Never Be Free. *Communications of the ACM, 53*(5), 62. doi:10.1145/1735223.1735242

Fitzsimmons, H. (2010, October). Cloud.com Selected as Cloud Computing Platform for Korea's First Large-Scale Private ClouFkoread. *Computers, Networks & Communications, 158.*

Gatewood, B. (2009). Clouds on the Information Horizon: How to Avoid the Storm. *Information Management Journal, 43*(4), 32–36.

Golden, B. (2009). Cloud Computing: "Be Prepared. *EDUCAUSE Review, 44*(4), 64.

Greengard, S., & Kshetri, N. (2010). Cloud Computing and Developing Nations. *Communications of the ACM, 53*(5), 18. doi:10.1145/1735223.1735232

Hayes, B. (2008). Cloud Computing. *Communications of the ACM, 51*(7), 9. doi:10.1145/1364782.1364786

International Telecommunications Union. (2009). *Measuring the Information Society: The ICT Development Index.* Geneva, Switzerland: Author.

King, J. (2010). Clearing the Air on Cloud Computing. *EDUCAUSE Review, 45*(3), 64.

Louridas, P. (2010). Up in the Air: Moving Your Applications to the Cloud. *IEEE Software, 27*(4), 6–11. doi:10.1109/MS.2010.109

Lucky, R. (2009). Cloud Computing. *IEEE Spectrum, 46*(5), 27. doi:10.1109/MSPEC.2009.4907382

May, M. (2010). Forecast calls for clouds over biological computing. *Nature Medicine, 16*(1), 6. doi:10.1038/nm0110-6a

Mell, P., & Grance, T. (2010). The NIST Definition of Cloud Computing. *Communications of the ACM, 53*(6), 50.

Nevin, R. (2009). Supporting 21st Century Learning through Google Apps. *Teacher Librarian, 37*(2), 35–38.

O'Brien, K. J. (2010, September 19). Cloud Computing Hits a Snag. *The New York Times.*

Thilmany, J. (2009). In the Clouds. *Mechanical Engineering (New York, N.Y.), 131*(7), 16.

VersionOne. (2009). *Cloud Confusion Amongst IT Professionals.*

Wang, C., Ren, K., Lou, W., & Li, J. (2010). Toward Publicly Auditable Secure Cloud Data Storage Services. *IEEE Network, 24*(4), 5. doi:10.1109/MNET.2010.5510914

Woo, M., & Dieckmann, M. (2010). The Multiple Personalities of Cloud Computing. *EDUCAUSE Review, 45*(3), 12.

This work was previously published in International Journal of Enterprise Information Systems, edited by Madjid Tavana, pp. 55-68, Volume 6, Issue 4, copyright 2010 by IGI Publishing (an imprint of IGI Global).

Section 3
Emerging Software Development Technologies

Chapter 13
A Good Role Model
for Ontologies:
Collaborations

Michael Pradel
Technische Universität Dresden, Germany

Jakob Henriksson
Technische Universität Dresden, Germany

Uwe Aßmann
Technische Universität Dresden, Germany

ABSTRACT

Although ontologies are gaining more and more acceptance, they are often not engineered in a compo-nent-based manner due to, among various reasons, a lack of appropriate constructs in current ontology languages. This hampers reuse and makes creating new ontologies from existing building blocks difficult. We propose to apply the notion of roles and role modeling to ontologies and present an extension of the Web Ontology Language OWL for this purpose. Ontological role models allow for clearly separating different concerns of a domain and constitute an intuitive reuse unit.

1. INTRODUCTION

Ontology languages are emerging as the de facto standard for capturing semantics on the web. One of the most important ontology languages today is the Web Ontology Language (OWL), standard-ized and recommended by the World Wide Web Consortium (W3C) (Patel-Schneider et al., 2004). One issue currently addressed in the research community is how to define reusable ontologies or ontology parts. In more general terms, how to construct an ontology from possibly independently developed components.

OWL natively provides some facilities for reusing ontologies and ontology parts. First, a feature inherited from RDF (Hayes et al., 2004), upon which OWL is layered, is *linking*—loosely referencing distributed web content and other ontologies using URIs. Second, OWL provides an owl:imports construct which syntactically

DOI: 10.4018/978-1-4666-1761-2.ch013

includes the complete referenced ontology into the importing ontology. The linking mechanism is convenient from a modeling perspective, but is semantically not well-defined—there is no guarantee that the referenced ontology or web content exists. Furthermore, the component (usually an ontology class) is small and often hard to detach from the surrounding ontology in a semantically well-defined way. Usually a full ontology import is required since it is unclear which other classes the referenced class depends on. The owl:imports construct can only handle complete ontologies and does not allow for partial reuse. This can lead to inconsistencies in the resulting ontology due to conflicting modeling axioms. Overall, OWL seems to be inflexible in the kind of reuse provided, especially regarding the granularity of components.

Existing approaches addressing these issues often refer to *modular ontologies* and, in general terms, aim at enabling the reuse of ontology parts or fragments in a well-defined way (for some work in this direction, see Cuenca Grau et al., 2006, 2007a, 2007b). That is, investigate how only certain parts of an ontology can be reused and deployed elsewhere. While it is interesting work and allows for reuse, we believe that such extracted ontological units fail to provide an intuitive meaning of why those units should constitute *components*—they were not designed as such.

The object-oriented software community has long discussed new ways of modeling software. One interesting result of this research is the notion of *role modeling* (Reenskaug et al., 1996). The main argument is that today's class-oriented modeling mixes two related but ultimately different notions: *natural types* and *role types*. Natural types capture the identity of its instances, while a role type describes their interactions. Intuitively, an object cannot discard its natural type without losing its identity while a role type can be changed depending on the current context of the object. *Person* for example, is a natural type while *Parent* is a role type. Parent is a *role* that can be played by

persons. A role type thus only models one specific aspect of its related natural types. Related role types can be joined together into a *role model* to capture and separate one specific concern of the modeled whole.

In this paper we introduce role modeling to ontologies. Role modeling can bring several benefits to ontologies and ontological modeling. Roles provide:

- More natural ontological modeling by separating roles from classes
- An appropriate notion and size of reusable ontological components—role models
- Separation of concerns by capturing a single concern in a role model

We believe that role models constitute useful and natural units for component-based ontology engineering. Role models are developed as components and intended to be deployed as such, in contrast to existing approaches aimed at extracting ontological units from ontologies not necessarily designed to be modular. While we argue that modeling with roles is beneficial to ontological modeling and provides a new kind of component not previously considered for ontologies, the transition from object-orientation is not straightforward. The contribution of this paper is the introduction of modeling primitives to support roles in ontologies and a discussion of the main differences for role modeling between ontologies and object-oriented models (henceforth, the latter are simply referred to as models). The semantics of the new modeling primitives is provided by translation into the assumed underlying ontological formalism of Description Logics (DLs) (Baader et al., 2003). That way, existing tools can be reused for modeling with roles. To convince the reader of the usefulness of role models, we demonstrate their use on two examples. The first example shows separation of concerns and the second example demonstrates reuse of role models in different contexts.

The remaining part of the paper is structured as follows. Section 2 introduces roles as used and understood in object-orientation and discusses the main differences between models and ontologies. Section 3 introduces role models to ontologies and gives examples of their use. Section 4 discusses related work to component-based ontology modeling and Section 5 concludes the paper and discusses open issues.

2. FROM ROLES IN SOFTWARE MODELING TO ONTOLOGIES

The OOram software engineering method (Reenskaug et al., 1996) was the first to introduce roles in object-orientation. The innovative idea was that objects can actually be abstracted in two ways: classifying them according to their inherent properties and focusing on how they work together with other objects (collaborate). While the use of classes as an object abstraction is a cornerstone in object-oriented modeling, focusing on object collaborations using roles has not been given the attention it deserves (however, for some work addressing these issues, see CaesarJ (Aracic et al., 2006) and ObjectTeams (Herrmann, 2002)).

There are different views on what roles are in the object-oriented community (Steimann, 2000; Steimann, 2005). However, some basic concepts seem to be accepted by most authors:

Roles and role types. A role describes the behavior of an object in a certain context. In this context the object is said to play the role. One object may play several roles at a time. A set of roles with similar behavior is abstracted by a role type (just as similar objects are abstracted by a class).

Collaborations and role models. Roles focus on the interaction between objects and consequently never occur in isolation, but rather in collaborations. This leads to a new abstraction not available for classes—the role model. It describes a set of role types that relate to each other and thus as a whole characterizes a common collaboration (a common goal or functionality).

Open and bound role types. Role types are bound to classes by a *plays* relation, e.g. *Person plays Father* (a person can play the role of being a father). However, not all role types of a role model must be bound to a class. Role types not associated with a class are called open and intuitively describe missing parts of a collaboration.

It is important to note that class modeling and role modeling do not replace each other, but are complementary. A purely class-based approach arguably leads to poor modeling by enforcing the representation of role types by classes and thus disregards reuse possibilities based on object collaborations. However, roles cannot replace classes entirely since this would disallow modeling of properties that are not related to a specific context.

Adapting Roles for Ontology Modeling

There is currently no consensus on the exact relationship between models and ontologies, although the question is a current and important one (see e.g. (Aßmann et al., 2006)). There is however some agreement upon fundamental differences between models and ontologies which will have an impact on transferring the notion of roles from models to ontologies.

One difference is that models often describe something dynamic, for example a system to be implemented. In contrast, ontologies are static entities. Even though an ontology may evolve over time, the entities being modeled do not have the same notion of time. Models often describe systems that are eventually to be executed, while ontologies do not (although some approaches exist that compile ontologies to Java; see for example, http://www.aifb.uni-karlsruhe.de/WBS/aeb/onto-java). The dynamism and notion of executability in modeling is closely connected to functionality (or behavior). A collaboration in object-oriented modeling often captures a separate and reusable functionality. For example, a realization of depth-first traversal over graph structures may require several collaborating methods in different classes for its implementation. The collection of all the related dependencies between the classes constitutes a collaboration and thus implements this *functionality* (Smaragdakis & Batory, 2002). Because of the non-existence of dynamism and behavior in ontologies, roles and collaborations necessarily capture something different. Instead of describing the *behavior* of an object using the notion of a role, ontological roles describe context-dependent *properties*.

Definition 1 (Ontological roles and role types). *An ontological role describes the properties of an individual in a certain context. A set of roles with similar properties is abstracted by an ontological role type.*

Based on this we define what we consider a role model (collaboration) to be in an ontological setting.

Definition 2 (Ontological collaborations and role models). *An ontological role model describes a set of related ontological role types and as such encapsulates common relationships between ontological roles.*

For example, an ontology may describe the concept *Person*. If *john*, *mary* and *sarah* are said to be persons, but in fact belong to a family, the needed associations may be encoded in a *Family* collaboration describing relationships such as parents having children. The existing *Family* collaboration could then simply be imported and employed to encode that *john* and *mary* are the parents of *sarah*.

Another difference between models and ontologies are their implicit assumptions. In models, classes are assumed to be disjoint, which is, however, not the case for ontologies. This implies that role-playing individuals may belong

to classes to which the corresponding role type is not explicitly bound. To avoid unintended role bindings, the ontology engineer explicitly has to constrain them in the ontology.

3. USING ROLE MODELS IN ONTOLOGIES

Class-based modeling, as used in ontologies today, has proven to be successful, but experience in object-orientation has lead to role modeling as a complementary paradigm. This section shows how roles and role models can beneficially be used in ontologies. One of our main motivations is to promote role models as a useful ontological unit—a component—in ontological modeling. We therefore show how role models can be incorporated and reused in class-based ontologies.

The following example is intended to demonstrate how classes can be split into separate concerns where each concern is modeled by employing a different role model. Figure 1 shows parts of a wine ontology modeled with roles. Classes are represented by gray rectangles while white rectangles with rounded corners denote role types. The definition of a role type is specified inside its rectangle (in standard DL syntax). In addition, role types are tagged with the name of their role model, e.g. *(Product)*. Labeled arrows represent binary properties between types.

The ontology in Figure 1 models three natural types (classes): *Wine*, *Winery* and *Food*. In a class-based version of the ontology in Figure 1, the concerns of wine both being a product and a drink (to be had with a meal) would be intermingled in a single class definition of *Wine*. The most natural way of modeling this would be to state that *Wine* is a subclass of the classes *Product* and *Drink*. However, this would not be ideal since a wine does not always have to be a product. Rather, we would like to express that a wine *can* be seen as a product (in the proper context). This can be expressed using roles where these concerns

Figure 1. Different concerns of the Wine class are separated by the role types Product and Drink

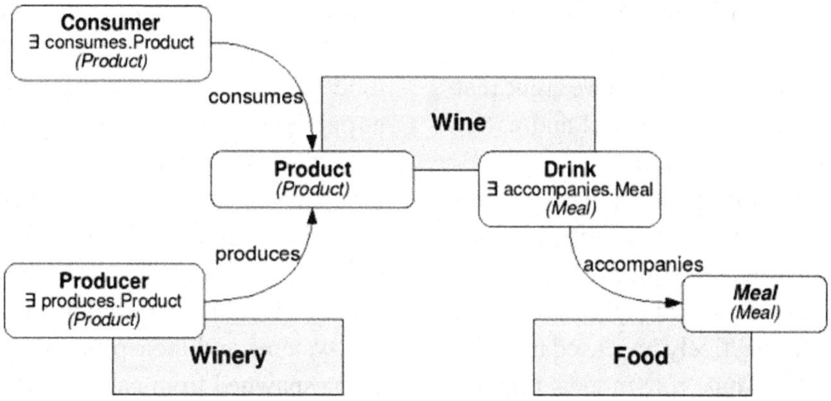

are instead explicitly separated into the role types *Product* and *Drink*. The motivation from a modeling perspective is that wines are always wines (that is, wine is a natural type). A wine may however be seen differently in different contexts: As a product to be sold, or as a drink being part of a meal. Modeling the role-based ontology from Figure 1 in a more concrete syntax could look like this (based on Manchester OWL syntax in Horridge et al., 2006):

```
import http://ontology-rolemodels.
org/product.rm as p
import http://ontology-rolemodels.
org/meal.rm as m

Class: Wine
       Plays: p#Product
       Plays: m#Drink

Class: Winery
       Plays: p#Producer

Class: Food
       Plays: m#Meal
```

The import statements import the needed role models and the Plays primitive binds roles to classes. The translation of the ontology into standard DL giving the ontology meaning is discussed below in Section *Semantics of Role-Modeled Ontologies*.

The above mentioned modeling distinction can also be helpful in other situations. Imagine the existence of an ontology with the classes *Person* and *PolarBear* (naturally) stated to be disjoint. The modeler now wants to introduce the concept of *Parent* and decides that parents are persons. Furthermore, while being focused on polar bears for a while decides that since obviously not all polar bears are parents, the opposite should hold and states that parents are also polar bears. This unfortunate and unintentional mistake makes the class *Parent* unsatisfiable (i.e. it is always empty). A more natural way to solve this problem would be to import a *Family* role model (modeling notions such as parents etc.) and state that *Persons* can play the role of *Parent* and *PolarBears* can do the same. Thus, instead of intermingling a *class Parent* with the definitions of *Person* and *PolarBear*, possibly causing inconsistencies, the *role type Parent* cross-cuts the different involved (natural) classes as a separate concern. Doing this will prevent the role type *Parent* from being empty. This example has shown that employing roles can be more natural than using classes to describe non-inherent properties of individuals.

Note that we do not claim that it is not possible to solve the above mentioned modeling problem strictly using classes as it is done today. In fact, we very much recognize this fact by giving role-based ontologies a translational semantics to standard DL semantics (see Section *Semantics of Role-Modeled Ontologies*). Instead we argue that modeling with roles is more natural and easier from the perspective of the modeler.

Apart from the rather philosophical distinction between classes and roles described above, roles are important in collaborations. A set of collaborating roles may be joined together in a role model, which may effectively be reused in many different ontologies. Thus, role models provide an interesting *reuse unit* for ontologies.

Figure 2 shows an example of reusability. There are two class-based ontologies, one modeling wines and the other pizzas. Both the concept of *Wine* and *Pizza* in the different ontologies can in certain contexts be considered as products (as one concern). To capture this concern and the relationships the role of being a product has with other roles, for example being a producer, we reuse the *Product* role model introduced in Figure 1.

The example shows how a set of related relationships (for example *produces* and *consumes*) can be encapsulated in a role model and reused for different domains. Not only relationships are encapsulated, but also the related role types that act as ranges and domains for the relationships.

As another example we can again consider the previously mentioned *Family* role model where relationships such as *hasChild* and *hasParent* are modeled. This role model may not only be used in an ontology catered to modeling persons. Consider for instance the same notions being needed in an ontology modeling tree data structures. There, possible relationships between nodes may also be modeled by reusing the same role model. Another example would be an ontology describing operating systems and their processes, new processes being spawned from parent processes, etc.

After having looked at some examples of ontologies being modeled using role models, we will in the following section discuss their semantics.

Semantics of Role-Modeled Ontologies

We argue that modeling with roles should be enabled by introducing new ontological modeling primitives. Roles allow modelers to separate concerns in an intuitive manner and provide useful ontological units (components). At the same time, current class-based ontology languages (e.g. OWL) are already very expressive. Thus, we believe that there is no lack in expressiveness, but rather in modeling primitives and reuse. We therefore aim for a translational approach where

Figure 2. The Product role model reused in two different ontologies

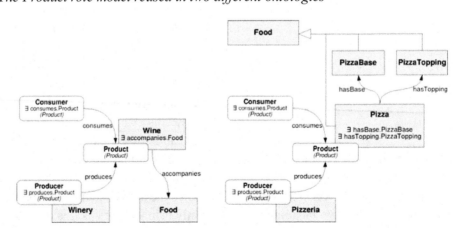

role-based ontologies may be compiled to standard (DL-based) ontologies. A great advantage is that this permits to reuse existing tools, in particular already well-developed reasoning engines.

A class-based ontology is considered to be a set of DL axioms constructed using class descriptions (or simply classes), property descriptions (or properties), and individuals. For supporting roles, we enhance the syntax with role types and role properties. For the sake of simplicity, we restrict role types to be conjuncts of existential restrictions limited to atomic role types. That is, of the form where R_i are role types and p_i are role properties. Role properties simply define their domain and range (both have to be role types). Classes (respectively properties) and role types (respectively role properties) are built from disjoint sets of names. This disjointness corresponds to the underlying difference of natural types and role types.

To support role modeling, we introduce two new axioms. The first axiom expresses that individuals of a class *can* play a role: $R \rhd C$ (*role binding*) binds role type R to class C. The second axiom expresses that some specific individual plays a role: $R(a)$ (*role assertion*), where R is a role type and a an individual. Additionally, we add syntax for ontologies to import role models.

The extended syntax may now be translated to the underlying ontology language by the following algorithm. Role properties and role property assertions are left out here but can be easily integrated into the syntax extensions and the translation algorithm as follows.

Make all imported role type definitions available as classes in the ontology.

For each role type R used in the ontology:

1. Let $\{C_1, \ldots, C_n\}$ be the set of classes to which R is bound ($R \rhd C_i$). Then add axiom to the ontology.
2. For each role assertion $R(a)$, make the same assertion available in the resulting ontology,

now referring to the class-representative for the role type R.

Remove import and Plays statements.

This translation captures the *can-play* semantics of roles by defining role types as subtypes of classes. It implies that an open role R may not be played by any individual since would be added to the ontology (i.e. R is always interpreted as the empty set). The semantics of our role modeling extension is an immediate consequence of the translation by using the standard semantics of DLs.

We will now look at an example of how a role-based ontology is compiled to a standard class-based ontology. The ontology from Figure 1 imports the role models *Product* and *Meal*. The *Product* role model could for example be defined by the following (where the definitions of the role properties *produces* and *consumes* are left out):

RoleModel: http://ontology-rolemodels.org/product.rm
Role: Producer
EquivalentTo: produces some Product
Role: Consumer
EquivalentTo: consumes some Product
Role: Product

To illustrate the impact of binding one role type to multiple classes, we assume that the *Product* role type is also bound to the class *Food* in Figure 1 (and in the subsequent listing). That is, also foods can be considered products in some contexts. Our translation as defined above results in the following class-based ontology (for the example disregarding the *Meal* role model):

```
Class: Wine
Class: Winery
Class: Food
Class: Producer
      EquivalentTo: produces some
Product
      SubClassOf: Winery
Class: Consumer
```

```
        EquivalentTo: consumes some
Product
        SubClassOf: owl:Nothing
Class: Product
        SubClassOf: Wine or Food
```

The resulting ontology consists of only standard OWL constructs and can thus be used by existing tools such as reasoners. A consequence of this resulting ontology is for example that an individual playing the role of a product has to be either a wine or a food. We can thus single out and study the concern of being a product, but not having to consider in detail what those products are. We could have done the same in a class-based ontology by stating that wines and foods are products, thus using *Product* as a super-class to both *Wine* and *Food*. However, as already mentioned, this would disregard the fact that wines and foods are not always products.

A consequence of the above-defined semantics is however that the resulting logic is non-monotonic. A logic is monotonic if adding a new axiom never falsifies assertions that were true before adding the axiom. The reason is that adding role bindings can redefine previous knowledge. Consider the example from Figure 1, with *Food* declared to be disjoint from *Wine*, and individual *pasta* to be a *Food*, that is, *Food(pasta)*. Since the role type *Product* is (only) bound to *Wine*, $\neg Product(pasta)$ follows from the ontology. But if we then also bind *Product* to *Food*, we can no longer conclude $\neg Product(pasta)$, hence we have to retract previously established knowledge. We discuss this further in (Henriksson et al., 2008).

4. RELATED WORK

OntoClean, a methodology proposed by Guarino and Welty (2002), aims at identifying common misuses of the subsumption relationship using meta-properties for ontological classes. There are two basic meta-properties: *essence* and *rigidity*. Properties of a class belong to its essence, if they *must* hold for an instance (in contrast, for example, to properties of a role type, which *can* hold). Rigidity means that the properties of the class must hold for all instances. These meta-properties provide a categorization of types, which is similar to our approach. Essential and rigid classes correspond to natural types; non-essential and non-rigid classes correspond to role types. Furthermore, Guarino proposes to constrain subsumption based on meta-properties. For example, a rigid type should not be subsumed by a non-rigid type. We fulfill this requirement by translating the role binding axiom $R \triangleright C$ into , that is, a role type is always subsumed by a natural type.

Sunagawa et al. (2006) propose an ontology framework with support for roles. The work builds upon three notions: *role concepts*, which are similar to our role types, *potential players*, which roughly correspond to classes that are related to a role type via $\triangleright$, and *role holders*, that is, instances actually playing a role. The authors argue for organizing role types and classes in two separate type hierarchies. Moreover, the paper describes compound roles created from primitive roles, realizing ideas similar to roles playing roles as in (Steimann, 2000). The framework consists of a custom ontology language and appropriate tools (see http://www.hozo.jp). In contrast, we aim at embedding roles into existing ontology languages by translating syntactical extensions into the underlying language.

Spyns (2005) adopts the Object Role Modeling (ORM) method (Halpin, 1998) to ontology modeling by proposing a step-wise ontology engineering methodology. The author distinguishes an *ontology base*, containing intuitive conceptualizations of a domain, from *ontological commitments*, that is, sets of domain rules for a specific application. Unlike our work, the methodology abstracts from concrete formalisms, such as DLs. Moreover, ORM uses a different notion of roles, which is similar to DL properties.

Modularizing and reusing ontologies is also tackled on a more formal level. One work in this direction proposes a new import primitive: *semantic import* (Pan et al., 2006). Semantic import differs from owl:imports (referred to as syntactic import) by allowing to import partial ontologies and by additionally enforcing the existence of any referred external ontologies or ontology elements (classes, properties, individuals) by the notion of *ontology spaces*. The goal in this work is controlled partial reuse.

The work in Cuenca Grau et al. (2007b) defines a logical framework for modular integration of ontologies by allowing each ontology to define its *local* and *external* signature (that is, classes, properties, etc.). The external signature is assumed to be defined in another ontology. Two distinct restrictions are defined on the usage of the external signatures. The first syntactically disallows certain axioms which are considered harmful, while the second restriction generalizes the first by taking semantic issues into consideration. The general goal, apart from a formal framework, is to allow safe merger of ontologies.

The authors of (Cuenca Grau et al., 2006) also propose partial reuse of ontologies by allowing for automatically extracting ontological modules. One interesting requirement put on such an extracted module is that it should describe a well-defined subject matter, that is, be self-contained from a modeling perspective.

In contrast to these works on partial ontology reuse, in particular how to extract or modularize existing ontologies, our work aims at defining a more intuitive ontological unit—an ontological component that was defined as such.

5. CONCLUSION AND OUTLOOK

In this paper we have proposed an ontological unit able to improve modeling and provide a means for reuse—the ontological role model. The concept of roles has its roots in software modeling and we

have taken the first steps to transfer this notion to the world of ontologies. Role models provide a view on individuals and their relationships that is different from the abstractions provided by purely class-based approaches. As such, role models provide a reusable abstraction unit for ontologies. Furthermore, due to the translational semantics, the approach is compatible with existing formalisms and tools.

While OWL provides certain reuse possibilities via its owl:imports construct, it fails to provide a clear and intuitive notion of a *component*. In contrast, role models have more component-like characteristics; the role types defined in a role model can be seen as its interfaces. We think it is important to have a metaphorical understanding of why reusable entities belong together, which is given in our approach by the notion of roles and the binding of role types to natural types.

A so far unexplored opportunity for ontological role modeling concerns collaborative ontology development, that is, the situation where several engineers (perhaps over time) work on a common ontology. Explicitly describing which role types a concept relates to can help reduce misunderstandings of the concept. Thus, a role type can disambiguate the intended interpretation of a concept. Potentially, such reasoning could also be partly automated to help in ontology matching and merging. Further work is required to fully understand these opportunities, and realize their limitations.

As a next step we aim at integrating role modeling into tools, for example the Protégé ontology editor (Knublauch et al., 2004). This is important since we argue that ontology engineers should treat roles as first class members of their language and distinguish them from classes. Other issues also remain to be further clarified. The semantics of roles may be subject of discussion. Apart from focusing on *can-play* semantics, *must-play* may in some cases be desirable for role bindings. Another issue to clarify is the implication of applying one role model several times in an ontology. One could argue for multiple imports where each import is associated with a unique name space. However, this would disallow to refer to all instances of a certain role type, for instance to all products in an ontology. Finally, further investigations into the implications of the open-world semantics of ontologies relating to role bindings and role assertions should be performed.

In conclusion, we argue that role models provide an interesting reuse abstraction for ontologies and roles should be supported as an ontological primitive.

ACKNOWLEDGMENT

This research has been co-funded by the European Commission and by the Swiss Federal Office for Education and Science within the 6th Framework Programme project REWERSE No. 506779 (cf. http://rewerse.net).

REFERENCES

Aracic, I., Gasiunas, V., Mezini, M., & Ostermann, K. (2006). *An Overview of CaesarJ*. New York: Springer.

Aßmann, U., Zschaler, S., & Wagner, G. (2006). *Ontologies, Meta-Models, and the Model-Driven Paradigm*. New York: Springer.

Baader, F., Calvanese, D., McGuinness, D. L., Nardi, D., & Patel-Schneider, P. F. (Eds.). (2003). *The Description Logic Handbook*. Cambridge, UK: Cambridge University Press.

Cuenca Grau, B., Horrocks, I., Kazakov, Y., & Sattler, U. (2007a). Just the right amount: Extracting modules from ontologies. In *Proceedings of the Sixteenth International World Wide Web Conference (WWW 2007)*, Banff, Alberta, Canada (pp. 717-726).

Cuenca Grau, B., Kazakov, Y., Horrocks, I., & Sattler, U. (2007b). A logical framework for modular integration of ontologies. In *Proceedings of the 20th International Joint Conference on Artificial Intelligence (IJCAI 2007)* (pp. 298-303).

Cuence Grau, B., Parsia, B., Sirin, E., & Kalyanpur, A. (2006, June 2–5). Modularity and web ontologies. In P. Doherty, J. Mylopoulos, & C. A. Welty (Eds.), *Proceedings of KR2006: 20th International Conference on Principles of Knowledge Representation and Reasoning,* Lake District, UK, (pp. 198-209). Menlo Park, CA: AAAI Press.

Guarino, N., & Welty, C. A. (2002). Evaluating ontological decisions with OntoClean. *Communications of the ACM, 45*(2), 61–65. doi:10.1145/503124.503150

Halpin, T. (1998). Object-role modeling (ORM/NIAM). In *Handbook on Architectures of Information Systems*. New York: Springer.

Hayes, P., et al. (2004). *RDF Semantics*. Retrieved from http://www.w3.org/TR/rdf-mt/

Henriksson, J., Pradel, M., Zschaler, S., & Pan, J. Z. (2008). Ontology Design and Reuse with Conceptual Roles. In *Proceedings of the Second International Conference on Web Reasoning and Rule Systems (RR'08)* (LNCS 5341, pp. 104-118).

Herrmann, S. (2002). *Object teams: Improving modularity for crosscutting collaborations*. Paper presented at Net Object Days 2002.

Horridge, M., Drummond, N., Goodwin, J., Rector, A., Stevens, R., & Wang, H. (2006). *The manchester OWL syntax*. Paper presented at OWL: Experiences and Directions (OWLED 06).

Knublauch, H., Fergerson, R. W., Noy, N. F., & Musen, M. A. (2004). *The Protégé OWL plugin: An open development environment for semantic web applications*. Paper presented at the Third International Semantic Web Conference (ISWC).

Pan, J., Serafini, L., & Zhao, Y. (2006). *Semantic import: An approach for partial ontology reuse.* Paper presented at the ISWC2006 Workshop on Modular Ontologies (WoMO).

Patel-Schneider, P. F., Hayes, P., & Horrocks, I. (2004). *OWL web ontology language semantics and abstract syntax.* Retrieved from http://www.w3.org/TR/owl-semantics/

Reenskaug, T., Wold, P., & Lehne, O. (1996). *Working with Objects, The OOram Software Engineering Method.* Greenwich, CT: Manning Publications.

Smaragdakis, Y., & Batory, D. (2002). Mixin layers: An object-oriented implementation technique for refinements and collaboration-based designs. *ACM Transactions on Software Engineering and Methodology, 11*(2), 215–255. doi:10.1145/505145.505148

Spyns, P. (2005). Adapting the object role modelling method for ontology modelling. In *Proceedings of the International Symposium on Foundations of Intelligent Systems* (LNCS 3488, pp. 276-284).

Steimann, F. (2000). On the representation of roles in object-oriented and conceptual modelling. *Data & Knowledge Engineering, 35*(1), 83–106. doi:10.1016/S0169-023X(00)00023-9

Steimann, F. (2005). The role data model revisited. In *Proceedings of Roles, an interdisciplinary perspective, AAAI Fall Symposium* (pp. 128-135).

Sunagawa, E., Kozaki, K., Kitamura, Y., & Mizoguchi, R. (2006). Role organization model in Hozo. In *Proceedings of the International Conference on Managing Knowledge in a World of Networks (EKAW)* (LNCS 4248, pp. 67-81)

This work was previously published in International Journal of Enterprise Information Systems, edited by Madjid Tavana, pp. 1-11, Volume 6, Issue 1, copyright 2010 by IGI Publishing (an imprint of IGI Global).

Chapter 14
Linguistics–Based Modeling Methods and Ontologies in Requirements Engineering

Florian Lautenbacher
University of Augsburg, Germany

Bernhard Bauer
University of Augsburg, Germany

Tanja Sieber
University of Miskolc, Hungary

Alejandro Cabral
Oracle Strategic Program, Argentina

ABSTRACT

Developing new software based on requirements specifications created by business analysts often leads to misunderstanding and lack of comprehension, because of the different backgrounds of the people involved. If requirements specifications instead have a clearly defined structure and comprehensive semantics, this obstacle can be resolved. Therefore, we propose to structure the requirements specifications using existing linguistics-based modeling methods and annotate the used terms with ontologies to enhance the understanding and reuse of these documents during the software engineering process.

1. MOTIVATION

Not only normal software development, but also the upcoming research area semantic-based software development (de Cesare, 2007) typically has an iterative software development process starting with the requirements engineering and requirements analysis phase. Before beginning

with the development of software, the needs of the customer must be clarified and summarized into requirements specifications. These requirements contain all (or nearly most) of the details about the software product to be developed and are normally described in natural language. Some companies have therefore defined styleguides. However, most of the used terms are not defined in a concrete way which leads to misinterpretation

DOI: 10.4018/978-1-4666-1761-2.ch014

and incomprehension, i.e. the semantics are not defined clearly. Sometimes glossaries are used to describe the expressions, but even those can be interpreted differently by various readers/writers. Missing or not clearly defined requirements lead to change requests for the software product once it is tested or, in the worst case, when it is used by the customers. The customers might have thought of something different, but their requirement has not been described properly in the requirements specification. Therefore, it is critical to specify the requirements as precisely as possible in the first place to avoid unnecessary changes to the finished product afterwards and to build the product on time and in budget.

As stated in Rupp (2006), software (S) is a combination of documentation (D) and code (C), i.e $S=D+C$. The documentation should not only cover the source code and its comments itself, but also the description of using the product afterwards (software documentation), any kind of technical specification and documentations, like functional and non-functional aspects, UML diagrams or database descriptions, etc. In document engineering, which is concerned with these issues, internal and external document engineering can be distinguished. The former refers to the documentation produced during the whole software development process, while the latter refers to the documentation produced for the system's users after the product is released (Rueping, 2003). Requirements specifications can be seen as a typical example of internal documents, whereas user manuals are typical external document examples. There are some linguistics-based modeling methods that are widely used in external document engineering, which could also be used for internal document engineering, e.g. for gathering requirements. Using these modeling methods, the structure of documents and their underlying dependencies can already be reflected in the modeled segmentation of the documents, making it easier to be derived and annotated with semantic data afterwards. This semantic annotation is based on ontologies

and can be used to describe the meaning of the constructs in a way that computers can not only read but also interpret.

We will therefore show how the semantics of requirements specifications can be gathered using linguistics-based modeling methods and that an annotation of these documents with ontologies can foster reuse and personalization.

This article is structured as follows: in the next section we describe the challenges of current documents and the difference of understanding some data between sender and recipient. Additionally, we describe our definition of data and how the communication between different persons takes place. Afterwards, we show how different linguistics-based modeling methods can be used to clarify the underlying meaning of terms. We evaluate several linguistics-based modeling methods and show a summary of our evaluation. We then use an example to clarify the usage of the modeling methods as well as introduce the process and benefits of semantic annotation through the usage of ontologies. Subsequently, we show some related work before we conclude describing the benefits of using linguistics-based modeling methods and ontologies.

2. CHALLENGES OF SEMANTIC REQUIREMENTS ENGINEERING

In this section we introduce the basics of linguistics such as the Speech act theory, before we introduce models for the description of data and the process of communication that are required for understanding the problems in Requirements Engineering and possible solutions.

Speech Act Theory

John Langshaw Austin developed his Speech Act theory in such a way that today, more than 45 years later, we find it useful to conduct our research on semantics in requirements engineering with reference to the theory. In Austin (1962) he introduced an informal description of the idea of an illocutionary act that can be captured by emphasing that when we use language as more than a mere way to state things as true/false, we actually do the action being pronounced or denoted. A good example is when a minister joins two people in marriage saying: "*I pronounce you husband and wife*".

To further explain this theory, Austin declared three types of speech acts:

- **Locutionary acts:** saying something (the locution) with a certain meaning but not necessarily building a speech. It may be a word, sentence or sound. There are three different kinds of locutionary acts: It is at one level the production of certain noises and as such it is called the *phonetic* act; through the production of those noises the speaker produces words in syntactic arrangements and this act is called *phatic* act. Finally, through the production of words in syntactic arrangements, with certain intentions and in certain contexts, it conveys certain messages and is in this respect dubbed *rhetic* act.

- **Illocutionary acts:** the performance of an act in saying something, or basically the speaker's intent. John Searle developed further this category in 1969 (Searle, 1969) and identified five illocutionary points: *assertives* (true or false statements), *directives* (statements with a certain intent), *commisives* (statements which commit the speaker to a course of action), *expressives* (express the sincerity of the speech act) and *declaratives* (statements that connote a change of the world referred by representing as already changed).

- **Perlocutionary acts:** These acts have a direct effect on sensitive perception, feelings or actions of both the speaker and the receiver. These acts basically seek to change

a state of mind, an idea or feeling towards a representation.

Austin's analysis and contribution through his Speech Act theory went beyond the referencial theories during his time and considered the context in which language was actually used. He was the first to consider the context and the listener as a part of the communication equation, relying on the concept of *convention* to depict an illocution-perlocution distinction. For Austin, illocutionary acts are based on the existence of convention, while perlocutionary acts are not. By this, Austin opens a window to another dilemma: *meaning*, though he fails to further develop his Speech Act in this area, thus allowing others to criticize his work:

Grice (1967), Austin's Oxford colleague, developed his own theory on meaning and distinguished *natural* from *non-natural* meaning, in terms of whether or not there exists a natural connection between an utterance and what is actually meant by it. Logically, non-natural meaning refers to those cases where this natural connection does not exist. In other words the meaning of any utterance consists in its intentional use by the speaker to accomplish his or her desire to get the listener to do something by revealing to him/her the actual intention the speaker has, and this cannot be solely based on the *convention* concept that Austin explained.

Similar to Grice's analysis Strawson (1969) criticizes Austin's theory as well, as he describes Speech Acts as not really dependent on conventions working as connections between utterances and meanings. He explains that a person can act without actually using an existing convention all the time in order to accomplish or perform an act by uttering something. Both Grice and Strawson acknowledge the presence of a deeper concept than the one Austin introduced when naming conventions: they both refer to *intention*. Strawson additionally rejects the illocution-perlocution distinction that Austin based on the existence of convention as a context identifier and integrator.

All this analysis though could not be complete without Wittgenstein's referential theory on meaning, where he presents the idea that language cannot consist of or be a linguistic rule of the signifier and the signified. If that were the case, there would be a space where another rule connects the statement of the rule with what it really signifies. Wittgenstein (1973) declares the true importance of *context* to determine the meaning. In order to really understand what an utterance means, the context needs to be present, considered and integrated with the language that is being used.

All these categories created by Austin and afterwards developed by Searle, Grice, Strawson and Wittgenstein apply to languages as we see them: understanding that by language we imply a system of communication consisting of sounds, words or characters used by two sources/ destinations to exchange information. In the case of a written exchange we can speak about a scribal act instead of a phonetic act, but the spirit behind the Speech Act theory remains the same, which makes it quite interesting for documentation engineering purposes and henceforth also for requirements engineering.

Illocutionary acts are performed with intentions. They are communicatively successful if the speaker's/writer's illocutionary intention is recognized by the hearer/reader. Illocutionary acts are all intentional and are generally performed with the primary intention of achieving some perlocutionary effect.

By sending certain data in the form of words or written commands we issue not just an order or perlocutionary act. The content of the statement is imbued with a certain meaning. In spoken languages this meaning can be implied by the tone/ intonation used to communicate, or by different signs the speaker can send. Even if these are not used, a certain meaning can be transmitted if the speaker and the hearer know each other. The use of different codes and contexts help quite a bit: it is by them that a speaker constructs a statement, sends it as a message with an identified meaning, then a hearer receives it and using the codes already learned and identifying the context used to create this message, re-constructs the message received, imbuing it with another meaning that is analog to the one originally sent by the other source. In written documents this is much more difficult since the future reader is mostly not known and therefore the meaning must be made explicit in other ways. The challenges for written documents can be explained by using a semantic data model.

Semantic Data Model

When specifying requirements, these are summarized in some kind of requirements specification in a document containing *data*. But the term *data* is often used without any exact terminological definition. There are different definitions for this term and henceforth it is not used in a uniform way in papers and lectures. Therefore, we introduce our understanding of *data* following a semantic data model in order to describe the problems that occur between somebody who specifies the requirements (*sender*) and the person who reads the requirements specification (*receiver*).

According to the semantic data model introduced in Sieber and Kammerer (2006), data penetrates through various levels: it can have different *forms* (such as '13' and '*13*'), different kinds of *representation* (e.g. arabic numbers vs. roman numbers vs. textual description) and different *semantics* (for example the number '13' can describe the age of a person or the number of a house).

- At the level of form all data are called *data instances,* where a data instance itself is a semiotic entity in terms of Peirce. That is, it can appear as icon, index or symbol. The semantic data model bridges the existing gap between the understanding of data and the semiotics.

- At the level of representatives data appear in an abstract form and are then called *data representatives*.
- At the level of meaning data appear again in a more abstract version and are then called *data items*. These data items can even be split into smaller meaningful components (*complex data items*) or are not dividable (*atomic data items*).

Figure 1 shows the semantic data model in a graphical way: there are several data instances for '13' which belong to different data representatives and all to the atomic data item *house number* which might be part of the complex data item *address*.

Sender-Recipient Model

If someone wants to specify the *house number* as a data item, then it can happen that somebody else sees the concrete data instances, but understands something different by it. Henceforth, it does not happen at the same level of knowledge. Data instances are the only part of the semantic data model which appear outside of a human being in a concrete form (as icon, index or symbol), all other levels of abstraction are intra-personal. Following this understanding of data the consequence is that meaning or semantics is also to be understood as something intra-personal and we are captured in our lingual possibilities to talk about it.

Every communication based on data instances between two parties has to consider that each person has a different background and different knowledge (compare Figure 2) and will derive from a data instance maybe different meanings. Therefore, the data instances have to be specified in a way the recipient can understand what they are meant for. If the sender wants to specify the number of a house and the recipient only recognizes the data instance '13', then he might think of it as the age of a person (compare Figure 3).

Figure 1. Semantic data model (according to Sieber & Kovács, 2005) for the data item "house number"

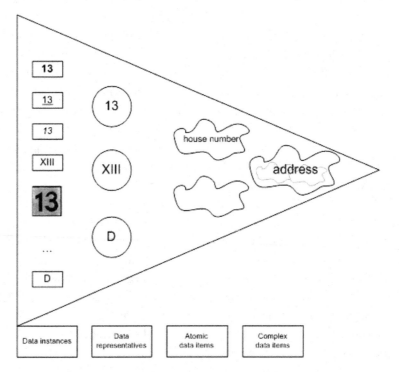

Figure 2. Sender-Recipient model of Sieber & Kovács (2005)

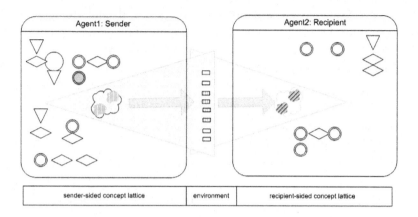

Semantic Communication Model

To describe what actually happens when a message is exchanged between different persons, we developed a semantic communication model considering existing communication models such as Shannon and Weaver (1964), Berlo (1960), Bühler (1965), Schramm (1954) or Flensburg (2007).

Therefore, we relate the Sender-Recipient model with the semantic data model and combine them using *messages*. In principal, each person has a different background and knowledge. Each time a document (e.g. a requirements specification) is written, the background and knowledge of the target recipients have to be considered in order to

enable the recipient to understand the document. In spoken language this is quite easy since the recipients are (normally) known, but in written documents the future readers are unknown and their expected specific attributes are estimated by intentional group analysis. A *message* (cf. Figure 4) consists of data instances that are either on an objectlevel, describing the message itself, or at a metalevel, adding additional data to the data instances on objectlevel (such as filetype, creation date, target audience, etc.). A message is transmitted from the sender to the receiver. Both parties may have a different background and knowledge. Therefore, the message must be structured in a way that allows for an easy

Figure 3. Sender-Recipient model for the data instance "13"

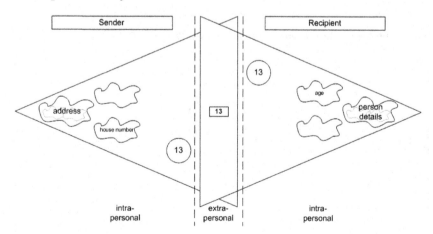

abstraction process. Linguistics-based modeling methods are one way to achieve such a structure of documents and will be introduced and explored in the following sections.

According to Shannon and Weaver (1964) there is always the problem of *noise* when transmitting messages (and can be extended to *semantic noise* according to Berlo (1960)). This semantic noise needs to be reduced drastically in order to allow for a faultless interpretation of the data instances.

3. LINGUISTICS-BASED MODELING METHODS

Requirements specifications are most of the times simple text files. In order to cover the intended semantics when writing them (according to the Speech Act theory), it is necessary to describe the constructs in a way in which the reader can capture the purpose of the words used by the writer. In addition it is possible to rely on existing text files of an ontology or one can start one step earlier and use existing linguistics-based modeling methods to ensure capturing the semantics into the future documents. Modeling methods are mostly used for creating structures in technical documentation and for information structuring.

Using natural language processing techniques would be another possibility. But as they are very time-consuming, we focus on the usage of modeling methods and ontologies instead. The most prominent modeling methods that are used in the context of external technical documentation for that purpose are the functional-positional segmentation method, the function design™ method, information mapping™, information structuring in XML/SGML (Lobin, 2000) and DITA. In the following we give a more detailed overview about the method of functional positional segmentation, the function design™ method as well as DITA, before we compare them.

The Functional-Positional Segmentation Method

Wiegand (1989) described the process of how a structural analysis of dictionary articles can be performed. He developed a segmentation method consisting of the method of functional segmentation and the method of functional-positional segmentation. The functional segmentation (e.g. of dictionary articles) includes the identification of functional text elements which is also interesting for modeling all kinds of documents and henceforth also for requirements specifications. The requirements specification should already exist in order to apply the functional-positional segmentation method.

Functional segmentation determines typographical and non-typographical structure pointers

Figure 4. Semantic communication model (Sieber & Lautenbacher, 2007)

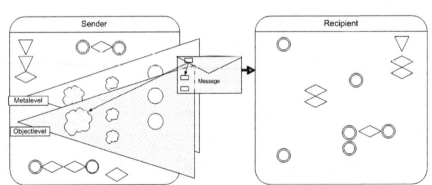

that assist the user in perceiving the structure of the article and of parts of an article that belong together. Typical typographical structure pointers are the font type and the font styles. Examples for non-typographical structure pointers are punctuation marks, brackets and arrows. Exhaustive functional text-segmentation is described as the incremental segmentation of a dictionary article by considering statements and structure pointers together with a presentation as whole-part relationships in a formally defined description language. This leads to a segmentation of the text in which all elements are defined and can be associated to be part of a bigger context. (Figure 5)

On the other hand, the functional-positional segmentation does not only force the segmentation of the text, but also includes the position of all text segments in a linear order. The determined hierarchical structure of articles can then be presented as a tree-like partitive structure graph.

The Function Design Method

The function design™ method (Muthig & Schäflein-Armbruster, 1999) is a universal and flexible technology for structuring technical documentation. It has been developed on the basis of theoretical thoughts upon the Speech Act: each spoken sentence contains information and serves a communicative function. Nevertheless, there is no clear 1:1 correlation between a sentence and its communicative function. Most of the times the meaning of a sentence is transported using meta-spoken ways such as pronounciation as described

previously. This must be achieved differently in printed documents.

Based on that, the goal of the function design™ theory is that each sentence of a text needs to have a unique identifiable function. The function design™ method can be divided into macro and micro levels: on the macro level the kind of document is classified and on the micro level this document is further segmented into sequence patterns, functional entities and tags. Therefore, the developer must put himself in the position of the recipient of a text, for example the reader of a warning. The reader of a warning needs answers such as "what is the danger?"; "how big is the danger?"; "how can I avoid the danger?"; etc.

The intentions and existing knowledge of the target group must be kept in mind during the whole specification process. The created document should answer the questions a possible reader may have. Therefore, the data items in the document can be captured in functional entities such as warning, notices, preconditions etc. These functional entities must answer the questions that a potential reader might be thinking of (for example, "what do I need to consider when doing some task?"). Each functional entity is described with the following data items:

- Name and (optional) abbreviation
- Purpose
- Sequential order
- Inner structure and formulation
- Layout and design

Figure 5. Functional-positional segmentation after Wiegand without tree structure

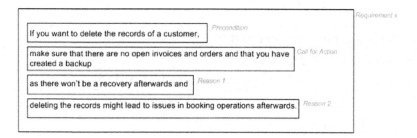

Basic functional entities can be grouped into structural patterns which have a common purpose or function. This fosters reuse of data in the function design.

The function design™ method needs to be applied while creating a new document (unlike Wiegand's method where an existing document is a precondition). The functional entities need to have the same form in the whole document. For example, a deletion action of customer records can simply be written in plain text such as "If you want to delete the records of a customer, make sure that there are no open invoices and orders and that you have created a backup as there won't be a recovery afterwards and deleting the records might lead to issues in booking operations afterwards." or it can be presented in the following (Figure 6):

DITA

The Darwin Information Typing Architecture (DITA) (OASIS, 2007) is an information architecture based on XML especially developed for the area of technical documentation. DITA defines a set of information types that can be created and managed related to specific topics. DITA allows the authoring, producing and delivering of technical information and specifies basic elements such as topics and maps. A topic is an information entity including a title and content that is short enough to be specific to a single subject, but long enough to be self-understandable without additional references. Maps are documents that help to organize relationships to other topics.

One focus in DITA is laid on specialization (that was the reason for refering to Charles Darwin who was investigating inheritance during his studies about the theory of evolution). Inheritance and specialization allow defining new information whereas existing design is reused as much as possible. Figure 7 shows the same example as in the preceeding sections modeled in DITA.

Comparison of Different Linguistics-Based Modeling Methods

As there are some more linguistics-based modeling methods (e.g. Ament, 2003; Ley, 2007; Lobin, 2000) as described in the previous sections, we evaluated them according to several criteria. These criteria were divided into five sections: structure and documentation of the modeling method, experiences when applying the modeling method to an example, evaluation of the result after applying the modeling method, how can the instances be personalized and how can they be reused in another context. The questions in the evaluation were developed similarly to other evaluation approaches such as Hevner et al. (2004), Hong et al. (1993) and Moodey & Shanks (1994). The results are only summarized here, the detailed evaluation can be found in Sieber and Lautenbacher (2007).

Concerning the comprehensibility of each modeling method, the function design™ method stands out with 37 of 40 possible evaluation points. This is probably due to the teaching of the method at universities for 10 years. DITA catches up when considering the application of the modeling

Figure 6. Function design method example

Deleting customer records!
No recovery afterwards.
Possible issues in booking invoices and orders.
- Check open invoices and orders first.   - Create backup of records.

Figure 7. Example written in DITA

```
<task id="deletingRecords">
        <title>Deleting customer records</title>
        <taskbody>
                <context>If a customer has not contacted the company for more than 10
                        years, his/her records can be deleted</context>
                <prereq>
                        <ul>
                                <li>Check open invoices and orders first</li>
                                <li>Create backup</li>
                        <ul>
                </prereq>
                <steps>
                        <step>Confirm the deletion</step>
                </steps>
                <result>
                        <ul>
                                <li>Recovery not possible anymore</li>
                                <li>Issues in booking operations possible afterwards</li>
                        </ul>
                </result>
        </taskbody>
</task>
```

method (92 of 105 possible evaluation points) as well as evaluating the quality of the results (33 of 50 evaluation points). Personalization is not really possible with any of the modeling methods (the best one had 14 of 40 evaluation points); however, DITA assists the user in reuse being nearly optimal (66 of 70 evaluation points) through a high degree of standardization as well as the use of modules that can be reused in different contexts. Concluding, DITA came first in this evaluation (with 236 of 305 possible evaluation points) ahead of function design™ (203) and information mapping (192).

4. APPLYING LINGUISTICS-BASED MODELING METHODS AND ONTOLOGIES TO REQUIREMENTS ENGINEERING

In this section we demonstrate how linguistics-based modeling methods can be used in requirements engineering and how the resulting specifications can be used as a comprehensive human-understandable basis for semantic annotation further on.

Applying DITA to an Example of a Requirements Specification

First, we introduce an example that describes requirements for a typical customer relationship management (CRM) system. In this system, personal details about customers as well as their orders are stored, created, modified and deleted. The requirements of the creation process for a new customer order (compare Metz et al., 2003) can be modeled in a textual editor (e.g. an Office product with predefined templates) as follows:

Name of scenario: Register new customer order
Description: A new customer order is entered into the CRM system.
Context: A sales clerk with a non-processed customer order.

Main scenario:

1. The sales clerk enters the customer's ID.
2. The system displays the customer's profile.
3. The sales clerk confirms that the customer's credit rating is sufficient and the order can be processed.
4. The system assigns an order ID.

5. The sales clerk registers the desired trade items.

…

Preconditions: Customer has been stored in system, trade items are available in system.

- ○ System has initiated an order for the customer
- ○ System has documented payment information
- ○ System has registered request with the customer
- ○ System has logged all failures
- ○ System has logged transaction date and time

Actors involved: Sales clerk, CRM system

After the requirements have been entered in the editor, they can be stored in DITA XML-format as shown in Figure 8.

Annotating the Example by a Requirements Ontology

Linguistics-based modeling methods allow a modular access based on the defined functional entities, but they have strong limitations regarding

automated processing. Therefore, it is necessary to describe the used constructs in a way machines can 'understand' (similar to Grice's description of *meaning*). That's where the Semantic Web and ontologies come into play.

Similar to Bauer and Roser (2006) where the usage of ontologies in the context of software engineering and development is described, annotating the constructs of a requirements specification on the basis of a requirements ontology can assist the computer to process the used vocabulary. Therefore, an ontology in the Web Ontology Language (OWL; W3C, 2004) can be used and new knowledge can be gathered through the process of reasoning on this ontology. There are many approaches for annotating documents (Web pages, videos, etc.) as a means to use this data for further processing (see Euzenat, 2002; Missikoff et al., 2003). Having annotated the requirements with semantic data, this knowledge can also be used in further parts of the software engineering process as well as in document engineering.

An ontology has been defined as "a (formal) explicit specification of a (shared) conceptualization" (Gruber, 1993). There are different kinds of ontologies: Guarino (1997) differentiates between

Figure 8. Customer creation requirements in DITA

```
<task id="registerNewCustomerOrder">
        <title>Register new customer order</title>
        <taskbody>
                <context>A sales clerk with a non-processed customer order</context>
                <prereq>
                        <ul>
                                <li>Customer has been stored in system</li>
                                <li>Trade items are available in the system</li>
                        </ul>
                </prereq>
                <steps>
                        <step>The sales clerk enters the customer's ID</step>
                        <step>The system displays the customer's profile</step>
                        <step>The sales clerk confirms that the customer's credit rating
is sufficient and the order can be processed.</step>
                        <step>The system assigns an order ID</step>
                        <step>The sales clerk registers the desired trade items</step>
                        <step>I</step>
                </steps>
                <result>
                        <ul>
                                <li>System has initiated an order for the customer</li>
                                <li>System has documented payment information</li>
                                <li>System has registered request with the customer</li>
                                <li>System has logged all failures</li>
                                <li>System has logged transaction date and time</li>
                        </ul>
                </result>
        </taskbody>
</task>
```

application ontologies that contain the definitions specific to a particular application, while *reference ontologies* refer to ontological theories whose focus is to clarify the intended meaning of terms used in specific domains. Kassal (2008) developed a reference ontology for the domain of requirements engineering that allows to capture the knowledge of all stakeholders at the beginning of a project in a formal notation. Therefore, the ontology focuses on the stakeholder (together with the complementary stakeholder knowledge), but also considers intentions, documents, business concepts or influence factors. Figure 9 shows the ontology with the entailed concepts in greater detail.

The requirements ontology has been instantiated with the previous example and does now contain the description of all roles and users (such as sales clerk) and the goals that were defined within a project (e.g. Register new customer order). By using this ontology (an excerpt in XML-format is shown in Figure 10) we can now annotate the customer order example in DITA.

Thereby, we use additional tags referencing parts of the ontology in analogy to current Semantic Web service standards such as SAWSDL (Kopecky et al., 2007). With these *ref*-tags, we can point from one word or a whole passage in the requirements specifications to some concepts in the ontology. This allows for improved computer processing. The result is shown in Figure 11. There, the person sales clerk is referenced to a similar named concept in the ontology or the description that the rating is sufficient is connected to the concept Rating_Sufficient in the ontology.

Benefits

Using DITA it is now easily possible to derive a technical documentation for the product, since DITA has been developed exactly for this purpose. With the semantic annotations one can automatically query existing projects as to whether there

had been similar use cases and how they were implemented. Looking for existing components which implement one of the mentioned requirements is also possible. Henceforth, the reuse of existing components can be further extended. A software developer does not need to know which components have been implemented in earlier projects, but using their semantic descriptions he can simply search for keywords and find the existing components and their descriptions and use them in the new project. This is possible due to the semantic annotation that has been integrated into the requirements. With the use of an inference engine the system can now compute similarities and equalities between requirements based on their described concepts. This enables one to find corresponding components and other use cases based on semantics and not only their syntax.

For example, one might search for all processes in which the identification of a customer is requested or modified. "Entering_Customer_ID" in the ontology includes the concepts "Enter" and "Customer_ID" which themselves might be inherited by "Insert" and "identification". Since "Insert" is a kind of modification and identification fits to the request, the PC can compute that this step, and hence the whole use case, must be considered.

Another benefit is the possibility to check for inconsistencies: if several requirements have been entered, they might describe different behaviors of a single system or several concepts of a domain that do not fit together. One requirement might say that every customer has exactly one address whereas the other says that the shipping address of the customer might be different than the address where the person lives or the organization is located.

Additionally, it is now possible to personalize a system to the user: since the ontology can, for example, represent the low level of computer expertise of the sales clerk, the human-machine interface can be adapted and made as simple as required.

Figure 9. The requirements ontology ON-EREQ (Kassal, 2008)

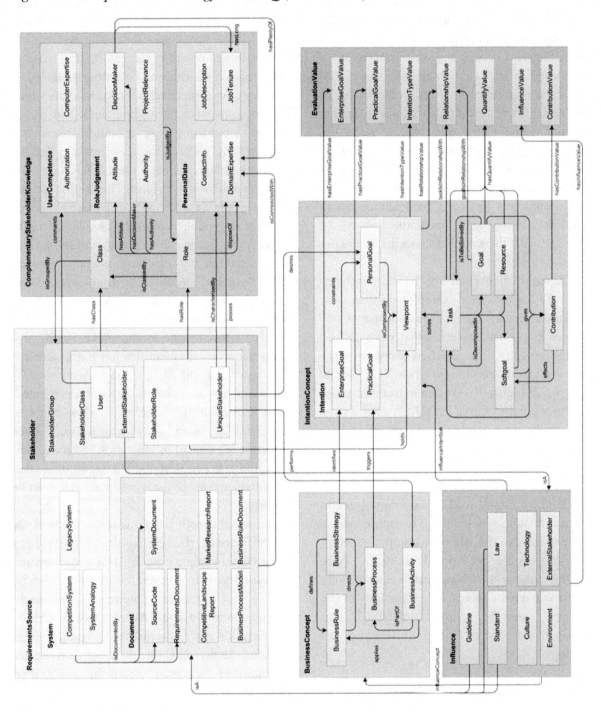

Figure 10. An excerpt of the requirements ontology

```
<User rdf:about="#Sales_Clerk">
     <hasAuthorization rdf:resource="#Operator"/>
     <hasClass rdf:resource="#OperationalBusinessUser"/>
     <hasComputerExpertise rdf:resource="#Novice"/>
</User>
<Goal rdf:about="#Register_new_Customer_Order">
     <isToBeSolvedBy rdf:resource="#Entering_Customer_ID"/>
     <isToBeSolvedBy rdf:resource="#Register_Trade_Items"/>
</Goal>
<Task rdf:about="#Entering_Customer_ID">
     <isDecomposedIn rdf:resource="#Rating_Sufficient"/>
     <isDecomposedIn rdf:resource="#Customer_Profile"/>
</Task>
```

Figure 11. Customer creation requirements in DITA with semantic annotations

```
<task id="registerNewCustomerOrder">
   <title ref="&ONEREQ;Register_new_Customer_Order">
     Register new customer order</title>
   <taskbody>
     <context ref="&ONEREQ;Sales_Clerk">A sales clerk with a non-processed
       customer order</context>
     <prereq>
       <ul>
         <li>Customer has been stored in system</li>
         <li>Trade items are available in the system</li>
       </ul>
     </prereq>
     <steps>
       <step ref="&ONEREQ;Entering_Customer_ID">The sales clerk enters the customer's
         ID</step>
       <step>The system displays the customer's profile</step>
       <step ref="&ONEREQ;Rating_Sufficient">The sales clerk confirms that the
         customer's credit rating is sufficient and the order can be
         processed</step>
       <step>The system assigns an order ID</step>
       <step ref="&ONEREQ;Register_Trade_Items">The sales clerk registers the desired
         trade items</step>
       <step>I</step>
     </steps>
     <result>
       <ul>
         <li>System has initiated an order for the customer</li>
         <li>System has documented payment information</li>
         <li>System has registered request with the customer</li>
         <li>System has logged all failures</li>
         <li>System has logged transaction date and time</li>
       </ul>
     </result>
   </taskbody>
</task>
```

5. RELATED WORK

The combination of requirements engineering and Semantic Web technologies was already studied in Selberg and Austin (2003). There, the Internet is described as a virtual, chaotic system which is similar to the study of requirements and the authors have shown which parts of requirements engineering could be realized with each tier of the Semantic Web layer cake. In their following report (Mayank et al., 2004) they describe how components could be semantically annotated and how this semantic annotation could be implemented. Similarly, Kinary (2003) shows how semantic an-

notated components could be composed to solve a problem, but there is no adoption of Semantic Web languages- Java is used instead.

Kaiya and Saeki (2005) represent a framework for the ontology-based analysis of requirements, but many technical details are missing as the report is quite high-level. Additionally, Lin et al. (1996) summarize all requirements in an ontology in order to deduce additional information and to check the consistency of the requirements. This ontology does not only cover quality of service aspects, but also organizational, structural or functional aspects. Dobson & Sawyer (2006) state that the basics for ontology-based requirements analysis has already been laid through the Requirements Modeling Language (RML) in the 1980s and how RML could be combined with current Semantic Web languages.

6. CONCLUSION AND OUTLOOK

In this article we have shown that linguistics-based modeling methods need to be considered and applied to requirements engineering. As in many other areas, multidisciplinarity is typical for this domain: in times of offshoring there are different cultures involved, there are always people with different apprenticeships (business analysts, software engineers, documentation engineers, etc.) which hinders a common understanding of the terms used. Only with the application of linguistics-based modeling methods and a semantic annotation of the terms adopted in requirements specifications these obstacles can be overcome.

The modeling methods allow for a clear structure of the document: already during writing of the requirements specifications the author is forced to think about how the content can best be presented to the future reader. Linguistics-based modeling methods are based on research on linguistics and Speech Acts which have already been used in the area of technical documentation for years. The usage of these techniques in Requirements Engineering seems therefore more than natural.

When the requirement documents are not only human-understandable, but become 'machine-understandable', then their reuse will grow intensively. Many tasks can be automated and documents for the next software engineering phase could be automatically generated with the usage of the model-driven architecture (MDA™) (Frankel, 2003). For example, semantically described requirements specifications could be used to generate semantic business process models (Hepp et al., 2005) which could then be further refined and finally executed.

The semantic annotation can also lead to further personalization of the developed software: if the person who is responsible for some requirements can be traced back, it is possible to personalize the software to the needs of each individual person as described in the requirements specification (e.g., in a developed requirements profile). By using an ontology that covers the profile of the requestor, it is possible to personalize the application to the needs of each specific user later on.

REFERENCES

W3C. (2004). *OWL Web Ontology Language Reference*. Retrieved from http://www.w3.org/TR/owl-ref/

Ament, K. (2003). *Single Sourcing: Building Modular Documentation*. Norwich, NY: William Andrew Publishing.

Austin, J. L. (1962). *How to Do Things with Words*. Cambridge, MA: Harvard University Press.

Bauer, B., & Roser, S. (2006). Semantic-enabled Software Engineering and Development. In *Proceedings of Informatik 2006* (LNI P-94, pp. 293-296). Bonner Köllen Verlag.

Berlo, D. K. (1960). *The Process of Communication*. New York: Holt, Rinehart, and Winston.

Bühler, K. (1965). *Sprachtheorie: Die Darstellungsform der Sprache*. Stuttgart, Germany: Verlang UTB.

de Cesare, S., Holland, G., Holtmann, C., & Lycett, M. (2007). Semantic-based systems development. In *OOPSLA Companion* (pp. 760).

Dobson, G., & Sawyer, P. (2006). *Revisiting Ontology-Based Requirements Engineering in the age of the Semantic Web*. Paper presented at the International Seminar Dependable Requirements Engineering of Computerised Systems at NPPs, Halden.

Euzenat, J. (2002). Eight Questions about Semantic Web Annotations. *IEEE Intelligent Systems, 17*(2), 55–62.

Flensburg, P. (2007, August 11-14). *An enhanced communication model*. Paper presented at the 30th Information Systems Research Seminar in Scandinavia (IRIS), Tampere, Finland.

Frankel, D. S. (2003). *Model Driven Architecture – Applying MDA™ to Enterprise Computing*. New York: Wiley.

Gašević, D., Kaviani, N., & Milanović, M. (in press). Ontologies and Software Engineering. In S. Staab & R. Studer (Eds.), *Handbook on Ontologies*.

Grice, H. P. (1967). Logic and Conversation. In A. P. Martinich (Ed.), *Philosophy of Language*. New York: Oxford University Press.

Gruber, T. R. (1993). A Translation Approach to Portable Ontology Specifications. *Knowledge Acquisition, 5*(2), 199–220. doi:10.1006/knac.1993.1008

Guarino, N. (1997). Understanding, building and using ontologies. *International Journal of Human-Computer Studies, 46*(2-3), 293–310. doi:10.1006/ijhc.1996.0091

Hepp, M., Leymann, F., Domingue, J., Wahler, A., & Fensel, D. (2005, October 18-20). Semantic Business Process Management: A Vision Towards Using Semantic Web Services for Business Process Management. In *Proceedings of IEEE ICEBE,* Beijing, China (pp. 535-540).

Hevner, A. R., March, S. T., Park, J., & Ram, S. (2004). Design Science in Information Systems Research. *MIS Quarterly, 28*(1), 75–105.

Hong, S., Goor, G., & Brinkkemper, S. (1993). A Formal Approach to the Comparison of Object-Oriented Analysis and Design Methodologies. In J. F. Nunamaker & R. H. Sprague (Eds.), *Information Systems of HICCS* (pp. 689-698).

Kaiya, H., & Saeki, M. (2005). *Ontology Based Requirements Analysis: Lightweight Semantic Processing Approach*. Paper presented at the International Conference on Quality Software (QSIC), Melbourne, Australia.

Kassal, S. (2008). *Semantic Requirements – Ontologie-basierte Modellierung von Anforderungen im Software Engineering*. Master thesis, University of Augsburg.

Kiniry, J. R. (2003). *Semantic Component Composition*. Paper presented at ECOOP, Darmstadt, Germany.

Kopecky, J., Vitvar, T., Bournez, C., & Farrell, J. (2007). SAWSDL: Semantic Annotations for WSDL and XML Schema. *IEEE Internet Computing, 11*(6), 60–67. doi:10.1109/MIC.2007.134

Ley, M. (2006). Aspekte der Informationsstrukturierung: Über Strukturierungsprinzipien, die Ebenen der Textstruktur und Dokumentgrammatiken. *Technische Kommunikation, 28*(4), 51–53.

Lin, J., Fox, M. S., & Bilgic, T. (1996). A Requirement Ontology for Engineering Design. *Concurrent Engineering, 4*(3), 279–291. doi:10.1177/1063293X9600400307

Lobin, H. (2000). *Informationsmodellierung in XML und SGML*. Berlin Heidelberg, Germany: Springer-Verlag.

Mayank, V., Kositsyna, N., & Austin, M. (2004). *Requirements Engineering and the Semantic Web – Part II* (Tech. Rep. 2004-14). College Park, MD: Institute for Systems Research.

Metz, P., O'Brien, J., & Weber, W. (2003). Specifying Use Case Interaction: Types of Alternative Courses. *Journal of Object Technology JOT, 2*(2).

Missikoff, M., Schiappelli, F., & Taglino, F. (2003, October). A Controlled Language for Semantic Annotation and Interoperability in e-Business Applications. In *Proceedings of the Semantic Integration Workshop (SI-2003)*, Sanibel Island, FL (Vol. 82, 13). CEUR-WS.

Moodey, D. L., & Shanks, S. (1994). What makes a good data model? Evaluating the Quality of Entity Relationship Models. In P. Loucopoulos (Ed.), *Entity-Relationsship Approach – Proceedings of ER'94, Business Modelling and Re-Engineering* (pp. 94-111).

Muthig, J., & Schäflein-Armbruster, R. (1999). *Funktionsdesign: eine universelle und flexible Standardisierungstechnik*. Augsburg, Germany: WEKA-Verlag.

OASIS. (2007). *DITA Version 1.1, Architectural Specification*. Boston: Author.

Rueping, A. (2003). *Agile Documentation: A Pattern Guide to Producing Lightweight Documents for Software Projects*. New York: Wiley Software Patterns Series.

Rupp, C. (2007). *Requirements Engineering und Management – Professionelle, iterative Anforderungsanalyse für die Praxis*. Munich, Germany: Hanser Verlag.

Schramm, W. (1954). How communication works. In W. Schramm (Ed.), *The Process and Effects of Mass Communication* (pp. 5-6). Urbana, IL: University of Illinois Press.

Searle, J. (1969). *Speech Acts: An Essay in the Philosophy of Language*. Cambridge, UK: Cambridge University Press.

Selberg, S. A., & Austin, M. (2003). *Requirements Engineering and the Semantic Web – Part I*, (Tech. Rep. 2003-20). College Park, MD: Institute for Systems Research.

Shannon, C. F., & Weaver, W. (1964). *The Mathematical Theory of Communication*. Urbana, IL: University of Illinois Press.

Sieber, T., & Kammerer, M. (2006). Sind Metadaten bessere Daten? *Technische Dokumentation, 5/2006*, 56–58.

Sieber, T., & Kovács, L. (2005). Technical documentation: Terms, problems and challenges in managing data, information and knowledge. In Proceedings of the *University of Miskolc's 5th International Conference of PhD Students* (pp. 165-170).

Sieber, T., & Lautenbacher, F. (2007). *Enterprise Content Integration: Documentation, Implementation and Syndication using Intelligent Metadata (ECIDISI)* (Tech. Rep. 2007-17). Augsburg, Germany: University of Augsburg, Germany. Retrieved from http://www.ds-lab.org/publications/reports/2007-17.html

Strawson, P. F. (1969). Intention and Convention in Speech Acts. In K. T. Fann (Ed.), *Symposium on J. L. Austin, International Library of Philosophy and Scientific Method*. New York: Humanities Press.

Tetlow, P., Pan, J. Z., Oberle, D., Wallace, E., Uschold, M., & Kendall, E. (2006). *Ontology Driven Architectures and Potential Uses of the Semantic Web in Systems and Software Engineering*. Cambridge, MA: W3C.

Wiegand, H. E. (1989). Aspekte der Makrostruktur im allgemeinen einsprachigen Wörterbuch: alphabetische Anordnungsformen und ihre Probleme. In F. J. Hausmann, O. Reichmann, H. E. Wiegand, & L. Zgusta (Eds.), *Wörterbücher* (Vol. 1, pp. 371-409). Berlin, Germany: Springer.

Wiegand, H. E. (1989). Der Begriff der Mikrostruktur: Geschichte, Probleme, Perspektiven. In F. J. Hausmann, O. Reichmann, H. E. Wiegand, & L. Zgusta (Eds.), *Wörterbücher* (Vol. 1, pp. 409-462). Berlin, Germany: Springer.

Wittgenstein, L. (1973). *Philosophical investigations*. Upper Saddle River, NJ: Prentice Hall.

This work was previously published in International Journal of Enterprise Information Systems, edited by Madjid Tavana, pp. 12-28, Volume 6, Issue 1, copyright 2010 by IGI Publishing (an imprint of IGI Global).

Chapter 15
Semantic User Interfaces

Károly Tilly
Oracle, Hungary

Zoltán Porkoláb
Eötvös Lóránd University, Hungary

ABSTRACT

Semantic User Interfaces (SUIs), are sets of interrelated, static, domain specific documents having layout and content, whose interpretation is defined through semantic decoration. SUIs are declarative in nature. They allow program composition by the user herself at the user interface level. The operation of SUI based applications follow a service oriented approach. SUI elements referenced in user requests are automatically mapped to reusable service provider components, whose contracts are specified in domain ontologies. This assures semantic separation of user interface components from elements of the underlying application system infrastructure, which allows full separation of concerns during system development; real, application independent, reusable components; user editable applications and generic learnability. This article presents the architecture and components of a SUI framework, basic elements of SUI documents and relevant properties of domain ontologies for SUI documents. The basics of representation and operation of SUI applications are explained through a motivating example.

INTRODUCTION

Creating and editing static documents is one of the most common computer skills. The required abilities, entering and editing text, importing figures, defining layout and decorating pieces of contents seem to be learnable by any literate person. If we take a look at the user interface of

DOI: 10.4018/978-1-4666-1761-2.ch015

an application system, we just see sets of text and figures representing menus, toolbars, controls and pieces of content. There is seemingly nothing there, which could not have been arranged by a teenage student, who knows, how to edit static web pages using a fancy HTML editor.

In fact teenage students are currently not able to create user interfaces. Let us see, why. User interfaces contain pieces of contents with specific semantic meaning known by the user.

This knowledge is the *user's mental model* of the application. On the other hand, semantic meaning is encoded by implementors into program components and data structures according to information gained about the application domain during system analysis and design. Human computer interaction is basically a mapping between the user's mental model and the internal representations of domain knowledge incorporated in the application system. This mapping is nowadays implemented by hardcoded, application specific associations between user interface- and application level components using event handlers and relatively simple protocols. We call this feature *strong semantic coupling* between user interfaces and underlying application layers. It results that it is not enough for a teenage student to understand user interface level concepts and components, but she should also be familiar with the methods of creating and activating application components for executing user requests.

We argue that strong semantic coupling is one of the main reasons, which currently holds back domain experts from creating applications by themselves. If we could *semantically separate* the user interface from underlying components, it would lead to significant advantages, among others full separation of concerns between stakeholders during system development; real, application independent, reusable components; user editable applications and generic learnability.

To characterize *semantic separation*, we distinguish it first from *modular* and *spatial* separation.

Modular separation is related to application design by clearly isolating user interface functionalities from pieces of application logic at the implementation source code level. This kind of separation is successfully implemented in state of the art GUI libraries, generally based on a form of the Model-View-Controller pattern.

Spatial separation is mainly related to application deployment. It allows user interface components and application logic components to be executed on physically different devices.

Spatial separation is fundamental in web based environments, where user interface components are rendered by web browsers, while the execution layer is embodied in application logic and database tier components activated through application servers. Spatial separation supports platform- and device independence as well.

Modular and spatial separation do not prevent strong semantic coupling, however, so the user interface and the underlying application logic is still designed, implemented and operated as a single, monolithic unit.

Semantic separation is about explicitly separating domain concepts of the user's mental model from user interface components and application components. The set of separated domain concepts allow a dynamic mapping between elements of user interface documents and underlying application components. In the following it is supposed that domain concepts are organized and stored in *domain ontologies*.

The power of semantic separation is demonstrated by hyperlinks in static HTML pages. From our current point of view a hyperlink offers a *service* with a predefined, simple *contract*, which says that the associated target is navigated, whenever the user clicks the hyperlink object on the screen. This contract is fixed in HTML/HTTP standards, and implemented by web browsers and HTTP servers. Anybody can assemble websites from static HTML pages, because it is enough to know the contents of the document, and the hyperlink contract, but it is not necessary to know anything about the underlying application environment (in this case the HTTP server).

To generalize the above described nice properties of hyperlinks, we introduce Semantic User Interfaces (SUIs) and SUI Documents (SUIDs). A SUI is a user interface, which implements semantic separation. SUIDs are static, user editable documents for describing SUIs. SUIDs can contain references to arbitrary services, whose contracts are specified in domain ontologies. The purpose of SUIDs is to empower domain experts to create applications by editing sets of static documents, while IT professionals design and implement reusable user interface components and service provider components based on standard specifications stored in domain ontologies. To achieve this, as a first step we need an execution environment and a description language for SUI Documents.

According to this scenario section 2 introduces an infrastructure for interpreting SUI Documents while section 3 explains the primitives and main elements of SUIDs and an experimental language, SIDL, for describing SUIDs. Section 4 summarizes the most important features of domain ontologies supporting semantic separation. Section 5 outlines the development process of SUI applications. The relationships of our work to other research are analyzed in section 6 before closing conclusions in section 7.

INTERPRETING SEMANTIC USER INTERFACE DOCUMENTS

SUI applications work in a *request/response* style. A *request* is defined as a list of objects, where each object has an associated semantic meaning. Formally a *request* is a set of $r_n=\{(O_i, \rho_j)\}$ pairs of $O_i \in O$ *objects* and associated $\rho_j \in \rho$ *roles*, where O is a universe of objects, ρ is a universe of *roles*, and an *object* is an entity having its own identity, behavior, internal state and lifespan according to traditional object oriented terminology, while a *role* is a possible semantic meaning of an object.

Roles are categorized in *domain ontologies*. The most significant role is *service*, which specifies the requested operation. Any request must contain exactly one object associated to the role *service*. The role of all remaining objects in a request is *argument*. Specific roles categorized as arguments, like *source* or *target* are domain dependent.

Each SUID object has a *content type*, which determines its interpretation, internal structure, and rendering behavior. E.g. an object representing

the character sequence "*document.txt*" can have a content type of *fileName* or *text*. If the request r = {(*delete,service*),("*document.txt*",*argument*)} is formulated by the user, the actual content type of "*document.txt*" determines, whether the piece of text or the appropriate file will be deleted. Content types are categorized in *domain ontologies*.

Requests are executed by service providers, which implement activities with predefined contracts stored in domain ontologies. Service provider contracts have a structure similar to requests, though they refer to *content types* instead of objects. Formally a *service provider contract* is a set of $c_n=\{(T_i, \rho_j)\}$ pairs of $T_i \in T$ *content types* and associated $\rho_j \in \rho$ *roles*, where T is a universe of content types, and ρ is a universe of *roles*. In this context a content type is an *object class* according to traditional object oriented terminology, and a *role* is a possible semantic meaning of a class.

Architectural elements and operation of an infrastructure for SUI applications are explained in the next paragraphs according to Figure 1.

Service provider contracts are categorized in *Domain Ontologies* and associated to service providers in the Service *Provider Registry*.

The *SUI Document Browser* renders SUIDs containing objects with specific *content types* registered in domain ontologies.

User interaction through SUIs is based upon a simple interaction model, which we call the *presentation-navigation-selection-activation* cycle. According to this model the user interface *presents* a set of *content objects*. The user assembles *requests* in the following way: he *navigates* desired objects, *selects* them, *assigns a semantic role* to each of them, and finally performs a *terminating gesture* to initiate request execution. Terminating gestures, like pressing the *Enter* key, signal the SUID Browser that the user has assembled a request, which should be forwarded for execution. The system *executes* the request, and returns a result, which is combined by the SUID Browser (Figure 1) with the actually displayed pieces of contents.

Figure 1. Architectural elements of a SUI framework

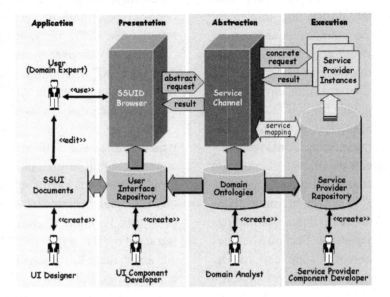

Semantic separation is assured by the *Service Channel*, which dynamically matches requests to service provider contracts according to the roles and content types of request objects. The Service Channel determines the actual provider contract from the request, retrieves the providers offering the given contract from the Provider Registry, and selects one of them to execute. Selection is made according to user preferences and heuristics.

Mapping abstract requests to concrete service provider instances results a kind of parametric polymorphism at the user interface level. It allows the user to formulate requests by combining a specific service with objects having different content types and roles. According to domain ontology specifications the user interface always presents a specific service the same way independently of its arguments. For example, if service *copy* has an associated shortcut *Ctrl+C*, it can be used to copy selected content to the clipboard (as usual), but it can also be used to copy a source to a target argument independently of the fact, whether the content type of the arguments are local file, URL or even two files with different formats (which requires implicit conversion). This way the user can formulate semantically similar requests in the

same way, while the execution of requests may need providers drastically different in complexity and resource requirements. This feature highly simplifies learning and using SUID applications, and leads to a level of user interface consistency unseen before (Baranyi, Hercegfi & Tilly, 2003).

REPRESENTING SEMANTIC USER INTERFACE DOCUMENTS

This section summarizes the basics of Semantic Interface Definition Language (SIDL) for describing layout and structure of SUI Documents. SIDL offers a set of declarative language primitives simple enough to be understood and learnt by anyone, while still allowing users to specify each and every aspects of user interface components according to the Model-View-Controller pattern.

SIDL is built around a set of atomic components, which form a *user interface pattern language* according to (Mahemoff & Johnston, 1998). These components can be orthogonally combined to create higher level constructs to define arbitrary user interface features. It was a demanding task for us to define the language primitives, since *widgets* are not appropriate for this purpose. We found that widgets, the elementary components of state of the art graphical user interfaces, are compound, intuitively specified components with functional overlaps. See (Johnson, 1992) for additional details.

To see why widgets are not appropriate, let us consider a simple example. Current GUI libraries offer among others popup lists and combo lists for list based selection. The model behind these widgets is basically the same: labels are associated to a list of values. The labels are displayed, and when selected by the user, the associated value is assigned to the list component.

The above mentioned widgets result from static bindings of slightly different presentations with a single model. It would be much better to separate view and controller related features from the model, so that users could arbitrarily recombine them according to their needs.

A similar problem is that widgets offer a set of predefined properties (like font, color or size) for the user to change component behavior. Since the number of properties is limited for ergonomical and technical reasons, state of the art systems demand the creation of programmatic extensions (typically event handlers), when a specific widget functionality is not supported through setting property values. For example what if the user wants to change the popup list's filtering or value checking behavior? At this point the popup list (and in generally widgets) loose declarative configurability, and functionalities must be added as pieces of procedural code, implementing, say, Java vetoable change event handlers. This is surely not meant for domain experts.

It implies that the required granularity of atomic components of SUIDs is necessarily finer than widgets. We found that atomic interface components can be classified into two main categories: *Axes* for describing the model part and *Atomic Interface Components* (AICs) for describing the view and controller part of compound interface components.

The following sections explain main characteristics of axes and atomic interface components, and show a simple example for the description and operation of an SIDL text field.

Axes

Axes are lists of objects, which define the model (DOM) of SUI Documents. Axes directly represent high level concepts understood and applied by domain experts. Axes can be categorized as *content axes*, *request axes*, *attribute axes* and *semantic axes*.

Content axes hold pieces of contents, which must be rendered (e.g. plain text characters). A content axis contains pure, undecorated, uninterpreted data, originally entered by the user, or directly defined as part of a SUID.

Request axes define dimensions of requests. Request objects form an *n dimensional vector space* called the *request space* structured by *n different semantic dimensions* called *request axes*, along which simple, atomic navigation or selection operations can be performed. A request axis is a domain dependent concept, which determines a *view* of the objects along another axis. In most cases objects along a request axis form ordered sequences. For example the request axes of the text document domain are among others *character*, *word*, *line* or *paragraph*. Request axes decompose the request space into several hierarchical views, which drastically reduce the complexity of navigation, selection and in general request formulation.

Attribute axes associate a property to objects of another axis. An attribute axis can e.g. store font, color or selection state of a content axis' individual characters.

Semantic axes determine the interpretation of another axis in a specific context. A semantic axis can e.g. define the roles of objects along another axis.

This approach decomposes the model of a SUI Document into four, clearly separated parts. Content axes hold *document content*, attribute axes hold *formatting and style* information, request axes hold *controller related data*, while semantic axes define the *semantic interpretation* of specific pieces in the document. The user is free to add, delete or modify any kinds of axes when editing SUIDs.

Atomic Interface Components (AIC)

According to the applied *presentation-navigation-selection-activation* user interaction model we identified four basic classes of AICs: *viewers*, *navigators*, *selectors* and *combinators* explained in the following paragraphs.

Viewers implement the *presentation* and *input acquisition* part of an AIC pattern by rendering and displaying objects through associated screen areas or modalities like audio channels, while sensing and forwarding gestures and user input.

Navigators enable the user to have access to presentations of objects. Navigation occurs along specific request axes of an n-dimensional request space.

Selectors mark objects as arguments of a request along a set of request axes.

Combinators process terminating gestures through assembling requests from pieces of selected contents in a set of associated viewers, initiating request execution, and merging request results into the contents of related viewers.

Higher level user interface components can be created as AIC compounds built around viewers according to Figure 2. Each viewer renders an associated content axis containing objects of arbitrary content types (even viewers). Viewers are categorized in *domain ontologies* according to their layout, so e.g. *row viewers* render base axis objects into a horizontal line, *column viewers* render base axis objects into a vertical column, while *table viewers* render base axis objects into a table with a set of rows and columns. By embedding viewers into base axes of other viewers, it is possible to implement any traditional part-whole GUI layout structures. Besides content rendering,

viewers sense user gestures and they can also offer services, like inserting or deleting objects along their base axis.

A viewer can have an arbitrary number of associated navigators and selectors, which allow specific kinds of navigation and selection operations along request axes associated to the content axis of the viewer. Navigators and selectors are categorized in Domain Ontologies according to the algorithm they use. E.g. *linear navigators* can navigate the previous, next, first or last object along the navigation axis relative to an actual navigation position, while *random navigators* allow the user to pick an arbitrary object along the navigation axis. Linear and random selectors can be defined accordingly, but in this case the result of the operations is not just setting the navigation position, but also selecting objects. Notice that linear navigators and selectors describe operations mainly related to keyboard type input devices, while random navigators and selectors describe operations mainly related to pointing devices (e.g. mouse).

Event Nets

To keep SUIDs fully declarative and to allow full semantic separation, SIDL hides all details of traditional event handling. This is achieved through *event nets*, which are simple, user definable data flow networks that determine the activation order of specific components.

Potential events can be specified in SIDL in the form of services and user gestures associated to AICs. User gestures are sensed by viewers through attached device dependent *sensor* components like *MouseSensor* or *KeyboardSensor*. Viewers receive focus according to usual rules. If a sensor detects a user event, it transforms it into a *generic event object*, and passes it to the viewer having the current focus. The event object is processed by the viewer using its associated event net.

Event nets are data flow networks, whose nodes are AICs, and whose edges can be labeled

Figure 2. Composition relations of atomic interface components

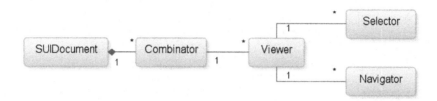

by three different conditions: "*ifNotProcessed*", "*ifProcessed*" and "*always*". These conditions require that the next AIC in the network is activated, whenever the previous AIC has not processed the gesture ("*ifNotProcessed*"), has processed the gesture ("*ifProcessed*") or all the time respectively ("*always*"). If the user does not specify event processing order, viewers have a default event net, where component order is determined by the lexical order of the AIC components in the SIDL description, and edges are labeled with "*ifNotProcessed*" conditions. Users can create event nets by explicitly specifying the order and conditions of activation for each components related to a viewer. Event nets are scheduled by the SUID Browser, which activates AICs one by one accordingly. Items signal the scheduler, if they have processed an event or not.

Describing User Interface Components in SIDL

Using axes and AICs it is possible to *reproduce* any current user interface functionalities like menus, radio buttons, popup lists, buttons and hyperlinks.

SIDL interface documents are built around a set of viewers. Each viewer has a *content axis*, which holds the set of undecorated objects that a viewer must render. Content axes are referenced by *request axes*, which tokenize content axes into specific pieces. Content and request axes can have associated attribute- and semantic axes. Viewers can have associated navigators and selectors. Viewers, navigators and selectors can offer services along their associated axes.

As an example Figure 3 shows the AIC pattern of a text field. The figure uses UML class diagram notations with somewhat different interpretations. Class boxes denote *AIC* and *axis instances*, lines denote *associations* and notes show values of instance properties.

The central (view) part of the text field pattern is *RowViewer*, which renders the characters of its base axis (*CharacterAxis*) in a horizontal line. *RowViewer* offers two services: *new* allows the user to add new characters, while *delete* allows the user to delete selected pieces of contents.

The controller part is defined by a linear navigator and a linear selector. Both of them allow navigation/selection of the *next/previous* object along the *character* and *word* request axes. Navigation is also possible to the *first/last* characters. *It is very important to notice that the parts presented in Figure 3 can all freely be changed by the user in SIDL, and it is enough for the user to name a service to be able to execute it later.*

The following code sample shows the SIDL source of the text field example in Figure 3:

```
<unit name="TextField">
  <content name="Root" type="Text"/>
    <viewer name="TextFieldViewer"
type="RowViewer" sensor="KBSensor
MSensor" >
    <view of="Root"
axis="CharacterAxis" service="New
Delete"
        gesture="Shortcut"
name="TextFieldContent"/>
      <attribute of="TextFieldContent"
```

Figure 3. AIC pattern of a text field

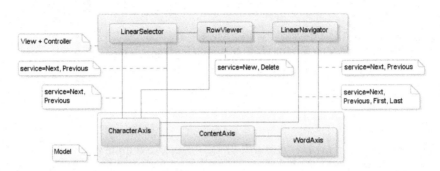

```
axis="FontAxis" name="Font"/>
    <navigator
type="LinearNavigator">
        <view axis   ="CharacterAxis"
service="Next Previous First Last"
            gesture="Shortcut"/>
        <view axis="WordAxis"
service="Next Previous"
gesture="Shortcut"/>
    </navigator>
    <selector type="LinearSelector">
        <view axis="CharacterAxis"
service="Next Previous"
gesture="Shortcut"/>
        <view axis="WordAxis"
service="Next Previous"
gesture="Shortcut"/>
    </selector>
  </viewer>
</unit>
```

SIDL contains a set of keywords (in the example typed in bold) for defining language primitives like atomic interface components and axes, furthermore SIDL allows the user to include names of ontology concepts (in the example typed in italic). One of the most important features of SIDL is that it defines a small language core, which can be extended by direct references to names of domain ontology concepts. Domain experts should learn the language core (which is

simple), and they can extend core functionalities by referring to familiar and stable domain concepts. The actual specification of SIDL is less than twenty pages, which allows us to assume, that it is a suitable core domain language to be learned by application domain experts.

The top level SIDL construct is a *unit*, which defines a named reusable module (in our example *TextField*).

The definition contains the base axis called *Root*, with content type *Text*, the field called *TextFieldViewer*, which is a *RowViewer*, and a linear navigator and linear selector to perform appropriate operations above the text field. Ontology concepts are directly referenced by name in the SIDL source (e.g. gesture="*Shortcut*", or service="*Next Previous*"). For example in the case of *LinearNavigator*, the definition says that the interface should allow navigation to the previous/next/first/last character of the viewer's base axis using keyboard shortcuts. Service attributes used to present and activate a service, like *shortcut*, *label*, *command* or *icon* are associated to services at the level of domain ontologies.

In the example the user does not have to define shortcuts for specific services (in fact she is not even allowed to do so), because the shortcut of, say, navigating to the next position along an axis is specified as *right arrow* in the ontology, and it is not supposed to change. Similarly the user does not have to define a component, which is supposed to execute the navigate next service along the character axis, because service provider mappings are automatically performed by the SUID Browser and Service Channel of the SUI infrastructure. This feature gives SIDL high descriptive power while assuring consistency of interfaces across different documents and platforms (Baranyi, Hercegfi & Tilly 2003).

SIDL uses special attributes to define relationships between axes. The *of* attribute defines the base axis of another axis. E.g. <**view of**="Root" **axis**="*CharacterAxis*"...> tokenizes the axis named *Root* into characters. The base view associated to request axes of navigators and selectors is implicitly specified, and it is always the base view of the viewer to which the navigator or selector belongs. Axes can also be defined by a *reference* to another axis using the *is* attribute (not demonstrated in our example).

SIDL Components on the Move

This section introduces the operation of an AIC pattern through our previous text field example.

When the SUID Browser renders the text field, it builds an internal representation according to

Figure 4. The figure shows the model, view and controller parts. Arrows denote relationships between axes and atomic interface components. Whenever the user performs a gesture, the *Event-Net* component activates one or more interface components. Meanwhile the contents of underlying axes are automatically synchronized by the SUID Browser.

The SUID Browser first activates RowViewer, which, according to its rendering rule, displays the characters of the base axis in a horizontal line. As all SIDL viewers, the RowViewer combines the contents of its base axis with the contents of associated attribute- and request axes, so in our case the characters will be shown with their actual selection highlight and font.

The user may first press a literal key, say "*a*". It will be processed by the RowViewer by inserting character *a* after the actual navigation position along *Content Axis*. The contents of referencing axes (*Character Axis* and *Word Axis*) are automatically updated by the SUID Browser, and the viewer is activated again to reflect the changes to the user.

If the user presses a control key, say right arrow, which is the gesture associated to navigat-

Figure 4. The operation of a text field

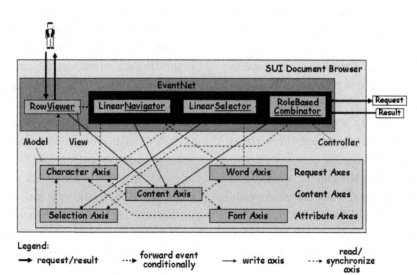

ing to the next navigation position, the EventNet activates RowViewer again, which replies with *NotProcessed*, so EventNet passes the event object to *LinearNavigator*. *LinearNavigator* determines the actual navigation axis (*Character Axis* or *Word Axis*), and updates the navigation position in *Content Axis* accordingly by moving the navigation marker token to the correct position. Changes of *Content Axis* are automatically reflected by *RowViewer* again. Selection gestures are processed in a similar fashion by *LinearSelector* through updating the contents of *Selection Axis*. If the user performs a terminating gesture (say she presses the *enter* key), the combinator will process the event, assembles a request using the actual contents of *Selection Axis*, forwards the request, receives the reply, and updates *Content Axis* accordingly. Changes will be automatically reflected by *RowViewer* again.

This example extends the view of SUI application operation presented in section 2, since it shows details of *request assembly*, which is performed by the SUID Browser itself.

DOMAIN ONTOLOGIES

The foundations for semantic separation are Domain Ontologies, which contain classifications and attributes of all relevant concepts outlined in the previous sections for building and using SUI Documents.

Even the most fundamental user interface is domain dependent, so the highest level concepts stored in domain ontologies are *domains*. For example when modifying a document containing text and figures in a text editor, there are at least three related domains: the *meta-document domain*, which describes the concepts related to documents as entities, the *text document domain*, which defines the concepts related to text editing, and the *graphics document domain*, which defines the concepts related to creating layouts and 2D drawings.

The core domain is the *SUI domain*, which contains the concepts *axis*, *role*, *content type* and *service provider contract*. It defines the set of atomic interface components as specific content types, and classifies services and argument types as specific roles. Services are stored along with their names, lexical specifications and user interface attributes like *label*, mouse- and keyboard *gestures* and *icon*. This guarantees that services can be referenced in SUI Documents in a platform and device independent way using ontology concept names.

For all other domains analysis must result a set of domain specific axes, roles, content types and service provider contracts.

CREATING SEMANTIC USER INTERFACE APPLICATIONS

According to Figure 1. SUI applications are created as follows.

As a first step domain expert *domain analysts* analyze relevant application domains, and create ontological specifications. For example the *text document domain*, which describes how to edit text, and the *meta-document domain*, which defines how to handle files, both contain the abstract service *"copy"* with specifications, like: *"if a single piece of text is copied, its characters must be copied to the clipboard"*; *"if copy has two file arguments, then the contents of the source file is copied to the destination file"*; or *"if copy has a file as a source and a URL as a target, the source file contents must be uploaded to the target location"*.

The knowledge gathered during domain analysis is distilled in *Domain Ontologies* as a set of user interface components, roles (first of all services), axes, content types and service provider contracts as discussed in sections 3 and 4.

Service provider component developers and *user interface component developers* are IT experts, who implement service providers and user interface components based upon the specification of services and user interface components defined in domain ontologies.

An application in our approach is just an interrelated set of static SUI Documents created and edited by *interface designers* or *users*. A user can be an interface designer as well, but a user is supposed to have domain expertise, while an interface designer is more a user interface design expert. None of them needs special IT knowledge unless using a SUID editor (not shown in Figure 1), which is just a special document editor. Notice that creating SIDL is just editing text, layout and decoration – which may be semantic decoration as well, where the semantic role of certain components must be specified.

According to Figure 1 domain ontologies assure perfect separation of high level concerns between *user interface designers (users), UI component developers, service provider component developers* and *domain analysts*. In our scenario domain analysts perform *analysis*, user interface designers perform *design* and user interface- and service provider component developers perform *implementation*. In theory they do not have to directly communicate with each others, since every relevant pieces of information is stored in domain ontologies, which they can read, thus all can do his own task without knowing anything about the task of the others.

RELATED WORK

Our work suggests that user interfaces can be considered the top level of the interface hierarchy of components. This point is clearly supported by the fact that however the presented request structure and axiomatic user interface components were derived from our simple user interaction model based upon a fully user centric view, there is a strong analogy between requests, contracts and *forms* described by (Lumpe & Schneider, 2005) applied in composition languages like Piccola (Nierstrasz & Achermann, 2003). We strongly

conjecture that SUI Documents can be formalized using constructs similar to the Piccola calculus of Nierstrasz and Achermann (Nierstrasz & Achermann, 2003). This can lead to very interesting results, like a unified theory of interfaces, and generic, sound rules of interface design including user interfaces, formally verifiable user interfaces or a minimal set of axiomatic, composable user interface components.

SIDL is *end user centric*, so SUIDs are interpreted at the user interface level, while known composition languages all follow a *developer oriented approach*, which results code that mainly executes at the application logic level (not excluding user interfaces) (Wuyts & Ducasse, 2001). This statement is even valid for high level approaches, like that of (Pahl, 2007) for semantic model based generation of service oriented software systems using ontology-based transformation and reasoning techniques. Human computer interaction admits request-response style operation, where components participating an application communicate with the user, but they do not directly communicate with each others. The connection between SUI application components is established by the set of *axes* forming the *model layer* of the user interface as explained in section *"Describing User Interface Components in SIDL"*. That is why SUIDs do not contain any glue code or adaptors, as required in known compositional environments (Gschwind, 2002). On the other hand dynamic service provider mapping performed by the Service Channel shows similarities with type based composition proposed by (Gschwind, 2002), and in the future it will benefit from using more sophisticated service provider lookup solutions like COLOS suggested by (Bay, Eugster & Oriol, 2006). Because of the independent nature of service activation, SUIs nicely support *independent extensibility* according to (Szypersky, 2002, pp. 95).

SIDL is not generative (Czarnecki & Eisenecker, 2000) and does not rely on meta-programming methods successfully applied for program composition among others by (Assmann, 2000) or

(Lumpe & Schneider, 2005). It is again possible because of the user centric, request response nature of SIDL. On the other hand, at a later stage of SUI research, generative or meta programming techniques may become useful in automatic generation of SUIDs derived from high level specifications.

SIDL is a domain specific language (Czarnecki & Eisenecker, 2000), though our experiences show that domain experts in general are very rarely willing to learn any kind of programming languages. In spite of the possibilities of encoding domain knowledge using language constructs (e.g. in the form of aspects as suggested by (D'Hondt & D'Hondt, 1999), we think that Domain Ontologies is the simplest and most straightforward way of defining and using domain knowledge. That is why SIDL captures a simple core domain (SUI components), which can be extended through domain ontology concepts that do not complicate the set of language constructs. That is why SIDL as a language becomes domain independent, and stays simple, while still allowing the description of arbitrary domain dependent user interfaces.

SIDL shows similarities to *user interface markup languages*, like UIML (Helms, 2008), or Xforms (Boyer, 2007), which all generalize HTML using XML, and support declarative, document based user interface development. An interesting example is the Views system (Bishop & Horspool 2004), which goes beyond other UI markup languages by clearly separating event handling from UI descriptions, this way establishing the way to separating user interface elements from application code. We also think that the separation of event handling is crucial, which is implemented in SIDL using event nets. (Saravan, 2000) claims *XMLterm* to be a UI markup language for "*semantic user interfaces*". At this point it is important to notice that UI markup languages (including Views and XMLterm) are domain specific XML languages, which focus on the definition, layout, rendering and event handling of traditional, widget-like interface components. They emphasize the importance of XML represen-

tation for easy content exchange between different platforms, but none of them goes beyond spatial separation. The fundamental feature of SIDL is semantic separation and not XML, which means that SIDL *generalizes semantic contracts, not* the *set of tags*. SIDL has an XML syntax just for the sake of easy experimental implementation. We did our best to eliminate redundancies and clumsiness resulting from XML syntax when defining SIDL.

Component based application development languages, like Java Server Pages (JSR 245, 2006), do not perform semantic separation as well, since they use explicit references to application components, not to mention their complicated syntax, which no domain expert would ever accept.

SUIDs rely on fine grained service provider components like *copy*, *delete* or *move* in a user interface. It seemingly contradicts the "*maximizing reuse minimizes use*" principle of (Szyperski, 2002, pp. 45), which says that to minimize context dependency problems, components should be large grained (i.e. more universal). In our case reusability is guaranteed by careful domain analysis and semantic separation, which largely eliminate service provider configuration issues.

Portal frameworks offer users to customize or even build their own interfaces. The main building block of portal interfaces are instances of portlets (JSR168, 2003), which are user interface components with predefined and documented functionalities. According to the OASIS Web Services for Remote Portlets standard (WSRP, 2003) even web services can be used as portlets. Portlets however do not support semantic separation, since they bundle pieces of code for application logic with UI generator elements (mainly through dynamic HTML), which is assembled into pages by portal engines. Currently there are no standard ontological methods applied for categorizing portlet functionality, so portlet semantics is arbitrary.

At last but not least the semantic web has apparent relationships to our work. The semantic web, however, concentrates on high level information integration, while SUI tries to capture axiomatic components of human-computer interaction. Known efforts for *semantic portal frameworks* (Stojanovic et al., 2001) or even *semantic user interfaces* (Saravan, 2000) address the problems of the semantic web, which follows a top down approach compared to our bottom-up view.

CONCLUSION AND FURTHER WORK

In this article we presented semantic user interfaces as a new approach for building applications. We implemented an experimental proof of concept SUI framework kernel according to Figure 1 in Java. The kernel contains a basic set of AIC and service provider components, handles domain ontologies, interprets and renders SIDL interface descriptions, builds and handles orthogonal service requests, performs service mappings and result merging. We worked out the elements of three domain ontologies for testing: the SUI domain, the text document domain and the graphics document domain. We used Protégé (Protégé, 2008) for building, and OWL description format for loading domain ontologies into our kernel.

Our experiments verify that the concept is viable. In our simple test domains AIC decomposition is appropriate for generating familiar interface functionalities.

The power of SUIs lays in domain ontologies. It is assumed that the structure and concepts of a well established ontology becomes stable and generic over time. Creating stable ontologies is however difficult even for the simplest domains (Dublin Core, 2007). On the other hand the approach may work even without stable ontologies, in the fashion of developing and publishing vendor dependent component libraries nowadays. There is much work ahead, which is however reasonable, because of the following important advantages of SUIDs.

Separation of concerns between stakeholders: domain users can directly edit SUI Documents related to their own field of expertise, while component developers can work in an application independent way. It admits the appearance of a large number of small development companies creating reusable components for specialized subdomains, even single services. E.g. *copy.com* could specialize for implementing copy providers for different operations ranging from simple text copy inside documents, through file conversion to migration between different kinds of databases.

SUIs are platform and device independent, because component specifications and service attributes, like gestures, icons or labels are fixed in domain ontologies.

Abstract requests simplify user interaction: gestures only depend on the abstract service (e.g. Ctrl+C in the case of copy), and they are independent of the content type of the arguments. If an SUI user knows, what he wants (e.g. to copy a source object to a destination object), he will perform the same gestures, independently of the fact whether he wants to copy text, download a document or migrate content between two databases (though the latter case will definitely require more than two arguments).

Learnability: Stable domain ontologies admit teaching new generations of software users for *applying concepts* instead of applying *concrete applications*, i.e. we can teach them how to *edit text* instead of how to *use MS Word* or *Open Office* (Baranyi, Hercegfi & Tilly 2003).

Reusability: this property follows from the proposed service oriented architecture and the assumption that domain ontologies can reach a stable, steady state.

Our next important goal is to create a high level SUI editor based upon SIDL and our SUI framework, and to test its capabilities in practice on real users. To make the approach practically efficient, AIC compound libraries must be worked out for important user interface patterns, like picker, slider or color chooser.

REFERENCES

Assmann, U. (2000). *Meta-programming Composers in Second Generation Component Systems*, Technical Report 17/97, University of Karlsruhe, Dept. of Computer Science

Baranyi, S., Hercegfi, K., & Tilly, K. (2003). Invariant User Interfaces. *Periodica Polytechnica, 47*(4), 297–310.

Bay, T. G., Eugster, P., & Oriol, M. (2006). *Generic Component Lookup*, Proc. of the 9th Int. SIGSOFT Symp. on Component Based Software Engineering, CBSE 2006, LNCS, vol. 4063, (pp. 182-197), Springer

Bishop, J., & Horspool, N. (2004). Developing principles of GUI programming using Views. *Proceedings of SIGCSE, 04*, 373–377. doi:10.1145/1028174.971429

Boyer, J. M. (2007). *Xforms1.1, W3C Working Draft*, Retrieved July 24, 2008 from the W3C Web Site: http://www.w3.org/TR/2007/WD-xforms11-20070222

Czarnecki, K., & Eisenecker, U. (2000) *Generative Programming: Methods, Tools, and Applications*, Addison-Wesley

D'Hondt, M., & D'Hondt, T. (1999). *Is Domain Knowledge an Aspect?* Proc. of the Workshop on Object-Oriented Technology, LNCS; vol. 1743, (pp. 293-294), Springer

Dublin Core Metadata Initiative (2007). Retrieved July 24, 2008 from the Dublin Core Web Site: http://dublincore.org/

Gschwind, T. (2002). *Adaptation and Composition Techniques for Component Based Software Engineering*, PhD Thesis, Technical University of Vienna

Helms, J. (Ed.). (2008). *User Interface Markup Language (UIML) Specification, Committee Draft 4.0*, Retrieved July 24, 2008 from the OASIS Web Site: http://www.oasis-open.org/committees/download.php/28457/uiml-4.0-cd01.pdf

Johnson, J. (1992). *Selectors: Going Beyond User-Interface Widgets*, Proc. of CHI 92: Conference on Human Factors in Computing Systems, (pp. 273-279), May 3-7, Monterey, California

JSR168. *Portlet Specification* (2003). Retrieved July 24, 2008 from the Java Community Process Web Site: http://jcp.org/en/jsr/detail?id=168

JSR 245: JavaServer™ Pages 2.1 (2006). Retrieved July 24, 2008 from the Java Community Process Web Site: http://www.jcp.org/en/jsr/detail?id=245

Lumpe, M., & Schneider, J. G. (2005). A Form-based Meta-model for Software Composition. *Science of Computer Programming, 56*, 59–78. doi:10.1016/j.scico.2004.11.005

Mahemoff, M. J., & Johnston, L. J. (1998) *Principles for a Usability-Oriented Pattern Language*, Proc. of OZCHI '98: Australasion Computer Human Interaction Conference, (pp. 132-139.), Nov. 30- Dec. 4. Adalaide, South Australia

Nierstrasz, O., & Achermann, F. (2003). *A Calculus for Modeling Software Components*, Proc. of the First Int. Symp. on Formal Methods for Components and Objects, LNCS, vol. 2852, (pp. 339-360), Springer

Pahl, C. (2007). Semantic Model-Driven Architecting of Service-Based Software Systems. *Information and Software Technology, 49*(8), 838–850. doi:10.1016/j.infsof.2006.09.007

Protégé Ontolology Editor and Knowledge Acquisition System. (2008), Retrieved July 24, 2008 from Protégé Web Site: http://protege.stanford.edu

Quan, D. A., & Karger, R. (2004). *Semantic Interfaces and OWL Tools: How to Make a Semantic Web Browser*, Proc. of the 13th Int. Conf. on World Wide Web, WWW '04, (pp. 255-265), ACM

Saravan, R. (2000). *XMLterm: A Mozilla-based Semantic User Interface*, Retrieved July 24, 2008 from the O'Reilly XML.com Web Site: http://www.xml.com/pub/a/2000/06/07/ xmlterm/index.html

Stojanovic, N., Maedche, A., Staab, S., Studer, R., & Sure, Y. (2001). *SEAL – A Framework for Developing Semantic Portals*, Proc. of First Int. Conf. on Knowledge Capture, Victora, B. C., Canada, LNCS, vol. 2097, (pp. 1-22), Springer

Szyperski, C. (2002). *Component Software – Beyond Object Oriented Programming*, Addison Wesley

Windows Presentation Foundation (2006) Retrieved July 24, 2008 from the Wikipedia Web Site: http://en.wikipedia.org/wiki/Windows_Presentation_Foundation

WSRP. *OASIS Web Services for Remote Portlets* (2003). Retrieved July 24, 2008 http://www.oasis-open.org/ committees/tc_home.php?wg_abbrev=wsrp

Wuyts, R., & Ducasse, S. (2001). *Composition Languages for Black Box Components*, Proc. of Roel, First OOPSLA Workshop on Language Mechanisms for Programming Software Components.

This work was previously published in International Journal of Enterprise Information Systems, edited by Madjid Tavana, pp. 29-43, Volume 6, Issue 1, copyright 2010 by IGI Publishing (an imprint of IGI Global).

Chapter 16
Drivers of Organizational Participation in XML-Based Industry Standardization Efforts

Rubén A. Mendoza
Saint Joseph's University, USA

T. Ravichandran
Rensselaer Polytechnic Institute, USA

ABSTRACT

XML-based vertical standards are an emerging compatibility standard for describing business processes and data formats in specific industries that have emerged in the past decade. Vertical standards, typically implemented using eXtensible Markup Language (XML), are incomplete products in constant evolution, continually adding functionality to reflect changing business needs. Vertical standards are public goods because they are freely obtained from sponsoring organizations without investing resources in their development, which gives rise to linked collective action dilemmas at the development and diffusion stages. Firms must be persuaded to invest in development without being able to profit from the output, and a commitment to ensure the diffusion of the standard must be secured from enough potential adopters to guarantee success. In this paper, the authors explore organizational drivers for participation in vertical standards development activities for supply- and demand-side organizations (i.e., vendors and end-user firms) in light of the restrictions imposed by these dilemmas.

INTRODUCTION

Standards play a major role in a firm's competitive position, often making the difference between success and failure (Mitchell, 1994). Compatibility standards define physical and technical interfaces between products and information systems (David, 1987) and are developed in various ways, of which committee-led efforts are most desirable when coordination, not competition, is the primary concern (Farrell & Saloner, 1988). A new class of compatibility standards known as vertical

DOI: 10.4018/978-1-4666-1761-2.ch016

standards has emerged in the last decade. Vertical standards focus on business processes and data formats specific to individual industries (Markus et al., 2003), and are generally implemented using the eXtensible Markup Language (XML) due to its flexibility and extensibility. XML-based vertical standards are incomplete products, in a constant state of evolution and growth, which permits firms to continually add functionality to reflect changing business processes and data formats not originally included in the standard. While some adopters may be satisfied with the initial version of an XML-based vertical standard, others will continue to participate in further development and push for increased functionality. XML-based vertical standards exhibit public goods (Olson, 1971) properties, since they can be obtained free of cost from the sponsoring consortium or standards-developing organization (SDO) without having to invest resources in their development. This gives rise to two linked collective action dilemmas at the development and diffusion stages (Markus et al., 2006) which consortia must identify and solve in their specific industries. At the development stage, firms must be persuaded to invest in XML-based vertical standards development even when copyright policies of the sponsoring consortium or SDO typically prevent the commercial appropriation of the results of the development process by any participant. At the diffusion stage, a commitment from enough potential adopters is crucial to ensuring an XML-based vertical standard's success (Markus et al., 2003). Thus, developers must make a potentially irrecoverable investment, and a critical mass of adopters must be recruited from firms without a stake in the success of the standard. This paper adds to the growing literature on vertical standards by exploring the motivation for participation in the development of vertical standards for supply- and demand-side organizations, i.e., vendors and end-user firms, in the face of these linked dilemmas. We test two linear regression models using constructs that explore the effect of resource and interest heterogeneity

in the participation of demand- and supply-side firms in XML-based vertical standards development activities

Literature Review

IT standards are common technical specifications that define product or system interface and compatibility characteristics (David & Greenstein, 1990). Standards are subject to network externalities (Rohlfs, 1974), and are vulnerable to start-up and discontinuance problems (Markus, 1987) due to high consumer adoption costs when a dominant standard does not exist (Axelrod et al., 1995). Dominant standards may emerge as the result of free-market forces (*de facto*), by legislative mandate (*de jure*), or through coordinated sponsorship by consortia or SDOs (consensus; Farrell & Saloner, 1988; David & Greenstein, 1990). In general, the emergence of dominant standards is subject to three well-understood effects (Quelin et al., 2001): increasing returns, path dependence, and irreversibility. Increasing returns make the utility of a standard greater for the (n+1)th user than it was for the nth user (Rohlfs, 1974; Arthur, 1994). Path dependence is the degree to which standardization outcomes are influenced by small-event history in the development and diffusion of a standard (Arthur, 1994), and can trap firms into the wrong technical platform. Irreversibility refers to inflexion points in the cumulative diffusion curve which make a change to any other outcome not possible for long periods of time (Henry, 1974). All these effects play a role in the decision by members of an industry to standardize on a single technology. Increasing returns affect all non-legislated standards types, but consensus standards have been argued to be more likely to enlist supporters than proprietary technologies seeking to become de facto standards (Greenstein, 1992). Consensus standards allow firms to participate and control development, offering a chance to reduce path dependence, but increased participation increases standards complexity (Markus et al., 2006). As the number of participants in a standardization process increases, competition with other standardization efforts is reduced (Axelrod et al., 1995), eventually tipping the market and making diffusion processes irreversible.

Vertical standards focus on business processes and data formats specific to a single industry (Markus et al., 2003). Vertical standards are dynamic, changing, modular standards which, much like EDI (Lyytinen & Damsgaard, 2001), are complex abstract innovations, create interorganizational dependencies, and require extensive expertise to deploy successfully.

Vertical standards built on XML are extensible, scalable, and built for modularity. Since their functionality is constantly in the process of being upgraded, vertical standards are incomplete products. This minimalist approach (Nelson et al., 2005) permits the standard to continue to add business process descriptions, data structures and formats, and other business functionality not included in the original standard. While some participants may be satisfied with the initial version, others will continue to actively participate in its development and push for increased functionality.

Vertical standards exhibit public goods properties (Olson, 1971) because a firm's decision to participate in development activities and the decision to adopt any version of the vertical standard are independent of each other. Vertical standards development efforts are vulnerable to free-rider problems (Olson, 1971) but successful diffusion requires a critical mass (Markus, 1987) of adopters. Thus, lack of participation at the development stage may negatively affect diffusion stage processes, linking two collective-action dilemmas (Markus et al., 2006) which industries must identify and solve separately.

Most of the emerging research on vertical standards focuses on organizational adoption or on the policies and processes governing development activities. The organizational incentives for individual firms to participate in these development activities, however, have not yet been investigated.

Participation benefits the firm by spreading total development costs over all participants and by combining technical and other expertise of all participants (David & Greenstein, 1990). As the development network grows, a firm's utility from joining also grows (Axelrod et al., 1995). Size of the development network is positively associated with the total network effect "pull" of a vertical standard and to an "insider" participation effect (Xia et al., 2003). While participation contributes to substantial expertise and social capital gains for contributing firms (Xia et al., 2008), competitor presence reduces the overall utility of participation for individual firms (Teece, 1992). To solve this participation dilemma, SDOs create bylaws to ensure weak appropriability of the results by any firm (Farrell, 1989) and to prevent development efforts from splintering. Diverging interests resulting in fractured standardization efforts have led to failures in the automotive industry (Gerst & Bunduchi, 2005), electricity markets (Wareham et al., 2005), and financial services sector (Chang & Jarvenpaa, 2005; Gogan, 2005).

Organizational Drivers of Participation

Firms may participate in vertical standards development to ensure industry coordination (Nelson et al., 2005), avoid being locked out of a market (Schilling, 1998), reduce orphaning risk (Besen, 1995), or increase organizational expertise (Gosain, 2003). Development participants may behave collaboratively by contributing to a standard to best meet industry needs, or non-collaboratively by seeking to maintain competitive advantage, going so far as engaging in process sabotage (Besen, 1995), potentially leading to incomplete standard adoption in an industry. Participants in vertical standards development processes are unable to directly appropriate standardization effort results (Benkler, 2002) so participation incentives must be other than direct rents extraction from the vertical standard itself. As such, organizational incentives for collaborative behavior will differ between potential adopters (demand-side organizations) and software vendors and enterprise system integrators offering complementary products and services (supply-side organizations). The availability of resources and expertise will incentivize demand- and supply-side firms equally and direct proportion to their existence within each firm.

In this paper, we examine two categories of participation incentives based on the heterogeneity of available resources for potential participants, such as capital, assets, firm capabilities, and prior related expertise (Daft, 1983), and on the heterogeneity of interests in the outcome of the standardization process. Resource heterogeneity plays a large role in the firm's ability to obtain competitive advantage (Barney, 1991), and interest heterogeneity has been identified as a potential detriment to the success of vertical standards development efforts (Markus et al., 2006). Research suggests differences in resource and interest heterogeneity may influence the solution to the linked collective action dilemmas (standards-development and diffusion) vertical standards are subject to. We concentrate on the standards-development dilemma and propose constructs to help explain what motivates organizational participation in the face of coordination and free-rider problems. We group our constructs into these two categories (*Resource Heterogeneity* and *Interest Heterogeneity*) to examine their significance on standards development participation by supply- and demand-side

organizations. Figure 1 illustrates the regression models used to test the hypotheses described below for both supply- and demand-side organizations. In the rest of this section, we provide a detailed description of these constructs, the items used to measure them, and offer testable hypotheses for each. The constructs are summarized in Table 1, and Table 2 shows the measurement items used for each construct.

Organizational Participation

We define organizational participation in vertical standards development activities as the level of capital and human resource investment in the various activities necessary to support development activities. We measure this construct using six items to gauge the level of participation in technical development, governance, administrative, and information-sharing activities in support of vertical standard development, and the level of capital and human resource investment in these activities by the organization.

Resource Heterogeneity

Available Resources

Varying levels of resources and capabilities available to the firm have a profound impact on organizational performance (Wernerfelt, 1984). Resource availability affects the firm's ability to

Table 1. Organizational participation constructs

Supply-side	Demand-side
Resource Heterogeneity	
• Available Resources • Knowledge Stock	• Available Resources • Knowledge Stock
Interest Heterogeneity	
• Emerging & Supporting Technology Investment • Risk Hedging • Market Opportunity	• Emerging & Supporting Technology Investment • Risk Hedging • Legacy Technology Embeddedness • Benefits • Organizational Compatibility • Adoption Convergence

Figure 1. Organizational participation in development activities

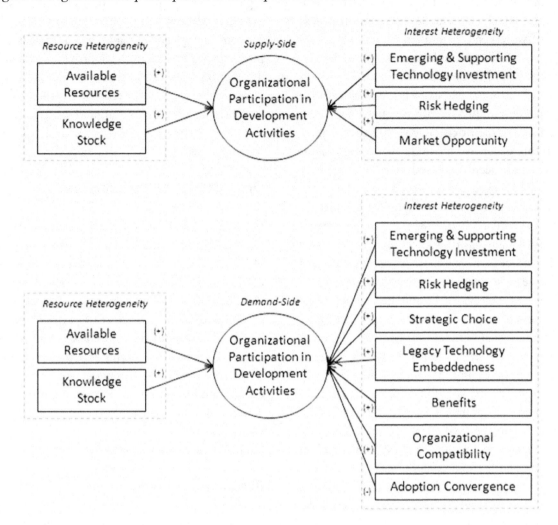

exploit information technology to support its core competencies (Ravichandran, 2005). Consistent with existing research (DeLone, 1981), we use revenue as a proxy for capital and human resources available for participation in development activities for demand-side and supply-side firms, and posit that higher resource availability allows firms to participate more actively in vertical standards development activities. Thus,

Hypothesis 1a: For supply-side organizations, available resources have a positive effect on participation in vertical standards development activities.

Hypothesis 1b: For demand-side organizations, available resources have a positive effect on participation in vertical standards development activities.

Knowledge Stock

Absorptive capacity is the firm's ability to identify, acquire, assimilate and exploit new information, and is a function of prior related knowledge (Cohen & Levinthal, 1990). Firms develop internal expertise before adopting IT-related innovations (Attewell, 1992) and insufficient investment in its development may stall prospects of developing

Table 2. Measurement items

Resource Heterogeneity
(Supply- and Demand-side)
• Available Resources
◦ What was your company's total revenue [last fiscal year]?
• Knowledge Stock
◦ Our company has the necessary technical expertise to implement vertical standards?
◦ It will not take a long time for our company to acquire the necessary technical expertise needed to implement vertical standards
◦ Our company has the necessary project management expertise to implement vertical standards?
◦ It will not take a long time for our company to acquire the necessary project management expertise needed to implement vertical standards
Interest Heterogeneity
(Supply- and Demand-side)
• Emerging & Supporting Technology Investment
◦ Prior to the adoption of a vertical standard, our company had a significant total dollar investment in Internet technologies
◦ Prior to the adoption of a vertical standard, our company had a significant total dollar investment in XML technologies
◦ Prior to the adoption of a vertical standard, our company had significant technical expertise with Internet technologies
◦ Prior to the adoption of a vertical standard, our company had significant technical expertise with XML technologies
• Risk Hedging
◦ How many different vertical standards are available in your industry?
◦ How many different vertical standards compete directly with any vertical standards your company has adopted?
◦ How many different vertical standards has your organization adopted?
(Supply-side only)
• Market Opportunity
◦ An adequate number of external software products exist to support the vertical standards our company has adopted
◦ External software products that support the vertical standards our company has adopted are of high quality
◦ An adequate number of external consulting services exist to support the vertical standards our company has adopted
◦ External consulting services that support the vertical standards our company has adopted are of high quality
(Demand-side only)
• Legacy Technology Embeddedness
◦ Prior to the adoption of vertical standards data exchange technologies were important to our company's business operations
◦ Prior to the adoption of vertical standards data exchange technologies contributed significantly to the integration of our company's internal business processes
◦ Prior to the adoption of vertical standards data exchange technologies contributed significantly to the integration of our company's external business processes
◦ Prior to the adoption of vertical standards data exchange technologies contributed significantly to the automation of our company's internal business processes
◦ Prior to the adoption of vertical standards data exchange technologies contributed significantly to the automation of our company's external business processes
◦ Prior to the adoption of vertical standards data exchange technologies contributed significantly to quality improvement in our company's internal business processes
◦ Prior to the adoption of vertical standards data exchange technologies contributed significantly to quality improvement in our company's external business processes
◦ Prior to the adoption of vertical standards data exchange technologies enabled our company to develop new internal business processes
◦ Prior to the adoption of vertical standards data exchange technologies enabled our company to develop new external business processes
• Benefits
◦ Vertical standards adopted by our company already deliver significant business benefits to our company
• Organizational Compatibility
◦ Vertical standards adopted by our company are compatible with our internal business processes
◦ Vertical standards adopted by our company are compatible with our external business processes
◦ Vertical standards adopted by our company are compatible with our internal data formats
◦ Vertical standards adopted by our company are compatible with our external data formats
• Adoption Convergence
◦ Our company has adopted the same vertical standard as most of our major customers
◦ Our company has adopted the same vertical standard as most of our major suppliers
◦ Our company has adopted the same vertical standard as most of our industry's major participants

future expertise (Cohen & Levinthal, 1990). A firm's level of related expertise (knowledge stock) is a key driver of complex innovation assimilation (Ravichandran, 2005). Participation in vertical standards development activities help develop a firm's knowledge stocks ahead of its competitors, increase internal expertise with developing vertical standards features, and increase the rate of vertical standard assimilation into the firm's business fabric. The more knowledge stock a firm possesses, the likelier it is to identify, acquire, assimilate, and exploit new information related to vertical standards development activities and its own participation in those activities. We measure knowledge stock using four measures that assess a firm's levels of technical and project management expertise with vertical standards technologies and related processes for both demand- and supply-side organizations. We offer that greater levels of knowledge stock lead to greater participation in development activities, and

Hypothesis 2a: For supply-side organizations, knowledge stock has a positive effect on participation in vertical standards development activities.

Hypothesis 2b: For demand-side organizations, knowledge stock has a positive effect on participation in vertical standards development activities.

Interest Heterogeneity

Vertical standards development is problematic due to conflicting interests of participating organizations (Markus et al., 2006) including maintaining control over the developing technology (Gerst & Bunduchi, 2005), protecting existing investment by ensuring compatibility with legacy technologies (Wareham et al., 2005), managing competitor presence in the development process (Chang & Jarvenpaa, 2005), and dealing with potentially negative structural changes in the industry as a

result of the emergence of a dominant standard (Wigand et al., 2005). Ensuring broad stakeholder development collaboration requires solving the free-rider problem of public goods while avoiding fragmentation (Wareham et al., 2005). Reaching critical mass (Markus, 1987) of potential adopters requires the right mix of incentives to avoid excess inertia (Farrell & Saloner, 1985) and a stalling of network effects during diffusion.

Emerging & Supporting Technology Investment

Firms have been using XML and vertical standards technologies for internal purposes for several years (Mendoza & Jahng, 2003; Steinfield et al., 2004), and internal use of interorganizational technologies has been found to spur bandwagon effects (Steinfield et al., 2004), favoring their diffusion. Firms with significant investments in Internet technologies and XML-based applications are likely to attempt to maximize business benefits from those investments. Low-risk investment in Internet infrastructure technologies and emerging XML-based applications provide the organization with the appropriate infrastructure and expertise to support vertical standards deployment (Gosain, 2003; Ravichandran, 2005).

While standards enable and constrain future capabilities (Gosain, 2003), investment in emerging technologies like XML and Internet infrastructure technologies clearly enables future investment in vertical standards. Participation in vertical standards development helps the firm influence the developing standard to ensure maximum compatibility with any other emerging and supporting technology investment (Zhao et al., 2007). Levels of investment in emerging and supporting technologies are evaluated using four items that measure investment and technical expertise in Internet and XML technologies. We hypothesize that

Hypothesis 3a: For supply-side organizations, emerging and supporting technology investment has a positive effect on participation in vertical standards development activities.

Hypothesis 3b: For demand-side organizations, emerging and supporting technology investment has a positive effect on participation participation in vertical standards development activities.

Risk Hedging

When multiple standards compete for dominance firms minimize orphaning risks by waiting for a clear winner (Farrell & Saloner, 1985). Orphaning risk has been identified as a major impediment to the adoption of standards-based technologies (Dedrick & West, 2003), including vertical standards (Weitzel et al., 2006). Orphaning risk may create additional problems in hiring, availability of complementary products, lack of industry best practices, and vendor support (Fichman & Kemerer, 1993). Organizations mitigate these risks by participating in multiple development efforts (Gogan, 2005), which also help firms assess the standardization prospects for competing specifications. Supply-side organizations keep multiple market opportunities open (Nickerson & Muehlen, 2003; Steinfield et al., 2004) while building expertise required to develop products and services for the "winning" standard. When participating in multiple standardization efforts, demand-side firms engage in low-risk experimentation (Gosain, 2003) and develop new product and service offerings ahead of the competition (Steinfield et al., 2004) based on the developing standards. We use three items to measure the number of available vertical standards in the respondent's industry, the number of vertical standards adopted by the respondent, and the number of vertical standards in direct competition with any vertical standards the firm has adopted. Higher numbers of available, competing and adopted vertical standards increase uncertainty and may lead to greater interest on the

part of the firm to hedge against orphaning risks and to participate more actively in development activities for one or more vertical standards. Thus,

Hypothesis 4a: For supply-side organizations, risk hedging behavior leads to greater participation in vertical standards development activities.

Hypothesis 4b: For demand-side organizations, risk hedging behavior leads to greater participation in vertical standards development activities.

Market Opportunity

Early supply-side adoption of a vertical standard allows suppliers to modify products and services to match development path ahead of non-participating competitors (Steinfield et al., 2004). Suppliers also get an "insider" participation effect (Xia et al., 2003) that allows them to manipulate compatibility between complementary products to create customer lock-in (Chen & Forman, 2006). Firms are generally unable to use standards as competitive weapons (Zhao et al., 2005), but supply-side organizations may develop new product offerings (Steinfield et al., 2004) based on early knowledge of the vertical standard development path. Thus, market opportunities are unlikely primary motivators for demand-side organizations, and we use this construct as a predictor of development participation for supply-side organizations only. We use four items to measure the number and quality of vertical standards-compliant external software products and consulting services available to respondents. A higher number of products and services may be interpreted by supply-side organizations as a signal of a vibrant complementary products market, providing an incentive to participate in the development of one or more vertical standards. Therefore,

Hypothesis 5: For supply-side organizations, greater availability of complementary products and services that are vertical standards-compliant has a positive effect on participation in vertical standards development activities.

Legacy Technology Embeddedness

Legacy data exchange technologies are deeply embedded in the firm's business activities as they create value through automational, informational, and transformational effects on business processes (Mooney et al., 1996). As the assimilation cycle (Swanson & Ramiller, 1997) for legacy data exchange technologies deepens, organizational dependence on this investment grows.

Legacy investment can exert a drag (Fichman & Kemerer, 1999) on incompatible newer technologies, but the flexibility of vertical standards permits them to be a bridging technology (Hovav et al., 2004) that allows codified domain knowledge conversion, permitting continued leveraging of legacy assets. We use this construct only with demand-side organizations because it is more relevant to extending the use of deeply embedded legacy technologies than it is for supply-side firms. We measure legacy technology embeddedness with nine totals items assessing the contributions and importance of legacy data exchange technologies to automational, informational, and transformational effects (Mooney et al., 1996) on the firm's internal and external business processes.

Hypothesis 6: For demand-side organizations, higher levels of legacy technology embeddedness have a positive effect on participation in vertical standards development activities.

Benefits

Organizations derive output and process benefits from participating in standards-development activities (Xia et al., 2008). Output benefits are obtained from the use of the vertical standard itself as a source of competitive advantage, whereas process benefits come from the development process itself and include expertise acquisition and social capital in the firm's business network (Xia et al., 2008). Output benefits are difficult to obtain because competition based on standards is much less desirable, but process benefits are unilateral and much more predictable (Xia et al., 2008), making development process participation incentives likelier to come from process rather than output benefits. Research shows higher process benefits are strongly correlated with higher valuation of output (Xia et al., 2008) and overall benefits are greater for development process participants than for non-participants (Zhao et al., 2007). Enterprise information system integration and process optimization provide the highest benefits for complex technology adopters (Swatman et al., 1994) but extracting these benefits is a function of vertical standards value perception, and how well adopters identify and exploit this value internally, since external implementation of vertical standards in an industry is homogeneous. As organizations are better able to understand and predict the potential and actual value of vertical standards, participation incentives also increase (Zhao et al., 2007). We measure business benefits of vertical standards with a single item that asks about the level of significant business benefits delivered to the organization by vertical standards, and propose that

Hypothesis 7: For demand-side organizations, higher levels of benefits delivered by vertical standards have a positive effect on participation in vertical standards development activities.

Organizational Compatibility

Research suggests that resource homogeneity is not a source of sustained competitive advantage (Mata et al., 1995). Since vertical standards are homogeneously available in an industry and their external implementation is identical in all cases, or the standard's industry benefits are diluted, the evaluation of vertical standards benefits should consider only internal differentiators, such as their compatibility with existing business processes and data formats. Internal compatibility is a major positive factor in the success of collaborative products (Dedrick & West, 2003). Compatibility with internal- or external-facing business processes and existing data formats is a function of each adopting organization's dexterity at exploiting its own unique characteristics (Barney, 1991), and waiting until a vertical standard is completed to learn what changes to business processes and data formats are needed increases adoption costs (Coney, 2007). Participation in development activities makes a standard valuable earlier to the firm, and research shows payoffs increase with the intrinsic value of a technology to the firm (Zhao et al., 2007). Greater organizational fit of vertical standards incentivizes firms to participate in development activities, and we measure this construct using four items asking about the compatibility of vertical standards with internal and external business processes and data formats.

Hypothesis 8: For demand-side organizations, higher levels of compatibility of developing vertical standards have a positive effect on participation in vertical standards development activities.

Adoption Convergence

Research suggests the existence of leading developers and passive adopters in collaborative standardization efforts (Zhao et al., 2007). Leading developers participate actively in consortium activities, which may help reduce their implementation costs for the standard (Zhao et al., 2007) and accrue social capital with their business partners (Xia et al., 2008). Passive adopters deploy the final standard but choose not to participate in its development, and may interpret business partner

adoption as a signal of the legitimacy of the standard and of its industry acceptance. An artifact is legitimized when a social network develops norms and prescriptions for its use (Emerson, 1962).

We define adoption convergence as the increasing perception of a specific vertical standard as a legitimate option in an industry. Exposure to peer and vendor signaling (Ravichandran, 2005) reduces uncertainty about the standard's future and passive adopters may interpret influential business partner adoption behaviors as legitimation signals. A cascading process of influence in a business network drives further adoption, leading to convergence. Passive adopters let active developers bear the burden of development costs, and avail themselves of the results, in line with the public-goods nature of vertical standards. Increased business partner convergence reduces the need to invest in development activities for passive adopters, resulting in lower participation in development activities. We measure adoption convergence using three items to assess the firm's intent to adopt the same vertical standards as its influential business partners.

Hypothesis 9: For demand-side organizations, higher levels of adoption convergence with business partners have a negative effect on participation in vertical standards development activities.

Data Collection and Analysis

Data was collected by surveying members of the Association for Cooperative Operations Research and Development (ACORD.org), the leading consortium for the development and promotion of standards related to conducting business in the insurance, reinsurance and related financial services industries. ACORD's standards have evolved from paper forms (1970s) to EDI (1980s) and XML (1990s). Its XML standards are continually updated by volunteer member committees serving three line-of-business categories: Life,

Annuity & Health (LAH); Property & Casualty/ Surety (PCS); and Reinsurance and Large Commercial (RLC). The initial electronic invitation resulted in 747 responses self-classified as either primarily in the LAH, PCS, or RLC categories, as well as suppliers and agents/brokers to any LAH, PCS, or RLC firms. Companies in LAH, PCS, or RLC are the primary users for vertical standards generating demand for their development, and were grouped as *demand-side* firms. All firms identifying themselves as suppliers were grouped as *supply-side* organizations, with agents/brokers forming a third group. This resulted in 534 firms classified as demand-side, and 153 as supply-side. Sixty responses, 52 from Agent/Brokers and 8 lacking any identifying information, were not dropped from further data analysis.

A Kaiser-Meyer-Olkin (KMO) coefficient of 0.794 (which exceeds the minimum recommended 0.500; Kaiser 1970) indicated that factor analysis is appropriate with this data set, so we completed a principal components analysis to validate the measurement items used. In addition, Bartlett's test of sphericity was significant (p<0.000), indicating correlation amongst our items and confirming the appropriateness of factory analysis (Bartlett, 1950). Table 3 shows all items load on their assigned construct with much larger coefficients than on all other constructs, indicating convergent and discriminant validity of the constructs. Items in the Organizational Compatibility construct suggest two separate but theoretically-related constructs and were retained as a single construct in the data analysis based also on the results of the scale reliability analysis. Two single-item constructs show no evidence of loading on any other constructs and were kept from scale reliability analysis. All Cronbach's Alpha (Cronbach, 1951) scale reliability measures are seen to exceed the minimum recommended levels.

The average scores of the six items forming the organizational participation in vertical standards development activities construct for demand-side (μ=3.86, σ=1.52) and supply-side (μ=4.66, σ=1.53) firms were significantly different (p<0.001), confirming the main structural difference in our model. Thus, supply-side participation in vertical standards development activities is found to be significantly higher than demand-side participation.

We evaluated two linear regression models (Figure 1) to help explain participation levels for demand- and supply-side firms using only surveys completed at a minimum of 50%. The model tested for supply-side organizations was as follows:

$$P = \beta_0 + (\beta_1 * AR) + (\beta_2 * KS) + (\beta_3 * ESTI) + (\beta_4 * RH) + (\beta_5 * MO) + \varepsilon, \text{ where}$$

P = Organizational participation
AR = Available resources
KS = Knowledge stock
ESTI = Emerging & supporting technology investment
RH = Risk hedging
MO = Market opportunity

Our results, summarized in Table 4, show tolerance coefficients were above 0.30 and the variance inflation factor (VIF) was below 3.0, indicating a lack of multicollinearity in the variables (Marquardt, 1970). The regression coefficients for Market Opportunity (β=0.511, p<0.006) and Knowledge Stock (β=0.364, p<0.016) are positive and strongly significant, suggesting supply-side participation in development activities is driven primarily by commercial interests, and that resource heterogeneity plays an important role in the participation decision. Combined with the significant participation difference with demand-side firms, these results signal supply-side firms find ample opportunities and incentive to benefit from vertical standards development despite the difficulties posed by standards-based competition. The participation difference between supply- and demand-side firms suggests supply-side firms

Table 3. Instrument validity & reliability

Construct	Items	Factor Loadings									α
Organizational Participation in Development Activities	P1	**.830**	.115	.151	.030	-.007	.200	.066	.061	-.128	0.931
	P2	**.847**	.049	.067	.050	-.005	.179	.133	-.006	-.025	
	P3	**.815**	.012	.144	.007	-.025	.095	.088	.008	.043	
	P4	**.788**	.062	.109	.060	.136	.082	.027	.154	-.157	
	P5	**.855**	.053	.068	.076	.106	.217	.069	.109	-.054	
	P6	**.827**	.049	.116	.011	.100	.212	.160	.087	-.094	
Knowledge Stock	KS1	.101	**.802**	.152	-.025	-.082	.154	.062	.073	-.078	0.924
	KS2	.136	**.834**	.203	-.002	.090	.079	.068	.062	-.068	
	KS3	.029	**.886**	.056	.056	.044	.150	.117	.039	-.169	
	KS4	.011	**.853**	.016	.053	.077	.095	.094	.014	-.239	
Emerging & Supporting Technology Investment	ESTI1	.212	.010	**.732**	.025	.051	.252	-.047	.136	-.114	0.850
	ESTI2	.175	.047	**.827**	.132	.002	.155	.065	.004	.160	
	ESTI3	.122	.188	**.723**	.030	.013	.271	-.010	.045	-.174	
	ESTI4	.122	.229	**.863**	.156	.035	.089	.000	-.013	.070	
Risk Hedging	RH1	.046	.005	.093	**.857**	-.040	.139	.011	.059	.054	0.827
	RH2	.059	-.077	.073	**.817**	.060	.023	.062	-.080	.074	
	RH3	.069	.168	.120	**.827**	.008	.191	-.101	.100	.074	
Market Opportunity	MO1	-.012	-.014	-.002	.080	**.772**	.050	.153	.118	.038	0.882
	MO2	.067	.027	.071	-.043	**.833**	.156	.220	.066	-.028	
	MO3	.069	.044	.007	.026	**.834**	.098	-.057	.053	-.043	
	MO4	.097	.056	.017	-.038	**.850**	.111	.116	.008	-.055	
Legacy Technology Embeddedness	LTE1	.183	-.001	.179	.004	-.005	**.806**	-.063	-.010	-.097	0.960
	LTE2	.114	.088	.012	.055	.049	**.848**	.218	-.147	.015	
	LTE3	.137	.087	.108	.040	.058	**.876**	-.094	.212	-.058	
	LTE4	.092	.057	.123	.083	.104	**.835**	.133	-.116	-.011	
	LTE5	.130	.069	.161	-.044	.107	**.838**	-.091	.179	-.070	
	LTE6	.097	.078	.053	.058	.083	**.868**	.189	-.133	.015	
	LTE7	.124	.086	.122	.056	.061	**.873**	-.039	.157	-.074	
	LTE8	.163	.130	.039	.215	.091	**.787**	.207	-.164	.037	
	LTE9	.141	.102	.143	.091	.082	**.810**	-.031	.156	-.036	
Organizational Compatibility	OC1	.176	.086	-.056	-.031	.172	.092	**.840**	.096	.001	0.860
	OC2	.170	.137	.018	.024	.131	.089	**.878**	.027	-.007	
	OC3	.169	.087	.158	.001	.209	.065	.358	**.736**	-.202	
	OC4	.137	.089	.181	.009	.141	.129	.408	**.725**	-.174	
Adoption Convergence	AC1	-.116	-.207	-.033	.073	-.064	-.014	-.074	-.058	**.911**	0.954
	AC2	-.131	-.131	.040	.072	.013	-.101	-.026	.025	**.890**	
	AC3	-.083	-.189	-.029	.075	-.039	-.052	-.039	-.087	**.915**	
Benefits	B1	.230	.204	.011	.006	.220	.016	.551	.297	-.232	n/a
Available Resources	AR1	.168	.071	-.114	.089	.037	-.094	-.294	.513	.242	n/a

Table 4. Summary of results

Supply-side Participation n=52, r^2=0.360, Adj. r^2=0.292, Power=0.9893			
Construct	**β**	**Tolerance**	**VIF**
Resource Heterogeneity			
Available Resources	0.127	0.847	1.181
Knowledge Stock	0.364[2]	0.842	1.188
Interest Heterogeneity			
Emerging & Supporting Technology Investment	0.036	0.729	1.371
Risk Hedging	0.049	0.680	1.470
Market Opportunity	0.511[3]	0.927	1.078
Demand-side Participation n=168, r^2=0.212, Adj. r^2=0.173, Power=0.9995			
Resource Heterogeneity			
Available Resources	0.078	0.972	1.029
Knowledge Stock	-0.076	0.738	1.355
Interest Heterogeneity			
Emerging & Supporting Technology Investment	0.283[3]	0.803	1.246
Risk Hedging	0.058	0.912	1.096
Legacy Technology Embeddedness	0.074	0.771	1.298
Benefits	0.021	0.503	1.986
Organizational Compatibility	0.238[2]	0.494	2.023
Adoption Convergence	-0.158[1]	0.768	1.302

1 p<0.10, 2 p<0.05, 3 p<0.010

have opportunity to influence vertical standards development to benefit existing products and services ahead of competitors, and also suggests vendors have a tremendous advantage in development path expertise and may be able to manipulate vertical standards compatibility to their benefit. All other constructs behave as theorized, but none reached any level of statistical significance.

The regression model used for explaining demand-side participation in vertical standards development was:

$$P = \beta_0 + (\beta_1 * AR) + (\beta_2 * KS) + (\beta_3 * ESTI) + (\beta_4 * RH) + (\beta_5 * LTE) + (\beta_6 * B) + (\beta_7 * OC) + (\beta_8 * AC) + \varepsilon, \text{ where}$$

P = Organizational participation
AR = Available resources
KS = Knowledge stock
ESTI = Emerging & supporting technology investment
RH = Risk hedging
LTE = Legacy technology embeddedness
B = Benefits
OC = Organizational compatibility
AC = Adoption convergence

Our results, summarized in Table 4, show tolerance coefficients were above 0.30 and the variance inflation factor (VIF) was below 3.0, indicating a lack of multicollinearity in the variables (Marquardt, 1970). Results show compatibility with existing business processes and data formats (Organizational Compatibility, β=0.238, p<0.05) and with existing technology investment (Emerging & Supporting Technology Investment, β=0.283, p<0.001) are strong demand-side participation motivators. This confirms the importance of development participation to ensure demand-side firms can influence standard development for greater fit with their existing business and technical technology investment and business process and data format environments.

The Adoption Convergence construct is mildly significant (β=-0.158, p<0.10) and in the hypothesized direction, suggesting that demand-side firms are passive adopters. ACORD's intellectual property (IP) policies protect demand-side organizations from the threat of standards appropriation (Benkler, 2002) by supply-side firms, allowing demand-side organizations to uncouple process from output benefits (Xia et al., 2008) in the development process. Thus, demand-side organizations are shown to be passive adopters of vertical standards, leaving the role of active participants to supply-side firms. Resource availability does not drive development participation for demand-side organizations which appear to allow supply-side firms to take the lead on technical and project management issues related to vertical standards development. Demand-side organizations look to the adoption behaviors of critical business partners, and supplier leadership in standards development makes adopting the ACORD standards their influential partners are invested in the easiest and safest solution. All other constructs behave as theorized, with the exception of Knowledge Stock, but none reached any level of statistical significance. The negative Knowledge Stock coefficient (β=-0.076) is very small, but suggests that demand-side organizations with higher expertise levels actively allow supply-side firms to bear the development costs of the standard and plan on reaping the benefits of adoption once a working version of the standard is issued. This is consistent with the passive-adopter role of demand-side firms and with the public goods nature of vertical standards.

DISCUSSION AND IMPLICATIONS

End-user participation in development activities is a key feature of vertical standards. Our results show there may be greater vendor influence in vertical standards development than previously understood, even as end-users retain strategic control of the development path. For practitioners, this is a double-edged benefit. As long as ACORD's IP policies continue to prevent supply-side appropriation of the vertical standard, demand-side organizations may feel at ease with supplier leadership during development. However, ongoing vigilance is required to avoid undue vendor influence over the technical path of vertical standards. It is particularly critical to make sure customization and extensions in support of the standard, but outside its domain, are not used by suppliers to lock end-users in, as has been observed in the case of physical networking products (Chen & Forman, 2006).

The significance of compatibility with existing investment as a motivator of participation in development activities by demand-side firms suggests that the bridging capabilities of vertical standards are being exploited heavily by these firms. XML-based vertical standards are ideally suited to this task because XML permits the development of custom tags to embed semantic information into data payloads, and to "reskin" data and end-user interfaces to meet any business requirement. This increases the importance of vigilance on undue supply-side development influence and on the manipulation of customization and non-standard extensions to create lock-in. This is especially important when a demand-side firm lacks prior related expertise (knowledge stock) to work directly with vertical standard technologies and the work has to be outsourced or contracted to a third-party vendor.

Clear non-appropriation IP policies preserve diverging competitive interests necessary to ensure widespread cooperation (David & Greenstein, 1990), and ACORD's high levels of supply-side development participation are a successful example. While ACORD's IP policy and participation and membership guidelines are clearly defined to protect against appropriation of the results of development activities, it is still unclear how much control of the strategic direction of these activities demand-side organizations actually retain, given the significant difference in participation between demand- and supply-side firms.

While supply-side participation seems driven by commercial business interests, demand-side involvement is motivated by protecting compatibility with existing investments in business processes and data formats, while minimizing investment. Our data provides empirical confirmation of the presence of passive adopters in vertical standards development (Zhao et al., 2007), an important finding for supply-side organizations because it confirms their participation in standards development efforts can generate business opportunities before standards completion. Suppliers can become sources of expertise to demand-side organizations to help them understand the applicability and functionality of the emerging standard, reducing barriers to later diffusion.

Confirmation of the existence of passive adopter behavior is also important for demand-side organizations because passive adoption may allow supply-side firms to take control of the strategic direction of vertical standards development activities, or to manipulate vertical standards compatibility to introduce switching costs, as has been observed with physical products (Chen & Forman, 2006).

Additional research is necessary to determine how SDOs solve resource problems when faced with passive adopters. It is possible passive adopters withhold participation and resources in exchange for a commitment to adopt the end result, without which the adoption stage may fail. These findings may also be of interest to SDOs because they show that it is possible to exploit industry standards based on open technologies, such as XML, for competitive advantage *during* the development cycle, and not only during or after the adoption stage.

CONCLUSION

Our results provide evidence of the existence of passive adopters (Zhao et al., 2007) in vertical standards development activities, and highlight the need for further work to understand the extent of supply-side influence in development activities. The availability of commercial opportunities for supply-side firms in development activities is also shown. While this result may seem unsurprising at first, it is notable because existing theory states it is difficult to extract rents from vertical standards due to their public goods nature and to the low levels of appropriability of the output of development activities due to IP policies put in place by SDOs. Still, suppliers are finding it advantageous to invest in vertical standards development activities at a significantly higher level than potential adopters do. By contrast, the participation of demand-side organizations in development activities appears aligned more with protectionist behaviors than with an active drive to modify the emerging standard to suit future business needs. It is unclear whether these two combined results are a function of the level of control demand-side firms have on the development process, or a result of savvy penetration of an SDO by supply-side firms in order to place themselves in the best possible competitive position.

Identifying and describing the specific strategy ACORD is using to solve the linked collective action dilemmas (Markus et al., 2006) at the development and diffusion stages would be quite useful to other consortia, but falls outside the scope of our work. Lastly, the usefulness of investigating resource and interest heterogeneity as motivators for participation in development activities is confirmed in our approach.

ACKNOWLEDGMENT

The authors gratefully acknowledge the help from the review team in improving the final version of this paper. Thanks also to Dr. Tavana for helping us manage the review process quickly and effectively.

REFERENCES

Arthur, W. B. (1994). *Increasing returns and path dependence in the economy.* Ann Arbor, MI: University of Michigan.

Attewell, P. (1992). Technology Diffusion and Organizational Learning: The Case of Business Computing. *Organization Science*, *3*(1), 1–19. doi:10.1287/orsc.3.1.1

Axelrod, R., Mitchell, W., Thomas, R. E., Bennett, D. S., & Bruderer, E. (1995). Coalition Forming in Standard-Setting Alliances. *Management Science*, *41*(9), 1493. doi:10.1287/mnsc.41.9.1493

Barney, J. (1991). Firm Resources and Sustained Competitive Advantage. *Journal of Management*, *17*(1), 99–120. doi:10.1177/014920639101700108

Bartlett, M. S. (1950). Tests of significance in factor analysis. *The British Journal of Psychology*, *3*, 77.

Benkler, Y. (2002). Coase's Penguin, or, Linux and The Nature of the Firm. *The Yale Law Journal*, *112*(3), 369. doi:10.2307/1562247

Besen, S. M. (1995). The Standards Processes in Telecommunication and Information Technology. In Hawkins, R., Mansell, R., & Skea, J. (Eds.), *Standards, Innovation, and Competitiveness: the Politics and Economics of Standards in Natural and Technical Environments*. Cheltenham, UK: Edward Elgar.

Chang, C., & Jarvenpaa, S. (2005). Pace of Information Systems Standards Development and Implementation: The Case of XBRL. *Electronic Markets*, *15*(4), 365–377. doi:10.1080/10196780500303029

Chen, P.-Y., & Forman, C. (2006). Can Vendors Influence Switching Costs and Compatibility in an Environment with Open Standards? *Management Information Systems Quarterly*, *30*, 541–562.

Cohen, W. M., & Levinthal, D. A. (1990). Absorptive capacity: A new perspective on learning and innovation. *Administrative Science Quarterly*, *35*(1), 128. doi:10.2307/2393553

Coney, B. (2007). *Business Process Change: Migrating from MS-Word to XML to meet Board of Health Requirements and Business Process Needs*. Paper presented at the On Philadelphia XML Users Group Speaker Series, Philadelphia.

Cronbach, L. J. (1951). Coefficient Alpha and the Internal Structure of Tests. *Psychometrika*, *16*, 297–334. doi:10.1007/BF02310555

Daft, R. L. (1983). *Organization Theory and Design*. New York: West.

David, P. A. (1987). Some new standards for the economics of standardization in the information age. In Dasgupta, P., & Stoneman, P. (Eds.), *Economic policy and technological performance* (pp. 206–239). Cambridge, UK: Cambridge University Press. doi:10.1017/CBO9780511559938.010

David, P. A., & Greenstein, S. (1990). The economics of compatibility standards: an introduction to recent research. *Economics of Innovation and New Technology*, *1*, 3–41. doi:10.1080/10438599000000002

Dedrick, J., & West, J. (2003, December 12-14). *Why Firms Adopt Open Source Platforms: A Grounded Theory of Innovation and Standard Adoption.* Paper presented at the International Conference on IS Special Workshop on Standard Making sponsored by MISQ, Seattle, WA.

DeLone, W. H. (1981). Firm Size and the Characteristics of Computer Use. *Management Information Systems Quarterly*, 65–77. doi:10.2307/249328

Emerson, R. M. (1962). Power Dependence Relations. *American Sociological Review, 27*(1), 31–41. doi:10.2307/2089716

Farrell, J. (1989). Standardization and Intellectual Property. *Jurimetrics Journal, 30*, 35–50.

Farrell, J., & Saloner, G. (1988). Coordination Through Committees and Markets. *The Rand Journal of Economics, 19*(2), 235. doi:10.2307/2555702

Fichman, R. G., & Kemerer, C. F. (1993). Adoption of Software Engineering Process Innovations: The Case of Object Orientation. *Sloan Management Review, 34*(2), 7–22.

Fichman, R. G., & Kemerer, C. F. (1999). The Illusory Diffusion of Innovation: An Examination of Assimilation Gaps. *Information Systems Research, 10*(3), 255–275. doi:10.1287/isre.10.3.255

Gerst, M., & Bunduchi, R. (2005). Shaping IT Standardization in the Automotive Industry - The Role of Power in Driving Portal Standardization. *Electronic Markets, 15*(4), 335–343. doi:10.1080/10196780500302872

Gogan, J. L. (2005). Punctuation and Path Dependence: Examining a Vertical IT Standard-Setting Process. *Electronic Markets, 15*(4), 344–354. doi:10.1080/10196780500302880

Gosain, S. (2003, December 12-14). *Realizing the Vision for Web Services: Strategies for Dealing with Imperfect Standards.* Paper presented at the International Conference on IS Special Workshop on Standard Making sponsored by MISQ, Seattle, WA.

Greenstein, S. (1992). Invisible Hand versus Invisible Advisors: Coordination Mechanisms in Economic Networks. *Journal of the American Society for Information Science American Society for Information Science, 43*(8), 538–249. doi:10.1002/(SICI)1097-4571(199209)43:8<538::AID-ASI4>3.0.CO;2-2

Henry, C. (1974). Investment Decisions Under Uncertainty: The "Irreversibility Effect". *The American Economic Review, 64*(6), 1006–1012.

Hovav, A., Patnayakuni, R., & Schuff, D. (2004). A model of Internet standards adoption: the case of IPv6. *Information Systems Journal, 14*(3), 265. doi:10.1111/j.1365-2575.2004.00170.x

Kaiser, H. F. (1970). A second generation little jiffy. *Psychometrika, 35*, 401–416. doi:10.1007/BF02291817

Lyytinen, K., & Damsgaard, J. (2001, April 7-10). *What's Wrong With the Diffusion of Innovation Theory: The Case of a Complex and Networked Technology.* Paper presented at the International Federation for Information Processing (IFIP), Banff, Alberta, Canada.

Markus, M. L. (1987). Toward a "Critical Mass" Theory of Interactive Media. *Communication Research, 14*(5), 491–511. doi:10.1177/009365087014005003

Markus, M. L., Steinfield, C. W., & Wigand, R. T. (2003, December 12-14). *The Evolution of Vertical IS Standards: Electronic Interchange Standards in the US Home Mortgage Industry.* Paper presented at the International Conference on IS Special Workshop on Standard Making sponsored by MISQ, Seattle, WA.

Markus, M. L., Steinfield, C. W., Wigand, R. T., & Minton, G. (2006). Industry-Wide Information Systems Standardization As Collective Action: The Case of the U.S. Residential Mortgage Industry. *Management Information Systems Quarterly, 30*, 439–465.

Marquardt, D. W. (1970). Generalized Inverses, Ridge Regression, Biased Linear Estimation, and Nonlinear Estimation. *Technometrics, 12*(3), 605–607. doi:10.2307/1267205

Mata, F. J., Fuerst, W. L., & Barney, J. B. (1995). Information Technology and Sustained Competitive Advantage: A Resource-Based Analysis. *Management Information Systems Quarterly, 19*(4), 487–505. doi:10.2307/249630

Mendoza, R. A., & Jahng, J. J. (2003, August). *Adoption of XML Specifications: An Exploratory Study of Industry Practices.* Paper presented at the Americas Conference on Information Systems (AMCIS), Tampa, FL.

Mitchell, W. (1994). *Product Standards and Competitive Advantage.* Retrieved from http://faculty.fuqua.duke.edu/~willm/bio/cases%20&%20readings/Notes/Standards_note.pdf

Mooney, J. G., Gurbaxani, V., & Kraemer, K. L. (1996). A Process Oriented Framework for Assessing the Business Value of Information Technology. *The Data Base for Advances in Information Systems, 27*(2), 68–81.

Nelson, M. L., Shaw, M. J., & Qualls, W. (2005). Interorganizational System Standards Development in Vertical Industries. *Electronic Markets, 15*(4), 378–392. doi:10.1080/10196780500303045

Nickerson, J. V., & Muehlen, M. Z. (2003, December 12-14). *Defending the Spirit of the Web: Conflict in the Internet Standards Process.* Paper presented at the International Conference on IS Special Workshop on Standard Making sponsored by MISQ, Seattle, WA.

Olson, M. (1971). *Logic of Collective Action: Public Goods and the Theory of Groups* (2nd ed.). Cambridge, MA: Harvard University Press.

Quelin, B. V., Abdessemed, T., Bonardi, J.-P., & Durand, R. (2001). Standardisation of Network Technologies: Market Processes or the Result of Inter-Firm Cooperation? *Journal of Economic Surveys, 15*(4), 543–569. doi:10.1111/1467-6419.00148

Ravichandran, T. (2005). Organizational Assimilation of Complex Technologies: An Empirical Study of Component-Based Software Development. *IEEE Transactions on Engineering Management, 52*(2), 249–268. doi:10.1109/TEM.2005.844925

Rohlfs, J. (1974). A Theory of Interdependent Demand for a Communications Service. *The Bell Journal of Economics and Management Science, 5*(1), 16–37. doi:10.2307/3003090

Schilling, M. (1998). Technological Lockout: An Integrative Model of the Economic and Strategic Factors Driving Technology Success and Failure. *Academy of Management Review, 23*(2), 267–284. doi:10.2307/259374

Steinfield, C. W., Wigand, R. T., Markus, M. L., & Minton, G. (2004, May 13-14). *Promoting e-Business Through Vertical IS Standards: Lessons from the US Home Mortgage Industry.* Paper presented at the Workshop on Standards and Public Policy, Chicago.

Swanson, E. B., & Ramiller, N. C. (1997). The Organizing Vision in Information Systems Innovations. *Organization Science, 8*(5), 458–474. doi:10.1287/orsc.8.5.458

Swatman, P. M. C., Swatman, P. A., & Fowler, D. C. (1994). A model of EDI integration and strategic business reengineering. *The Journal of Strategic Information Systems, 3*(1), 41–60. doi:10.1016/0963-8687(94)90005-1

Teece, D. J. (1992). Competition, Cooperation, and Innovation: Organizational Arrangements for Regimes of Rapid Technological Progress. *Journal of Economic Behavior & Organization, 18*(1), 1–25. doi:10.1016/0167-2681(92)90050-L

Wareham, J., Rai, A., & Pickering, G. (2005). Standardization in Vertical Industries: An Institutional Analysis of XML-Based Standards Infusion in Electricity Markets. *Electronic Markets, 15*(4), 323–334. doi:10.1080/10196780500302849

Weitzel, T., Wendt, O., Beimborn, D., & Koenig, W. (2006). Network Effects and Diffusion Theory: Extending Economic Network Analysis. In Jakobs, K. (Ed.), *Advanced Topics in Information Technology Standards and Standardization Research* (*Vol. 1*, pp. 282–305). Hershey, PA: Idea Group.

Wernerfelt, B. (1984). A Resource-based View of the Firm. *Strategic Management Journal, 5*(2), 171–180. doi:10.1002/smj.4250050207

Wigand, R. T., Markus, M. L., & Steinfield, C. W. (2005). Preface to the Focus Theme Section: 'Vertical Industry Information Technology Standards and Standardization'. *Electronic Markets, 15*(4), 285–288. doi:10.1080/10196780500302641

Xia, M., Zhao, K., & Mahoney, J. T. (2008). *Enhancing Value via Cooperation: Firms' Process Benefits From Participation in a Consortium.* Unpublished Working Paper, University of Illinois.

Xia, M., Zhao, K., & Shaw, M. J. (2003, December 12-14). *Open E-Business Standard Development and Adoption: An Integrated Perspective.* Paper presented at the International Conference on IS Special Workshop on Standard Making sponsored by MISQ, Seattle, WA.

Zhao, K., Xia, M., & Shaw, M. J. (2005). Vertical E-Business Standards and Standards Developing Organizations: A Conceptual Framework. *Electronic Markets, 15*(4), 289–300. doi:10.1080/10196780500302690

Zhao, K., Xia, M., & Shaw, M. J. (2007). An Integrated Model of Consortium-Based E-Business Standardization: Collaborative Development and Adoption with Network Externalities. *Journal of Management Information Systems, 23*(4), 247–271. doi:10.2753/MIS0742-1222230411

This work was previously published in International Journal of Enterprise Information Systems, edited by Madjid Tavana, pp. 20-37, Volume 6, Issue 4, copyright 2010 by IGI Publishing (an imprint of IGI Global).

Chapter 17

An Empirical Evaluation of the Assimilation of Industry- Specific Data Standards Using Firm-Level and Community-Level Constructs

Rubén A. Mendoza
Saint Joseph's University, USA

T. Ravichandran
Rensselaer Polytechnic Institute, USA

ABSTRACT

Vertical standards focus on industry-specific product and service descriptions, and are generally implemented using the eXtensible Markup Language (XML). Vertical standards are complex technologies with an organizational adoption locus but subject to inter-organizational dependence and network effects. Understanding the assimilation process for vertical standards requires that both firm and industry-level effects be considered simultaneously. In this paper, the authors develop and evaluate a two-level model of organizational assimilation that includes both firm and industry-level effects. The study was conducted in collaboration with OASIS, a leading cross-industry standards-development organization (SDO), and with ACORD, the principal SDO for the insurance and financial services industries. Results confirm the usefulness of incorporating firm-level and community-level constructs in the study of complex networked technologies. Specifically, the authors' re-conceptualization of the classical DoI concepts of relative advantage and complexity are shown to be appropriate and significant in predicting vertical standards assimilation. Additionally, community-level constructs such as orphaning risk and standard legitimation are also shown to be important predictors of assimilation.

DOI: 10.4018/978-1-4666-1761-2.ch017

INTRODUCTION

Vertical standards are specifications that focus on industry-specific product and service descriptions, data structures, definitions, and formats, and that formalize and codify business processes for participating organizations (Markus et al., 2003). Researchers have begun to acknowledge their uniqueness and to integrate various applicable research streams to the study of their development, adoption, diffusion, assimilation, and value across industries. Vertical standards are often implemented via the eXtensible Markup Language (XML), play a critical role in inter-organizational data-sharing (Hills, 2000; Lim & Wen, 2002), and are expected to yield more influence than any previous inter-organizational system (Wareham et al. 2005). The emerging body of literature focusing on vertical standards uses concepts of classical diffusion of innovations theory (DoI; Rogers, 1983), augmented with ideas from various other theoretical streams. DoI theory focuses on relatively simple technologies subject to voluntary binary adoption by individual users. However, vertical standards are complex technologies with an organizational adoption locus and subject to inter-organizational dependence (Fichman, 1992; Lyytinen & Damsgaard, 2001). Understanding the nature of the assimilation process for vertical standards requires the consideration of industry-level effects, along with factors shown to predict organizational adoption and diffusion of technology-based innovations.

Our research adds to our understanding of the vertical standards assimilation phenomenon by proposing and evaluating a two-level model of organizational assimilation based on both firm- and community-level effects. The model uses the three firm-level DoI concepts most consistently found to be significant in predicting technological adoption and diffusion (Premkumar et al., 1997; Tornatzky & Klein, 1982). At the community level, assimilation of complex networked technologies has been shown to be subject to network externali-

ties (Wigand et al., 2005), which help technologies achieve the point of critical mass (Markus, 1987) at which a dominant platform emerges in a market. Network externalities have been shown to affect technology assimilation in various industries (Au & Kauffman, 2001; Kauffman et al., 2000). Thus, our model uses the concept of network externalities to develop the two community-level constructs labeled *orphaning risk* and *standard legitimation*.

To our knowledge, this is the first large-scale empirical study of organizational assimilation of vertical standards. The study was conducted with the ongoing collaboration of OASIS, a leading cross-industry standards-development organization (SDO), and of ACORD, the principal SDO for the insurance and financial services industries. Additionally, it is the first attempt to operationalize and measure the concepts of technology orphaning risk and standard legitimation as they relate to information technology (IT) assimilation. As previous research suggests, the changes with greatest longevity and impact will not be those inherent to the technology itself, but the behavioral changes the technology enables on a mass scale (Evans & Wurster, 1997). Understanding the factors that motivate the adoption and diffusion of vertical standards is critical to the understanding of any likely structural changes across industries.

LITERATURE REVIEW

In contrast to horizontal standards, which define basic connectivity specifications for use in multiple industries, vertical standards formally specify unique data structures, semantic definitions, document formats, and business processes for specific industries (Markus et al., 2003; Steinfield et al., 2004, 2005; Wigand et al., 2005). They are organizational-level technologies whose assimilation is complicated by community effects external to the organization's environment. The assimilation of vertical standards is still in its early stages (Wareham et al., 2005), which provides opportunities to make contributions of practical significance to their technical development and to industry practices moderating their assimilation. Vertical standards belong to a special category of technology innovations collectively known as complex networked technologies (Damsgaard & Lyytinen, 2001; Lyytinen & Damsgaard, 2001), which also includes EDI and whose assimilation is subject to significant organizational interdependence (Fichman, 1992).

Classical DoI theory, with its emphasis on the binary adoption of relatively simple technologies by individual users, remains a solid foundation for the study of vertical standards, but has been shown to be insufficient for the study of complex networked technologies (Lyytinen & Damsgaard, 2001). Since complex networked technologies are generally subject to network externalities (Lyytinen & Damsgaard, 2001), recent research on vertical standards has incorporated economic effects theory concepts into their study. While useful, economic effects theory treats the adoption decision-making process as a "black box" because the complexities of real-world adoption decisions are simply too difficult to model (Farrell & Saloner, 1985). Network exchange theory (Markovsky et al., 1988) introduces the concept of power in social network structures to the study of technological innovations, but does not explain the technical environment in which industry-specific standards are evaluated. For example, system compatibility and migration issues are not addressed, prior technology investment and knowledge barriers are not factored in and, in general, technology-specific issues that may affect the balance and execution of power in a social network are not considered. Lastly, theories of competitive advantage have not established a solid link between IT investment and competitive advantage (Brynjolfsson & Hitt, 1996, 1998; Johnson & Vitale, 1988). While several models have emerged that include IT in resource-based views of the firm (Bharadwaj, 2000; Mata et al., 1995), IT is often considered as an isolated artifact

in these research efforts. It is typically viewed as unable to interact and change with the demands of the environment that surrounds it, one of the key abilites of complex networked technologies, such as EDI (Damsgaard & Truex, 2000) and vertical standards (West, 2003). It is clear that, in order to understand the causes and effects of vertical standards assimilation by organizations and industries, systematic research must be conducted using an amalgamation of theories and methodologies (Wareham et al., 2005; Wigand et al., 2005). The research community has begun this process, and multiple avenues of research are now being explored.

The development of VS differs significantly from other IT standards due to heavy user involvement (Nickerson & Muehlen, 2003; Zhao et al., 2005), and to the ability of individual VS to adapt to the changing needs of their niche industries (West, 2003), and differences in technical development of standards have been found to significantly affect their adoption rates (Lyytinen & Fomin, 2002). Accordingly, the academic literature on VS has concentrated on technical development processes (Chang & Jarvenpaa, 2005; Nelson et al., 2005; Reimers & Li, 2005; Steinfield et al., 2004; Zhao et al., 2005), and has been largely qualitative in nature. The emerging literature on vertical standards has explored the various governance procedures used by SDOs (Steinfield et al., 2004), proposed a cross-industry Standards Development Cycle (Nelson et al., 2005), and developed an approach to technical development based on transaction cost theory (Reimers & Li, 2005). Zhao et al. (2005) propose a framework for further SDO-based research that is an adaptation of the Technology-Organization-Environment variable classification index previously used by Tornatzky and Fleischer (1990), while Chang and Jarvenpaa (2005) examine the change dynamics amongst XBRL standards-development participants within SDOs. Others explore the importance of individual relationships (Markus et al., 2003), technical compatibility and migration choices (Wigand et al., 2005), and potential industry structure effects of adoption (Steinfield et al., 2005) in the standards-development processes of the U.S. home mortgage industry. Path dependencies have also been explored in the U.S. home mortgage (Wigand et al., 2005), financial services (Gogan, 2005), and energy markets (Wareham et al. 2005), and the role of environmental factors has been documented for the financial industry (Ciganek et al., 2005). The failure of a vertical standards-based electronic exchange in the automotive industry (Gerst & Bunduchi, 2005), and the industry consequences of participation in a chemical industry exchange (Christiaanse & Rodon, 2005) have also received some attention.

Empirical studies of electronic commerce technology standards are few, and have been limited to general Internet technology adoption in German (Beck & Weitzel, 2005), New Zealand (Al-Qirim, 2005), and American (Wymer & Regan, 2005) SMEs. The potential impacts of the use of VS on organizational and industry structures have received much less attention (Wigand et al., 2005).

MODEL AND HYPOTHESES

We introduce a two-level model of organizational assimilation of vertical standards which includes firm- and community-level effects (Figure 1). Our firm-level constructs are grounded in the three variables in classical DoI theory found to be most consistently able to explain the diffusion of innovations across organizations: complexity, relative advantage, and compatibility (Premkumar et al., 1997; Tornatzky & Klein, 1982). The community-level constructs in the model reflect the propensity of vertical standards, as complex networked technologies, to be influenced by network externalities, and are divided into *demand-* and *supply-side* effects, reflecting their origins with either business partners or with suppliers of vertical standards products and services. Since vertical standards are developed for inter-organizational use, our unit of

analysis in this study is the organization, and not an individual user. Assimilation is conceptualized here as a multi-stage progression of appropriation of a technical innovation through which the technology becomes an integral part of the way the organization does business (Swanson, 1994). This definition reflects the well-known effect of wide technology acquisition with narrow dispersion within a firm (Fichman & Kemerer, 1999). To our knowledge, this is the first and, so far, only model of assimilation of vertical standards to have been empirically tested and validated on a large scale.

Assimilation Scale

We measure the assimilation of vertical standards using a 7-point Guttman scale adapted from previous work by Ettlie (1980), Fichman and Kemerer (1997), and Ravichandran (2005). Ettlie (1980) deployed a version of Guttman scaling to measure the extent of assimilation of innovations in the transportation industry. Fichman and Kemerer (1997) modified the Ettlie scale to suit the study of technological innovations in their work on the assimilation of software process innovations, and Ravichandran (2005) adapted this assimilation scale to study component-based software-development methodologies. Our scale contains measures that track an organization's experience with vertical standards from awareness through formal evaluation, limited or large-scale deployment, and even formal rejection of the innovation.

Complementary Technology Investment

Complementary technology investment is defined as existing capital investment in technologies that enable or facilitate interconnectivity between emerging vertical standards and important legacy technology investments made by an organization. The availability of complementary products and services has been shown to play a crucial role in

Figure 1. Model of organizational assimilation of vertical standards

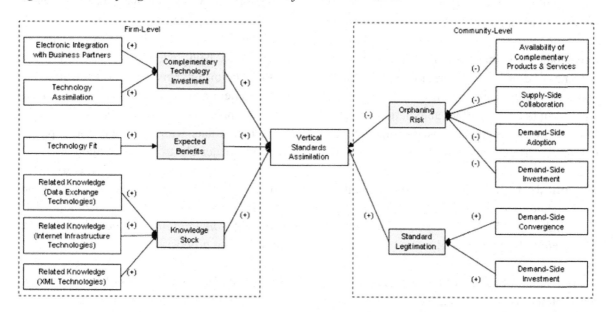

widespread technology adoption. In the insurance industry, prior investment in technical platforms that enable the deployment of newer technologies has been shown to accelerate their pace of deployment for an organization (Forman & Gron, 2005). In a cross-industry study, Schilling (1998, 2002) demonstrates that *compatibility* of existing technology investments with emerging platforms reduces technological lockout for the organization, making compatibility with future technologies an important criterion in the investment decision for *any* technology by an organization. Dedrick and West (2003) show that the compatibility of open source platforms with current technologies, skills and tasks greatly influences an organization's adoption decision.

Participants in this research effort were specifically asked about their respective organization's investment in electronic data interchange (EDI) systems, infrastructure Internet technologies, and proprietary applications of the base XML specification. Organizations with large existing investment in EDI systems are likely to attempt to extend its usable life by taking advantage of EDI's compatibility with emerging vertical

standards specifications. Vertical standards, by nature, utilize telecommunications infrastructure based on open Internet technologies. Therefore, any organizational investment in that infrastructure, while not made *explicitly* for the benefit of vertical standards, will enable and facilitate their deployment and assimilation. Similarly, vertical standards are generally implemented through the use of the XML specification approved in 1998 (XML Cover Pages, 2003), and research shows that many organizations began developing expertise with this base specification in anticipation of industry-wide standardization efforts (Mendoza & Jahng, 2003, 2004). Due to the expertise developed with the base XML specification, any investment in proprietary XML applications would facilitate the use of emerging vertical standards.

Fichman and Kemerer (1993, 1997) described capital investment in technology, and on the processes and procedures developed with its use, as exerting a *drag* on the organization's ability to adopt and assimilate emerging technical innovations. They explained that as legacy investment grows, this *prior technology drag* prevents the company from investing in unproven or unfamiliar technologies. We hypothesize that, due to the nature of vertical standards, prior investment in complementary technologies does not place an undue burden on their assimilation and does not become a "drag" for the organization. Instead, complementary technology investment provides a platform to enable further automation, integration, and transformation of business processes by emerging vertical standards. Thus,

Hypothesis 1: Investment in complementary technologies is positively associated with higher levels of assimilation of vertical standards by organizations.

The effects of the use of ITs between an organization and its business partners have been researched and described extensively. The electronic markets hypothesis (EMH, Malone et al., 1987) suggests that the emergence of electronically-coordinated markets between organizations along a specific supply chain or within an industry will reduce the overall size of a firm. The EMH also describes an *electronic integration* effect of IT on organizations and business processes, and defines it as the transformation and "tighter coupling of... the processes that create and use the information" processed by those ITs. Further, the *move to the middle* hypothesis (Clemons et al., 1993) recognizes that the increasing standardization and interconnectivity of information technology allow organizations to make greater relationship-specific investments in IT without a corresponding increase in risk. This reduces coordination costs for the firm and increases performance monitoring with its customers and suppliers, leading to lasting, more tightly-integrated linkages with a smaller number of external partners. In a study of the insurance industry, Zaheer and Venkatraman (1994) show that electronic integration significantly enhances interfirm relationships. Lastly, Wigand (1997) describes an electronic strategic networking effect of IT that facilitates the establishment of strategic technology-enabled links between organizations

designed to help them achieve joint goals towards a position of competitive advantage.

We make use of existing views of electronic integration as being externally-focused and acting on the relationship between an organization and its customers and suppliers. It is proposed that prior extensive use of information technologies to exchange data with customers and suppliers leads to greater electronic integration and to an increase in legacy investment. In order to protect and maximize returns on this investment, any additional IT investment by the organization will be made with *compatibility* in mind, which leads to the following proposition:

Hypothesis 1a: Higher levels of electronic integration with business partners is positively associated with increased investment in complementary technologies.

Classical diffusion of innovations theory defines compatibility of an innovation as its degree of fit with a potential adopter's norms and processes (Rogers, 1983). As the innovation and its technical capabilities, impacts on business processes, and organizational structures are absorbed into the firm, a cycle of *assimilation* (Swanson & Ramiller, 1997) begins and deepens, and the technological innovation becomes a part of the fabric of the company as it demonstrates its value. Mooney et al. (1996) suggested that an information technology creates business value through three separate but complementary effects on business processes and labeled them automational, informational, and transformational effects.

Automational effects are *efficiency* gains experienced from the substitution of information technology for human labor to routinize processes and embed them in technology. One of the biggest expected benefits of vertical standards is the routinization of data exchange across inter-organizational system boundaries. Automated business processes using legacy technologies represent a significant "soft" investment for the organization. Such codification of domain knowledge (Wareham et al., 2005) in legacy systems that have been deeply assimilated leave organizations with a large investment to protect and extend. Informational effects are reflected in the ability of a technological innovation to enable better-informed decision-making processes through its ability to collect, store, process, and share data with greater efficiency. Other researchers have previously identified these capabilities as creating *electronic integration* effects, which not only speed communication, but also lead to closer coupling of processes and organizational structures within and across firms (Malone et al., 1987; Zaheer & Venkatraman, 1994). Firms are also interested in protecting these strategic informational linkages. Lastly, transformational effects of information technology allow for the development of new processes and streamlined organizational structures to take advantage of the technology's capabilities. Researchers have identified an *electronic strategic networking* effect (Wigand, 1997; Wigand et al., 1997) that complements the integration, communication, and brokerage effects identified by Malone et al. (1987). An electronic strategic network is the deliberate use and strategic deployment of technology-enabled linkages and data exchange networks among business partners to support joint goals in the marketplace. This is one more example of a soft investment based on legacy, deeply-assimilated technologies that firms are interested in protecting.

Companies participating in this research effort were specifically asked about the degree to which data exchange technologies contributed to automate, inform, and transform business processes prior to the adoption of a vertical standard. It is logical to expect that the longer a legacy system has been in use in a company, the higher the level of assimilation with business processes and organizational structures it has reached through automational, informational, and transformational effects. The accumulation of these effects leaves

organizations with large soft investments and with incentive to capitalize on technology assimilation by utilizing 'bridge' technologies to extend their reach and usefulness. Accordingly, it is hypothesized here that

Hypothesis 1b: Higher levels of technology assimilation by an organization are positively associated with increased investment in complementary technologies.

Expected Benefits

The link between technology investment, productivity, and competitive advantage remains unclear despite much work in the area (Bakos & Treacy, 1986; Brynjolfsson & Hitt, 1998; Clemons & Row, 1991; King et al., 1989; Porter & Millar, 1985; and many others). Despite the finding that *relative advantage* consistently provides significant predictive power in studies of the diffusion of technological innovations (Tornatzky & Klein, 1982), research yields mixed evidence to support that claim for complex networked technologies. Research has found that the greatest contribution of complex networked IOS like EDI is the facilitation of internal systems integration and business process reengineering (Johnson & Vitale 1988; Ramamurthy et al., 1999; Swatman et al., 1994).

In the case of web services, an XML-based technology, evidence of their contribution to gains in relative advantage has been weak to non-existent (Ciganek et al., 2005, 2006). This may be because web services are infrastructure technologies whose benefits are neither readily observable nor measurable, and may only develop after a suitable period of time, making their connection to benefits difficult to identify. Vertical standards are another infrastructure technology whose external benefits are not immediately obvious in the marketplace, making it difficult to establish a link to relative advantage. Since the external implementation of vertical standards by an organization is homogeneous throughout the industry in which they are applicable (or they would not *be* standards), it is appropriate to measure the relative advantage they offer to an organization in terms of internal, indirect business benefits. Participants in our research effort were asked about the degree to which vertical standards will deliver business benefits, the importance of the transactions they will support, and impact on existing infrastructure currently or after their adoption. Overall, a positive correspondence is expected between higher expected benefits and assimilation stage for vertical standards. We posit that

Hypothesis 2: Higher expected benefits of the use of vertical standards are positively associated with higher levels of assimilation of vertical standards by organizations.

Other than software vendors, users of electronic business standards rarely compete on the basis of standards implementation (Zhao et al., 2005), so their deployment for external use can only lead to competitive parity (Barney, 1991; Mata et al., 1995), in the best of cases. Resource-based views suggest that the benefits obtained through the use of a technological innovation are most easily transformed into competitive advantage by the users if the innovation makes use of resources unique to the firm (Barney, 1991; Brynjolfsson & Hitt, 1998), but technologies that support processes become standardized as the processes themselves become standardized (Carr, 2004). For the vast majority of participants in any given industry, standardization of vertical standards technologies takes place *prior* to the standardization of business processes and data formats to support them internally. Therefore, it is fitting to conceptualize benefits as the level of fit between vertical standards and *existing* processes and data formats used by organizations. A study of the deployment of MRP in the U.S. manufacturing sector shows that a high level of fit between technology and existing business processes helps explain organizational adoption (Cooper & Zmud, 1990). Also, in a sample of over

350 Fortune 1000 firms, Tanriverdi (2006) found that complementarities among IT infrastructure technologies and IT management processes create super-additive value synergies. We suggest that the most appropriate way to evaluate business value to an organization from its use of vertical standards is to determine the degree to which they are compatible with existing business processes and data formats supporting both internal and external transactions. In this way, the organization may exploit resources unique to itself while maintaining the external compatibility vertical standards provide. We offer the following hypothesis:

Hypothesis 2a: Higher levels of fit between vertical standards and an organization's existing business processes and data formats increase levels of expected benefits obtained from vertical standards by an organization.

Knowledge Stock

Diffusion of Innovations theory defines the *complexity* of an innovation as the degree of difficulty in understanding it and putting it to use (Rogers, 1983), and studies have shown its importance in their diffusion and assimilation. Moore and Benbasat (1991) showed that ease of use, a construct equivalent to complexity is a significant predictor of intent to use personal computers by individuals in organizations. Work based on a series of interviews with MIS managers showed that complexity was a consistent criterion for the adoption of the Linux open-sourced operating system (Dedrick & West, 2003), and empirical work with MIS executives on the adoption of customer-based inter-organizational systems supports the role of complexity in their adoption (Grover, 1993). When confronted with complexity in a technological innovation, firms delay its assimilation until sufficient internal expertise exists to overcome the knowledge barrier and to successfully deploy and exploit it (Attewell, 1992). The knowledge barrier created by the complexity of an innovation slows diffusion, an effect which has been observed with individual adoption of personal workstations (Davis, 1989), and in organizational adoption of Manufacturing Resource Planning (MRP) systems (Cooper & Zmud, 1990) and of corporate travel reservation systems (Chircu et al., 2001).

Nambisan and Wang (1999) described three kinds of knowledge barriers presented by complex technologies which must be overcome in order to assist the spread of web-based technologies: technology-, project-, and application-related. Technology-related knowledge barriers reflect the organization's lack of expertise with necessary infrastructure component and features to assimilate a technology innovation. Project-related barriers are insufficient understanding regarding financial and human resources required to develop and deploy these solutions. Lastly, application-related barriers echo the firm's inability to maximize business benefits of the technology. In a study of the assimilation of component-based software development, Ravichandran (2005) defined *knowledge stock* as knowledge developed by an organization with a specific technology in all these areas, and found empirical confirmation that higher knowledge stock is associated with increased assimilation of component-based software development. We retain this definition of knowledge stock and include not only technical expertise but also evaluative and exploitative skills, project management, and change management expertise that allows an organization to derive value from its information technology investments. Our survey instrument specifically asked about organizational knowledge stock levels related to these types of skills. The following hypothesis is offered regarding the relationship between knowledge stock and the assimilation of vertical standards:

Hypothesis 3: Higher levels of knowledge stock are positively associated with higher levels of assimilation of vertical standards by organizations.

The role of organizational learning in the assimilation of complex technologies has been shown to be significant in studies of the use of software process innovations and component-based software development methodologies by organizations (Fichman & Kemerer, 1997; Ravichandran, 2005). Cohen and Levinthal (1990) conceptualized a firm's ability to realize the value of new, external knowledge, assimilate it, and exploit it as the organization's absorptive capacity which Zahra and George (2002) further defined as a function of prior related knowledge. Absorptive capacity has been shown to be a significant factor in explaining high levels of use of IT in organizations (Boynton et al., 1994). Fichman and Kemerer (1997) demonstrated that existing related knowledge and greater diversity of technical expertise and activities contribute significantly to the assimilation of software process innovations such as object-oriented programming languages, validating the organizational learning approach to innovation assimilation.

Organizations with significant investment in Electronic Data Interchange (EDI) applications will have already developed absorptive capacity in the area of electronic data exchange applications and will find it less challenging to put those transferable skills to use working with XML-based vertical standards. Thus, the *soft* investment in technical, project management, evaluative, and exploitative skills developed with legacy data exchange technologies and systems, such as EDI, are likely to contribute directly to an increase in deployable knowledge stock for the firm. Thus, we offer that

Hypothesis 3a: Higher levels of related knowledge with data exchange technologies, such as EDI, are positively associated with higher levels of knowledge stock.

Similarly, capital and soft investment in Internet technologies allows the organization to build knowledge stock with the technology platforms necessary to successfully deploy vertical standards. A link between deployment of Internet technologies and other complex networked technologies has been found in the insurance industry (Forman & Gron, 2005). Accordingly, we hypothesize that

Hypothesis 3b: Higher levels of related knowledge with Internet infrastructure technologies are positively associated with higher levels of knowledge stock.

Vertical standards are complex inter-organizational technologies that require the participation of industry players to identify appropriate domain knowledge, i.e., industry-specific data and business processes, to formalize and codify (Nelson & Nelson, 2003; Wareham et al., 2005). Gosain (2003) suggested that low-risk experimentation by firms anticipating making an investment in web service-based technologies can help mitigate the risk presented by knowledge barriers and increase the organization's knowledge stock. This is precisely the kind of experimentation observed in the insurance, financial services, aerospace, telecommunications, and other industries with XML-based applications and web service technologies (Ciganek et al., 2005, 2006; Mendoza & Jahng, 2003). Ciganek et al. (2005) found a similar approach to reducing knowledge barriers related to web services in the financial services industry and in a separate cross-industry study (Ciganek et al., 2006). The body of expertise gained by these organizations in developing custom solutions to data format and exchange needs, and in the codification of internal and external business processes, makes a contribution towards the development of knowledge stock related to XML-based standards. Thus, it is hypothesized that

Hypothesis 3c: Higher levels of related knowledge with XML technologies are positively associated with higher levels of knowledge stock.

Orphaning Risk

Orphaning risk is defined as the possibility that, by adopting a technical specification before it becomes the dominant standard in an industry, an organization may be left stranded with an inferior, non-standard, or even incompatible technology (Besen, 1992, 1995). Orphaning risk has been shown to be a significant motivator in the adoption of open-sourced software such as the Linux operating system (Dedrick & West, 2003), and various server-side and web-based applications (Miralles et al., 2005). Interestingly, in their study of open-sourced adoption practices by CIOs in industries as varied as pharmaceutical, banking, beauty care, telecommunications, and steel, Miralles et al. (2005) discovered that avoidance of orphaning risk and its attendant lock-in were considered primary criteria for the selection of open-sourced software *even by non-adopters*. A study of the failure of two mutually enabling vertical standards in the financial services industry (eCheck and Financial Services Markup Language, or FSML) shows that orphaning risk is a real concern for vertical standards assimilation and merits study (Gogan, 2005).

For complex networked technologies like vertical standards, network externalities postpone the adoption decision to allow a dominant technology to emerge (Damsgaard & Lyytinen, 2001). However, at an industry level, this approach can lead to excess inertia (Farrell & Saloner, 1985), a market-wide situation in which all participants wait for someone else to bear the costs of early adoption before they follow suit (David & Greenstein, 1990). Using an agent-based simulation approach, Weitzel et al. (2006) showed that the level of optimization regarding the choice of technology as a dominant standard reached in a centralized model is better than that reached by a decentralized model. We suggest that an organization will perceive greater orphaning risks in the adoption of a specification which does not count with the formal backing of an established standards-development organization (SDO) in its industry, regardless of how widely the specification may have spread throughout the industry or with the company's influential business partners. In short,

Hypothesis 4: Higher orphaning risks reduce levels of assimilation of vertical standards by organizations.

Schilling (1998) proposed that, for technologies subject to network externalities and which require complementary goods, a lack of the same will increase the likelihood of being locked out of the market, and later confirmed it in a cross-industry empirical study of technological lock out (Schilling, 2002). In the same study, it was shown that a positive relationship exists between the installed base of a technology and the availability of complementary goods. In the U.S. home video game industry, companies with a strong network of complementary products for their gaming platforms have claimed or share market leadership (Gallagher & Park, 2002). Wareham et al. (2005) showed that the structure and size of complementary markets played an important role in the failure of a vertical standard to be assimilated by companies in the energy market.

The availability of complementary products and services signal a commitment from suppliers to the standard, and may also reinforce the commitment to the standard by adopters (Dedrick & West, 2003) by indicating the standard has become or is on its way towards a dominant position in the industry (Fichman & Kemerer, 1993). As their numbers increase, complementary products and services generate their own bandwagon effects, and the number of suppliers entering the market also increases, raising the pool of technical, project management, support, and maintenance expertise (Hills, 2000). Thus, it is expected that complementary products and services, in combination with technical support and consulting services provided by a growing development community, greatly reduce the risk of technology orphaning

to potential adopters. Formally, we state that this *supply-side* effect reduces perceived orphaning risks, and we extend the following hypothesis

Hypothesis 4a: Higher availability of complementary products and services are associated with lower levels of orphaning risk.

An overabundance of specifications vying to become the dominant standard has been detrimental to the emergence of an industry standard in technologies ranging from ERP to EDI, XML, and XML-based web services (Benjamin et al., 1990; Chen et al., 2003; Damsgaard & Lyytinen, 2001; Damsgaard & Truex, 2000; Lucy-Bouler & Morgenstern, 2003; Nickerson & Muehlen, 2003; Sumner, 2000). One of the many ways to remedy this problem is for suppliers of vertical standards-based products and services to seek to collaborate to establish a single dominant platform upon which to compete. This strategy, known as coopetition (Brandenburger & Nalebuff, 1996), entails the combination of cooperative behaviors between customers, suppliers, and complementary product producers aimed at expanding the initial size of a market, with competitive strategies to become the dominant player once it has been established. Vendor behavior during development activities and in the initial adoption stages of technical standards has been suggested as an important variable in the development and establishment of technical specification as industry standards (Besen, 1995). The authors identify collaborative strategies, which require participants agree to develop and select the technical specification that best serves the needs of their industry, as well as non-collaborative strategies, which include a vendor's preference for its own specification or none at all over a competing one, and process sabotage designed to maintain industry incompatibility for its own advantage. Only collaborative strategies send market signals interpreted by potential adopters as capable of reducing orphaning risk (Ravichandran, 2005). Empirical evidence supports the superiority of free-market collaboration behaviors over any other standards-development activity (Farrell & Saloner, 1988). Since this collaborative behavior involves *suppliers* of products and services related to vertical standards, we label it a *supply-side* effect and submit that

Hypothesis 4b: Higher levels of supply-side collaboration in development activities are associated with lower levels of orphaning risk.

Empirical work on EDI assimilation has revealed the predictive significance of the adoption decision of important business partners on potential EDI adopters (Bouchard, 1993). The study argues that the advantages offered by EDI are not in the innovation *per se*, but rather in the investment and use of EDI by influential partners relative to the potential adopter. This finding was echoed in a multiple case-based study of small businesses supplying the provincial government of British Columbia, Canada (Iacovou et al., 1995) in which external pressure from the provincial government, their most significant business partner, was cited as the strongest explanatory factor. Thus,

Hypothesis 4c: Higher levels of demand-side adoption are associated with lower levels of orphaning risk.

The concept of reciprocal investment has been used to explain the importance of asset-specific investment by one member of a business dyad in the continuance of the relationship (Son et al., 1999; Zaheer & Venkatraman, 1994). We extend this concept to include investment in non-specific system assets, i.e., standards-based systems and suggest that significant investment in (any) vertical standards by major customers and suppliers is a signal to a partner that a similar investment will not be lost and that the partner will not be stranded with a useless asset. Therefore, organizational assimilation of the standard(s) in question does not expose the organization to as much risk as it

otherwise would. Since the investment in question involves *influential business partners* of potential adopters, we label it a *demand-side* effect and offer the following two hypotheses

Hypothesis 4d: Higher levels of demand-side investment in vertical standards are associated with lower levels of orphaning risk.

Standard Legitimation

Another manifestation of the power of network externalities is in an effect we call *standard legitimation*. Legitimation refers to the collective development of norms and prescriptions for the accepted use of an artifact in a social network (Emerson, 1962). The legitimation signal is as simple as the visible act of adoption by an organization, and further assessments by potential adopted about the efficiency, productivity gains or improvements in competitive position afforded by an innovation may not be necessary. This signal becomes a cue for business partners that the innovation is "legitimate" and that, in fact, *not* adopting it presents a risk of abnormality or illegitimacy to external stakeholders, and spurs its adoption (Abrahamson & Rosenkopf, 1993; Meyer & Rowan, 1977). For information technology-based products and systems, legitimation is the development of an underlying rationale for the assimilation of a technology by an organization as part of what Swanson and Ramiller (1997) termed the *organizing vision* of a community of potential adopters. This organizing vision helps a community of would-be technology adopters *interpret* the nature and purpose of the innovation, *legitimize* it as appropriate to meeting their business needs, and to *mobilize* the necessary market mechanisms to enable its assimilation in the community. Since legitimation is a community process, the coalescence of various interests is required for the development of the importance of vertical standards and the acceptance of a single dominant one in the industry (Lyytinen &

Damsgaard, 2001). We extend the existing social concept of legitimation to denote the community-based process through which a vertical standard becomes accepted by industry members through its assimilation by influential business partners. More properly, it is stated that

Hypothesis 5: Higher levels of standard legitimation for any given vertical standard are positively associated with higher levels of assimilation of vertical standards by organizations.

As has been observed with EDI (Bouchard, 1993), the adoption of technological innovations by business partners is theorized to play an important role in the assimilation of vertical standards. As influential business partners adopt and converge on a dominant standard, a market signal about its likelihood of success is interpreted by the rest of the industry (Keil, 2002), and its legitimacy in the industry increases. Agent-based simulations have shown that adoption decisions by autonomous agents are influenced by the adoption decisions of the most significant members of the adopter's overall network (Weitzel et al., 2006). We define the concept of *convergence* as the process through which a single vertical standard emerges as the dominant or winning industry standard and is acknowledged as such by industry members. In a cascading process of influence, deployment decisions by major industry players or influential business partners generate imitation behaviors in peripheral industry members (Abrahamson & Fombrun, 1994; Abrahamson & Rosenkopf, 1997), leading to convergence. We refer once again to our previous definition of demand-side effects and hypothesize that

Hypothesis 5a: Higher levels of demand-side convergence are positively associated with higher levels of standard legitimation.

In a similar manner, the participation of major or influential business partners in the technical development activities of vertical standards may be interpreted by organizations as signals of their intent to adopt. The investment of time, capital, and human resources of major business partners to the development of vertical standards for the industry is a strong sign of their commitment to the diffusion of the vertical standard in the industry. The reasons for individual organizations to participate in the development activities of standards-making bodies in their industries are varied and include the need to develop technical expertise (Chwelos et al., 2001; Kowalski & Karcher, 1994), maintain control of a technology for their own competitive benefit (Gerst & Bunduchi, 2005), the sharing costs related to the standard development life cycle (Nelson et al., 2005), and avoiding lock-out or late market entry (Nickerson & Muehlen, 2003). Independent of the reason for joining an effort, increased participation by influential business partners increases legitimation of a vertical standard in the eyes of potential adopters. Stated in terms of demand-side effects,

Hypothesis 5b: Higher levels of demand-side investment in vertical standards are positively associated with higher levels of standard legitimation.

METHODOLOGY

Data for this effort were collected via the use of online surveys and in partnership with the Organization for the Advancement of Structured Information Standards (OASIS-Open.org), the International Digital Enterprise Alliance (IDEAlliance.org), and of the Association for Cooperative Operations Research and Development (ACORD.org). OASIS is a nonprofit, international, independent consortium driving the development, convergence, and adoption of e-business standards. OASIS has over 5,000 individual members representing more than 600 organizations in 100 countries and is widely recognized as one of the leading SDOs in e-business and Internet-related technologies and standards. IDEAlliance is an industry organization dedicated to developing and validating best practices in publishing and information technology. ACORD is a global, nonprofit association whose mission is to facilitate the development and use of standards specifically for the insurance, reinsurance and related financial services industries. The instrument was tested and validated using data collected from OASIS and IDEAlliance memberships, and the validated instrument was administered to the general membership of ACORD.

Two rounds of tests were conducted with OASIS. The first trial was designed to test the process of administering the survey online, and the face validity, wording, logical flow, and clarity of the instrument. Minimal changes were made to the survey on the basis of follow-up conversations with several participants. Data from the second round of testing was combined with data from printed surveys collected at The XML Conference, a leading industry conference sponsored by IDE-Alliance, and was used to validate the instrument.

Assimilation stages were identified using a seven-point Likert scale adapted from Fichman and Kemerer's (1997) software process innovation assimilation scale, as described previously. We performed a principal components analysis (PCA) with SPSS v14.0 for scale validation. Components with eigenvalues greater than or equal to 1.0 were extracted, and scree plots and the existing literature were used to guide the final number of components. Varimax rotation was employed to maximize the loadings. The results of the PCA support the use of the constructs shown in Figure 1. Scale reliability was determined using Cronbach's Alpha and found to be at or above 0.70, the recommended minimum score for the scales to be considered reliable (Nunnally, 1978). The validated instrument was administered to the general membership of ACORD. The electronic

invitation to complete the survey was sent via an internal newsletter to individuals representing over 500 organizations with membership in ACORD. Identifying information for the individual responses was not available to the authors of this paper. Surveys not completed to at least a 75% level were discarded, leaving a total of 234 surveys for further analysis. Three of those surveys were from organizations which indicated no interest in the use of vertical standards, and were accordingly excluded from the rest of the analysis, resulting in 231 usable surveys.

DATA ANALYSIS AND RESULTS

The model was tested using the Partial Least Squares (PLS) method supported by PLS-Graph software (beta version 3.0, Build 1126). PLS is recommended in causal-predictive analysis for complex models with low theoretical information (Joreskog & Wold 1982), and is particularly well-suited for predicting dependent variables from a large number of independent variables (Abdi, 2003). PLS is well recognized as an appropriate tool in theory development, particularly when it involves new measurement items (Chin, 1995, 1998), as is the case in this study. Since significance tests are not provided directly by the PLS method, they were estimated using a bootstrapping technique with 100 samples, common practice with PLS-based studies.

Of the 231 surveys in the final PLS-Graph analysis, 60% come from members in the Life, Personal & Commercial insurance, and Financial Services areas, while 26% are from software and IT services providers. 67% of the surveys come from individuals at the Director, President, or Chief Executive level, and 53% of all respondents state their role in vertical standards adoption decisions for their companies was *Significant* to *Very Significant* on our 7-point Likert scale. This final number provides the study with reasonable assurance that the data obtained has adequate organizational-level perspective on the assimilation of vertical standards and their importance to ACORD members. Sixty percent of respondents estimate that between 66-100% of the organization's future data transactions will be conducted through the use of vertical standards, and that these transactions will be of a critical nature for the company's business. These numbers are significant because they reflect the external focus of data exchange based on vertical standards, and their future importance to company transactions. Revenue for participating organizations during FY 2004-2005 is normally distributed, with an average in the range of US$100-500 Million, and standard deviation of between US$5-50 Million. More than half the respondents (54%) state that vertical standards are in partial or full deployment in their organizations, while 18% indicate their company is actively evaluating vertical standards for deployment. 22% point out their firm has no formal adoption or deployment plans, but is tracking their development and building internal expertise in anticipation of their use. Path coefficients for all constructs in the PLS-Graph model are shown in Figure 2. The numbers below each

variable name represent the r^2 values for each construct. All coefficient loadings are in the hypothesized directions, and all but two at both levels are significant at least at the 0.1 level.

At the organizational level, two of the three constructs based on DoI theory were found to be statistically significant, and the third was in the hypothesized direction. This confirms the usefulness of incorporating DoI concepts into the study of complex networked technologies. Specifically, our re-conceptualization of relative advantage in the *Expected Benefits* construct and of complexity in *Knowledge Stock* was shown to be appropriate. Complementary Technology Investment was the only first-level construct without statistical significance, although its path coefficient (0.069) was in the expected direction and the total variance accounted for was high (r^2=34.90%). While there was no statistical significance in the path coefficient, results for this construct do provide some confirmation that investment in technologies that enable or facilitate interconnectivity between emerging vertical standards and important legacy technology investments also facilitate the overall assimilation of vertical standards. Electronic in-

Figure 2. Path coefficients and r^2 values

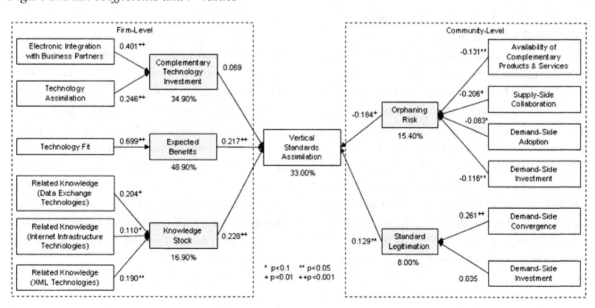

tegration with business partners (0.401, $p<0.001$) and technology assimilation (0.246, $p>0.001$) are both shown to be strong contributors to higher complementary technology investment. Most importantly, these results suggest that prior investment in legacy technologies does not necessarily constitute a technology *drag* on the assimilation of emerging technologies, as has been previously suggested.

Expected benefits were also found to be strong predictors of assimilation (0.217, $p<0.001$), and the level of fit of the technology with existing business processes and data formats (0.699, $p<0.001$) is a significant source of benefits. Our results provide empirical evidence that confirms qualitative findings in other studies (Nelson et al., 2005; Steinfield et al., 2004) regarding the nature of the competitive advantage afforded by these emerging technologies, i.e., that the primary benefit of the use of these technologies is interoperability within and across organizational boundaries. As our results suggest, compatibility with how the organization does business and codifies results is a significant contributor to overall benefits.

Our results also confirm that knowledge stocks (0.228, $p<0.001$) are a significant factor in increasing assimilation of vertical standards in organizations. Additionally, our data shows that expertise with related technologies such as EDI (0.204, $p<0.01$), Internet infrastructure (0.110, $p<0.1$), and the base XML specification (0.190, $p<0.05$) increase the organization's ability to identify, absorb, and exploit new knowledge to help them successfully deploy and use emerging technologies. The lack of statistical significance for related knowledge in the area of Internet infrastructure technologies may be due to the fact that, while a robust infrastructure based on Internet technologies is necessary to be able to deploy vertical standards, that infrastructure was not created *with vertical standards in mind*.

Both of the community-level constructs developed for this effort were strongly supported by our data. Further, four of the six second-level

variables representing supply- and demand-side effects were also strongly significant, and one of the remaining two had support at the 0.10 level. Overall, this confirms the validity of combining market-level influences with organizational-level factors in the study of the assimilation of emerging technologies.

Results for the orphaning risk construct (-0.184, $p<0.01$) show that the adoption and deployment of an industry specification *not* specifically endorsed by an established industry body or accredited SDO presents higher stranding risks for the organization, regardless of the popularity of the specification with the rest of the industry. Contributing to the reduction of these orphaning risks are two supply-side and two demand-side effects. The availability of complementary products and services (-0.131, $p<0.05$) and the collaboration of software vendors, systems integrators, and other players (-0.206, $p<0.01$) in the development of vertical standards and the provision of their associated services are crucial supply-side signals that contribute to a reduction in perceived orphaning risks for the organization. On the demand-side of the equation, adoption (-0.083, $p<0.1$) and investment (-0.116, $p<0.05$) by influential business partners also reduce orphaning risks in the eyes of potential adopters. It is interesting to note that actual investment in vertical standards is of greater significance than a simple adoption signal, which lends empirical support to the idea of assimilation gaps as described by Fichman and Kemerer (1999). The authors describe the potential for erroneous conclusions based on the cumulative gap created by the measuring of external acquisition signaling versus the extent of actual internal deployment of an innovation. Our data suggests that potential adopters assign greater credibility to measurable investment of various kinds, i.e., capital, human, complementary technologies, knowledge stock, etc. than to a potentially-misleading market signal of the adoption of a vertical standard not coupled with commitment on the part of influential business partners.

As hypothesized, standard legitimation (0.129, p<0.05) is a significant contributor to the assimilation of vertical standards by organizations. Demand-side convergence (0.261, p<0.001), signaled by the adoption of a single "winning" vertical standard by a potential adopter's influential business partners, is a powerful legitimator for a vertical standard, whereas their participation in standards-development activities (demand-side investment) does not achieve statistical significance with our data. These results are consistent with the results of demand-side effects for the orphaning risk construct, in that convergence signaling, i.e., business partner adoption, legitimizes a standard but does not contribute to a reduction in stranding risk for the organization to the same extent that investment does. Also, enriching the results of the supply-side collaboration effects in the orphaning risk construct, the collaborative nature of participation in standards-development activities by business partners may be viewed with suspicion by potential adopters. This may also point to a need for further refinement of the legitimacy construct to incorporate existing work that identifies several approaches to the concept of legitimacy (Suchman, 1995). Recent work that may also be helpful has shown that network topology, network density, and the extent of industry-wide coordination of standardization efforts have a substantial impact on technology-based standards diffusion and assimilation (Weitzel et al., 2006).

Overall, the results provide strong support for the proposed model, with thirteen of seventeen hypotheses strongly supported (p<0.05 or lower). Two additional hypotheses are supported at the p=0.10 level, and with the path coefficients for the two remaining hypothesis not reaching statistical significance in the hypothesized direction. The average variance accounted for by the five firm- and community-level constructs was just over 24%, with an r^2 of 33% for the dependent variable of assimilation.

DISCUSSION

The literature on adoption and diffusion of technological innovations has yielded a mix of significant findings at both the organizational and community levels (Ciganek et al., 2006). This study is the result of the first large-scale empirical contribution towards an integrative model of vertical standards assimilation, and the first to combine proven concepts from DoI theory with community-level network effects in an empirical effort. We show that community-level effects are, in fact, important to vertical standards assimilation, and that they can be categorized into demand-side and supply-side effects with some reliability. Further refining of the standard legitimation construct, incorporating the extant literature on the topic of organizational legitimacy, would help advance the distilment of influential factors in that process. Macro-level social processes variables such as power, influence, and dependence need to be addressed more in detail in the context of vertical standards assimilation. We have also found evidence to suggest that prior investment in technology should not be thought of as a homogeneous block exerting a drag that keeps organizations from assimilating emerging technologies. Rather, some investments are necessary to providing the right infrastructure to ensure the future integration of vertical standards with business processes and data exchange practices. In addition, the flexibility of XML as a base for developing and implementing vertical standards allows organizations to deploy XML in non-standard ways to create functionality bridges between legacy systems and vertical standards, reducing the drag of the legacy investment on vertical standards. Our results also show the usefulness of re-conceptualizing the classical view of competitive advantage in terms of technology fit and benefits. Additional work in this area would help identify the type and extent of fit with existing business processes and data formats, as well as the kinds of benefit an organization obtains from the deployment of vertical standards, and whether those benefits are primarily internal, external, or what mix of the two. The results for the community-level variables proposed in the model (orphaning risk and standard legitimation) hint at the possibility that network externalities effects on the assimilation of vertical standards may be more nuanced than currently thought, and that differentiating between demand- and supply-side as the origin of those effects may be useful.

Of practical importance, the significance of related knowledge with technologies similar to those used by vertical standards presents opportunities for SDOs to continue to expand their intermediary and mediating role as knowledge creators and disseminators. The formation of co-operative alliances between SDOs whose members experience an overlap of standards-development activities would accelerate the assimilation of vertical standards. SDOs would also benefit from allying with and obtaining official recognition from international bodies, as OASIS has done with UN/CEFACT and the ISO. For providers of products and services complementary to vertical standards, the importance of customer training as a catalyst for market growth is highlighted by the significance of knowledge stock in their assimilation. Vendors with leadership positions in their development will find a proper balance between intellectual property rights protection and collaboration with influential stakeholders to be a useful tool to maintaining their position of leadership. Consumers of vertical standards will continue to profit from developing internal expertise that will be useful when official legitimation of a single vertical standard in their industry occurs and industry-wide assimilation commences. Organizations enjoying asymmetrical power relationships with their business partners may consider the use of incentives to encourage them to assimilate the standards they have adopted. These incentives may take the shape of training, technical advice, cost-sharing strategies, and even service hosting.

CONCLUSION

The value of examining community-level factors in the assimilation of complex networked technologies like vertical standards is now apparent in the literature (Wareham et al., 2005; Wigand et al., 2005) and has been confirmed in this study. The operationalization and measurement of the orphaning risk and standard legitimation concepts described here must continue to be refined and systematically compared across industries. The present state of assimilation of vertical standards offers ample opportunity to make significant theoretical and practical contributions, and potentially influence standards-development processes and institutional policies.

The managerial implications of this study are perhaps clearer for supply-side organizations than for demand-side firms (e.g., users). Suppliers of products and services which complement and/or extend vertical standards functionality can fine-tune their offerings to emphasize the extent to which they can reduce the risk of future stranding for its customers while providing internal compatibility bridges to legacy technology investment. This kind of positioning would presumably entice customers to see a suppliers' products and services as not only a safe investment, but also as a way to maximize the customers' own ability to continue to extract value from older systems and applications. Suppliers can also highlight the extent to which they participate and collaborate in the development of vertical standards to position themselves as 'team players' with their customers. Suppliers can also take advantage of the importance of firm-level constructs on a firm's decision to assimilate vertical standards. Suppliers can ensure their expertise is readily available to their customers as the latter seek ways to continue to extract value from existing technology and business process investment with their business partners. Both suppliers and SDOs can also leverage their technical and development process expertise to provide training services to customer firms, further enhancing their ability to make themselves indispensable to the customer organization. By becoming a trusted, embedded source of expertise and technical development work for a customer, a supplier can also ensure that switching costs are built into the relationship, since competition based on standards makes it more difficult to extract rents from the standards-based product itself.

Demand-side organizations, i.e., those deploying and assimilating vertical standards, should experience an increase in the number and quality of available options for the provision of technical and project management expertise related to vertical standards. The customer firm, however, must be alert to any activities or product acquisitions that expand its dependence on a single provider in order to avoid future lock-in.

ACKNOWLEDGMENT

The authors gratefully acknowledge the help of the anonymous review team for the comments provided, which greatly improved the final version of this paper. We would also like to thank the Editor-in-Chief of the journal, Dr. Madjid Tavana, for his assistance in getting this paper through the review process in a simple and effective manner.

REFERENCES

Abdi, H. (2003). Partial Least Squares (PLS) Regression. In Lewis-Beck, M., Bryman, A., & Futing, T. (Eds.), *Encyclopedia of Social Sciences Research Methods* (pp. 1–7). Thousand Oaks, CA: Sage.

Abrahamson, E., & Fombrun, C. J. (1994). Macroculture: Determinants and Consequences. *Academy of Management Review, 19*(4), 728–755. doi:10.2307/258743

Abrahamson, E., & Rosenkopf, L. (1993). Institutional and Competitive Bandwagons: Using Mathematical Modeling as a Tool to Explore Innovation Diffusion. *Academy of Management Review, 18*(3), 487–517. doi:10.2307/258906

Abrahamson, E., & Rosenkopf, L. (1997). Social Network Effects on the Extent of Innovation Diffusion: A Computer Simulation. *Organization Science, 8*(3), 289–309. doi:10.1287/orsc.8.3.289

Al-Qirim, N. (2005). An Empirical Investigation of an e-commerce Adoption-Capability Model in Small Businesses in New Zealand. *Electronic Markets, 15*(4), 418–437. doi:10.1080/10196780500303136

Attewell, P. (1992). Technology Diffusion and Organizational Learning: The Case of Business Computing. *Organization Science, 3*(1), 1–19. doi:10.1287/orsc.3.1.1

Au, Y. A., & Kauffman, R. J. (2001). Should We Wait? Network Externalities, Compatibility, and Electronic Billing Adoption. *Journal of Management Information Systems, 18*(2), 47–63.

Bakos, J. Y., & Treacy, M. D. (1986). Information Technology and Corporate Strategy: A Research Perspective. *Management Information Systems Quarterly, 10*(2), 107–119. doi:10.2307/249029

Barney, J. (1991). Firm Resources and Sustained Competitive Advantage. *Journal of Management, 17*(1), 99–120. doi:10.1177/014920639101700108

Beck, R., & Weitzel, T. (2005). Some Economics of Vertical Standards: Integrating SMEs in EDI Supply Chains. *Electronic Markets, 15*(4), 313–322. doi:10.1080/10196780500302781

Benjamin, R. I., de Long, D. W., & Morton, M. S. S. (1990). Electronic Data Interchange: How Much Competitive Advantage? *Long Range Planning, 23*(1), 29–40. doi:10.1016/0024-6301(90)90005-O

Besen, S. M. (1992). AM versus FM: The Battle of the Bands. *Industrial and Corporate Change, 1*, 375–396. doi:10.1093/icc/1.2.375

Besen, S. M. (1995). The Standards Processes in Telecommunication and Information Technology In Hawkins, R., Mansell, R., & Skea, J. (Eds.), *Standards, Innovation, and Competitiveness: the Politics and Economics of Standards in Natural and Technical Environments*. Cheltenham, UK: Edward Elgar.

Bharadwaj, A. (2000). A Resource-Based Perspective on Information Technology Capability and Firm Performance: An Empirical Investigation. *Management Information Systems Quarterly, 24*(1), 169–197. doi:10.2307/3250983

Bouchard, L. (1993). *Decision Criteria in the Adoption of EDI*. Paper presented at the Fourteenth International Conference on Information Systems, Orlando, FL.

Boynton, A. C., Zmud, R. W., & Jacobs, G. C. (1994). The Influence of IT Management Practice on IT Use in Large Corporations. *Management Information Systems Quarterly, 18*(3), 299–318. doi:10.2307/249620

Brandenburger, A. M., & Nalebuff, B. J. (1996). *Co-Opetition. 1. A Revolutionary Mindset That Combines Competition and Cooperation. 2. The Game Theory Strategy That's Changing the Game of Business*. New York: Doubleday.

Brynjolfsson, E., & Hitt, L. (1996). Paradox Lost? Firm-Level Evidence on the Returns to Information Systems Spending. *Management Science, 42*(4), 541–558. doi:10.1287/mnsc.42.4.541

Brynjolfsson, E., & Hitt, L. M. (1998). Beyond the productivity paradox. *Communications of the ACM, 41*(8), 49–55. doi:10.1145/280324.280332

Carr, N. G. (2004, May 1). *The Argument Over IT*. Retrieved from http://www.cio.com/archive/050104/carr.html

Chang, C., & Jarvenpaa, S. (2005). Pace of Information Systems Standards Development and Implementation: The Case of XBRL. *Electronic Markets, 15*(4), 365–377. doi:10.1080/10196780500303029

Chen, A. N. K., LaBrie, R. C., & Shao, B. B. M. (2003). An XML Adoption Framework for Electronic Business. *Journal of Electronic Commerce Research, 4*(1), 1–14.

Chin, W. W. (1995). Partial Least Squares is to LISREL as principal components analysis is to common factor analysis. *Technology Studies, XXI*(2), 315–319.

Chin, W. W. (1998). Issues and Opinions on Structural Equation Modeling. *Management Information Systems Quarterly, 22*(1).

Chircu, A. M., Kauffman, R. J., & Keskey, D. (2001). Maximizing the Value of Internet-Based Corporate Travel Reservation Systems. *Communications of the ACM, 44*(11), 57–63. doi:10.1145/384150.384162

Christiaanse, E., & Rodon, J. (2005). A Multilevel Analysis of eHub Adoption and Consequences. *Electronic Markets, 15*(4), 355–364. doi:10.1080/10196780500302997

Chwelos, P., Benbasat, I., & Dexter, A. S. (2001). Research report: Empirical test of an EDI adoption model. *Information Systems Research, 12*(3), 304–321. doi:10.1287/isre.12.3.304.9708

Ciganek, A. P., Haines, M. N., & Haseman, W. D. (2005, January 3-6). *Challenges of Adopting Web Services: Experiences from the Financial Industry*. Paper presented at the Hawaii International Conference on System Sciences (HICSS 38), Waikoloa, HI.

Ciganek, A. P., Haines, M. N., & Haseman, W. D. (2006, January 4-7). *Horizontal and Vertical Factors Influencing the Adoption of Web Services*. Paper presented at the Hawaii International Conference on System Sciences (HICSS 39), Kauai, HI.

Clemons, E. K., Reddi, S. P., & Row, M. C. (1993). The Impact of Information Technology on the Organization of Economic Activity: The "Move to the Middle" Hypothesis. *Journal of Management Information Systems, 10*(2), 9–35.

Clemons, E. K., & Row, M. (1988). McKesson Drug Company: A Case Study of Economost - A Strategic Information System. *Journal of Management Information Systems, 5*(1), 36–50.

Cohen, W. M., & Levinthal, D. A. (1990). Absorptive capacity: A new perspective on learning and innovation. *Administrative Science Quarterly, 35*(1), 128. doi:10.2307/2393553

Cooper, R., & Zmud, R. (1990). Information Technology Implementation Research: A Technological Diffusion Approach. *Management Science, 36*(2), 123–139. doi:10.1287/mnsc.36.2.123

Damsgaard, J., & Lyytinen, K. (2001). The Role of Intermediating Institutions in the Diffusion of Electronic Data Interchange (EDI): How Industry Associations Intervened in Denmark, Finland, and Hong Kong. *The Information Society, 17*(3), 195–210. doi:10.1080/01972240152493056

Damsgaard, J., & Truex, D. (2000). Binary Trading Relations and the Limits of EDI Standards: The Procrustean Bed of Standards. *European Journal of Information Systems, 9*(3), 173–188. doi:10.1057/palgrave/ejis/3000368

David, P. A., & Greenstein, S. (1990). The economics of compatibility standards: an introduction to recent research. *Economics of Innovation and New Technology, 1*, 3–41. doi:10.1080/10438599000000002

Davis, F. D. (1989). Perceived Usefulness, Ease of Use, and User Acceptance of Information Technology. *Management Information Systems Quarterly, 13*(3), 319–340. doi:10.2307/249008

Dedrick, J., & West, J. (2003, Dec 12-14). *Why Firms Adopt Open Source Platforms: A Grounded Theory of Innovation and Standard Adoption*. Paper presented at the International Conference on IS Special Workshop on Standard Making sponsored by MISQ, Seattle, WA.

Emerson, R. M. (1962). Power Dependence Relations. *American Sociological Review, 27*(1), 31–41. doi:10.2307/2089716

Ettlie, J. E. (1980). Adequacy of Stage Models for Decisions on Adoption of Innovation. *Psychological Reports, 46*(8), 991–995.

Evans, P. B., & Wurster, T. S. (1997, September/October). Strategy and the New Economics of Information. *Harvard Business Review, 75*, 70–82.

Farrell, J., & Saloner, G. (1985). Standardization, compatibility, and innovation. *The Rand Journal of Economics, 16*(1), 70–83. doi:10.2307/2555589

Farrell, J., & Saloner, G. (1988). Coordination Through Committees and Markets. *The Rand Journal of Economics, 19*(2), 235. doi:10.2307/2555702

Fichman, R. G. (1992). *Information Technology Diffusion: A Review of Empirical Research*. Paper presented at the 13th International Conference on Information Systems (ICIS), New York.

Fichman, R. G., & Kemerer, C. F. (1993). Adoption of Software Engineering Process Innovations: The Case of Object Orientation. *Sloan Management Review, 34*(2), 7–22.

Fichman, R. G., & Kemerer, C. F. (1994). *Toward a Theory of the Adoption and Diffusion of Software Process innovations*. Paper presented at the Diffusion, Transfer and Implementation of IT, Elsevier Sciences, North Holland.

Fichman, R. G., & Kemerer, C. F. (1997). The Assimilation of Software Process Innovations: An Organizational Learning Perspective. *Management Science, 43*(10), 1345–1363. doi:10.1287/mnsc.43.10.1345

Fichman, R. G., & Kemerer, C. F. (1999). The Illusory Diffusion of Innovation: An Examination of Assimilation Gaps. *Information Systems Research, 10*(3), 255–275. doi:10.1287/isre.10.3.255

Forman, C., & Gron, A. (2005, January 3-6). *Vertical Integration and Information Technology Adoption: A Study of the Insurance Industry*. Paper presented at the Hawaii International Conference on System Sciences (HICSS 38), Waikoloa, HI.

Gallagher, S., & Park, S. H. (2002). Innovation and Competition in Standard-Based Industries: A Historical Analysis of the U.S. Home Video Game Market. *IEEE Transactions on Engineering Management, 49*(1), 67–82. doi:10.1109/17.985749

Gerst, M., & Bunduchi, R. (2005). Shaping IT Standardization in the Automotive Industry - The Role of Power in Driving Portal Standardization. *Electronic Markets, 15*(4), 335–343. doi:10.1080/10196780500302872

Gogan, J. L. (2005). Punctuation and Path Dependence: Examining a Vertical IT Standard-Setting Process. *Electronic Markets, 15*(4), 344–354. doi:10.1080/10196780500302880

Gosain, S. (2003, Dec 12-14). *Realizing the Vision for Web Services: Strategies for Dealing with Imperfect Standards*. Paper presented at the International Conference on IS Special Workshop on Standard Making sponsored by MISQ, Seattle, WA.

Grover, V. (1993). An Empirically Derived Model for the Adoption of Customer-based Interorganizational Systems. *Decision Sciences, 24*(3), 603–640. doi:10.1111/j.1540-5915.1993.tb01295.x

Hills, B. (2000). Common message standards for electronic commerce in wholesale financial markets. *Bank of England Quarterly Bulletin, 40*(3), 274–285.

Iacovou, C. L., Benbasat, I., & Dexter, A. S. (1995). Electronic Data Interchange and Small Organizations: Adoption and Impact of Technology. *Management Information Systems Quarterly*, 465–484. doi:10.2307/249629

Johnson, R., & Vitale, M. (1988). Creating competitive advantage with interorganizational information systems. *Management Information Systems Quarterly, 12*(2), 153–165. doi:10.2307/248839

Joreskog, K. G., & Wold, H. (Eds.). (1982). *Systems Under Indirect Observation: Causality, Structure and Prediction*. Amsterdam: North-Holland.

Kauffman, R. J., McAndrews, J., & Wang, Y.-M. (2000). Opening the "Black Box" of Network Externalities in Network Adoption. *Information Systems Research, 11*(1), 61–82. doi:10.1287/isre.11.1.61.11783

Keil, T. (2002). De-facto Standardization Through Alliances - Lessons From Bluetooth. *Telecommunications Policy, 26*(3-4), 205–213. doi:10.1016/S0308-5961(02)00010-1

King, W. R., Grover, V., & Hufnagel, E. H. (1989). Using Information and Information Technology for Sustainable Competitive Advantage: Some Empirical Evidence. *Information & Management, 17*(2), 87–93. doi:10.1016/0378-7206(89)90010-4

Kowalski, V. J., & Karcher, B. (1994, Mar). Industry Consortia in Open Systems. *StandardView, 2*, 34–40. doi:10.1145/224145.224150

Lim, B. B. L., & Wen, H. J. (2002). The Impact of Next Generation XML. *Information Management & Computer Security, 10*(1), 33–40. doi:10.1108/09685220210417490

Lucy-Bouler, T., & Morgenstern, D. (2003, Dec 12-14). *Is Digital Medicine a Standards Nightmare?* Paper presented at the International Conference on IS Special Workshop on Standard Making sponsored by MISQ, Seattle, WA.

Lyytinen, K., & Damsgaard, J. (2001, April 7-10). *What's Wrong With the Diffusion of Innovation Theory: The Case of a Complex and Networked Technology.* Paper presented at the International Federation for Information Processing (IFIP), Banff, Alberta, Canada.

Lyytinen, K., & Fomin, V. (2002). Achieving high momentum in the evolution of wireless infastructures: the battle over the 1G solutions. *Telecommunications Policy, 26*(3-4), 149–170. doi:10.1016/S0308-5961(02)00006-X

Malone, T. W. (1987). Modeling Coordination in Organizations and Markets. *Management Science, 33*(10), 1317–1332. doi:10.1287/mnsc.33.10.1317

Malone, T. W., Yates, J., & Benjamin, R. I. (1987). Electronic Markets and Electronic Hierarchies. *Communications of the ACM, 30*(6), 484–497. doi:10.1145/214762.214766

Markovsky, B., Willer, D., & Patton, T. (1988). Power Relations in Exchange Networks. *American Sociological Review, 53*, 220–236. doi:10.2307/2095689

Markus, M. L. (1987). Toward a "Critical Mass" Theory of Interactive Media. *Communication Research, 14*(5), 491–511. doi:10.1177/009365087014005003

Markus, M. L., Steinfield, C. W., & Wigand, R. T. (2003, December 12-14). *The Evolution of Vertical IS Standards: Electronic Interchange Standards in the US Home Mortgage Industry.* Paper presented at the International Conference on IS Special Workshop on Standard Making sponsored by MISQ, Seattle, WA.

Mata, F. J., Fuerst, W. L., & Barney, J. B. (1995). Information Technology and Sustained Competitive Advantage: A Resource-Based Analysis. *Management Information Systems Quarterly, 19*(4), 487–505. doi:10.2307/249630

Mendoza, R. A., & Jahng, J. (2004). An Exploratory Study on Adoption of Complex Networked Technologies: The Case of the eXtensible Markup Language (XML) Specifications. *Seoul Journal of Business, 10*(2).

Mendoza, R. A., & Jahng, J. J. (2003, August). *Adoption of XML Specifications: An Exploratory Study of Industry Practices.* Paper presented at the Americas Conference on Information Systems (AMCIS), Tampa, FL.

Meyer, J., & Rowan, B. (1977). Institutionalized organizations: Formal structure as myth and ceremony. *American Journal of Sociology, 83*, 340–363. doi:10.1086/226550

Miralles, F., Sieber, S., & Valor, J. (2005, May). *CIO Herds and User Gangs in the Adoption of Open Source Software.* Paper presented at the Thirteenth European Conference on Information Systems (ECIS), Regensburg, Germany.

Mooney, J. G., Gurbaxani, V., & Kraemer, K. L. (1996). A Process Oriented Framework for Assessing the Business Value of Information Technology. *The Data Base for Advances in Information Systems, 27*(2), 68–81.

Moore, G. C., & Benbasat, I. (1991). Development of an Instrument to Measure the Perceptions of Adopting an Information Technology Innovation. *Information Systems Research, 2*(3), 192–222. doi:10.1287/isre.2.3.192

Nambisan, S., & Wang, Y.-M. (1999). Roadblocks to Web technology adoption? *Communications of the ACM, 42*(1), 98–101. doi:10.1145/291469.291482

Nelson, K. M., & Nelson, J. H. (2003, December 12-14). *The Need for a Strategic Ontology.* Paper presented at the International Conference on IS Special Workshop on Standard Making sponsored by MISQ, Seattle, WA.

Nelson, M. L., Shaw, M. J., & Qualls, W. (2005). Interorganizational System Standards Development in Vertical Industries. *Electronic Markets, 15*(4), 378–392. doi:10.1080/10196780500303045

Nickerson, J. V., & Muehlen, M. z. (2003, December 12-14). *Defending the Spirit of the Web: Conflict in the Internet Standards Process.* Paper presented at the International Conference on IS Special Workshop on Standard Making sponsored by MISQ, Seattle, WA.

Nunnally, J. C. (1978). *Psychometric Theory* (2nd ed.). New York: McGraw-Hill.

Porter, M. E., & Millar, V. E. (1985). How Information Gives you Competitive Advantage. *Harvard Business Review, 63*(4), 149.

Premkumar, G., Ramamurthy, K., & Crum, M. R. (1997). Determinants of EDI adoption in the transportation industry. *European Journal of Information Systems, 6*(2), 107–121. doi:10.1057/palgrave.ejis.3000260

Ramamurthy, K., Premkumar, G., & Crum, M. R. (1999). Organizational and interorganizational determinants of EDI diffusion and organizational performance: A Causal Model. *Journal of Organizational Computing and Electronic Commerce, 9*(4), 253–285. doi:10.1207/S153277440904_2

Ravichandran, T. (2005). Organizational Assimilation of Complex Technologies: An Empirical Study of Component-Based Software Development. *IEEE Transactions on Engineering Management, 52*(2), 249–268. doi:10.1109/TEM.2005.844925

Reimers, K., & Li, M. (2005). Antecedents of a Transaction Cost Theory of Vertical IS Standardization Processes. *Electronic Markets, 15*(4), 301–312. doi:10.1080/10196780500302740

Rogers, E. M. (1983). *Diffusion of Innovations* (3rd ed.). New York: The Free Press.

Schilling, M. (1998). Technological Lockout: An Integrative Model of the Economic and Strategic Factors Driving Technology Success and Failure. *Academy of Management Review, 23*(2), 267–284. doi:10.2307/259374

Schilling, M. A. (2002). Technology success and failure in winner-take-all markets: Testing a model of technological lock out. *Academy of Management Journal, 45*(2), 387–398. doi:10.2307/3069353

Son, J.-Y., Narasimhan, S., & Riggins, F. J. (1999, 1999). *Factors Affecting the Extent of Electronic Cooperation Between Firms: Economic and Sociological Perspectives.* Paper presented at the International Conference on Information Systems (ICIS).

Steinfield, C. W., Markus, M. L., & Wigand, R. T. (2005). Exploring interorganizational systems at the industry level of analysis: evidence from the US home mortgage industry. *Journal of Information Technology, 20*, 224–233. doi:10.1057/palgrave.jit.2000051

Steinfield, C. W., Wigand, R. T., Markus, M. L., & Minton, G. (2004, May 13-14). *Promoting e-Business Through Vertical IS Standards: Lessons from the US Home Mortgage Industry.* Paper presented at the Workshop on Standards and Public Policy. Federal Reserve Bank of Chicago, Chicago, IL.

Suchman, M. C. (1995). Managing Legitimacy: Strategic and Institutional Approaches. *Academy of Management Review, 20*(3), 571–610. doi:10.2307/258788

Sumner, M. (2000). Risk factors in enterprise-wide/ ERP projects. *Journal of Information Technology, 15*(4), 317–327. doi:10.1080/02683960010009079

Swanson, E. B. (1994). Information Systems Innovations Among Organizations. *Management Science, 40*(9), 1069–1091. doi:10.1287/mnsc.40.9.1069

Swanson, E. B., & Ramiller, N. C. (1993). Information Systems Research Thematics: Submissions to a New Journal. *Information Systems Research, 4*(4), 299–330. doi:10.1287/isre.4.4.299

Swanson, E. B., & Ramiller, N. C. (1997). The Organizing Vision in Information Systems Innovations. *Organization Science, 8*(5), 458–474. doi:10.1287/orsc.8.5.458

Swatman, P. M. C., Swatman, P. A., & Fowler, D. C. (1994). A model of EDI integration and strategic business reengineering. *The Journal of Strategic Information Systems, 3*(1), 41–60. doi:10.1016/0963-8687(94)90005-1

Tanriverdi, H. (2006). Performance Effects of Information Technology Synergies in Multibusiness Firms. *Management Information Systems Quarterly, 30*(1), 57–77.

Tornatzky, L. G., & Fleischer, M. (1990). *The Processes of Technology Innovation.* Lexington, MA: Lexington Books.

Tornatzky, L. G., & Klein, K. J. (1982). Innovation Characteristics and innovation Adoption-Implementation: A Meta Analysis of Findings. *IEEE Transactions on Engineering Management, EM-29*(1), 28–45.

Tornatzky, L. G., & Klein, K. J. (1982). Innovation Characteristics and innovation Adoption-Implementation: A Meta Analysis of Findings. *IEEE Transactions on Engineering Management, EM-29*(1), 28–45.

Wareham, J., Rai, A., & Pickering, G. (2005). Standardization in Vertical Industries: An Institutional Analysis of XML-Based Standards Infusion in Electricity Markets. *Electronic Markets, 15*(4), 323–334. doi:10.1080/10196780500302849

Weitzel, T., Beimborn, D., & Konig, W. (2006). A Unified Economic Model of Standard Diffusion: The Impact of Standardization Cost, Network Effects, and Network Topology. *Management Information Systems Quarterly, 30*, 489–514.

West, J. (2003, December 12-14). *The Role of Standards in the Creation and Use of Information Systems.* Paper presented at the International Conference on IS Special Workshop on Standard Making sponsored by MISQ, Seattle, WA.

Wigand, R. T., Picot, A., & Reichwald, R. (1997). *Information, organization and management: Expanding markets and corporate boundaries.* Chichester, England: Wiley.

Wigand, R. T., Steinfield, C. W., & Markus, M. L. (2005). Information Technology Standards Choices and Industry Structure Outcomes: The Case of the U.S. Home Mortgage Industry. *Journal of Management Information Systems, 22*(2), 165–191.

Wymer, S. A., & Regan, E. A. (2005). Factors Influencing e-commerce Adoption and Use by Small and Medium Businesses. *Electronic Markets, 15*(4), 438–453. doi:10.1080/10196780500303151

Zaheer, A., & Venkatraman, N. (1994). Determinants of Electronic Integration in the Insurance Industry: An Empirical Test. *Management Science, 40*(5), 549–566. doi:10.1287/mnsc.40.5.549

Zahra, S. A., & George, G. (2002). Absorptive Capacity: A Review, Reconceptualization, and Extension. *Academy of Management Review, 27*(2), 185. doi:10.2307/4134351

Zhao, K., Xia, M., & Shaw, M. J. (2005). Vertical E-Business Standards and Standards Developing Organizations: A Conceptual Framework. *Electronic Markets, 15*(4), 289–300. doi:10.1080/10196780500302690

Chapter 18
Toward UML–Compliant Semantic Web Services Development

Diana M. Sánchez
Rey Juan Carlos University, Spain

César J. Acuña
Rey Juan Carlos University, Spain

José María Cavero
Rey Juan Carlos University, Spain

Esperanza Marcos
Rey Juan Carlos University, Spain

ABSTRACT

The emerging Semantic Web and, in particular, Semantic Web services (SWS), demands the inclusion of new components in applications involving this technology. Therefore, Web development methodologies must be tailored to support the systematic development of such new components. In previous works we presented a UML profile, which extends the SOD-M method for service oriented Web Information System development of the MIDAS model-driven framework, to address the development of Semantic Web Services using WSMO (Web Service Modeling Ontology). The UML profile allows for the modeling of the new elements required by WSMO Web Services. This paper focuses on studying the possibility of improving the proposed UML profile, including the OCL (Object Constraint Language), for the representation of WSMO logical axioms through three case studies. This would allow developers, whose knowledge does not extend beyond UML, to develop applications that use Semantic Web services.

DOI: 10.4018/978-1-4666-1761-2.ch018

INTRODUCTION

Many different Web development methodologies have been proposed to address different aspects of Web application development since the Web appeared. These methodologies were later adapted with the evolution of the Web and its underlying technologies. For example, with Web services existing methodologies were modified to include new models of WSDL document generation (Lausen, de Brujin, Polleres, & Fensel, 2005), new models of service composition, and so on. Semantic Web Services (SWS) expand the capabilities of a Web service by associating a semantic description of the service in order to enable automatic search, discovery, selection, composition, and integration (Dimitrov, Simov, Momtchev, & Ognyanov, 2005). Semantic Web services technology demands the inclusion of new components in the applications involving them. Nevertheless, current Web development methodologies do not include specific techniques or models to develop the new elements required to build SWS-based applications. In general, SWS should be included in Web application development methodologies for several reasons. Most importantly: (a) to enable the systematic development of new required components and (b) to promote the widespread adoption of SWS. Unfortunately, for the average software developer, the learning curve for semantically rich languages, used to describe SWS, can be steep. This fact provides a barrier to the adoption and widespread use of such technologies (Gannod & Timm, 2004). To be widely adopted by users and to succeed in real-world applications, SWS development must be aligned with mainstream software trends such as Model Driven Architecture (Miller & Mukerji, 2001).

Based on the above reasons, in Acuña and Marcos (2006), we presented a UML profile for modeling the new elements required by SWS-based applications. This profile was developed as an extension of the SOD-M (Service Oriented Development Method) (De Castro, Marcos, & López, 2006) included in the MIDAS framework.

MIDAS is an MDA framework for Service-Oriented Web Information Systems Development. The motivation for that work was the lack of specific techniques and methodological approaches to develop SWS. Our proposal is developed within the MDA framework in order to reap the benefits that the framework already provides.

The first version of the SWS UML profile enables the modeling of SWS based on the WSMO (Web Services Modeling Ontology) proposal (Grønmo, Jaeger, & Hoff, 2005). In WSMO, a SWS description requires the definition of four basic components: ontologies, Semantic Web services, goals and mediators. As a consequence, the profile contains four models at a Platform Specific level, one for each WSMO modeling element. Starting from the UML models defined to model the SWS and generating the corresponding XMI description (Object Management Group, 2005), the WSML description of each element of WSMO could be generated through the implementation of mappings rules.

Although the UML profile enables the modeling of those four main elements, WSMO axioms were modeled by means of UML notes and using WSML code directly on the models. In this work we focus on the improvement of the UML profile with the aim of making Semantic Web services development fully UML-compliant. We propose to complete the profile by using the Object Constraint Language (OCL) (Object Management Group, 2006) for the representation of the WSMO axioms. Note that OCL is a language familiar to the average software developer. We analyze three case studies in which we have tried to convert an axiom, expressed in WSML, using OCL expressions.

The rest of the paper is structured as follows. The following section discusses related work and provides a background to this study. Definitions of concepts required in order to set up the context of this research are then provided. This is followed by a description of the three case studies. Finally, conclusions are presented along with directions for future research.

RELATED WORK

This section presents related work in the area of the development of Semantic Web services, more specifically the following focus will be placed on (1) tools for generating SWS and (2) methodological approaches for building SWS.

Tools for Generating Semantic Web Services

Tools for SWS represent the area with the greatest number of initiatives; however such initiatives tend to be limited to code generation. Examples of such tools include the Web Services Modeling Toolkit (WSMT) (Jaeger, Engel, & Geihs, 2005) and WSMO Studio (Dimitrov et al., 2005) for the automatic generation of Web services using WSML. There are also tools for the generation of the elements necessary to develop OWL-S based Web service representations. Examples of such tools include the OWL-S Editor (Elenius et al., 2005) and the OWL-S Editor II (Scicluna, Abela, & Montebello, 2004).

These tools use their own notation for modeling the different components of SWS and only develop one aspect of the applications. As they are ad-hoc tools concentrating exclusively on generating semantic descriptions in OWL-S or WSMO, they provide no way of integrating SWS development within a methodological framework.

UML for Semantic Web Services

As one of the most common modeling languages in software development, UML has been used in an attempt to contribute in the area of the development of Semantic Web services. Authors, such as Wang, He, He, and Qian (2006) and Grønmo et al. (2005), have investigated the benefits of building SWS in UML instead of using other complex semantic languages. Both proposals launch a UML profile for building SWS, however the starting point in both cases is OWL-S instead of WSMO.

They create mappings between OWL-S constructs and those UML elements required for modeling a specific SWS.

Timm and Gannod (2007) focused on Web service composition and proposed the use of UML and OCL for specifying this composition. The authors presented an MDA based approach for specifying SWS compositions through the use of a specific UML profile. This profile is used in transformations for building the OWL-S specifications from UML diagrams.

In relation to the e-business domain, Ha and Lee (2006) proposed the use of UML as a bridge between an ontology framework, represented in OWL, and a Web service, represented in WSDL. For improving the discovery service of a Web service, the authors created an ontology for relating a Web service to a UML model. The UML model is the middle layer that intermediates between OWL and WSDL enabling the communication between these two layers.

Methodological Approaches to the Development of Semantic Web Services

Proposals of methodologies for the systematic development of SWSs are limited due to the immature state of SWS technology. A few initiatives in this area are however worth mentioning.

Gannod and Timm (2004) propose a model-driven approach for administering and generating SWSs following the OWL-S proposal, with a set of UML extensions to represent different aspects of the SWSs so that, by applying transformation rules expressed in XSLT, the OWL-S code may be generated automatically. UML extensions made via profiles are used to facilitate the transformation process and stereotypes help to identify the classes to be generated as descriptions in OWL-S. The aims of Gannod and Timm (2004) are similar to those of our research, however while Gannod and Timm only look into the generation of semantic descriptions for Web services, our work aims to integrate the development of SWS with other aspects of a Web information system. Our intention is to provide a more comprehensive methodological framework allowing for the analysis and description of the relations of SWSs with other components of a Web information system along with the definition of the necessary interaction among various components.

Jaeger et al. (2005) present a three-step process for generating OWL-S specifications. The initial phase is the creation of templates using existing software artifacts (for example, software models and WSDL documents) followed by the automated identification of ontologies related to the Web services and, finally, Web services are classified according to these ontologies. This proposal is interesting as it seeks to define the OWL-S specifications of SWSs by means of applying transformation rules applied to other models of the system. It may therefore be considered as a model-driven approach.

PREVIOUS CONCEPTS

This section introduces some previous concepts required in order to frame this work. A brief presentation of SOD-M (a method for the service-oriented development of Web Information Systems) is provided followed by a description of WSMO, adopted here for semantically describing Web services. Subsequently the final subsection presents the UML profile for SWS modeling.

SOD-M: A Service Oriented Development Method

SOD-M is a method for the service oriented development of WIS. It follows a service oriented approach for the modeling and development of WIS. SOD-M provides a set of business and behavioral models at different levels of abstraction. SOD-M also provides a set of mapping rules to navigate between the different levels of abstrac-

tion. In this way, starting from a high-level business model, SOD-M allows us to obtain specific models for different services technologies (for example, Web services). The work presented in Acuña and Marcos (2006) and its improvement presented in this work intends to extend SOD-M for the inclusion of the SWS technology.

SOD-M is part of the MIDAS framework, which is an MDA framework for WIS development. SOD-M focuses on the behavioral aspect of the MIDAS framework, although MIDAS also manages other aspects of WIS modeling (De Castro, Marcos, & Cáceres, 2004; Marcos, Vela, & Cavero, 2003; Vela, Acuña, & Marcos, 2004).

WSMO: Web Service Modeling Ontology

WSMO is a Semantic Web services description proposal submitted to the W3C by DERI[1]. WSMO is an ontology for describing various aspects related to SWS. The conceptual grounding of WSMO (Grønmo et al., 2005) defines four main components:

1. **Ontologies:** are the key to linking conceptual real-world semantics defined and agreed upon by communities of users.
2. **Goals:** Goals are representations of an objective for which fulfillment is sought through the execution of a Web service.
3. **Web Services:** WSMO Web service descriptions consist of functional, non-functional and behavioral aspects of a Web service. A Web service is a computational entity which is able (by invocation) to achieve a user's objective. A service, in contrast, is the actual value provided by this invocation.
4. **Mediators:** describe elements that overcome interoperability problems between different WSMO elements. Mediators are the core concept to resolve incompatibilities on the data, process and protocol level, i.e. in order to resolve mismatches between differ-

ent terminologies used (data level), in the way communication occurs between Web services (protocol level) as well as in the way Web services (and goals) are combined (process level).

Within the WSMO proposal, the Web Service Modeling Language (WSML) aims at providing the means to formally describe all the elements defined in WSMO.

A UML Profile for Semantic Web Service Modeling

When modeling SWS with WSMO, the UML profile includes four models, one model for each of WSMO's main elements: Ontology Model, Web Service Model, Goal Model and Mediator Model. Figure 1 shows the relationship of such models with respect to the MDA four-layer metamodeling architecture. The Meta-Object Facility (MOF) (Scicluna et al., 2004) specification is used to specify the WSMO metamodel placed at the metamodel layer (M2). The metamodels of the four new models are placed at the same level. These metamodels refine the WSMO metamodel elements. The different metamodels allow the representation, through the M1 models, of all WSMO elements, with their own particularities.

In order to make use of UML's graphical modeling capabilities, each model has a corresponding UML Profile. These profiles support the UML notation and enable graphical editing of WSMO elements using UML diagrams. For reasons of clarity the UML profiles were not included in Figure 1 but belong to the M2 level of the metamodeling architecture. The instances of the defined models, that is, the concrete ontologies, goals, Web services and mediators, are placed at level M0.

From now on, as an example, we partially present the profile by introducing the Ontology Model, the idea is to use this model in order to show how it can be improved using the Object Constraint Language (OCL).

To model the WSMO ontologies we have decided to split its modeling into two related models: The *ontology context model* and the *ontology content model*s. This separation is due to WSML's ontology definition where we can clearly distinguish contextual information of ontologies from content information.

The *ontology context model*, extends the UML package diagram and collects information about the context of the ontology, that is to say, information about namespaces, imported ontologies and used mediators. Figure 2 shows the *Ontology context metamodel.*

The *ontology content model* represents the different elements of the modeled ontology: classes, properties, instances, axioms, etc. The *ontology content model* extends the UML class diagram. Figure 3 shows the corresponding metamodel.

In the ontology content meta-model the axioms were originally represented by UML class stereotyped with <<*Axiom*>> with the axiom definition as a tagged value of type string (see the dotted area in Figure 3). The axiom definition typically includes a portion of WSML code representing the axiom. In order to fill this tagged value for each axiom definition, the developer still needs to know about WSML in order to write the axiom definition, this is precisely the aspect we will try to solve in this work by using OCL to represent the axioms.

USING OCL TO REPRESENT WSMO AXIOMS

The aim of this section is to analyze if it is possible to complete the UML Profile by adding OCL as way to represent axioms. It is important to remind the reader that this profile is intended to be used by people who are familiar with the UML and want to use it to represent SWS. By using this profile, with the improvements discussed here, the developers whose knowledge does not extend

Figure 1. Model architecture for WSMO elements modeling

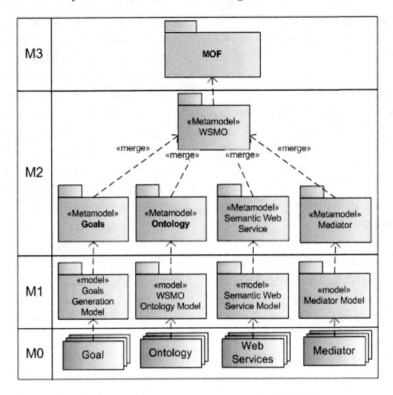

beyond UML should be able to develop applications that use Semantic Web services.

Axioms in WSMO are written in WSML (WSMO, n.d.) and they are used to specify a logical expression which helps to formalize one or several features of SWSs. WSML is a formal language created following the WSMO proposal in

order to define a syntax that enables one to define ontologies and Web services. WMSL has been developed taking as starting point three logical formalisms: Description Logics, First-Order Logic and Logic Programming; however this language has four variants. Each variant is based or extends a specific part of those formalisms. For example,

Figure 2. Ontology context meta-model

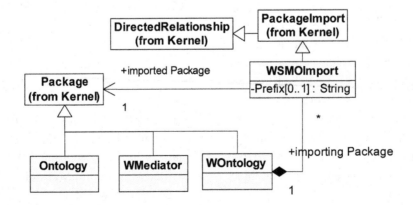

Figure 3. Ontology content meta-model

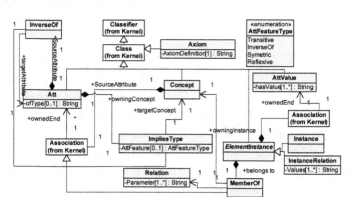

WSML-Core (the smallest version of WSML) is based on a part of Description Logic (a part of First-Order Logic) that describe types. The remaining versions of WSML extend the language from First-Order Logic or Logic Programming according to the desired level of expressiveness (WSMO, n.d.).

Axioms represent constraints which act over SWS elements and which must be satisfied. Axioms provide completeness to the SWS model and, in the scope of WSMO, they are typically used for: a) to restrict an attribute into a concept, b) to define or restrict the extension of a concept, c) to extend relations and define functions and d) to define preconditions, postconditions, assumptions and effects of a Web service capability. So, our proposal is to obtain a good and easy way to represent *these* axioms.

WSML is a formal language that has recently been developed. Developers require concrete solutions that allow them create SWS, therefore, the main requirement to on how to represent axioms is to be able to represent everything that can be represented using WSML.

The Object Constraint Language (OCL) has been created to complete the UML and provide it with improved expressive capabilities. Expressions written with OCL are used to specify invariant conditions that must hold for the system being modeled or queries over objects described in a model (Object Management Group, 2006).

Since OCL belongs to the UML family, OCL is quite easy to read and write. So, people without a strong mathematical o logical background are able to write constraints in OCL easier than in other formal logic-based languages. OCL is useful in the following cases: a) as a query language, b) to specify invariants on classes and types, c) to specify type invariant for stereotypes, d) to describe pre- and post conditions on operations and methods, e) to specify target (sets) for messages and actions, f) to specify constraints on operations, g) to specify derivation rules for attributes for any expression over a UML model.

The OCL is based on First-Order Logic and Set Theory. Therefore both languages, OCL and WSML, are linked to each other through First-Order Logic. Both have similar notations and are based on the same part of First-Order Logic to define their main elements: concepts in WSML and sets in the case of OCL.

If we compare the different uses listed for the axioms in WSMO and for OCL in UML we find some equivalence between them, so it is possible to think that OCL is a suitable manner to express axioms in our profile. However, in order to check the suitability of OCL to express all aspects that could be expressed in WSML, we propose to analyze some case studies. These case studies have been chosen taking into account the different uses given to the axioms in WSMO. So three WSML codes are studied and an attempt is made to convert these to OCL code. These case studies help us to know if it is possible to use OCL to represent WSML axioms.

Case Studies

The following case study scenarios have been classified according to the role and the function of an axiom in the Ontology Model: axioms that define or restrict a concept, axioms that specify a relation or function between concepts and axioms that define capabilities.

The starting point for each case study is WSML code in which axioms are declared. Next, the UML Profile presented previously is applied to represent the concepts and attributes. Finally we translate the axioms expressed in WSML to OCL, preserving their meaning. Case studies were obtained from the WSMO Primer (WSMO, 2005), a document written by WMSL creators that presents WSMO and some examples about this proposal. We chose these examples because we consider the book as a reliable source for WSML examples. Each case study is introduced by a brief explanation of the scenario and of the axioms. Then, the WSML code and its translation into OCL are shown.

Case 1: Axioms that Define or Restrict a Concept

Here, the axiom is used to explicitly express the meaning of a concept. This scenario represents a concept called *tripFromAustria*, which is a sub-concept of the *trip* concept. The *trip* concept is composed of four attributes: origin and destination (of type *location*), and arrival and departure (of type *date*). The *location* type is defined in an external ontology that is referenced by the *loc* expression. Here, the way to specify the features that describe the new concept is through an axiom that specifies particular conditions of the concept. The WSML code and its conversion to OCL code is shown in Figure 4.

Case 2: Axioms that Specify a Relation or a Function

In this case, the logical expression contained in the axiom expresses a relation. A relation describes interrelation between a set of parameters while a function is a special kind of relation where one parameter returns the result of a function (WSMO, 2005). The example presents the rela-

Figure 4. An axiom that specifies a new concept

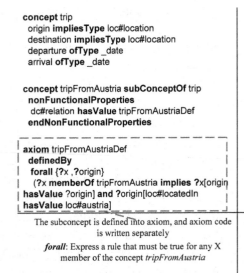
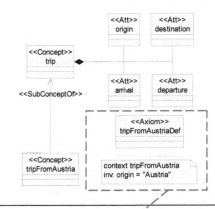

The subconcept is defined into axiom, and axiom code is written separately

forall: Express a rule that must be true for any X member of the concept *tripFromAustria*

The OCL code must be associated to an element of the model and an Axiom element. The code is written by means of a note

inv: express a condition that must be true into its context (in this case *tripFromAustria*)

Figure 5. An axiom that is used to specify a relation

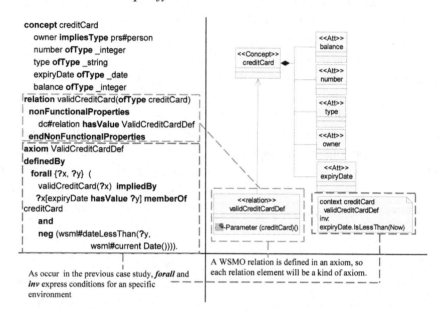

tion *validCreditCard* that is applied on the *credit card* concept. A credit card is considered valid up to its expiry date.

In this case, the OCL code is not associated to an *<<Axiom>>* element, but to a *<<relation>>* element. The WSMO proposal defines relations in terms of logical expressions, so a relation is a kind of axiom that describes interrelation between a set of parameters. WSML allows two ways to write the code of a relation: a) inside the definition of a relation or b) in an axiom defined outside of the relation definition, but that is associated to the relation. In this case the axiom is defined outside of the relation. The WSML code and its equivalence in our profile using OCL are shown in Figure 5.

Case 3: Axioms that Define Capabilities

Another use of axioms is to define capabilities. Capabilities describe the functionality of SWS in terms of preconditions, postconditions, assumptions and effects (WSMO, 2005). This case shows the capability to book a ticket where all parts of a capability are showed. In WSML, the first part of a capability is the definition of variables, the second part specifies preconditions, then assump-

tions and finally postconditions. In this case we analyze each part separately. At the end of the case we show all parts together.

The first part of capability shows the definition of five variables; these variables are used in the *precondition* to validate the integrity of information as it is shown in the description tag of the WSML code:

```
capability BookTicketCapability
sharedVariables { ?creditCard, ?ini-
tialBalance, ?trip, ?reservationHold-
er, ?ticket}
precondition
        definedBy
            ?reservationRequest [res-
ervationItem hasValue ?trip,  reser-
vationHolder hasValue ?reservation-
Holder
        ] memberOf
tr#reservationRequest   and ?trip
memberOf tr#tripFromAustria
and ?creditCard [balance has-
Value ?initialBalance] memberOf
po#creditCard.
```

This WSML code shows that three attributes of the concept *reservationRequest* and one attribute of the concept *creditCard* must have a valid value. In OCL, the initialization of a variable is done by an ***init*** expression and the specification of a set of preconditions is done using the ***pre*** expression. Here, the preconditions cover the validation of valid values for some attributes. An equivalent OCL code to represent this precondition is as follows:

```
context r: reservation::bookTicket(
iB:Integer, rH:String, t: trip, k:
ticket)
init: self.reservationRequest.reser-
vationItem = t
init: self.reservationRequest.reser-
vationHolder= rH
init: self.creditCard.balance = iB;
pre: c.balance <> `'" and t <> `' and
rH <> `'
```

On the basis of the WSML code the next section is the *assumption* part, in which conditions that must be true are specified and they must be known before starting the execution of the capability. In this example, the credit card presented by a requester must be one of two possible cards:

```
assumption
definedBy
po#validCreditCard(?creditCard) and
(?creditCard[type hasValue "Plas-
ticBuy"]
or ?creditCard[type hasValue "Golden-
Card"]).
```

As with cases 1 and 2, a condition that must be true can be written in OCL using an ***inv*** (invariant) expression. So, this assumption can be re-written in OCL as:

```
inv: self.creditCard.validCredit-
Card() and
```

```
(self.creditCard.type = 'Plas-
ticBuy' or self.creditCard.c.type =
'GoldenCard')
```

The next parts of the WSML code are the *postcondition* and the *effect*. Postconditions show the result of the execution of the SWS. In our case, postconditions tell us that a reservation has correct information and a reservation holder is created. The effect is that the price of a ticket is deducted from the credit card. The WSML code for the postcondition and effect parts is as follows:

```
postcondition
definedBy
?reservation memberOf tr#reservation
[ reservationItem hasValue ?ticket,
reservationHolder hasValue ?reserva-
tionHolder] and ?ticket[trip hasValue
?trip] memberOf tr#ticket.
effect
definedBy
ticketPrice(?ticket, "euro", ?ticket-
Price) and ?finalBalance= (?initial-
Balance - ?ticketPrice)
and ?creditCard[po#balance hasValue
?finalBalance ] .
```

Postconditions are expressed in OCL using the ***post*** expression. This block must always be at the end of the code. On the other hand, the *effect* block describes actions that change the state of some elements, so it is possible to group these actions in a ***body*** block in OCL. So, taking into account that the order of blocks must be changed for language specifications, this code could be re-written in OCL as follows:

```
body: c.initialBalance =
c.initialBalance - tk.ticketPrice
post:self.reservationItem = k and
self.reservationHolder = rH and self.
ticket.trip = t
```

Figure 6. Axioms to specify the capability of a SWS

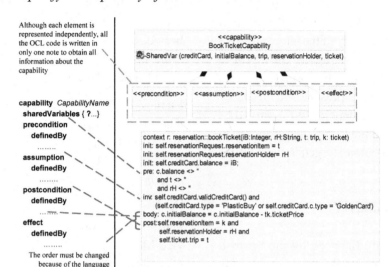

Figure 6 shows a complete representation of how this capability can be represented in our profile. The left side shows general parts of WSML code to specify the capability; however the dots of each section can be replaced by the WSML code presented in this case. The right side shows the representation of the capability using our profile. As in case 2, the OCL code is not associated to an <<Axiom>> element specifically. Instead the code is associated to *precondition*, *assumption*, *postcondition* and *effect* elements since in WSML all axioms that define these elements are written into each one.

Taking into account that the previous case studies represent the common uses of axioms in WSMO, we can conclude that there is a wide set of cases in which OCL can be used to define axioms as in WSMO without the loss of expressivity and maintaining the semantics of the restriction.

CONCLUSION AND FUTURE WORK

Applications involving Semantic Web service technology require the inclusion of new components. Therefore, Web development methodolo-gies must be tailored to support the systematic development of such new components. In previous works we presented a UML profile, which extends the SOD-M of the MIDAS model-driven framework to address the development of Semantic Web services using WSMO (Web Service Modeling Ontology). The UML profile allows for the modeling of the new elements required by WSMO Web Services.

In this paper we have focused on the study of OCL as a tool to refine such UML profile in order to represent the axiom definition using a language closer to the perspective of software developers as opposed to WSML. As part of the UML family, we consider OCL to be a good choice as a means to represent logical expressions.

The adoption of OCL for the representation of WSMO axioms has been validated through several case studies. The selected case studies represent different uses of the axioms. For each case the conversion to OCL was possible in a straightforward manner. As a result of this study we have concluded that there is a wide set of cases in which it is possible to write WMSO axioms using OCL and without having in depth knowledge of WMSL rules.

In terms of future research we will attempt to build a correspondence between WSML and OCL through a formal study of the languages. We are also working on integrating the UML profile for SWS development and the correspondences between OCL and WSML presented in this paper in M2DAT (Timm & Ginnon, 2007), an MDA tool that integrates all the techniques proposed in MIDAS for the semi-automatic generation of WIS.

ACKNOWLEDGMENT

This work is partially financed by the Spanish Ministry of Education and Science under the project MODEL CAOS (TIN2008-03582) and by the Spanish project "Agreement Technologies" (CONSOLIDER CSD2007-0022, INGENIO 2010)

REFERENCES

Acuña, C., & Marcos, E. (2006). Modeling Semantic Web Services: A Case Study. In D. Wolber, N. Calder, C. Brooks, & A. Ginije (Ed.), *Proceedings of the 6th International Conference on Web Engineering* (pp 32-39). ACM Publishing.

De Castro, V., Marcos, E., & Cáceres, P. (2004). A User Service Oriented Method to Model Web Information Systems. In X. Zhou et al. (Eds.), *Proceedings of the Web Information System Engineering Conference 2004 (WISE 2004)* (LNCS 3306, pp. 41-52).

De Castro, V., Marcos, E., & López, M. (2006). A model driven method for service composition modelling: A case study. *International Journal of Web Engineering and Technology*, *2*(4), 335–353. doi:10.1504/IJWET.2006.010419

Dimitrov, M., Simov, A., Momtchev, V., & Ognyanov, D. (2005). WSMO Studio - An Integrated Service Environment for WSMO. In *Proceedings of the WIW 2005 Workshop on WSMO Implementations*. Retrieved from http://www.wsmostudio.org

Elenius, D., Denker, G., Martin, D., Gilham, F., Khouri, J., Sadaati, S., et al. (2005, May). The owl-s editor - a development tool for Semantic Web services. In *Proceedings of the Second European Semantic Web Conference* (LNCS 3532, pp. 78-92)

Fensel, D., & Bussler, C. (2002). The Web Service Modeling Framework WSMF. *Electronic Commerce Research and Applications*, *1*(2). doi:10.1016/S1567-4223(02)00015-7

Gannod, G., & Timm, J. (2004). *An MDA-based Approach for Facilitating Adoption of Semantic Web Service*. Paper presented at the IEEE EDOC Workshop on Model-Driven Semantic Web (MDSW 04).

Grønmo, R., Jaeger, M. C., & Hoff, H. (2005). Transformations between UML and OWL-S. In *Model Driven Architecture – Foundations and Applications* (LNCS 3748, pp. 269-283).

Ha, Y., & Lee, R. (2006, June 19-20). Semantic Web Service Modeling using UML for e-business environment. In *Proceedings of the Seventh ACIS International Conference on Software Engineering, Artificial Intelligence, Networking, and Parallel/Distributed Computing (SNPD '06)* (pp. 368-374).

Jaeger, M., Engel, L., & Geihs, K. (2005). *A methodology for developing owl-s descriptions*. Paper presented at the First International Conference on Interoperability of Enterprise Software and Applications Workshop on Web Services and Interoperability.

Kerrigan, M. D9.1v0.1 Web Service Modeling Toolkit (WSMT). Working Draft Retrieved from: http://www.wsmo.org/TR/d9/d9.1/v0.1/20050127/, 2005

Lausen, H., de Brujin, J., Polleres, A., & Fensel, D. (2005, April). WSML - a Language Framework for Semantic Web Services. In *Proceedings of the W3C Rules Workshop,* Washington DC. Retrieved from http://www.w3.org/2004/12/rules-ws/paper/44/

Lausen, H., Polleres, A., & Roman, D. (Eds.). (2005). *Web Service Modeling Ontology Submission.* Retrieved from http://www.w3.org/Submission/WSMO/

Marcos, E., Vela, B., & Cavero, J. M. (2003). Methodological Approach for Object-Relational Database Design using UML. *Journal on Software and Systems Modeling, 2,* 59–72. doi:10.1007/s10270-002-0001-y

Miller, J., & Mukerji, J. (Eds.). (2001). *OMG Model Driven Architecture* (Document No. ormsc/2001-07-01). Retrieved from http://www.omg.com/mda

Object Management Group (OMG). (2002). *Meta-Object Facility, version 1.4.* Retrieved from http://omg.org/technology/documents/formal/mof.htm

Object Management Group (OMG). (2005). *XML Metadata Interchange (XMI).* Retrieved from http://ww.omg.org/technology/documents/formal/xmi.htm

Object Management Group (OMG). (2006). *OCL 2.0 Specification.* Retrieved from http://www.omg.org/docs/ptc/05-06-06.pdf

Scicluna, J., Abela, C., & Montebello, M. (2004, October). *Visual modeling of owl-s services.* Paper presented at the IADIS International Conference on WWW/Internet.

Timm, J. T. E., & Gannod, G. C. (2007, July 9-13). Specifying Semantic Web Service Compositions using UML and OCL. In *Proceedings of the IEEE International Conference on Web Services (ICWS'07)* (pp. 521-528).

Vara, J. M., De Castro, V., & Marcos, E. (2005). WSDL automatic generation from UML models in a MDA framework. *International Journal of Web Services Practices, 1*(1-2), 1–12.

Vela, B., Acuña, C., & Marcos, E. (2004). A Model Driven Approach for XML Database Development. In *Proceedings of the 23rd International Conference on Conceptual Modeling (ER2004)* (LNCS 3288, pp. 780-794).

Wang, C., He, K., He, Y., & Qian, W. (2006). Mappings from OWL-s to UML for Semantic Web Services. *Research and Practical Issues of Enterprise Information Systems, 205,* 397-406. ISBN: 1571-5736. WSMO. (n.d.). *WSML Final Draft 5. DERI.* Retrieved from http://www.wsmo.org/TR/d16/d16.1/v0.21/#sec:wsml-xml

WSMO. (2005). *WSMO Primer.* Retrieved from http://www.wsmo.org/TR/d3/d3.1/v0.1/

ENDNOTE

[1]   Digital Enterprise Research Institute. http://www.deri.org

This work was previously published in International Journal of Enterprise Information Systems, edited by Madjid Tavana, pp. 44-56, Volume 6, Issue 1, copyright 2010 by IGI Publishing (an imprint of IGI Global).

Chapter 19
Integrating Web Portals with Semantic Web Services:
A Case Study

César J. Acuña
Rey Juan Carlos University, Spain

Mariano Minoli
Rey Juan Carlos University, Spain

Esperanza Marcos
Rey Juan Carlos University, Spain

ABSTRACT

Several systems integration proposals have been suggested over the years. However these proposals have mainly focused on data integration, not allowing users to take advantage of services offered by Web portals. Most of the mentioned proposals only provide a set of design principles to build integrated systems and lack in suggesting a systematic way of how to develop systems based on the integration architecture they propose. In previous work we have developed PISA (Web Portal Integration Architecture)—a Web portal integration architecture for data and services—and MIDAS-S, a methodological approach for the development of integrated Web portals, built according to PISA. This work shows, by means of a case study, how both proposals fit together integrating Web portals.

INTRODUCTION

The World Wide Web (or just Web) is now the most popular information source. Besides well-known sources such as static and dynamic Web portals, digital libraries, etc., there are a large number of Web portals that offer users not only data, but

services like bookstores or theatre and flight ticket booking in addition. These services must also be considered as part of any integration efforts. Current integration proposals, however, do not allow users to take advantage of services offered by Web portals. Traditional integration proposals, based on materialized approaches or mediation schemas, have focused on just data integration (see Acuña, Gómez, Marcos, & Bussler, 2005;

DOI: 10.4018/978-1-4666-1761-2.ch019

Collet, Huhns, & Shen, 1991; Eyal & Milo, 2001; Mena, Kashyap, Sheth, & Illarramendi, 1996). Some implementations in these works only focus on querying the data available on Web portals and mostly ignore operational aspects offered by Web portals. Moreover, most of the noted proposals only provide a set of design principles to build integration systems and lack in providing a systematic way for building such integrated systems using the architecture they propose.

In previous work, we have presented a complete proposal for integration-oriented Web portal development. This proposal includes both a generic software architecture for the Web portal integration called PISA (Web Portal Integration Architecture) (Acuña, Gómez, Marcos, & Bussler, 2005) and a set of software engineering techniques for the development of integration-oriented Web portals based on the PISA proposal, called MIDAS-S (Acuña & Marcos, 2006).

PISA is a software architecture which defines the main components needed to build integration-oriented Web portals. This architecture takes into account not only data, but also the behaviour offered by Web portals. PISA was defined following a Model-Driven Architecture (MDA) approach (Miller & Mukerji, 2001) as described in Marcos et al. (2006). In that work, a PISA Platform Independent Model (PIM) represents those abstract components required by any integration-oriented system from a conceptual point of view: The PISA Platform Specific Model (PSM) is an instance of PISA-PIM using a specific platform. In the case study developed in this paper, PISA-PSM uses Semantic Web Services technology implemented using the Web Services Modeling Ontology (WSMO) proposal.

MIDAS-S complements prior work on PISA by providing a set of software engineering techniques to ease the development of an integration-oriented Web portal, built using PISA. In turn, MIDAS-S is based on the MIDAS framework (Cáceres, Marcos, & Vela, 2003), which is an MDA framework for Web information systems development that allows the development of integration-oriented Web portals. MIDAS-S adds a semantic aspect to MIDAS and uses two orthogonal dimensions. First, MIDAS-S gauges the platform dependence degree (following a MDA approach) and specifies the whole system by Computation Independent Models (CIMs), Platform Independent Models (PIMs) and Platform Specific Models (PSMs). Second, MIDAS-S models the system according to three basic aspects—hypertext, content and behavior. In addition, MIDAS-S uses the UML as the only notation for modeling both PIMs and PSMs.

At the PIM level of MIDAS-S, techniques and models proposed by a Service Oriented Development Method (SOD-M) (De Castro, Marcos, & López Sanz, 2006) have been followed to develop the behavioural aspect. A Hypertext Modeling Method or MIDAS (HM[3]) (Cáceres, De Castro, & Marcos, 2004) was used for the development of Hypertext.

This paper demonstrates how PISA and MIDAS-S fit together to develop integration-oriented Web portals via a case study. In achieving this aim the paper is structured as follows. The following section describes case study, which brings together Web portals employed by Madrid City Hall. Subsequently the main components of the PISA architecture are described. The integrated Web portal development process is then presented in detail. Finally the main conclusions are drawn and directions for future work discussed.

CASE STUDY STATEMENT: INTEGRATING MADRID CITY HALLS WEB PORTALS

Madrid City Hall offers a number of Web Portals containing information about the city, its various Government departments and cultural offerings. The purpose of the integration approach here, therefore, is developing a tool that provides users with the capability of searching across the different City Hall Web portals and booking of theatre play tickets without needing to have the knowledge of or interacting with those Web portals. The essence of the case study is captured in the following scenario:

Imagine a person who lives in the south of Madrid, Spain. This person is interested in enquiring about the cultural events scheduled for the coming weeks in different cities in his area. On one hand, each local government in Madrid has its own Web portal, formed by a set of HTML pages which offer information about the cultural events (cinema sessions, theatre performances, etc), among others. On the other hand there are specialized portals which offer theatre ticket purchase services.

To attend to a specific cultural event, this person must (a) access each local government Web portal to retrieve information about cultural events and (b) look for another Web portal which offers a theatre ticket sale service. Consequently, it is clear that it would be benficial for the user to interact with an integrated Web portal that offers information for several cities, alongside the possibility of purchasing tickets for any plays of interest.

It is of importance that the integration problem remains hidden to users. Note that in this case study, integration of services and data are combined. On the one hand city hall portals offer cultural events information (data); on the other, the ticket sale service is offered by other specialized portals.

CASE STUDY ARCHITECTURE IN PISA

This section describes case study architecture using PISA, which is an architectural model defining the main components required by an integration-oriented system. PISA has been defined following the MDA, so it achieves the benefits of an MDA approach (see Marcos, Acuña, & Cuesta,

2006). First, an architectural model at PIM level called PISA-PIM is defined. Services involved in PISA-PIM can be split into two groups: *Core Services Group* composed of mandatory services to achieve integration; and *Access Services Group*, composed of *external* services used to wrap the data or services in the Web portals.

Integration components can be implemented by different technologies depending on specific needs, available technologies, etc. Starting from PISA-PIM, multiple architectural models can be obtained according to chosen platform. In this work, the decision was taken to implement the architecture by means of Semantic Web Services (SWS) following the Web Services Modeling Ontology (WSMO) approach (Bruijn, Bussler, Domingue, & Fensel, 2005).

The resulting architecture is shown in Figure 1. Note that the integration level is implemented using the Web Services Execution Environment (WSMX), which is an execution environment for semantic Web services provided by WSMO. In broad terms this architecture works as follows, A User Interface (UI) creates a requirement and translates it into a WSML message consisting of a goal that describes what WSMX should execute. The goal is then sent to WSMX for execution. Before WSMX can execute the goal, however, WSML descriptions of the Web services offering the capability that matches the service requirement, the ontologies these Web services use, and the source format ontology must have been created and compiled to WSMX. When WSMX receives the WSML message with a specific goal, it discovers the WS that best matches that goal, mediates the service requirement data using mapping rules between the source format ontology and the ontology of the discovered Web service, and finally invokes it, providing the data to it in the concepts and formats it expects.

Development has been guided by MIDAS-S, which accounts for the PISA-PSM model. The tasks addressed were:

Figure 1. PISA architecture for study case

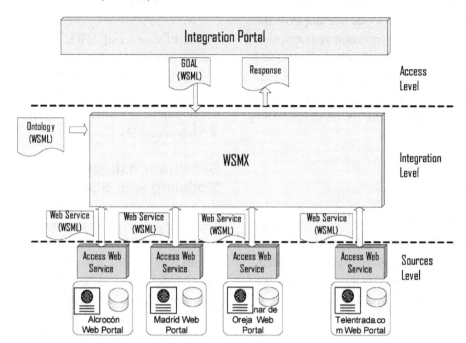

1. **Selection of Web Portals to integrate:** This aspect includes the task of selecting which City Hall portals to integrate. Two Web Portals corresponding to Madrid and Colmenar de Oreja City Halls were selected on the basis of the amount of information they offered (about the city in general, the government, etc). For reference, both portals are almost totally static sites. A focus placed on the information provided by the Cultural Council and, in particular, that in the cultural events section. A ticket sales Web portal called Telentrada.com was also taken into account for the integration Web portal, which specialises in cultural events. Although this site has been developed for human interaction, our Access Services provides adequate interfaces that allow the integration portal to use it services.

2. **Access services construction:** Several Web services were developed in order to expose the existing portal services. As part of this task, WSMX ontologies, goals and service descriptions were developed and the semantic aspects are described later herein. Details about *how* those Web Services were developed are omitted for reasons of space.

Figure 2. Business process model

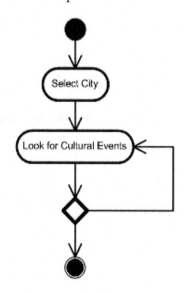

3. **Integration Portal development:** The Web portal was developed starting from the services requiring integration. A description of the MIDAS-S modelling techniques used to model the integration portal behaviour and hypertext aspects are described below. Detail at the PSM level are out of the scope of this paper.

MIDAS-S CIM

At the CIM-level of MIDAS-S, two models may be developed using SOD-M (De Castro, Marcos, & López Sanz, 2006), covering value and business process repectively. For this case study we have used the Business Process Model, which is now discussed.

Business Process Modeling with SOD-M

The business process model uses UML Action-State figures to expose high-level *business services*. Illustrated in Figure 2, these business services allow the user to select a city and them look for cultural events in that city. This process continues until the desired event is found.

MIDAS-S PIM

At the PIM-level of MIDAS-S, techniques and models proposed by SOD-M (De Castro, Marcos, & López Sanz, 2006) were followed to develop the behavioural aspect. HM³ was used for the development of Hypertext (Cáceres, De Castro, & Marcos, 2004).

Behaviour Aspect Modeling with SOD-M

The behavioural analysis starts from business models at the PIM-level, which are omitted here. Figure 3 shows the Integration Web Portal Use Case Model. In this model, the Integration Portal user is represented as an actor alongside the business services offered by portal.

The Use Case Model is extended with other functionality required to achieve the business services. Figure 4 shows the extended Use Case model for the "Look for Cultural Events" Use Case, both cases have been stereotyped with <<BS>> which means they are Basic Uses Cases (not Composed ones). In the following sections, only models related to "Look for Cultural Events" use case have been included.

Once required functionality has been identified, the service process model is used to represent the work flow (see Figure 5).

Figure 6 illustrates the Service Composition Model for "Look for Cultural Events". In this

Figure 3. Integration Web portal use case model

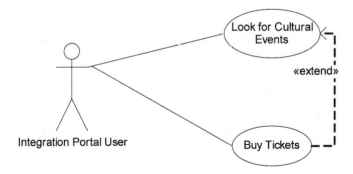

Figure 4. Extended use case model "look for cultural events"

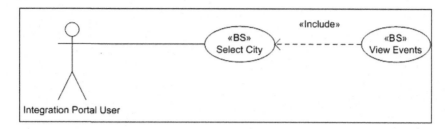

Figure 5. Service process model for "look for cultural events"

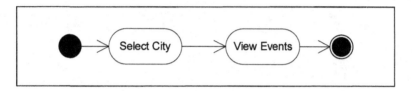

Figure 6. Service composition model for "look for cultural events" business service

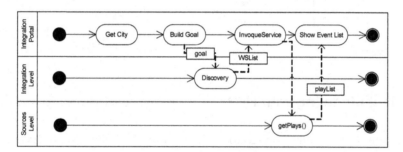

Figure 7. Extended service composition model for "look for cultural events"

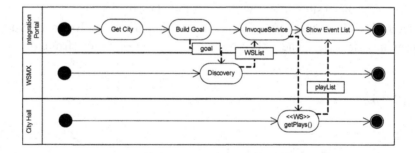

model, two collaborators have been identified. Those collaborators represent two different levels in PISA-PIM levels.

An extended service composition model is then developed, which allows the representation of Web Services platform specific details. Figure 7 shows the Extended Service composition model for "Look for Cultural Events" and actions that will be implemented as Web Services have been identified.

Figure 8. Extended use case model for business service "look for cultural events"

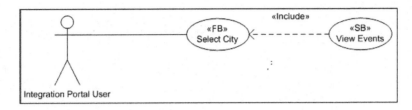

Figure 9. Extended navigation model for the integration Web portal

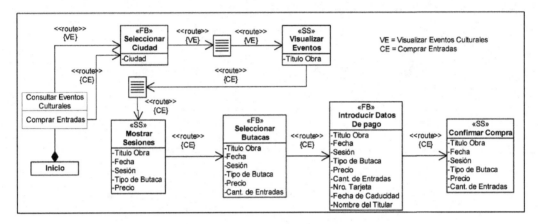

Hypertext Aspect Modeling with HM³

The HM³ method is used to obtain a Navigation Model (see Cáceres, De Castro, & Marcos, 2004). In Figure 8 an extended Use Case model for the business service "Look for Cultural Events" is presented. Use cases have been stereotyped with <<SB>> for Structural Use Cases, where functionality is only to provide a data view, and <<FB>> for Functional Use Case when interaction with the user is needed.

Figure 9 shows an Extended Navigation Model for the Integration Web Portal, where the part corresponding to the "Look for Cultural Event" business services is highlighted by the dotted oval.

This model (an Extended Slice) is created by adding information from the Service Process

Figure 10. MIDAS-S framework

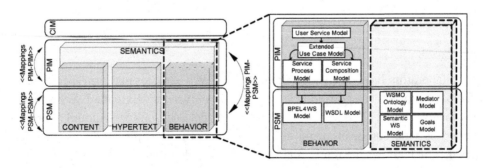

Figure 11. Ontology context model for theatre tickets ontology

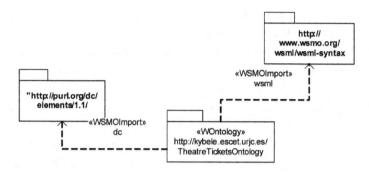

Model (in order to obtain routes), and from the Conceptual Data Model (in order to obtain attributes). The Extended Navigation Model is obtained by adding navigational structures like menus and guided tours.

MIDAS-S PSM

At the PSM-level, MIDAS-S has been used to model semantic descriptions of Access Services. In defining the semantic aspect MIDAS-S adds new elements (see Acuña & Marcos, 2006 for full details). Note that semantics aspect of MIDAS-S is encompassing in that it covers all of the aspects

previously considered in MIDAS – primarily because it is desirable to add semantics to any aspect when needed. Figure 10 shows how semantic elements fit together in MIDAS-S Framework and the process of modelling the semantic aspects of the Web Integration Portal with MIDAS-S is now considered.

Semantic Aspect Modeling with MIDAS-S

In order to semantically describe Web services used as Access Services by the Web Integration Portal, semantic elements have been created such as ontologies, service descriptions and goals. In

Figure 12. Ontology content model for theatre tickets ontology

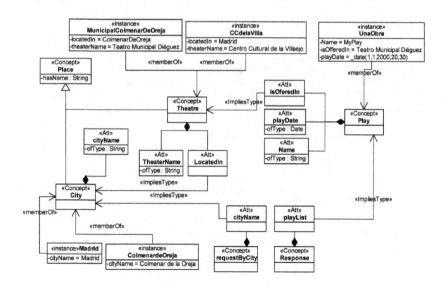

MIDAS-S, these elements are described using UML Profiles. Figure 11 shows the Ontology Context Model for Theatre Tickets Ontology (demonstrating the use of namespaces for import).

Figure 12 shows the Ontology Content Model for Theatre Tickets Ontology. In this model, concepts are defined alongside their attributes and instances.

Semantic Web Services are thus Web Services extended via semantic description. As an example, Figure 12 shows the semantic description for *getplays()* method. This method is used to get a play list.

Figure 13 illustrates the Context Model (top) and Content Model (bottom) for the Web service. The Content Model has a *capability* governed by a precondition to receive a request by city (*?request*) and a post condition defined through the *Response* concept.

Goals are last elements developed and represent an objective for which fulfilment is sought through the execution of a Web service. Figure 14 shows the generic structure of goals used by Integration Web Portal. This generic structure is used by replacing *?theCity* variable, which allows the discovery of all services that are able to retrieve

Figure 13. Web service context and content model

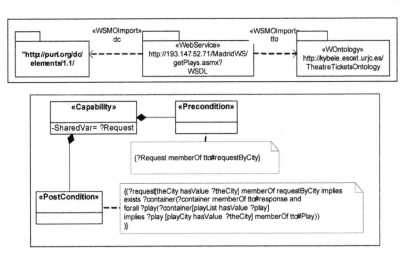

Figure 14. Context and content model for generic goal

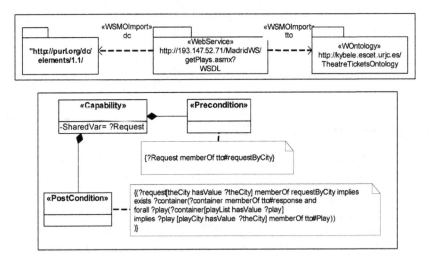

a list of plays located in a particular City by referencing a concept instance.

Finished semantic descriptions are loaded into WSMX repository. The next step in construction of Web integration portal is coding the Web pages that interact with users and invocate the corresponding Web services. The resulting Web portal thus integrates information and services from various sites by making semantic searches and invoking different Web services.

CONCLUSION AND FUTURE WORK

This work has presented the development process for an integration-oriented Web portal that builds on prior technology and methodological developments (ie.e., MIDAS, PISA, SOD-M and HM³). PISA and MIDAS form a complete proposal for Web portal integration: PISA sets up design principles to develop integration Web portals, defining a set of components to achieve the integration; MIDAS provides a set of techniques, especially MIDAS-S, to systematically build integration Web portals based on PISA. This work has shown, by means of a case study, how both proposals combine to develop a Web portal to integrate information from several City Hall Web portals. For PISA implementation at PSM-level, semantic Web services have been used. As part of the future work, we are developing more integration Web portals, in order to refine and validate in depth our proposal.

ACKNOWLEDGMENT

This work is partially founded by the following research projects: GOLD (TIN 2005-0010) financed by the Spanish Ministry of Education and Sciences; Agreement Technologies" (CONSOLIDER CSD2007-0022, IN-GENIO 2010), and FOMDAS (URJC-CM-2006-CET-0387) financed by the Rey Juan Carlos University and the Local Government of Madrid. We also want to thank Elisa Herrmann for it valuable help in the last minute English revision of this work.

REFERENCES

Acuña, C., Gómez, J. M., Marcos, E., & Bussler, C. (2005). Towards Web Portal Inte-gration through Semantic Web Services. In D. Wolber, N. Calder, C. Brooks, & A. Ginige (Ed.), *Proceedings of the International Conference on Next Generation Web Services Practices (NWeSP '05)* (pp. 223-228). Washington, DC: IEEE Computer Society.

Acuña, C., & Marcos, E. (2006). Modeling semantic Web services: A case study. In D. Wolber, N. Calder, C. Brooks, & A. Ginige (Eds.), *Proceedings of the 6th International Conference on Web Engineering (ICWE 2006)* (pp. 32-39). ACM Publishing.

Bayardo, R. J., Jr., Bohrer, W., Brice, R., Cichocki, A., Flower, J., Helal, A., et al. (1997). Infosleuth: Agent-Based Semantic Integration of Information in Open and Dynamic Environments. In *Proceeding of the ACM SIGMOD International Conference on Management of Data* (pp. 195-206).

Bruijn, J. D., Bussler, C., Domingue, J., & Fensel, D. (2005). *WSMO*. Retrieved May 10, 2008, from http://www.w3.org/Submission/WSMO/

Cáceres, P., De Castro, V., & Marcos, E. (2004). Navigation Modeling from a User Services Oriented Approach. In *Proceedings of the 3rd Biennial International Conference in Advanced in Information Systems (ADVIS 2004)* (LNCS 3271, pp. 150-160).

Cáceres, P., Marcos, E., & Vela, B. (2003). *A MDA-Based Approach for Web Information System Development*. Paper presented at the Workshop in Software Model Engineering.

Collet, C., Huhns, N., & Shen, W. (1991). Resource Integration using large knowledge base in Carnot. *IEEE Computer,* 55-62.

De Castro, V., Marcos, E., & Cáceres, P. (2004). A User Services Oriented Method to model Web Information Systems. In X. Zhou, S. Su, M. Papazoglou, M. Orlowska, & K. Jeffery (Ed.), *Proceedings of the 5th International Conference on Web Information Systems Engineering (WISE 2004)* (LNCS 3306, pp. 41-52).

De Castro, V., Marcos, E., & López Sanz, M. (2006). A Model Driven Method for Service Composition Modeling: A Case Study. *International Journal of Web Engineering and Technology, 2*(4), 335–353. doi:10.1504/IJWET.2006.010419

Eyal, A., & Milo, T. (2001). Integrating and customizing heterogeneous e-commerce applications. *The VLDB Journal, 10,* 16–38.

Levy, A., Rajaraman, A., & Ordille, J. (1996). Querying heterogeneous information sources using sources descriptions. In *Proceedings of the 22th International Conference on Very Large Data Bases,* Bombay, India (pp. 251-262).

Marcos, E., Acuña, C., & Cuesta, C. (2006). Integrating Software Architecture into a MDA Framework. In V. Gruhn & F. Oquendo (Eds.), *Proceedings of the 3rd European Workshop on Software Architectures (EWSA 2006)* (pp. 127-143).

Mena, E., Kashyap, V., Sheth, A., & Illarramendi, A. (1996). *Observer: An approach for query processing in global information systems based on interoperation across pre-existing ontologies.* Paper presented at the International Conference on Cooperative Information Systems (CoopIS '96).

Miller, J., & Mukerji, J. (2001). *Model Driven Architecture.* Retrieved May 8, 2008, from http://www.omg.com/mda

This work was previously published in International Journal of Enterprise Information Systems, edited by Madjid Tavana, pp. 57-67, Volume 6, Issue 1, copyright 2010 by IGI Publishing (an imprint of IGI Global).

Chapter 20
Semantics for Accurate Conflict Detection in SMoVer:
Specification, Detection and Presentation by Example

Kerstin Altmanninger
Johannes Kepler University Linz, Austria

Wieland Schwinger
Johannes Kepler University Linz, Austria

Gabriele Kotsis
Johannes Kepler University Linz, Austria

ABSTRACT

In collaborative software development, the utilization of Version Control Systems (VCSs) is a must. For this, a multitude of pessimistic as well as optimistic VCSs for model artifacts emerged. Pessimistic approaches follow the lock-edit-unlock paradigm whereas optimistic approaches allow parallel editing of one resource, which are therefore the preferred ones. To be flexible for the ever increasing variety of modeling environments and languages such tools should be independent of the modeling environment and applicable to various modeling languages. Those VCS characteristics may implicate a lack of information for the conflict detection method by virtue of firstly receiving solely the state of an artifact without concrete editing operations and secondly due to unavailable knowledge about the semantics of a modeling language. However, in optimistic VCSs concurrent changes can result in conflicts and inconsistencies. In environment and language independent VCSs inconsistencies would even arise more often due to information losses. Hence, accurate conflict detection methods are indispensable for the realization of such VCSs. To tackle this task, the "Semantically enhanced Model Version Control System" SMoVer is presented. With SMoVer it is possible to specify the semantics of a modeling language, needed for conflict detection in order to provide more accurate conflict reports than other current environment and language independent VCSs. In this work, it is exemplified how semantics of a specific modeling language can be specified in SMoVer, how those specifications can improve the accuracy of conflict reports and finally how those can be presented to modelers.

DOI: 10.4018/978-1-4666-1761-2.ch020

INTRODUCTION

The shift from code-centric to model-centric software development places models as first class artifacts in Model-Driven Engineering (MDE). A major prerequisite for the wide acceptance of MDE are proper methods and tools which are available for traditional software development, such as build tools, test frameworks or Version Control Systems (VCSs). Considering the latter, VCSs are particularly essential to enable collaborative editing and sharing of *model artifacts* like UML, ER or Domain Specific Modeling Language (DSML) models.

Different systems use different strategies to provide collaborative editing. With the utilization of *pessimistic* VCSs, modelers can work on the same set of model artifacts. Parallel editing of the same artifact is prevented by locking. *Optimistic* VCSs instead are crucial when the development process proceeds in parallel. Those systems enable each modeler to work on a personal copy of a model artifact, which may result in conflicting modifications. Such conflicting modifications need to be resolved and finally merged by appropriate techniques for model comparison, conflict detection, conflict resolution and merging.

Generic VCSs like CVS (2008) or Subversion (Tigris, 2008) are not applicable to model artifacts since they apply text-based comparison in a line-based manner and therefore cannot provide adequate conflict reports. To preserve the logical structure of model artifacts *graph-based* techniques need to be utilized instead.

Most current optimistic, graph-based VCSs for model artifacts are bounded to a specific modeling environment, e.g., the IBM Rational Software Architect (2008) also known as RSA. Such environment specific VCSs are therefore not widely applicable. Hence, modelers can not utilize the modeling environment of preference but need to use the one for which version control functionalities are provided and the whole model development team is using. So-called *environment*

independent VCSs, like Odyssey-VCS (Murta et al., 2008), instead, are preferable. Such systems allow modelers to use their modeling environment of preference for editing their model versions which leads to a better acceptance of the VCS.

In view of the fact that MDE is not only about UML and in the light of a growing number of DSMLs, VCSs which are solely applicable on specific modeling languages are often not usable. For example, if modelers evolve models for different application areas they might require to employ different modeling languages, for each application area the most appropriate one. To allow parallel editing in a team of the artifacts under development, language specific modeling environments with included version control functionalities can be utilized in some cases. Beside the drawbacks as already mentioned, for many modeling language no language specific VCS exists. Hence, often generic VCSs like Subversion (Tigris, 2008) are utilized. Examples for modeling language specific VCS approaches which provide solely versioning capabilities for e.g., UML models are Cicchetti and Rossini (2007), Oda and Saeki (2005) and RSA (2008). Therefore, the number of supported modeling languages of a VCS is an important characteristic. A *modeling language independent* (e.g., MOF-based) VCS like Odyssey-VCS (Murta et al., 2008) is desirable. Thus, the utilization of an environment and language independent VCS is of interest for modelers since they can choose their preferred modeling environment for editing model artifacts and furthermore can use the VCS for a number of modeling languages and different application areas.

Such a system needs to provide an *accurate conflict detection method* to achieve a merged, consistent model artifact. A conflict, however, represents inconsistencies between different parallel evolved model versions. To identify the accuracy of the conflict detection method, the definition of Leser and Naumann (2006, pp. 331-333), to determine the *effectiveness* of a method, can be conducted. Therefore, the results gained from the conflict detection method, and the actual perception of conflicts in reality, are considered. With the result *true-positive*, a conflict has been detected by the conflict detection method and in reality. Accordingly, the result *true-negative* states that a conflict has neither been detected by the method nor in reality. Those two results depict the optimum equate to accurate conflict detection. The accuracy of the method can be declined by *false-positive* and *false-negative* results. These are conflicts reported by the method and not conflicts in reality or those conflicts that have not been detected by the method.

For dealing with concurrent modifications on models, in an environment independent and language independent VCS, the concentration on the reduction of false-positive and false-negative results is particularly challenging. Firstly, environment independent VCS can only operate on the state of a model artifact whereas environment specific VCSs can trace the modification performed by the modelers. Since environment specific VCSs receive an editing history, these systems dispose of more information for the conflict detection method than environment independent VCSs for which editing operations of modelers are often not present (Lippe & Oosterom, 1992). Secondly, VCSs for specific languages can provide language specific conflict reports since the conflict detection method dispose of language specific features. Hence, those systems gain more accuracy in conflict detection opposed to language independent VCS approaches. This insufficiency of language independent VCS can be ascribed to the fact that the conflict detection method has too little information about the meaning of the model artifacts under comparison. Thus, it is necessary not only to consider the logical structure of models in terms of a graph-based representation, but also to *understand the model's semantics* in order to provide a more accurate identification of conflicts (cf. Edwards, 1997). Consequently, the focus of this work is laid on the description of how the accuracy of the conflict detection pro-

cess, in an environment and language independent VCS called SMoVer (SMOVER, 2008), can be improved by the utilization of semantics. This description extends previous work (Altmanninger et al., 2008) in this context by a more in-depth discussion about semantic specifications for conflict detection in SMoVer and corresponding comprehensive examples.

This article is organized as follows. The following section describes the semantically enhanced model VCS SMoVer from a conceptual and implementation point of view. Subsequently it is exemplified, by means of WSBPEL (Web Services Business Process Execution Language, 2007), how semantics can be specified to improve the accuracy of conflict detection and finally how conflicts can be reported to the modeler in SMoVer. Related work concerning conflict detection mechanisms in VCSs for models is then discussed and finally a conclusion and an overview of further prospects are provided.

THE SEMANTICALLY ENHANCED MODEL VERSION CONTROL SYSTEM (SMoVer)

In the following the conceptual design of the semantically enhanced model VCS SMoVer is introduced starting with a scenario for the description of the workflow in an optimistic, graph-based, environment and language independent VCS for model artifacts. Finally, the implementation of SMoVer is described.

Conceptual Design

In Figure 1 a scenario is visualized in which two modelers, Sally and Harry are parallel editing the same model artifact by utilizing an optimistic VCS. Therefore Sally and Harry create personal working copies of a model artifact out of the repository and both want to commit their version later back to the repository. After editing the personal working copy in a modeling environment Sally commits her edited working copy of the model artifact to the repository first. The commit process can proceed since the current revision in the repository (Revision 1) is the direct ancestor of the incoming working copy. Harry edited his working copy with a different modeling environment and attempts to commit his model artifact later. Since the last revision in the repository is not the one he has checked-out previously his commit fails and returns with an "out of date" message. Hence he has to apply an update to retrieve a merged version of his edited model artifact and Sally's checked-in version which is now the last revision in the repository. If no other modeler committed a model artifact in the meanwhile Harry can commit the merged artifact to the repository.

The update Harry applied, however, consists of four phases: Comparison, conflict detection, conflict resolution and merge. In SMoVer, in the first phase, the edited model versions of Sally (V') and Harry (V") have to be compared with respect to their common ancestor version (V) which is called a 3-way comparison (Mens, 2002; Ohst et al., 2003). This comparison process is based on a graph-based structural difference computation (Lin et al., 2007; Rivera & Vallecillo, 2008; Toulmé, 2006) between the model versions. The interpretation of the resulting structural differences then yield to the identification of conflicts. To make explicit this process of the

computation of conflicts between concurrently edited versions (V' and V") of a common model artifact (V), the following Object Constraint Language (OCL) (Object Management Group, 2005) expressions define the derivation of the conflict sets. In more detail, the conflict set (Con) contains all conflicting model elements and is a union of three sets that represent update-update (UpdCon), create-create (CrCon) and update-delete (DelCon) conflicts accordingly. Whereas the isUpdated function determines updated model elements and the function areNotEqual checks for the equality (as opposed to the identity) of two model elements.

```
Creates'=(V'-V)
Creates"=(V"-V)
Updates'=V->select(e|e.
isUpdated(V,V')
Updates"=V->select(e|e.
isUpdated(V,V")
Deletes'=(V-V')
Deletes"=(V-V")

CrCon =Creates'-
>intersection(Creates")->select(e|e.
areNotEqual(V',V"))
UpdCon=Updates'-
>intersection(Updates")->select(e|e.
areNotEqual(V',V"))
DelCon=(Updates'-
```

Figure 1. Workflow showing the utilization of a VCS for model artifacts

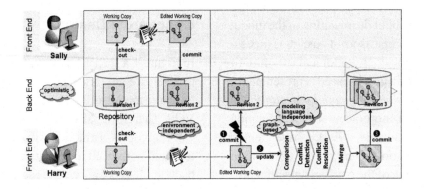

```
>intersection(Deletes"))-
>union(Updates"->
intersection(Deletes'))

Con=UpdCon->union(CrCon-
>union(DelCon))
```

LISTING 1.1. OCL CONSTRAINTS FOR THE DETERMINATION OF CONFLICTS SETS

By inspecting the structural features, namely the attributes and references of a model element, one can determine whether the model element as a whole has been updated. In particular four different *update strategies* to detect structural changes in a graph that are of interest for conflicts detection are considered:

- **Attribute update (ATT):** The value of an attribute has been changed.
- **Reference update (REFS):** The set of referenced model elements has been changed. Model elements have been either created or deleted by modelers whereas the following combinations can be identified: Create-Create (CC), Create-Delete (CD), Delete-Create (DC), Delete-Delete (DD).
- **Role update (ROL):** A model element is referenced or de-referenced by another model element. Again, the four possible combinations of create and delete can be enumerated (CC, CD, DC, DD).
- **Referenced element update (REF):** A referenced model element has undergone an update.

If all update strategies are regarded conjunctively on the concepts provided by the modeling language for the identification of structural differences, this may lead to a report of any structural changes leading to a huge amount of conflicts except particular ones of static and behavioral semantics. Moreover, the update-strategy ROL results out of REFS updates and the update-strategy REF results out of ATT, REFS and ROL updates which assist to define updates more precisely where needed.

Disabling update-strategies on specific model elements may restrict the reported conflicts to those which are valuable. For example, no conflict should be reported due to a REF update of a package element for which two modeler updated/added/deleted contained elements. Thus, the setting of those strategies on the elements of the modeling language which should be versioned is an essential task which needs to be defined in advance and thus can be considered as the first step in providing semantically enhanced conflict detection.

The second and more powerful step is the construction of *semantic view definitions* of interest (cf. Figure 2) for semantically enhanced conflict detection. Therefore various possibilities exist with which false-positive and false-negative conflict detection results can be reduced. In the following a categorization according to three main semantic aspects important for accurate conflict detection, namely equivalent concepts, static semantics and behavioral semantics, is proposed.

The first category, *equivalent concepts*, tackles apparent conflicts resulting from modeling diversities in that most modeling languages offer concepts allowing the expression of identical meaning in different ways to achieve convenient modeling and readability. Thus, through such modeling diversities false-positive results may arise. This means that a conflict has been detected by the method which does not constitute a conflict in reality. For example, one modeler updates a part of a model and the resulting model holds the same meaning than the original version. So (s)he used an equivalent way to express the semantics of constructs by using different, semantically equivalent modeling concepts. The second modeler edits the same model but adds, updates or deletes elements that are part of the

Figure 2. Reference schema of SMoVer

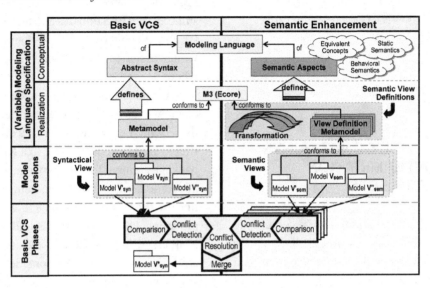

elements edited by the first modeler and which would result in a conflict. Hence, view definitions for equivalent concepts can be defined in SMoVer to avoid false-positive results. Modelers, however, receive a notification about such avoided conflicts and can make a decision in the representation for storage. The definition for equivalent concepts, however, also serves to detect conflicts more precisely.

Whereas equivalent concepts may give rise to false-positive results, *static semantic* and *behavioral semantic conflicts* may not be detected by pure structural comparison and conflict detection between model versions. For example, concurrent modifications on a model may not result in an obvious conflict when syntactically different parts of the model (e.g., different model elements) were edited. Nevertheless, they may interfere with each other due to side effects (Mens, 2002; Shao et al., 2007; Thione & Perry, 2005), thus yielding an actual conflict, which, without considering the model's semantics, would remain hidden. Reasons could be, firstly, the violation of constraints (Object Management Group, 2005), relationships or context conditions (*static semantics*) which cannot be operated on by utilizing a solely struc-

tural difference computation algorithm. Secondly, also concurrent changes of the behavior (e.g., data and control flow) of a model artifact could affect a merged model artifact not incorporating behavioral side-effects (*behavioral semantics*). For the detection of such conflicts, techniques such as denotational semantics, program slicing and dependence graphs are proven to be useful in software development (Mens, 2002; Shao et al., 2007; Thione & Perry, 2005). Hence, some of those techniques can be utilized for the creation of semantic view definitions.

A semantic view definition consists of two parts, namely a *view definition metamodel* and a corresponding *model transformation* (cf. Figure 2). The former, which defines the abstract syntax of the semantic view, can either be represented by a subset of the source metamodel (syntactical level) for expressing equivalent concepts, a domain specific view definition metamodel (like a metamodel of a dependency graph) or a metamodel of a different modeling language (Ryndina et al., 2007) to tackle static & behavioral semantics. A semantic mapping between the source and the target metamodel (metamodel of the semantic view definition) is defined by a model transformation. Therefore, this approach is similar to the concept of translational semantics (Harel & Rumpe, 2004; Slonegger & Kurz, 1995), which maps the constructs of one language onto constructs of another, usually simpler language such as machine instructions. The output of such a transformation is another model which conforms to the metamodel representing the semantic view definition of interest. As a consequence of the transformation realizing a semantic mapping, conflict detection can be carried out now on both, model versions in the *syntactical view* (V_{syn}, V'_{syn} and V''_{syn}) and *semantic views* (V_{sem}, V'_{sem} and V''_{sem}), by means of a structural comparison. Hence, a conflict determined purely upon the comparison of three versions of a model is called *syntactic conflict* whereas a *semantic conflict* is a conflict that is detected between model versions which have been transformed in a semantic view.

Implementation

In order to define the abstract syntax of a modeling language and a desired semantic view definition, a metamodeling architecture is needed. Therefore the "Eclipse Modeling Framework" (EMF) provides Ecore (Eclipse Foundation, 2008), which is a simplified version of MOF that constitutes the M3 layer, that has been chosen for the realization of SMoVer. EMF covers persistence support with an XMI serialization mechanism and a reflective API for manipulating EMF models. The creation of a semantic view from a model artifact is realized through the "Atlas Transformation Language" (ATL) (Allilaire et al., 2006), which is a QVT-like model-to-model transformation language. Accordingly, the top of Figure 2 shows the usage of this metamodeling stack in the context of the implementation architecture.

The comparison of the concurrently edited model versions (V' and V") with their common ancestor version (V) is carried out on a generic graph representation of the respective models and views by using persistent unique identifiers (IDs) and heuristics, e.g., for matching equivalent concepts. For model comparison, however, the EMF reference implementation of "Service Data Objects" (SDO) (Eclipse Foundation, 2008) is utilized. SDO is a general framework to realize standardized access to potentially heterogeneous data sources such as databases, XML files or models serialized in XMI. SDO allows to create datagraphs from EMF models, which are convenient for comparison purposes as SDO offers a mechanism to establish the difference between two graphs. These so called "change summaries" are used in SMoVer to store modifications between versions, which are then used by the actual conflict detection mechanism. Hence, the underlying algorithm implements the aforementioned update strategies for the comparison phase and establishes the relevant sets of conflicting elements. The comparison, conflict detection and merge components of the implementation are realized using Java, SDO, EMF and ATL. ATL, however, serves for model transformations in the semantic view(s) and to produce a consistent merged model version.

SEMANTIC SPECIFICATION, CONFLICT DETECTION AND PRESENTATION BY EXAMPLE

In the following subsections the process of semantic specification, conflict detection and conflict report presentation for each of the previously mentioned semantic aspects (equivalent concepts, static & behavioral semantics) is exemplified by means of WSBPEL (2007) examples.

Semantic Specification

Before inspecting the defined semantic view definitions (cf. Figure 3), and the related examples in detail, the setting of the update strategies is explained in the following. Both tasks, however, are part of the semantic specification possibilities in SMoVer to adapt the conflict detection method to a specific modeling language to improve the accuracy of the method.

In the center of Figure 3 the metamodel of WSBPEL (2007) is visualized for which a possible setting of the update strategies, as the first step to adapt the conflict detection method in SMoVer to a specific modeling language, is shown. To start with, the attribute comment in the element NamedElement is neglected as conflicting value update of an attribute (ATT) because it supposably does not influence the semantics of the model. Considering the REF update, for WSBPEL it is not advisable to report a conflict in, for example, a Process, Sequence or Flow element. Otherwise those elements would always report a conflict if concurrent modifications, which do not affect each other, have been performed in the same Process, Sequence or Flow. Similarly, no conflict should be reported if two modelers created or deleted Activity elements from/to a Flow/Sequence (REFS update) except in one case if two modelers added an Activity to the same position in a Sequence. To limit the amount of falsely

indicated conflicts (false-positive results) reported in the syntactical view, a semantic view definition has been established (cf. Static Semantic View Definition in Figure 3). Accordingly, a conflict is only reported if a user interaction is required. Finally, regarding ROL updates, they can be neglected for the computation of To and From elements because they cannot exist without the element Copy and in turn can only be referenced by a single Copy element.

Semantic Conflict Detection

In the following for each of the three semantic aspects an example is given in order to describe the semantically enhanced conflict detection process.

Equivalent Concepts

Considering the example as shown in Figure 4, it describes two activities (Assign1, Assign2) referenced by two ConditionalLink nodes (CondLink1, CondLink2) defining preconditions for the execution of an activity. Sally has changed

Figure 3. Subset of a WSBPEL metamodel and associated semantic view definitions

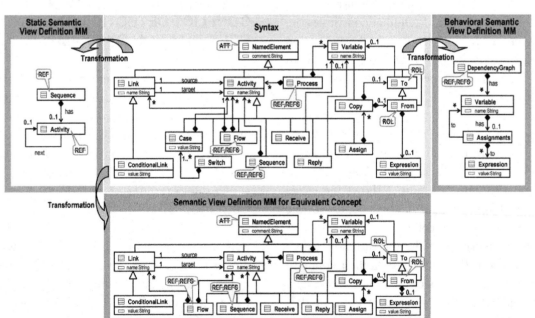

her working copy by adapting the condition in CondLink1. Harry has replaced the concept of utilizing a Flow and according ConditionalLink nodes by a Switch with two Case statements in his working copy. Regarding the modified working copies, a purely structural comparison would report a conflict during the check-in process, since CondLink1 has been updated by Sally and deleted by Harry. A modeler, however, would identify the parallel edited model versions as consistent to each other after inspecting their semantics since the conflict in the syntactical view results due to the utilization of two different, semantically equivalent concepts.

Therefore, a semantic view definition (cf. Semantic View Definition for Equivalent Concept in Figure 3), constituting a subset of the WSBPEL metamodel is defined. Notice, the concept of Switch and Case has been excluded in the semantic view definition metamodel. Accordingly, modeling diversities of the WSBPEL language, since each Switch statement with Case nodes can also be expressed through a Flow with ConditionalLink nodes, are reduced. The above mentioned

fact is covered by the semantic mapping, in that each Switch statement with Case nodes become transformed into a Flow with ConditionalLink nodes conveying the same meaning. Due to the fact that no semantic conflict can be found, a previously falsely indicated syntactic conflict has been avoided. Notice, this gives rise to a major benefit that employing semantic view definitions may be utilized to reduce the amount of reported conflicts to a modeler, which results in a more effective conflict detection.

Reflecting the above explicated example, a syntactic but no semantic conflict is reported. The knowledge gained conveys that the different model versions comprise equivalent concepts and therefore are consistent to each other. Imagine a slightly different scenario in which Harry modified the Case1 element which is transformed to a CondLink1 element in the semantic view, a semantic conflict is reported as well additionally to the syntactic one. In this case, the semantic conflict detection conveys the information about the origin of the semantic conflict in the equivalent concept. Therefore, with the help of semantic

Figure 4. Syntactic conflict resulting from semantic equivalent concepts

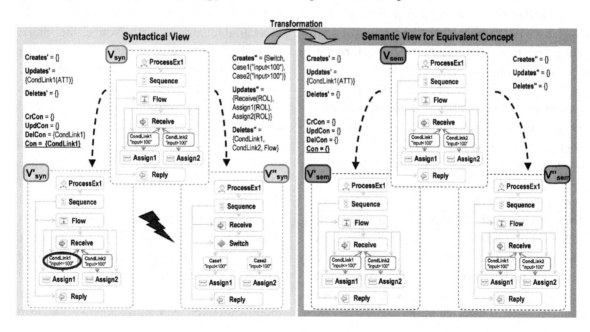

view definitions for equivalent concepts, semantic conflicts in equivalent concepts can be detected and appropriately reported to modelers.

Static Semantic Conflicts

In the syntactical view in Figure 5, a WSBPEL model is given (V_{syn}) describing a Sequence containing Activity nodes which are subject to an order. If Sally and Harry concurrently insert the Activities ReplyOut and ReplyFin at the same position in the Sequence, this gives rise to a conflict due to the fact that a decision is required about the order of the created activities to generate a merged version.

However, the above mentioned specific case of a REFS:CC update can also be detected in the syntax by applying the REFS:CC strategy, but using a semantic view definition is more powerful. The reason for that is twofold. Firstly, by simply using the REFS:CC strategy for the conflict detection in the syntax, many falsely indicated conflicts may be detected as well (e.g., creation of activities at different positions) and secondly, the conflicting model element can not be identified as precisely as with a semantic view definition. Using a REFS:CC strategy in the syntax does not make available the model element which actually causes the conflict, since the relationship of activities is merely expressed implicitly through the Sequence element.

Therefore, to make explicit the relationship of Activity elements, a static semantic view definition is established (cf. Figure 3) describing an ordering relation of activities. Looking at the model transformation, by realizing the semantic mapping, a Sequence containing Activity elements is mapped to a connected chain of Activity elements each Activity pointing to its successor, whereas the Sequence element itself becomes mapped to a Sequence element in the semantic view metamodel, pointing to the first Activity in the chain. Coming back to Figure 5 a static semantic conflict is detected in the semantic view

due to the reference property next of the Assign Activity. Summing up, this static semantic view definition strongly increases the accuracy of the conflict detection report in this setting because a conflict is only reported if the modeler's interaction is needed.

Behavioral Semantic Conflicts

While all parallel changes, performed by modelers, are intended to affect a model semantically, it may occur that no syntactic conflict is reported but semantic interferences, caused by e.g., behavioral side effects, exist. To tackle the emergence of behavioral semantic conflicts an example for a view definition is explained in the following.

The presented example, as shown in Figure 6 visualizes a Process for the derivation of postal charges for the payment (Variable sum) during online shopping. If the payment is smaller than the value 200 additional postal charges are added (Assign3). Sally has changed the charging calculation process through adapting the noCharge limit and increasing the charge, whereas Harry has modified the same process slightly different. Due to the fact that Harry has inserted a second charge limit (redCharge, Assign4) the modifications of both modelers (Harry and Sally) implicitly affect the Variable sum as well. Notice, the interference of the Variable sum can not be recognized by conflict detection on the syntax. However, it might still be of interest for Sally and Harry, since a merged version would conform to none of the modeler's intents.

Therefore, a behavioral semantic view definition (cf. Figure 3) is used exploiting the concept of a dependency graph, to make explicit the data flow in the model versions. Considering the semantic mapping, each Variable is mapped to a Variable referencing a container element Assignments, which stores references to all values (Variable and Expression elements) relevant to the current Variable. Consequently, concurrent modifications concerning assigning values to one

Figure 5. Detection of a static semantic conflict

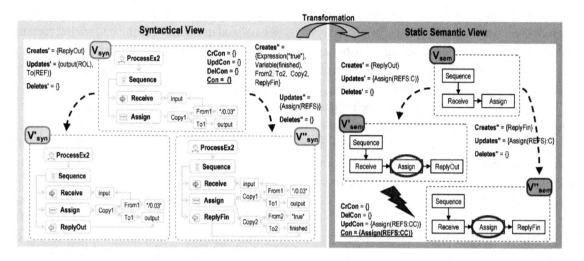

Figure 6. Detection of a behavioral semantic conflict

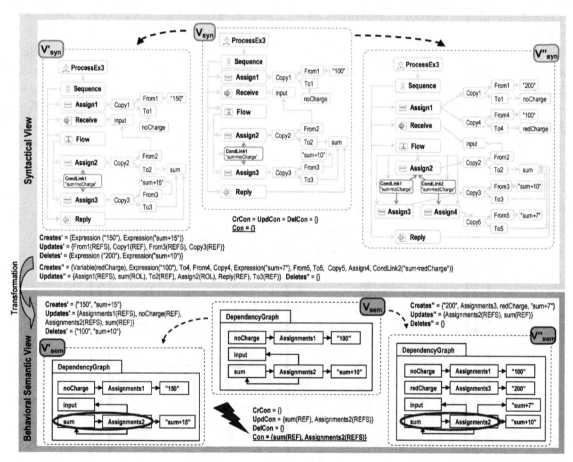

and the same Variable can be detected. Thus, the REF update upon the Variable sum indicates that both modelers performed implicit changes to this Variable resulting in the detection of a behavioral semantic conflict. Reflecting on the example, the amount of reported conflicts can be increased and therefore false-negative results are reduced realized by the utilization of behavioral semantic views. Hence unintended side effects can be detected and consequently wrongly merged versions encapsulated with a time consuming bug fixing process can be avoided.

Presentation of Conflict Reports

In order to assist modelers during the conflict resolution phase the result of the conflict detection phase should be presented as supportive as possible.

In Figure 7 the possible outcomes of the conflict detection phase are visualized. The presentation of detected conflicts is by default reported for each view in which they are detected, in the syntactic and semantic views. Nevertheless, this presentation has some drawbacks. First, if a semantic view

definition comprising an equivalent concept and a specific scenario has turned out as conceptually visualized in Figure 7, in the bottom left rectangle (C), the equivalent concept needs to be traced back to the syntactical view to eliminate the wrongly identified conflict. Secondly, semantic views are specific abstract views comprising checks for semantic interferences between the model versions. If a conflict is detected in such a view it might be difficult for the modeler to figure out the changes he has to apply on his model in the syntactic view to resolve a conflict. Summing up, it is essential to collect all information retrieved out of the conflict detection phase in one view, the syntactical one to assist the modeler as best as possible in the conflict resolution phase. Therefore, a technique is essential to *trace back* semantic conflicts as well as information on equivalent concepts into the syntactical view.

Considering the previous example of the semantic view definition for an equivalent concept (cf. Figure 4) the elements in the semantic view which have been transformed in an equivalent presentation can be traced back by their ID to the elements in the syntactical view. This mechanism

Figure 7. Possible outcomes of the conflict detection phase

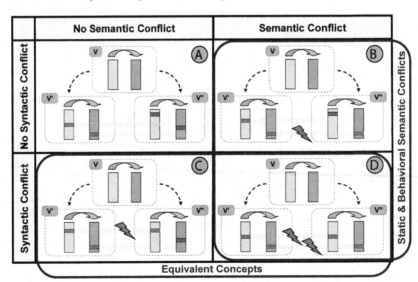

is needed to indicate the falsely detected conflicts due to equivalent concepts in the syntactic view. The modeler, however, can choose between the equivalent concepts. If (s)he does not choose one, the committed representation is taken for the storage in the repository.

In the second previously described example (cf. Figure 5), for a static semantic view definition the presentation of the static semantic conflict in the syntactical view is simply done by tracing back the conflicting elements in the semantic view by the elements IDs.

In the last example (visualized in Figure 6) the conflict for the element sum can be traced back according to a 1:1 mapping by the element's ID. The Assignment2 element in the behavioral semantic view is not present in the syntactical view (0:1) and therefore (a) WSBPEL metamodel element(s) can be specified for which a conflict should be displayed. Hence, it can be defined that all elements to which Assignments2 points should be traced back. Finally, behavioral semantic conflicts are displayed in the syntactical view in V' for the elements sum, input and "sum+15" and in V" for the elements sum, input, "sum+7" and "sum+10".

RELATED WORK

Versioning is a major subcategory of the broad field of *software configuration management* (Conradi & Westfechtel, 1998), the discipline of handling the evolution of complex software systems. Emerging in the field of *software engineering*, the first versioning system was implemented in the early 1970s and was based on the simple idea that each time a file was changed, a new version was created. At that time, already multi-user management was supported, but only in a pessimistic manner. Since locking imposes limitations on concurrent editing *optimistic approaches* came up. Generic VCSs like CVS (2008) and Subversion (Tigris, 2008) provide comparison and merge algorithms which take neither the structure nor the semantics

of the artifact under consideration into account. With those systems any kind of artifact can be versioned but they are too weak to support the underlying data model of e.g., model artifacts, program source code files and RDF graphs. Based on this observation, the quest for more expressive data models was guided not only in the area of software engineering but also in model-driven engineering and ontology engineering. Here, the shift from line-based to tree-based, and finally to graph-based data models took place. Since the natural representation of artifacts in software engineering, model-driven engineering and ontology engineering are graphs, the focus of the following related approaches (cf. Table 1) is laid on *graph-based* VCSs. Those related approaches are checked against the proposed VCS characteristics environment independent, language independent and accuracy improvement. VCSs with accuracy improvement techniques, like modeling environment specific VCSs which improve the accuracy by logging of editing operations or refactoring operations or VCSs which can solely provide accuracy improvements for a specific modeling language, are not considered.

As visualized in Table 1 the number of *environment independent* VCSs is rare. Solely Odyssey-VCS and CoObRA provide interfaces which allow the integration in arbitrary modeling environments. Odyssey-VCS provides a web service interface for the VCS functionalities check-out, commit and update by streaming the model artifacts XMI serialization. Thus, the integration in any modeling environment can be achieved easily. CoObRA is incorporated in the Fujaba tool (Schneider & Zündorf, 2007) and SMoVer is incorporated in Eclipse. Both VCS explicitly define interfaces which have to be implemented in any environment in order to use the backend. The rest of the approaches, mentioned in Table 1, are either not fully realized (cf. Cicchetti & Rossini and Alanen & Porres), are part of a modeling environment or provide plug-ins for specific modeling environments, IDEs and editors.

Table 1. Related Approaches checked against the proposed VCS characteristics

Area	Approach	Environment Independent	Language Independent	Accuracy Improvement
Model Engineering	Cicchetti & Rossini (2007)	✗	✗	✓
	Odyssey-VCS (Murta et al., 2008)	✓	✓	✗
	CoObRA (Schneider & Zündorf, 2007)	✓	✓	✗
	Alanen & Porres (2003)	✗	✓	✗
	CAME (Oda & Saeki, 2005)	✗	✗	✗
	RSA (2008)	✗	✗	✗
Software Engineering	MolhadoRef (Dig et al., 2008)	✗	✗	✗
	Ekman & Asklund (2004)	✗	✗	✗
Ontology Engineering	SemVersion (Völkel, 2006)	✗	✗	✓

For example, CAME and RSA have version control functionalities implemented, MolhadoRef as well as the approach of Ekman & Asklund are plug-ins for Eclipse and SemVersion can be used within Protégé.

Modeling language independent VCS are rare. To start with, Odyssey-VCS as well as the presented VCS SMoVer support versioning functionalities for MOF-based model artifacts and therefore offer much flexibility in the utilization of the VCS. Another language flexible system is CoObRA which works with object-oriented data models. Over and above, Alanen & Porres do not provide difference calculation and merging algorithms with which the functionality of a VCS for MOF-based models can be realized. By contrast, the approach of Cicchetti & Rossini and RSA solely provide versioning functionalities for UML model artifacts and the modeling environment CAME supports additionally ER models. Additionally, MolhadoRef and the approach of Ekman & Asklund are solely applicable on the programming language Java. Finally, SemVersion is limited to RDS based languages and therefore also does not provide the flexibility of being reused in the modeling domain.

Only two approaches exist which provide semantic specification possibilities to *improve* *the accuracy* of the conflict detection method. In the area of model engineering Cicchetti & Rossini propose to leverage conflict detection and resolution by adopting design-oriented descriptions endowed with custom conflict specifications. Hence, several conflicting situations, which cannot be captured by a priori structural conflict detection mechanisms, can be specified that they refer to as "domain specific conflicts". The VCS administrators, however, are forced to enumerate all wrong cases in the form of weaving models, which negatively affects the usability and scalability of the approach. Therefore, in the work of Cicchetti & Rossini each modification is not allowed to preserve a design pattern and the design pattern itself has to be specified in a weaving pattern (as they exemplified for the singleton design pattern). Anyway, this approach focuses on the detection of previously undiscovered conflicts in terms of domain specific conflicts only, whereas behavioral semantic conflicts and the detection of previously falsely indicated conflicts as provided by SMoVer are not considered. In the area of ontology engineering, SemVersion performs semantic difference calculations on the basis of the semantics of the used ontology language. SemVersion is proposing the separation of language specific features (e.g., semantic difference) from general features (e.g., structural difference or branch and merge). Therefore, assuming the use of RDF Schema as the ontology language and two versions (A and B) of an RDFS ontology, SemVersion uses RDF Schema entailment on model A and B and infers all possible triples. Now, a structural difference on A and B can be calculated in order to obtain the semantic difference.

Summarizing, currently (2008) no optimistic, graph-based, environment and language independent VCS (besides SMoVer) exist which provides techniques to improve the accuracy of the conflict detection method. Nevertheless, accuracy improvement techniques are especially essential for such systems to tackle eventual information lacks opposed to environment and language specific VCSs (cf. Lippe & Oosterom, 1992).

CONCLUSION AND FUTURE WORK

In this paper a semantically enhanced VCS called SMoVer is presented in an exemple-based manner. SMoVer encapsulates the characteristics of an optimistic, graph-based, environment and language independent VCS which provides semantic specification possibilities to ensure more accurate conflict detection during the check-in process. This process of semantic specification in SMoVer is exemplified in terms of the modeling language WSBPEL. Therefore, firstly, the semantic specification possibilities by means of three semantic aspects (equivalent concepts, static and behavioral semantics) are elaborated. Secondly, the semantic conflict detection method and finally the presentation of the result of the conflict detection phase are exemplified and explained. This approach, however, benefits by establishing the necessary update strategies and view definitions (transformations and according view definition metamodels) besides increasing effectiveness in the conflict detection phase also in enabling to maintain consistency between concurrently edited model versions in syntax and semantics.

Future research, in a short distant prospect, will focus on the finalization of possible semantic view definitions in the form of a catalogue for the modeling languages WSBPEL and UML Activity Diagrams (AD). Both selected modeling languages are behavioral modeling languages and therefore all three semantic aspects can be exploited. Those two modeling languages have been selected since an *evaluation* conducted on solely one specific general purpose language or DSML is not significant. Thus, the evaluation will encompass an inspection of the expressiveness and number for semantic view definition possibilities for the DSML WSBPEL and the subset of the general purpose language UML AD. After the completion of this catalogue a comprehensive evaluation of the effectiveness of the conflict detection method, in terms of accuracy, realized in SMoVer will be conducted. Therefore SMoVer is going to be compared to other VCSs for model artifacts like Odyssey-VCS (Murta et al., 2008) and RSA (2008).

In the current implementation of SMoVer (2008) no graphical conflict resolution component exists and conflict reports are only available in text-based manner, separately for all views. Hence, it will be investigated in the implementation of advanced techniques for the presentation of the result of the conflict detection phase in SMoVer.

In a longer prospect, it is planned to integrate the support for metamodel versioning in SMoVer. Moreover, research in the area of VCSs for model artifacts will focus on building a VCS called AMOR (Altmanninger et al., 2008) which comprises the characteristics of SMoVer and additional mechanisms. Firstly, to further improve the accuracy of the conflict detection method, AMOR will provide supplementary to semantically enhanced conflict detection an operation-based conflict detection mechanism with which logged operations can be imported to the environment independent VCS. Secondly, AMOR will also support intelligent conflict resolution support, specifically aiming at techniques for the representation of differences between model versions and relieving modelers from repetitive tasks by suggesting proper resolution strategies, thus enhancing productivity and consistency of versioning.

REFERENCES

Alanen, M., & Porres, I. (2003). Difference and union of models. In P. Stevens, J. Whittle, and G. Booch (Ed.), *UML 2003 – The Unified Modeling Language* (LNCS 2863, pp. 2-17).

Allilaire, F., Bézivin, J., Jouault, F., & Kurtev, I. (2006). *ATL – Eclipse support for model transformation*. Paper presented at the Eclipse Technology eXchange Workshop (eTX) at the ECOOP Conference.

Altmanninger, K. (2008). Models in conflict – towards a semantically enhanced version control system for models. In H. Giese (Ed.), *Models in Software Engineering* (LNCS 5002, pp. 293-304).

Altmanninger, K., Kappel, G., Kusel, A., Retsch-itzegger, W., Schwinger, W., Seidl, M., et al. (2008). *AMOR – towards adaptable model versioning*. Paper presented at the 1st International Workshop on Model Co-Evolution and Consistency Management (MCCM) at the ACM/IEEE 11th International Conference on Model Driven Engineering Languages and Systems (MoDELS).

Cicchetti, A., Di Ruscio, D., & Pierantonio, A. (2007). A metamodel independent approach to difference representation. *Journal of Object Technology. Special Issue on TOOLS EUROPE*, *6*(9), 165–185.

Cicchetti, A., & Rossini, A. (2007). Weaving models in conflicts detection specifications. In *Proceedings of the ACM Symposium on Applied Computing* (pp. 1035-1036). ACM Publishing.

Conradi, R., & Westfechtel, B. (1998). Version models for software configuration management. *ACM Computing Surveys*, *30*(2), 232–282. doi:10.1145/280277.280280

Dig, D., Manzoor, K., Johnson, R., & Nguyen, T. N. (2008). Effective software merging in the presence of object-oriented refactorings. *IEEE Transactions on Software Engineering*, *34*(3), 321–335. doi:10.1109/TSE.2008.29

Eclipse Foundation. (2008). *Eclipse Modeling Framework Project (EMF)*. Retrieved August 29, 2008, from http://www.eclipse.org/modeling/emf/

Edwards, W. (1997). Flexible conflict detection and management in collaborative applications. In *Proceedings of the 10th Annual ACM Symposium on User Interface Software and Technology* (pp. 139-148).

Ekman, T., & Asklund, U. (2004). Refactoring-aware versioning in Eclispe. *Electronic Notes in Theoretical Computer Science*, *107*, 57–69. doi:10.1016/j.entcs.2004.02.048

Harel, D., & Rumpe, B. (2004). Meaningful model-ing: What's the semantics of "semantics"? *Computer*, *37*(10), 64–72. doi:10.1109/MC.2004.172

IBM. (2008). *IBM Rational Software Architect*. Retrieved August 29, 2008, from http://www-306. ibm.com/software/awdtools/architect/swarchitect

Leser, U., & Naumann, F. (2006). *Informationsin-tegration: Architekturen und Methoden zur Inte-gration verteilter und heterogener Datenquellen*. Heidelberg, Germany: Dpunkt Verlag.

Lin, Y., Gray, J., & Jouault, F. (2007). DSMDiff: A differentiation tool for domain-specific mod-els. *European Journal of Information Systems*, *16*, 349–361. doi:10.1057/palgrave.ejis.3000685

Lippe, E., & Oosterom, N. (1992). Operation-based merging. *ACM SIGSOFT Software Engineering Notes*, *17*(5), 78–87. doi:10.1145/142882.143753

Mens, T. (2002). A state-of-the-art survey on software merging. *IEEE Transactions on Software Engineering, 28*(5), 449–462. doi:10.1109/TSE.2002.1000449

Murta, L., Corrêa, C., Prudêncio, J. G., & Werner, C. (2008). Towards Odyssey-VCS 2: improvements over a UML-based version control system. In *Proceedings of the International Workshop on Comparison and Versioning of Software Models* (pp. 25-30).

OASIS. (2007). *Web Services Business Process Execution Language Version 2.0.* Retrieved August 29, 2008, from http://docs.oasis-open.org/wsbpel/2.0/wsbpel-v2.0.pdf

Object Management Group. (2005). *OCL 2.0 Specification.* Retrieved August 29, 2008, from http://www.omg.org/docs/ptc/05-06-06.pdf

Oda, T., & Saeki, M. (2005). Generative technique of version control systems for software diagrams. In *Proceedings of the 21st IEEE International Conference on Software Maintenance* (pp. 515-524). Washington, DC: IEEE Computer Society.

Ohst, D., Welle, M., & Kelter, U. (2003). Differences between versions of UML diagrams. *ACM SIGSOFT Software Engineering Notes, 28*(5), 227–236. doi:10.1145/949952.940102

Rivera, J. E., & Vallecillo, A. (2008). Representing and operating with model differences. In R. F. Paige & B. Meyer (Eds.), *Proceedings of Objects, Components, Models and Patterns: 46th International Conference, TOOLS EUROPE* (LNBIP 11, pp. 141-160).

Ryndina, K., Küster, J. M., & Gall, H. (2007). Consistency of business process models and object life cycles. In T. Kühne (Ed.) *Models in Software Engineering* (LNCS 4364, pp. 80-90).

Savannah. (2008). *Concurrent Versions System (CVS).* Retrieved August 29, 2008, from http://www.nongnu.org/cvs/

Schneider, C., & Zündorf, A. (2007). *Experiences in using optimistic locking in Fujaba.* Paper presented at the Workshop on Comparison and Versioning of UML Models.

Shao, D., Khurshid, S., & Perry, D. E. (2007). Evaluation of semantic interference detection in parallel changes: An exploratory experiment. In *Proceedings of the 23rd IEEE International Conference on Software Maintenance (ICSM)* (pp. 74-83).

Slonegger, K., & Kurtz, B. (1995). *Formal syntax and semantics of programming languages: a laboratory based approach.* Boston: Addison-Wesley Longman.

SMOVER. (2008). *SMoVer: A Semantically Enhanced Version Control System for Models.* Retrieved August 29, 2008, from http://smover.tk.uni-linz.ac.at/

Thione, G. L., & Perry, D. E. (2005). Parallel changes: Detecting semantic interferences. In *Proceedings of the 29th Annual International Computer Software and Applications Conference (COMPSAC)* (Vol. 1, pp. 47-56). Washington, DC: IEEE Computer Society.

Tigris. (2008). *Subversion.* Retrieved August 29, 2008, from http://subversion.tigris.org/

Toulmé, A. (2006). *Presentation of EMF compare utility.* Paper presented at the Eclipse Modeling Symposium.

Völkel, M. (2006). *D2.3.3.v2 SemVersion – versioning RDF and ontologies.* Retrieved August 29, 2008, from http://www.aifb.uni-karlsruhe.de/Publikationen/showPublikation?publ_id=1163

This work was previously published in International Journal of Enterprise Information Systems, edited by Madjid Tavana, pp. 68-84, Volume 6, Issue 1, copyright 2010 by IGI Publishing (an imprint of IGI Global).

Compilation of References

Abas Business Software. (2003). *ERP Survey 2003/2004*. Retrieved from ftp://ftp.abas.de/pub/marketing/download/eng_konradin2003.pdf

Abdi, H. (2003). Partial Least Squares (PLS) Regression. In Lewis-Beck, M., Bryman, A., & Futing, T. (Eds.), *Encyclopedia of Social Sciences Research Methods* (pp. 1–7). Thousand Oaks, CA: Sage.

Abdinnour-Helm, S., Lengnick-Hall, M., & Lengnick-Hall, C. (2003). Pre-implementation attitudes and organizational readiness for implementing and Enterprise Resource Planning system. *European Journal of Operational Research*, 146(2), 258–273. doi:10.1016/S0377-2217(02)00548-9

Aberdeen Group. (2009). *Business Adoption of Cloud Computing*. Boston: Author.

Abrahamson, E., & Fombrun, C. J. (1994). Macroculture: Determinants and Consequences. *Academy of Management Review*, 19(4), 728–755. doi:10.2307/258743

Abrahamson, E., & Rosenkopf, L. (1993). Institutional and Competitive Bandwagons: Using Mathematical Modeling as a Tool to Explore Innovation Diffusion. *Academy of Management Review*, 18(3), 487–517. doi:10.2307/258906

Abrahamson, E., & Rosenkopf, L. (1997). Social Network Effects on the Extent of Innovation Diffusion: A Computer Simulation. *Organization Science*, 8(3), 289–309. doi:10.1287/orsc.8.3.289

Achanga, P., Shehab, E., Rajkumar, R., & Nelder, G. (2006). Critical success factors for lean implementation within SMEs. *Journal of Manufacturing Technology Management*, 4(17), 460–471. doi:10.1108/17410380610662889

Ackoff, R. L. (1989). From data to wisdom. *Journal of Applied Systems Analysis*, 16, 3–9.

Acuña, C., & Marcos, E. (2006). Modeling Semantic Web Services: A Case Study. In D. Wolber, N. Calder, C. Brooks, & A. Ginije (Ed.), *Proceedings of the 6th International Conference on Web Engineering* (pp 32-39). ACM Publishing.

Acuña, C., Gómez, J. M., Marcos, E., & Bussler, C. (2005). Towards Web Portal Inte-gration through Semantic Web Services. In D. Wolber, N. Calder, C. Brooks, & A. Ginige (Ed.), *Proceedings of the International Conference on Next Generation Web Services Practices (NWeSP'05)* (pp. 223-228). Washington, DC: IEEE Computer Society.

Adams, D. A., Nelson, R. R., & Todd, P. A. (1992). Perceived Usefulness, Ease of Use and Usage Information Technology. *Management Information Systems Quarterly*, 16(2), 227–250. doi:10.2307/249577

Aguinis, H. (2004). *Regression Analysis for Categorical Moderators*. New York: The Guilford Press.

Ajzen, I., & Fishbein, M. (1980). *Understanding Attitudes and Predicting Social Behavior*. Englewood Cliffs, NJ: Prentice-Hall.

Aken, A., & Michalisin, M. (2007) The Impact of the Skills Gap on the Recruitment of MIS Graduates. In *Proceedings of the 2007 ACM SIGMIS CPR conference on Computer personnel research: The global information technology workforce* (pp. 105-111).

Akkerman, H., & Van Helden, K. (2002). Vicious and Virtuous Cycles in ERP Implementation: A Case Study of Interrelations Between Critical Success Factors. *European Journal of Information Systems*, 11(1), 35–46. doi:10.1057/palgrave/ejis/3000418

Aladwani, M. A., & Palvia, P. C. (2002). Developing and validating instrument for measuring user perceived web quality. *Information & Management, 39*(6), 467–476. doi:10.1016/S0378-7206(01)00113-6

Alanen, M., & Porres, I. (2003). Difference and union of models. In P. Stevens, J. Whittle, and G. Booch (Ed.), *UML 2003 – The Unified Modeling Language* (LNCS 2863, pp. 2-17).

Alcacer, J. (2006). Location Choices Across the Value Chain: How Activity and Capability Influence Collocation. *Management Science, 52*(10), 1457–1471. doi:10.1287/mnsc.1060.0658

Alegria, J., Carvalho, T., & Ramalho, R. (2004). *Uma experiência open source para tomar o pulso e ter pulso sobre a função sistemas e tecnologias de informação.* Paper presented at the 5ª CAPSI, Conferência da Associação Portuguesa de Sistemas de Informação, Lisboa, Portugal.

Al-kaabi, H., Potter, A., & Naim, M. (2007). An Outsourcing Decision Model for Airlines MRO Activities. *Journal of Quality in Maintenance Engineering, 13*(3), 217–227. doi:10.1108/13552510710780258

Allen, D., Kern, T., & Havenhand, M. (2002). ERP critical success factors: an exploration of the contextual factors in public sector institutions. In *Proceeding of the 35th Hawaii International Conference on System Sciences*.

Allen, D., Kern, T., & Mattison, D. (2002). Culture, Power, and Politics in ICT Outsourcing in Higher Education Institutions. *European Journal of Information Systems, 11*, 159–173. doi:10.1057/palgrave/ejis/3000425

Allen, R. S., & Helms, M. M. (2006). Linking Strategic Practices and Organizational Performance to Porter's Generic Strategies. *Business Process Management Journal, 12*(4), 433–454. doi:10.1108/14637150610678069

Allilaire, F., Bézivin, J., Jouault, F., & Kurtev, I. (2006). *ATL – Eclipse support for model transformation.* Paper presented at the Eclipse Technology eXchange Workshop (eTX) at the ECOOP Conference.

Al-Mashari, M. (2003). Enterprise resource planning (ERP) systems: A research agenda. *Industrial Management + Data Systems, 103*(1-2), 22-27.

Al-Mashari, M., & Al-Mudimigh, A. (2003). ERP implementation: lessons from a case study. *Information Technology & People, 1*, 21–33. doi:10.1108/09593840310463005

Al-mashari, M., Al-mudimigh, A., & Zairi, M. (2003). Enterprise Resource Planning: A Taxonomy of Critical Factors. *European Journal of Operational Research, 146*(1), 352–364. doi:10.1016/S0377-2217(02)00554-4

Al-Mashari, M., & Zairi, M. (1999). BPR implementation process: an analysis of key success and failure factors. *Business Process Management Journal, 5*(1), 87–112. doi:10.1108/14637159910249108

Al-Qirim, N. (2005). An Empirical Investigation of an e-commerce Adoption-Capability Model in Small Businesses in New Zealand. *Electronic Markets, 15*(4), 418–437. doi:10.1080/10196780500303136

Al-Qirim, N. A. (2003). The strategic outsourcing decision of IT and eCommerce: the case of small businesses in New Zealand. *Journal of Information Technology Cases and Applications, 5*(3), 32–56.

Al-Somali, S. A., Gholami, R., & Clegg, B. (2009). An investigation into the acceptance of online banking in Saudi Arabia. *Technovation, 29*(2), 130–141. doi:10.1016/j.technovation.2008.07.004

Altmanninger, K. (2008). Models in conflict – towards a semantically enhanced version control system for models. In H. Giese (Ed.), *Models in Software Engineering* (LNCS 5002, pp. 293-304).

Altmanninger, K., Kappel, G., Kusel, A., Retschitzegger, W., Schwinger, W., Seidl, M., et al. (2008). *AMOR – towards adaptable model versioning.* Paper presented at the 1st International Workshop on Model Co-Evolution and Consistency Management (MCCM) at the ACM/IEEE 11th International Conference on Model Driven Engineering Languages and Systems (MoDELS).

Alwabel, S. A., Zairi, M., & Gunasekaran, A. (2006). The Evolution of ERP and Its Relationship with e-Business. *International Journal of Enterprise Information Systems, 2*(4), 58–76.

Ament, K. (2003). *Single Sourcing: Building Modular Documentation.* Norwich, NY: William Andrew Publishing.

Amin, H. (2007). Internet banking adoption among young intellectuals. *Journal of Internet Banking and Commerce, 12*(3), 1–13.

Amoako-Gyampah, K. (2004). ERP implementation factors A comparison of managerial and end-user perspectives. *Business Process Management Journal, 2*(10), 171–183. doi:10.1108/14637150410530244

Amoako-Gyampah, K. (2007). Perceived usefulness, user involvement and behavioral intention: an empirical study of ERP implementation. *Computers in Human Behavior, 23*(3), 1232–1248. doi:10.1016/j.chb.2004.12.002

Amoako-Gyampah, K., & Salam, A. F. (2004). An extension of the technology acceptance model in an ERP implementation environment. *Information & Management, 41*(6), 731–745. doi:10.1016/j.im.2003.08.010

Anderson, E., & Weitz, B. (1992). The use of pledge to build and sustain commitment in distribution channels. *JMR, Journal of Marketing Research, 29*(1), 18–34. doi:10.2307/3172490

Angell, I., & Smithson, S. (1991). *Information Systems Management.* London: Macmillan Information Systems Series.

Antonucci, Y., Corbitt, G., Stewart, G., & Harris, A. (2004). Enterprise systems education: where are we? Where are we going? *Journal of Information Systems Education, 15*(3), 227–234.

Aracic, I., Gasiunas, V., Mezini, M., & Ostermann, K. (2006). *An Overview of CaesarJ.* New York: Springer.

ARC Advisory Group. (2003). *ERP Market Opportunities Change While Remaining Strong Overall at $8.9 Billion.* Retrieved from http://www.arcweb.com/Community/arcnews/arcnews.asp?ID=328

Armbrust, M., Fox, A., Griffith, R., Joseph, A., Katz, R., & Konwinski, A. (2010). A View of Cloud Computing. *Communications of the ACM, 53*(4), 50. doi:10.1145/1721654.1721672

Arnold, W. (2010, October 10) Regulations and Security Concerns Hinder Asia's Move to Cloud Computing. *The New York Times.*

Arslan, O., & Er, I. D. (2008). SWOT Analysis for Safer Carriage of Bulk Liquid Chemicals in Tankers. *Journal of Hazardous Materials, 154*(1-3), 901–913. doi:10.1016/j.jhazmat.2007.10.113

Arthur, W. B. (1994). *Increasing returns and path dependence in the economy.* Ann Arbor, MI: University of Michigan.

Artz, K. W. (1999). Buyer-Supplier Performance: The Role of Asset Specificity, Reciprocal Investments and Relational Exchange. *British Journal of Management, 10*, 113–126. doi:10.1111/1467-8551.00114

Ash, C., & Burn, J. M. (2003). Strategic framework for the management of E-ERP change. *European Journal of Operational Research, 46*(2), 374–387. doi:10.1016/S0377-2217(02)00556-8

Assmann, U. (2000). *Meta-programming Composers in Second Generation Component Systems*, Technical Report 17/97, University of Karlsruhe, Dept. of Computer Science

Aßmann, U., Zschaler, S., & Wagner, G. (2006). *Ontologies, Meta-Models, and the Model-Driven Paradigm.* New York: Springer.

Attewell, P. (1992). Technology Diffusion and Organizational Learning: The Case of Business Computing. *Organization Science, 3*(1), 1–19. doi:10.1287/orsc.3.1.1

Aurrecoechea, C., Campbell, A., & Hauw, L. (1996). A survey of qos architectures. *Multimedia Systems Journal, 6*, 138–151. doi:10.1007/s005300050083

Austin, J. L. (1962). *How to Do Things with Words.* Cambridge, MA: Harvard University Press.

Au, Y. A., & Kauffman, R. J. (2001). Should We Wait? Network Externalities, Compatibility, and Electronic Billing Adoption. *Journal of Management Information Systems, 18*(2), 47–63.

Axelrod, R., Mitchell, W., Thomas, R. E., Bennett, D. S., & Bruderer, E. (1995). Coalition Forming in Standard-Setting Alliances. *Management Science, 41*(9), 1493. doi:10.1287/mnsc.41.9.1493

Baader, F., Calvanese, D., McGuinness, D. L., Nardi, D., & Patel-Schneider, P. F. (Eds.). (2003). *The Description Logic Handbook.* Cambridge, UK: Cambridge University Press.

Bacheldor, B. (2006). Process Improvement Drives Manufacturers' RFID Implementations. *RFID Journal*. Retrieved July 1, 2008, from http://www.rfidjournal.com/article/articleview/2903/1/1/

Baets, W. R. J. (1998). *Organizational Learning and Knowledge Technologies in a Dynamic Environment*. Norwell, MA: Kluwer Academic Publishers. doi:10.1007/978-1-4615-5773-9

Bagchi, S., Kanungo, S., & Dasgupta, S. (2003). Modeling use of enterprise resource planning systems: A path analytic study. *European Journal of Information Systems*, *12*(2), 142–158. doi:10.1057/palgrave.ejis.3000453

Bailey, R. (2004). *Mathematics – Applications and Concepts (Course 2)*. New York: McGraw-Hill.

Baker, R. (2005). Enterprise Information Systems and B2B E-Commerce: The Significance of XML. *International Journal of Enterprise Information Systems*, *1*(1), 53–64.

Bakos, J. Y., & Brynjolfsson, E. (1993). Information technology, incentives, and the optimal number of suppliers. *Journal of Management Information Systems*, *10*(2), 37–53.

Bakos, J. Y., & Treacy, M. D. (1986). Information Technology and Corporate Strategy: A Research Perspective. *Management Information Systems Quarterly*, *10*(2), 107–119. doi:10.2307/249029

Baranyi, S., Hercegfi, K., & Tilly, K. (2003). Invariant User Interfaces. *Periodica Polytechnica*, *47*(4), 297–310.

Barker, T., & Frolick, M. (2003). ERP implementation failure: a case study. *Information Systems Management*, *20*(4), 43–49. doi:10.1201/1078/43647.20.4.20030901/77292.7

Barnes, F. (2010). Putting a lock on Cloud-Based Information. *Information Management Journal*, *44*(4), 26–30.

Barney, J. (1991). Firm Resources and Sustained Competitive Advantage. *Journal of Management*, *17*(1), 99–120. doi:10.1177/014920639101700108

Barratt, M., & Choi, T. (2007). Mandated RFID and institutional responses: cases of decentralized business units. *Production and Operations Management*, *16*(5), 569–585.

Bartlett, M. S. (1950). Tests of significance in factor analysis. *The British Journal of Psychology*, *3*, 77.

Bauer, B., & Roser, S. (2006). Semantic-enabled Software Engineering and Development. In *Proceedings of Informatik 2006* (LNI P-94, pp. 293-296). Bonner Köllen Verlag.

Bay, T. G., Eugster, P., & Oriol, M. (2006). *Generic Component Lookup*, Proc. of the 9th Int. SIGSOFT Symp. on Component Based Software Engineering, CBSE 2006, LNCS, vol. 4063, (pp. 182-197), Springer

Bayardo, R. J., Jr., Bohrer, W., Brice, R., Cichocki, A., Flower, J., Helal, A., et al. (1997). Infosleuth: Agent-Based Semantic Integration of Information in Open and Dynamic Environments. In *Proceeding of the ACM SIGMOD International Conference on Management of Data* (pp. 195-206).

Becerra-Fernandez, I., Murphy, K. E., & Simon, S. J. (2000). Enterprise resource planning: Integrating ERP in the business school curriculum. *Communications of the ACM*, *43*(4), 41. doi:10.1145/332051.332066

Beck, R., & Weitzel, T. (2005). Some Economics of Vertical Standards: Integrating SMEs in EDI Supply Chains. *Electronic Markets*, *15*(4), 313–322. doi:10.1080/10196780500302781

Benbasat, I., Goldstein, D. K., & Mead, M. (1987). The Case Research Strategy in Studies of Information Systems. *Management Information Systems Quarterly*, *11*(3), 368–386. doi:10.2307/248684

Bendoly, E., & Schoenherr, T. (2005). ERP system and implementation-process benefits: implications for B2B e-procurement. *International Journal of Operations & Production Management*, *25*(4), 304–319. doi:10.1108/01443570510585516

Benjamin, R. I., de Long, D. W., & Morton, M. S. S. (1990). Electronic Data Interchange: How Much Competitive Advantage? *Long Range Planning*, *23*(1), 29–40. doi:10.1016/0024-6301(90)90005-O

Benkler, Y. (2002). Coase's Penguin, or, Linux and The Nature of the Firm. *The Yale Law Journal*, *112*(3), 369. doi:10.2307/1562247

Berlo, D. K. (1960). *The Process of Communication*. New York: Holt, Rinehart, and Winston.

Besen, S. M. (1992). AM versus FM: The Battle of the Bands. *Industrial and Corporate Change, 1*, 375–396. doi:10.1093/icc/1.2.375

Besen, S. M. (1995). The Standards Processes in Telecommunication and Information Technology In Hawkins, R., Mansell, R., & Skea, J. (Eds.), *Standards, Innovation, and Competitiveness: the Politics and Economics of Standards in Natural and Technical Environments*. Cheltenham, UK: Edward Elgar.

Bharadwaj, A. (2000). A Resource-Based Perspective on Information Technology Capability and Firm Performance: An Empirical Investigation. *Management Information Systems Quarterly, 24*(1), 169–197. doi:10.2307/3250983

Bhargava, H. (2007). Building Smart RFID Networks. *RFID Journal*. Retrieved July 7, 2008, from http://www.rfidjournal.com/article/articleview/3387/1/82/

Bhattacherjee, A. (2000). Beginning SAP R/3 Implementation at Geneva Pharmaceuticals. *Communications of the Association for Information Systems, 4*(2).

Biehl, M. (2005). Selecting internal and external supply chain functionality: the case of ERP systems versus electronic marketplaces. *Journal of Enterprise Information Management, 18*(4), 441–457. doi:10.1108/17410390510609590

Biehl, M., & Kim, H. (2003). Electronic marketplaces versus enterprise resource planning: a comparison and decision methodology for supply chain management. International Journal of Technology. *Policy & Management, 3*(3/4), 262–284.

Bingi, P., Sharma, M., & Godla, J. (1999). Critical issues affecting an ERP implementation. *Information Systems Management, 16*(3), 7–14. doi:10.1201/1078/43197.16.3.19990601/31310.2

Bishop, J., & Horspool, N. (2004). Developing principles of GUI programming using Views *Proceedings of SIGCSE, 04*, 373–377. doi:10.1145/1028174.971429

Black, J. A., & Farias, G. (2000). Dynamic Strategies: Emergent Journeys. *Emergence, 2*(1), 101–113. doi:10.1207/S15327000EM0201_07

Blanchard, D. (2008, May). Wal-Mart Lays Down the Law. *Industry Week*, 71–74.

Blossom, P. (2005, January 24). Levels of RFID Maturity, Part 2. *RFID Journal*. Retrieved July 5, 2008, from http://www.rfidjournal.com/article/articleview/1347/1/82/

Boon, O., Wilkin, C., & Corbitt, B. (2003). *Towards A Broader Based Is Success Model – Integrating Critical Success Factors and the Deleon AND McLean's Is Success Model*. Retrieved from www. deakin.edu.ac

Bouchard, L. (1993). *Decision Criteria in the Adoption of EDI*. Paper presented at the Fourteenth International Conference on Information Systems, Orlando, FL.

Bowling, T., Licul, E. D., & Hammond, V. (2007). *Global Data Synchronization: Building a flexible approach*. Retrieved December 12, 2009, from ftp://ftp.software.ibm.com/software/integration/wpc/library/ge-5103990.pdf

Boyer, J. M. (2007). *Xforms1.1, W3C Working Draft*, Retrieved July 24, 2008 from the W3C Web Site: http://www.w3.org/TR/2007/WD-xforms11-20070222

Boykin, R., & Martz, W. Jr. (2004). The integration of ERP into a logistics curriculum: applying a systems approach. *Journal of Enterprise Information Management, 17*(1), 45–55. doi:10.1108/09576050410510944

Boykin, R., Martz, W., & Mensching, J. (1999). The integration of enterprise information systems in the operations management curriculum. *Journal of Computer Information Systems, 39*(4), 45–55.

Boyle, T. (2007). Technical-Oriented Enterprise Resource Planning (ERP) Body of Knowledge for Information Systems Programs: Content and Implementation. *Journal of Education for Business, 82*(5), 267–274. doi:10.3200/JOEB.82.5.267-275

Boynton, A. C., Zmud, R. W., & Jacobs, G. C. (1994). The Influence of IT Management Practice on IT Use in Large Corporations. *Management Information Systems Quarterly, 18*(3), 299–318. doi:10.2307/249620

Bozarth, C. (2006). ERP implementation efforts at three firms Integrating lessons from the SISP and IT-enabled change literature. *International Journal of Operations & Production Management, 11*, 1223–1339. doi:10.1108/01443570610705836

Bradely, J., & Lee, C. C. (2007). ERP and user satisfaction: A case study. *International Journal of Enterprise Information Systems, 3*(4), 33–50.

Brandenburger, A. M., & Nalebuff, B. J. (1996). *Co-Opetition. 1. A Revolutionary Mindset That Combines Competition and Cooperation. 2. The Game Theory Strategy That's Changing the Game of Business*. New York: Doubleday.

Bristow, R., Dodds, T., Northam, R., & Plugge, L. (2010). Cloud Computing and the Power to Choose. *EDUCAUSE Review, 45*(3), 14.

Brochner, J., Adolfsson, P., & Johansson, M. (2002). Outsourcing facilities management in the process industry: a comparison of Swedish and UK patterns. *Journal of Facilities Management, 1*(3), 265–271. doi:10.1108/14725960310807953

Bromiley, P., & Cummings, L. L. (1991). *Transaction Costs in Organizations with Trust (Tech. Rep.)*. University of Minnesota, Department of Strategic Management and Organization.

Brown, C. V., & Vessey, I. (2003). Managing the Next Wave of Enterprise Systems: Leveraging Lessons from ERP. *MIS Quarterly Executive, 2*(1), 65–77.

Bruijn, J. D., Bussler, C., Domingue, J., & Fensel, D. (2005). *WSMO*. Retrieved May 10, 2008, from http://www.w3.org/Submission/WSMO/

Brynjolfsson, E., & Hitt, L. (1996). Paradox Lost? Firm-Level Evidence on the Returns to Information Systems Spending. *Management Science, 42*(4), 541–558. doi:10.1287/mnsc.42.4.541

Brynjolfsson, E., & Hitt, L. M. (1998). Beyond the productivity paradox. *Communications of the ACM, 41*(8), 49–55. doi:10.1145/280324.280332

Brynjolfsson, E., Hofmann, P., & Jordan, J. (2010). Economic and Business Dimensions Cloud Computing and Electricity: Beyond the Utility Model. *Communications of the ACM, 53*(5), 32. doi:10.1145/1735223.1735234

Bueno, S., & Salmeron, J. L. (2008). TAM-based success modeling in ERP. *Interacting with Computers, 20*(6), 515–523. doi:10.1016/j.intcom.2008.08.003

Bühler, K. (1965). *Sprachtheorie: Die Darstellungsform der Sprache*. Stuttgart, Germany: Verlang UTB.

Bunker, D. (2000). *Enterprise Resource Planning System Tools: The Context of their Creation and Use within the Technology Transfer Process*. Paper presented at the Americas Conference on Information Systems, AMCIS, Long Beach, CA.

Burnes, J. (1996). *Using ISCM to create a competitive edge in the year 2000*. Cambridge, MA: MIT Center for Transportation Studies.

Burn, J., & Ash, C. (2005). A dynamic model of e-business strategies for ERP enabled Organizations. *Industrial Management & Data Systems, 105*(8), 1084–1095. doi:10.1108/02635570510624464

Burns, M. (2006). *Accounting System/ERP Customer Survey*. Retrieved from http://www.180systems.com/ERPCustomerSurvey.php

Burns, M. (2008). *Accounting/ERP Comparison*. Retrieved from http://www.180systems.com/ERPsystem-comparison.php

Burt, D. N., Dobler, D. W., & Starling, S. L. (2003). *World-Class Supply Management: The Key to Supply Chain Management*. New York: McGraw-Hill.

Cáceres, P., De Castro, V., & Marcos, E. (2004). Navigation Modeling from a User Services Oriented Approach. In *Proceedings of the 3rd Biennial International Conference in Advanced in Information Systems (ADVIS 2004)* (LNCS 3271, pp. 150-160).

Cáceres, P., Marcos, E., & Vela, B. (2003). *A MDA-Based Approach for Web Information System Development*. Paper presented at the Workshop in Software Model Engineering.

Calisir, F., & Calisir, F. (2004). The relation of interface usability characteristics, perceived usefulness, and perceived ease of use to end-user satisfaction with enterprise recourse planning (ERP) systems. *Computers in Human Behavior, 20*(4), 505–515. doi:10.1016/j.chb.2003.10.004

Calisir, F., Gumussoy, C. A., & Bayram, A. (2009). Predicting the behavioral intention to use enterprise resource planning systems: An exploratory extension of the technology acceptance model. *Management Research News, 32*(7), 597–613. doi:10.1108/01409170910965215

Callaway, E. (2000). *ERP – The Next Generation: ERP is Web Enabled for E-business*. Charleston, SC: Computer Technology Research.

Calza, F., & Passaro, R. (1997). EDI network and logistics management at Unilever-Sagit. *Supply Chain Management, 2*(4), 158–170. doi:10.1108/13598549710191322

Cannon, A. R., Reyes, P. M., Frazier, G. V., & Prater, E. L. (2008). RFID in the contemporary supply chain: multiple perspectives on its benefits and risks. *International Journal of Operations & Production Management, 28*(5), 433–545. doi:10.1108/01443570810867196

Caputo, M., & Zirpoli, F. (2002). Supplier involvement in automotive component design: outsourcing strategies and supply chain management. *International Journal of Technology Management, 23*(1, 2, & 3), 129-154.

Carr, N. G. (2004, May 1). *The Argument Over IT.* Retrieved from http://www.cio.com/archive/050104/carr.html

Carton, F., Frederic, A., & Sammon, D. (2007). Project management: a case study of a successful ERP implementation. *International Journal of Managing Projects in Business, 1*(1), 106–124. doi:10.1108/17538370810846441

Caruso, J., & King, P. (2002). *Enterprise Systems at Three University Systems: California State University, University System of Georgia, University of Wisconsin System.* Boulder, CO: Educase Center for Applied Research.

Čerić, V. (2001). Building the Knowledge Economy. *Journal of Computing and Information Technology, 9*(3), 177–183. doi:10.2498/cit.2001.03.02

Cervone, F. H. (2010). An overview of virtual and cloud computing. *OCLC Systems & Services, 26*(3), 162–165. doi:10.1108/10650751011073607

Chang, C., & Jarvenpaa, S. (2005). Pace of Information Systems Standards Development and Implementation: The Case of XBRL. *Electronic Markets, 15*(4), 365–377. doi:10.1080/10196780500303029

Chang, H.-H. (2008). Intelligent agent's technology characteristics applied to online auctions task: A combined model of TTF and TAM. *Technovation, 28*(9), 564–577. doi:10.1016/j.technovation.2008.03.006

Chang, K., Jackson, J., & Grover, V. (2003). E-commerce and corporate strategy: an executive perspective. *Information & Management, 40*(7), 663–675. doi:10.1016/S0378-7206(02)00095-2

Chang, M.-K., Cheung, W., Cheng, C.-H., & Yeung, J. H. Y. (2008). Understanding ERP system adoption from the user's perspective. *International Journal of Production Economics, 113*(2), 928–942. doi:10.1016/j.ijpe.2007.08.011

Chang, Y., Cheng, Y., & Lin, B. (2007). An efficient web services –enabled architecture for radio frequency identification environment. *International Journal of Mobile Communications, 5*(6), 646–660. doi:10.1504/IJMC.2007.014179

Chatfield, A. T., & Yetton, P. (2000). Strategic payoff from EDI as a function of EDI embeddedness. *Journal of Management Information Systems, 16*(4), 195–224.

Chau, P. Y. K. (2001). Influence of computer attitude and self-efficacy on IT usage behavior. *Journal of End User Computing, 13*(1), 26–33.

Chen, A. N. K., LaBrie, R. C., & Shao, B. B. M. (2003). An XML Adoption Framework for Electronic Business. *Journal of Electronic Commerce Research, 4*(1), 1–14.

Chen, P.-Y., & Forman, C. (2006). Can Vendors Influence Switching Costs and Compatibility in an Environment with Open Standards? *Management Information Systems Quarterly, 30*, 541–562.

Cherry, S. (2009). Forecast for Cloud Computing: Up, Up, and Away. *IEEE Spectrum, 46*(10), 68. doi:10.1109/MSPEC.2009.5268002

Chiang, I. R., & Mookerjee, V. S. (2004). A fault threshold policy to manage software development projects. *Information Systems Research, 15*(1), 3–21. doi:10.1287/isre.1040.0012

Chin, W. W. (1995). Partial Least Squares is to LISREL as principal components analysis is to common factor analysis. *Technology Studies, XXI*(2), 315–319.

Chin, W. W. (1998). Issues and Opinions on Structural Equation Modeling. *Management Information Systems Quarterly, 22*(1).

Chircu, A. M., Kauffman, R. J., & Keskey, D. (2001). Maximizing the Value of Internet-Based Corporate Travel Reservation Systems. *Communications of the ACM, 44*(11), 57–63. doi:10.1145/384150.384162

Chiu, Y. (2010). Taiwan Sees Clouds in Its Forecast. *IEEE Spectrum*, *47*(8), 13. doi:10.1109/MSPEC.2010.5520615

Chou, H. W. (2001). Effects of training method and computer anxiety on learning performance and self-efficacy. *Computers in Human Behavior*, *17*(1), 51–69. doi:10.1016/S0747-5632(00)00035-2

Chow, W. (2004). An exploratory study of the success factors for extranet adoption in e-supply chain. *Journal of Global Information Management*, *12*(1), 60–67. doi:10.4018/jgim.2004010104

Choy, K. L., & Lee, W. B. (2002). A generic tool for the selection and management of supplier relationships in an outsourced manufacturing environment: the application of case based reasoning. *Logistics Information Management*, *15*(4), 235–253. doi:10.1108/09576050210436093

Christiaanse, E., & Rodon, J. (2005). A Multilevel Analysis of eHub Adoption and Consequences. *Electronic Markets*, *15*(4), 355–364. doi:10.1080/10196780500302997

Chuang, M.-L., & Shaw, W. H. (2008). An empirical study of enterprise resource management systems implementation From ERP to RFID. *Business Process Management Journal*, *5*(14), 675–693. doi:10.1108/14637150810903057

Chuck, C. H., & Ngai, E. W. T. (2007). ERP systems adoption: An exploratory study of the organizational factors and impacts of ERP success. *Information & Management*, *44*, 418–432. doi:10.1016/j.im.2007.03.004

Chwelos, P., Benbasat, I., & Dexter, A. S. (2001). Research report: Empirical test of an EDI adoption model. *Information Systems Research*, *12*(3), 304–321. doi:10.1287/isre.12.3.304.9708

Cicchetti, A., & Rossini, A. (2007). Weaving models in conflicts detection specifications. In *Proceedings of the ACM Symposium on Applied Computing* (pp. 1035-1036). ACM Publishing.

Cicchetti, A., Di Ruscio, D., & Pierantonio, A. (2007). A metamodel independent approach to difference representation. *Journal of Object Technology*. *Special Issue on TOOLS EUROPE*, *6*(9), 165–185.

Ciganek, A. P., Haines, M. N., & Haseman, W. D. (2005, January 3-6). *Challenges of Adopting Web Services: Experiences from the Financial Industry*. Paper presented at the Hawaii International Conference on System Sciences (HICSS 38), Waikoloa, HI.

Ciganek, A. P., Haines, M. N., & Haseman, W. D. (2006, January 4-7). *Horizontal and Vertical Factors Influencing the Adoption of Web Services*. Paper presented at the Hawaii International Conference on System Sciences (HICSS 39), Kauai, HI.

Clemons, E. K., Reddi, S. P., & Row, M. C. (1993). The Impact of Information Technology on the Organization of Economic Activity: The "Move to the Middle" Hypothesis. *Journal of Management Information Systems*, *10*(2), 9–35.

Clemons, E. K., & Row, M. (1988). McKesson Drug Company: A Case Study of Economost - A Strategic Information System. *Journal of Management Information Systems*, *5*(1), 36–50.

Cleverley, M. (2009). Emerging Markets How ICT Advances Might Help Developing Nations. *Communications of the ACM*, *52*(9), 30. doi:10.1145/1562164.1562177

Cohen, N. H. (2000). A Java Framework for Mobile Data Synchronization. In O. Etzion & P. Scheuermann (Eds.), *Cooperative Information Systems* (LNCS 1901, pp. 287-298). Berlin: Springer.

Cohen, W. M., & Levinthal, D. A. (1990). Absorptive capacity: A new perspective on learning and innovation. *Administrative Science Quarterly*, *35*(1), 128. doi:10.2307/2393553

Collet, C., Huhns, N., & Shen, W. (1991). Resource Integration using large knowledge base in Carnot. *IEEE Computer*, 55-62.

Collins, R., & Bechler, K. (1999). Outsourcing in the chemical and automotive industries: choice or competitive imperative? *Journal of Supply Chain Management*, *35*(4), 4–10. doi:10.1111/j.1745-493X.1999.tb00239.x

Collins, R., Bechler, K., & Pires, S. (1997). Outsourcing in the automotive industry: from JIT to modular consortia. *European Management Journal*, *15*(5), 498–508. doi:10.1016/S0263-2373(97)00030-3

Compeau, D. R., & Higgins, C. A. (1995). Computer Self-Efficacy: Development of a Measure and Initial Test. *Management Information Systems Quarterly, 19*(2), 89–211. doi:10.2307/249688

Coney, B. (2007). *Business Process Change: Migrating from MS-Word to XML to meet Board of Health Requirements and Business Process Needs.* Paper presented at the On Philadelphia XML Users Group Speaker Series, Philadelphia.

Conradi, R., & Westfechtel, B. (1998). Version models for software configuration management. *ACM Computing Surveys, 30*(2), 232–282. doi:10.1145/280277.280280

Cook, W. J. (2000). *Strategies: The Art of Science of Holistic Strategy.* Westport, CT: Quorem.

Cooper, R., & Zmud, R. (1990). Information Technology Implementation Research: A Technological Diffusion Approach. *Management Science, 36*(2), 123–139. doi:10.1287/mnsc.36.2.123

Corswant, F., & Fredriksson, P. (2002). Sourcing trends in the car industry: a survey of car manufacturers' and suppliers' strategies and relations. *International Journal of Operations & Production Management, 22*(7/8), 741–758. doi:10.1108/01443570210433526

Cover, T. M., & Thomas, J. A. (1991). *Elements of information theory.* New York: John Wiley and Sons Inc. doi:10.1002/0471200611

Cox, J. (2007, May 8). ERP, Security Among Top Concerns for Higher-Ed IT Pros. *CIO.*

Creeger, M. (2010). Moving to the Edge: A CTO Roundtable on Network Virtualization. *Communications of the ACM, 53*(8), 55. doi:10.1145/1787234.1787251

Cronbach, L. J. (1951). Coefficient Alpha and the Internal Structure of Tests. *Psychometrika, 16*, 297–334. doi:10.1007/BF02310555

Cuenca Grau, B., Horrocks, I., Kazakov, Y., & Sattler, U. (2007a). Just the right amount: Extracting modules from ontologies. In *Proceedings of the Sixteenth International World Wide Web Conference (WWW 2007),* Banff, Alberta, Canada (pp. 717-726).

Cuenca Grau, B., Kazakov, Y., Horrocks, I., & Sattler, U. (2007b). A logical framework for modular integration of ontologies. In *Proceedings of the 20th International Joint Conference on Artificial Intelligence (IJCAI 2007)* (pp. 298-303).

Cuence Grau, B., Parsia, B., Sirin, E., & Kalyanpur, A. (2006, June 2–5). Modularity and web ontologies. In P. Doherty, J. Mylopoulos, & C. A. Welty (Eds.), *Proceedings of KR2006: 20th International Conference on Principles of Knowledge Representation and Reasoning,* Lake District, UK, (pp. 198-209). Menlo Park, CA: AAAI Press.

Cusumano, M. (2010). Technology Strategy and Management Cloud Computing and SaaS as New Computing Platforms. *Communications of the ACM, 53*(4), 27. doi:10.1145/1721654.1721667

Czarnecki, K., & Eisenecker, U. (2000) *Generative Programming: Methods, Tools, and Applications,* Addison-Wesley

D'Hondt, M., & D'Hondt, T. (1999). *Is Domain Knowledge an Aspect?* Proc. of the Workshop on Object-Oriented Technology, LNCS; vol. 1743, (pp. 293-294), Springer

Daft, R. L. (1983). *Organization Theory and Design.* New York: West.

Damanpour, F. (2001). E-businesse e-commerce evolution: perspective and strategy. *Managerial Finance, 27*(7), 16–34. doi:10.1108/03074350110767268

Damsgaard, J., & Lyytinen, K. (2001). The Role of Intermediating Institutions in the Diffusion of Electronic Data Interchange (EDI): How Industry Associations Intervened in Denmark, Finland, and Hong Kong. *The Information Society, 17*(3), 195–210. doi:10.1080/01972240152493056

Damsgaard, J., & Truex, D. (2000). Binary Trading Relations and the Limits of EDI Standards: The Procrustean Bed of Standards. *European Journal of Information Systems, 9*(3), 173–188. doi:10.1057/palgrave/ejis/3000368

Davenport, T. H. (1993). *Process Innovation: Reengineering Work Through Information Technology.* Boston, MA: Harvard Business School Press.

Davenport, T. H. (1998). Putting the enterprise into the enterprise system. *Harvard Business Review, 76*(4), 121–131.

Davenport, T. H. (2000). *Mission Critical: Realizing the Promise of Enterprise Systems*. Boston: Harvard Business School Press.

Davenport, T. H., & Prusak, L. (2000). *Working Knowledge: How Organizations Share What They Know*. Boston, MA: Harvard Business School Press.

David, C., & Coker, W. (2006). *Lessons Learned from the Army's Largest ERP Implementation*. Retrieved from khyde@corpcomminc.com

David, P. A. (1987). Some new standards for the economics of standardization in the information age. In Dasgupta, P., & Stoneman, P. (Eds.), *Economic policy and technological performance* (pp. 206–239). Cambridge, UK: Cambridge University Press. doi:10.1017/CBO9780511559938.010

David, P. A., & Greenstein, S. (1990). The economics of compatibility standards: an introduction to recent research. *Economics of Innovation and New Technology*, *1*, 3–41. doi:10.1080/10438599000000002

Davidson, S. B., Garcia-Molina, H., & Skeen, D. (1985). Consistency in partitioned networks. *ACM Computing Surveys*, *17*, 341–370. doi:10.1145/5505.5508

Davis, C., & Comeau, J. (2004). Enterprise integration in business education: Design and outcomes of a capstone ERP-based undergraduate e-business management course. *Journal of Information Systems Education*, *15*(3), 287–299.

Davis, F. D. (1989). Perceived usefulness, perceived ease of use, and user acceptance of information technology. *Management Information Systems Quarterly*, *13*(3), 319–340. doi:10.2307/249008

Davis, F. D. (1993). User acceptance of information technology: System characteristics, user perceptions and behavioural impacts. *International Journal of Man-Machine Studies*, *38*(3), 475–387. doi:10.1006/imms.1993.1022

Davis, F. D., Bagozzi, R. P., & Warshaw, R. P. (1989). User acceptance of computer technology: A comparison of two theoretical models. *Management Science*, *35*(8), 982–1003. doi:10.1287/mnsc.35.8.982

Day, M., Magnan, G., Webb, M., & Hughes, J. (2006, April). Strategic Supplier Relationship Management. *Supply Chain Management Review*, 40-48.

de Búrca, S., Fynes, B., & Marshall, D. (2005). Strategic technology adoption: extending ERP across the supply chain. *Journal of Enterprise Information Management*, *18*(4), 427–440. doi:10.1108/17410390510609581

De Castro, V., Marcos, E., & Cáceres, P. (2004). A User Service Oriented Method to Model Web Information Systems. In X. Zhou et al. (Eds.), *Proceedings of the Web Information System Engineering Conference 2004 (WISE 2004)* (LNCS 3306, pp. 41-52).

De Castro, V., Marcos, E., & López Sanz, M. (2006). A Model Driven Method for Service Composition Modeling: A Case Study. *International Journal of Web Engineering and Technology*, *2*(4), 335–353. doi:10.1504/IJWET.2006.010419

de Cesare, S., Holland, G., Holtmann, C., & Lycett, M. (2007). Semantic-based systems development. In *OOPSLA Companion* (pp. 760).

Dedrick, J., & West, J. (2003, Dec 12-14). *Why Firms Adopt Open Source Platforms: A Grounded Theory of Innovation and Standard Adoption*. Paper presented at the International Conference on IS Special Workshop on Standard Making sponsored by MISQ, Seattle, WA.

Deelman, E. (2010). Grids and Clouds: Making Workflow Applications Work in Heterogeneous Distributed Environments. *International Journal of High Performance Computing Applications*, *24*(3), 284. doi:10.1177/1094342009356432

DeFelice, A., & Leon, J. (2010). Cloud Computing. *Journal of Accountancy*, *210*(4), 50–55.

DeLone, W. H. (1981). Firm Size and the Characteristics of Computer Use. *Management Information Systems Quarterly*, 65–77. doi:10.2307/249328

DeLone, W. H., & McLean, E. R. (2003). The DeLone and McLean Model of Information Systems Success: A Ten-Year Update. *Journal of Management Information Systems*, *19*(4), 9–30.

Denoual, E., & Imag, C. G. (2006). A method to quantify corpus similarity and its application to quantifying the degree of literality in a document. *International Journal of Technology and Human Interaction*, *2*, 51–66.

deVaus, D. (1991). *Surveys in Social Research* (3rd ed.). Sydney, Australia: Allen and Unwin.

Dey, D., Zhang, Z. J., & De, P. (2006). Optimal synchronization policies for data warehouses. *Journal on Computing, 18*(2), 229–242.

Dig, D., Manzoor, K., Johnson, R., & Nguyen, T. N. (2008). Effective software merging in the presence of object-oriented refactorings. *IEEE Transactions on Software Engineering, 34*(3), 321–335. doi:10.1109/TSE.2008.29

Dimitrov, M., Simov, A., Momtchev, V., & Ognyanov, D. (2005). WSMO Studio - An Integrated Service Environment for WSMO. In *Proceedings of the WIW 2005 Workshop on WSMO Implementations*. Retrieved from http://www.wsmostudio.org

Ding, F., & Stoner, A. (2004). An evaluation procedure for material service centers. *Supply Chain Management, 9*(2), 197–203. doi:10.1108/13598540410527088

Dobson, G., & Sawyer, P. (2006). *Revisiting Ontology-Based Requirements Engineering in the age of the Semantic Web*. Paper presented at the International Seminar Dependable Requirements Engineering of Computerised Systems at NPPs, Halden.

Doll, W. J., Hendrickson, A., & Deng, X. (1998). Using Davis's perceived usefulness and ease of-use instruments for decision making: A confirmatory and multi group invariance analysis. *Decision Sciences, 29*(4), 840–869. doi:10.1111/j.1540-5915.1998.tb00879.x

Dong, L. (2008). Exploring the Impact of Top Management Support of Enterprise Systems Implementation Outcomes. *Business Process Management Journal, 14*(2), 204–218. doi:10.1108/14637150810864934

Donovan, R. M. (n.d.). Retrieved from www.rmdonovan.com

Douglas, A. F. (1999). *Mastering the digital marketplace: practical strategies for competitiveness in the new economy*. New York: John Wiley & Sons.

Dublin Core Metadata Initiative (2007). Retrieved July 24, 2008 from the Dublin Core Web Site: http://dublincore.org/

Durkee, D. (2010). Why Cloud Computing Will Never Be Free. *Communications of the ACM, 53*(5), 62. doi:10.1145/1735223.1735242

Dyer, J. H. (1996). Does governance matter? Keiretsu alliances and asset specificity as sources of Japanese competitive advantage. *Organization Science, 7,* 649–666. doi:10.1287/orsc.7.6.649

Dyer, J. H., & Singh, H. (1998). The Relational View: Cooperative Strategy and Sources of Interorganizational Competitive Advantage. *Academy of Management Review, 23*(4), 660–679. doi:10.2307/259056

Eason, K. (1988). *Information technology and organizational change*. London: Taylor & Francis.

Eclipse Foundation. (2008). *Eclipse Modeling Framework Project (EMF)*. Retrieved August 29, 2008, from http://www.eclipse.org/modeling/emf/

Edwards, W. (1997). Flexible conflict detection and management in collaborative applications. In *Proceedings of the 10th Annual ACM Symposium on User Interface Software and Technology* (pp. 139-148).

Ekman, T., & Asklund, U. (2004). Refactoring-aware versioning in Eclispe. *Electronic Notes in Theoretical Computer Science, 107,* 57–69. doi:10.1016/j.entcs.2004.02.048

El Sawah, S., El Fattah, T., Assem, A., & Rasmy, M. H. (2008). A quantitative model to predict the Egyptian ERP implementation success index. *Business Process Management Journal, 3*(14), 288–306. doi:10.1108/14637150810876643

Elenius, D., Denker, G., Martin, D., Gilham, F., Khouri, J., Sadaati, S., et al. (2005, May). The owl-s editor - a development tool for Semantic Web services. In *Proceedings of the Second European Semantic Web Conference* (LNCS 3532, pp. 78-92)

Elliott, M. (2005). Yellow light, green light. *Industrial Engineer, 37,* 6.

Ellis, R. J. (1988). *Managing Strategy in the Real-World: Conclusions and Frameworks for Field Studies of Business Practice*. Lexington, MA: Lexington Books.

Emerson, R. M. (1962). Power Dependence Relations. *American Sociological Review, 27*(1), 31–41. doi:10.2307/2089716

Endo, S., Miyamoto, T., Kumagai, S., & Fujii, T. (2004). A Data Synchronization Method for Peer-to-Peer Collaboration Systems. In *Proceedings of International Symposium on Communications and Information Technologies* (pp. 368-373). Washington, DC: IEEE.

Erat, S., & Kavadias, S. (2006). Introduction of New Technologies to Competing Industrial Customers. *Management Science, 52*(11), 1675–1688. doi:10.1287/mnsc.1060.0561

ERP Implementation Guidelines. (2002). *ERP Executive Steering Committee.*

Essex, D. (1999). Get into Web Portal. Computerworld. Retrieved April 15, 2010, from http://www.informationweek.com

Esteves, J., & Pastor, J. (2001). Analysis of Critical Success Factors Relevance along SAP Implementation Phases. In *Proceedings of the Seventh Americas Conference ON Information Systems.*

Esteves, J., Casanovas, J., & Pastor, J. (2003).Modeling with Partial Least Squares Critical Success Factors Interrelationships in ERP Implementations. In *Proceedings of the Ninth Americans conference on Information systems.*

Ettlie, J. E. (1980). Adequacy of Stage Models for Decisions on Adoption of Innovation. *Psychological Reports, 46*(8), 991–995.

Eurostat. (2009). Retrieved from http://ec.europa.eu/eurostat/ramon/index.cfm?TargetUrl=DSP_PUB_WELC

Euzenat, J. (2002). Eight Questions about Semantic Web Annotations. *IEEE Intelligent Systems, 17*(2), 55–62.

Evans, M. G. (1985). A Monte Carlo study of the effects of correlated method variance in moderated multiple regression analysis. *Organizational Behavior and Human Decision Processes, 36*, 302–323. doi:10.1016/0749-5978(85)90002-0

Evans, P. B., & Wurster, T. S. (1997, September/October). Strategy and the New Economics of Information. *Harvard Business Review, 75*, 70–82.

Eyal, A., & Milo, T. (2001). Integrating and customizing heterogeneous e-commerce applications. *The VLDB Journal, 10*, 16–38.

Fan, Y. (2000). Strategic outsourcing: evidence from British companies. *Marketing Intelligence & Planning, 18*(4), 213–220. doi:10.1108/02634500010333398

Farrell, J. (1989). Standardization and Intellectual Property. *Jurimetrics Journal, 30*, 35–50.

Farrell, J., & Saloner, G. (1985). Standardization, compatibility, and innovation. *The Rand Journal of Economics, 16*(1), 70–83. doi:10.2307/2555589

Farrell, J., & Saloner, G. (1988). Coordination Through Committees and Markets. *The Rand Journal of Economics, 19*(2), 235. doi:10.2307/2555702

Feeny, D., & Willcocks, L. (1998). Core IS capabilities for exploring IT. *Sloan Management Review, 39*(3), 9–21.

Fensel, D., & Bussler, C. (2002). The Web Service Modeling Framework WSMF. *Electronic Commerce Research and Applications, 1*(2). doi:10.1016/S1567-4223(02)00015-7

Ferguson, R. B. (2006). RFID loses reception: high tag costs are still putting the kibosh on returns on investment. *e-Week, 23*(10), 11-12.

Fertalj, K., & Kalpić, D. (2004). ERP Software Evaluation and Comparative Analysis. *Journal of Computing and Information Technology, 12*(3), 195–209. doi:10.2498/cit.2004.03.02

Fichman, R. G. (1992). *Information Technology Diffusion: A Review of Empirical Research.* Paper presented at the 13th International Conference on Information Systems (ICIS), New York.

Fichman, R. G., & Kemerer, C. F. (1994). *Toward a Theory of the Adoption and Diffusion of Software Process innovations.* Paper presented at the Diffusion, Transfer and Implementation of IT, Elsevier Sciences, North Holland.

Fichman, R. G., & Kemerer, C. F. (1993). Adoption of Software Engineering Process Innovations: The Case of Object Orientation. *Sloan Management Review, 34*(2), 7–22.

Fichman, R. G., & Kemerer, C. F. (1997). The Assimilation of Software Process Innovations: An Organizational Learning Perspective. *Management Science, 43*(10), 1345–1363. doi:10.1287/mnsc.43.10.1345

Fichman, R. G., & Kemerer, C. F. (1999). The Illusory Diffusion of Innovation: An Examination of Assimilation Gaps. *Information Systems Research, 10*(3), 255–275. doi:10.1287/isre.10.3.255

Filman, R. E. (1999). *Achieving ilities*. Paper presented at the Workshop on Compositional Software Architectures, Monterey, CA.

Fine, C. H. (2000). Clockspeed-based strategies for supply chain design. *Production and Operations Management, 9*(3), 213–221. doi:10.1111/j.1937-5956.2000.tb00134.x

Finney, S., & Corbett, M. (2007). ERP implementation:a compilation and analysis of critical success factors. *Business Process Management Journal, 3*(13), 329–347. doi:10.1108/14637150710752272

Fishbein, M., & Ajzen, I. (1975). *Belief, attitude, Intention and behavior: An introduction to research and theory.* Reading, MA: Addison-Wesley.

Fitzsimmons, H. (2010, October). Cloud.com Selected as Cloud Computing Platform for Korea's First Large-Scale Private ClouFkoread. *Computers, Networks & Communications, 158*.

Flensburg, P. (2007, August 11-14). *An enhanced communication model.* Paper presented at the 30th Information Systems Research Seminar in Scandinavia (IRIS), Tampere, Finland.

Folinas, D., Vlachopoulou, M., Manthou, V., & Sigala, M. (2004). Modeling the e-volution of supply chain: Cases and best practices. *Electronic Networking Applications and Policy, 14*(4), 274–283. doi:10.1108/10662240410555298

Forman, C., & Gron, A. (2005, January 3-6). *Vertical Integration and Information Technology Adoption: A Study of the Insurance Industry.* Paper presented at the Hawaii International Conference on System Sciences (HICSS 38), Waikoloa, HI.

Fornell, C., & Larcker, D. (1981). Structural equation models with unobservable variables and measurement error. *JMR, Journal of Marketing Research, 18*(1), 39–50. doi:10.2307/3151312

Foster, J. N., Greenwald, M. B., Kirkegaard, C., Pierce, B. C., & Schmitt, A. (2007). Exploiting schemas in data synchronization. *Journal of Computer and System Sciences, 73*, 669–689. doi:10.1016/j.jcss.2006.10.024

Frankel, D. S. (2003). *Model Driven Architecture – Applying MDA™ to Enterprise Computing.* New York: Wiley.

Fui, F., Nah, H., Zuckweiler, K. M., Lee, J., & Lau, S. (2003). ERP Implementation: Chief Information Officers' Perceptions of Critical Success Factors. *International Journal of Human-Computer Interaction, 1*(16), 5–22.

Fui-Hoon Nah, F., Zuckweiler, K. M., & Lee-Shang, J. L. (2003). ERP Implementation: Chief Information Officer's Perceptions of Critical Success Factors. *International Journal of Human-Computer Interaction, 16*(1), 5–22. doi:10.1207/S15327590IJHC1601_2

Fuller, M., Sankar, C. S., & Raju, P. K. (2009). Design and development of the data synchronization case study. *Computers in Education Journal, 19*(4), 22–31.

Gable, G., Scott, J., & Davenport, T. H. (1998, September 29-October 2). Cooperative ERP life cycle knowledge management. In *Proceedings of the 9th Australasian Conference on Information Systems,* Sydney, Australia (pp. 227-240).

Gable, G. (1998). Large package software: A neglected technology. *Journal of Global Information Management, 6*(3), 3–4.

Gallagher, S., & Park, S. H. (2002). Innovation and Competition in Standard-Based Industries: A Historical Analysis of the U.S. Home Video Game Market. *IEEE Transactions on Engineering Management, 49*(1), 67–82. doi:10.1109/17.985749

Gannod, G., & Timm, J. (2004). *An MDA-based Approach for Facilitating Adoption of Semantic Web Service.* Paper presented at the IEEE EDOC Workshop on Model-Driven Semantic Web (MDSW 04).

Garcia-Sanchez, N., & Perez-Bernal, L. E. (2007). Determination of Critical Success Factors in Implementing an ERP System: A Field Study in Mexican Enterprises. *Information Technology for Development, 13*(3), 293–309. doi:10.1002/itdj.20075

Gargeya, V. B., & Brady, C. (2005). Success and failure factors of adopting SAP in ERP system implementation. *Business Process Management Journal, 11*(5), 501–516. doi:10.1108/14637150510619858

Gašević, D., Kaviani, N., & Milanović, M. (in press). Ontologies and Software Engineering. In S. Staab & R. Studer (Eds.), *Handbook on Ontologies*.

Gatewood, B. (2009). Clouds on the Information Horizon: How to Avoid the Storm. *Information Management Journal, 43*(4), 32–36.

Gaukler, G. M., Seifert, R. W., & Hausman, W. H. (2007). Item-level RFID in the retail supply chain. *Production and Operations Management, 16*(1), 65–76.

Gefen, D. (2004). What makes an ERP implementation relationship worthwhile: linking trust mechanisms and ERP usefulness. *Journal of MIS, 21*(1), 263–288.

Gerst, M., & Bunduchi, R. (2005). Shaping IT Standardization in the Automotive Industry - The Role of Power in Driving Portal Standardization. *Electronic Markets, 15*(4), 335–343. doi:10.1080/10196780500302872

Ghazinoory, S., Zadeh, A. E., & Memariani, A. (2007). Fuzzy SWOT Analysis. *Journal of Intelligent and Fuzzy Systems, 18*(1), 99–108.

Ghemawat, P., & Cassiman, B. (2005). Special Issue on Strategic Dynamics: Call for papers. *Management Science*. Retrieved January 2, 2007, from http://mansci.pubs.informs.org/special_issues/Special_Issue_on_Strategic_Dynamics.pdf

Ghemawat, P. (2006). *Strategy and the Business Landscape* (2nd ed.). Upper Saddle River, NJ: Pearson Education, Inc.

Gist, M. E. (1987). Self-efficacy: implications for organizational behavioral and human resource management. *Academy of Management Review, 12*(3), 472–485. doi:10.2307/258514

Goel, S., Sharda, H., & Taniar, D. (2003). Message-Oriented-Middleware in a Distributed Environment. In T. Böhme, G. Heyer, & H. Unger (Eds.), *Innovative Internet Community Systems* (LNCS 2877, pp. 93-103). Berlin: Springer.

Gogan, J. L. (2005). Punctuation and Path Dependence: Examining a Vertical IT Standard-Setting Process. *Electronic Markets, 15*(4), 344–354. doi:10.1080/10196780500302880

Golden, B. (2009). Cloud Computing: "Be Prepared. *EDUCAUSE Review, 44*(4), 64.

Gosain, S. (2003, December 12-14). *Realizing the Vision for Web Services: Strategies for Dealing with Imperfect Standards.* Paper presented at the International Conference on IS Special Workshop on Standard Making sponsored by MISQ, Seattle, WA.

Grant, G. G. (2003). Strategic alignment and enterprise systems implementation: the case of Metalco. *Journal of Information Technology, 18*, 159. doi:10.1080/0268396032000122132

Grant, R. (1996, July/August). Prospering in dynamically competitive environments: Organizational capability as knowledge integration. *Organization Science, 7*(4), 375–387. doi:10.1287/orsc.7.4.375

Greenfield, A., Patel, J., & Fenner, J. (2001). Online Invoicing for Business-to-Business Users. *Information Week, November, 863,* 80-82.

Greengard, S., & Kshetri, N. (2010). Cloud Computing and Developing Nations. *Communications of the ACM, 53*(5), 18. doi:10.1145/1735223.1735232

Greenstein, S. (1992). Invisible Hand versus Invisible Advisors: Coordination Mechanisms in Economic Networks. *Journal of the American Society for Information Science American Society for Information Science, 43*(8), 538–249. doi:10.1002/(SICI)1097-4571(199209)43:8<538::AID-ASI4>3.0.CO;2-2

Grice, H. P. (1967). Logic and Conversation. In A. P. Martinich (Ed.), *Philosophy of Language*. New York: Oxford University Press.

Grieger, N. (2002). Electronic marketplaces: a literature review and a call for supply chain management research. *European Journal of Operational Research, 144,* 280–294. doi:10.1016/S0377-2217(02)00394-6

Grønmo, R., Jaeger, M. C., & Hoff, H. (2005). Transformations between UML and OWL-S. In *Model Driven Architecture – Foundations and Applications* (LNCS 3748, pp. 269-283).

Grover, V. (1993). An Empirically Derived Model for the Adoption of Customer-based Interorganizational Systems. *Decision Sciences, 24*(3), 603–640. doi:10.1111/j.1540-5915.1993.tb01295.x

Gruber, T. R. (1993). A Translation Approach to Portable Ontology Specifications. *Knowledge Acquisition, 5*(2), 199–220. doi:10.1006/knac.1993.1008

Gruman, G. (2006, December). Four Stages of Enterprise Architecture. *CIO Magazine*, 67-76.

Gschwind, T. (2002). *Adaptation and Composition Techniques for Component Based Software Engineering*, PhD Thesis, Technical University of Vienna

Guarino, N. (1997). Understanding, building and using ontologies. *International Journal of Human-Computer Studies, 46*(2-3), 293–310. doi:10.1006/ijhc.1996.0091

Guarino, N., & Welty, C. A. (2002). Evaluating ontological decisions with OntoClean. *Communications of the ACM, 45*(2), 61–65. doi:10.1145/503124.503150

Guerrero, F. M., Lozano, M., & Rueda-Cantuche, J. M. (2008). Spain's Greatest and Most Recent Mine Disaster. *Disasters, 32*(1), 19–40. doi:10.1111/j.1467-7717.2007.01025.x

Gupta, O., Priyadarshini, K., Massoud, S., & Agrawal, S. (2004). Enterprise resource planning: a case of a blood bank. *Industrial Management + Data Systems, 104*(7), 589-603.

Ha, Y., & Lee, R. (2006, June 19-20). Semantic Web Service Modeling using UML for e-business environment. In *Proceedings of the Seventh ACIS International Conference on Software Engineering, Artificial Intelligence, Networking, and Parallel/Distributed Computing (SNPD'06)* (pp. 368-374).

Ha¨kkinen, L., & Hilmola, O.-P. (2008). Life after ERP implementation Long-term development of user perceptions of system success in an after-sales environment. *Journal of Enterprise Information Management, 3*(21), 285–309. doi:10.1108/17410390810866646

Hair, J. F., Black, W., Babin, B., Anderson, R. E., & Tatham, R. L. (2006). *Multivariate Data analysis*. Upper Saddle River, NJ: Prentice-Hall.

Halla, F. (2007). A SWOT Analysis of Strategic Urban Development Planning: The Case of Dar es Salaam city in Tanzania. *Habitat International, 31*(1), 130–142. doi:10.1016/j.habitatint.2006.08.001

Halpin, T. (1998). Object-role modeling (ORM/NIAM). In *Handbook on Architectures of Information Systems*. New York: Springer.

Hammer, M., & Champy, J. (1993). *Reengineering the Corporation: A Manifesto for Business Revolution*. London: N. Brealey.

Hamner, M., & Qazi, R. U. R. (2009). Expanding the technology acceptance model to examine personal computing technology utilization in government agencies in developing countries. *Government Information Quarterly, 26*(1), 128–136. doi:10.1016/j.giq.2007.12.003

Harel, D., & Rumpe, B. (2004). Meaningful modeling: What's the semantics of "semantics"? *Computer, 37*(10), 64–72. doi:10.1109/MC.2004.172

Ha, S., & Stoel, L. (2009). Consumer e-shopping acceptance: Antecedents in a technology acceptance model. *Journal of Business Research, 62*(5), 565–571. doi:10.1016/j.jbusres.2008.06.016

Hasan, B. (2006). Delineating the effects of general and system-specific computer self-efficacy beliefs on IS acceptance. *Information & Management, 43*(5), 565–571. doi:10.1016/j.im.2005.11.005

Hasan, B. (2007). Examining the Effects of Computer Self-Efficacy and System Complexity on Technology Acceptance. *Information Resources Management Journal, 20*(3), 77–88.

Hausman, A. V., & Siekpe, J. S. (2009). The effect of web interface features on consumer online purchase intentions. *Journal of Business Research, 62*(1), 5–13. doi:10.1016/j.jbusres.2008.01.018

Hawking, P. (1999). The teaching of enterprise resource planning systems (SAP R/3) in Australian Universities. In *Proceedings Pan-Pacific Conference XVI*, Fiji.

Hawking, P., Ramp, A., & Shackleton, P. (2001). IS'97 model curriculum and enterprise resource planning systems. *Business Process Management Journal, 7*(3), 225–233. doi:10.1108/14637150110392700

Hayen, R., Holmes, M., & Cappel, J. (2000). A framework for SAP R/3 enterprise software instruction. *Journal of Computer Information Systems, 40*(2), 79–85.

Hayes, P., et al. (2004). *RDF Semantics*. Retrieved from http://www.w3.org/TR/rdf-mt/

Hayes, B. (2008). Cloud Computing. *Communications of the ACM, 51*(7), 9. doi:10.1145/1364782.1364786

Heide, J. B. (1994). Interorganizational governance in marketing channels. *Journal of Marketing, 58*(1), 71–85. doi:10.2307/1252252

Heikkila, J., & Cordon, C. (2002). Outsourcing: a core or non-core strategic management decision. *Marketing Intelligence & Planning, 11*(4), 183–193.

Helms, J. (Ed.). (2008). *User Interface Markup Language (UIML) Specification, Committee Draft 4.0*, Retrieved July 24, 2008 from the OASIS Web Site: http://www.oasis-open.org/committees/download.php/28457/uiml-4.0-cd01.pdf

Henderson, R., Podd, J., Smith, M., & Varela-Alvarez, H. (1995). An examination of four user-based software evaluation methods. *Interacting with Computers, 7*(4), 412–432. doi:10.1016/0953-5438(96)87701-0

Henriksson, J., Pradel, M., Zschaler, S., & Pan, J. Z. (2008). Ontology Design and Reuse with Conceptual Roles. In *Proceedings of the Second International Conference on Web Reasoning and Rule Systems (RR'08)* (LNCS 5341, pp. 104-118).

Henry, C. (1974). Investment Decisions Under Uncertainty: The "Irreversibility Effect". *The American Economic Review, 64*(6), 1006–1012.

Hepp, M., Leymann, F., Domingue, J., Wahler, A., & Fensel, D. (2005, October 18-20). Semantic Business Process Management: A Vision Towards Using Semantic Web Services for Business Process Management. In *Proceedings of IEEE ICEBE,* Beijing, China (pp. 535-540).

Her Wu, J., & Min Wang, Y. (2006). Measuring ERP success: the ultimate users' view. *International Journal of Operations & Production Management, 8*(26), 882–903.

Hernandez, B., Jimenez, J., & Martin, M. J. (2008). Extending the technology acceptance model to include the IT decision-maker: A study of business management software. *Technovation, 28*(3), 112–121. doi:10.1016/j.technovation.2007.11.002

Herrmann, S. (2002). *Object teams: Improving modularity for crosscutting collaborations*. Paper presented at Net Object Days 2002.

Heumer, G., Schilling, M., & Latoschik, M. E. (2005). Automatic data exchange and synchronization for knowledge-based intelligent virtual environments. *IEEE Virtual Reality*, 43-50.

Heuss, T., Gillespie, S., & Kapczynski, J. (1994). *Robert Bosch: His Life and Achievements*. New York: Henry Holt & Co.

Hevner, A. R., March, S. T., Park, J., & Ram, S. (2004). Design Science in Information Systems Research. *MIS Quarterly, 28*(1), 75–105.

Hills, B. (2000). Common message standards for electronic commerce in wholesale financial markets. *Bank of England Quarterly Bulletin, 40*(3), 274–285.

Hill, T., & Westbrook, R. (1997). SWOT Analysis: It's Time for a Product Recall. *Long Range Planning, 3*, 46–52. doi:10.1016/S0024-6301(96)00095-7

Ho, C., Wu, W., and Tai, W. (2004). Strategies for the adaptation of ERP systems. *Industrial Management + Data Systems, 104*(3-4), 234-251.

Hoek, R. I. (1998). Logistics and virtual integration postponement, outsourcing and the flow of information. *International Journal of Physical Distribution & Logistics Management, 28*(7), 508–523. doi:10.1108/09600039810247498

Hoek, R. I. (1999). Postponement and the reconfiguration challenge for food supply chains. *Supply Chain Management, 4*(1), 18–34. doi:10.1108/13598549910255068

Holland, C., Light, B., & Gibson, N. (1998, August 14-16). Global ERP implementation. In *Proceedings of the American Conference of Information Systems (AMCIS '98), Global Information Technology and Global Electronic Commerce Mini-Track*, Baltimore, MD.

Holland, C. P., & Light, B. (1999). A Critical Success Factors Model for ERP Implementation. *IEEE Software, 16*(3), 30–36. doi:10.1109/52.765784

Holland, D., Light, B., & Gibson, N. (1999). A critical success factors model for ERP implementation. *IEEE Software, 16*(3), 30–36. doi:10.1109/52.765784

Holloway, S. (2006). *Potential of RFID in the Supply Chain*. Chicago, IL: Solidsoft Ltd.

Hong, S., Goor, G., & Brinkkemper, S. (1993). A Formal Approach to the Comparison of Object-Oriented Analysis and Design Methodologies. In J. F. Nunamaker & R. H. Sprague (Eds.), *Information Systems of HICCS* (pp. 689-698).

Hong, K., & Kim, Y. (2002). The critical success factors for ERP implementation: an organizational fit perspective. *Information & Management*, *40*(1), 25–40. doi:10.1016/S0378-7206(01)00134-3

Horridge, M., Drummond, N., Goodwin, J., Rector, A., Stevens, R., & Wang, H. (2006). *The manchester OWL syntax*. Paper presented at OWL: Experiences and Directions (OWLED 06).

Hovav, A., Patnayakuni, R., & Schuff, D. (2004). A model of Internet standards adoption: the case of IPv6. *Information Systems Journal*, *14*(3), 265. doi:10.1111/j.1365-2575.2004.00170.x

Huang, S.-M., Chang, I.-C., Han, L. S., & Tong, M. (2004). Assessing risk in ERP projects: identify and prioritize the factors. *Industrial Management & Data Systems*, *8*(104), 681–688. doi:10.1108/02635570410561672

Hung, S. Y., & Liang, T. P. (2001). Effect of computer self-efficacy on the use of executive support systems. *Industrial Management & Data Systems*, *101*(5), 227–237. doi:10.1108/02635570110394626

Hu, P. J. H., Clark, T. H. K., & Ma, W. W. (2003). Examining technology acceptance by school teachers: A longitudinal study. *Information & Management*, *41*(2), 227–241. doi:10.1016/S0378-7206(03)00050-8

Hwang, Y. (2005). Investigating enterprise systems adoption: uncertainty avoidance, intrinsic motivation, and the technology acceptance model. *European Journal of Information Systems*, *14*(2), 150–161. doi:10.1057/palgrave.ejis.3000532

Iacovou, C. L., Benbasat, I., & Dexter, A. S. (1995). Electronic Data Interchange and Small Organizations: Adoption and Impact of Technology. *Management Information Systems Quarterly*, 465–484. doi:10.2307/249629

IBM. (2008). *IBM Rational Software Architect*. Retrieved August 29, 2008, from http://www-306.ibm.com/software/awdtools/architect/swarchitect

IDC. (2000). *The Integrated Enterprise Resource Management Software Application Market in Croatia, 1999-2004*. Czech Republic: IDC East Central Europe.

Ifinedo, P. (2008). Impacts of Business Vision, Top Management Support, and External Expertise on ERP Success. *Business Process Management Journal*, *14*(4), 551–568. doi:10.1108/14637150810888073

Igbaria, M., & Iivari, J. (1995). The effects of self-efficacy on computer usage. *Omega*, *23*(6), 587–605. doi:10.1016/0305-0483(95)00035-6

Igbaria, M., Parasuraman, S., & Baroudi, J. (1996). A motivational model of microcomputer usage. *Journal of Management Information Systems*, *13*(1), 127–143.

Iidaka, T., Matsumoto, A., Nogawa, J., Yamamoto, Y., & Sadato, N. (2006). *Front parietal Network Involved in Successful Retrieval from Episodic Memory. Spatial and Temporal Analyses Using fMRI and ERP*. Oxford, UK: Oxford University Press.

International Business Machines Corp. (2009). *WebSphere MQ*. Retrieved December 12, 2009, from http://www-01.ibm.com/software/integration/wmq/

International Telecommunications Union. (2009). *Measuring the Information Society: The ICT Development Index*. Geneva, Switzerland: Author.

Italiano, I. C., & Ferreira, J. E. (2006). Synchronization options for data warehouse designs. *Computer*, *39*(3), 53–57. doi:10.1109/MC.2006.104

Jaeger, M., Engel, L., & Geihs, K. (2005). *A methodology for developing owl-s descriptions*. Paper presented at the First International Conference on Interoperability of Enterprise Software and Applications Workshop on Web Services and Interoperability.

Jakupović, A., Pavlić, M., & Fertalj, K. (2009). Analysis and Classification of ERP Producers by Business Operations. *Journal of Computing and Information Technology*, *17*(3), 239–258.

Jankowska, A. M., Kurbel, K., & Schreber, D. (2007). An architecture for agent-based mobile supply chain management. *International Journal of Mobile Communications*, *5*(3), 243–258. doi:10.1504/IJMC.2007.012393

Jaruwachirathanakul, B., & Fink, D. (2005). Internet Banking Adoption Strategies for a Developing Country: The Case of Thailand. *Internet Research*, *15*(3), 295–311. doi:10.1108/10662240510602708

Jaspers, M. W. M., Steen, T., Bos, C. V. D., & Geenen, M. (2004). The think aloud method-a guide to user interface design. *Medical Informatics*, *73*(11-12), 781–795. doi:10.1016/j.ijmedinf.2004.08.003

Jaynes, E. T. (1954). Information theory and statistical mechanics. *Physical Review*, *106*, 620–630. doi:10.1103/PhysRev.106.620

Johnson, J. (1992). *Selectors: Going Beyond User-Interface Widgets*, Proc. of CHI 92: Conference on Human Factors in Computing Systems, (pp. 273-279), May 3-7, Monterey, California

Johnson, M. E. (2001). Learning from toys: lessons in managing supply chain risk from the toy industry. *California Management Review*, *43*(3), 106–123.

Johnson, R., & Vitale, M. (1988). Creating competitive advantage with interorganizational information systems. *Management Information Systems Quarterly*, *12*(2), 153–165. doi:10.2307/248839

Jones, M. C., & Young, R. (2006). ERP Usage in Practice: An Empirical Investigation. *Information Resources Management*, *19*(1), 23–42. doi:10.4018/irmj.2006010102

Joreskog, K. G., & Wold, H. (Eds.). (1982). *Systems Under Indirect Observation: Causality, Structure and Prediction*. Amsterdam: North-Holland.

Joshi, A. W., & Stump, R. L. (1999). Determinants of commitment and opportunism: Integrating insights from transaction cost analysis and relational exchange theory. *Canadian Journal of Administrative Sciences*, *16*(4), 334–352.

JSR 245: JavaServer™ Pages 2.1 (2006). Retrieved July 24, 2008 from the Java Community Process Web Site: http://www.jcp.org/en/jsr/detail?id=245

JSR 168. *Portlet Specification* (2003). Retrieved July 24, 2008 from the Java Community Process Web Site: http://jcp.org/en/jsr/detail?id=168

Ju, T. L., Ju, P. H., & Sun, S. Y. (2008). A strategic examination of Radio Frequency Identification in Supply Chain Management. *International Journal of Technology Management*, *43*(4), 349–436. doi:10.1504/IJTM.2008.020555

Kaiser, H. F. (1970). A second generation little jiffy. *Psychometrika*, *35*, 401–416. doi:10.1007/BF02291817

Kaiya, H., & Saeki, M. (2005). *Ontology Based Requirements Analysis: Leightweight Semantic Processing Approach*. Paper presented at the International Conference on Quality Software (QSIC), Melbourne, Australia.

Kakabadse, N., & Kakabadse, A. (2000). Critical review-outsourcing: a paradigm shift. *Journal of Management Development*, *19*(8), 670–728. doi:10.1108/02621710010377508

Kallio, J., Saarinen, T., & Tinnila, M. (2002). Efficient change strategies. *Business Process Management Journal*, *8*(1), 80–93. doi:10.1108/14637150210418647

Karimi, J., Somers, T. M., & Bhattacherjee, A. (2007). The Impact of ERP Implementation on Business Process Outcomes: A Factor-Based Study. *Journal of Management Information Systems*, *24*(1), 101–134. doi:10.2753/MIS0742-1222240103

Karsak, E., & O' zogul, O. (2009). An integrated decision making approach for ERP system selection. *Expert Systems with Applications*, *36*, 660–667. doi:10.1016/j.eswa.2007.09.016

Kassal, S. (2008). *Semantic Requirements – Ontologie-basierte Modellierung von Anforderungen im Software Engineering*. Master thesis, University of Augsburg.

Katerattanakul, P., Hong, S., & Lee, J. (2006). Enterprise resource planning survey of Korean manufacturing firms. *Management Research News*, *12*(29), 820–837. doi:10.1108/01409170610717835

Kauffman, R. J., McAndrews, J., & Wang, Y.-M. (2000). Opening the "Black Box" of Network Externalities in Network Adoption. *Information Systems Research*, *11*(1), 61–82. doi:10.1287/isre.11.1.61.11783

Keen, P., & Mackintosh, R. (2001). *The freedom economy: Gaining the m-commerce edge in the era of wireless internet.* New York: Osborne-McGraw Hill.

Keil, T. (2002). De-facto Standardization Through Alliances - Lessons From Bluetooth. *Telecommunications Policy, 26*(3-4), 205–213. doi:10.1016/S0308-5961(02)00010-1

Kenevissi, F. (2006). *Multi-criteria decision making (Tech. Rep.).* Newcastle Upon Tyne, UK: Newcastle University, Newcastle Engineering Design Centre.

Kerrigan, M. D9.1v0.1 Web Service Modeling Toolkit (WSMT). Working Draft Retrieved from: http://www.wsmo.org/TR/d9/d9.1/v0.1/20050127/, 2005

Ke, W., & Wei, K. K. (2008). Organizational culture and leadership in ERP implementation. *Decision Support Systems, 45,* 208–218. doi:10.1016/j.dss.2007.02.002

Khan, N., & Fitzgerald, G. (2004). Dimensions of offshore outsourcing business models. *Journal of Information Technology Cases and Applications, 6*(3), 35–50.

Khoury, G. R. (2007). *A unified approach to enterprise architecture modeling.* Unpublished doctoral dissertation, Faculty of Information Technology, University of Technology, Sydney.

Kim, E. Y., Ko, E., Kim, H., & Koh, C. E. (2008, October). Comparison of benefits of radio frequency identification: Implications for business strategic performance in the U.S. and Korean retailers. *Industrial Marketing Management, 37*(7), 797–806. doi:10.1016/j.indmarman.2008.01.007

Kim, Y., Hsu, J., & Stern, M. (2006). An Update on the IS/IT Skills Gap. *Journal of Information Systems Education, 17*(4), 395–402.

Kim, Y., Lee, Z., & Gosain, S. (2005). Impediments to successful ERP implementation process. *Business Process Management Journal, 2*(11), 158–170. doi:10.1108/14637150510591156

King, J. (2010). Clearing the Air on Cloud Computing. *EDUCAUSE Review, 45*(3), 64.

King, W. (2005). Ensuring ERP implementation success. *Information Systems Management, 22*(3), 83–84. doi:10.1201/1078/45317.22.3.20050601/88749.11

King, W. R., Grover, V., & Hufnagel, E. H. (1989). Using Information and Information Technology for Sustainable Competitive Advantage: Some Empirical Evidence. *Information & Management, 17*(2), 87–93. doi:10.1016/0378-7206(89)90010-4

Kiniry, J. R. (2003). *Semantic Component Composition.* Paper presented at ECOOP, Darmstadt, Germany.

Kinsella, B. (2003). The Wal-Mart factor. *Industrial Engineer, 35,* 32.

Kinsner, W. (2007). Is entropy suitable to characterize data and signals for cognitive informatics? *International Journal of Cognitive Informatics and Natural Intelligence, 1,* 34–57.

Knublauch, H., Fergerson, R. W., Noy, N. F., & Musen, M. A. (2004). *The Protégé OWL plugin: An open development environment for semantic web applications.* Paper presented at the Third International Semantic Web Conference (ISWC).

Koch, C. (2007). *Getting Started with Enterprise Resource Planning (ERP): CIO.* Retrieved December 5, 2007, from www.cio.com/article/40323/3

Koch, C. (2008). *The ABCs of ERP.* Retrieved from http://www.cio.com/article/40323/ERP_Definition_and_Solutions

Kopecky, J., Vitvar, T., Bournez, C., & Farrell, J. (2007). SAWSDL: Semantic Annotations for WSDL and XML Schema. *IEEE Internet Computing, 11*(6), 60–67. doi:10.1109/MIC.2007.134

Koskimies, O. (2005). Using data item relationships to adaptively select data for synchronization. In L. Kutvonen & N. Alonistioti (Eds.), *Distributed Applications and Interoperable Systems* (LNCS 3543, pp. 220-225). Berlin: Springer.

Kowalski, V. J., & Karcher, B. (1994, Mar). Industry Consortia in Open Systems. *StandardView, 2,* 34–40. doi:10.1145/224145.224150

Kumar, K., & Van Hillegersberg, J. (2000). ERP experiences and evolution. *Communications of the ACM, 43*(4), 22–26. doi:10.1145/332051.332063

Kumar, V., Maheshwari, B., & Kumar, U. (2002). ERP systems implementation: best practices in Canadian government organizations. *Government Information Quarterly, 19*, 147–172. doi:10.1016/S0740-624X(02)00092-8

Kumar, V., Maheshwari, B., & Kumar, U. (2003). An investigation of critical Management issues in ERP implementation: empirical evidence from Canadian organizations. *Technovation, 23*, 793–807. doi:10.1016/S0166-4972(02)00015-9

Kuo, F. Y., Chu, T. H., Hsu, M. H., & Hsieh, H. S. (2004). An investigation of effort–accuracy trade-off and the impact of self-efficacy on Web searching behaviors. *Decision Support Systems, 3*(3), 331–342. doi:10.1016/S0167-9236(03)00032-0

Kwahk, K.-Y., & Lee, J.-N. (2008). The role of readiness for change in ERP implementation: Theoretical bases and empirical validation. *Information & Management, 45*, 474–481. doi:10.1016/j.im.2008.07.002

Lai, C. A., & Rivera, J. C. Jr. (2006). Using a Strategic Planning Tool as a Framework for Case Analysis. *Journal of College Science Teaching, 36*(2), 26–30.

LaLonde, B. (1998). Supply chain evolution by the numbers. *Supply Chain Management Review, 2*(1), 7–8.

Langenbach, M., Vaughn, C., & Aagaard, L. (1994). *An Introduction to Educational Research.* Needham Heights, MA: Allyn & Bacon.

Lankhorst, M., et al. (2005). *Enterprise Architecture at Work - Modelling, Communication, and Analysis.* New York: Springer. ISBN-10: 3-540-24371-2

Laudon, J., & Laudon, K. (2009). *Management Information Systems: Managing the Digital Firm* (10th ed.). Upper Saddle River, NJ: Prentice Hall. ISBN-10: 013607846X

Laughlin, S. P. (1999). An ERP game plan. *The Journal of Business Strategy, 20*(1), 32–37. doi:10.1108/eb039981

Lausen, H., de Brujin, J., Polleres, A., & Fensel, D. (2005, April). WSML - a Language Framework for Semantic Web Services. In *Proceedings of the W3C Rules Workshop,* Washington DC. Retrieved from http://www.w3.org/2004/12/rules-ws/paper/44/

Lausen, H., Polleres, A., & Roman, D. (Eds.). (2005). *Web Service Modeling Ontology Submission.* Retrieved from http://www.w3.org/Submission/WSMO/

Law, C. C. H., & Ngai, E. W. T. (2007). ERP systems adoption: An exploratory study of the organizational factors and impacts of ERP success. *Information & Management, 44*, 418–432. doi:10.1016/j.im.2007.03.004

Law, C. H., & Ngai, E. W. T. (2007). An investigation of the relationships between organizational factors, business process improvement, and ERP success. *Benchmarking: An International Journal, 3*(14), 387–406. doi:10.1108/14635770710753158

Leavy, B. (2001). Supply strategy what to outsource and where. *Irish Marketing Review, 14*(2), 46–52.

Lee, Y. S., Kim, Y. S., & Choi, H. (2004). Conflict resolution of data synchronization in mobile environment. In A. Laganà, M. L. Gavrilova, V. Kumar, Y. Mun, C. J. K. Tan, & O. Gervasi (Eds.), *Computational Science and its Applications* (LNCS 3044, pp. 196-205). Berlin: Springer.

Lee, C., & Han, H. (2008). Analysis of Skills Requirement for Entry-Level Programmer/Analysts in Fortune 500 Corporations. *Journal of Information Systems Education, 19*(1), 17–27.

Lee, D., & Park, J. (2008). RFID-based traceability in the supply chain. *Industrial Management & Data Systems, 108*(6), 713–725. doi:10.1108/02635570810883978

Lee, D., Trauth, E., & Harwell, D. (1995). Critical skills and knowledge requirements of IS professionals: A Joint Academic/Industry Investigation. *Management Information Systems Quarterly, 19*(3), 313–340. doi:10.2307/249598

Lee, H. L., Padmanabhan, V., & Whang, S. (1997). Information Distortion in Supply chain: The Bullwhip Effect. *Management Science, 43*(4), 546–558. doi:10.1287/mnsc.43.4.546

Lee, J., Hyunh, M. Q., Kwok, R. C., & Pi, S. (2003). IT outsourcing evolution-past, present, and future. *Communications of the ACM, 46*(5), 84–88. doi:10.1145/769800.769807

Lee, K., & Lin, S. (2008). A Fuzzy Quantified SOWT Procedure for Environmental Evaluation of an International Distribution Center. *Information Sciences, 178*(2), 531–549. doi:10.1016/j.ins.2007.09.002

Lee, S., & Fang, X. (2008). Perception Gaps About Skills Requirement for Entry-Level IS Professionals Between Recruiters And Students: An Exploratory Study. *Information Resources Management Journal, 21*(3), 39–63. doi:10.4018/irmj.2008070103

Lee, T. J., Lee, K. H., & Oh, K. (2007). Strategic Environments for Nuclear Energy Innovation in the Next Half Century. *Progress in Nuclear Energy, 49*(5), 397–408. doi:10.1016/j.pnucene.2007.05.002

Lee, Y. M., Feng, C., & Ying, T. L. (2009, February). A quantitative view on how RFID can improve inventory management in a supply chain. *International Journal of Logistics: Research & Applications, 12*(1), 23–43. doi:10.1080/13675560802141788

Leser, U., & Naumann, F. (2006). *Informationsintegration: Architekturen und Methoden zur Integration verteilter und heterogener Datenquellen.* Heidelberg, Germany: Dpunkt Verlag.

Levy, A., Rajaraman, A., & Ordille, J. (1996). Querying heterogeneous information sources using sources descriptions. In *Proceedings of the 22th International Conference on Very Large Data Bases,* Bombay, India (pp. 251-262).

Ley, M. (2006). Aspekte der Informationsstrukturierung: Über Strukturierungsprinzipien, die Ebenen der Textstruktur und Dokumentgrammatiken. *Technische Kommunikation, 28*(4), 51–53.

Li, X. M., & Wang, H. (2007). The Model of the Active Differential Data Synchronization for the Heterogeneous Data Source Integration Systems. In *Proceedings of the First International Symposium on Information Technologies and Applications in Education* (pp. 572-574). Washington, DC: IEEE.

Lian, J. (2001). *A study of Prerequisites for Successful ERP Implementations From The project Management, Perspective.* Retrieved from www.canias.com/enterprise/articles/20080604

Li, C. (1999). ERP packages: What's next? *Information Systems Management, 16*(3), 31–36. doi:10.1201/1078/43197.16.3.19990601/31313.5

Lieb, R., & Bentz, B. A. (2005). The use of third-party logistics services by large American manufacturers: the 2004 survey. *Transportation Journal, 44*(2), 5–15.

Lim, B. B. L., & Wen, H. J. (2002). The Impact of Next Generation XML. *Information Management & Computer Security, 10*(1), 33–40. doi:10.1108/09685220210417490

Lindholm, T., Kangasharju, J., & Tarkoma, S. (2009). Syxaw: Data Synchronization Middleware for the Mobile Web. *Mobile Networks and Applications, 14*(5), 661–676. doi:10.1007/s11036-008-0146-1

Lin, H.-F. (2007). Measuring Online Learning Systems Success: Applying the Updated DeLone and McLean Model. *Cyberpsychology & Behavior, 10*(6), 817–820. doi:10.1089/cpb.2007.9948

Lin, H.-Y., Hsu, P.-Y., & Ting, P.-H. (2006). ERP Systems Success: An Integration of IS Success Model and Balanced Scorecard. *Journal of Research and Practice in Information Technology, 38*(3), 215–228.

Lin, J., Fox, M. S., & Bilgic, T. (1996). A Requirement Ontology for Engineering Design. *Concurrent Engineering, 4*(3), 279–291. doi:10.1177/1063293X9600400307

Lin, Y., Gray, J., & Jouault, F. (2007). DSMDiff: A differentiation tool for domain-specific models. *European Journal of Information Systems, 16*, 349–361. doi:10.1057/palgrave.ejis.3000685

Lippe, E., & Oosterom, N. (1992). Operation-based merging. *ACM SIGSOFT Software Engineering Notes, 17*(5), 78–87. doi:10.1145/142882.143753

Lobin, H. (2000). *Informationsmodellierung in XML und SGML.* Berlin Heidelberg, Germany: Springer-Verlag.

Lockamy, A. III, & McCormack, K. (2004). The development of a supply chain management process maturity model using the concepts of business process orientation. *Supply Chain Management: An International Journal, 9*(4), 272–278. doi:10.1108/13598540410550019

Logistics Today. (2008, March). Wal-Mart Says Use RFID Tags or Pay Up. 4.

Lois, F., & Gerald, J. (2003). *The Role of Governance in ERP System Implementation.* Retrieved from www.elsevier.com.

Lonsdale, C. (1999). Effective managing vertical supply relationships: a risk management model for outsourcing. *Supply Chain Management, 4*(4), 176–183. doi:10.1108/13598549910284499

López-Garay, H. (2003). Extending checkland's phenomenological approach to information systems. In *Critical reflections on information systems: a systemic approach* (pp. 46-64). ISBN: 1-59140-040-6

Louridas, P. (2010). Up in the Air: Moving Your Applications to the Cloud. *IEEE Software, 27*(4), 6–11. doi:10.1109/MS.2010.109

Luarn, P., & Lin, H. H. (2005). Toward an understanding of the behavioral intention to use mobile banking. *Computers in Human Behavior, 21*(6), 873–891. doi:10.1016/j.chb.2004.03.003

Lucas, H. C. Jr. (2002). *Strategies for Electronic Commerce and the Internet.* Cambridge, MA: MIT Press.

Lucky, R. (2009). Cloud Computing. *IEEE Spectrum, 46*(5), 27. doi:10.1109/MSPEC.2009.4907382

Lucy-Bouler, T., & Morgenstern, D. (2003, Dec 12-14). *Is Digital Medicine a Standards Nightmare?* Paper presented at the International Conference on IS Special Workshop on Standard Making sponsored by MISQ, Seattle, WA.

Luftman, J., & McLean, E. (2004, June). Key Issues for IT Executives. *MISQ Executive,* 269-295.

Luh, Y. P., Pan, C. C., & Wei, C. R. (2008). An Innovative Design Methodology for the Metadata in Master Data Management System. *International Journal of Innovative Computing. Information and Control, 4*(3), 627–637.

Lumpe, M., & Schneider, J. G. (2005). A Form-based Meta-model for Software Composition *Science of Computer Programming, 56*, 59–78. doi:10.1016/j.scico.2004.11.005

Lyytinen, K., & Damsgaard, J. (2001, April 7-10). *What's Wrong With the Diffusion of Innovation Theory: The Case of a Complex and Networked Technology.* Paper presented at the International Federation for Information Processing (IFIP), Banff, Alberta, Canada.

Lyytinen, K., & Fomin, V. (2002). Achieving high momentum in the evolution of wireless infastructures: the battle over the 1G solutions. *Telecommunications Policy, 26*(3-4), 149–170. doi:10.1016/S0308-5961(02)00006-X

Mabert, V. A., Soni, A., & Venkataramanan, M. A. (2000). Enterprise resource planning survey of U.S. manufacturing firms. *Production and Inventory Management Journal, 41*(2), 52–58.

Mabert, V. A., & Venkatraman, M. A. (1998). Special Research Focus on Supply Chain Linkages: Challenges for Design and Management in the 21st Century. *Decision Sciences, 29*(3), 537–550. doi:10.1111/j.1540-5915.1998.tb01353.x

Magalhães, R., Sousa, P., & Tribolet, J. (2008). The role of business processes and entreprise architectures in the development of organizational self-awareness. *TECKNE - Revista de Estudos Politecnicos, 6*(9), 9-30.

Mahemoff, M. J., & Johnston, L. J. (1998) *Principles for a Usability-Oriented Pattern Language,* Proc. of OZCHI '98: Australasion Computer Human Interaction Conference, (pp. 132-139.), Nov. 30- Dec. 4. Adalaide, South Australia

Maitland, M., & Blitzer, D. M. (2002). *A GICS Overview for Standard & Poor's U.S. Indices.* Retrieved from www2.standardandpoors.com/spf/pdf/index/GICSIndexDocument.PDF

Malhotra, A., Gosain, S., & El Sawy, O. A. (2005, March). Absorptive Capacity Configurations in Supply Chains: Gearing for Partner-Enabled Market Knowledge Creation. *Management Information Systems Quarterly, 29*(1), 145–187.

Malone, T. W. (1987). Modeling Coordination in Organizations and Markets. *Management Science, 33*(10), 1317–1332. doi:10.1287/mnsc.33.10.1317

Malone, T. W., Yates, J., & Benjamin, R. I. (1987). Electronic Markets and Electronic Hierarchies. *Communications of the ACM, 30*(6), 484–497. doi:10.1145/214762.214766

Mangan, J., Lalwani, C., & Butcher, T. (2008). *Global Logistics and Supply Chain Management.* Hoboken, NJ: John Wiley & Sons, Inc.

Manufacturing Business Technology. (2006, August). RFID really does reduce stock-outs. 52.

Ma, Q., & Liu, L. (2004). The technology acceptance model: A meta-analysis of empirical findings. *Journal of Organizational and End User Computing, 16*(1), 59–72.

Marakas, G. M., Yi, M. Y., & Johnson, R. D. (1998). The multilevel and multifaceted character of computer self-efficacy: toward clarification of the construct and an integrative framework for research information. *Information Systems Research*, 9(2), 126–163. doi:10.1287/isre.9.2.126

Marcos, E., Acuña, C., & Cuesta, C. (2006). Integrating Software Architecture into a MDA Framework. In V. Gruhn & F. Oquendo (Eds.), *Proceedings of the 3rd European Workshop on Software Architectures (EWSA 2006)* (pp. 127-143).

Marcos, E., Vela, B., & Cavero, J. M. (2003). Methodological Approach for Object-Relational Database Design using UML. *Journal on Software and Systems Modeling*, 2, 59–72. doi:10.1007/s10270-002-0001-y

Markovsky, B., Willer, D., & Patton, T. (1988). Power Relations in Exchange Networks. *American Sociological Review*, 53, 220–236. doi:10.2307/2095689

Markus, M. L., Steinfield, C. W., & Wigand, R. T. (2003, December 12-14). *The Evolution of Vertical IS Standards: Electronic Interchange Standards in the US Home Mortgage Industry*. Paper presented at the International Conference on IS Special Workshop on Standard Making sponsored by MISQ, Seattle, WA.

Markus, M. L. (1987). Toward a "Critical Mass" Theory of Interactive Media. *Communication Research*, 14(5), 491–511. doi:10.1177/009365087014005003

Markus, M. L., Steinfield, C. W., Wigand, R. T., & Minton, G. (2006). Industry-Wide Information Systems Standardization As Collective Action: The Case of the U.S. Residential Mortgage Industry. *Management Information Systems Quarterly*, 30, 439–465.

Markus, M. L., Tanis, C., & Fenema, P. (2000). Multisite ERP implementations. *Communications of the ACM*, 43(4), 42–46. doi:10.1145/332051.332068

Marnewick, C. (2005). A conceptual model for enterprise resource planning (ERP). *Information Management & Computer Security*, 2(13), 144–155. doi:10.1108/09685220510589325

Marquardt, D. W. (1970). Generalized Inverses, Ridge Regression, Biased Linear Estimation, and Nonlinear Estimation. *Technometrics*, 12(3), 605–607. doi:10.2307/1267205

Martin, M. (1998). An electronics firm will save big money by replacing six people with one and lose all the paperwork, using enterprise resource planning software. But not every company has been so lucky. *Fortune*, 137(2), 149–151.

Mason, S. J., Cole, M. H., Ulrey, B. T., & Yan, L. (2003). Improving electronics manufacturing supply chain agility through outsourcing. *International Journal of Physical Distribution & Logistics Management*, 32(7), 610–620. doi:10.1108/09600030210442612

Masud, M. M., & Kiringa, I. (2007). Collaborative Data Synchronization in an Instance-Mapped P2P Data Sharing System. In R. Meersman, Z. Tari, P. Herrero, et al. (Eds.), *On the Move to Meaningful Internet Systems* (LNCS 4805, pp. 7-8). Berlin: Springer.

Mata, F. J., Fuerst, W. L., & Barney, J. B. (1995). Information Technology and Sustained Competitive Advantage: A Resource-Based Analysis. *Management Information Systems Quarterly*, 19(4), 487–505. doi:10.2307/249630

Matos, M. (2007). Organizational engineering: An overview of current perspectives. Unpublished master's thesis, Instituto Superior Técnico, Technical University of Lisbon, Lisbon, Portugal.

Mauerhofer, V. (2008). 3-D Sustainability: An Approach for Priority Setting in Situation of Conflicting Interests towards a Sustainable Development. *Ecological Economics*, 64(3), 496–506. doi:10.1016/j.ecolecon.2007.09.011

Maxwell, J. A. (2005). *Qualitative Research Design: An Interactive Approach*. Thousand Oaks, CA: Sage Publications Inc.

Mayank, V., Kositsyna, N., & Austin, M. (2004). *Requirements Engineering and the Semantic Web – Part II* (Tech. Rep. 2004-14). College Park, MD: Institute for Systems Research.

May, M. (2010). Forecast calls for clouds over biological computing. *Nature Medicine*, 16(1), 6. doi:10.1038/nm0110-6a

McAdam, R., & Galloway, A. (2005). Enterprise resource planning and organisational innovation: a management perspective. *Industrial Management & Data Systems, 105*(3), 280–290. doi:10.1108/02635570510590110

McCormack, K., & Johnson, B. (2001, October). Business process orientation, supply chain management, and the e-corporation. *IIE Solutions,* 33-37.

McCormack, K. P., & Johnson, W. C. (2003). *Supply Chain Networks and Business Process Orientation.* Boca Raton, FL: St. Lucie Press.

McFarlan, F. W., & Nolan, R. L. (1995). How to manage an IT outsourcing alliance. *Sloan Management Review, 36*(2), 9–23.

McGuinness, T., & Morgan, R. E. (2005). The Effect of Market and Learning Orientation on Strategy Dynamics. *European Journal of Marketing, 39*(11-12), 1306–1326. doi:10.1108/03090560510623271

McIvor, R. (2003). Outsourcing: insights from the telecommunications industry. *Supply Chain Management, 8*(3/4), 380–394.

McKersie, R. B., & Walton, R. E. (1991). Organizational Change. In Morton, M. S. S. (Ed.), *The Corporation of the 1990s: Information Technology and Organizational Transformation* (pp. 244–277). New York: Oxford University press.

McMurtrey, M., Downey, J., Zeltmann, S., & Friedman, W. (2008). Critical Skill Sets of Entry-Level IT Professionals. *An Empirical Examination of Perceptions from Field Personnel Journal of Information Technology Education, 7,* 101–120.

Mell, P., & Grance, T. (2010). The NIST Definition of Cloud Computing. *Communications of the ACM, 53*(6), 50.

Mena, E., Kashyap, V., Sheth, A., & Illarramendi, A. (1996). *Observer: An approach for query processing in global information systems based on interoperation across pre-existing ontologies.* Paper presented at the International Conference on Cooperative Information Systems (CoopIS '96).

Mendoza, R. A., & Jahng, J. (2004). An Exploratory Study on Adoption of Complex Networked Technologies: The Case of the eXtensible Markup Language (XML) Specifications. *Seoul Journal of Business, 10*(2).

Mendoza, R. A., & Jahng, J. J. (2003, August). *Adoption of XML Specifications: An Exploratory Study of Industry Practices.* Paper presented at the Americas Conference on Information Systems (AMCIS), Tampa, FL.

Menet, L., & Lamolle, M. (2009). A Model Driven Engineering Approach Applied to Master Data Management. In R. Meersman, P. Herrero, & T. Dillon (Eds.), *On the Move to Meaningful Internet Systems* (LNCS 5872, pp. 19-28). Berlin: Springer.

Mengel, M., Sis, B., & Halloran, P. F. (2007). SWOT Analysis of Banff: Strengths, Weaknesses, Opportunities, and Threats of the International Banff Consensus Process and Classification System for Renal Allograft Pathology. *American Journal of Transportation, 7*(1), 2221–2226. doi:10.1111/j.1600-6143.2007.01924.x

Mens, T. (2002). A state-of-the-art survey on software merging. *IEEE Transactions on Software Engineering, 28*(5), 449–462. doi:10.1109/TSE.2002.1000449

Mentzer, J. T., DeWitt, W., Keebler, J. S., Min, S., Nix, N. W., & Smith, C. D. (2001). Defining supply chain management. *Journal of Business Logistics, 22*(1), 1–25.

Merhout, J., Havelka, D., & Hick, S. (2009). Soft Skills versus Technical Skills: Finding the Right Balance for an IS Curriculum. In *Proceedings of Americas Conference on Information Systems (AMCIS) AMCIS 2009* (pp. 1-8).

Mertens, D. M. (2005). *Research and Evaluation in Education and Psychology.* Thousand Oaks, CA: Sage Publications, Inc.

Metaxiotis, K., Zafeiropoulos, I., Nikolinakou, K., & Psarras, J. (2005). Goal directed project management methodology for the support of ER implementation and optimal adaptation procedure. *Information Management & Computer Security, 1*(13), 55–71. doi:10.1108/09685220510582674

Metz, P., O'Brien, J., & Weber, W. (2003). Specifying Use Case Interaction: Types of Alternative Courses. *Journal of Object Technology JOT, 2*(2).

Meyer, J., & Rowan, B. (1977). Institutionalized organizations: Formal structure as myth and ceremony. *American Journal of Sociology, 83,* 340–363. doi:10.1086/226550

Microsoft. (2009). Retrieved from: http://www.microsoft.com/industry/default.mspx

Mikkola, J. H. (2003). Modularity, component outsourcing, and inter-firm learning. *R & D Management, 33*(4), 439–454. doi:10.1111/1467-9310.00309

Mikkola, J. H., & Skjott-Larson, T. (2004). Supply-chain integration: implications for mass customization, modularization, and postponement strategies. *Production Planning and Control, 15*(4), 352–361. doi:10.1080/0953728042000238845

Milgrom, P., & Roberts, J. (1986). Relying on the information of interested parties. *The Rand Journal of Economics, 17*, 18–32. doi:10.2307/2555625

Miller, B. (2003). "What is ERP?" *CIO*. Retrieved from http://www2.cio.com/analyst/report2003.html

Miller, J., & Mukerji, J. (2001). *Model Driven Architecture*. Retrieved May 8, 2008, from http://www.omg.com/mda

Miller, J., & Mukerji, J. (Eds.). (2001). *OMG Model Driven Architecture* (Document No. ormsc/2001-07-01). Retrieved from http://www.omg.com/mda

Mingers, J. (2001). Embodying information systems: the contribution of phenomenology. *Information and Organization, 11*(2), 103–128. doi:10.1016/S1471-7727(00)00005-1

Miralles, F., Sieber, S., & Valor, J. (2005, May). *CIO Herds and User Gangs in the Adoption of Open Source Software*. Paper presented at the Thirteenth European Conference on Information Systems (ECIS), Regensburg, Germany.

Mirzaee, M. (2007). ERP Experiment in Unilever Company. In *Proceedings of the second conference of experiment on ERP implementation*. Retrieved from www.irerp.com.

Missikoff, M., Schiappelli, F., & Taglino, F. (2003, October). A Controlled Language for Semantic Annotation and Interoperability in e-Business Applications. In *Proceedings of the Semantic Integration Workshop (SI-2003)*, Sanibel Island, FL (Vol. 82, 13). CEUR-WS.

Mitchell, W. (1994). *Product Standards and Competitive Advantage*. Retrieved from http://faculty.fuqua.duke.edu/~willm/bio/cases%20&%20readings/Notes/Standards_note.pdf

Møller, C. (2005). Unleashing the Potential of SCM: Adoption of ERP in Large Danish Enterprises. *International Journal of Enterprise Information Systems, 1*(1), 39–52.

Moodey, D. L., & Shanks, S. (1994). What makes a good data model? Evaluating the Quality of Entity Relationship Models. In P. Loucopoulos (Ed.), *Entity-Relationsship Approach – Proceedings of ER'94, Business Modelling and Re-Engineering* (pp. 94-111).

Mooney, J. G., Gurbaxani, V., & Kraemer, K., L. (1996). A Process Oriented Framework for Assessing the Business Value of Information Technology. *The Data Base for Advances in Information Systems, 27*(2), 68–81.

Moore, G. C., & Benbasat, I. (1991). Development of an Instrument to Measure the Perceptions of Adopting an Information Technology Innovation. *Information Systems Research, 2*(3), 192–222. doi:10.1287/isre.2.3.192

Moore, J. (2000). One Road to Turnover: An Examination of Work Exhaustion in Technology Professionals. *Management Information Systems Quarterly, 24*(1), 141–168. doi:10.2307/3250982

Moore, K. R. (1998). Trust and relationship commitment in logistics alliances: a buyer perspective. *International Journal of Purchasing and Materials Management, 34*(2), 211–237.

Morgan, R. M., & Hunt, S. D. (1994). The commitment-trust theory of relationship marketing. *Journal of Marketing, 58*(3), 20–38. doi:10.2307/1252308

Motwani, J., Mirchandani, D., & Gunasekaran, A. (2002). Successful implementation of ERP projects: Evidence from two case studies. *International Journal of Production Economics, 75*, 83–96. doi:10.1016/S0925-5273(01)00183-9

Moyaux, T., & Chaib-draa, B. (2007, May). Information sharing as a coordination mechanism for reducing the bullwhip effect in supply chain. *IEEE Transactions on Systems, Man, and Cybernetics, 37*(3), 396–409. doi:10.1109/TSMCC.2006.887014

Mukhopadhyay, T., & Kekre, S. (2002, October). Strategic and Operational Benefits of Electronic Integration in B2B Procurement Processes. *Management Science, 48*(10), 1301–1313. doi:10.1287/mnsc.48.10.1301.273

Murta, L., Corrêa, C., Prudêncio, J. G., & Werner, C. (2008). Towards Odyssey-VCS 2: improvements over a UML-based version control system. In *Proceedings of the International Workshop on Comparison and Versioning of Software Models* (pp. 25-30).

Muscatello, J. R., Small, M. H., & Chen, I. J. (2003). Implementing enterprise resource planning (ERP) systems in small and midsize manufacturing firms. *International Journal of Operations & Production Management, 8*(23), 850–871. doi:10.1108/01443570310486329

Muscatello, J., & Chen, I. (2008). Enterprise Resource Planning (ERP) Implementations: Theory and Practice. *International Journal of Enterprise Information Systems, 4*(1), 63–78. doi:10.4018/jeis.2008010105

Muthig, J., & Schäflein-Armbruster, R. (1999). *Funktionsdesign: eine universelle und flexible Standardisierungstechnik*. Augsburg, Germany: WEKA-Verlag.

Nah, F. F., & Delgado, S. (2006). Critical success factors for enterprise resource planning implementation and upgrades. *Journal of Computer Information Systems, 46*(5), 99–113.

Nah, F. F., Lau, J. L., & Kuang, J. (2001). Factors for successful implementation of enterprise systems. *Business Process Management Journal, 7*(3), 285–296. doi:10.1108/14637150110392782

Nah, F. F., Lau, J. L.-S., & Kuang, J. (2001). Critical Factors for Successful Implementation of Enterprise Systems. *Business Process Management Journal, 7*(3), 285–296. doi:10.1108/14637150110392782

Nah, F. F., Tan, X., & The, S. H. (2004). An empirical investigation on end-user's acceptance of enterprise systems. *Information Resources Management Journal, 17*(3), 32–53.

Nah, F. F., Zuckweiler, K., & Lau, J. L. (2003). ERP implementation: chief information officers' perceptions of critical success factors. *International Journal of Human-Computer Interaction, 16*(1), 5–22. doi:10.1207/S15327590IJHC1601_2

Nah, F., & Delgado, S. (2006). Critical Success Factors for Enterprise Resource Planning Implementation and Upgrade. *Journal of Computer Information Systems, 46*(5), 99–114.

Nah, F., Lou, J., & Kuang, J. (2001). Critical Factors for Successful Implementation of Enterprise Systems. *Business Process Management Journal, 3*(7), 285–296. doi:10.1108/14637150110392782

Nambisan, S., & Wang, Y.-M. (1999). Roadblocks to Web technology adoption? *Communications of the ACM, 42*(1), 98–101. doi:10.1145/291469.291482

Nelson, K. M., & Nelson, J. H. (2003, December 12-14). *The Need for a Strategic Ontology*. Paper presented at the International Conference on IS Special Workshop on Standard Making sponsored by MISQ, Seattle, WA.

Nelson, M. L., Shaw, M. J., & Qualls, W. (2005). Interorganizational System Standards Development in Vertical Industries. *Electronic Markets, 15*(4), 378–392. doi:10.1080/10196780500303045

Nevin, R. (2009). Supporting 21st Century Learning through Google Apps. *Teacher Librarian, 37*(2), 35–38.

Newell, S., Huang, J., & Tansley, C. (2006). ERP Implementation: A knowledge Integration Challenge for the Project Team. *Knowledge and Process Management, 4*(13), 227–238. doi:10.1002/kpm.262

Newman, R. (2008, November 11). *Here Comes a Bankruptcy Boom*. Retrieved January 23, 2009, from http://www.usnews.com/blogs/flowchart/2008/11/11/here-comes-a-bankruptcy-boom.html

Ngai, E. W. T., Law, C. C. H., & Wat, F. K. T. (2008). Examining the critical success factors in the adoption of enterprise resource planning. *Computers in Industry, 59*(58), 548–564. doi:10.1016/j.compind.2007.12.001

Nickerson, J. V., & Muehlen, M. Z. (2003, December 12-14). *Defending the Spirit of the Web: Conflict in the Internet Standards Process*. Paper presented at the International Conference on IS Special Workshop on Standard Making sponsored by MISQ, Seattle, WA.

Nielsen, J. (1997). *The need for speed*. Retrieved from http://www.useit.com/alertbox/ 9703a.html

Nielsen, J. (1999). User interface directions for the Web. *Communications of the ACM, 42*(1), 65–72. doi:10.1145/291469.291470

Nierstrasz, O., & Achermann, F. (2003). *A Calculus for Modeling Software Components*, Proc. of the First Int. Symp. on Formal Methods for Components and Objects, LNCS, vol. 2852, (pp. 339-360), Springer

Noekkenved, C. (2000). *Collaborative processes in e-supply networks: towards collaborative community B2B marketplaces*. New York: PricewaterhouseCoopers.

Nonaka, I. (1994). Dynamic theory of organizational knowledge creation. *Organization Science, 5*, 14–37. doi:10.1287/orsc.5.1.14

Norris, G., Hurley, J. R., Hartley, K. M., & Dunleavy, J. R. (2000). *E-Business and ERP: Transforming the Enterprise*. London: John Wiley & Sons Inc.

Novak, S., & Eppinger, S. D. (2001). Sourcing by design: product complexity and supply chain. *Management Science, 47*(1), 189–203. doi:10.1287/mnsc.47.1.189.10662

Nunnally, J. C. (1978). *Psychometric Theory* (2nd ed.). New York: McGraw-Hill.

Nunnally, J. C., & Bernstein, I. H. (1994). *Psychometric theory* (3rd ed.). New York: McGraw Hill.

OASIS. (2007). *DITA Version 1.1, Architectural Specification*. Boston: Author.

OASIS. (2007). *Web Services Business Process Execution Language Version 2.0*. Retrieved August 29, 2008, from http://docs.oasis-open.org/wsbpel/2.0/wsbpel-v2.0.pdf

Object Management Group (OMG). (2002). *Meta-Object Facility, version 1.4*. Retrieved from http://omg.org/technology/documents/formal/mof.htm

Object Management Group (OMG). (2005). *XML Metadata Interchange (XMI)*. Retrieved from http://ww.omg.org/technology/documents/formal/xmi.htm

Object Management Group (OMG). (2006). *OCL 2.0 Specification*. Retrieved from http://www.omg.org/docs/ptc/05-06-06.pdf

Object Management Group. (2005). *OCL 2.0 Specification*. Retrieved August 29, 2008, from http://www.omg.org/docs/ptc/05-06-06.pdf

O'Brien, K. J. (2010, September 19). Cloud Computing Hits a Snag. *The New York Times.*

Oda, T., & Saeki, M. (2005). Generative technique of version control systems for software diagrams. In *Proceedings of the 21st IEEE International Conference on Software Maintenance* (pp. 515-524). Washington, DC: IEEE Computer Society.

Ohst, D., Welle, M., & Kelter, U. (2003). Differences between versions of UML diagrams. *ACM SIGSOFT Software Engineering Notes, 28*(5), 227–236. doi:10.1145/949952.940102

Okhuysen, G. A., & Eisenhardt, K. M. (2002, August). Integrating knowledge in groups: How formal interventions enable flexibility. *Organization Science, 13*(4), 370–386. doi:10.1287/orsc.13.4.370.2947

Okrent, M. D., & Vokurka, R. J. (2004). Process mapping in successful ERP implementations. *Industrial Management & Data Systems, 104*(8), 637–643. doi:10.1108/02635570410561618

Olhager, J., & Selldin, E. (2003). Enterprise resource planning survey of Swedish manufacturing firms. *European Journal of Operational Research, 146*(2), 365–373. doi:10.1016/S0377-2217(02)00555-6

Olson, M. (1971). *Logic of Collective Action: Public Goods and the Theory of Groups* (2nd ed.). Cambridge, MA: Harvard University Press.

OMG. (2005). *UML profile for schedulability, performance, and time specification*. Needham, MA: Object Management Group.

Ong, C. S., Lai, J. Y., & Wang, Y. S. (2004). Factors affecting engineers' acceptance of asynchronous e-learning systems in high-tech companies. *Information & Management, 41*(6), 795–804. doi:10.1016/j.im.2003.08.012

On-Line Consultant. (2009). Retrieved from http://www.health-infosys-dir.com/top%20ERP%20vendors.htm

Open Mobile Alliance Ltd. (2009). *Data Synchronization Working Group*. Retrieved December 12, 2009, from http://www.openmobilealliance.org/Technical/DS.aspx

Orlikowski, W. J. (2002, May/June). Knowing in practice: Enacting a collective capability in distributed organizing. *Organization Science, 13*(3), 249–273. doi:10.1287/orsc.13.3.249.2776

Osei-Bryson, K.-M., Dong, L., & Ngwenyama, O. (2008). Exploring managerial factors affecting ERP implementation: An investigation of the Klein-Sorra model using regression splines. *Information Systems Journal*, *18*(5), 499–527. doi:10.1111/j.1365-2575.2008.00309.x

Ozen, C., & Basoglu, N. (2007, August 5-9) Exploring the Contribution of Information Systems User Interface Design Characteristics to Adoption Process. In *PICMET 2007 Proceedings,* Portland, OR (pp. 951-958).

Pagarkar, M., Natesan, M., & Prakash, B. (2005). *RFID in Integrated Order Management Systems*. Chennai, India: Tata Consultancy Services.

Pahl, C. (2007). Semantic Model-Driven Architecting of Service-Based Software Systems. *Information and Software Technology*, *49*(8), 838–850. doi:10.1016/j.infsof.2006.09.007

Pairat, R., & Jungthirapanich, C. (2005). A Chronological Review of ERP Research: An Analysis of ERP Inception, Evolution, and Direction. In *Proceedings of Engineering Management Conference, 2005 IEEE International* (Vol. 1, pp. 288-292).

Pan, J., Serafini, L., & Zhao, Y. (2006). *Semantic import: An approach for partial ontology reuse*. Paper presented at the ISWC2006 Workshop on Modular Ontologies (WoMO).

Paquin, J.-P., & Koplyay, T. (2007). Force Field Analysis and Strategic Management: A Dynamic Approach. *Engineering Management Journalm*, *19*(1), 28–37.

Parker, G. G., & Anderson, E. G. Jr. (2002). From buyer to integrator: the transformation of the supply-chain manager in the vertically disintegrating firm. *Production and Operations Management*, *11*(1), 75–91. doi:10.1111/j.1937-5956.2002.tb00185.x

Parr, A. N., & Shanks, G. (2000). A Taxonomy of ERP Implementation Approaches. In *Proceedings of the 33rd Hawaii International Conference on System Sciences.*

Patel-Schneider, P. F., Hayes, P., & Horrocks, I. (2004). *OWL web ontology language semantics and abstract syntax*. Retrieved from http://www.w3.org/TR/owl-semantics/

Patnayakuni, R., Rai, A., & Seth, N. (2006). Relational Antecedents of Information Flow Integration for Supply Chain Coordination. *Journal of Management Information Systems*, *23*(1), 13–49. doi:10.2753/MIS0742-1222230101

Patni Americas, Inc. (2008). *Thought Paper: Global Data Synchronization: A Foundation Block for Realizing RFID Potential.* Cincinnati, OH: Patni Americas, Inc. Retrieved July 24, 2008, from http://www.patni.com/resource-center/collateral/RFID/tp_RFID_Global-Data-Synchronization.html

Peslak, A. (2005a). A twelve-step, multiple course approach to teaching enterprise resource planning. *Journal of Information Systems Education*, *16*(2), 147–155.

Peslak, A. (2005b). Incorporating Business Processes and Functions: Addressing The Missing Element In Information Systems Education. *Journal of Computer Information Systems*, *45*(4), 56–61.

Peslak, A. R. (2006). Enterprise resource planning success. *Industrial Management & Data Systems*, *9*(106), 1288–1303. doi:10.1108/02635570610712582

Piplani, R., Pokharel, S., & Tan, A. (2004). Perspective on the use of information technology at third party logistics service providers in Singapore. *Asia Pacific Journal of Marketing and Logistics*, *16*(1), 27–41. doi:10.1108/13555850410765113

Piprani, B. (2009). A Model for Semantic Equivalence Discovery for Harmonizing Master Data. In R. Meersman, P. Herrero, & T. Dillon (Eds.), *On the Move to Meaningful Internet Systems* (LNCS 5872, pp. 649-658). Berlin: Springer.

Pires, S. R. I. (1998). Managerial implications of the modular consortium model in a Brazilian automotive plant. *International Journal of Operations & Production Management*, *18*(3), 221–232. doi:10.1108/01443579810368290

Pollalis, Y. A. (2003). Patterns of Co-Alignment in Information-Intensive Organizations: Business Performance Through Integration Strategies. *International Journal of Information Management*, *23*, 469–492. doi:10.1016/S0268-4012(03)00063-X

Pollalis, Y. A., & Frieze, I. H. (1993). A New Look at Critical Success Factors in IT. *Information Strategy: The Executive's Journal, 10*(1), 24–34.

Porter, M. E., & Millar, V. E. (1985). How Information Gives you Competitive Advantage. *Harvard Business Review, 63*(4), 149.

Powell, T. C., & Dent-Micaleff, A. (1997). Information technology as competitive advantage: the role of human, business, and technology resources. *Strategic Management Journal, 18*(5), 375–405. doi:10.1002/(SICI)1097-0266(199705)18:5<375::AID-SMJ876>3.0.CO;2-7

Premkumar, G., Ramamurthy, K., & Crum, M. R. (1997). Determinants of EDI adoption in the transportation industry. *European Journal of Information Systems, 6*(2), 107–121. doi:10.1057/palgrave.ejis.3000260

Protégé Ontolology Editor and Knowledge Acquisition System. (2008), Retrieved July 24, 2008 from Protégé Web Site: http://protege.stanford.edu

Ptak, C. A., & Schragenheim, E. (1999). *ERP – Tools, Techniques and Applications for Integrating the Supply Chain*. Boca Raton, FL: St. Lucie Press/ APICS.

Quan, D. A., & Karger, R. (2004). *Semantic Interfaces and OWL Tools: How to Make a Semantic Web Browser*, Proc. of the 13th Int. Conf. on World Wide Web, WWW '04, (pp. 255-265), ACM

Quebec Inc. (2007). Retrieved from http://templates.rfpbuilder.com/ERP1/ERPvendors.htm

Quelin, B. V., Abdessemed, T., Bonardi, J.-P., & Durand, R. (2001). Standardisation of Network Technologies: Market Processes or the Result of Inter-Firm Cooperation? *Journal of Economic Surveys, 15*(4), 543–569. doi:10.1111/1467-6419.00148

Radhakrishnan, A., Zu, X., & Grover, V. (2008). A process-oriented perspective on differential business value creation by information technology: An empirical investigation. *Omega, 36*, 1105–1125. doi:10.1016/j.omega.2006.06.003

Rai, A., Patnayakuni, R., & Seth, N. (2006, June). Firm Performance Impacts of Digitally Enabled Supply Chain Integration Capabilities. *Management Information Systems Quarterly, 30*(2), 225–246.

Ramamurthy, K., Premkumar, G., & Crum, M. R. (1999). Organizational and interorganizational determinants of EDI diffusion and organizational performance: A Causal Model. *Journal of Organizational Computing and Electronic Commerce, 9*(4), 253–285. doi:10.1207/S153277440904_2

Ramayah, T., & Aafaqi, B. (2004). Role of self-efficacy in e-library usage among student of a public university in Malaysia. *Malaysia Journal of Library and Information Science, 9*(1), 39–57.

Ramayah, T., & Chiun Lo, M. (2007). Impact of shared beliefs on "perceived usefulness" and "ease of use" in the implementation of an enterprise resource planning system. *Management Research New, 6*(30), 40–431.

Ramayah, T., & Jantan, M. (2004). Internet usage among Malaysian students: The role of demographic and motivational variables. *PRANJANA: The Journal of Management Awareness, 7*(2), 59–70.

Rao, K., & Young, R. (1994). Global supply chains: factors influencing outsourcing logistics functions. *International Journal of Physical Distribution & Logistics, 24*(6), 11–19. doi:10.1108/09600039410066141

Ravichandran, T. (2005). Organizational Assimilation of Complex Technologies: An Empirical Study of Component-Based Software Development. *IEEE Transactions on Engineering Management, 52*(2), 249–268. doi:10.1109/TEM.2005.844925

Recker, J., & Niehaves, B. (2008). Epistemological perspectives on ontology-based theories for conceptual modeling. *Applied Ontology, 3*(1/2), 111-130. ISSN: 1570-5838

Reenskaug, T., Wold, P., & Lehne, O. (1996). *Working with Objects, The OOram Software Engineering Method.* Greenwich, CT: Manning Publications.

Reimers, K., & Li, M. (2005). Antecedents of a Transaction Cost Theory of Vertical IS Standardization Processes. *Electronic Markets, 15*(4), 301–312. doi:10.1080/10196780500302740

Remus, U. (2007). Critical success factors for implementing enterprise portals A comparison with ERP implementations. *Business Process Management Journal, 4*(13), 538–552. doi:10.1108/14637150710763568

Research, A. M. R. (n.d.). *AMR Research Predicts ERP Market will Reach $66.6 Billion by2003*. Retrieved May 5, 2008 from http://www.amrresearch.com/Content/View.asp?pmillid=13280

Rivera, J. E., & Vallecillo, A. (2008). Representing and operating with model differences. In R. F. Paige & B. Meyer (Eds.), *Proceedings of Objects, Components, Models and Patterns: 46ᵗʰ International Conference, TOOLS EUROPE* (LNBIP 11, pp. 141-160).

Robert Bosch Gmb, H. (2008). *Structure and business sectors*. Retrieved October 15, 2008, from http://www.bosch.com/content/language2/html/2153.htm

Roberti, M. (2005). Wal-Mart to expand RFID tagging requirement. *RFID Journal*. Retrieved April 9, 2007, from http://www.rfidjournal.com/article/articleview/1930/1/1/

Roberti, M. (2008). Laying the Foundation for RFID. *RFID Journal*. Retrieved August 10, 2008, from http://www.rfidjournal.com/article/articleview/3524/1/435/

Roberts, H. J., & Barrar, P. R. N. (1992). MRP II implementation: key factors for success. *Computer Integrated Manufacturing Systems*, *5*(1), 31–38. doi:10.1016/0951-5240(92)90016-6

Robey, D., Ross, J. W., & Boudreau, M. (2002). Learning to implement enterprise systems: an exploratory study of the dialectics of change. *Journal of Management Information Systems*, *19*(1), 17–46.

Robinovich, E., Windle, R., Dresner, M., & Corsi, T. (1999). Outsourcing of integrated logistics functions: an examination of industry practices. *International Journal of Physical Distribution & Logistics Management*, *29*(6), 353–373. doi:10.1108/09600039910283587

Rogers, E. M. (1983). *Diffusion of Innovations* (3rd ed.). New York: The Free Press.

Rohlfs, J. (1974). A Theory of Interdependent Demand for a Communications Service. *The Bell Journal of Economics and Management Science*, *5*(1), 16–37. doi:10.2307/3003090

Rossetti, C., & Choi, T. Y. (2005). On the dark side of strategic sourcing: experiences from the aerospace industry. *The Academy of Management Executive*, *19*(1), 46–60.

Rueping, A. (2003). *Agile Documentation: A Pattern Guide to Producing Lightweight Documents for Software Projects*. New York: Wiley Software Patterns Series.

Rupp, C. (2007). *Requirements Engineering und Management – Professionelle, iterative Anforderungsanalyse für die Praxis*. Munich, Germany: Hanser Verlag.

Ryndina, K., Küster, J. M., & Gall, H. (2007). Consistency of business process models and object life cycles. In T. Kühne (Ed.) *Models in Software Engineering* (LNCS 4364, pp. 80-90).

Saaty, L. (1990). *Decision making for leaders*. Pittsburgh, PA: RWS publications.

Sabbaghi, A., & Vaidyanathan, G. (2008). Effectiveness and efficiency of RFID technology in supply chain management: Strategic values and challenges. *Journal of Theoretical and Applied Electronic Commerce Research*, *3*(2), 71–81. doi:10.4067/S0718-18762008000100007

Salanova, M., Grau, R. M., Cifre, E., & Llorens, S. (2000). Computer training, frequency of usage and burnout: The moderating role of computer self-efficacy. *Computers in Human Behavior*, *16*(6), 575–590. doi:10.1016/S0747-5632(00)00028-5

Sankar, C. S., & Rau, K. (2006). *Implementation Strategies for SAP R/3 in a Multinational Organization*. Hershey, PA: Idea Group Inc.doi:10.4018/978-1-59140-776-8

SAP. (2009). Retrieved from http://www.sap.com/industries/index.epx

Saraf, N., Langdon, C. S., & Gosain, S. (2007, September). IS Application Capabilities and Relational Value in Interfirm Partnerships. *Information Systems Research, September, 18*(3), 320-339.

Saravan, R. (2000). *XMLterm: A Mozilla-based Semantic User Interface*, Retrieved July 24, 2008 from the O'Reilly XML.com Web Site: http://www.xml.com/pub/a/2000/06/07/ xmlterm/index.html

Sarker, S., & Lee, A. S. (2003). Using a case study to test the role of three key social enablers in ERP implementation. *Information & Management*, *40*, 414–425. doi:10.1016/S0378-7206(02)00103-9

Sarkis, J., & Sundarraj, R. P. (2000). Factors for strategic evaluation of enterprise information technologies. *International Journal of Physical Distribution & Logistics Management*, 30(3/4), 196–220. doi:10.1108/09600030010325966

Satyanarayanan, M., & Kistler, J. (1992). Disconnected operation in the Coda file system. *ACM Transactions on Computer Systems*, 10(1), 3–25. doi:10.1145/146941.146942

Sauer, C., & Willcocks, L. (2003). Establishing the Business of the Future: The Role of Organizational Architecture and Information Technologies. *European Management Journal*, 21(4), 497–508. doi:10.1016/S0263-2373(03)00078-1

Savannah. (2008). *Concurrent Versions System (CVS)*. Retrieved August 29, 2008, from http://www.nongnu.org/cvs/

Schilling, M. (1998). Technological Lockout: An Integrative Model of the Economic and Strategic Factors Driving Technology Success and Failure. *Academy of Management Review*, 23(2), 267–284. doi:10.2307/259374

Schilling, M. A. (2002). Technology success and failure in winner-take-all markets: Testing a model of technological lock out. *Academy of Management Journal*, 45(2), 387–398. doi:10.2307/3069353

Schmid, B. F. (1993). Electronic markets. *Wirtschaftsinformatik*, 35(5), 465–480.

Schneider, C., & Zündorf, A. (2007). *Experiences in using optimistic locking in Fujaba*. Paper presented at the Workshop on Comparison and Versioning of UML Models.

Schniederjans, M. J., & Kim, G. C. (2003). Implementing enterprise resource planning systems with total quality control and business process reengineering Survey results. *International Journal of Operations & Production Management*, 4(23), 418–429. doi:10.1108/01443570310467339

Schramm, W. (1954). How communication works. In W. Schramm (Ed.), *The Process and Effects of Mass Communication* (pp. 5-6). Urbana, IL: University of Illinois Press.

Schultze, U. (2000). A Confessional Account of an Ethnography about Knowledge Work. *Management Information Systems Quarterly*, 24(1), 3–41. doi:10.2307/3250978

Schutt, T., Schintke, F., & Reinefeld, A. (2003). Efficient synchronization of replicated data in distributed systems. In P. M. A. Sloot et al. (Eds.), *Computational Science (ICCS 2003)* (LNCS 2657, pp. 274-283). Berlin: Springer.

Scicluna, J., Abela, C., & Montebello, M. (2004, October). *Visual modeling of owl-s services*. Paper presented at the IADIS International Conference on WWW/Internet.

Scott, J., & Vessey, I. (2002). Managing risks in enterprise implementations. *Communications of the ACM*, 45(4), 74–81. doi:10.1145/505248.505249

Searle, J. (1969). *Speech Acts: An Essay in the Philosophy of Language*. Cambridge, UK: Cambridge University Press.

Selberg, S. A., & Austin, M. (2003). *Requirements Engineering and the Semantic Web – Part I*, (Tech. Rep. 2003-20). College Park, MD: Institute for Systems Research.

Seneler, C. O., Basoglu, N., & Daim, T. A. (2008, July 27-31). Taxonomy for Technology Adoption: A Human Computer Interaction Perspective. In *PICMET 2008 Proceedings*, Cape Town, South Africa (pp. 2208-2219).

Seng Woo, H. (2007). Critical success factors for implementing ERP: the case of a Chinese electronics manufacturer. *Journal of Manufacturing Technology Management*, 4(18), 431–442.

Seuring, S. A. (2003). Outsourcing into service factories: an exploratory analysis of facility operators in the German chemical industry. *International Journal of Operations & Production Management*, 23(10), 1207–1223. doi:10.1108/01443570310496634

Shannon, C. F., & Weaver, W. (1964). *The Mathematical Theory of Communication*. Urbana, IL: University of Illinois Press.

Shannon, C. E. (1948). A mathematical theory of communication. *The Bell System Technical Journal*, 27, 623–656.

Shao, D., Khurshid, S., & Perry, D. E. (2007). Evaluation of semantic interference detection in parallel changes: An exploratory experiment. In *Proceedings of the 23rd IEEE International Conference on Software Maintenance (ICSM)* (pp. 74-83).

Sharma, A. (n.d.). *Risks in ERP implementation*. Retrieved from www.AshutoshSharma.gov.in

Shergill, G. S., & Chen, Z. (2005). Web-based shopping: Consumers' attitudes towards online shopping in New Zealand. *Journal of Electronic Commerce Research*, 6(2), 79–94.

Shih, Y.-Y. (2004). A case study of the critical success factors in implementing enterprise resource planning. *Journal of Ming Hsin Institute of Technology, 30*, 159–169.

Shih, Y.-Y. (2006). The effect of computer self-efficacy on enterprise resource planning usage. *Behaviour & Information Technology, 25*(5), 407–411. doi:10.1080/01449290500168103

Shih, Y.-Y., & Huang, S.-S. (2009). The actual usage of ERP systems: An extended technology acceptance perspective. *Journal of Research and Practice in Information Technology, 41*(3), 263–276.

Shuai, C. (2008). China's New Cooperation Strategy with the World Food Programme: a SWOT Analysis. *Outlook on Agriculture, 37*(2), 111–117. doi:10.5367/000000008784648898

Shutzberg, L. (2004). Radio Frequency Identification (RFID). In *Consumer Goods Supply Chain: Mandated Compliance or Remarkable Innovation?* Norcross, GA: Rock-Tenn Company.

Sieber, T., & Kovács, L. (2005). Technical documentation: Terms, problems and challenges in managing data, information and knowledge. In Proceedings of the *University of Miskolc's 5th International Conference of PhD Students* (pp. 165-170).

Sieber, T., & Lautenbacher, F. (2007). *Enterprise Content Integration: Documentation, Implementation and Syndication using Intelligent Metadata (ECIDISI)* (Tech. Rep. 2007-17). Augsburg, Germany: University of Augsburg, Germany. Retrieved from http://www.ds-lab.org/publications/reports/2007-17.html

Sieber, T., & Kammerer, M. (2006). Sind Metadaten bessere Daten? *Technische Dokumentation, 5/2006*, 56–58.

Siemnieniuch, C. E., Waddell, F. N., & Sinclair, M. A. (1999, April). The role of 'partnership' in supply chain management for fast-moving consumer goods: A case study. *International Journal of Logistics, 2*(1), 87–101. doi:10.1080/13675569908901574

Sikavica, P., & Novak, M. (1993). *Poslovna organizacija*. Zagreb, Croatia: Informator.

Simchi-Levi, D., Kaminsky, P., & Simchi-Levi, E. (2004). *Managing the Supply Chain: The Definitive Guide for the Business Professional*. New York: McGraw-Hill.

Singh, A., & Wesson, J. (2009, October 12-14). Evaluation Criteria for Assessing the Usability of ERP Systems. In *Proceedings of the 2009 Annual Research Conference of the South African Institute of Computer Scientists and Information Technologists (SAICSIT'09)*, Riverside, Vanderbijlpark, South Africa (pp. 87-95).

Sislian, E., & Satir, A. (2000). Strategic sourcing: a framework and a case study. *Journal of Supply Chain Management, 36*(3), 4–11. doi:10.1111/j.1745-493X.2000.tb00246.x

Slonegger, K., & Kurtz, B. (1995). *Formal syntax and semantics of programming languages: a laboratory based approach*. Boston: Addison-Wesley Longman.

Smaragdakis, Y., & Batory, D. (2002). Mixin layers: An object-oriented implementation technique for refinements and collaboration-based designs. *ACM Transactions on Software Engineering and Methodology, 11*(2), 215–255. doi:10.1145/505145.505148

Smith, M. A., Mitra, S., & Narashimhan, S. (1998). Information systems outsourcing: a study of pre-event firm characteristics. *Journal of Management Information Systems, 15*(2), 61–93.

SMOVER. (2008). *SMoVer: A Semantically Enhanced Version Control System for Models*. Retrieved August 29, 2008, from http://smover.tk.uni-linz.ac.at/

Snider, B., da Silveira, G. J. C., & Balakrishnan, J. (2009). ERP implementation at SMEs: analysis of five Canadian cases. *International Journal of Operations & Production Management, 1*(11), 4–29. doi:10.1108/01443570910925343

Snir, E. M. (2001). Liability as a catalyst for product stewardship. *Production and Operations Management, 10*(2), 190–206. doi:10.1111/j.1937-5956.2001.tb00078.x

Software Finder. (2009). Retrieved from http://softwarefinder.mbtmag.com/

Soh, C., Kien, S. S., & Tay-Yap, J. (2000). Cultural fits and misfits: is ERP a universal solution?", Association for Computing Machinery. *Communications of the ACM, 43*, 47. doi:10.1145/332051.332070

Soja, P. (2006). Success factors in ERP systems implementations: lessons from practice. *Journal of Enterprise Information Management, 6*(19), 646–661. doi:10.1108/17410390610708517

Soja, P. (2008). Examining the Conditions of ERP Implementations: Lessons Learnt from Adopters. *Business Process Management Journal, 14*(1), 105–123. doi:10.1108/14637150810849445

Somers, T., & Nelson, K. (2001). The Impact of Critical Success Factors across the Stage of Enterprise Resource Planning Implementations. In *Proceeding of the 34ᵗʰ Hawaii International Conference on System Sciences.*

Somers, K. J., & Bhattarcherjee, T. M. (2007). The Role of Information Systems Resources in ERP Capability and Business Process Outcomes. *Journal of Management Information Systems, 24*(2), 221–260. doi:10.2753/MIS0742-1222240209

Somers, T. M., & Nelson, K. G. (2004). A taxonomy of players and activities across the ERP project life cycle. *Information & Management, 41*(3), 257–278. doi:10.1016/S0378-7206(03)00023-5

Son Yu, C. (2005). Causes influencing the effectiveness of the post-implementation ERP system. *Management & Data Systems, 1*(105), 115–131.

Son, J.-Y., Narasimhan, S., & Riggins, F. J. (1999, 1999). *Factors Affecting the Extent of Electronic Cooperation Between Firms: Economic and Sociological Perspectives.* Paper presented at the International Conference on Information Systems (ICIS).

Songini, M. L. (2007, February). Wal-Mart Shifts RFID Plans. *Computerworld, 26*, 14.

Son, J., Narasimhan, S., & Riggins, F. J. (2005). Effects of Relational Factors and Channel of Climate on EDI Usage in the Customer-Supplier Relationship. *Journal of Management Information Systems, 22*(1), 321–353.

Southwick, R., & Sawyer, S. (1999). Critical Views of Organization, Management, and Information Technology: Applying Critical Social Theory to Information System Research. Paper presented at the Americas Conference on Information Systems, Milwaukee, WI.

Spalding, J. O. (1998). Transportation industry takes the right-of-way in the supply chain. *IIE Solutions, 30*(7), 24–28.

Spyns, P. (2005). Adapting the object role modelling method for ontology modelling. In *Proceedings of the International Symposium on Foundations of Intelligent Systems* (LNCS 3488, pp. 276-284).

Stake, R. E. (1994). Case Studies. In Denzin, N. K., & Lincoln, Y. S. (Eds.), *Handbook of Qualitative Research* (pp. 236–247). Thousand Oaks, CA: Sage.

Stanford University. (2009). *Stanford encyclopedia of philosophy.* Retrieved June 2009, from http://plato.stanford.edu/

Steimann, F. (2005). The role data model revisited. In *Proceedings of Roles, an interdisciplinary perspective, AAAI Fall Symposium* (pp. 128-135).

Steimann, F. (2000). On the representation of roles in object-oriented and conceptual modelling. *Data & Knowledge Engineering, 35*(1), 83–106. doi:10.1016/S0169-023X(00)00023-9

Steinfield, C. W., Wigand, R. T., Markus, M. L., & Minton, G. (2004, May 13-14). *Promoting e-Business Through Vertical IS Standards: Lessons from the US Home Mortgage Industry.* Paper presented at the Workshop on Standards and Public Policy, Chicago.

Steinfield, C. W., Markus, M. L., & Wigand, R. T. (2005). Exploring interorganizational systems at the industry level of analysis: evidence from the US home mortgage industry. *Journal of Information Technology, 20*, 224–233. doi:10.1057/palgrave.jit.2000051

Stevens, G. C. (1990). Successful Supply Chain Management. *Management Decision, 28*(8), 25–30. doi:10.1108/00251749010140790

Stewart, G., & Rosemann, M. (2001). Industry-oriented design of ERP-related curriculum - An Australian initiative. *Business Process Management Journal, 7*(3), 234–242. doi:10.1108/14637150110392719

Stojanovic, N., Maedche, A., Staab, S., Studer, R., & Sure, Y. (2001). *SEAL – A Framework for Developing Semantic Portals*, Proc. of First Int. Conf. on Knowledge Capture, Victora, B. C., Canada, LNCS, vol. 2097, (pp. 1-22), Springer

Strawson, P. F. (1969). Intention and Convention in Speech Acts. In K. T. Fann (Ed.), *Symposium on J. L. Austin, International Library of Philosophy and Scientific Method*. New York: Humanities Press.

Subramani, M. (2004, March). How Do Suppliers Benefit From Information Technology Use in Supply Chain Relationships. *Management Information Systems Quarterly*, *28*(1), 45–73.

Subramani, M. R., & Venkatraman, N. (2003). Safeguarding Investments in Asymmetric Interorganizational Relationships: Theory and Evidence. *Academy of Management Journal*, *46*(1), 46–62. doi:10.2307/30040675

Suchman, M. C. (1995). Managing Legitimacy: Strategic and Institutional Approaches. *Academy of Management Review*, *20*(3), 571–610. doi:10.2307/258788

Suganthi, B., Balachandher, K. G., & Balachandran, S. (2001). Internet banking patronage: an empirical investigation of Malaysia. *Journal of Internet Banking and Commerce*, *6*(1). Retrieved from http://www.arraydev.com/commerce/jibc/0103_01.htm.

Sumner, M. (1999). Critical success factors in enterprise wide information management systems projects. In *Proceedings of the Americas Conference on Information Systems (AMCIS)* (pp. 232-234).

Sumner, M. (2000). Risk factors in enterprise-wide/ERP projects. *Journal of Information Technology*, *15*(4), 317–327. doi:10.1080/02683960010009079

Sunagawa, E., Kozaki, K., Kitamura, Y., & Mizoguchi, R. (2006). Role organization model in Hozo. In *Proceedings of the International Conference on Managing Knowledge in a World of Networks (EKAW)* (LNCS 4248, pp. 67-81)

Sun, Y., Bhattacherjee, A., & Ma, Q. (2009). Extending technology usage to work settings: The role of perceived work compatibility in ERP implementation. *Information & Management*, *46*(6), 351–356. doi:10.1016/j.im.2009.06.003

Svensson, G. (2001). The impact of outsourcing on inbound logistics flows. *International Journal of Logistics Management*, *12*(1), 21–35. doi:10.1108/09574090110806208

Swanson, E. B. (1994). Information Systems Innovations Among Organizations. *Management Science*, *40*(9), 1069–1091. doi:10.1287/mnsc.40.9.1069

Swanson, E. B., & Ramiller, N. C. (1993). Information Systems Research Thematics: Submissions to a New Journal. *Information Systems Research*, *4*(4), 299–330. doi:10.1287/isre.4.4.299

Swanson, E. B., & Ramiller, N. C. (1997). The Organizing Vision in Information Systems Innovations. *Organization Science*, *8*(5), 458–474. doi:10.1287/orsc.8.5.458

Swatman, P. M. C., Swatman, P. A., & Fowler, D. C. (1994). A model of EDI integration and strategic business reengineering. *The Journal of Strategic Information Systems*, *3*(1), 41–60. doi:10.1016/0963-8687(94)90005-1

Szyperski, C. (2002). *Component Software – Beyond Object Oriented Programming*, Addison Wesley

Tanriverdi, H. (2006). Performance Effects of Information Technology Synergies in Multibusiness Firms. *Management Information Systems Quarterly*, *30*(1), 57–77.

Tarn, J. M., Yen, D. C., & Beaumont, M. (2002). Exploring the rationales for ERP and SCM integration. *Industrial Management & Data Systems*, *102*(1), 26–34. doi:10.1108/02635570210414631

Tas, J., & Sunder, S. (2004). Financial services business process outsourcing. *Communications of the ACM*, *47*(5), 50–52. doi:10.1145/986213.986238

Taylor, S., & Todd, P. A. (1995). Understanding Information Technology Usage: A Test of Competing Models. *Information Systems Research*, *6*(2), 144–176. doi:10.1287/isre.6.2.144

Taylor, W., & Wright, G. (2004). Organizational readiness for successful knowledge sharing: challenges for public sector managers. *Information Resources Management Journal*, *17*(2), 22–37. doi:10.4018/irmj.2004040102

Teece, D. J. (1992). Competition, Cooperation, and Innovation: Organizational Arrangements for Regimes of Rapid Technological Progress. *Journal of Economic Behavior & Organization, 18*(1), 1–25. doi:10.1016/0167-2681(92)90050-L

Teo, T. S. H., & Ang, J. S. K. (1999). Critical Success Factors in the Alignment of IS Plans with Business Plans. *International Journal of Information Management, 19*, 173–185. doi:10.1016/S0268-4012(99)00007-9

Teo, T. S. H., & Ang, J. S. K. (2000). How Useful are Strategic Plans for Information Systems? *Behaviour & Information Technology, 19*(4), 275–282. doi:10.1080/01449290050086381

Teo, T. S. H., Ang, J. S. K., & Pavri, F. N. (1997). The State of Strategic IS Planning Practices in Singapore. *Information & Management, 33*, 13–23. doi:10.1016/S0378-7206(97)00033-5

Terrados, J., Almonacid, G., & Hontoria, L. (2007). Regional Energy Planning through SWOT Analysis and Strategic Planning Tools: Impact on Renewables Development. *Renewable & Sustainable Energy Reviews, 11*(6), 1275–1287. doi:10.1016/j.rser.2005.08.003

Terry, D. B., Theimer, M. M., Petersen, K., Demers, A. J., Spreitzer, M. J., & Hauser, C. H. (1995). Managing update conflicts in Bayou, a weakly connected replicated storage system. In *Proceedings of the fifteenth ACM symposium on Operating systems principles* (pp. 172-182). New York: ACM.

Tesch, D., Braun, G., & Crable, E. (2008). An Examination of Employers' Perceptions and Expectations of IS Entry-level Personal and Interpersonal Skills. *Information Systems Education Journal, 6*(1), 3–16.

Tesch, R. (1990). *Qualitative Research Analysis: Types and Software Tools*. New York: Falmer.

Tetlow, P., Pan, J. Z., Oberle, D., Wallace, E., Uschold, M., & Kendall, E. (2006). *Ontology Driven Architectures and Potential Uses of the Semantic Web in Systems and Software Engineering*. Cambridge, MA: W3C.

The Checklist for Successful ERP Implementation. (2002). Retrieved from www.buker.com

Thilmany, J. (2009). In the Clouds. *Mechanical Engineering (New York, N.Y.), 131*(7), 16.

Thione, G. L., & Perry, D. E. (2005). Parallel changes: Detecting semantic interferences. In *Proceedings of the 29th Annual International Computer Software and Applications Conference (COMPSAC)* (Vol. 1, pp. 47-56). Washington, DC: IEEE Computer Society.

Thong, J. Y. L., Hong, W. H., & Tam, K. R. (2002). Understanding user acceptance of digital libraries: What are the roles of interface characteristics, organizational context, and individual differences? *International Journal of Human-Computer Studies, 57*(3), 215–242. doi:10.1016/S1071-5819(02)91024-4

Tierney, S. (2003). Exciting times --- but what about all the data RFID generates? *Frontline Solutions, 12*, 50.

Tigris. (2008). *Subversion*. Retrieved August 29, 2008, from http://subversion.tigris.org/

Timm, J. T. E., & Gannod, G. C. (2007, July 9-13). Specifying Semantic Web Service Compositions using UML and OCL. In *Proceedings of the IEEE International Conference on Web Services (ICWS'07)* (pp. 521-528).

Torkzadeh, G., & van Dyke, T. P. (2001). Development and validation of an Internet self-efficacy scale. *Behaviour & Information Technology, 20*(4), 275–280. doi:10.1080/01449290110050293

Tornatzky, L. G., & Fleischer, M. (1990). *The Processes of Technology Innovation*. Lexington, MA: Lexington Books.

Tornatzky, L. G., & Klein, K. J. (1982). Innovation Characteristics and innovation Adoption-Implementation: A Meta Analysis of Findings. *IEEE Transactions on Engineering Management, EM-29*(1), 28–45.

Toulmé, A. (2006). *Presentation of EMF compare utility*. Paper presented at the Eclipse Modeling Symposium.

Trauth, E. M., Farwell, D. W., & Lee, D. (1993). The IS expectation gap: Industry expectations versus academic preparation. *Management Information Systems Quarterly, 17*(3), 293–308. doi:10.2307/249773

Trepper, C. (1999). *ERP project management is key to a successful implementation*. Retrieved from http://www.erphub.com/strategy

Trimmer, K. J., Pumphry, L. D., & Wiggins, C. (2002). ERP implementation in rural health care. *Journal of Management in Medicine, 2/3*(16), 113–132. doi:10.1108/02689230210434871

Tsai, W.-H., Fan, Y.-W., Leu, J.-D., Chou, L.-W., & Yang, C.-C. (2007). The Relationship Between Implementation Variables and Performance Improvements of ERP Systems. *International Journal of Technology Management, 38*(4), 350–373. doi:10.1504/IJTM.2007.013406

Umble, E. J., Haft, R. R., & Umble, M. M. (2003). Enterprise Resource Planning: Implementation Procedures and Critical Success Factors. *European Journal of Operational Research, 146*, 241–257. doi:10.1016/S0377-2217(02)00547-7

Uscher-Pines, L., Barnett, D. J., Sapsin, J. W., Bishai, D. M., & Balicer, R. D. (2008). A Systematic Analysis of Influenze Vaccine Shortage Policies. *Public Health, 122*(2), 183–191. doi:10.1016/j.puhe.2007.06.005

Van Den Hoven, J. (2004). Data architecture standards for the effective enterprise. *Information Systems Management, 21*(3), 61–64. doi:10.1201/1078/44432.21.3.20040601/82478.9

Van Everdingen, Y., Van Hillegersber, J., & Waarts, E. (2000). ERP adoption by European midsize companies. *Communications of the ACM, 43*(4), 27–31. doi:10.1145/332051.332064

Van Hoek, S. (2001). E-Supply chains – virtually non-existing. *Supply Chain Management: An International Journal, 6*(1), 21–28. doi:10.1108/13598540110694653

Vara, J. M., De Castro, V., & Marcos, E. (2005). WSDL automatic generation from UML models in a MDA framework. *International Journal of Web Services Practices, 1*(1-2), 1–12.

Vasconcelos, A. (2006). *CEO Framework for Information System Architecture: An UML profile* (Tech. Rep.). Retrieved from http://web.ist.utl.pt/ist14250/reports/CEOF_UML_Profile_v1_2.pdf

Vasconcelos, A., Caetano, A., Neves, J., Sinogas, P., Mendes, R., & Tribolet, J. (2001). *A Framework for Modeling Strategy, Business Processes and Information Systems.* Paper presented at the 5th International Enterprise Distributed Object Computing Conference EDOC, Seattle.

Vasconcelos, A., Mendes, R., & Tribolet, J. (2004). Using Organizational Modeling to Evaluate Health Care IS/IT Projects. In *Proceedings of the 37th Annual Hawaii International Conference on System Sciences (HICCS37)*, HI.

Vasconcelos, A., Sousa, P., & Tribolet, J. (2007). Information System Architecture Metrics: an Enterprise Engineering Evaluation Approach. *The Electronic Journal Information Systems Evaluation, 10*(1), 91-122. ISSN: 1566-6379

Vasconcelos, A., Sousa, P., & Tribolet, J. (2008). Enterprise Architecture Analysis: An Information System Evaluation Approach. *International Journal of Enterprise Modelling and Information Systems Architectures, 3*(2), 31-53. ISSN: 1860-6059

Vela, B., Acuña, C., & Marcos, E. (2004). A Model Driven Approach for XML Database Development. In *Proceedings of the 23rd International Conference on Conceptual Modeling (ER2004)* (LNCS 3288, pp. 780-794).

Venkatesh, V., & Davis, F. D. (1996). A model of the antecedents of perceived ease of use: Development and test. *Decision Sciences, 27*(3), 451–481. doi:10.1111/j.1540-5915.1996.tb01822.x

Venkatesh, V., & Davis, F. D. (2000). A Theoretical Extension of the Technology Acceptance Model: Four Longitudinal Field Studies. *Management Science, 46*(2), 186–204. doi:10.1287/mnsc.46.2.186.11926

Venkatesh, V., & Morris, M. G. (2000). Why Do Not Men Ever Stop to Ask for Directions? Gender, Social and their Role in Technology Acceptance and Usage Behaviour. *Management Information Systems Quarterly, 24*(1), 115–139. doi:10.2307/3250981

VersionOne. (2009). *Cloud Confusion Amongst IT Professionals.*

Verville, J., Bernadas, C., & Halingten, A. (2005). So you're thinking of buying an ERP? Ten critical factors for successful acquisitions. *Journal of Enterprise Information Management, 6*(118), 667–685.

Völkel, M. (2006). *D2.3.3.v2 SemVersion – versioning RDF and ontologies.* Retrieved August 29, 2008, from http://www.aifb.uni-karlsruhe.de/Publikationen/showPublikation?publ_id=1163

Vonk, G., Geertman, S., & Schot, P. (2007). A SWOT Analysis of Planning Support Systems. *Environment & Planning, 39*(7), 1699–1714. doi:10.1068/a38262

Vrček, N., Dobrović, Ž., & Kermek, D. (2007). Novel Approach to BCG Analysis in the Context of ERP System Implementation. In Župančič, J. (Ed.), *Advances in Information Systems Development (Vol. 1*, pp. 47–60). New York: Springer. doi:10.1007/978-0-387-70761-7_5

Vukšić, V. B., & Spremić, M. (2005). ERP System Implementation and Business Process Change: Case Study of a Pharmaceutical Company. *Journal of Computing and Information Technology, 13*(1), 11–24. doi:10.2498/cit.2005.01.02

W3C. (2004). *OWL Web Ontology Language Reference.* Retrieved from http://www.w3.org/TR/owl-ref/

Wagner, L. E., Scott, V. S., & Galliers, D. R. (2006). The creation of 'best practice' software: Myth, reality and ethics. *Information and Organization, 16*(3), 251–275. doi:10.1016/j.infoandorg.2006.04.001

Waiman, C., Chu, S. C., & Du, T. C. (2009). A technology roadmap for RFID adoption in supply chains. *International Journal of Electronic Business, 7*(1), 44–57. doi:10.1504/IJEB.2009.023608

Walliman, N. (2001). *Your research project.* London: Sage Publications.

Wang, C., He, K., He, Y., & Qian, W. (2006). Mappings from OWL-s to UML for Semantic Web Services. *Research and Practical Issues of Enterprise Information Systems, 205*, 397-406. ISBN: 1571-5736. WSMO. (n.d.). *WSML Final Draft 5. DERI.* Retrieved from http://www.wsmo.org/TR/d16/d16.1/v0.21/#sec:wsml-xml

Wang, C., Ren, K., Lou, W., & Li, J. (2010). Toward Publicly Auditable Secure Cloud Data Storage Services. *IEEE Network, 24*(4), 5. doi:10.1109/MNET.2010.5510914

Wang, E. T. G., & Wei, H. L. (2007, November). Interorganizational Governance Value Creation: Coordination for Information Visibility and Flexibility in Supply Chains. *Decision Sciences, 38*(4), 647–674.

Wang, Y. S., Wang, Y. M., Lin, H. H., & Tang, T. I. (2003). Determinants of User Acceptance of Internet Banking: An Empirical Study. *International Journal of Service Industry Management, 14*(5), 501–519. doi:10.1108/09564230310500192

Wareham, J., Rai, A., & Pickering, G. (2005). Standardization in Vertical Industries: An Institutional Analysis of XML-Based Standards Infusion in Electricity Markets. *Electronic Markets, 15*(4), 323–334. doi:10.1080/10196780500302849

Watson, E., & Schneider, H. (1999). Using ERP systems in education. *Communication of the Association for Information Systems, 1*(9). Retrieved from http://cais.isworld.org/articles/?vol=1&art=9

Wee, S. (2000). *Juggling toward ERP success: keep key success factors high.* Retrieved from http://www.erpnews.com/erpnews/erp904/02get.html

Wei Chou, S., & Chieh Chang, Y. (2008). The implementation factors that influence the ERP (enterprise resource planning) benefits. *Decision Support Systems, 46*, 149–157. doi:10.1016/j.dss.2008.06.003

Weitzel, T., Beimborn, D., & Konig, W. (2006). A Unified Economic Model of Standard Diffusion: The Impact of Standardization Cost, Network Effects, and Network Topology. *Management Information Systems Quarterly, 30*, 489–514.

Weitzel, T., Wendt, O., Beimborn, D., & Koenig, W. (2006). Network Effects and Diffusion Theory: Extending Economic Network Analysis. In Jakobs, K. (Ed.), *Advanced Topics in Information Technology Standards and Standardization Research (Vol. 1*, pp. 282–305). Hershey, PA: Idea Group.

Wernerfelt, B. (1984). A Resource-based View of the Firm. *Strategic Management Journal, 5*(2), 171–180. doi:10.1002/smj.4250050207

West, J. (2003, December 12-14). *The Role of Standards in the Creation and Use of Information Systems.* Paper presented at the International Conference on IS Special Workshop on Standard Making sponsored by MISQ, Seattle, WA.

WFMC. (1999). *Terminology & Glossary* (Document Number WFMC-TC-1011, 3.0).

Wheeler, B. C. (2002). NEBIC: a dynamic capabilities theory for assessing net-enablement. *Information Systems Research, 13*(2), 125–146. doi:10.1287/isre.13.2.125.89

Wiegand, H. E. (1989). Aspekte der Makrostruktur im allgemeinen einsprachigen Wörterbuch: alphabetische Anordnungsformen und ihre Probleme. In F. J. Hausmann, O. Reichmann, H. E. Wiegand, & L. Zgusta (Eds.), *Wörterbücher* (Vol. 1, pp. 371-409). Berlin, Germany: Springer.

Wiegand, H. E. (1989). Der Begriff der Mikrostruktur: Geschichte, Probleme, Perspektiven. In F. J. Hausmann, O. Reichmann, H. E. Wiegand, & L. Zgusta (Eds.), *Wörterbücher* (Vol. 1, pp. 409-462). Berlin, Germany: Springer.

Wigand, R. T., Markus, M. L., & Steinfield, C. W. (2005). Preface to the Focus Theme Section: 'Vertical Industry Information Technology Standards and Standardization'. *Electronic Markets, 15*(4), 285–288. doi:10.1080/10196780500302641

Wigand, R. T., Picot, A., & Reichwald, R. (1997). *Information, organization and management: Expanding markets and corporate boundaries.* Chichester, England: Wiley.

Wigand, R. T., Steinfield, C. W., & Markus, M. L. (2005). Information Technology Standards Choices and Industry Structure Outcomes: The Case of the U.S. Home Mortgage Industry. *Journal of Management Information Systems, 22*(2), 165–191.

Wilder, C., & Davis, B. (1998). False starts, Strong finishes. *Informationweek, 711,* 41–53.

Williamson, O. E. (1985). *The Economic Institutions of Capitalism.* New York: The Free Press.

Windows Presentation Foundation (2006) Retrieved July 24, 2008 from the Wikipedia Web Site: http://en.wikipedia.org/wiki/Windows_Presentation_Foundation

Wittgenstein, L. (1973). *Philosophical investigations.* Upper Saddle River, NJ: Prentice Hall.

Wood, T., & Caldas, M. P. (2001). Reductionism and Coplex thinking during ERP implementation. *Business Process Management Journal, 5*(7), 387–393. doi:10.1108/14637150110406777

Woo, M., & Dieckmann, M. (2010). The Multiple Personalities of Cloud Computing. *EDUCAUSE Review, 45*(3), 12.

WSMO. (2005). *WSMO Primer.* Retrieved from http://www.wsmo.org/TR/d3/d3.1/v0.1/

WSRP. *OASIS Web Services for Remote Portlets* (2003). Retrieved July 24, 2008 http://www.oasis-open.org/committees/tc_home.php?wg_abbrev=wsrp

Wu, J. H., & Wang, L. (2007). Measuring ERP success: the key-users' viewpoint of the ERP to produce a viable IS in the organization. *Computers in Human Behavior, 23*(3), 1582–1596. doi:10.1016/j.chb.2005.07.005

Wuyts, R., & Ducasse, S. (2001). *Composition Languages for Black Box Components,* Proc. of Roel, First OOPSLA Workshop on Language Mechanisms for Programming Software Components

Wymer, S. A., & Regan, E. A. (2005). Factors Influencing e-commerce Adoption and Use by Small and Medium Businesses. *Electronic Markets, 15*(4), 438–453. doi:10.1080/10196780500303151

Xia, M., Zhao, K., & Mahoney, J. T. (2008). *Enhancing Value via Cooperation: Firms' Process Benefits From Participation in a Consortium.* Unpublished Working Paper, University of Illinois.

Xia, M., Zhao, K., & Shaw, M. J. (2003, December 12-14). *Open E-Business Standard Development and Adoption: An Integrated Perspective.* Paper presented at the International Conference on IS Special Workshop on Standard Making sponsored by MISQ, Seattle, WA.

Xue, Y., Liang, H., Boulton, W. R., & Snyder, C. A. (2005). ERP Implementation Failures in China: Case Studies With Implications for ERP Vendors. *International Journal of Production Economics, 97*(3), 279–295. doi:10.1016/j.ijpe.2004.07.008

Xu, Q., & Ma, Q. (2008). Determinants of ERP implementation knowledge transfer. *Information & Management, 45,* 528–539. doi:10.1016/j.im.2008.08.004

Yan, H., Diao, X. C., & Jiang, G. Q. (2008). Research on Data Synchronization in Oracle Distributed System. In *Proceedings of 2008 International Seminar on Future Information Technology and Management Engineering* (pp. 540-542). Washington, DC: IEEE.

Yen, R. H., Li, E. Y., & Niehoff, B. P. (2008). Do organizational citizenship behaviors lead to information system success? Testing the mediation effects of integration climate and project management. *Information & Management, 45*, 394–402. doi:10.1016/j.im.2008.04.004

Yesilbas, L. G., & Lombard, M. (2004). Towards a knowledge repository for collaborative design process: focus on conflict management. *Computers in Industry, 55*(3), 335–350.

Yi, M., & Hwang, Y. (2003). Predicting the use of web-based information systems: self-efficacy, enjoyment, learning goal orientation, and the technology acceptance model. *International Journal of Human-Computer Studies, 59*(4), 431–449. doi:10.1016/S1071-5819(03)00114-9

Yin, R. K. (1994). *Case Study Research: Design and Methods* (5th ed.). Fort Worth, TX: Dryden press.

Yin, R. K. (2003). *Applications of Case Study Research*. Thousand Oaks, CA: Sage.

Yougberg, E., Olen, D., & Hauser, K. (2009). Determinants of professionally autonomous end-user acceptance in an enterprise resource planning systems environment. *International Journal of Information Management, 29*(2), 138–144. doi:10.1016/j.ijinfomgt.2008.06.001

Yu, C. (2005). Causes influencing the effectiveness of the post-implementation ERP system. *Industrial Management + Data Systems, 105*(1-2), 115-132.

Yuksel, I., & Dagdeviren, M. (2007). Using the Analytic Network Process (AHP) in a SWOT Analysis: A Case Study for a Textile Firm. *Information Sciences, 177*, 3364–3382. doi:10.1016/j.ins.2007.01.001

Yusuf, Y., Gunasekaran, A., & Abthorpe, M. (2004). Enterprise Information systems project implementation: A case study of ERP in Rolls-Royce. *International Journal of Production Economics, 87*, 251–266. doi:10.1016/j.ijpe.2003.10.004

Zaheer, A., & Venkatraman, N. (1994). Determinants of Electronic Integration in the Insurance Industry: An Empirical Test. *Management Science, 40*(5), 549–566. doi:10.1287/mnsc.40.5.549

Zaheer, A., & Venkatraman, N. (1995). Relational Governance as an Interorganizational Strategy: An Empirical Test of the Role of Trust in Economic Exchange. *Strategic Management Journal, 16*, 373–392. doi:10.1002/smj.4250160504

Zahra, S. A., & George, G. (2002). Absorptive Capacity: A Review, Reconceptualization, and Extension. *Academy of Management Review, 27*(2), 185. doi:10.2307/4134351

Zahra, S. A., & Gerard, G. (2002). The net-enabled business innovation cycle and the evolution of dynamic capabilities. *Information Systems Research, 13*(2), 147–151. doi:10.1287/isre.13.2.147.90

Zairi, M. (2003). *You're ERP Project Won't Fail. CAN YOU SEE it?* Retrieved from www.ibm.com

Zhang, P., & Dran, G. (2001, January 3-6). Expectations and Rankings of Website Quality Features: Results of Two Studies on User Perceptions. In *Proceedings of the 34th Annual Hawaii International Conference on System Sciences (HICSS-34)* (Volume 7).

Zhang, P., & Dran, G. (2000). Satisfiers and dissatisfiers: A two-factor model for website design and evaluation. *Journal of the American Society for Information Science American Society for Information Science, 51*(14), 1253–1268. doi:10.1002/1097-4571(2000)9999:9999<::AID-ASI1039>3.0.CO;2-O

Zhang, P., & Dran, G. (2002). User expectations and ranking of quality factors in different web site domains. *International Journal of Electronic Commerce, 6*(2), 9–33.

Zhao, K., Xia, M., & Shaw, M. J. (2005). Vertical E-Business Standards and Standards Developing Organizations: A Conceptual Framework. *Electronic Markets, 15*(4), 289–300. doi:10.1080/10196780500302690

Zhao, K., Xia, M., & Shaw, M. J. (2007). An Integrated Model of Consortium-Based E-Business Standardization: Collaborative Development and Adoption with Network Externalities. *Journal of Management Information Systems, 23*(4), 247–271. doi:10.2753/MIS0742-1222230411

Zhao, X., Huo, B., Flynn, B. B., & Yeung, J. H. Y. (2008). The impact of power and relationship commitment on the integration between manufacturers and customers in a supply chain. *Journal of Operations Management, 26,* 368–388. doi:10.1016/j.jom.2007.08.002

Zheng, S., Yen, D. C., & Tarn, M. J. (2000). The new spectrum of the cross-enterprise solution: the integration of supply chain management and enterprise resource-planning systems. *Journal of Computer Information Systems,* 84–93.

Ziaee, M., Fathian, M., & Sadjadi, S. J. (2006). A modular approach to ERP system selection. *Information Management & Computer Security, 5*(14), 485–495. doi:10.1108/09685220610717772

Zucker, S. G., & Wang, S. H. (2009). The impact of data synchronization adoption on organizations: A case study. *Journal of Electronic Commerce in Organizations, 7*(3), 44–64.

About the Contributors

Madjid Tavana is a Professor of Business Systems and Analytics and the Lindback Distinguished Chair of Information Systems and Decision Sciences at La Salle University where he served as Chairman of the Management Department and Director of the Center for Technology and Management. He has been a Distinguished NASA Research Fellow at Kennedy Space Center, Johnson Space Center, Naval Research Laboratory - Stennis Space Center, and Air Force Research Laboratory. He was recently honored with the prestigious Space Act Award by NASA. He holds an MBA, a PMIS, and a PhD in Management Information Systems and received his post-doctoral diploma in strategic information systems from the Wharton School of the University of Pennsylvania. He is the Editor-in-Chief for *Decision Analytics*, the *International Journal of Strategic Decision Sciences*, the *International Journal of Enterprise Information Systems*, and the *International Journal of Applied Decision Sciences*. He has published over one hundred research papers in academic journals such as *Decision Sciences, Information Systems, Interfaces, Annals of Operations Research, Omega, Information and Management, Expert Systems with Applications, European Journal of Operational Research, Journal of the Operational Research Society, Computers and Operations Research, Knowledge Management Research and Practice, Computers and Industrial Engineering, Applied Soft Computing, Journal of Advanced Manufacturing Technology*, and *Advances in Engineering Software*, among others.

* * *

C.J. Acuña received his Msc in computer science from the National Technological University (UTN), Resistencia, Argentina in 2000 and his European PhD in Computer Science from Rey Juan Carlos University in 2007. He was with the UTN as a teaching assistant and is currently associate professor at the Department of Computing Languages and Systems II at Rey Juan Carlos University. His current research interests include Semantic Web Services and services-oriented architectures.

Kerstin Altmanninger is a research and teaching assistant at the Department of Telecooperation at the Johannes Kepler University Linz, Austria. She received her master degree in computer science in 2006. From April 2006 to February 2007 she was working in the project ModelCVS: A Semantic Infrastructure for Model-based Tool Integration. Now she is evolved in the preceding project AMOR – Adaptable Model Versioning. In this context she is doing her PhD since 2006, entitled *Models in Conflict – A Semantically Enhanced Version Control System for Model Artifacts*. Her research interests focus on the area of model engineering in general, and on Version Control Systems (VCSs), model merging, and model transformations in particular.

Rebecca Angeles is Full Professor, Management Information Systems Area, Faculty of Business Administration, University of New Brunswick Fredericton, Canada. She has published in Information & Management, Decision Support Systems, Supply Chain Management: An International Journal, Industrial Management & Data Systems, International Journal of Integrated Supply Management, International Journal of Management and Enterprise Development, International Journal of Value Chain Management, International Journal of Physical Distribution & Logistics Management, Logistics Information Management, Journal of Business Logistics, among others. Her current research interests are in radio frequency identification, supply chain management issues, outsourcing and its consequences on supply chains, electronic trading partnership management issues, business-to-business exchanges, electronic trading partnerships, electronic data interchange (EDI), and innovative approaches to teaching Management Information Systems.

Murugan Anandarajan is Professor of Management Information Systems in the Management Department at Drexel University. His current research interests include social networking, cloud computing, and e-Research collaboration. His research has appeared in journals such as Behavior and Information Technology, Computers and Operations Research, Decision Sciences, Industrial Data Management Systems, Information and Management, International Journal of Information Management, Journal of Management Information Systems, Journal of Global Information Systems, Journal of International Business Studies, and the Omega-International Journal of Management Science, among others. He is the editor of "e-Research Collaboration", published by Springer in 2010.

Bay Arinze is Professor of Management Information Systems at Drexel University in Philadelphia. His current research focuses on cloud computing, online research, and social networking. He has published numerous articles in such information systems and operations management journals as Information and Management, Decision Sciences, Omega-International Journal of Management Science, and Journal of Management Information Systems. He has received many research grants from such agencies as the National Science Foundation and consulted widely in the information technology area.

Uwe Assmann holds the chair of software engineering at the Technische Universität Dresden. He is the inventor of invasive software composition (ISC), a technology for the composition of program fragments for extreme software reuse. ISC provides a unified technology for generic, connector-,view-, and aspect-based programming, and works for arbitrary program or modeling languages. The technology is demonstrated by the Reuseware environment (http://www.reuseware.org). Roles are in Prof. Assmann's research interest, because roles can be merged into classes so that they form a grey-box component model in the sense of invasive software composition.

Bernhard Bauer is professor and head of the programming of Distributed Systems Group at the University of Augsburg since 2003. He holds a diploma in computer science from the University of Passau, Germany, and a PhD. in computer science from the Technische Universität München, Germany. For more than 6 years Bauer has worked in industry. The focus of his research group at the university is on industrialization of software engineering and software operation. The main research areas are model-driven software development, semantic technologies as well as self-organizing systems to improve the automation of the software product lifecycle as well as the autonomy of software systems.

He has published more than 100 scientific papers in the area of agent-based systems and agent-oriented software engineering, compiler construction, (semantic-enabled) model-driven software engineering and autonomous systems.

Todd A. Boyle is an Associate Professor of Operations Management and Canada Research Chair (CRC) in Integrative IT Diffusion in Small and Medium-sized Enterprises at St. Francis Xavier University, Nova Scotia, Canada. Dr. Boyle's current research focuses the adoption of CQI and integrated information systems in community pharmacies, and is funded by the Social Sciences and Humanities Research Council of Canada (SSHRC), Canada Foundation for Innovation (CFI), Nova Scotia Research and Innovation Trust (NSRIT), and the Nova Scotia Health Research Foundation (NSHRF). Dr. Boyle teaches courses in enterprise systems, management information systems, and business research methods.

Shabnam Dadbin is doing her postgraduate research in Industrial Management Department at Allameh Tabataba'i University, Tehran, Iran. Her research interest revolves around integrated information systems, enterprise resource management, and customer relationship management.

João Duarte is an IT consultant at Portugal Comunicações, the leading Portuguese telecommunications company. He holds a M.Sc. and B.Sc. degrees in Computer Engineering and Information Systems from Technical University of Lisbon. He has worked in several projects concerning software and system engineering. His research interests include information system architecture, technological architecture, enterprise architecture and phenomenology.

D.M. Sánchez Fúquene received her BS in computer science from the Universidad Distrital "Francisco José de Caldas", Bogotá, Colombia in 2001 and MS degrees in Information Technology and Information Systems from Rey Juan Carlos University (URJC) in 2007. She is currently working towards her PhD degree in the URJC. Her research interests include ontologies and the Semantic Web.

Roya Gholami is a lecturer in Operations and Information Management Group, Aston Business School in Birmingham, UK. Her current research interests are IT business value, Green IT, Information Technology Adoption, Information Technology and Development. She has published in IEEE Transaction on Engineering Management, Information & Management, Journal of Global Information Management, Information Resource Management Journal, World Economy, and Journal of Electronic Commerce in Organizations, Technovation and Electronic Journal of Information Systems in Developing Countries.

Payam Hanafizadeh is an assistant professor of Industrial Management Department, Allameh Tabataba'i University, Tehran, Iran . He is also a member of Design Optimization under Uncertainty Group at the University of Waterloo, Canada. He pursues his research in Information Systems and Decision-making under Uncertainty. The results of his research appear in top tier academic journals such as: The Information Society, Journal of Global Information Management, Telecommunications Policy, Mathematical and Computer Modeling, Expert Systems with Applications, International Journal of Information Management, to name only a few.

Jakob Henriksson received his PhD from the Technical University of Dresden, Germany, investigating extensions to invasive software composition, and in particular software composition applications to Semantic Web languages. One of the backbones of Semantic Web technology are ontology languages, but composition techniques and modularization concepts for such languages are only starting to emerge. Henriksson started investigating modularization concepts and possibilities based on role modeling in his thesis work. He is currently working as a research scientist at Intelligent Automation, Inc. in Maryland, USA.

Alen Jakupovic is a professor at Business department of the Polytechnic of Rijeka. He received his Ph. D. in information science at the Faculty of Humanities and Social Sciences, University of Zagreb, Croatia (2010.) and M.Sc. in information science at the Faculty of Organization and Informatics, University of Zagreb, Croatia (2006.). His research interests are in information systems design methodology and measurement. Alen Jakupovic has published in proceedings of the conferences such as: International Conference on Information Systems Analysis and Synthesis (ISAS), The C* Conference on Computer Science and Software Engineering (C3S2E), International Conference on Enterprise Information Systems and Web Technologies (EISWT), International Conference on Software Engineering and Data Engineering (SEDE), International Multi-Conference on Computing in the Global Information Technology (ICCGI), and in Journal of Computing and Information Technology.

Seong-Jong Joo is an Associate Professor of Operations Management in Hasan School of Business at Colorado State University-Pueblo. He received his B.S. in Military Science from Korea Air Force Academy, Seoul, Korea and MBA and PhD in Business Administration from Saint Louis University, St. Louis, Missouri. Before joining the academia in 2003, he served in the Republic of Korea Air Force as a Supply Officer (Lt. Colonel) for twenty-one years. His research interests include logistics and supply chain management in general and supply chain strategies, purchasing/materials management, inventory management, performance measures/benchmarking in particular. His articles have appeared in various journals such as Benchmarking: An International Journal, European Journal of Operational Research, International Journal of Logistics Management, Journal of Management Studies, Supply Chain Management: An International Journal, the Service Industries Journal, and others.

Gabriele Kotsis received her master's degree and her PhD from the University of Vienna. After visiting professor positions at the Vienna University for Economics and Business Administration and at the Copenhagen Business School, she is currently holding a full professor position at the Telecooperation Department at the Johannes Kepler University of Linz. Her research interests include performance management of computer systems and networks, workgroup computing, mobile and internet computing, telemedia and telecooperation. Prof. Kotsis is author of numerous publications in international conferences and journals and is co-editor of several books. From April 2003 to April 2007 she was president of the Austrian Computer Society.

Ik-Whan G. Kwon is a Professor of Decision Sciences and MIS at the John Cook School of Business, St. Louis University. He is also the Director of the Center for Supply Chain Management Studies at the John Cook School of Business since 1998. He received his B.A. in Economics from Korea University and first PhD degree in Economics from University of Georgia. His second PhD degree in Health Service Research was awarded in 1990 from the School of Public Health, St. Louis University. Dr. Kwon has published more than 125 academic articles and professional papers in numerous journals including Journal of Supply Chain Management, Supply Chain Management: An International Journal, International Journal of Physical Distribution and Logistics Management, New England Journal of Medicine, American Journal of Medical Association, American Journal of Public Health, and others. He serves on the Editorial Board of several journals.

Florian Lautenbacher is researcher and Ph.D. student at the University of Augsburg, Germany, and holds a diploma in Computer Science from the same university. During his studies he has worked for Fujitsu Siemens Computers, a medical supply center as well as at the university. His current research interests are in applying semantic technologies to model-driven software engineering, in particular in workflow and business process technologies as well as service-oriented architectures. Florian is project co-lead of the Eclipse Technology project Java Workflow Tooling (JWT) which started in 2007 and is part of the current Eclipse Galileo distribution. Moreover he is involved in several other national and international projects mostly related to business process management and SOA. He has published more than 20 scientific papers.

Chang Won Lee is an Professor in the School of Business at Hanyang University, Korea. He earned his Masters and PhD from Saint Louis University. He was a SCM researcher at University of Michigan. His research areas include global supply chain and outsourcing management, technology and information management, and entrepreneurial studies. His papers are published in The Journal of Operational Research Society, European Journal of Operational Research, Information & Management, Supply Chain Management: An International Journal, and others. He serves as a guest editor of International Journal of Entrepreneurship and Innovation Management and the managing editor of Management Review: An International Journal.

E. Marcos Martínez is an associate professor of the Rey Juan Carlos University (URJC), Madrid, Spain and head of the Department of Computing Languages and Systems II of the School of Computer Science and Engineering of the URJC. She received her PhD in computer sciences from Technical University of Madrid (Spain) in 1997. Marcos has been visiting scholar at the Telecom University (Paris, France). She is co-author of several books and she has published several articles and book chapters. Her current research focuses on Databases and the field of Information Systems.

Rubén A. Mendoza is an Assistant Professor in the Decision & System Sciences Department of the E.K. Haub School of Business, Saint Joseph's University, Philadelphia, PA. Dr. Mendoza's research focuses on the development, diffusion, assimilation, and utilization of XML-based industry standards in support of semantic standards for specific industries (known formally as vertical standards), and in the deployment of business intelligence solutions. He also has an interest in health informatics and IT audit. His research has previously been presented at the Americas Conference on Information Systems (AMCIS), the European Conference on Information Systems (ECIS), and the Hawaii International Conference on System Sciences (HICSS), and has been published in the International Journal of Enterprise Information Systems, the International Journal of Business Intelligence Research, and the International Journal of Business Information Systems.

M. Minoli is a PhD student at Rey Juan Carlos University where he also received his MSc in information technologies and computing systems. He is currently a PhD student in information technology. His research interests include software engineering, model-driven software development, semantic web services and code generation. He received the informatics engineering degree from the Resistencia's National Technological University, Argentina where he taught for five years.

Samar Mouakket is an assistant professor at the MIS department in the University of Sharjah, UAE. She received her Ph.D. in 1996 in Management Information Systems from Sheffield University, UK. Her research interests include systems analysis and user requirements determination during systems development, and the deployment of web-based business applications.

Mina Naeli is a researcher of the Department of Entrepreneurship in the University of Tehran. She holds her BSc in Management and Information Systems from the London School of Economics and Political Sciences (LSE), and her MSc in Management and Information Systems: change and development from the University of Manchester, Institute for Development Policy and Management (IDPM). Her research interests include e-service, e-democracy, e-trust, Human factors in information systems.

Mile Pavlic is a professor of IS and data modeling on the Department of Informatics at the University of Rijeka. He is the author of 5 books and over 40 journal articles. His work focuses on the following methods: business system analysis, business process modeling, data modeling and software engineering. Mile Pavlic has published in proceedings of the conferences such as International Conference Non-formal adult education and informal adult learning, International DAAAM Symposium, International Symposium on Operational Research, International Conference on Information Systems Analysis and Synthesis (ISAS), The C* Conference on Computer Science and Software Engineering (C3S2E), International Conference on Enterprise Information Systems and Web Technologies (EISWT), International Conference on Software Engineering and Data Engineering (SEDE), Central European Conference on Information and Intelligent Systems (CECIIS), and in journals such as Journal of Computing and Information Technology, Journal of Information and Organizational Sciences, Informatologia, Journal of Maritime Studies.

Alan R. Peslak is an Associate Professor of Information Sciences and Technology at Penn State University Worthington Scranton campus. His research areas include information technology social, ethical, and economic issues, enterprise resource planning, information privacy, and information technology pedagogy. Publications include the Communications of the ACM, Information Resources Management Journal, Journal of Business Ethics, Journal of Computer Information Systems, and Industrial Management and Data Systems. He is on the editorial boards of numerous journals. He currently serves as Executive Vice President for the Educational Special Interest Group of the Association for Information Technology Professionals.

Zoltán Porkoláb is an associate lecturer in the Department of Programming Languages and Compilers at Eötvös Loránd University, Budapest, Hungary, where he received his MSc and his PhD in software technology. Among other industrial related projects he has participated in Charles Simonyi's research on intentional programming. His current research focuses on programming languages, especially on C++ template metaprogramming. He was the leader of the Hungarian translation of Bjarne Stroustrup's book *The C++ Language*, and the organizer of the biannual workshop series called Workshop on Generative Technologies, held as part of the ETAPS workshops. He gives lecture on programming languages in BSc level, and on Advanced C++ technologies in MSc level at Eötvös University and currently is theses advisor of six PhD students.

Michael Pradel graduated in computer science at Technical University in Dresden, Germany, in 2008. He also spent two years at Ecole Centrale Paris, France, and became a graduate engineer. After a visit to EPFL, he is now working towards a PhD at ETH Zurich, Switzerland. His primary research interests are in the area of software engineering and programming languages.

T. Ravichandran is a Professor in the Lally School of Management & Technology, Rensselaer Polytechnic Institute, Troy, NY. His long term research interests focus on understanding how organizations develop capabilities to manage information systems and the mechanisms to facilitate the effective design, development, assimilation and use of information systems within and across organizations. Dr. Ravichandran serves as a Department Editor for IEEE Transactions in Engineering Management, as an Associate Editor of Information Systems Research and as a Senior Editor of Information & Management. His research has appeared in the Management Information Systems Quarterly, IEEE Transactions on Engineering Management, and the Journal of Management Information Systems.

Chetan S. Sankar is a Professor of Management at Auburn University. He has received more than two million dollars from ten National Science Foundation grants to develop exceptional instructional materials that bring real-world issues into classrooms. He has won awards for research and teaching excellence from the Society for Information Management, NEEDS, Decision Sciences Institute, American Society for Engineering Education, American Society for Mechanical Engineering, International Network for Engineering Education & Research, and the Project Management Institute. He is the editor-in-chief of the Decision Sciences Journal of Innovative Education and the managing editor of the Journal of STEM Education: Innovations and Research.

Wieland Schwinger is senior researcher at the Department of Telecooperation (TK) of the Johannes Kepler University Linz (JKU), Austria. Prior to that, he was working as a senior researcher and project manager at the Software Competence Center Hagenberg. He graduated with a master's in computer science from the University of Skövde, Sweden, in 1995 and a master in business informatics from JKU, Austria, in 1997. 2001 he was awarded a PhD and 2008 the venia docendi by the JKU. His research interests comprise web engineering and model engineering leading to more than 55 publications. He was involved in several national and international projects amongst them the EU-funded projects: UWA, WEE-Net, and MEDINA. Currently, he is involved in the FWF-funded project TROPIC on model transformations, and two FFG funded research projects, namely, AMOR on model versioning and BeAware! on ontology-based situation-awareness for road traffic management.

Mahesh Srinivasan is an Assistant Professor in the Department of Management at the University of Akron. He received a Ph.D. in Business Administration and a Master of Science degree in Business Logistics from the Pennsylvania State University. He also has a BS degree in Mechanical Engineering from the University of Pune, India and over 5 years of industry experience working for a German MNC. His research interests include supply chain and logistics management with particular focus on the role of IT in supply chain collaboration and integration, logistics performance metrics, stochastic inventory modeling and inter-organizational relationships within supply chains. Dr. Srinivasan has made several regional, national and international conference presentations and his work has appeared in the *Journal of Business Logistics* and *Supply Chain Practice Journal.*

Nicholas Standage has completed an undergraduate degree in Computer and Management Sciences at the University of Warwick, United Kingdom as well as an MSc in International Business in Aston Business School, United Kingdom. Since then he has acquired substantial international experience by having worked for a vehicle tracking systems provider in Portugal as well as by assisting with the implementation of a Database Management system in a travel agency in Cyprus. Nicholas is particularly interested in Enterprise Resource Planning systems the impact they have on Multinational Corporations and the underlying critical success factors that ensure their successful implementation.

Károly Tilly received an MSEE (1985), postgraduate degree in Measurement and Control Engineering (1987) and PhD in informatics (1995) at Budapest University of Technology, Hungary, where he worked as an associate professor at the Department of Measurement and Information Systems. He led several MSC and PhD courses, among others on Digital Computers, Artificial Intelligence and Software Technology. In 2002 he joined Oracle as a software architect and instructor. He participated several industrial and research projects related to the application of artificial intelligence technologies for solving industrial process monitoring, diagnostics and testing problems and intelligent user interfaces. His current field of scientific interest is related to semantic specification methods of user interface components and services and architectural elements for creating semantically separated, orthogonal, invariant user interfaces.

André Vasconcelos is a Professor of Computer Engineering and Information Systems at Instituto Superior Técnico, Technical University of Lisbon, Portugal. He holds a Ph.D. degree in Computer Engineering and Information Systems from Technical University of Lisbon, and his education background (M.Sc. and B.Sc.) is on computer science and software engineering. He has worked in several international projects concerning software and system engineering. He currently plays an active role in the enterprise engineering area, being involved in both research and consultancy projects concerning enterprise engineering and architecture. His research interests include information system architecture, information system evaluation, enterprise architecture and business process modeling.

Neven Vrcek is a professor of Software Engineering and Electronic Business at the University of Zagreb, Faculty of Organization and Informatics. His work is focused on wide area of implementation and use of ICT in the modern organizations. Neven Vrcek has published in proceedings of the conferences such as International Symposium on Biomedical Engineering, International IMEKO Conference on Measurement in Clinical Medicine, European Medical & Biological Engineering Conference, Conference Business Information Technology Management, European Concurrent Engineering Conference, International Conference on Information Technology Interfaces, Mediterranean Conference on Medical and Biological Engineering and Computing (MEDICON), Americas Conference on Information Systems, International Symposium on Research Methods, and in journals such as Journal of Computing and Information Technology, Journal of Information and Organizational Sciences, Informatologia.

Dongjin Yu is currently a professor at Hangzhou Dianzi University, China. He received his Bachelor Degree and Master Degree in Computer Applications from Zhejiang University, and PhD in Management from Zhejiang Gongshang University. His current research efforts focus on information systems and software engineering, especially the novel approaches to constructing large enterprise systems effectively and efficiently by emerging advanced information technologies. The concern of his research closely relates with real applications of e-government and e-business. He has led a number of government funded projects, including the Rapid Application Development Framework, OLAP Middleware, and Service-based Decision Support Systems. He is also the vice director of Institute of Intelligent and Software Technology of Hangzhou Dianzi University.

Behrouz Zarei is an assistant professor and head of the Department of Entrepreneurship in the University of Tehran. He holds his Ph.D. in Management Science from Lancaster University Management School, United Kingdom. His research areas are strategic Information System, E-government, and Business Process Reengineering.

Index